MASAHIRO HIKOKUBO

I wrote the story, but the anime served as the blueprint for our work on the manga, and now we've brought it to completion! I'm grateful to everyone who was involved, and I'd like to thank all the readers!!!

MASASHI SATO

It's the final volume!! I learned a lot over these full five years and nine months!! Thank you to everyone who supported me!!

Volume 9
SHONEN JUMP Manga Edition

Story by **MASAHIRO HIKOKUBO**
Art by **MASASHI SATO**
Production Assistance **STUDIO DICE**

Translation & English Adaptation **TAYLOR ENGEL AND IAN REID, HC LANGUAGE SOLUTIONS**
Touch-up Art & Lettering **JOHN HUNT**
Designer **SHAWN CARRICO**
Editor **MIKE MONTESA**

Published by VIZ Media, LLC
P.O. Box 77010
San Francisco, CA 94107

10 9 8 7 6 5 4 3 2 1
First printing, April 2016

www.viz.com

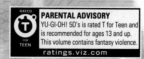

PARENTAL ADVISORY
YU-GI-OH! 5D's is rated T for Teen and
is recommended for ages 13 and up.
This volume contains fantasy violence.
ratings.viz.com

www.shonenjump.com

VOLUME 9
ETERNAL TURBO DUELIST!!

Story by **MASAHIRO HIKOKUBO**
Art by **MASASHI SATO**
Production Assistance **STUDIO DICE**

VOLUME 9
ETERNAL TURBO DUELIST!!

RIDE-61
DIVINE DUEL!!

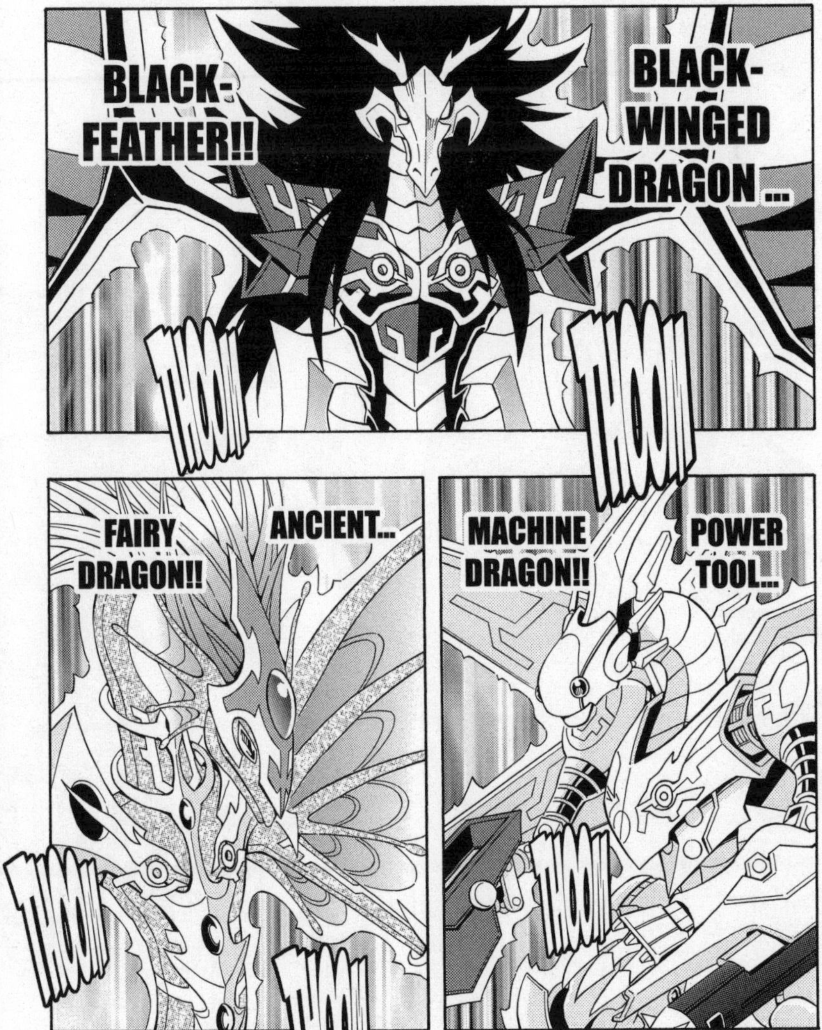
BLACK-WINGED DRAGON...
BLACK-FEATHER!!
THOOM
THOOM
POWER TOOL...
MACHINE DRAGON!!
THOOM
ANCIENT...
FAIRY DRAGON!!
THOOM
THOOM

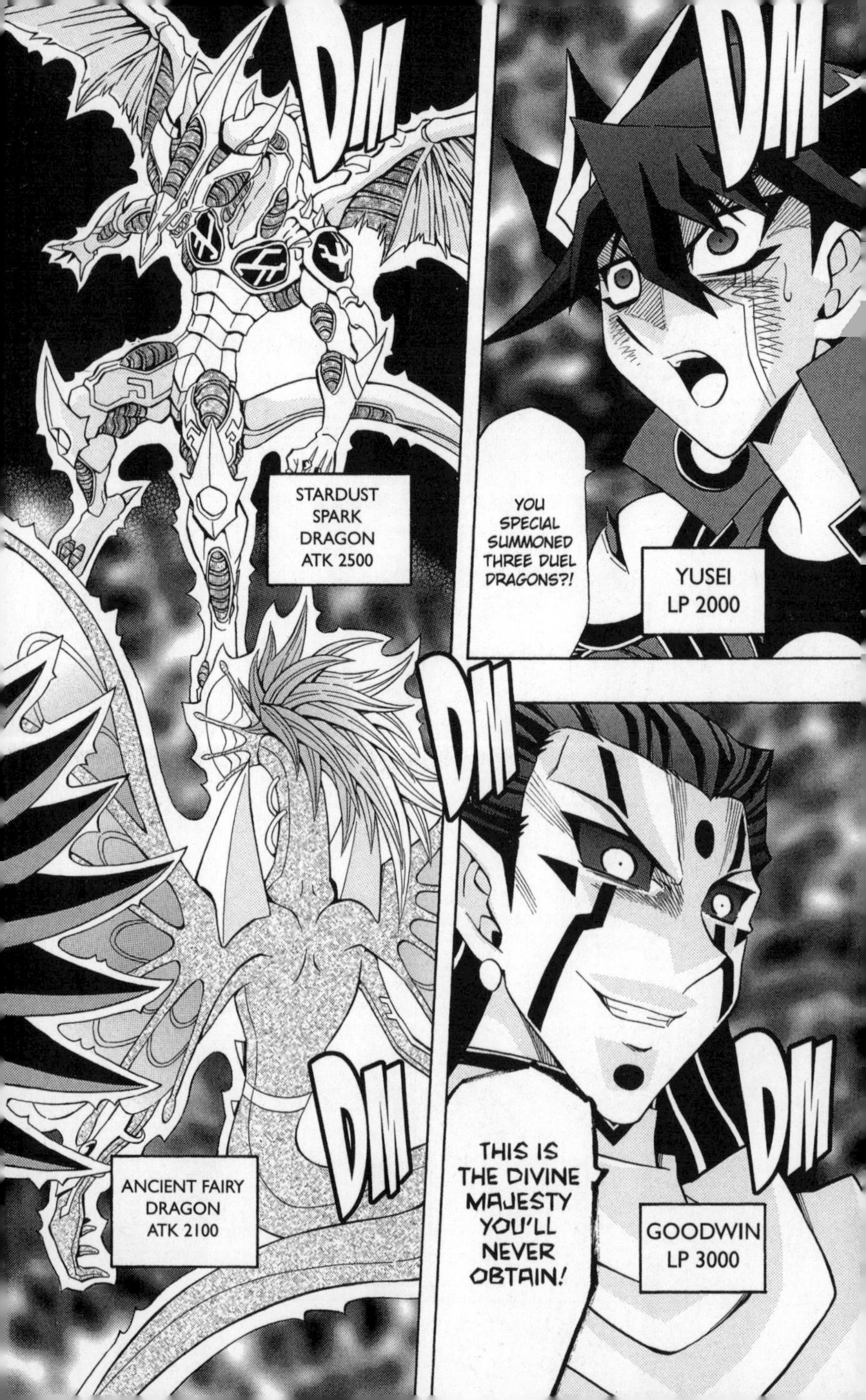
DM
YOU SPECIAL SUMMONED THREE DUEL DRAGONS?!
YUSEI LP 2000
DM
DM
THIS IS THE DIVINE MAJESTY YOU'LL NEVER OBTAIN!
GOODWIN LP 3000
DM
STARDUST SPARK DRAGON ATK 2500
DM
ANCIENT FAIRY DRAGON ATK 2100

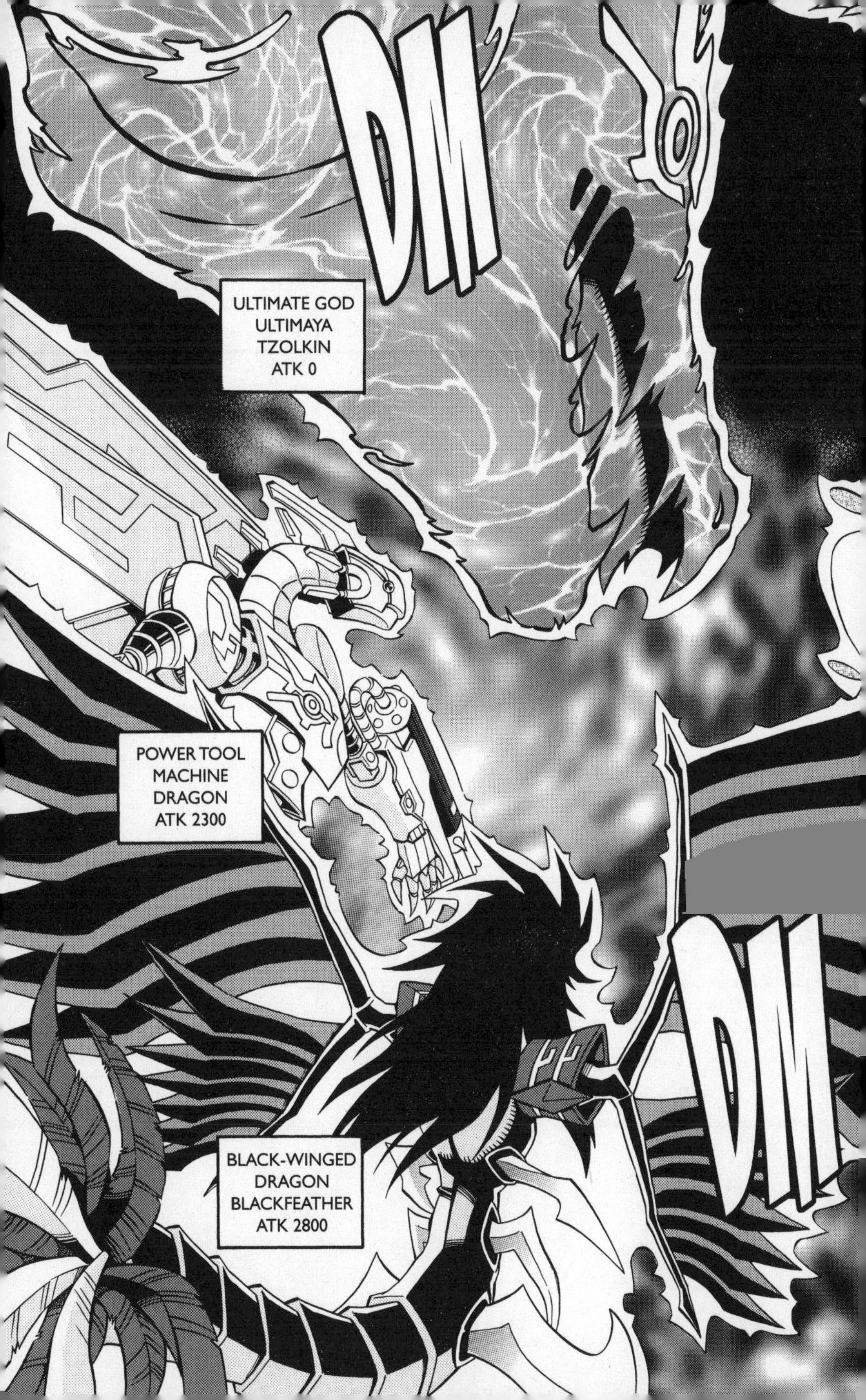
DM
ULTIMATE GOD ULTIMAYA TZOLKIN ATK 0
POWER TOOL MACHINE DRAGON ATK 2300
DM
BLACK-WINGED DRAGON BLACKFEATHER ATK 2800

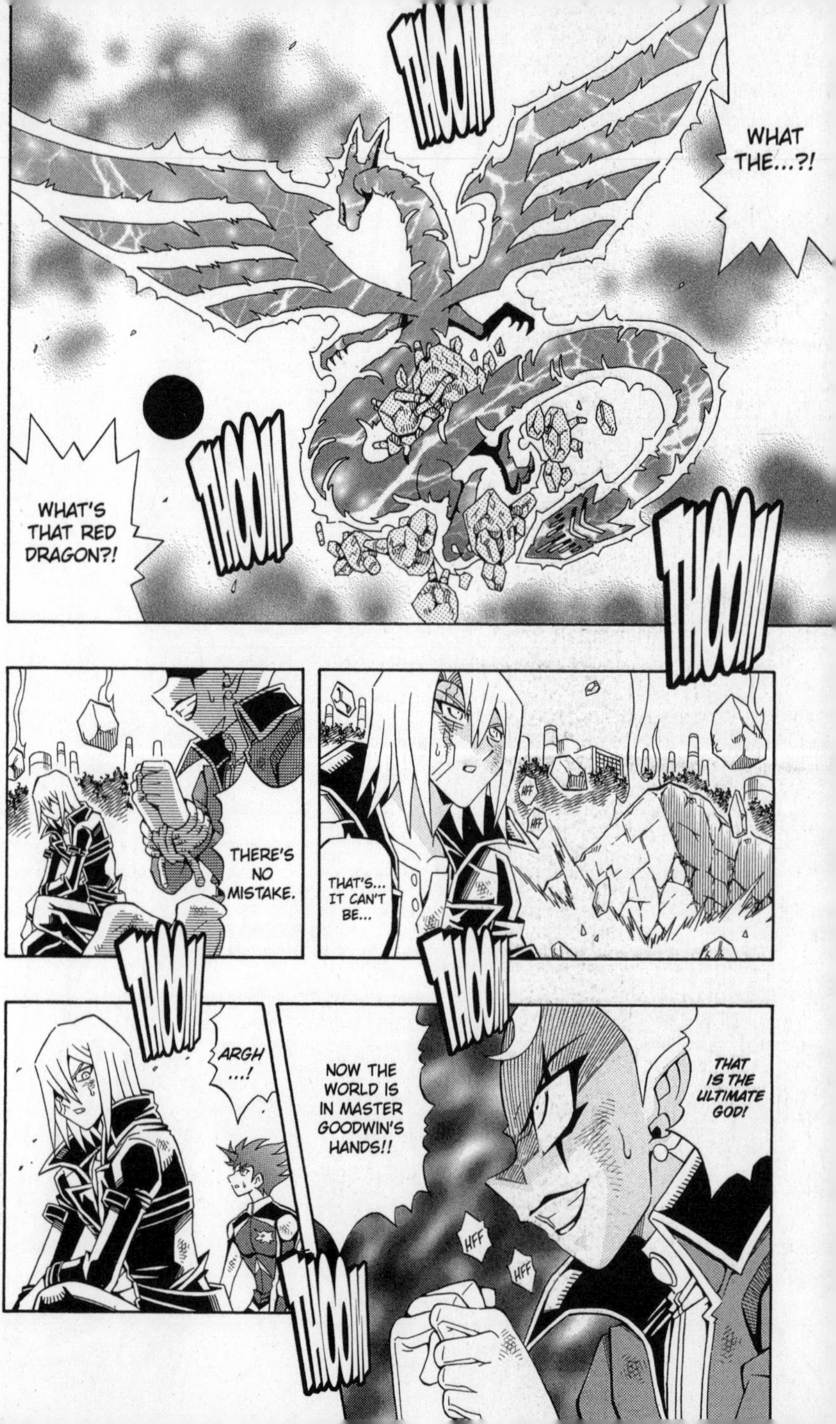
THOOM
WHAT THE...?!
THOOM
WHAT'S THAT RED DRAGON?!
THOOM
HFF
HFF
THAT'S... IT CAN'T BE...
THOOM
THERE'S NO MISTAKE.
THOOM
THAT IS THE ULTIMATE GOD!
NOW THE WORLD IS IN MASTER GOODWIN'S HANDS!!
HFF
HFF
THOOM
ARGH ...!

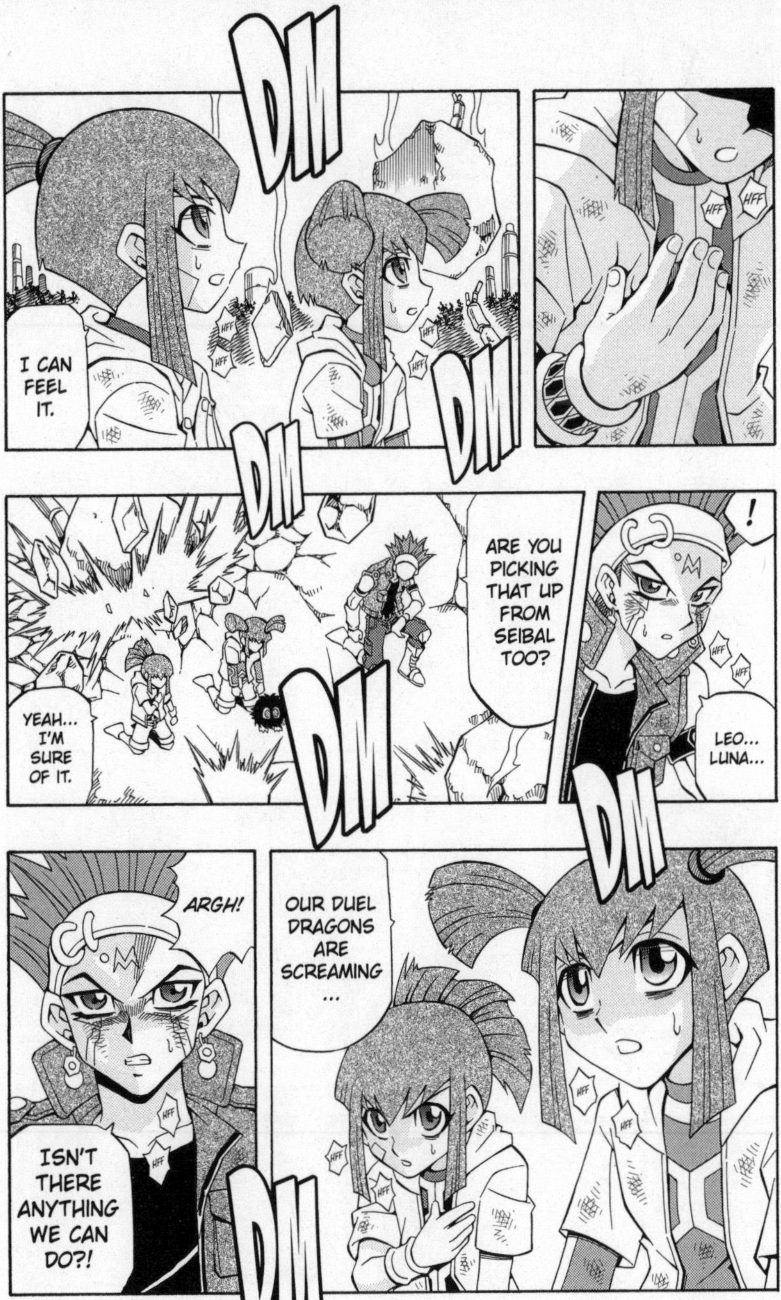
HFF
HFF
DM
DM
I CAN FEEL IT.
HFF
HFF
HFF
HFF
DM
!
LEO... LUNA...
HFF
HFF
ARE YOU PICKING THAT UP FROM SEIBAL TOO?
DM
YEAH... I'M SURE OF IT.
DM
OUR DUEL DRAGONS ARE SCREAMING...
HFF
HFF
HFF
HFF
ARGH!
HFF
HFF
ISN'T THERE ANYTHING WE CAN DO?!
DM

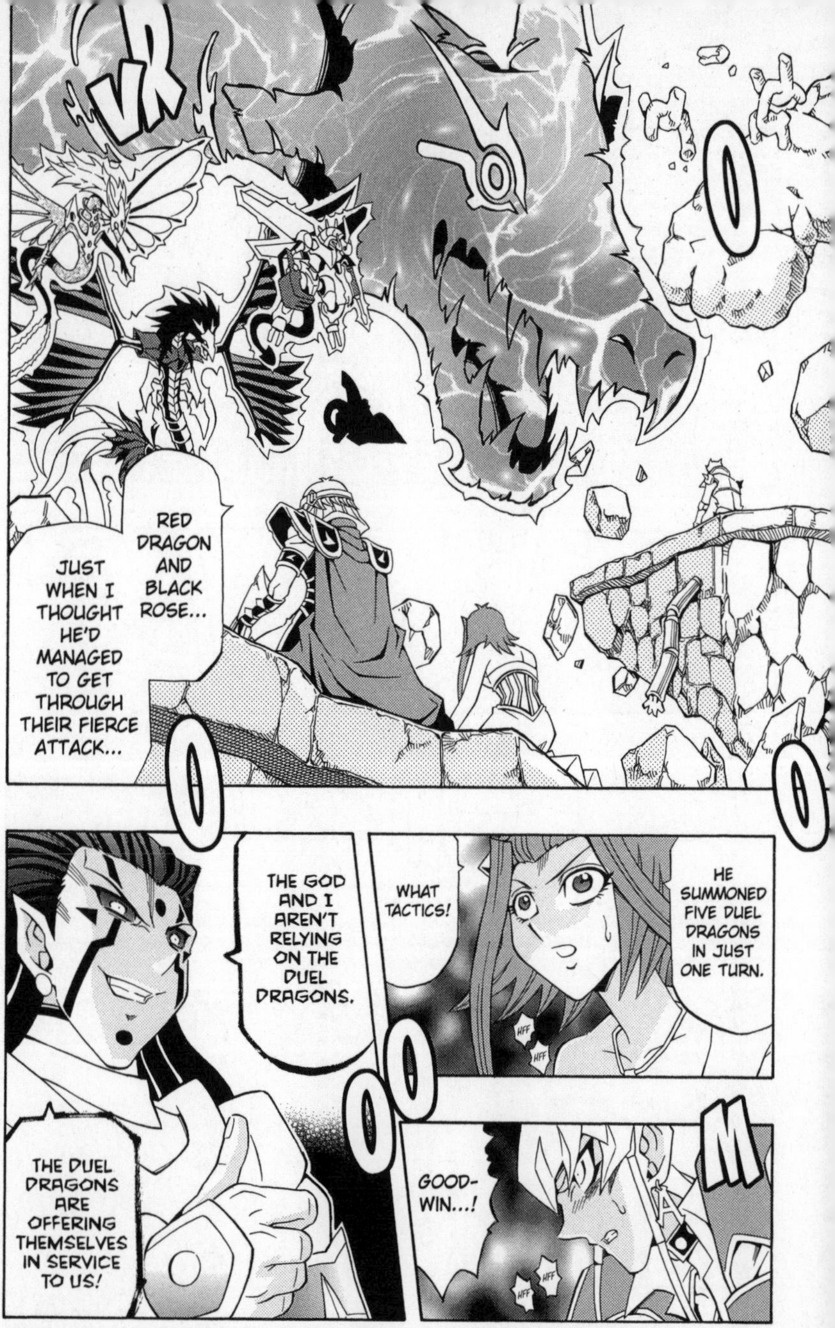
VR
RED DRAGON AND BLACK ROSE...
JUST WHEN I THOUGHT HE'D MANAGED TO GET THROUGH THEIR FIERCE ATTACK...
HE SUMMONED FIVE DUEL DRAGONS IN JUST ONE TURN.
WHAT TACTICS!
HFF
HFF
M
GOOD-WIN...!
HFF
HFF
HFF
THE GOD AND I AREN'T RELYING ON THE DUEL DRAGONS.
THE DUEL DRAGONS ARE OFFERING THEMSELVES IN SERVICE TO US!

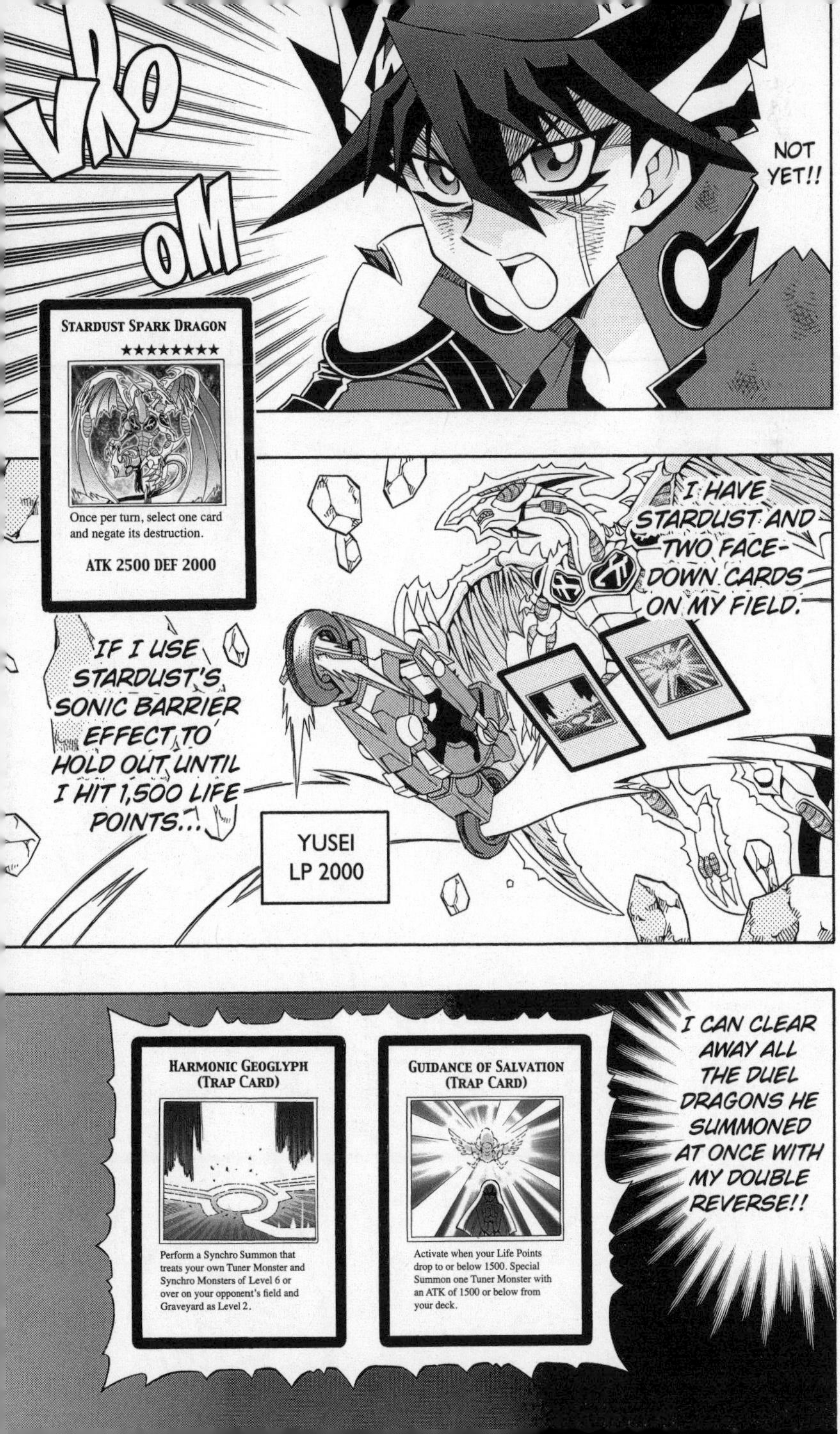
VROOM
NOT YET!!
STARDUST SPARK DRAGON
★★★★★★★★
Once per turn, select one card and negate its destruction.
ATK 2500 DEF 2000
I HAVE STARDUST AND TWO FACE-DOWN CARDS ON MY FIELD.
IF I USE STARDUST'S SONIC BARRIER EFFECT TO HOLD OUT UNTIL I HIT 1,500 LIFE POINTS...
YUSEI LP 2000
I CAN CLEAR AWAY ALL THE DUEL DRAGONS HE SUMMONED AT ONCE WITH MY DOUBLE REVERSE!!
GUIDANCE OF SALVATION (TRAP CARD)
Activate when your Life Points drop to or below 1500. Special Summon one Tuner Monster with an ATK of 1500 or below from your deck.
HARMONIC GEOGLYPH (TRAP CARD)
Perform a Synchro Summon that treats your own Tuner Monster and Synchro Monsters of Level 6 or over on your opponent's field and Graveyard as Level 2.

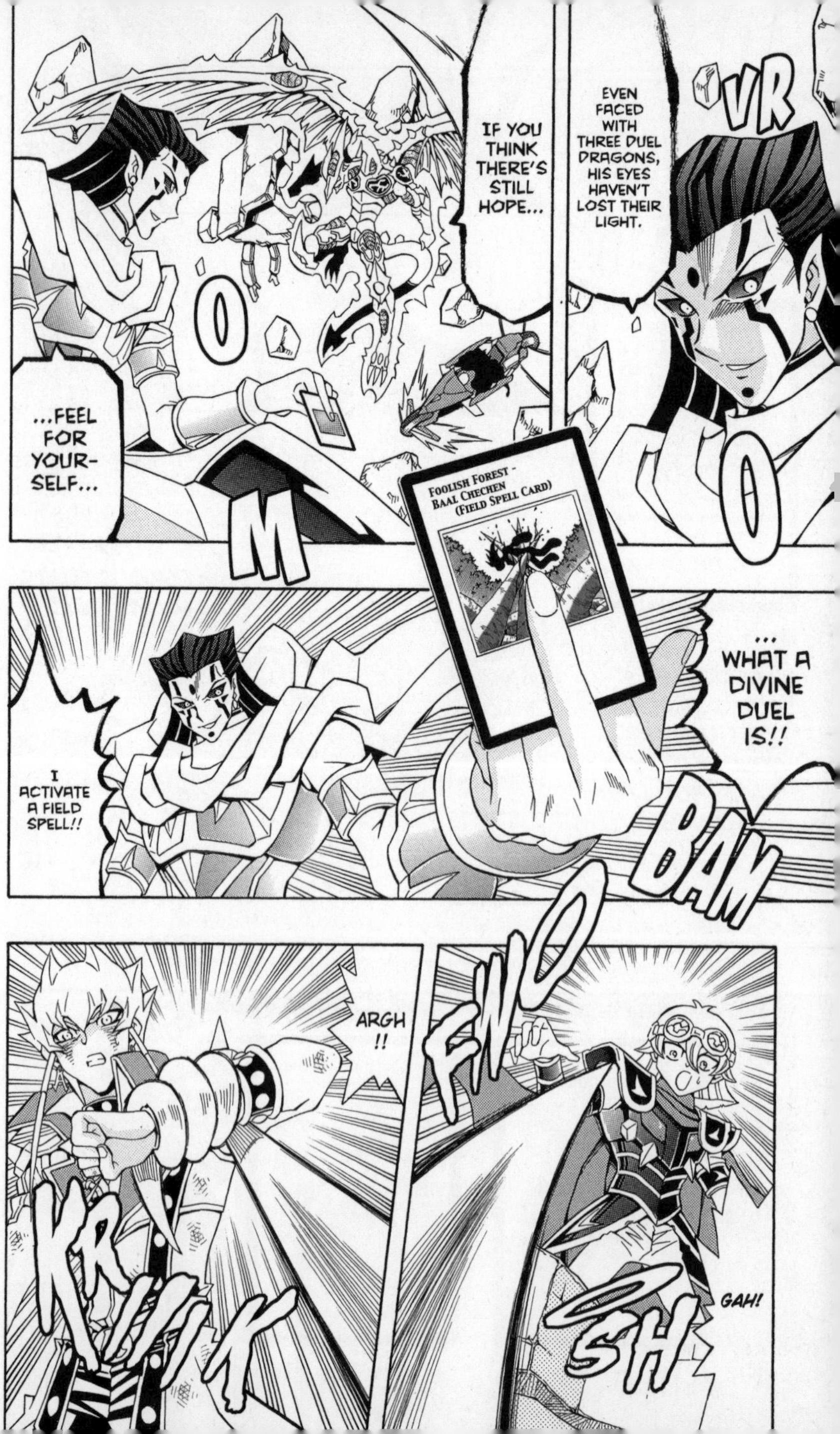
VR
EVEN FACED WITH THREE DUEL DRAGONS, HIS EYES HAVEN'T LOST THEIR LIGHT.
O
IF YOU THINK THERE'S STILL HOPE...
...FEEL FOR YOURSELF...
O
M
...WHAT A DIVINE DUEL IS!!
FOOLISH FOREST - BAAL CHECHEN (FIELD SPELL CARD)
BAM
I ACTIVATE A FIELD SPELL!!
FWO
GAH!
OSH
ARGH!!
KR
K

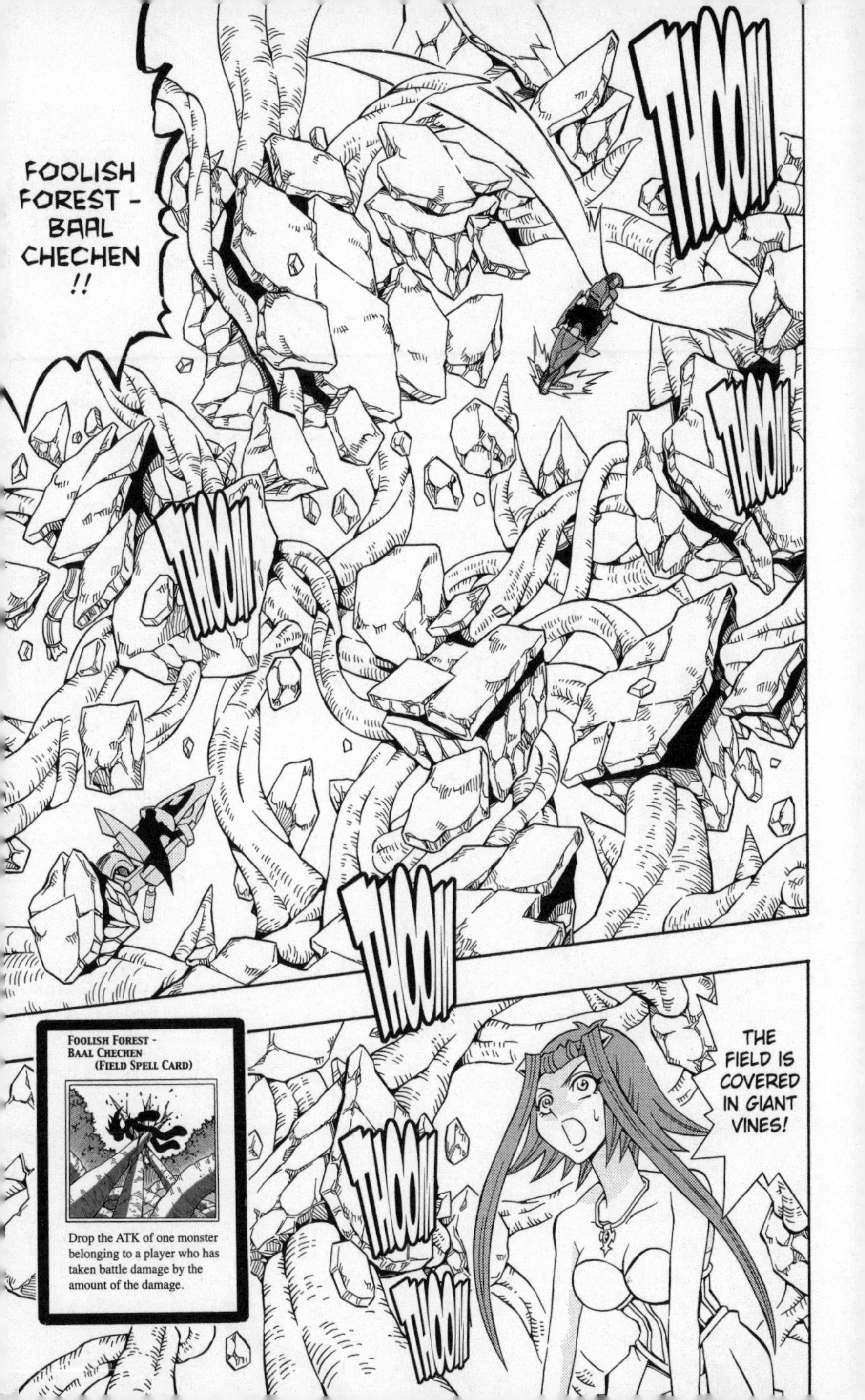
THOOM
FOOLISH FOREST - BAAL CHECHEN !!
THOOM
THOOM
THOOM
THE FIELD IS COVERED IN GIANT VINES!
THOOM
THOOM
Foolish Forest - Baal Chechen (Field Spell Card)
Drop the ATK of one monster belonging to a player who has taken battle damage by the amount of the damage.

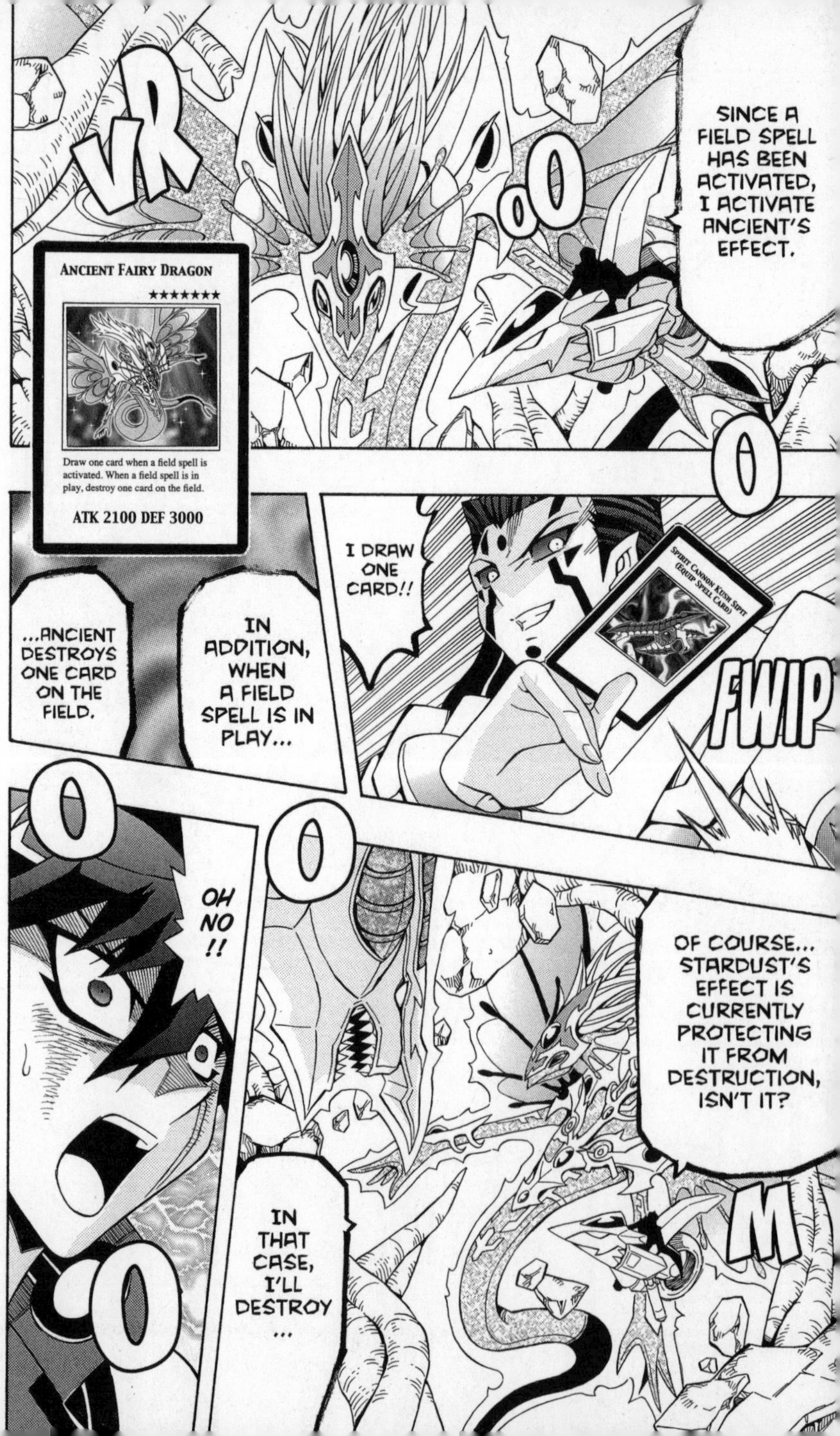
VR
SINCE A FIELD SPELL HAS BEEN ACTIVATED, I ACTIVATE ANCIENT'S EFFECT.
ANCIENT FAIRY DRAGON
Draw one card when a field spell is activated. When a field spell is in play, destroy one card on the field.
ATK 2100 DEF 3000
I DRAW ONE CARD!!
SPIRIT CANNON KUSH SIPIT (EQUIP SPELL CARD)
FWIP
IN ADDITION, WHEN A FIELD SPELL IS IN PLAY...
...ANCIENT DESTROYS ONE CARD ON THE FIELD.
OF COURSE... STARDUST'S EFFECT IS CURRENTLY PROTECTING IT FROM DESTRUCTION, ISN'T IT?
M
IN THAT CASE, I'LL DESTROY...
OH NO!!

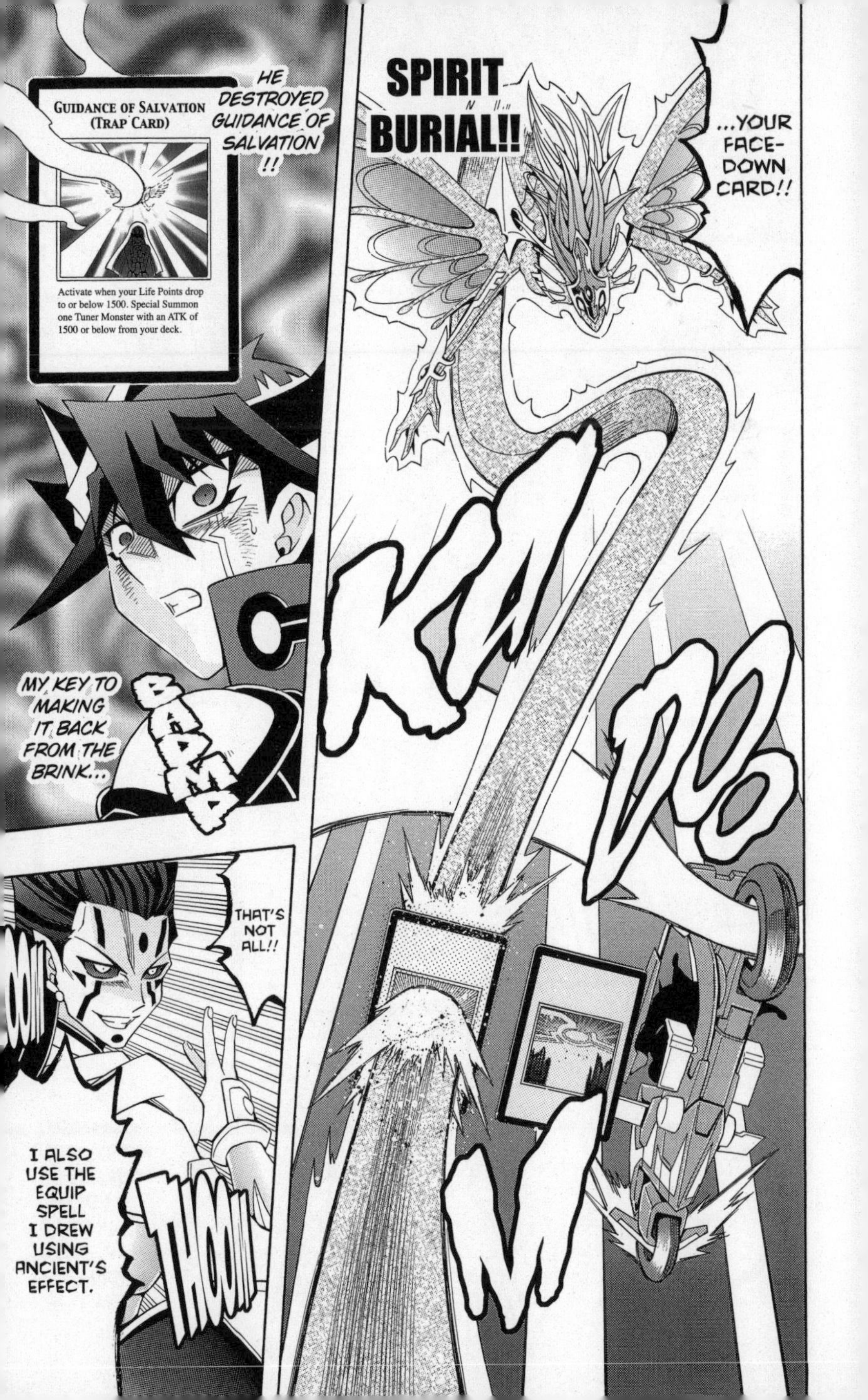
SPIRIT BURIAL!!
...YOUR FACE-DOWN CARD!!
HE DESTROYED GUIDANCE OF SALVATION!!
GUIDANCE OF SALVATION (TRAP CARD)
Activate when your Life Points drop to or below 1500. Special Summon one Tuner Monster with an ATK of 1500 or below from your deck.
MY KEY TO MAKING IT BACK FROM THE BRINK...
BAAM
THAT'S NOT ALL!!
I ALSO USE THE EQUIP SPELL I DREW USING ANCIENT'S EFFECT.
THOOM

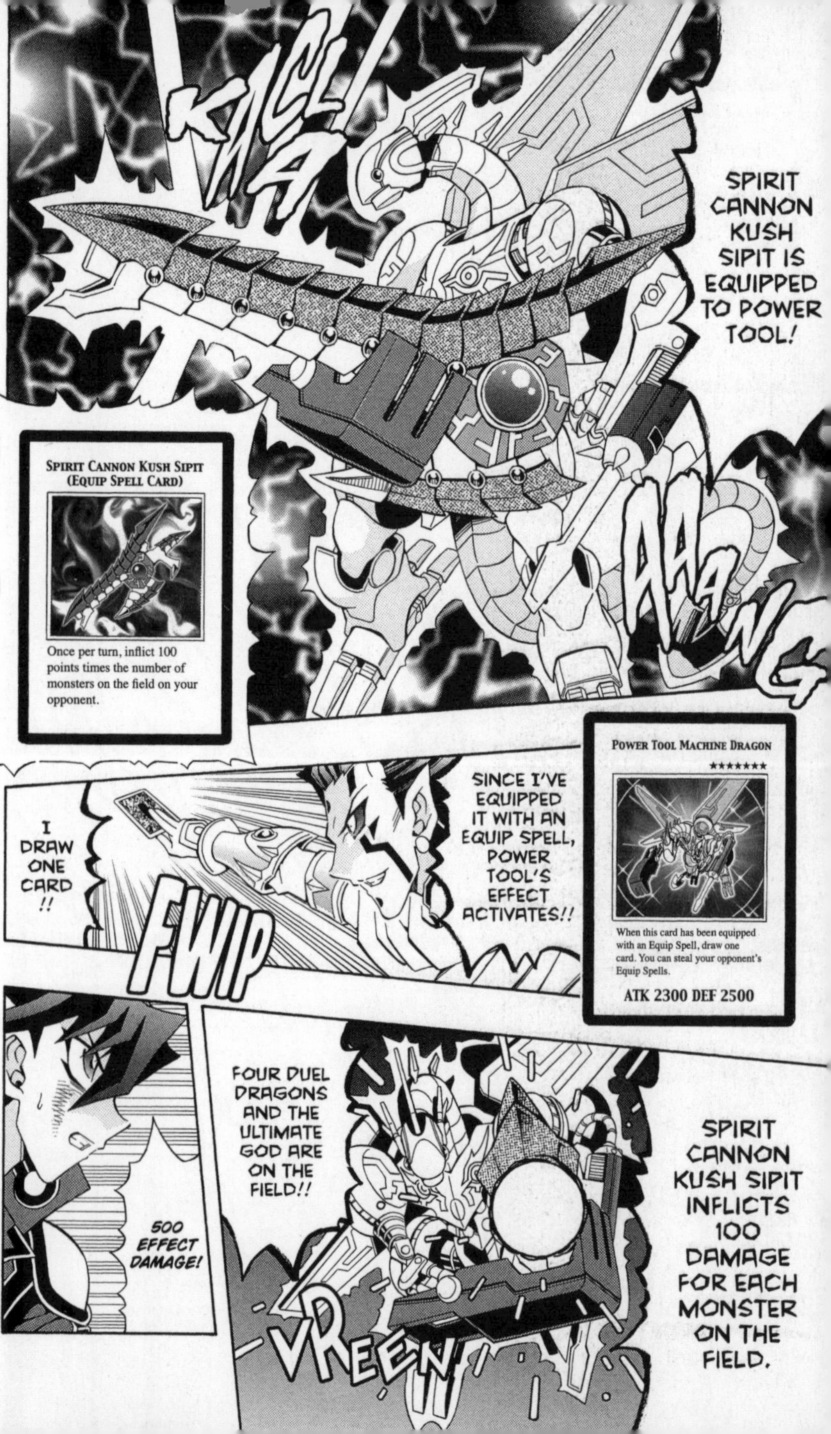
SPIRIT CANNON KUSH SIPIT IS EQUIPPED TO POWER TOOL!
SPIRIT CANNON KUSH SIPIT
(EQUIP SPELL CARD)
Once per turn, inflict 100 points times the number of monsters on the field on your opponent.
POWER TOOL MACHINE DRAGON
★★★★★★★
When this card has been equipped with an Equip Spell, draw one card. You can steal your opponent's Equip Spells.
ATK 2300 DEF 2500
SINCE I'VE EQUIPPED IT WITH AN EQUIP SPELL, POWER TOOL'S EFFECT ACTIVATES!!
I DRAW ONE CARD!!
FWIP
SPIRIT CANNON KUSH SIPIT INFLICTS 100 DAMAGE FOR EACH MONSTER ON THE FIELD.
FOUR DUEL DRAGONS AND THE ULTIMATE GOD ARE ON THE FIELD!!
VREEN
500 EFFECT DAMAGE!

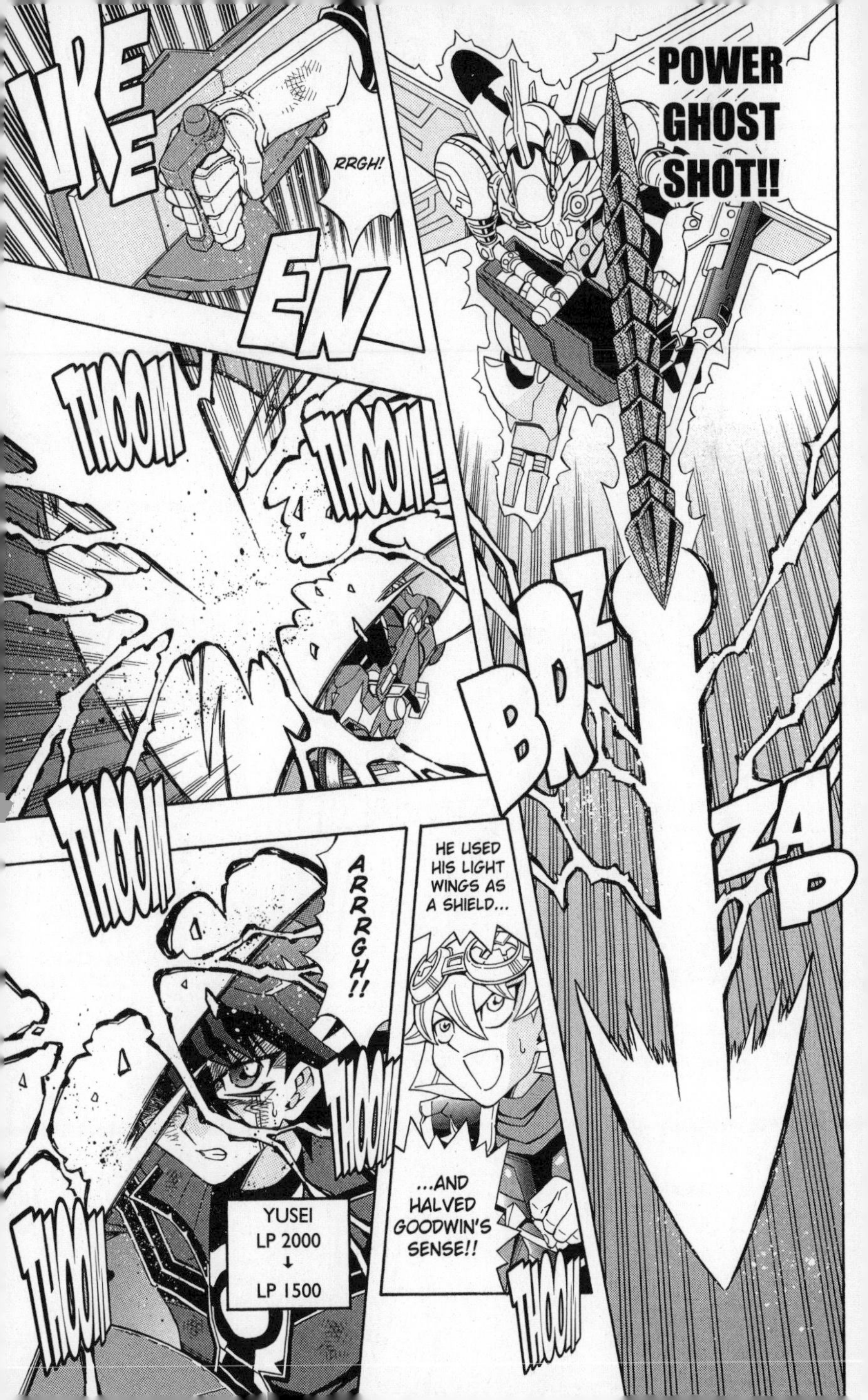

POWER GHOST SHOT!!
BRZ
ZAP
UKE
EN
RRGH!
THOOM
THOOM
HE USED HIS LIGHT WINGS AS A SHIELD...
...AND HALVED GOODWIN'S SENSE!!
THOOM
THOOM
ARRRGH!!
THOOM
YUSEI LP 2000 ↓ LP 1500
THOOM

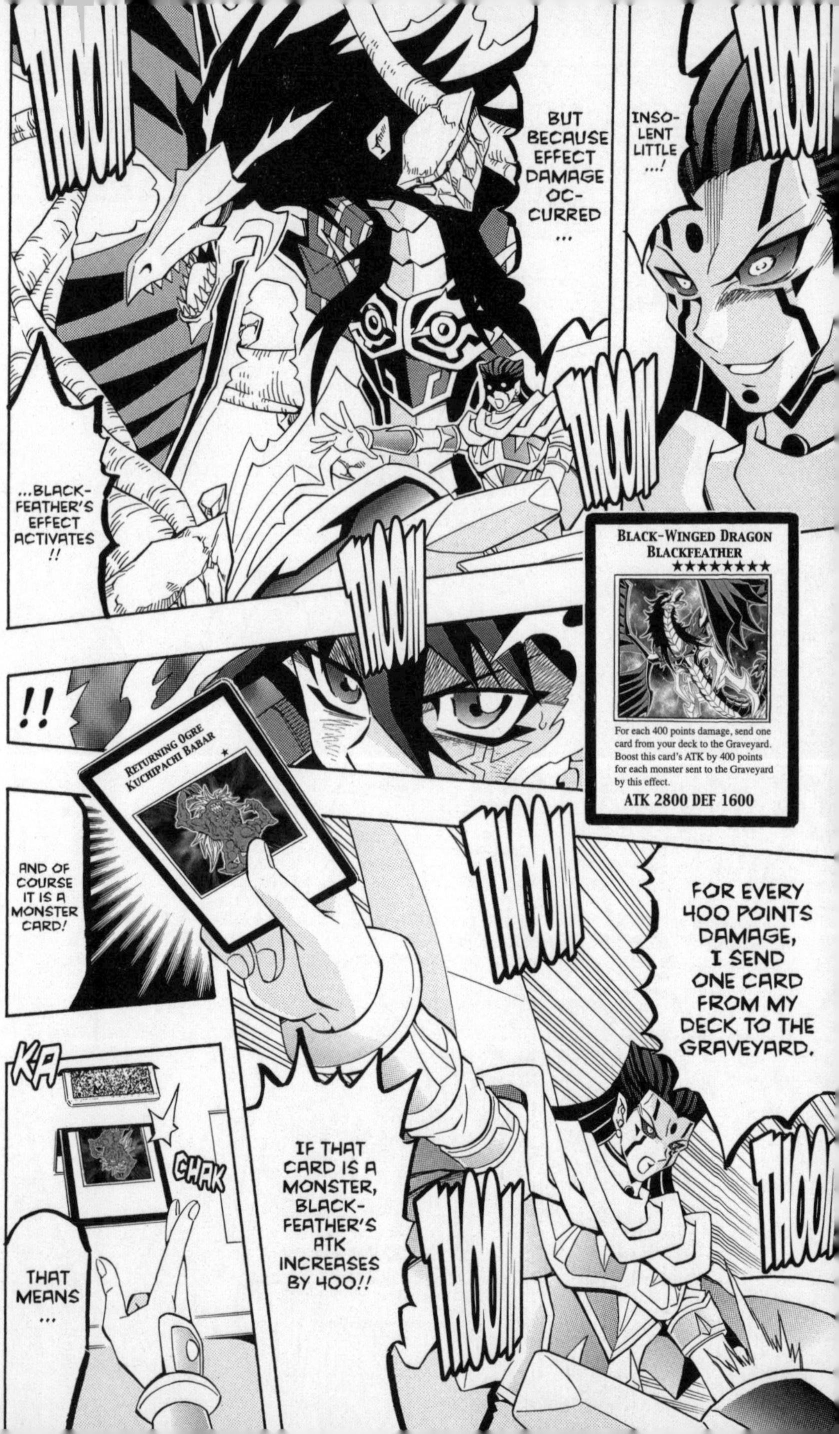
THOOM
INSO-LENT LITTLE ...!
THOOM
BUT BECAUSE EFFECT DAMAGE OC-CURRED ...
...BLACK-FEATHER'S EFFECT ACTIVATES!!
THOOM
THOOM
BLACK-WINGED DRAGON BLACKFEATHER
For each 400 points damage, send one card from your deck to the Graveyard. Boost this card's ATK by 400 points for each monster sent to the Graveyard by this effect.
ATK 2800 DEF 1600
THOOM
!!
RETURNING OGRE KUCHIPACHI BABAR
FOR EVERY 400 POINTS DAMAGE, I SEND ONE CARD FROM MY DECK TO THE GRAVEYARD.
THOOM
AND OF COURSE IT IS A MONSTER CARD!
THOOM
THOOM
IF THAT CARD IS A MONSTER, BLACK-FEATHER'S ATK INCREASES BY 400!!
K-A
CHAK
THAT MEANS ...

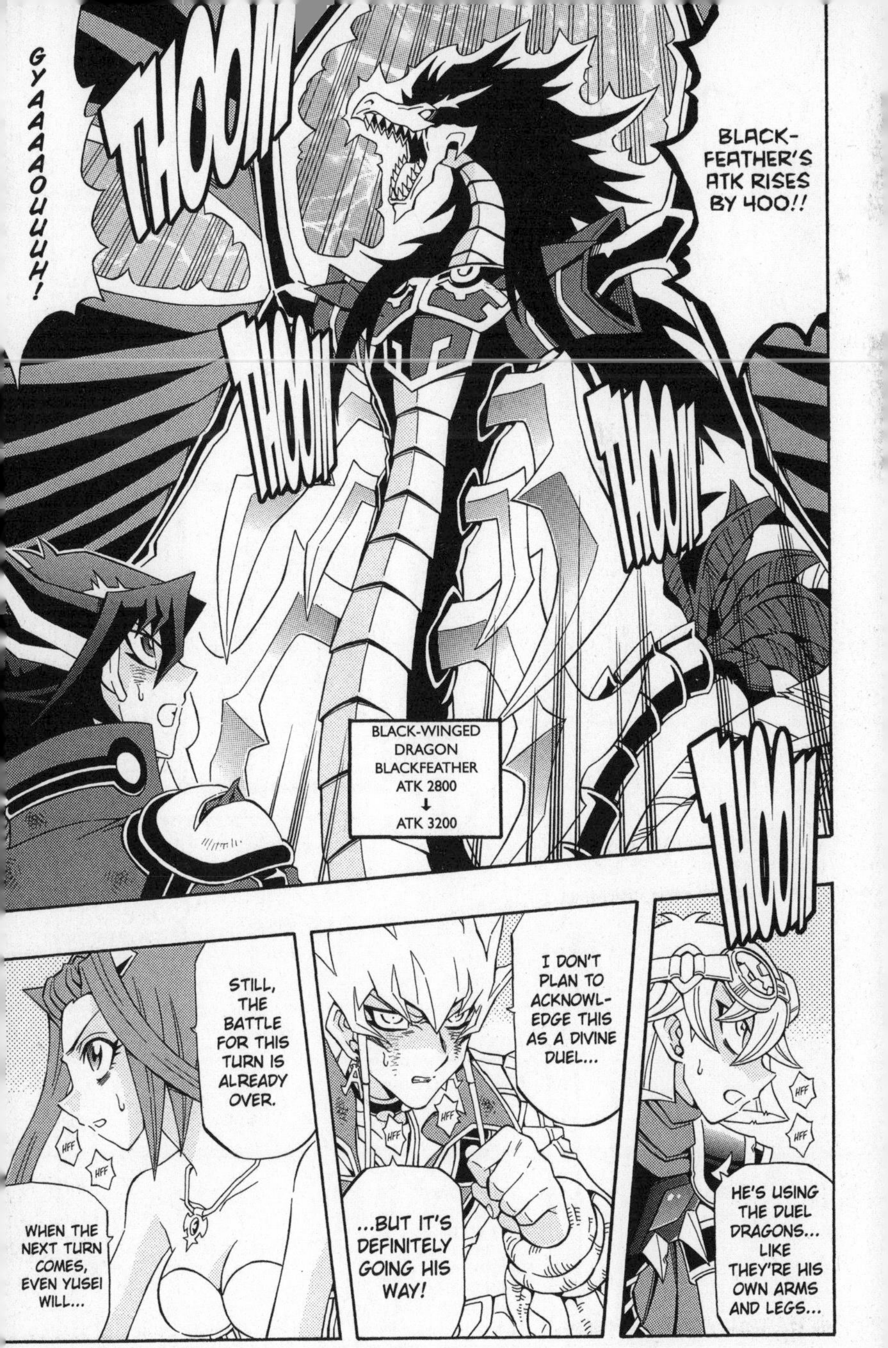
BLACK-FEATHER'S ATK RISES BY 400!!
THOOM
GYAAAAOUUUH!
THOOM
THOOM
BLACK-WINGED DRAGON BLACKFEATHER ATK 2800 ↓ ATK 3200
THOOM
HFF
HFF
HE'S USING THE DUEL DRAGONS... LIKE THEY'RE HIS OWN ARMS AND LEGS...
I DON'T PLAN TO ACKNOWLEDGE THIS AS A DIVINE DUEL...
HFF
HFF
...BUT IT'S DEFINITELY GOING HIS WAY!
STILL, THE BATTLE FOR THIS TURN IS ALREADY OVER.
HFF
HFF
WHEN THE NEXT TURN COMES, EVEN YUSEI WILL...

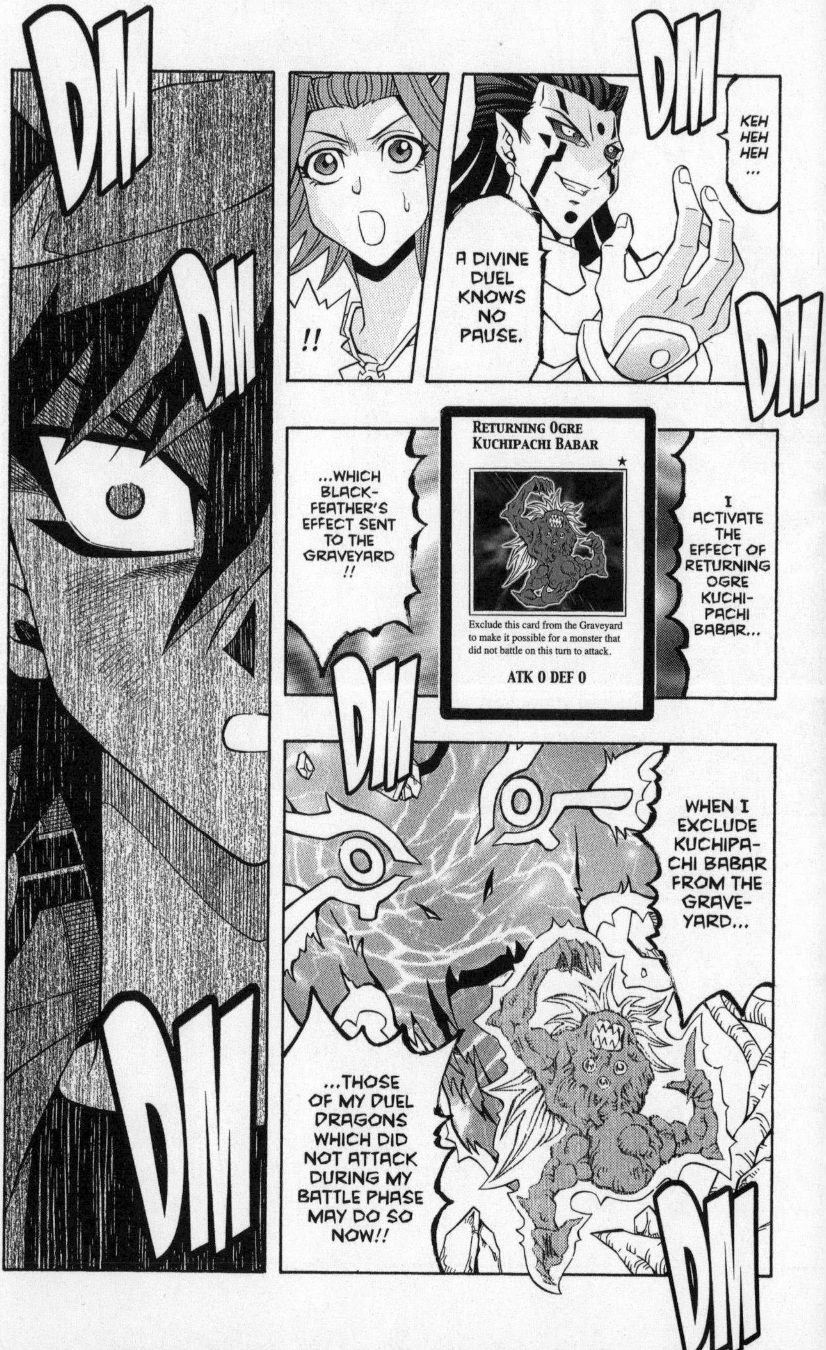
DM
KEH HEH HEH ...
A DIVINE DUEL KNOWS NO PAUSE.
DM
!!
I ACTIVATE THE EFFECT OF RETURNING OGRE KUCHIPACHI BABAR...
RETURNING OGRE KUCHIPACHI BABAR
★
Exclude this card from the Graveyard to make it possible for a monster that did not battle on this turn to attack.
ATK 0 DEF 0
...WHICH BLACK-FEATHER'S EFFECT SENT TO THE GRAVEYARD !!
DM
WHEN I EXCLUDE KUCHIPA-CHI BABAR FROM THE GRAVE-YARD...
...THOSE OF MY DUEL DRAGONS WHICH DID NOT ATTACK DURING MY BATTLE PHASE MAY DO SO NOW!!
DM
DM
DM
DM

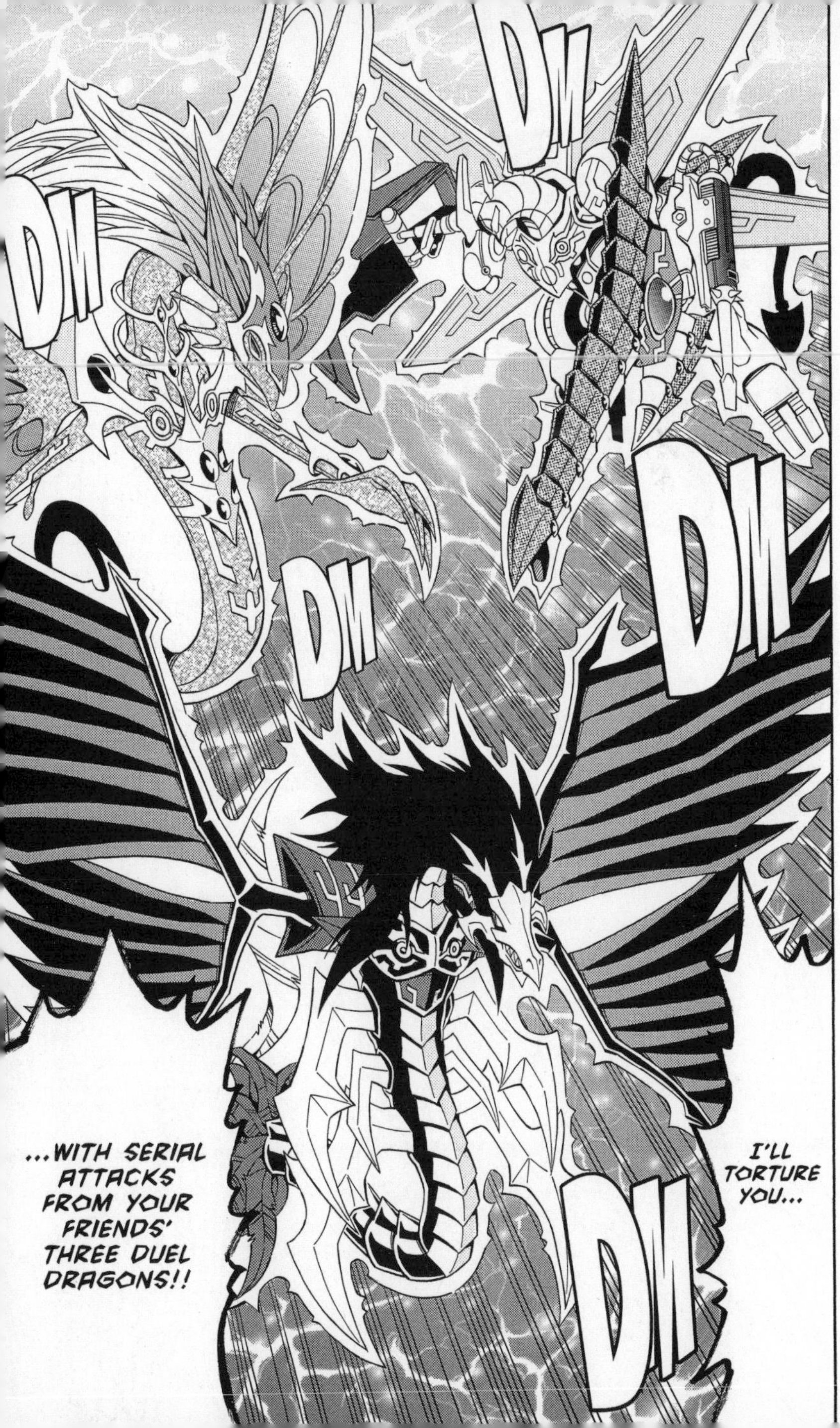
DM
DM
DM
DM
DM
DM
I'LL TORTURE YOU...
...WITH SERIAL ATTACKS FROM YOUR FRIENDS' THREE DUEL DRAGONS!!

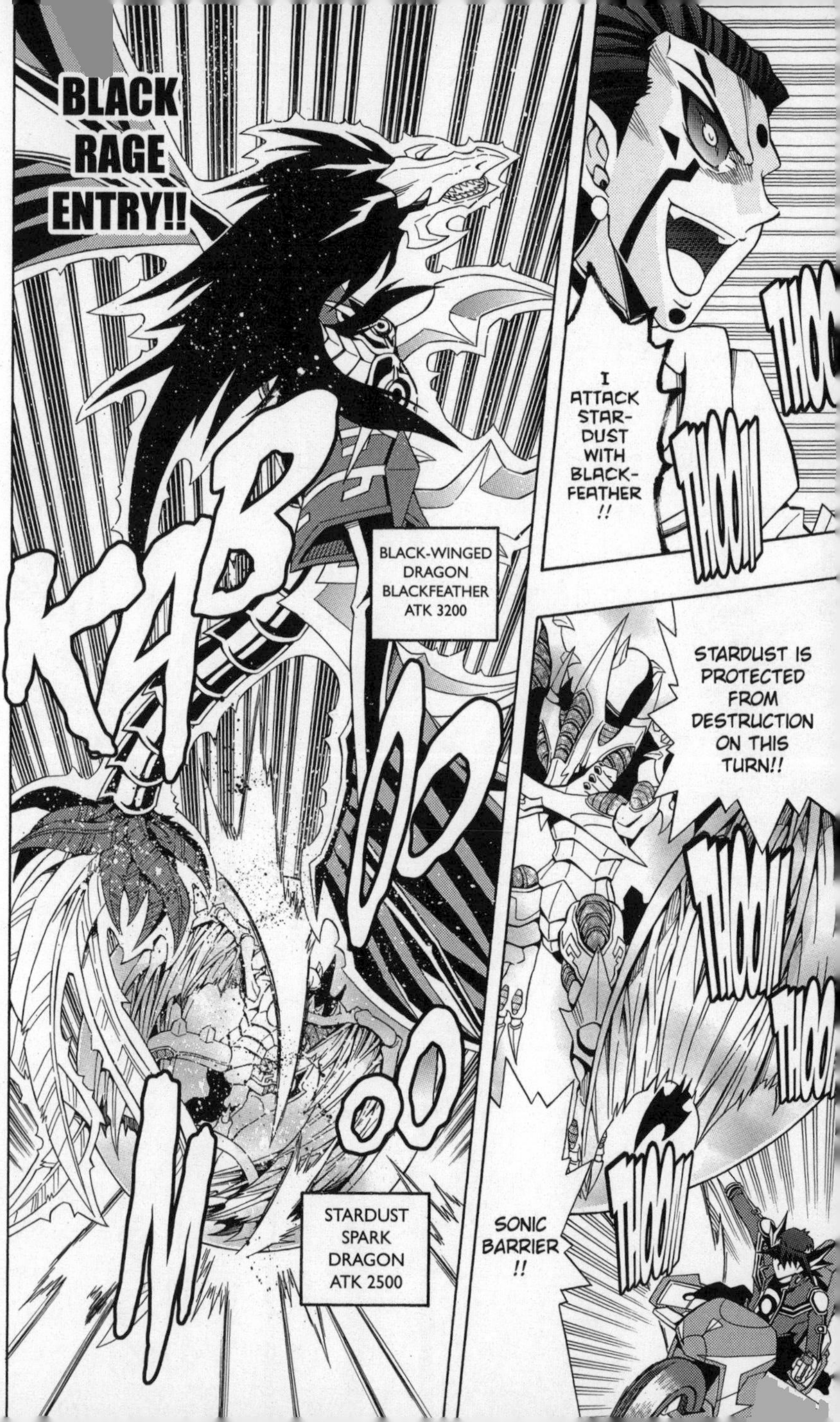
I ATTACK STAR-DUST WITH BLACK-FEATHER!!
THOO
THOOM
STARDUST IS PROTECTED FROM DESTRUCTION ON THIS TURN!!
THOOM
THOO
THOOM
SONIC BARRIER!!
BLACK RAGE ENTRY!!
BLACK-WINGED DRAGON BLACKFEATHER ATK 3200
KABOOOOM
STARDUST SPARK DRAGON ATK 2500

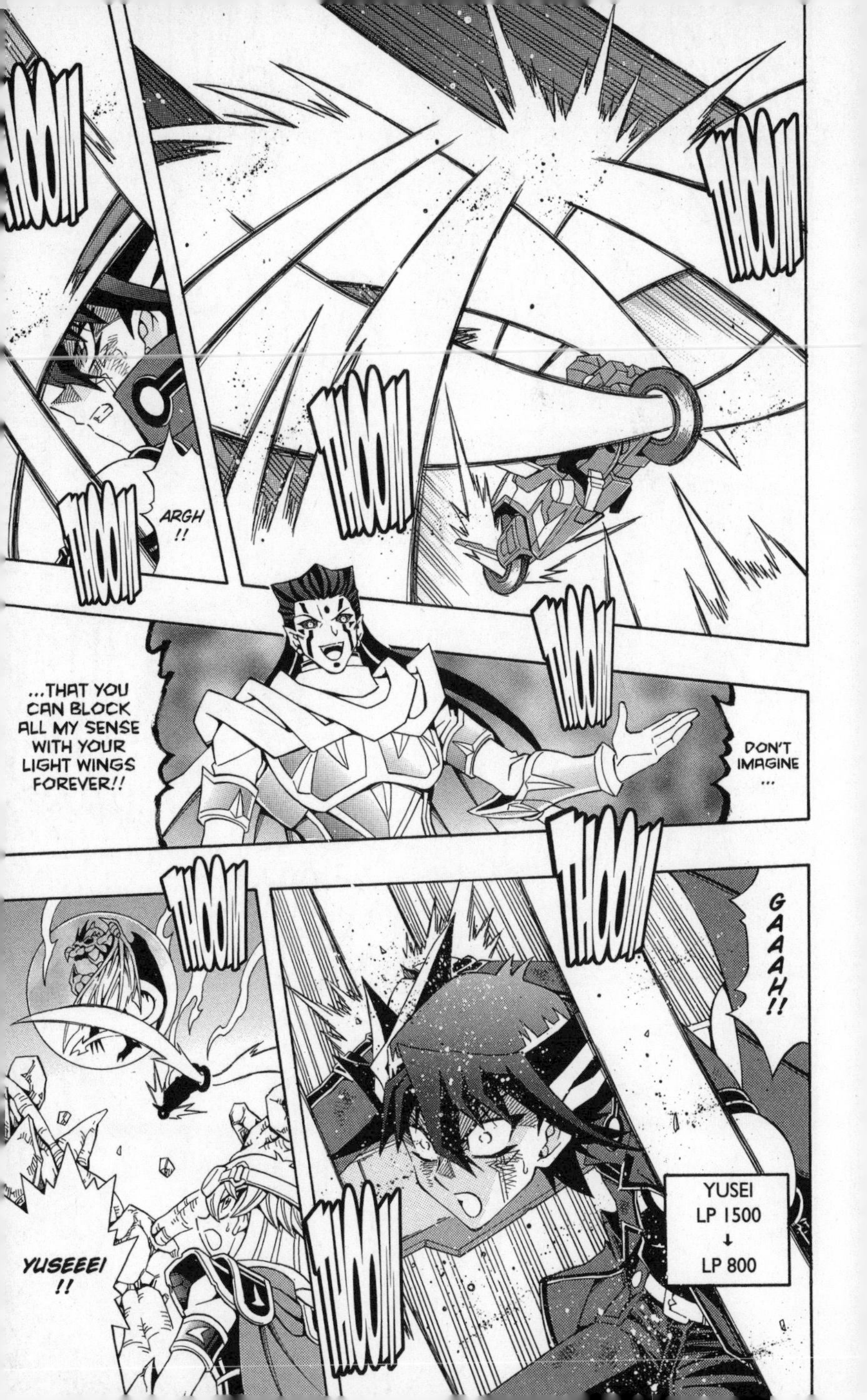
THOOM
THOOM
THOOM
THOOM
ARGH!!
THOOM
DON'T IMAGINE...
...THAT YOU CAN BLOCK ALL MY SENSE WITH YOUR LIGHT WINGS FOREVER!!
THOOM
GAAAAH!!
THOOM
THOOM
YUSEI LP 1500 ↓ LP 800
THOOM
YUSEEEI!!

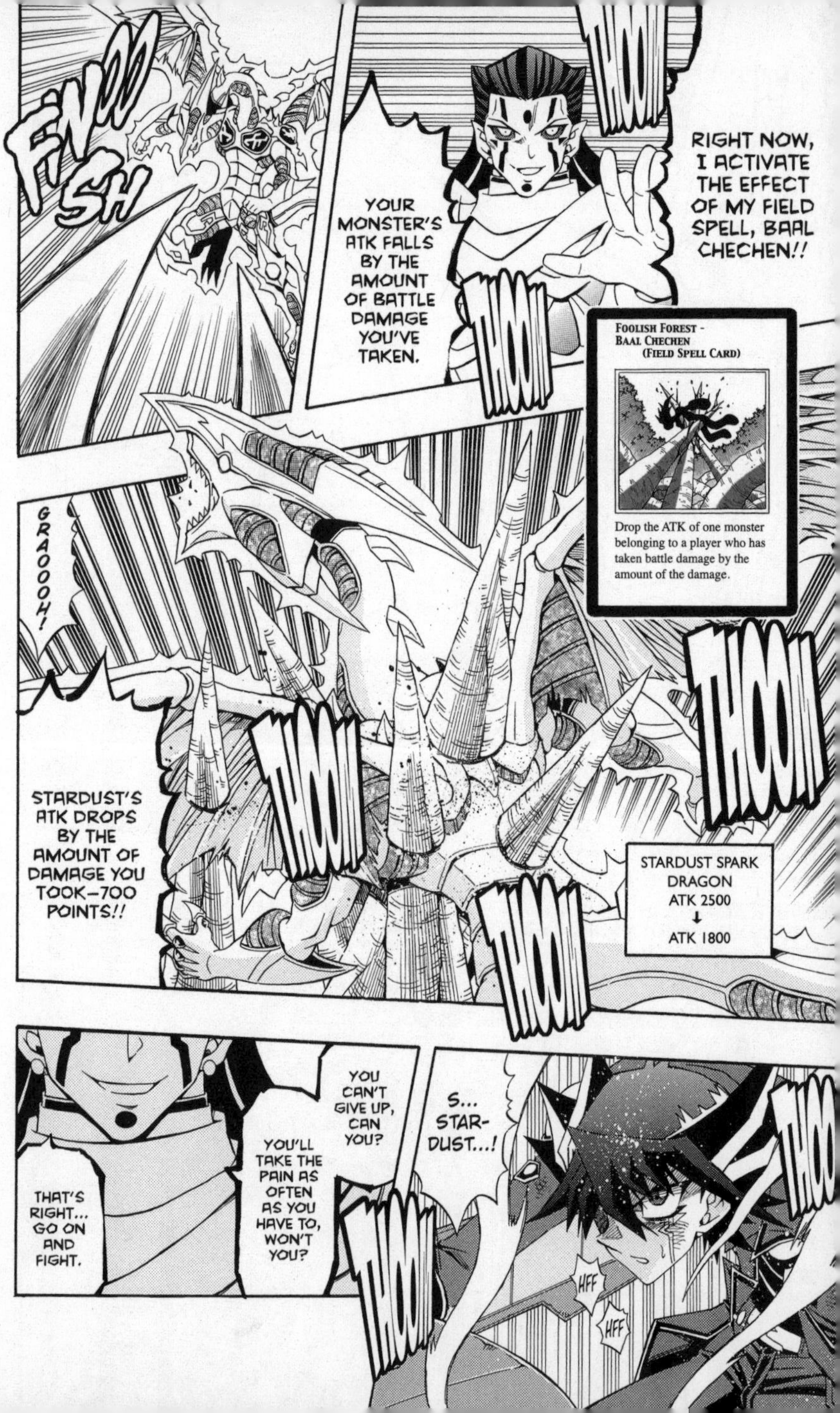

RIGHT NOW, I ACTIVATE THE EFFECT OF MY FIELD SPELL, BAAL CHECHEN!!
THOOM
YOUR MONSTER'S ATK FALLS BY THE AMOUNT OF BATTLE DAMAGE YOU'VE TAKEN.
THOOM
FINOOSH
FOOLISH FOREST - BAAL CHECHEN (FIELD SPELL CARD)
Drop the ATK of one monster belonging to a player who has taken battle damage by the amount of the damage.
THOOM
GRAOOOOH!
THOOM
STARDUST'S ATK DROPS BY THE AMOUNT OF DAMAGE YOU TOOK—700 POINTS!!
STARDUST SPARK DRAGON ATK 2500 ↓ ATK 1800
THOOM
THOOM
S... STAR-DUST...!
HFF
HFF
THOOM
YOU CAN'T GIVE UP, CAN YOU?
YOU'LL TAKE THE PAIN AS OFTEN AS YOU HAVE TO, WON'T YOU?
THAT'S RIGHT... GO ON AND FIGHT.

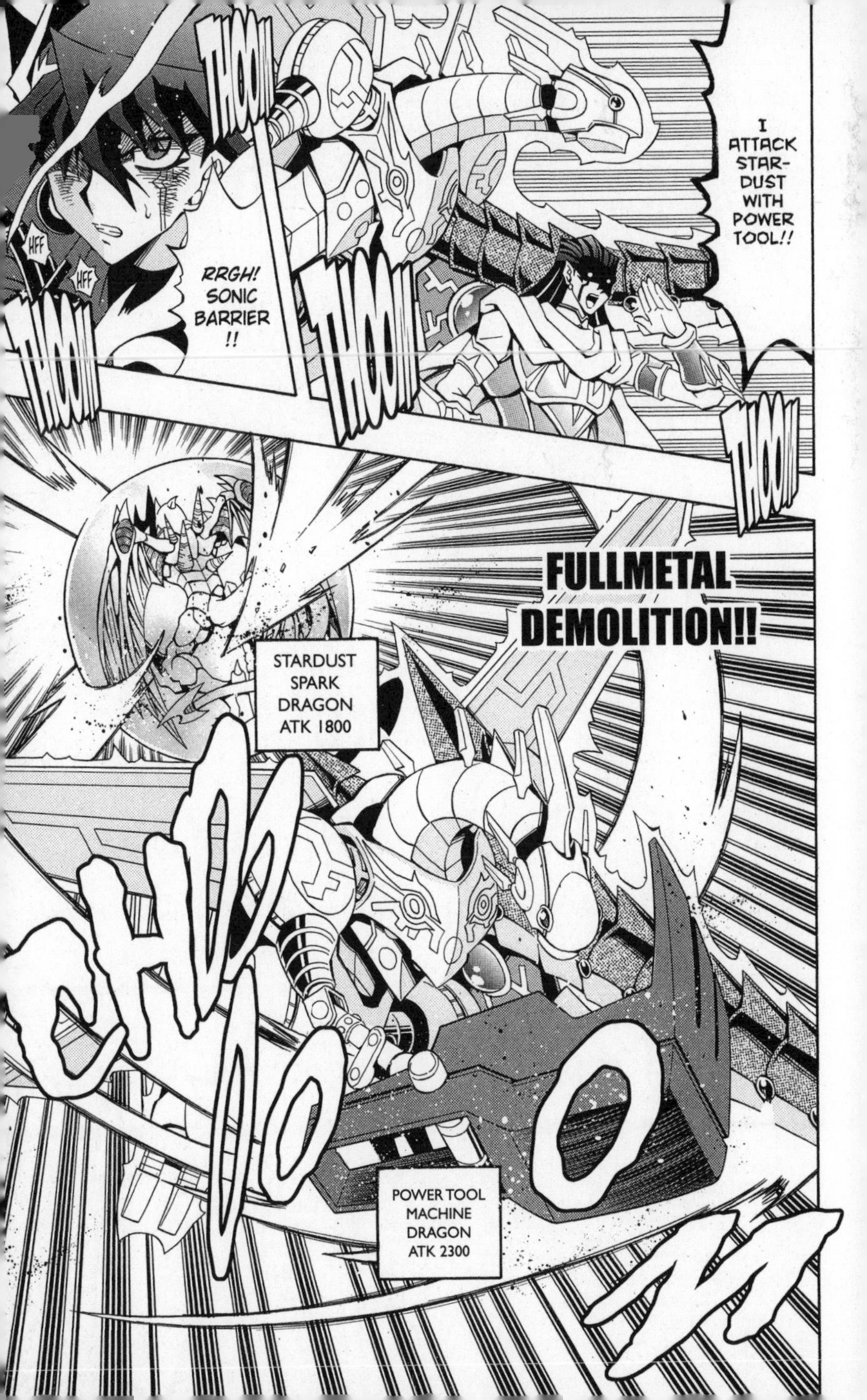
I ATTACK STARDUST WITH POWER TOOL!!
THOOM
THOOM
THOOM
HFF
HFF
RRGH! SONIC BARRIER!!
THOOM
FULLMETAL DEMOLITION!!
STARDUST SPARK DRAGON ATK 1800
POWER TOOL MACHINE DRAGON ATK 2300

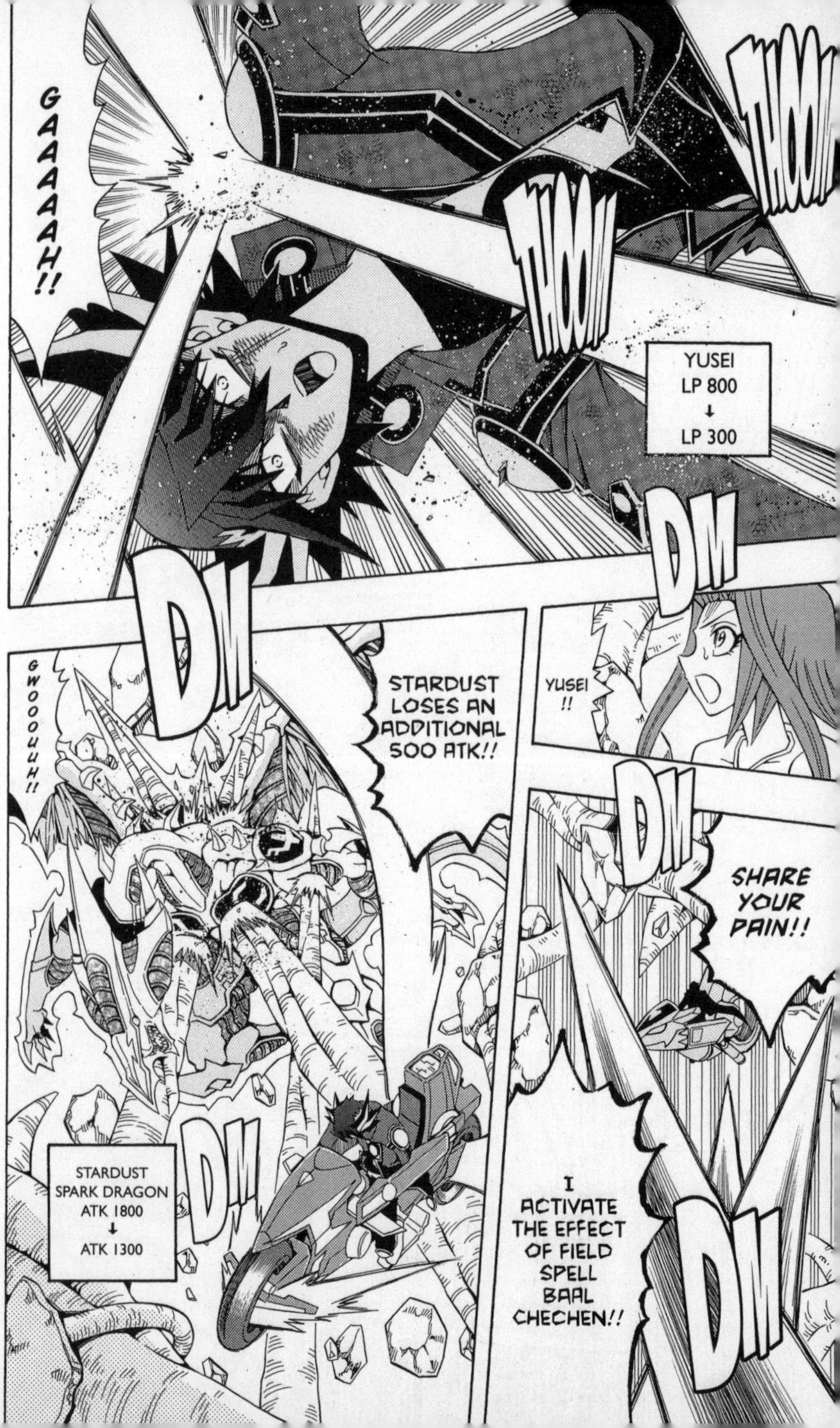

THOOM
THOOM
YUSEI
LP 800
↓
LP 300
GAAAAAAH!!
DM
DM
YUSEI!!
DM
SHARE YOUR PAIN!!
I ACTIVATE THE EFFECT OF FIELD SPELL BAAL CHECHEN!!
DM
STARDUST LOSES AN ADDITIONAL 500 ATK!!
GWOOOOUUH!!
STARDUST SPARK DRAGON
ATK 1800
↓
ATK 1300
DM

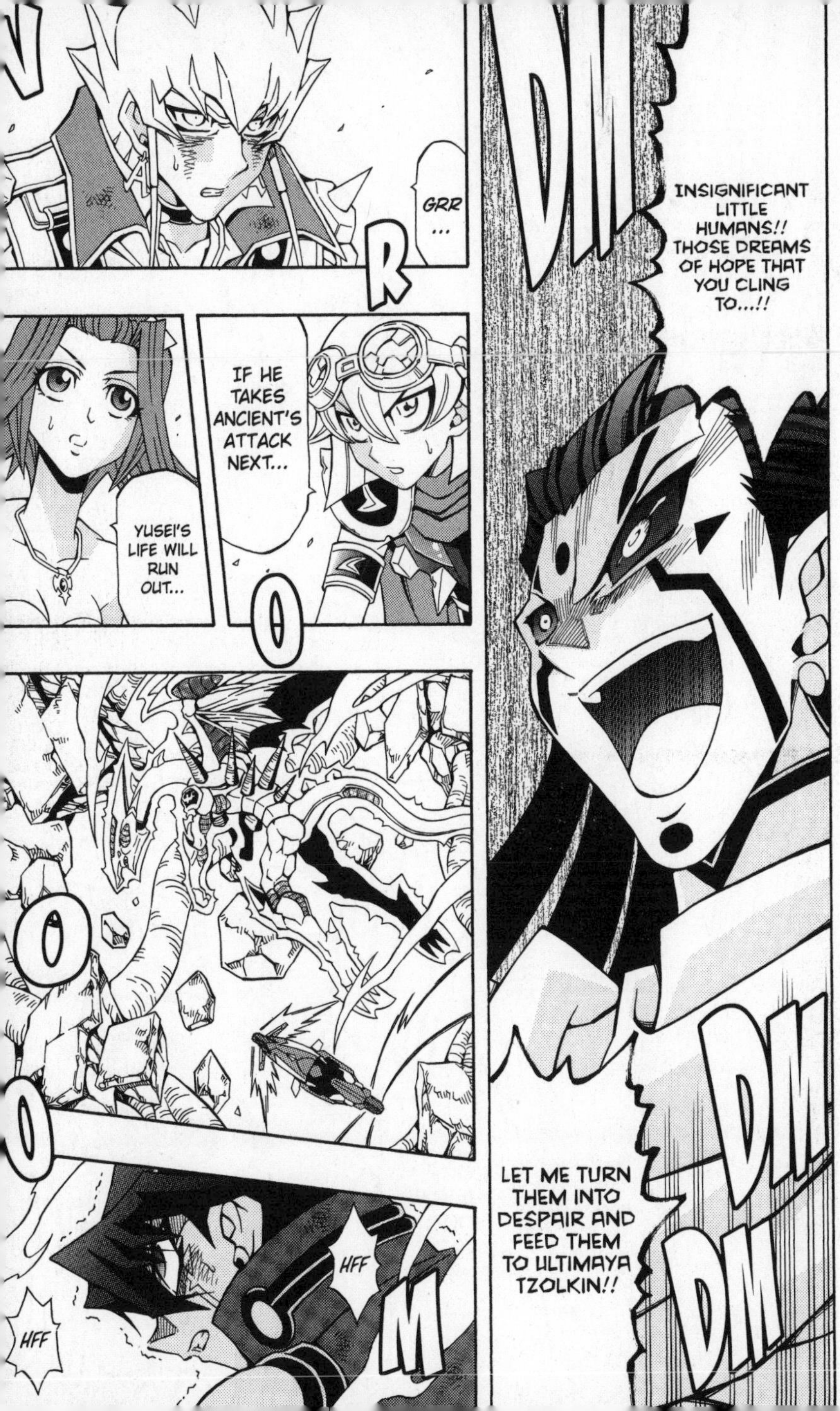

INSIGNIFICANT LITTLE HUMANS!! THOSE DREAMS OF HOPE THAT YOU CLING TO...!!
LET ME TURN THEM INTO DESPAIR AND FEED THEM TO ULTIMAYA TZOLKIN!!
DM
DM
GRR...
IF HE TAKES ANCIENT'S ATTACK NEXT...
YUSEI'S LIFE WILL RUN OUT...
HFF
HFF

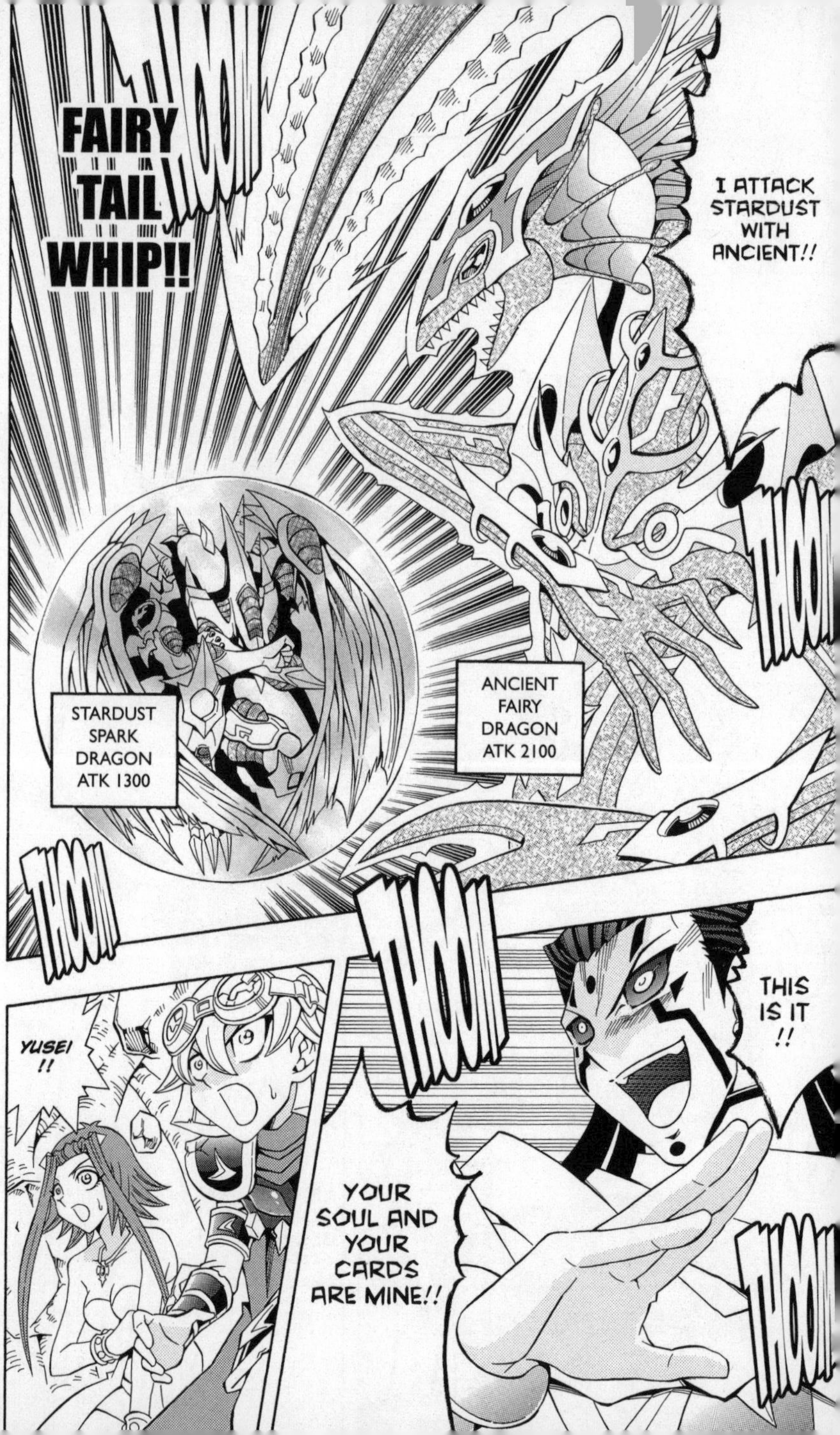
I ATTACK STARDUST WITH ANCIENT!!
FAIRY TAIL WHIP!!
THOOM
ANCIENT FAIRY DRAGON ATK 2100
STARDUST SPARK DRAGON ATK 1300
THOOM
THOOM
THIS IS IT!!
YOUR SOUL AND YOUR CARDS ARE MINE!!
THOOM
YUSEI!!

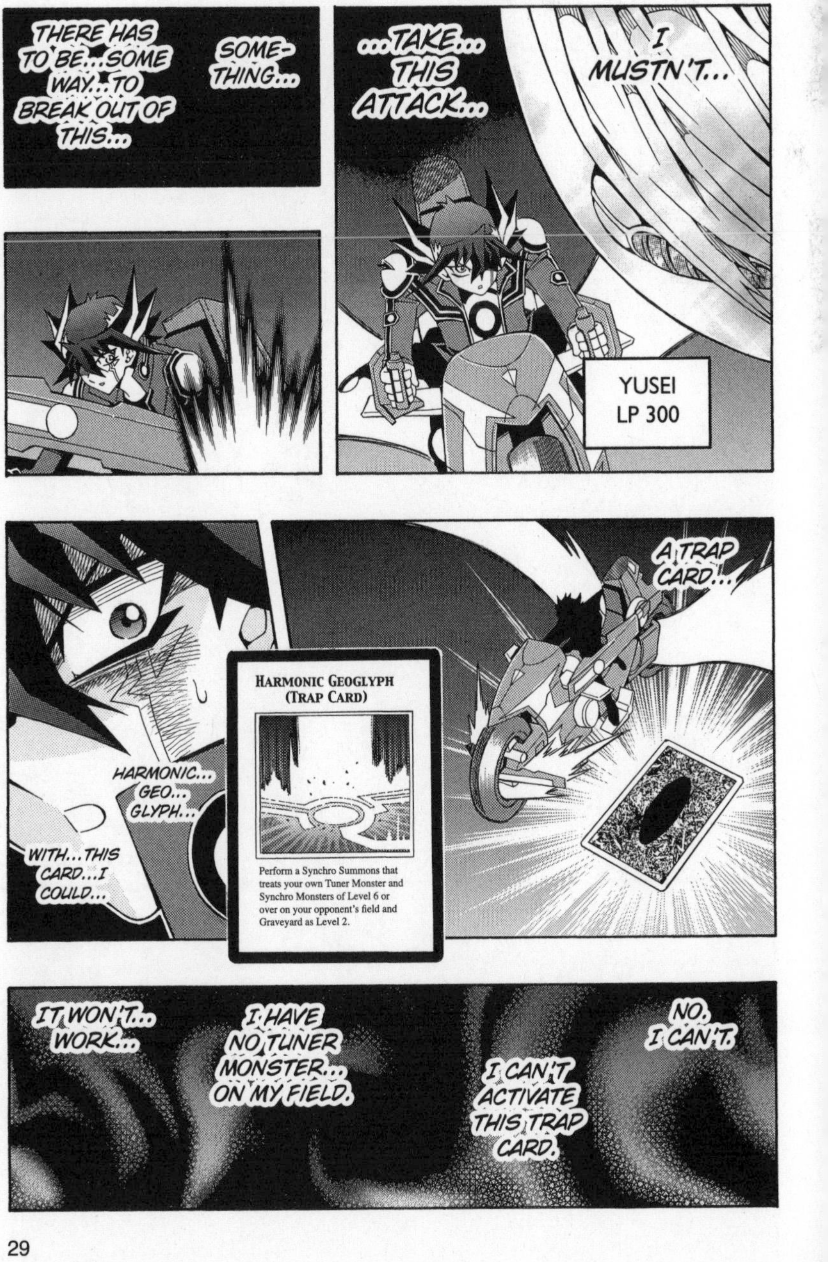
I MUSTN'T...
...TAKE... THIS ATTACK...
YUSEI LP 300
SOME-THING...
THERE HAS TO BE...SOME WAY...TO BREAK OUT OF THIS...
A TRAP CARD...
HARMONIC GEOGLYPH (TRAP CARD)
Perform a Synchro Summons that treats your own Tuner Monster and Synchro Monsters of Level 6 or over on your opponent's field and Graveyard as Level 2.
HARMONIC... GEO... GLYPH...
WITH...THIS CARD...I COULD...
NO. I CAN'T.
I CAN'T ACTIVATE THIS TRAP CARD.
I HAVE NO TUNER MONSTER... ON MY FIELD.
IT WON'T... WORK...

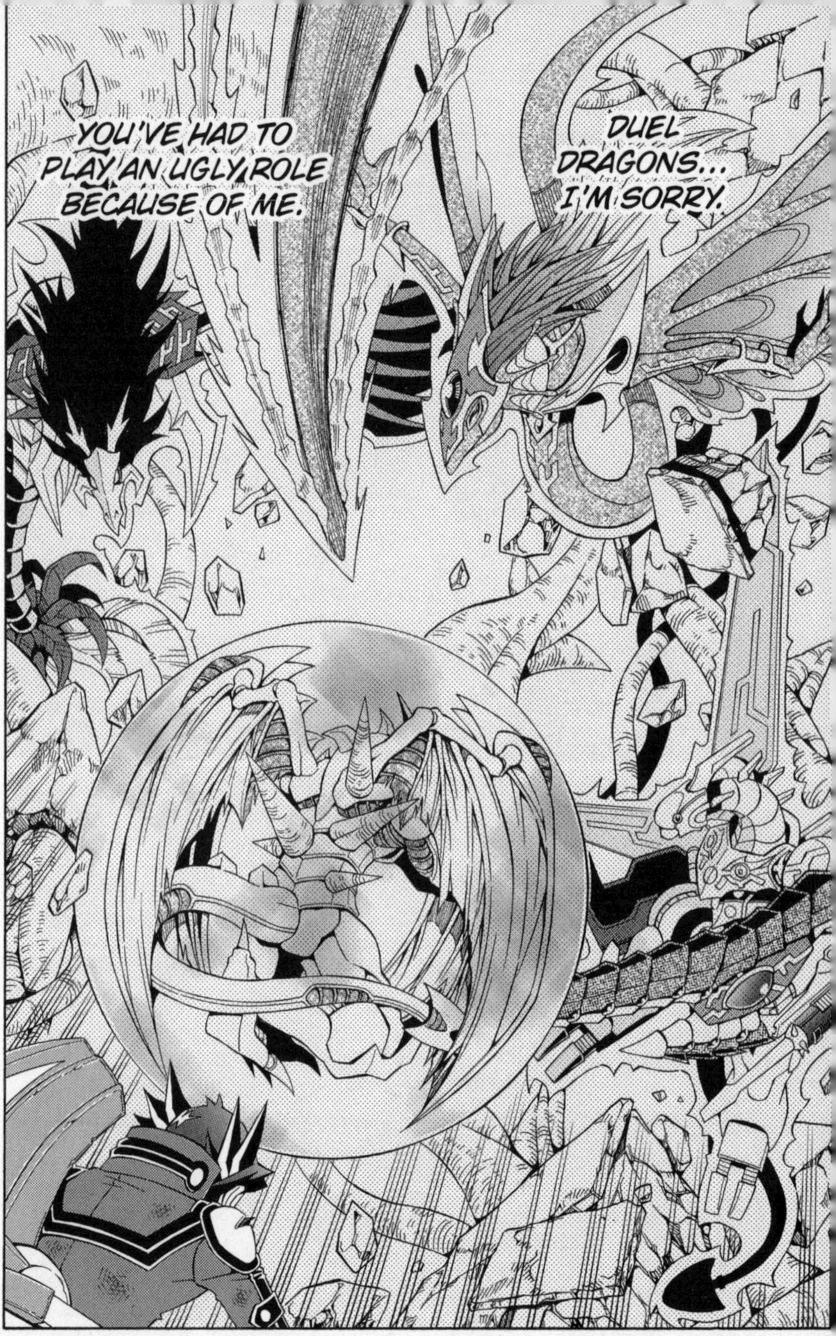
DUEL DRAGONS... I'M SORRY.
YOU'VE HAD TO PLAY AN UGLY ROLE BECAUSE OF ME.

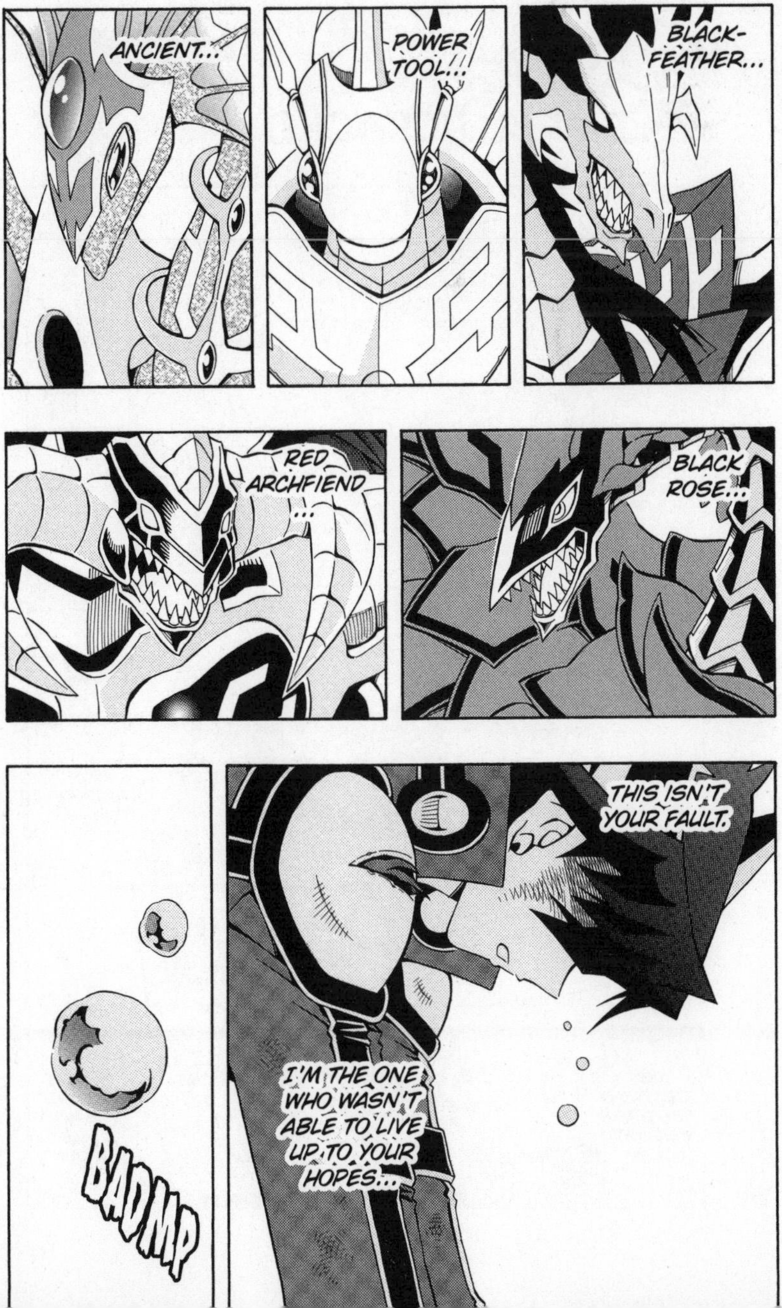
BLACK-
FEATHER...
POWER
TOOL...
ANCIENT...
BLACK
ROSE...
RED
ARCHFIEND
...
THIS ISN'T
YOUR FAULT.
I'M THE ONE
WHO WASN'T
ABLE TO LIVE
UP TO YOUR
HOPES...
BADMP

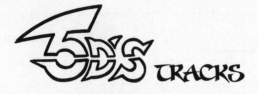

5D's TRACKS

THE 60TH

BY SATOMASA

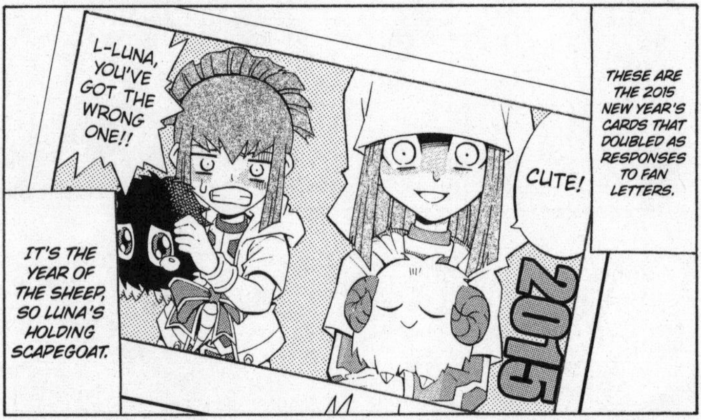
THESE ARE THE 2015 NEW YEAR'S CARDS THAT DOUBLED AS RESPONSES TO FAN LETTERS.
CUTE!
L-LUNA, YOU'VE GOT THE WRONG ONE!!
2015
IT'S THE YEAR OF THE SHEEP, SO LUNA'S HOLDING SCAPEGOAT.

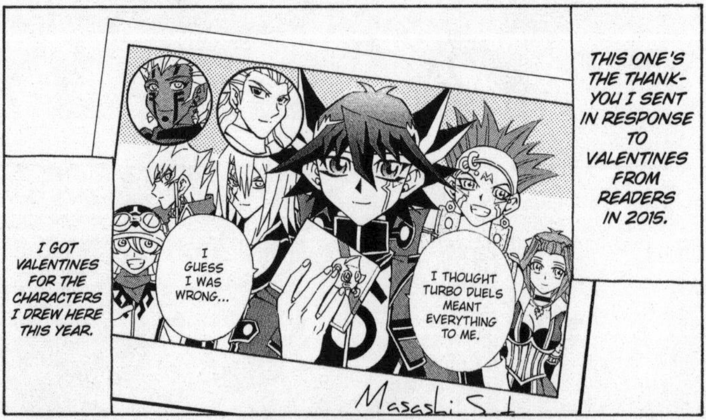
THIS ONE'S THE THANK-YOU I SENT IN RESPONSE TO VALENTINES FROM READERS IN 2015.
I THOUGHT TURBO DUELS MEANT EVERYTHING TO ME.
I GUESS I WAS WRONG...
I GOT VALENTINES FOR THE CHARACTERS I DREW HERE THIS YEAR.

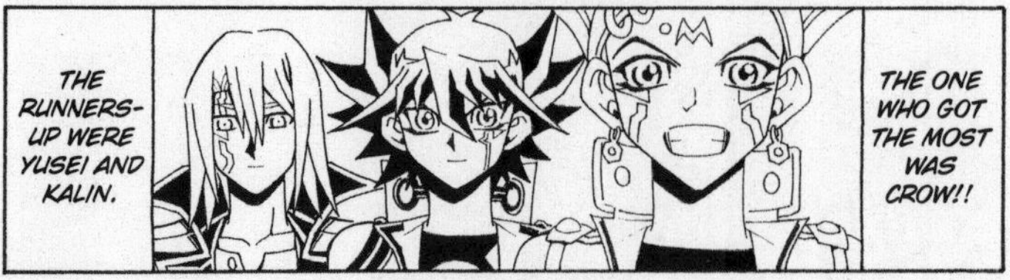
THE ONE WHO GOT THE MOST WAS CROW!!
THE RUNNERS-UP WERE YUSEI AND KALIN.

RIDE-62
PRAYERS!!

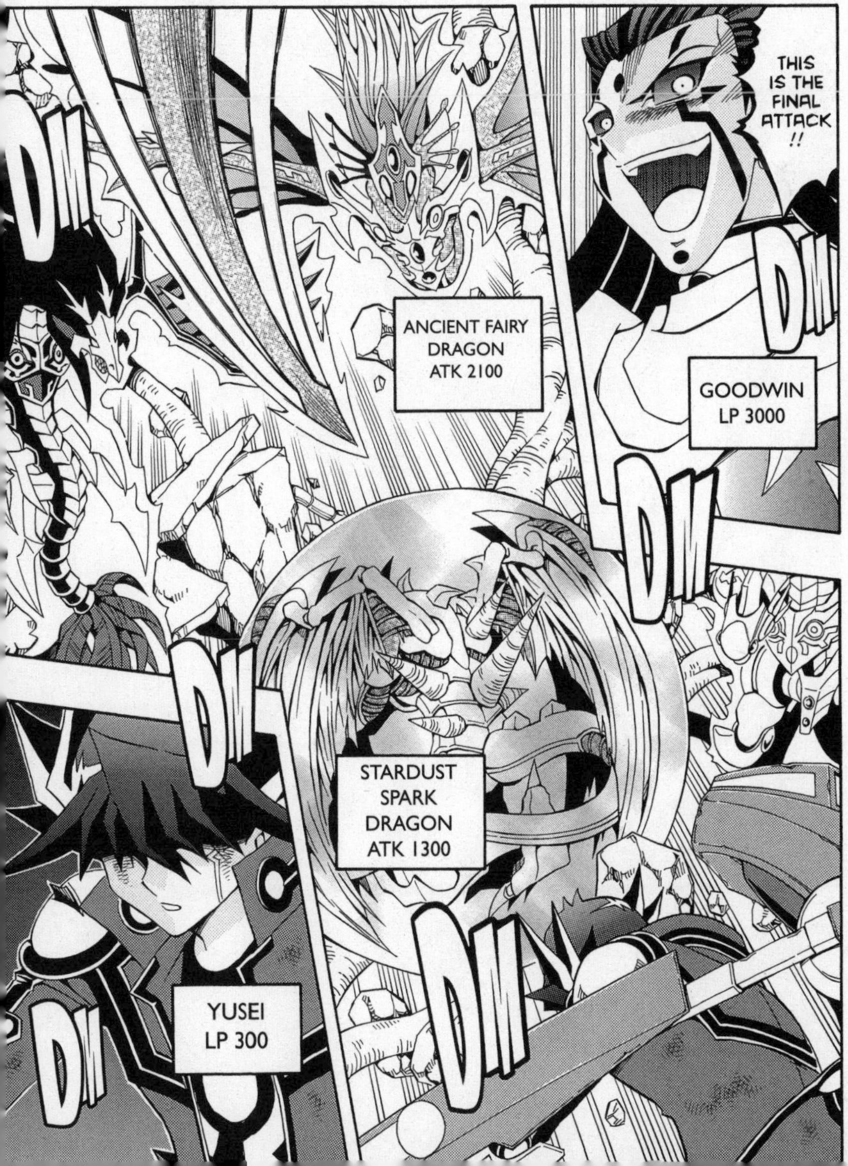
THIS IS THE FINAL ATTACK!!
DM
GOODWIN LP 3000
DM
DM
DM
ANCIENT FAIRY DRAGON ATK 2100
DM
STARDUST SPARK DRAGON ATK 1300
DM
DM
YUSEI LP 300
DM

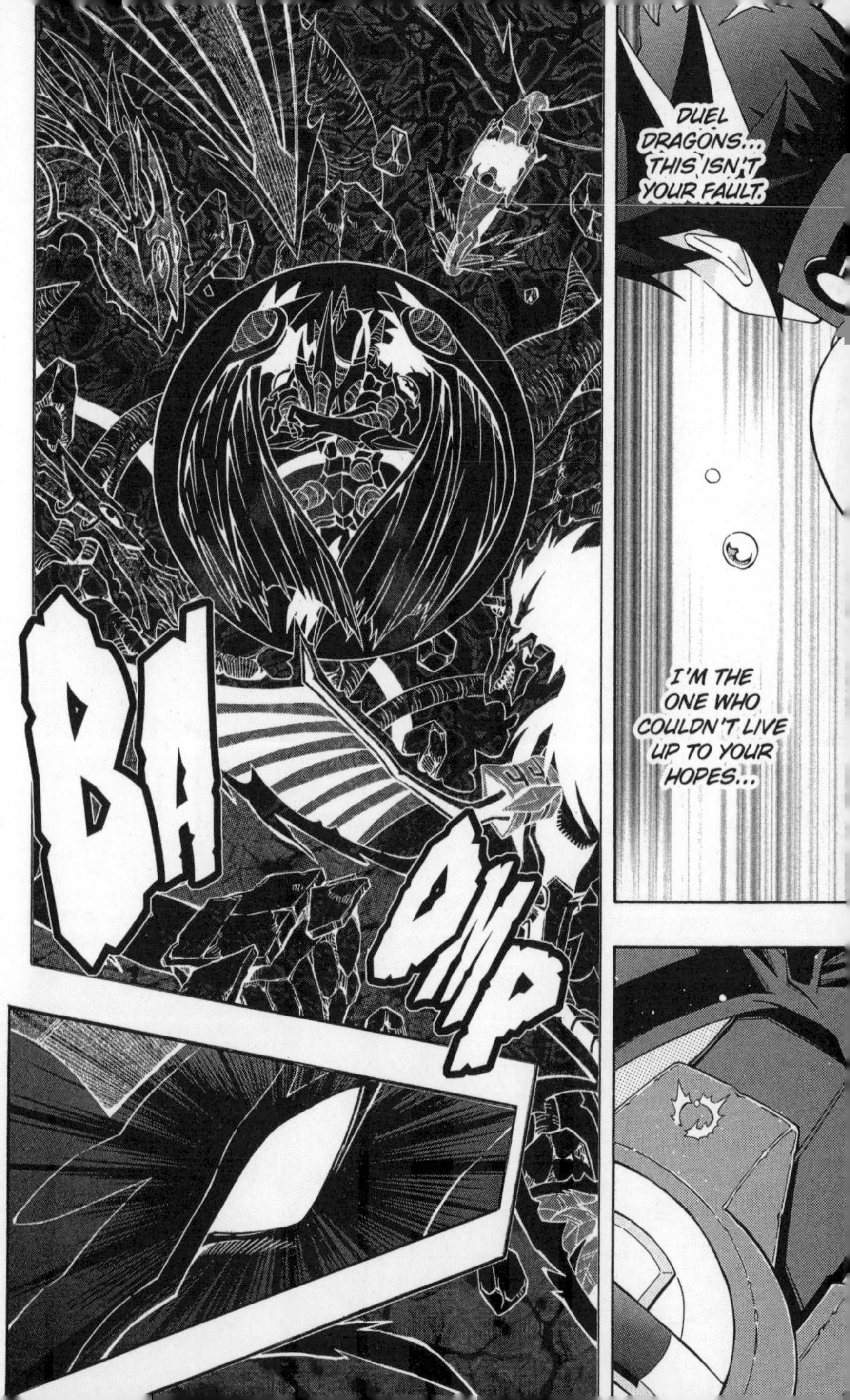
DUEL DRAGONS... THIS ISN'T YOUR FAULT.
I'M THE ONE WHO COULDN'T LIVE UP TO YOUR HOPES...
BA DMP

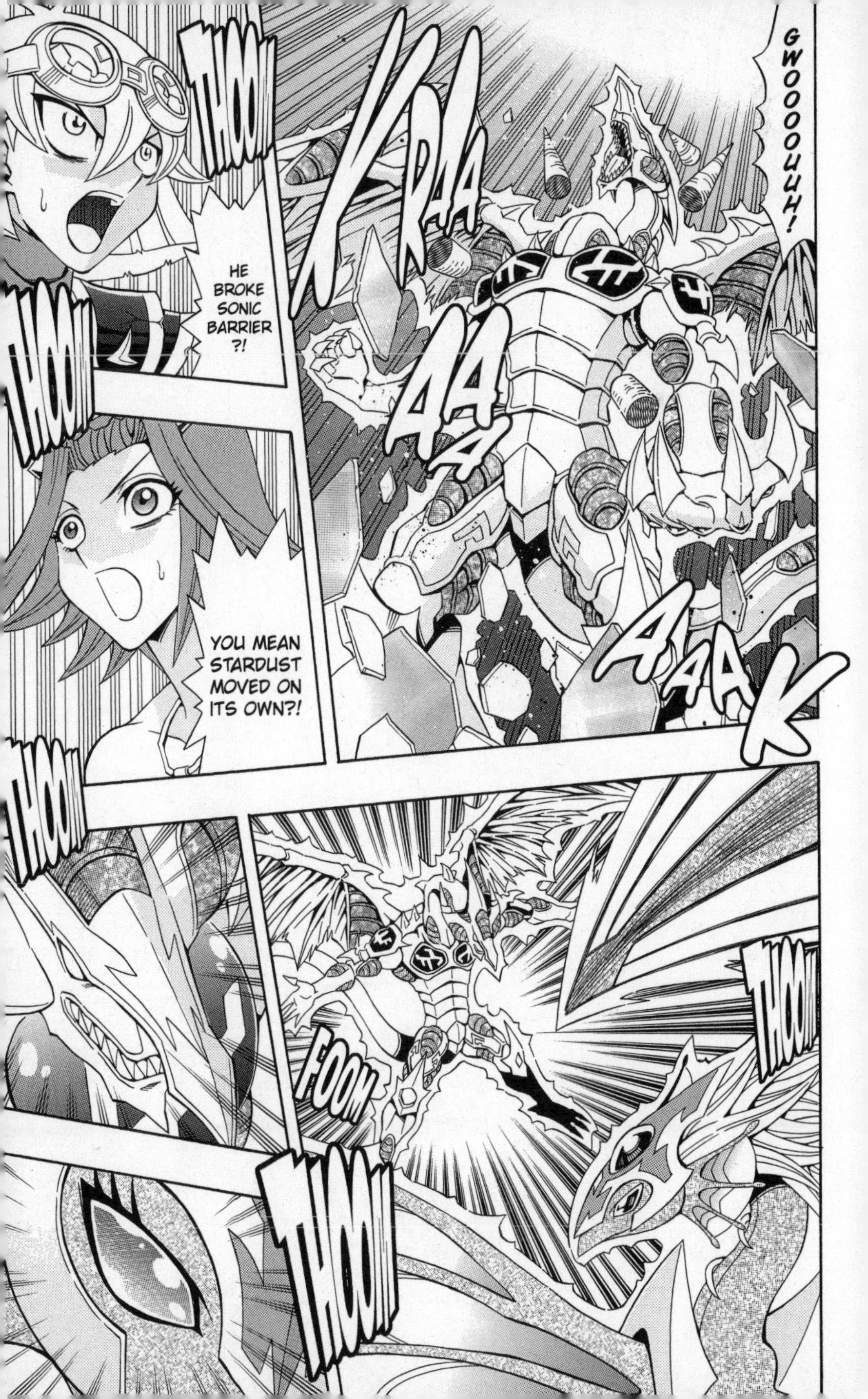
GWOOOOOUUH!
KRAAAAAAAAAK
THOOM
HE BROKE SONIC BARRIER?!
THOOM
YOU MEAN STARDUST MOVED ON ITS OWN?!
THOOM
THOOM
FOOM
THOOM
THOOM

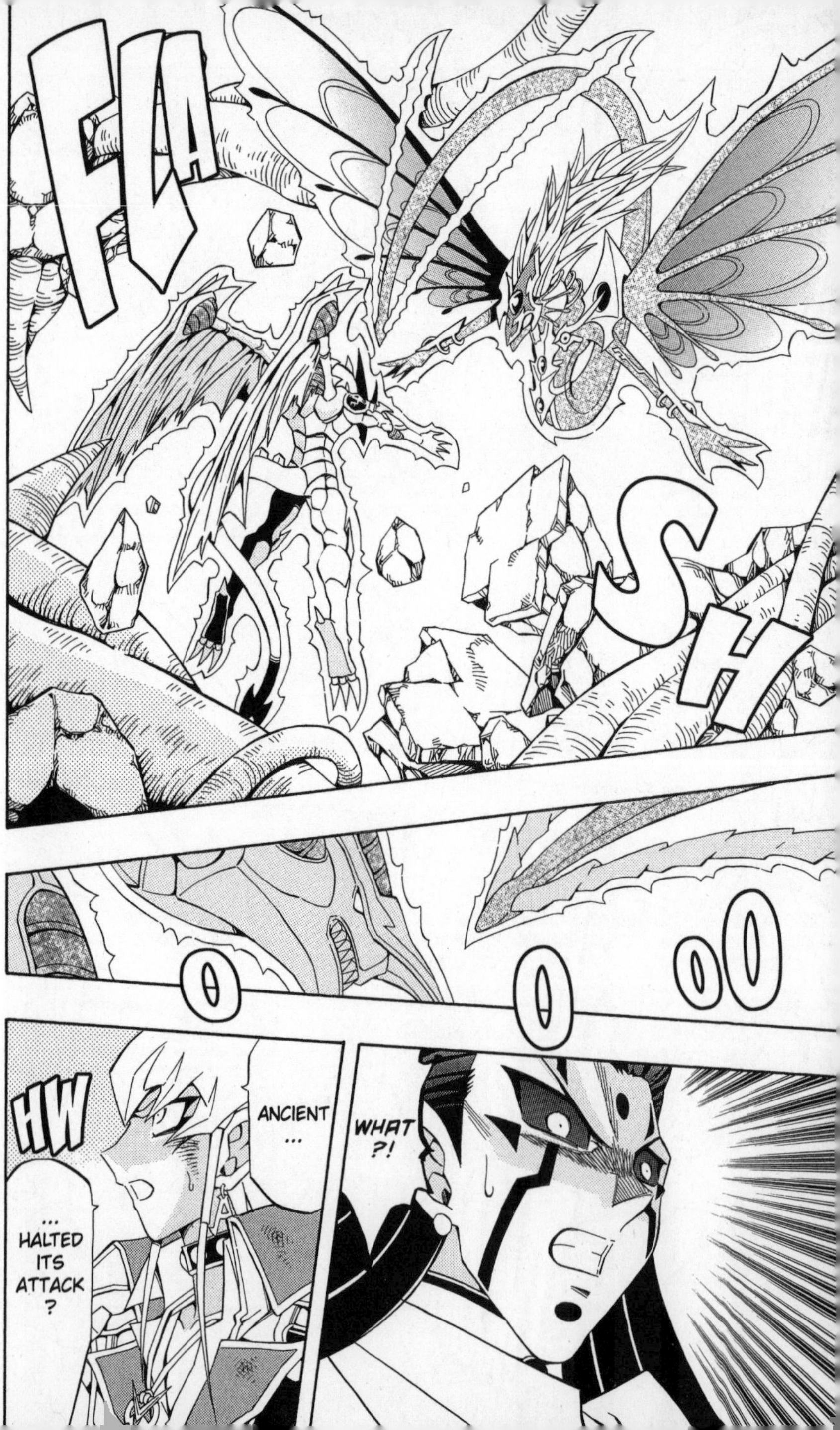
FLA
SH
O O OO
WHAT?!
ANCIENT...
...HALTED ITS ATTACK?
HW

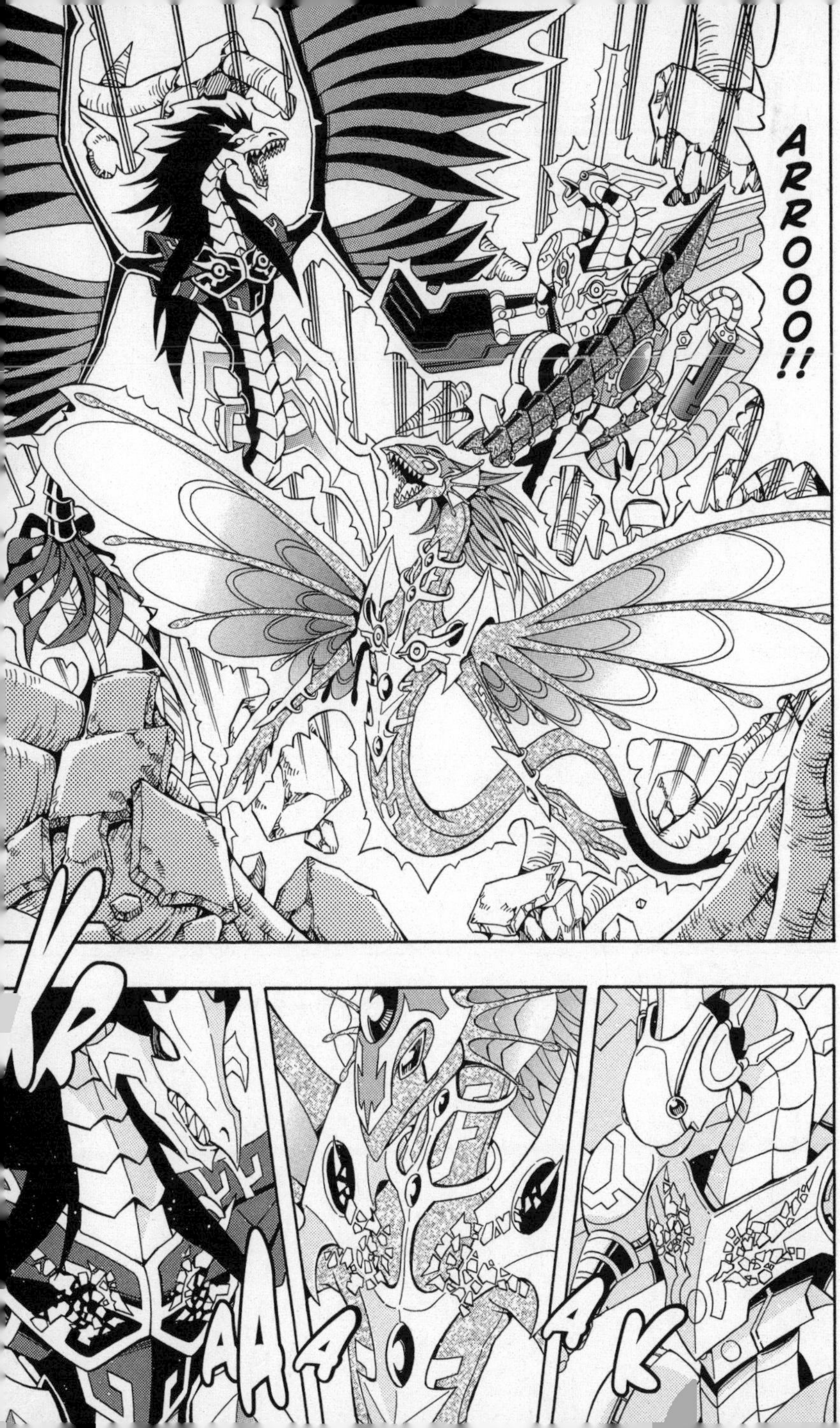
ARROOOO!!
RAAAAK

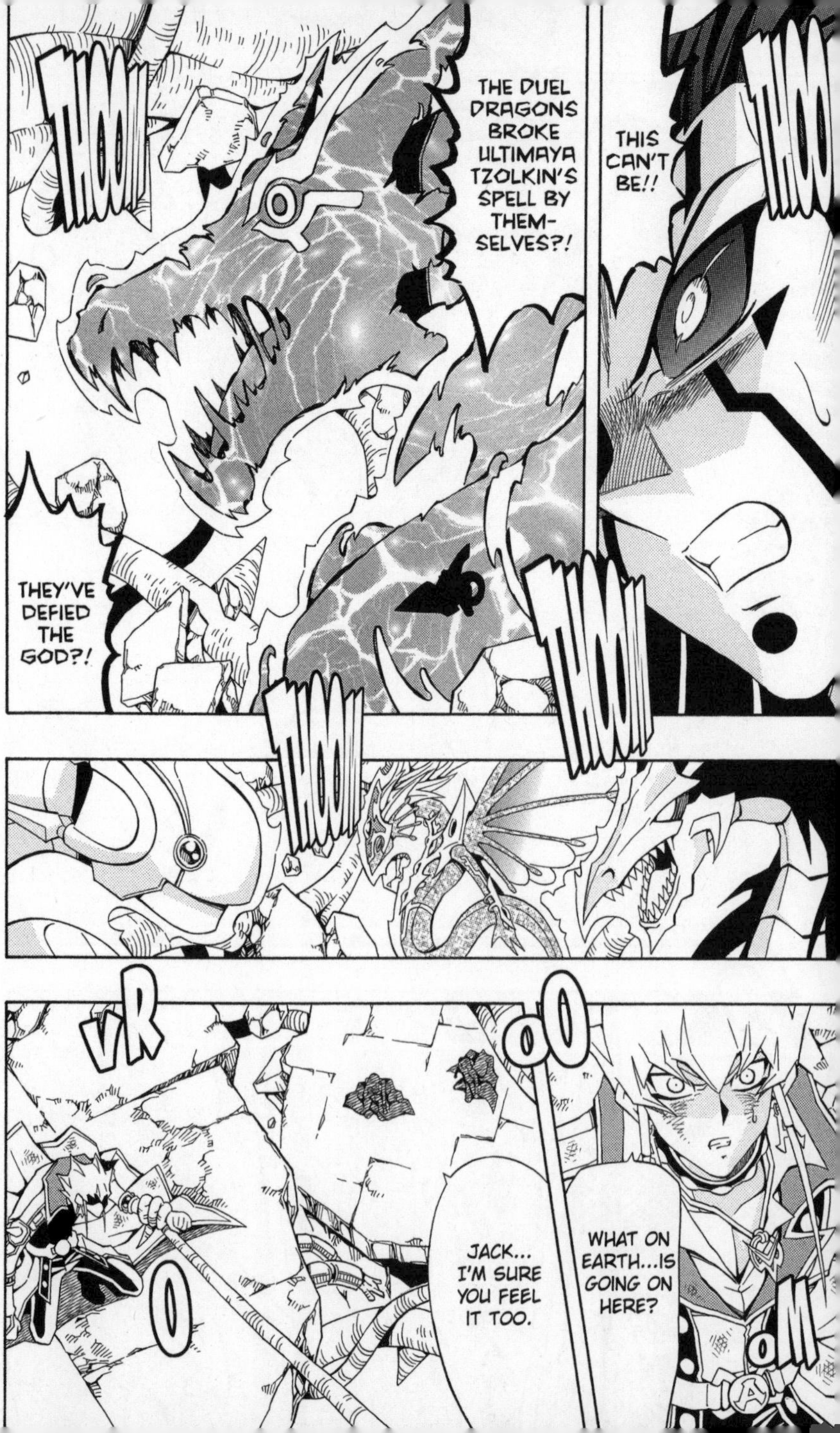
THOOM
THIS CAN'T BE!!
THOOM
THE DUEL DRAGONS BROKE ULTIMAYA TZOLKIN'S SPELL BY THEM-SELVES?!
THEY'VE DEFIED THE GOD?!
THOOM
THOOM
WHAT ON EARTH...IS GOING ON HERE?
JACK... I'M SURE YOU FEEL IT TOO.

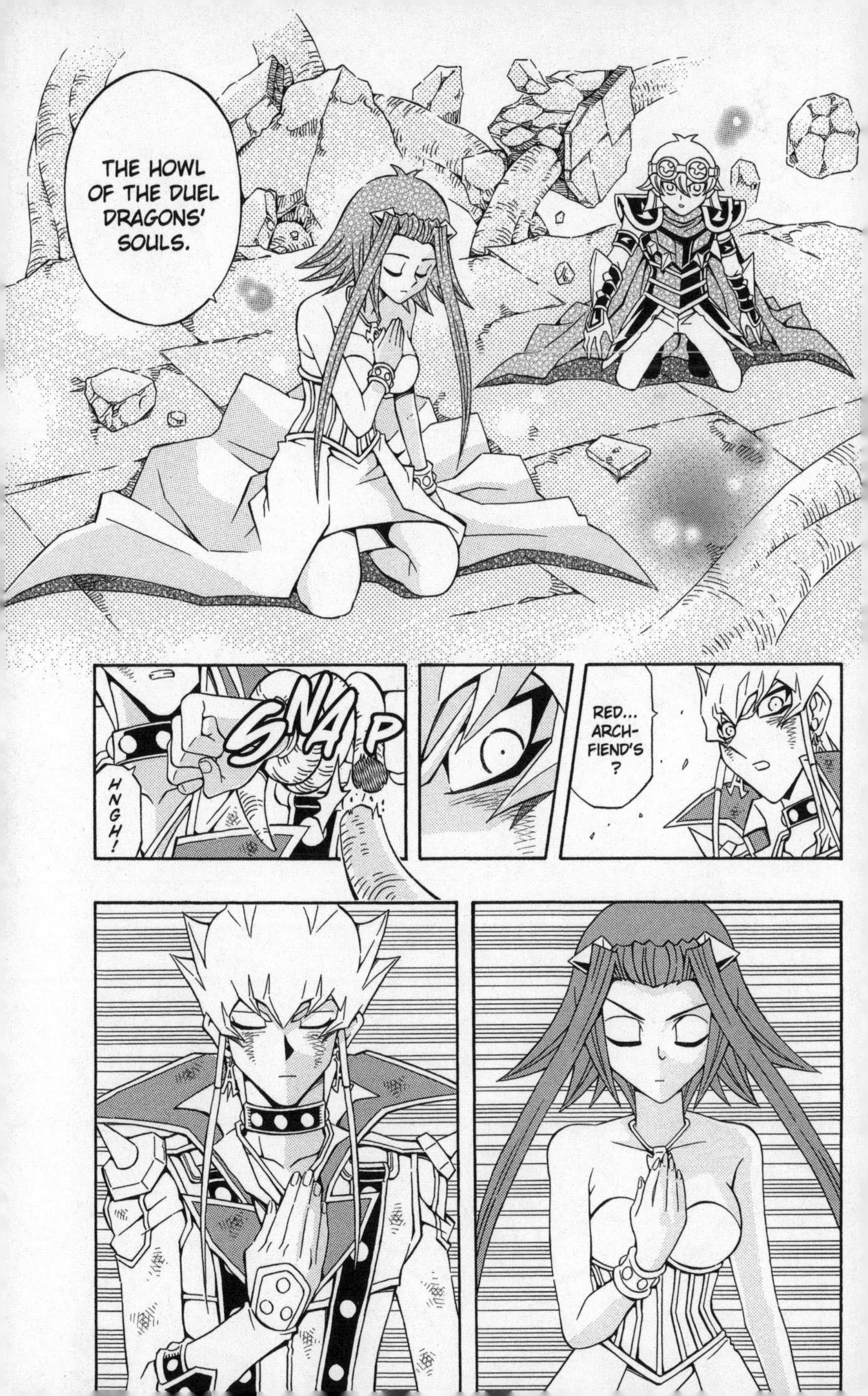
THE HOWL OF THE DUEL DRAGONS' SOULS.
RED... ARCH-FIEND'S?
SNAP
HNGH!

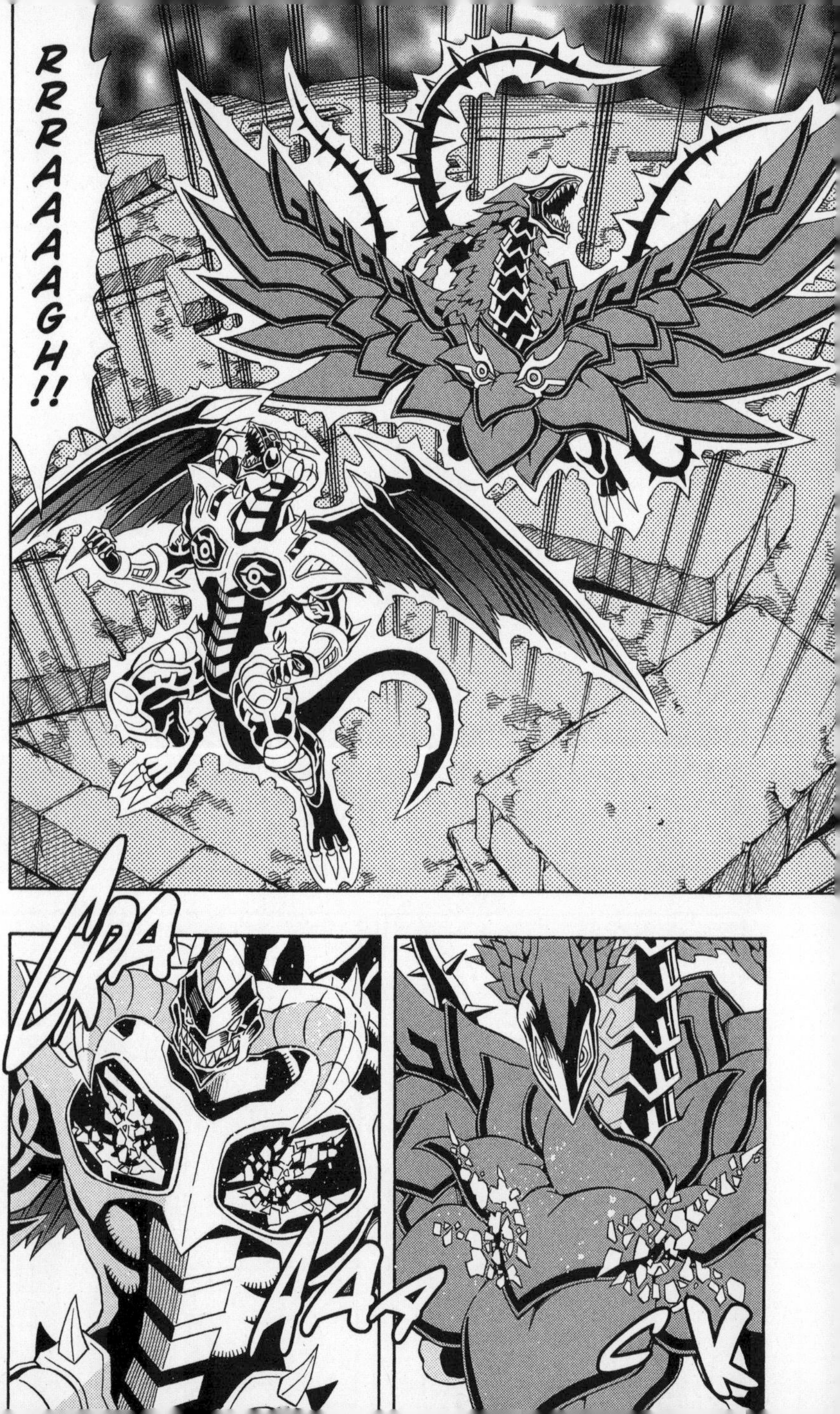
RRRAAAAAGH!!
CRA
AAA
CK

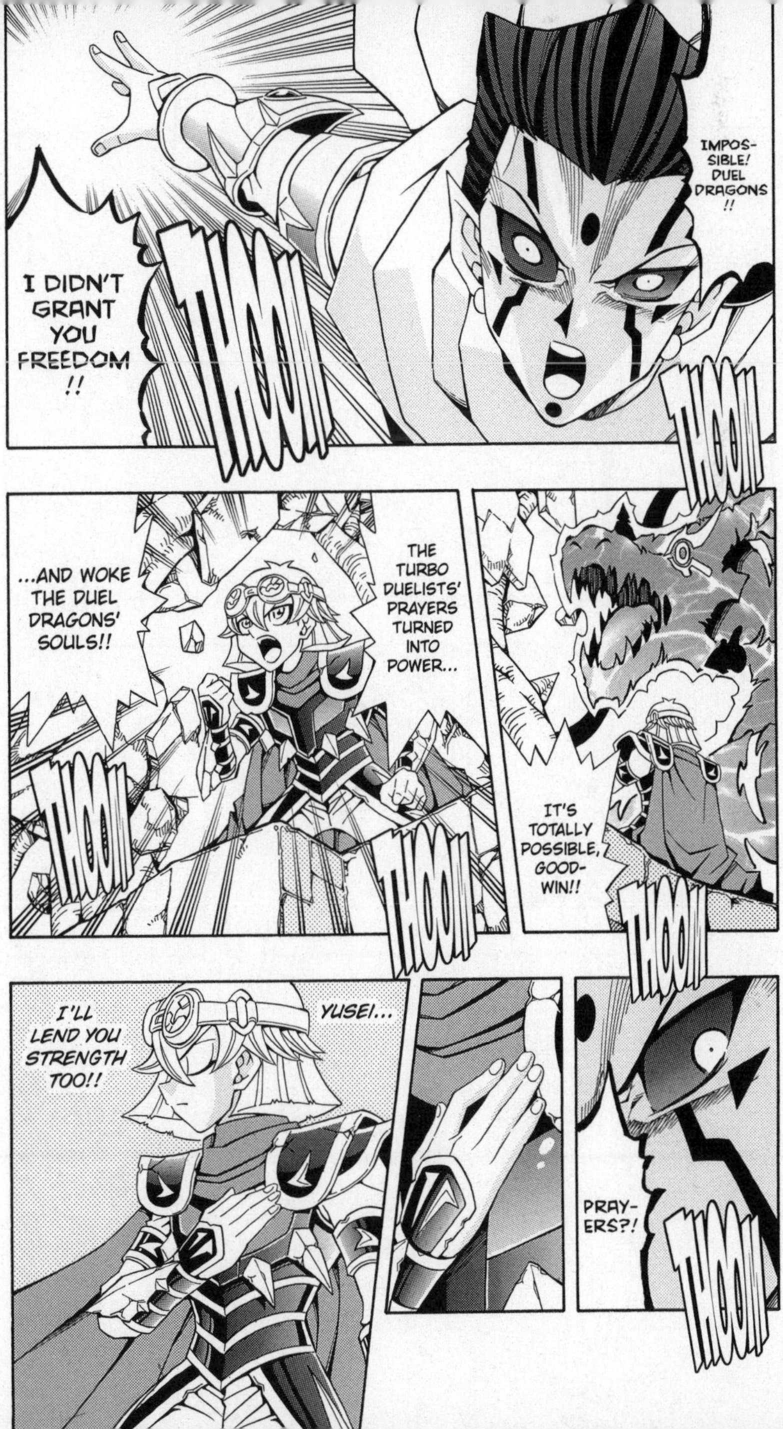
IMPOSSIBLE! DUEL DRAGONS!!
THOOM
I DIDN'T GRANT YOU FREEDOM!!
THOOM
IT'S TOTALLY POSSIBLE, GOODWIN!!
THOOM
THE TURBO DUELISTS' PRAYERS TURNED INTO POWER...
...AND WOKE THE DUEL DRAGONS' SOULS!!
THOOM
THOOM
PRAYERS?!
THOOM
YUSEI...
I'LL LEND YOU STRENGTH TOO!!

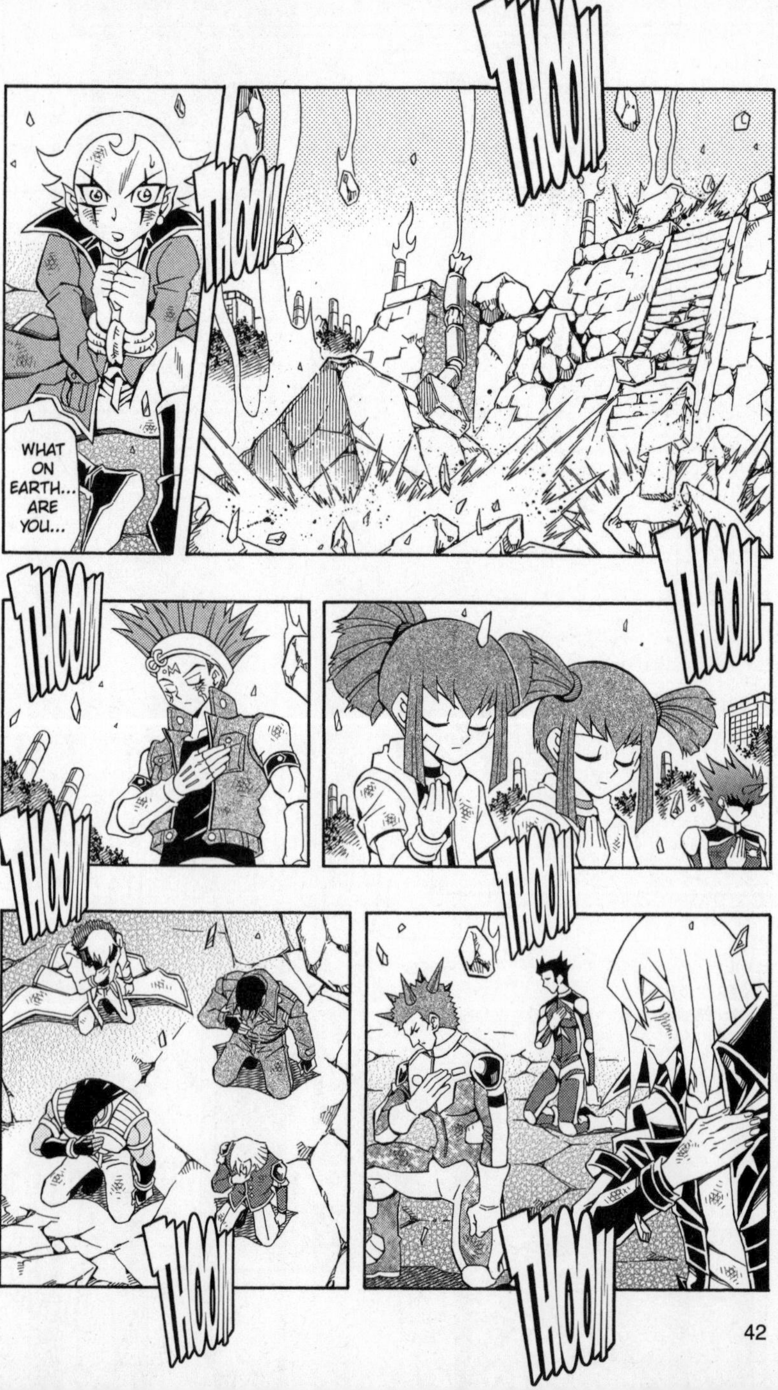
THOOM
THOOM
WHAT ON EARTH... ARE YOU...
THOOM
THOOM
THOOM
THOOM
THOOM
THOOM
THOOM

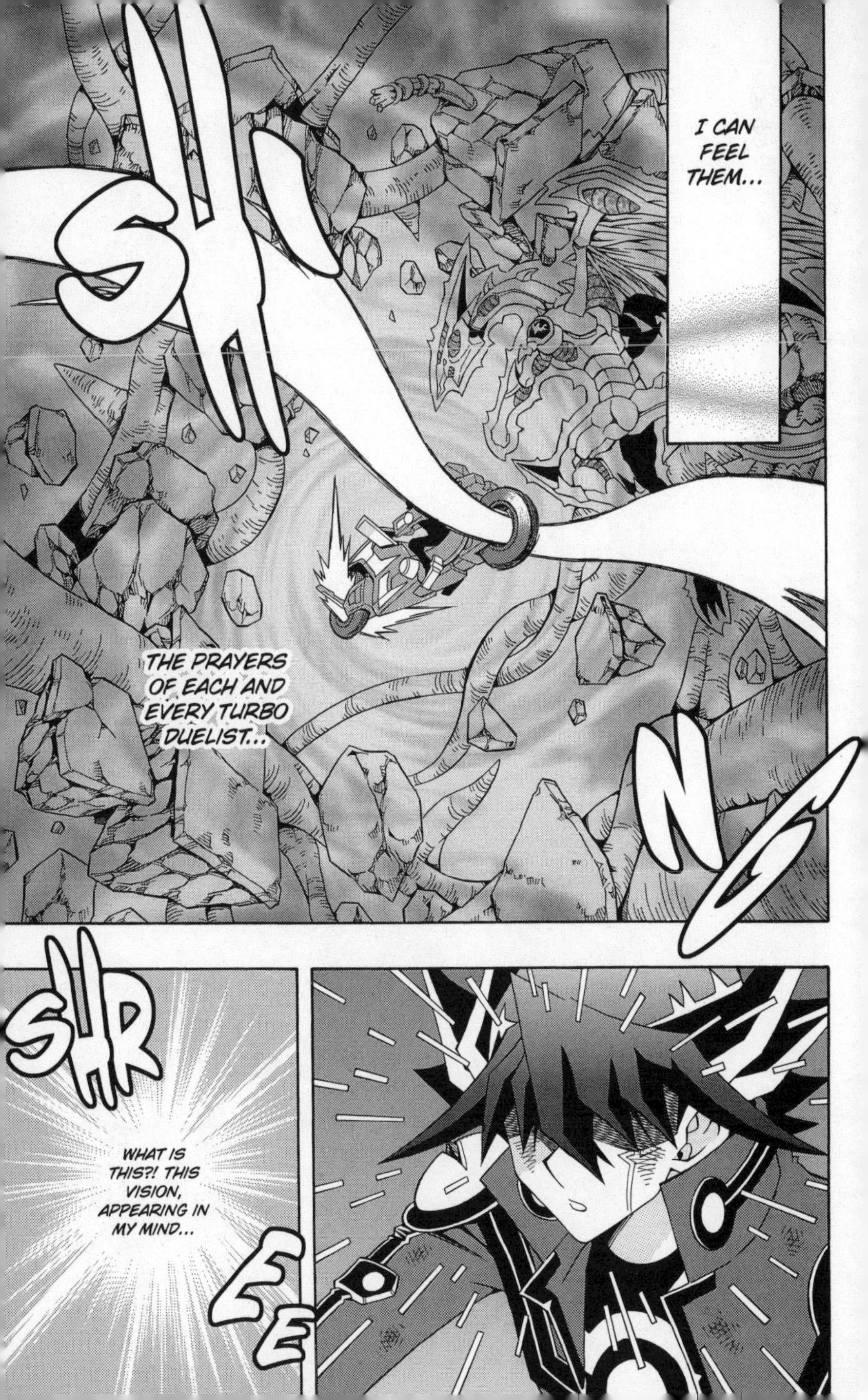

I CAN FEEL THEM...
SHH
THE PRAYERS OF EACH AND EVERY TURBO DUELIST...
NG
SHR
WHAT IS THIS?! THIS VISION, APPEARING IN MY MIND...
EE

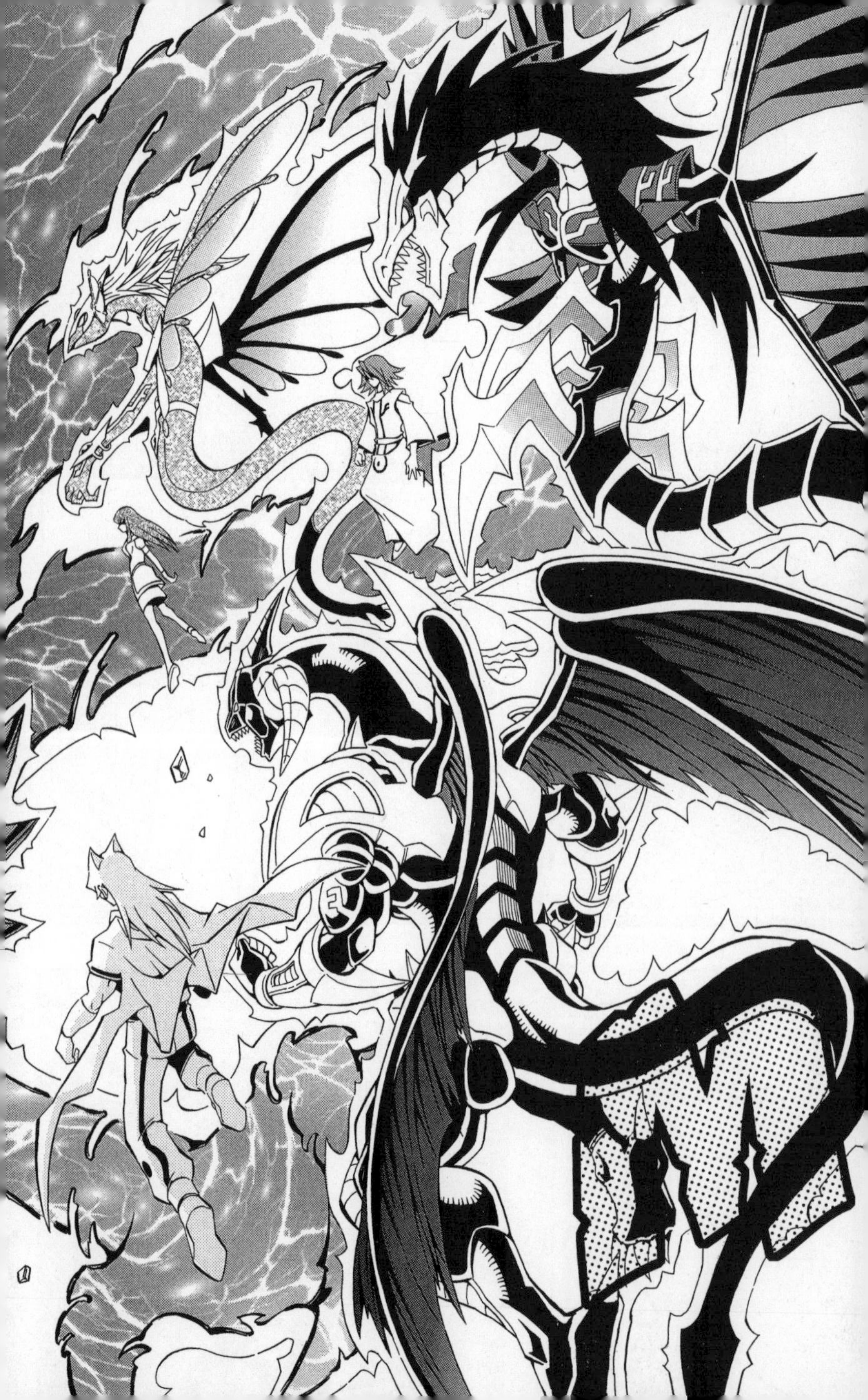

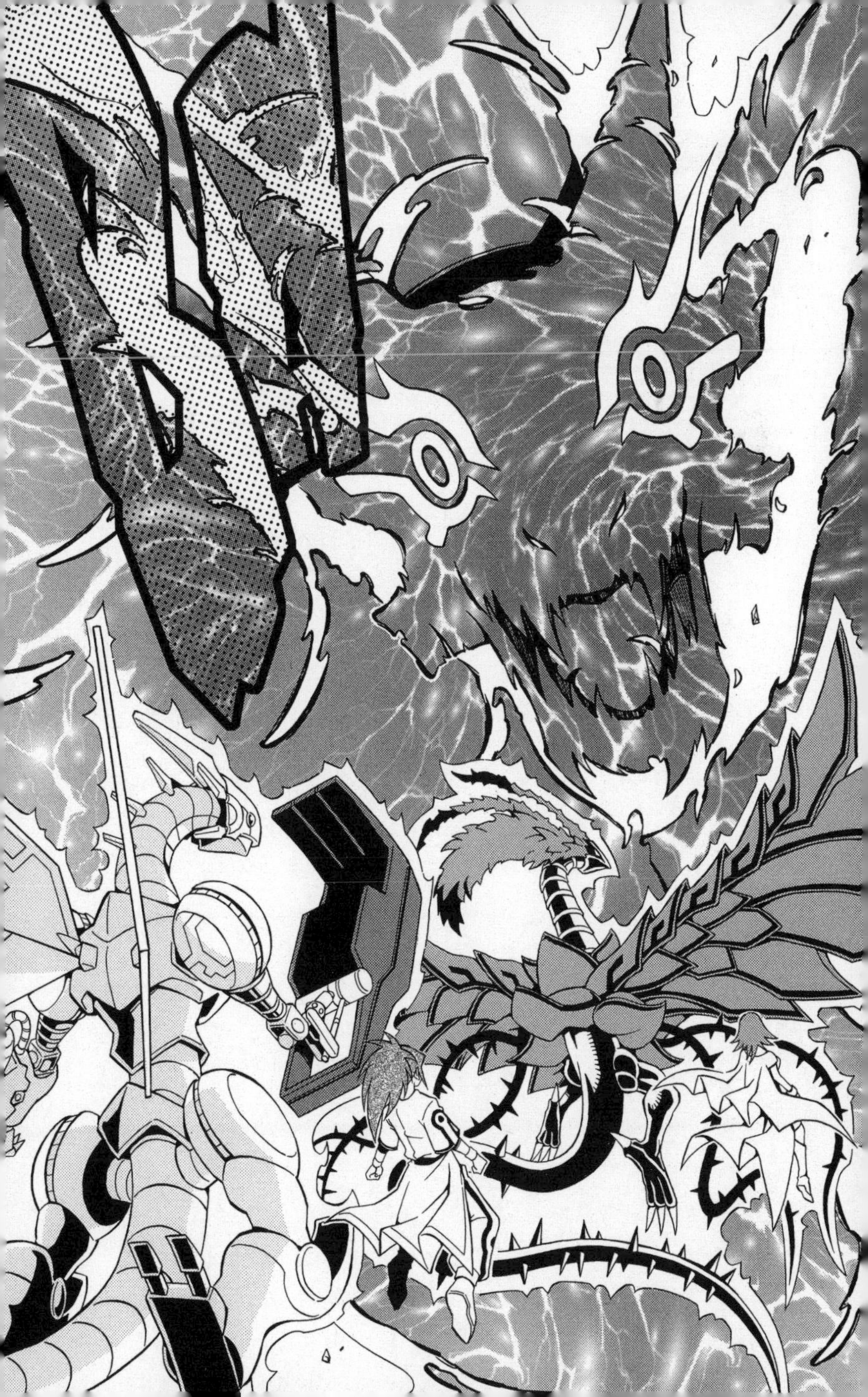

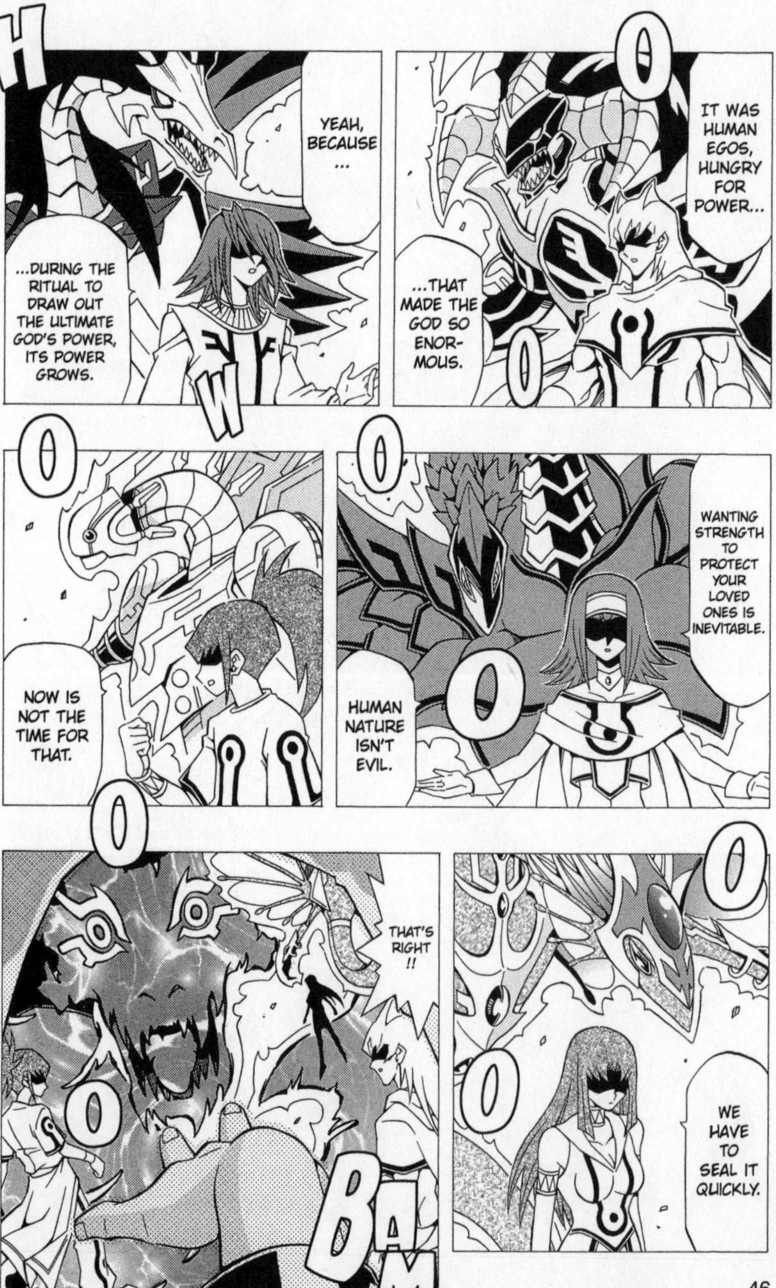
HWOOOOOOOOO
IT WAS HUMAN EGOS, HUNGRY FOR POWER...
...THAT MADE THE GOD SO ENOR-MOUS.
YEAH, BECAUSE ...
...DURING THE RITUAL TO DRAW OUT THE ULTIMATE GOD'S POWER, ITS POWER GROWS.
WANTING STRENGTH TO PROTECT YOUR LOVED ONES IS INEVITABLE.
HUMAN NATURE ISN'T EVIL.
NOW IS NOT THE TIME FOR THAT.
WE HAVE TO SEAL IT QUICKLY.
THAT'S RIGHT !!
BAM

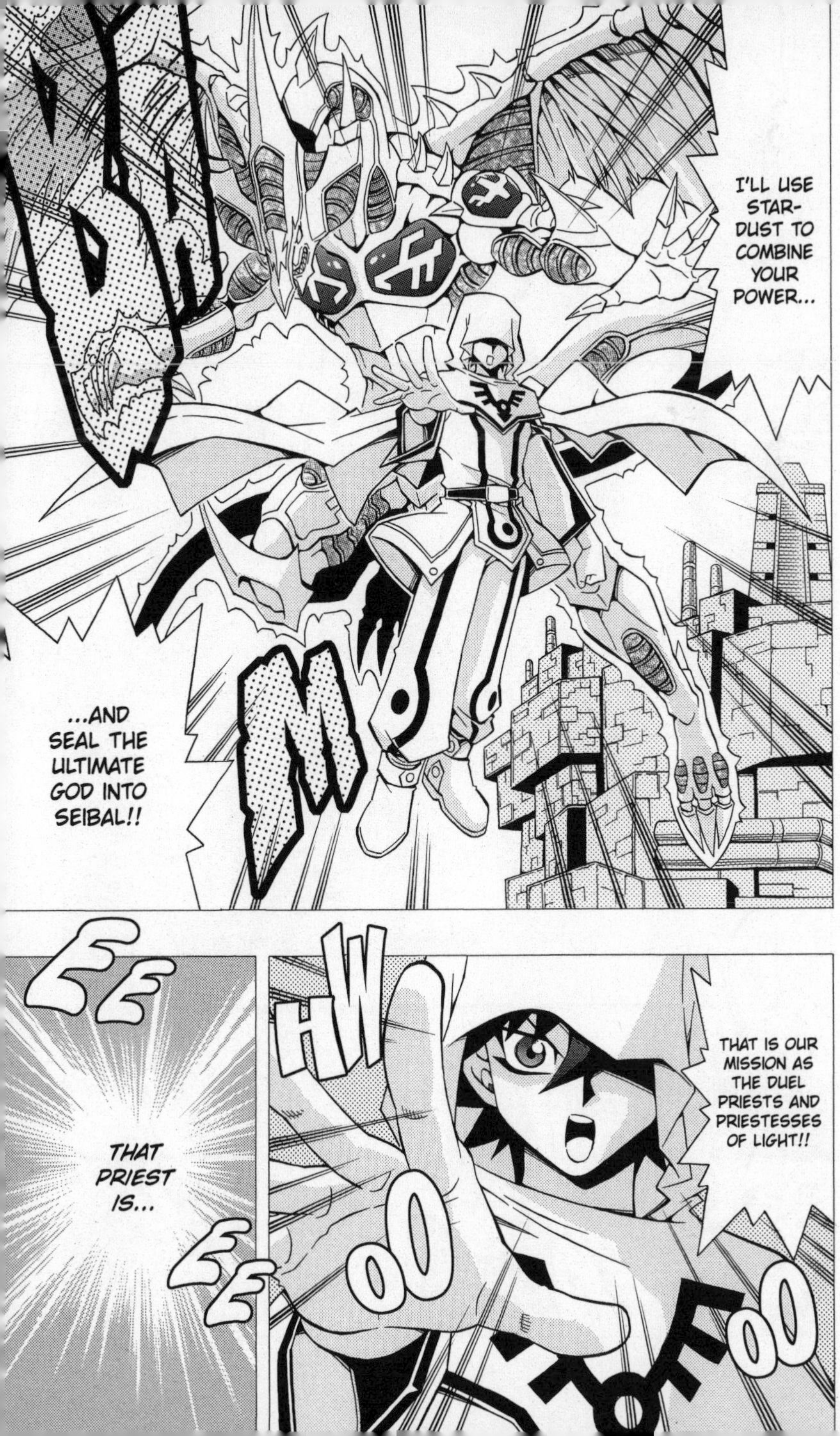
I'LL USE STAR-DUST TO COMBINE YOUR POWER...
...AND SEAL THE ULTIMATE GOD INTO SEIBAL!!
THAT IS OUR MISSION AS THE DUEL PRIESTS AND PRIESTESSES OF LIGHT!!
THAT PRIEST IS...

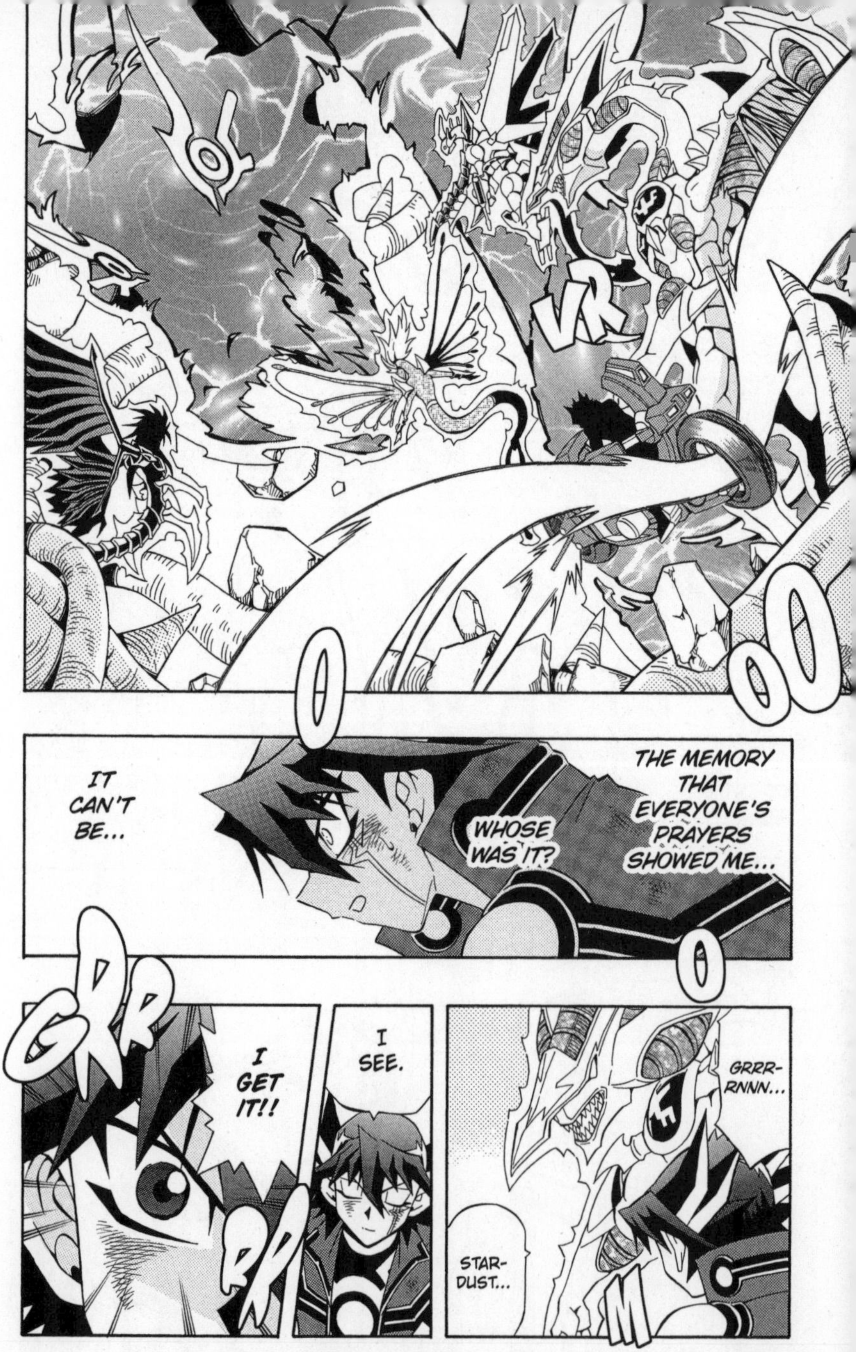
VR
OOOO
O
THE MEMORY THAT EVERYONE'S PRAYERS SHOWED ME...
WHOSE WAS IT?
IT CAN'T BE...
O
GRRR-RNNN...
STAR-DUST...
M
I SEE.
I GET IT!!
GRR
RR

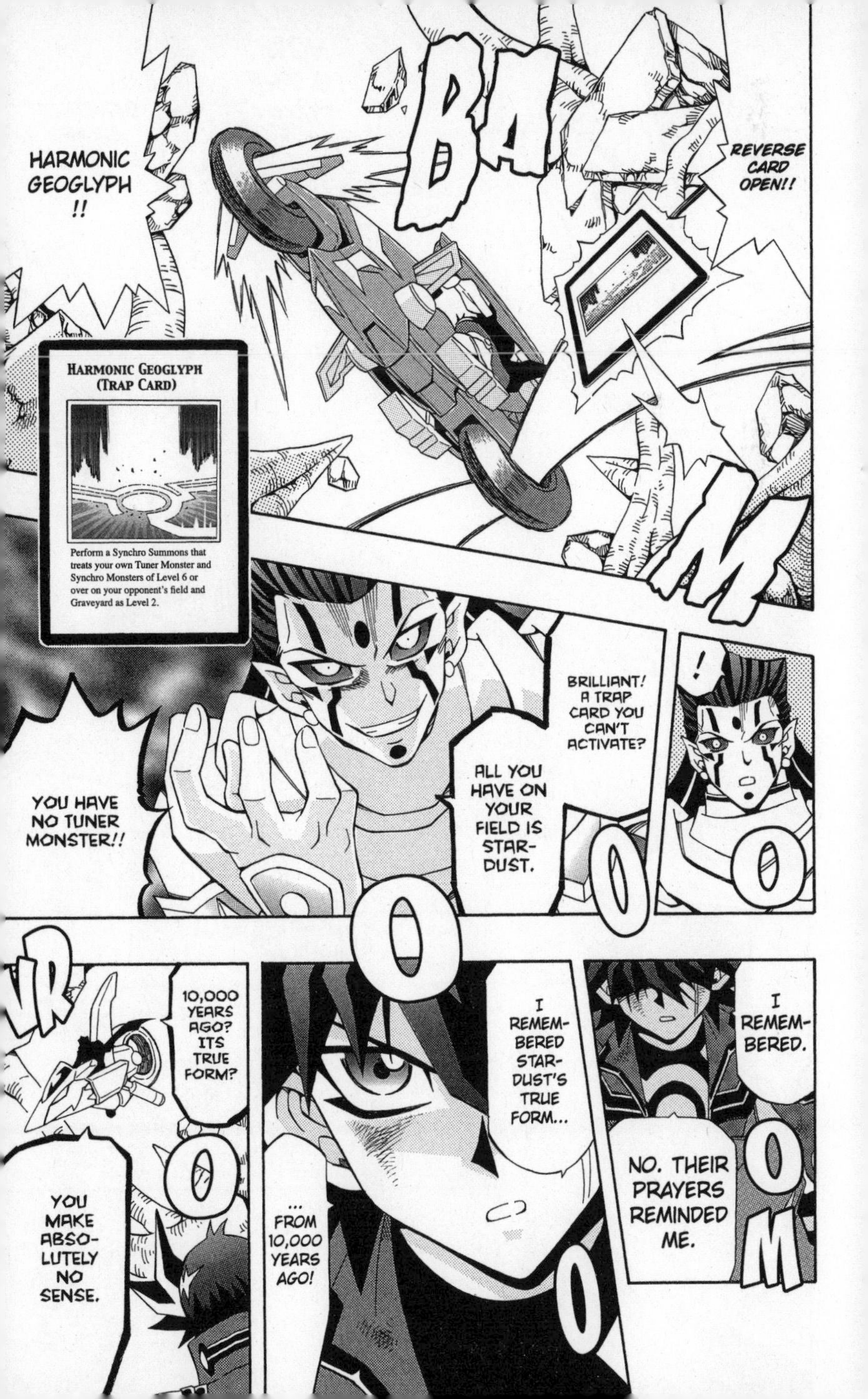

REVERSE CARD OPEN!!
BAM
HARMONIC GEOGLYPH!!
HARMONIC GEOGLYPH (TRAP CARD)
Perform a Synchro Summons that treats your own Tuner Monster and Synchro Monsters of Level 6 or over on your opponent's field and Graveyard as Level 2.
!
BRILLIANT! A TRAP CARD YOU CAN'T ACTIVATE?
ALL YOU HAVE ON YOUR FIELD IS STARDUST.
YOU HAVE NO TUNER MONSTER!!
VROOOOOOOM
I REMEMBERED.
NO. THEIR PRAYERS REMINDED ME.
I REMEMBERED STARDUST'S TRUE FORM...
...FROM 10,000 YEARS AGO!
10,000 YEARS AGO? ITS TRUE FORM?
YOU MAKE ABSOLUTELY NO SENSE.

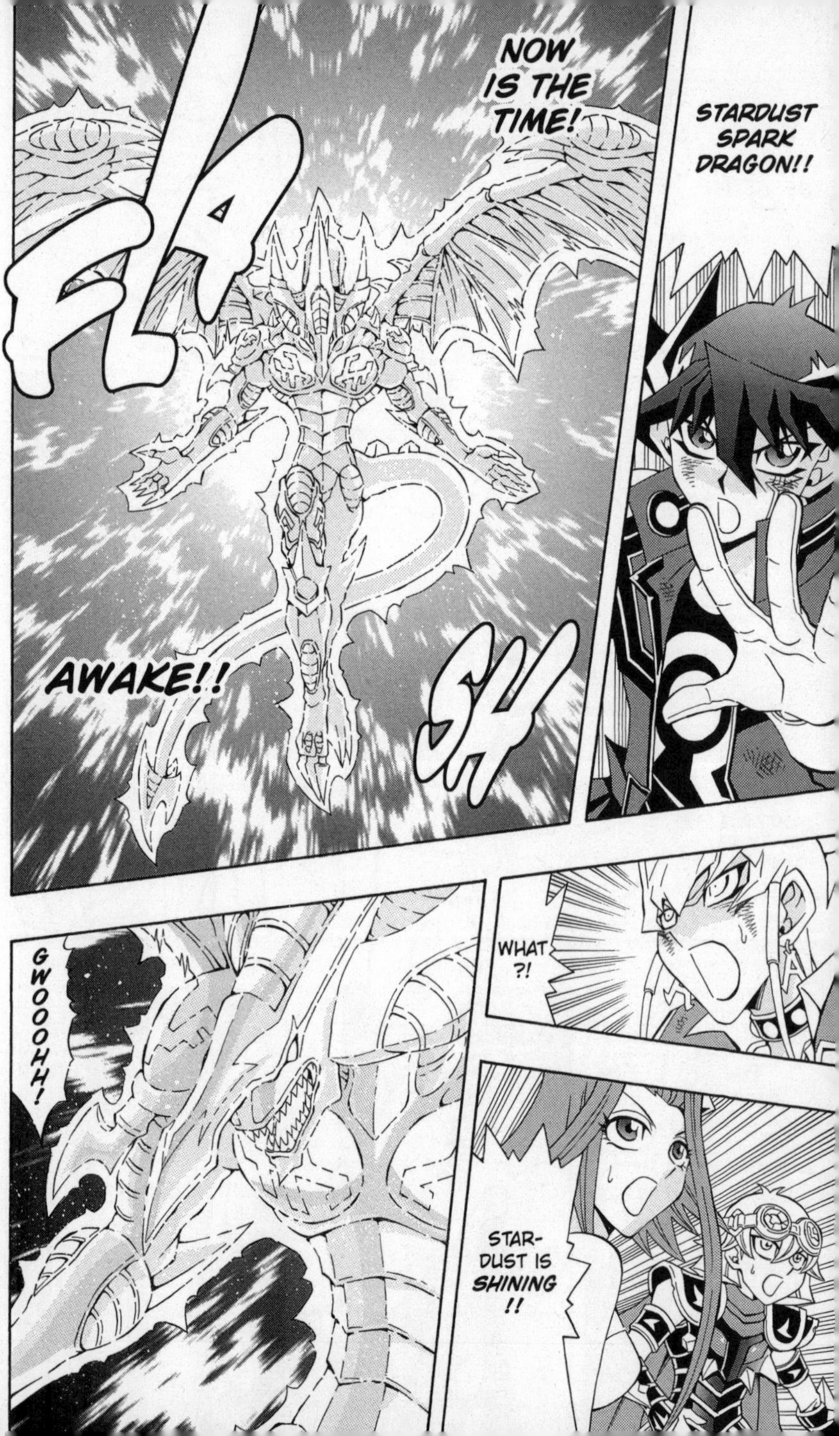
STARDUST SPARK DRAGON!!
NOW IS THE TIME!
FLA
SH
AWAKE!!
WHAT?!
STAR-DUST IS SHINING!!
GWOOOOHH!

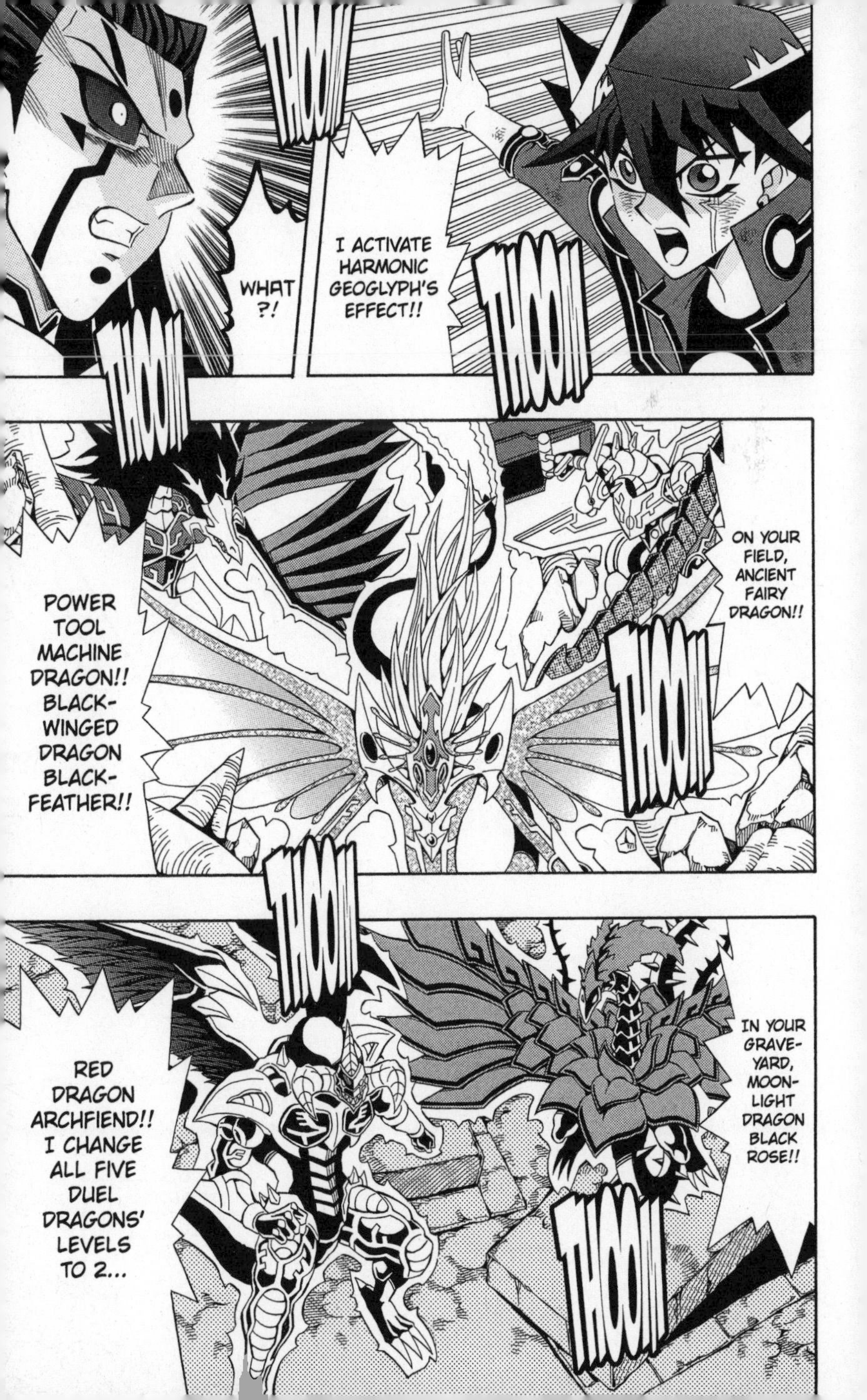
THOOM
I ACTIVATE HARMONIC GEOGLYPH'S EFFECT!!
THOOM
WHAT ?!
THOOM
ON YOUR FIELD, ANCIENT FAIRY DRAGON!!
THOOM
POWER TOOL MACHINE DRAGON!! BLACK-WINGED DRAGON BLACK-FEATHER!!
THOOM
IN YOUR GRAVE-YARD, MOON-LIGHT DRAGON BLACK ROSE!!
RED DRAGON ARCHFIEND!! I CHANGE ALL FIVE DUEL DRAGONS' LEVELS TO 2...
THOOM

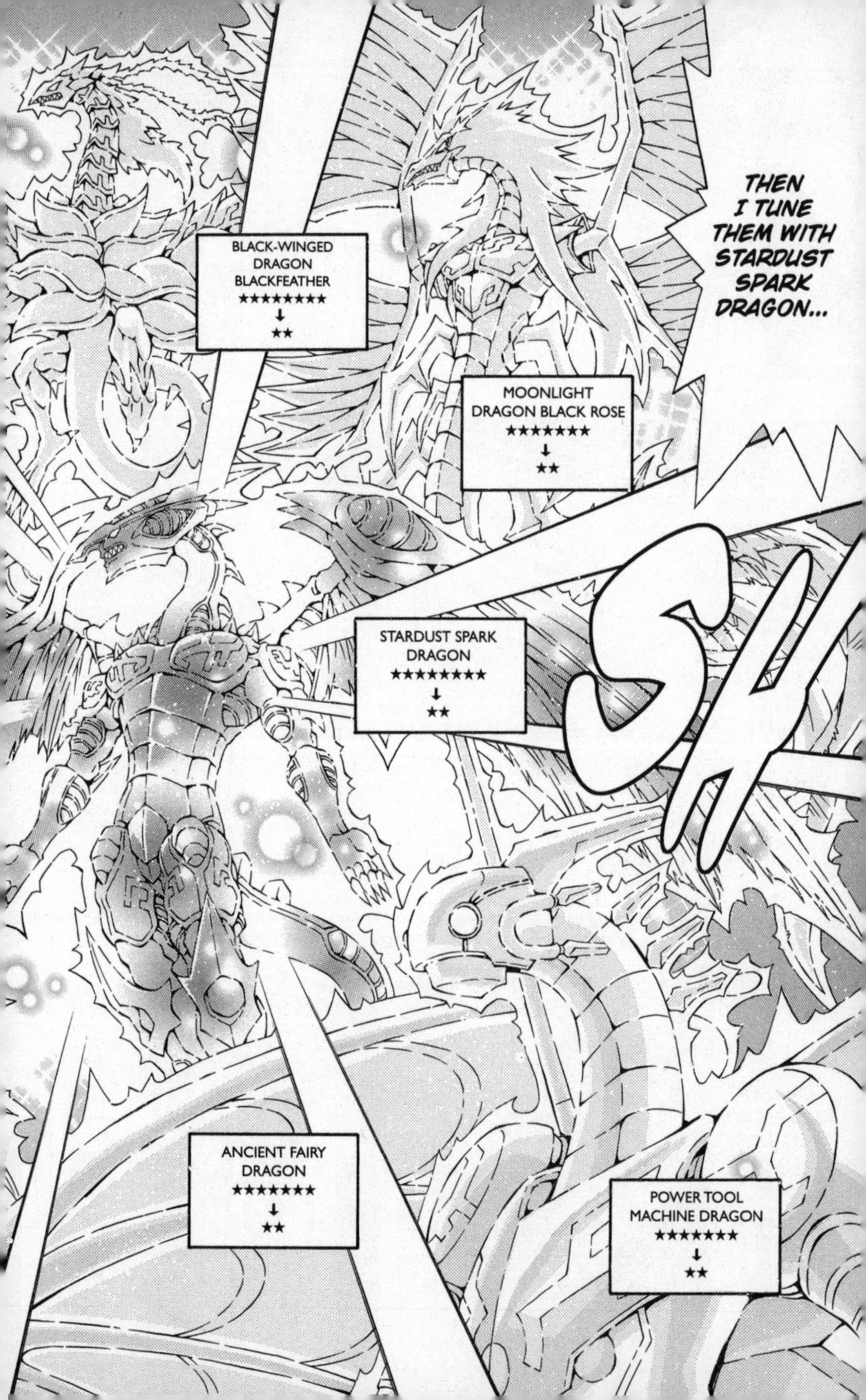
THEN I TUNE THEM WITH STARDUST SPARK DRAGON...
BLACK-WINGED DRAGON BLACKFEATHER ★★★★★★★★ ↓ ★★
MOONLIGHT DRAGON BLACK ROSE ★★★★★★★ ↓ ★★
SH
STARDUST SPARK DRAGON ★★★★★★★★ ↓ ★★
POWER TOOL MACHINE DRAGON ★★★★★★★ ↓ ★★
ANCIENT FAIRY DRAGON ★★★★★★★ ↓ ★★

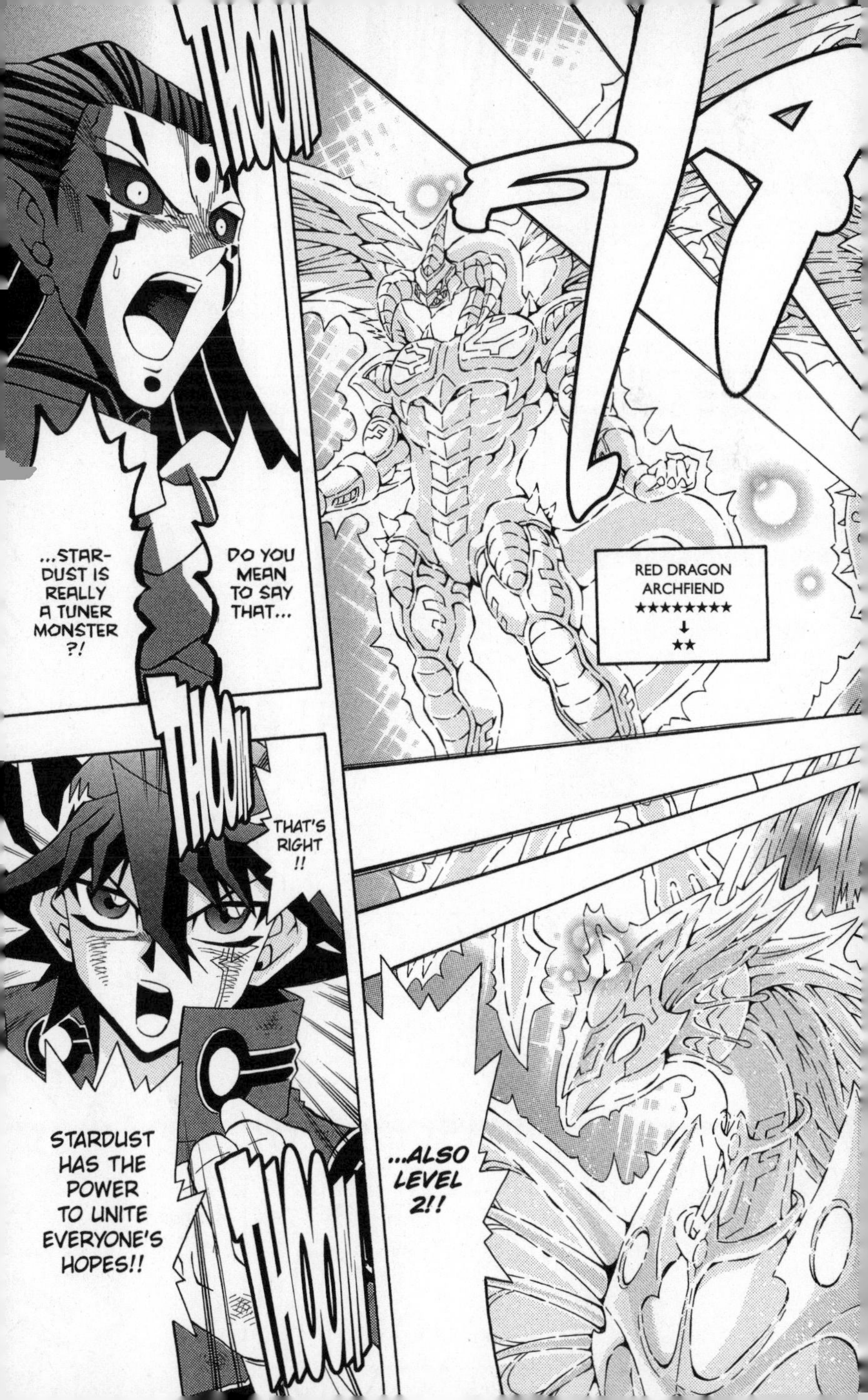
RED DRAGON ARCHFIEND
★★★★★★★★
↓
★★
THOOM
DO YOU MEAN TO SAY THAT...
...STARDUST IS REALLY A TUNER MONSTER ?!
...ALSO LEVEL 2!!
THOOM
THAT'S RIGHT !!
STARDUST HAS THE POWER TO UNITE EVERYONE'S HOPES!!
THOOM

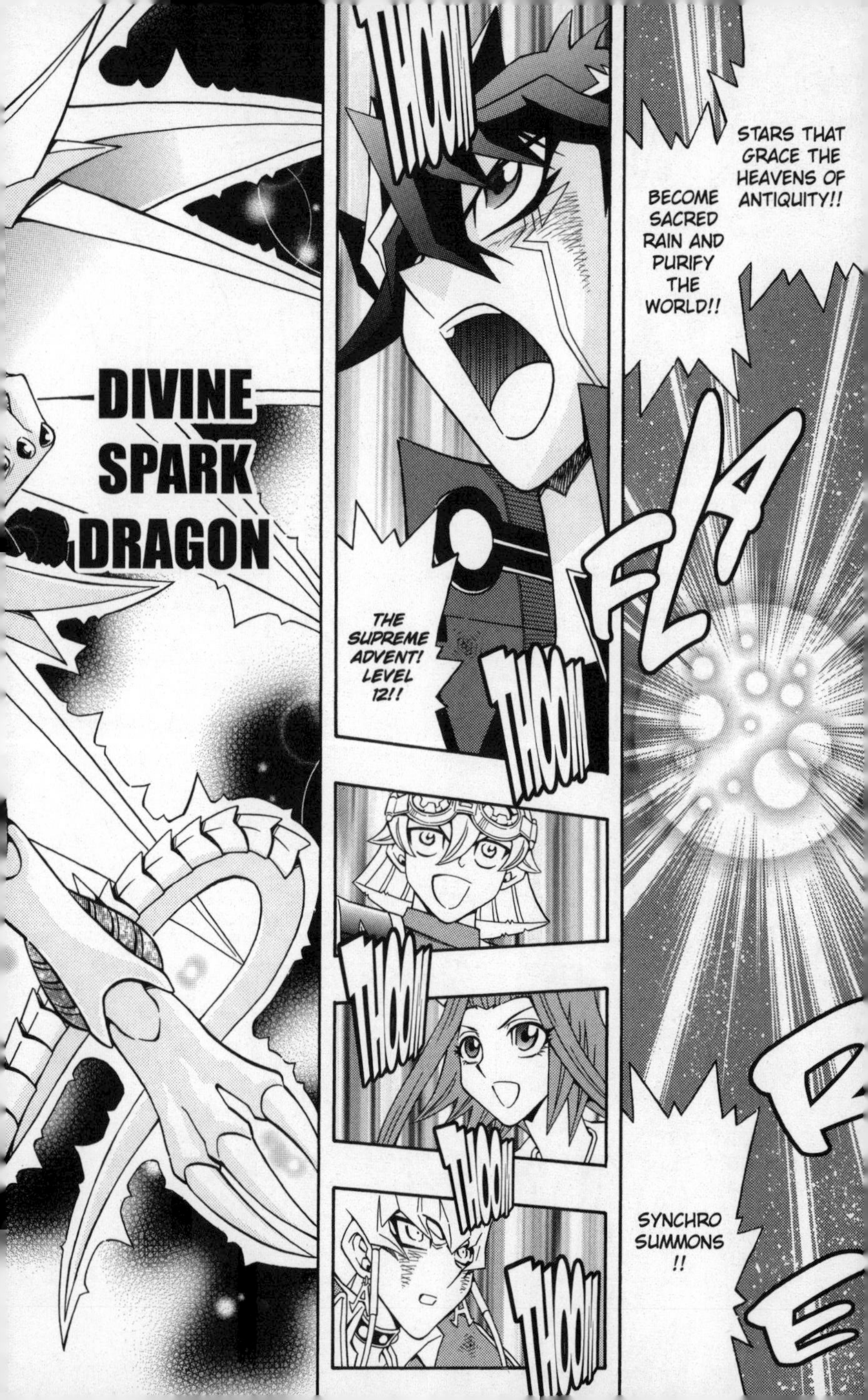
STARS THAT GRACE THE HEAVENS OF ANTIQUITY!!
BECOME SACRED RAIN AND PURIFY THE WORLD!!
FLA
SYNCHRO SUMMONS !!
THOOM
THE SUPREME ADVENT! LEVEL 12!!
THOOM
THOOM
THOOM
THOOM
DIVINE SPARK DRAGON

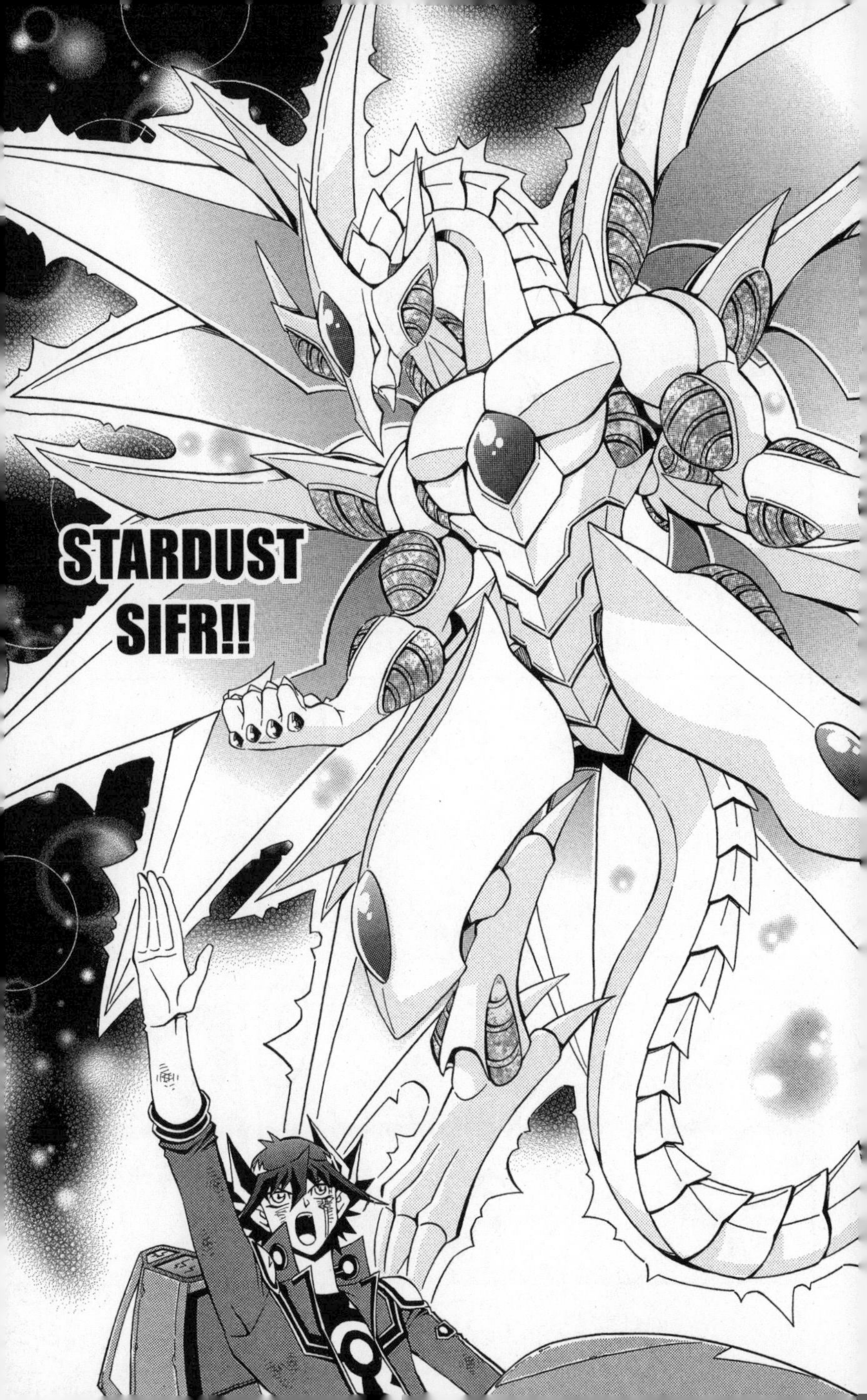
STARDUST SIFR!!

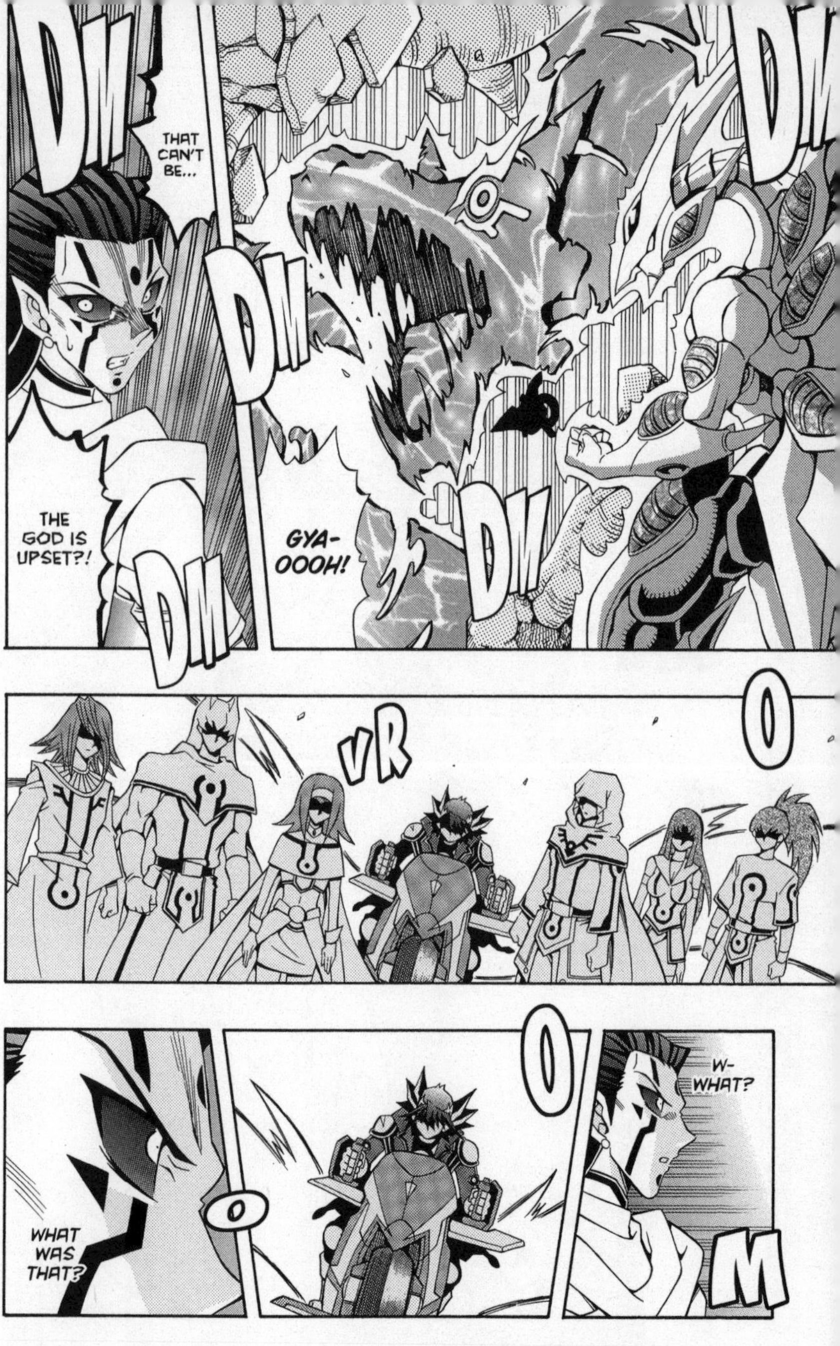
DM
DM
DM
GYA-OOOH!
DM
THAT CAN'T BE...
DM
THE GOD IS UPSET?!
DM
O
VR
O
W-WHAT?
M
O
WHAT WAS THAT?

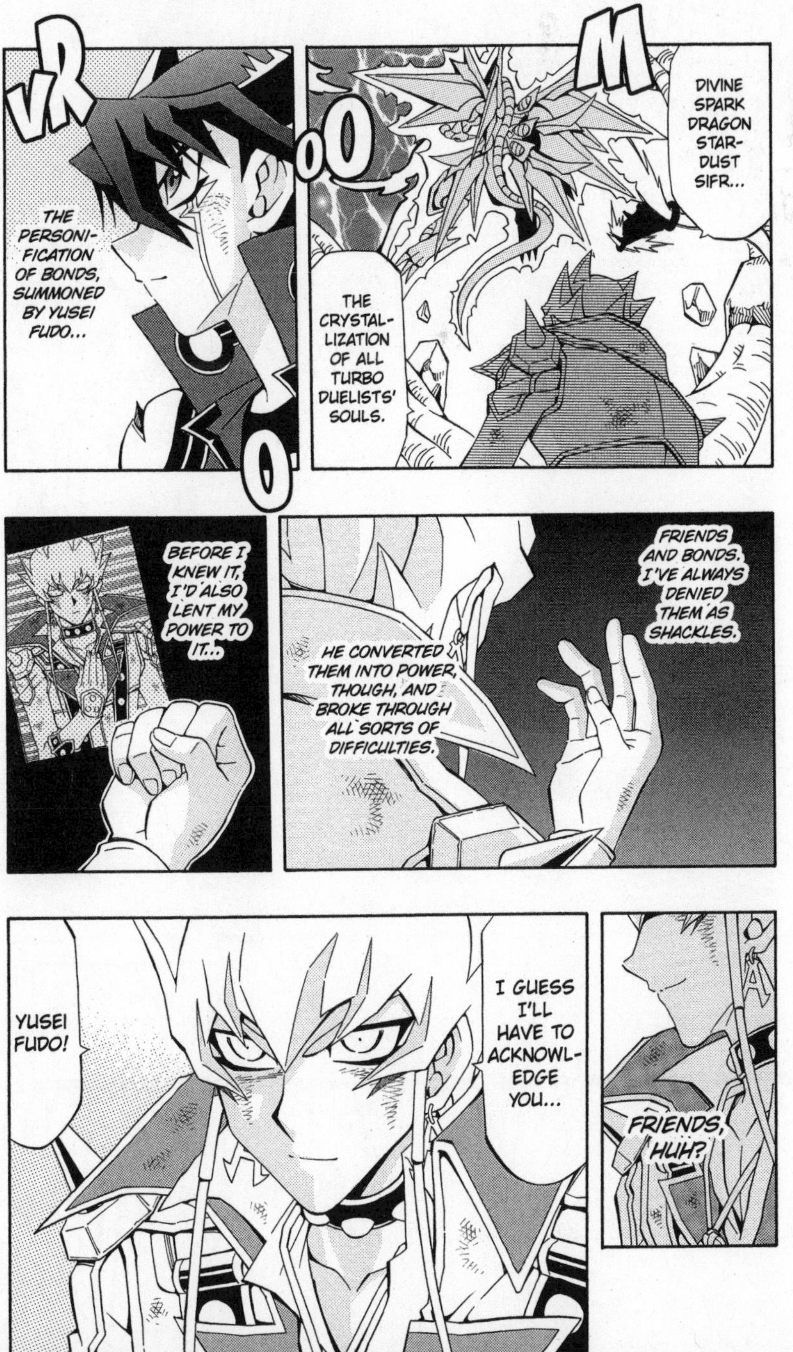
VROOOM
DIVINE SPARK DRAGON STARDUST SIFR...
THE CRYSTALLIZATION OF ALL TURBO DUELISTS' SOULS.
THE PERSONIFICATION OF BONDS, SUMMONED BY YUSEI FUDO...
FRIENDS AND BONDS. I'VE ALWAYS DENIED THEM AS SHACKLES.
HE CONVERTED THEM INTO POWER, THOUGH, AND BROKE THROUGH ALL SORTS OF DIFFICULTIES.
BEFORE I KNEW IT, I'D ALSO LENT MY POWER TO IT...
FRIENDS, HUH?
I GUESS I'LL HAVE TO ACKNOWLEDGE YOU...
YUSEI FUDO!

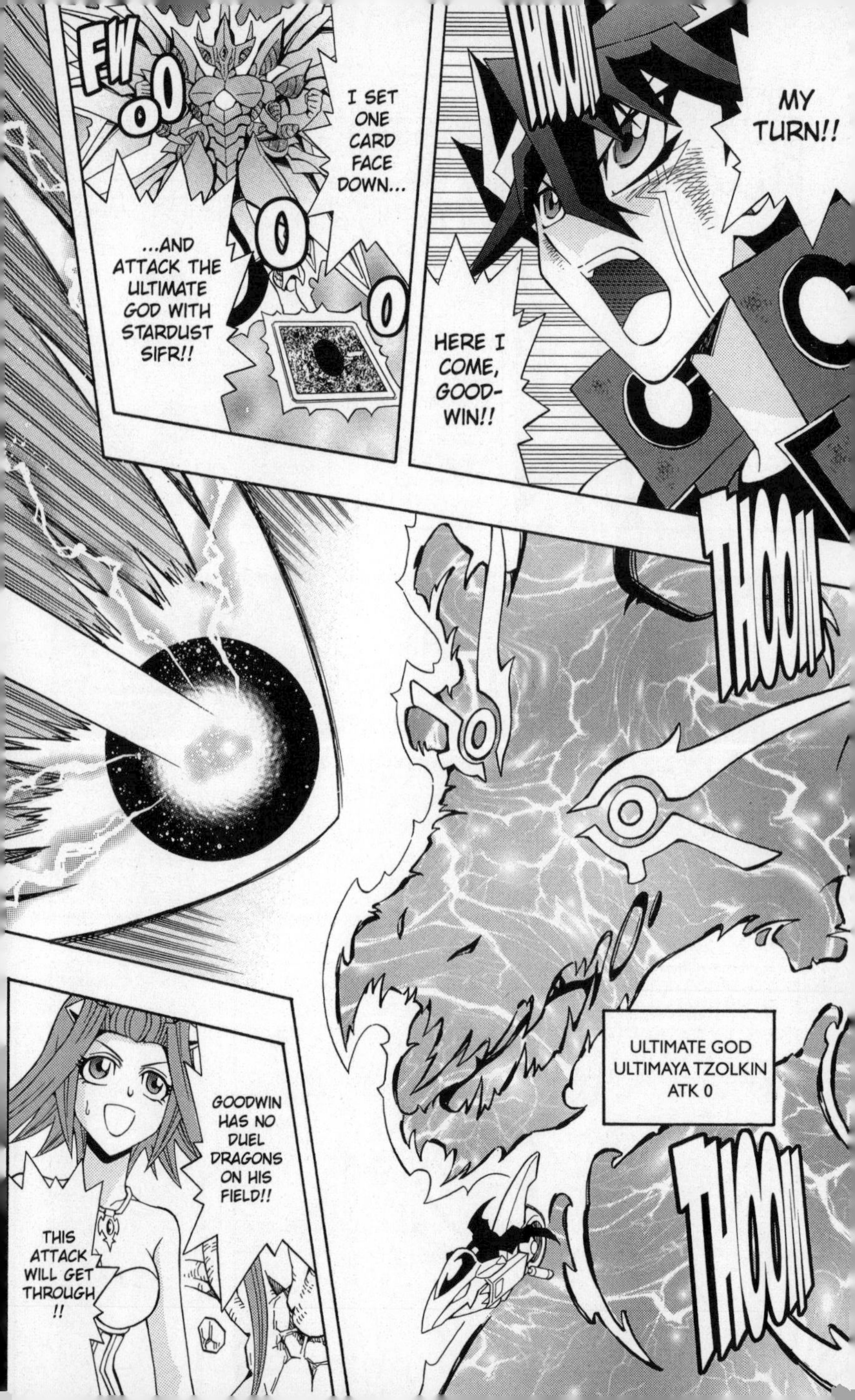
THOOM
MY TURN!!
HERE I COME, GOOD-WIN!!
FWOOOO
I SET ONE CARD FACE DOWN...
...AND ATTACK THE ULTIMATE GOD WITH STARDUST SIFR!!
THOOM
ULTIMATE GOD ULTIMAYA TZOLKIN ATK 0
THOOM
GOODWIN HAS NO DUEL DRAGONS ON HIS FIELD!!
THIS ATTACK WILL GET THROUGH !!

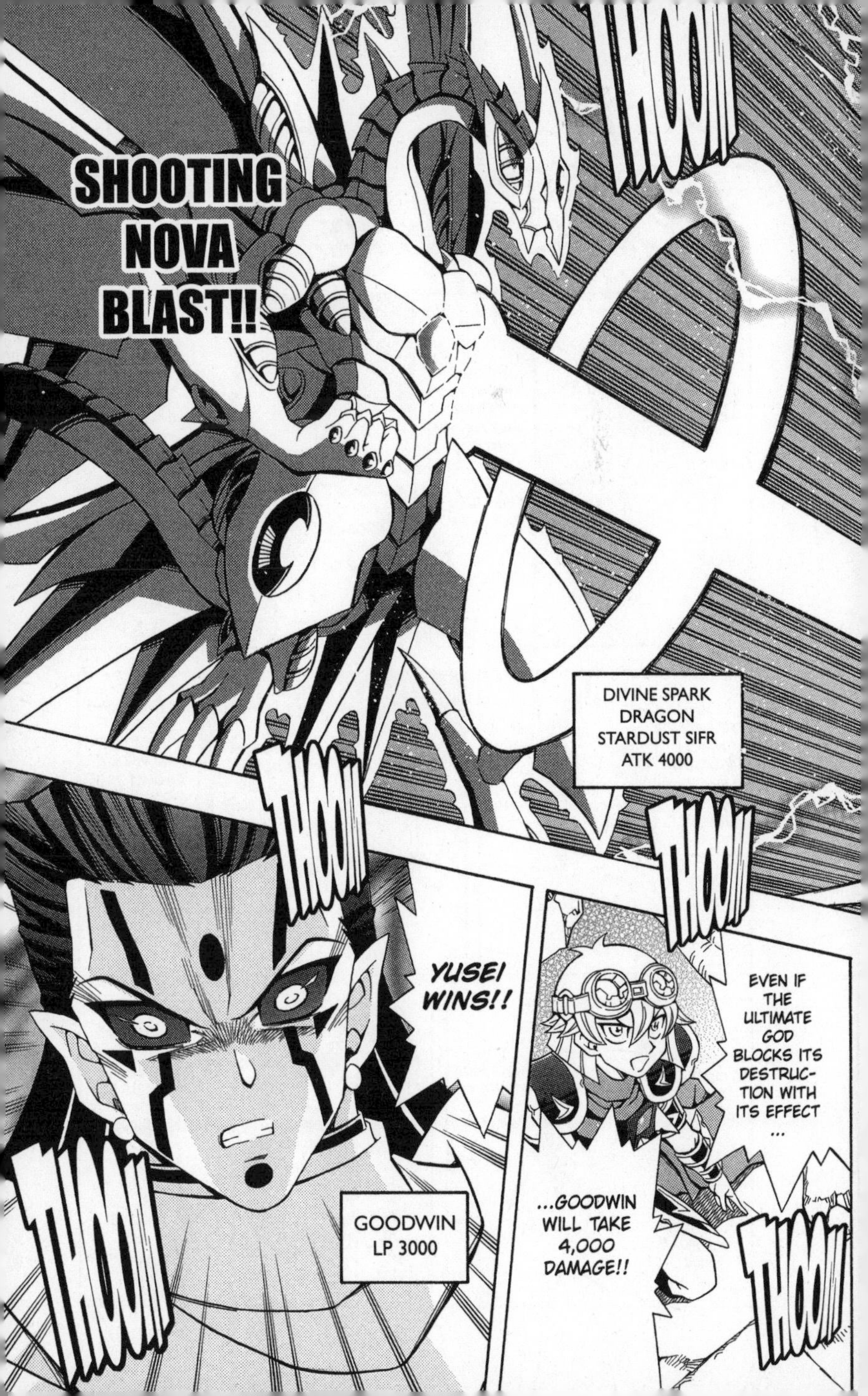
THOOM
SHOOTING NOVA BLAST!!
DIVINE SPARK DRAGON STARDUST SIFR ATK 4000
THOOM
THOOM
EVEN IF THE ULTIMATE GOD BLOCKS ITS DESTRUCTION WITH ITS EFFECT ...
...GOODWIN WILL TAKE 4,000 DAMAGE!!
THOOM
THOOM
YUSEI WINS!!
GOODWIN LP 3000
THOOM

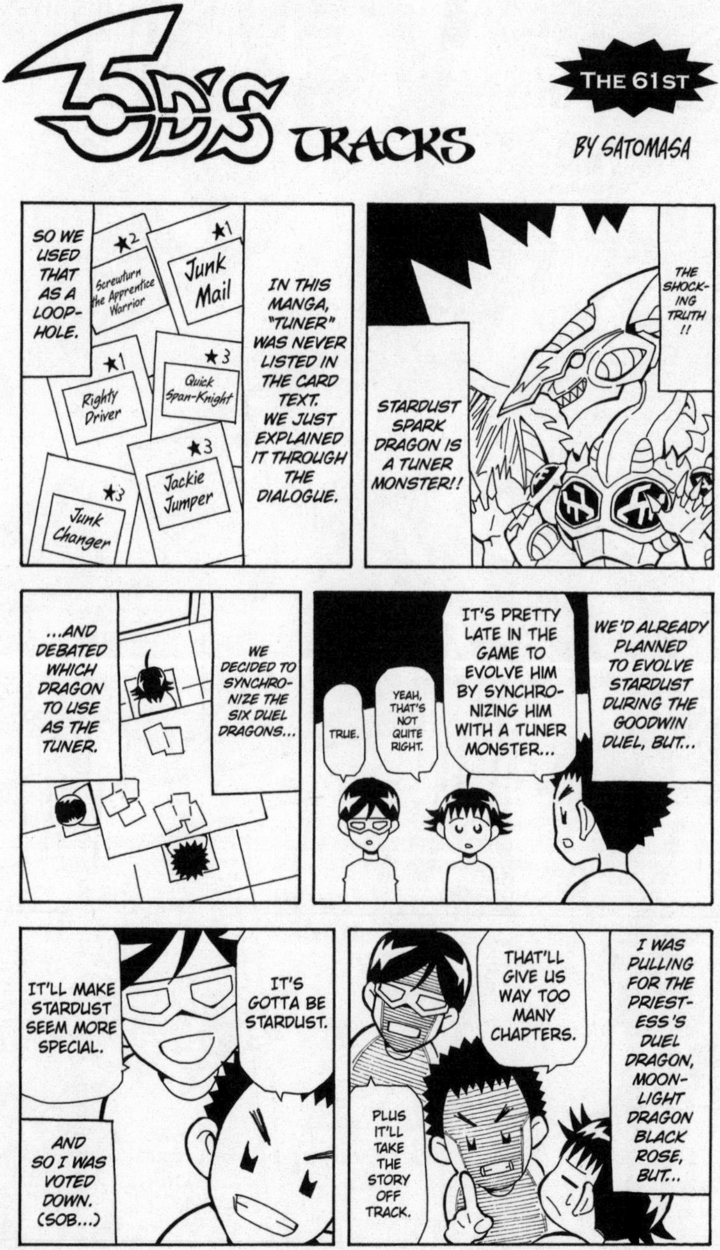
5D's TRACKS
THE 61ST
BY SATOMASA
THE SHOCKING TRUTH!!
STARDUST SPARK DRAGON IS A TUNER MONSTER!!
IN THIS MANGA, "TUNER" WAS NEVER LISTED IN THE CARD TEXT. WE JUST EXPLAINED IT THROUGH THE DIALOGUE.
★1 Junk Mail
★2 Screwturn the Apprentice Warrior
★3 Quick Span-Knight
★1 Righty Driver
★3 Jackie Jumper
★3 Junk Changer
SO WE USED THAT AS A LOOPHOLE.
WE'D ALREADY PLANNED TO EVOLVE STARDUST DURING THE GOODWIN DUEL, BUT...
IT'S PRETTY LATE IN THE GAME TO EVOLVE HIM BY SYNCHRONIZING HIM WITH A TUNER MONSTER...
YEAH, THAT'S NOT QUITE RIGHT.
TRUE.
WE DECIDED TO SYNCHRONIZE THE SIX DUEL DRAGONS...
...AND DEBATED WHICH DRAGON TO USE AS THE TUNER.
I WAS PULLING FOR THE PRIESTESS'S DUEL DRAGON, MOONLIGHT DRAGON BLACK ROSE, BUT...
THAT'LL GIVE US WAY TOO MANY CHAPTERS.
PLUS IT'LL TAKE THE STORY OFF TRACK.
IT'S GOTTA BE STARDUST.
IT'LL MAKE STARDUST SEEM MORE SPECIAL.
AND SO I WAS VOTED DOWN. (SOB...)

RIDE-63
ORIGIN OF REVENGE!!

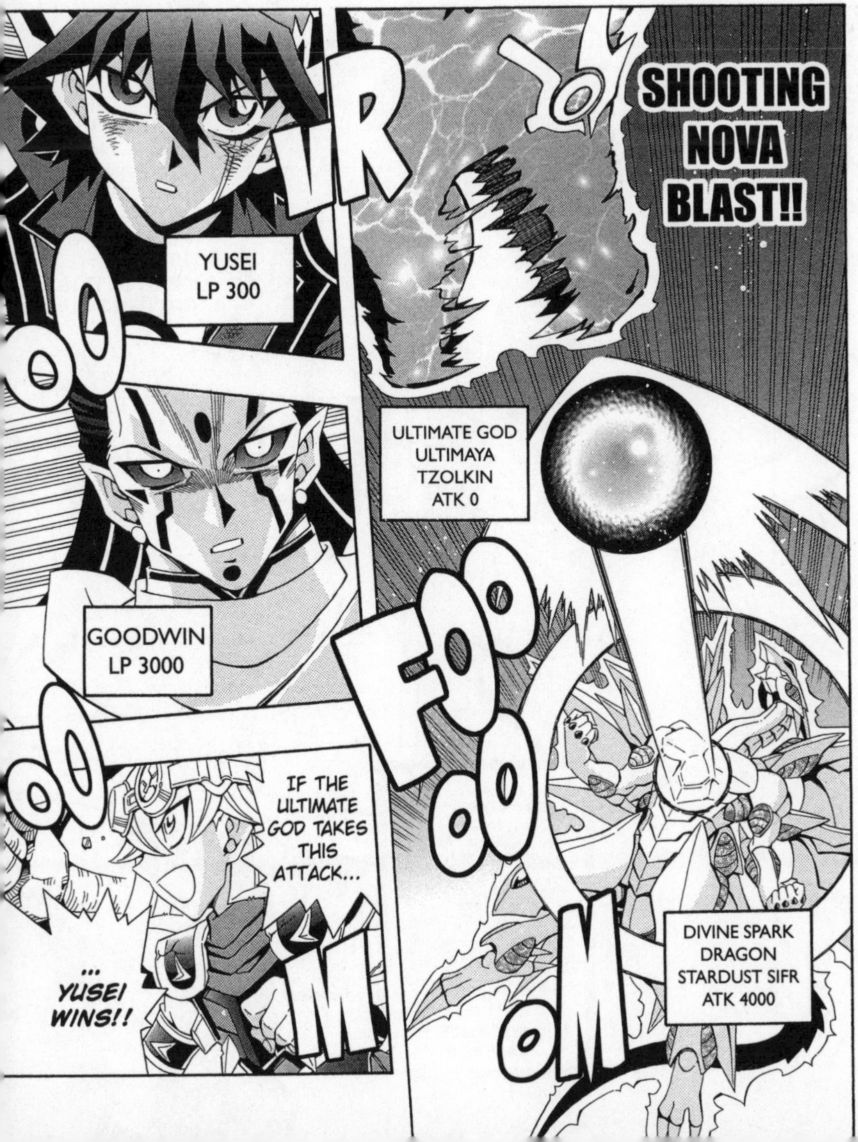
SHOOTING NOVA BLAST!!
ULTIMATE GOD ULTIMAYA TZOLKIN ATK 0
FOOOOOM
DIVINE SPARK DRAGON STARDUST SIFR ATK 4000
VROOOOOOM
YUSEI LP 300
GOODWIN LP 3000
IF THE ULTIMATE GOD TAKES THIS ATTACK...
...YUSEI WINS!!

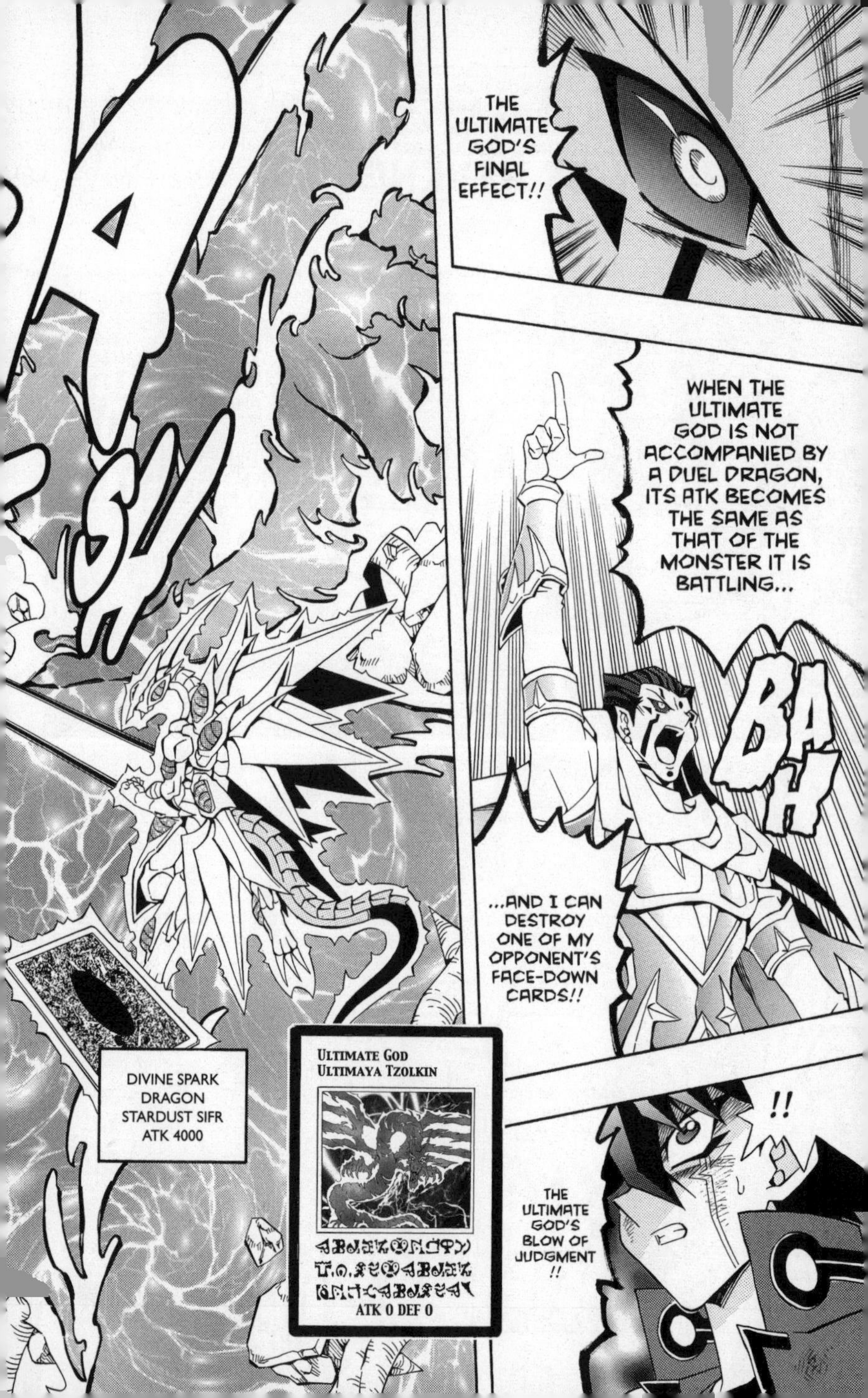
THE ULTIMATE GOD'S FINAL EFFECT!!
WHEN THE ULTIMATE GOD IS NOT ACCOMPANIED BY A DUEL DRAGON, ITS ATK BECOMES THE SAME AS THAT OF THE MONSTER IT IS BATTLING...
BAH
...AND I CAN DESTROY ONE OF MY OPPONENT'S FACE-DOWN CARDS!!
!!
THE ULTIMATE GOD'S BLOW OF JUDGMENT!!
ULTIMATE GOD ULTIMAYA TZOLKIN
ATK 0 DEF 0
DIVINE SPARK DRAGON STARDUST SIFR ATK 4000

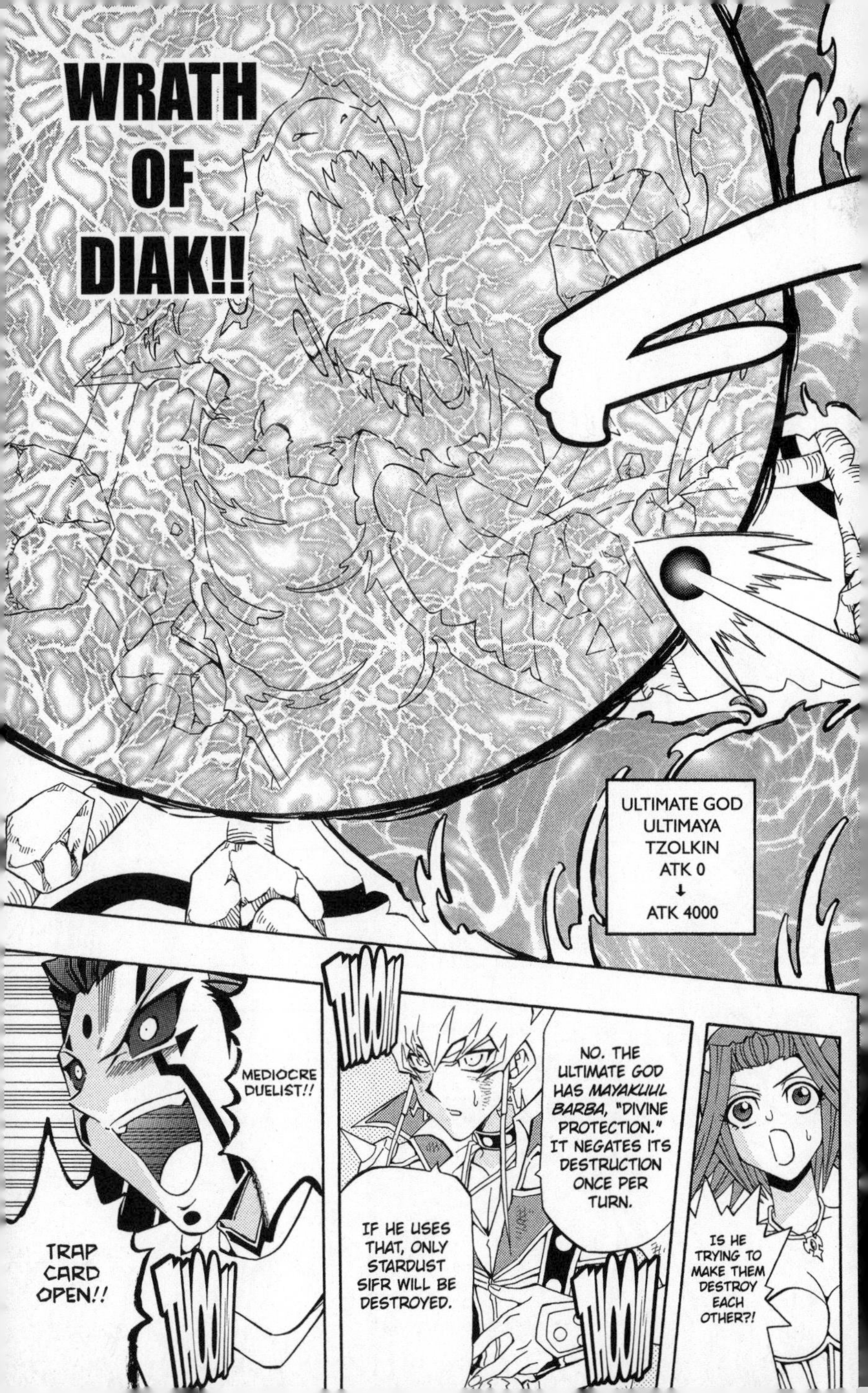
WRATH OF DIAK!!
ULTIMATE GOD ULTIMAYA TZOLKIN ATK 0 ↓ ATK 4000
IS HE TRYING TO MAKE THEM DESTROY EACH OTHER?!
THOOM
NO. THE ULTIMATE GOD HAS *MAYAKUUL BARBA*, "DIVINE PROTECTION." IT NEGATES ITS DESTRUCTION ONCE PER TURN.
IF HE USES THAT, ONLY STARDUST SIFR WILL BE DESTROYED.
THOOM
MEDIOCRE DUELIST!!
TRAP CARD OPEN!!
THOOM

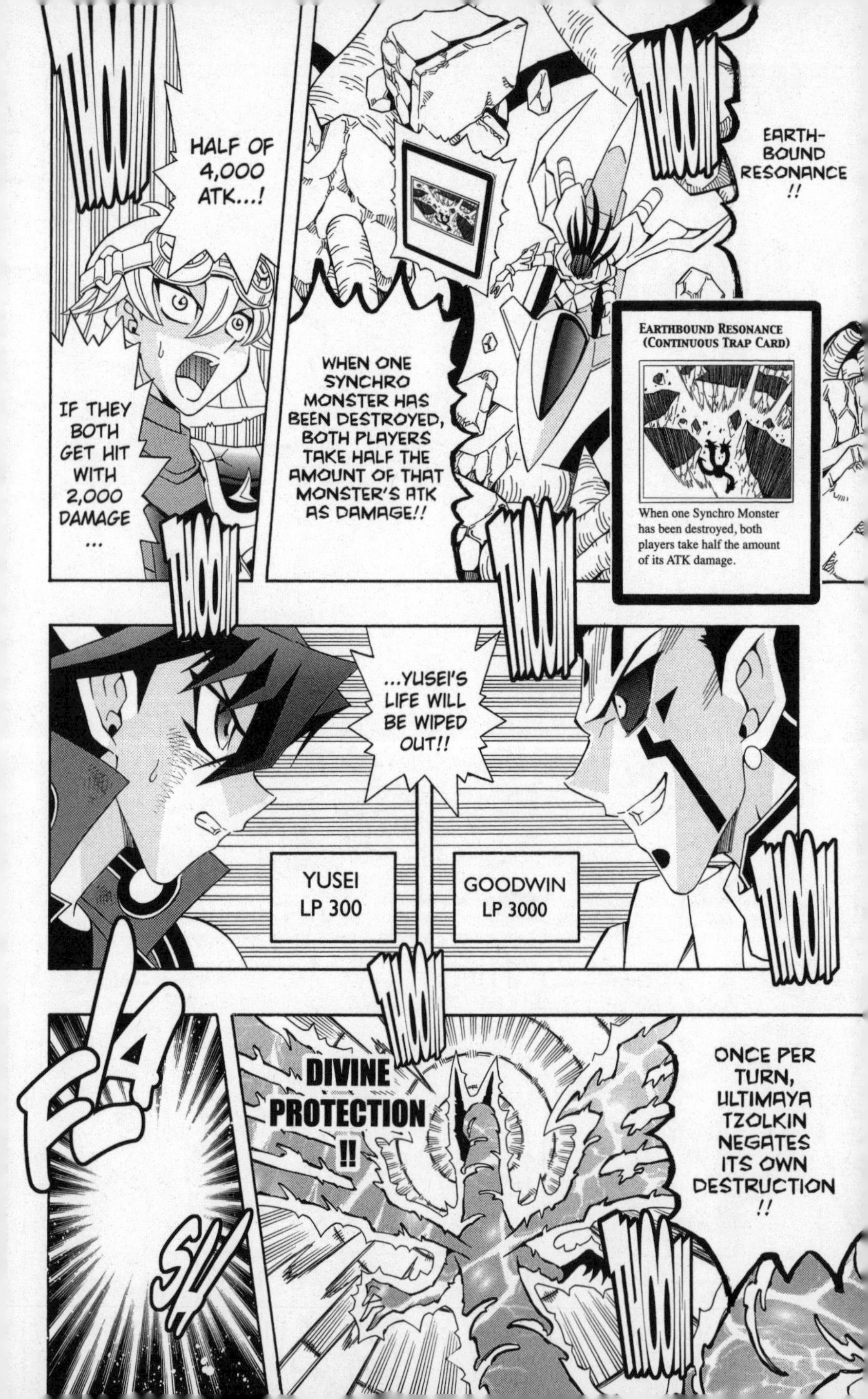
THOOM
EARTH-BOUND RESONANCE !!
WHEN ONE SYNCHRO MONSTER HAS BEEN DESTROYED, BOTH PLAYERS TAKE HALF THE AMOUNT OF THAT MONSTER'S ATK AS DAMAGE!!
EARTHBOUND RESONANCE (CONTINUOUS TRAP CARD)
When one Synchro Monster has been destroyed, both players take half the amount of its ATK damage.
THOOM
THOOM
HALF OF 4,000 ATK...!
IF THEY BOTH GET HIT WITH 2,000 DAMAGE ...
THOOM
THOOM
...YUSEI'S LIFE WILL BE WIPED OUT!!
GOODWIN LP 3000
YUSEI LP 300
THOOM
ONCE PER TURN, ULTIMAYA TZOLKIN NEGATES ITS OWN DESTRUCTION !!
DIVINE PROTECTION !!
THOOM
FLASH!

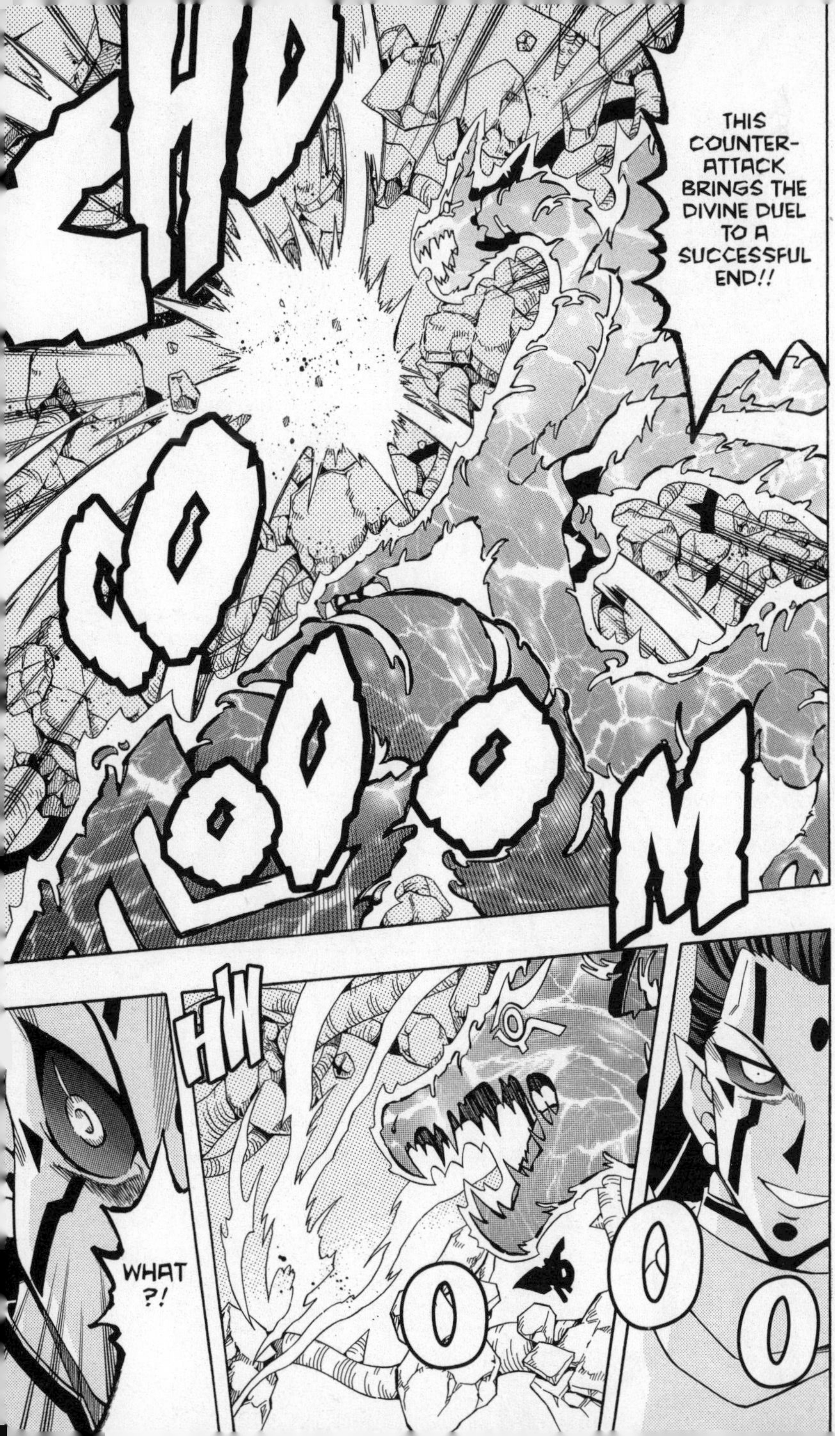
THIS COUNTER-ATTACK BRINGS THE DIVINE DUEL TO A SUCCESSFUL END!!
WHAT?!

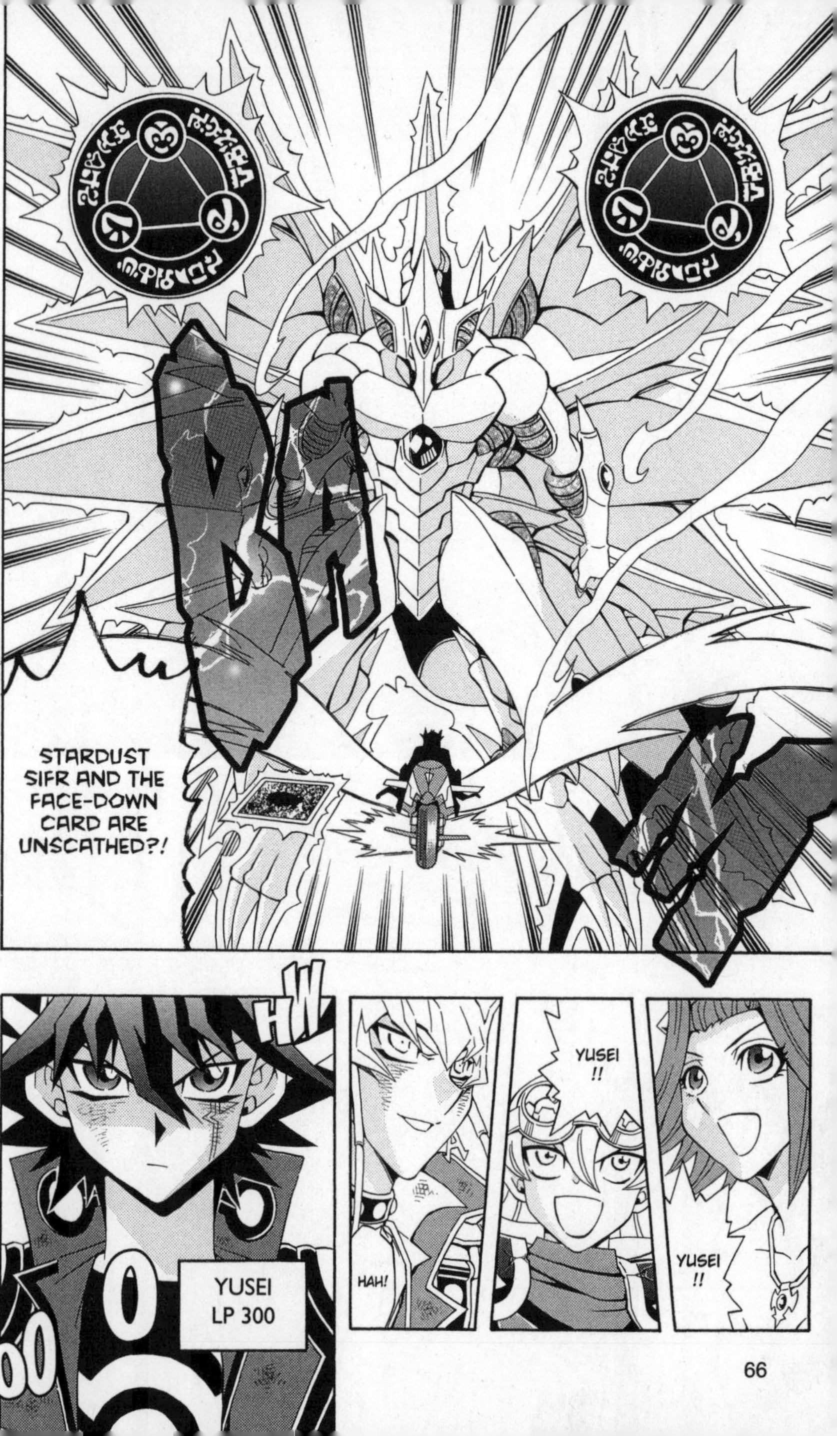
STARDUST SIFR AND THE FACE-DOWN CARD ARE UNSCATHED?!
YUSEI !!
YUSEI !!
HAH!
HW
YUSEI LP 300

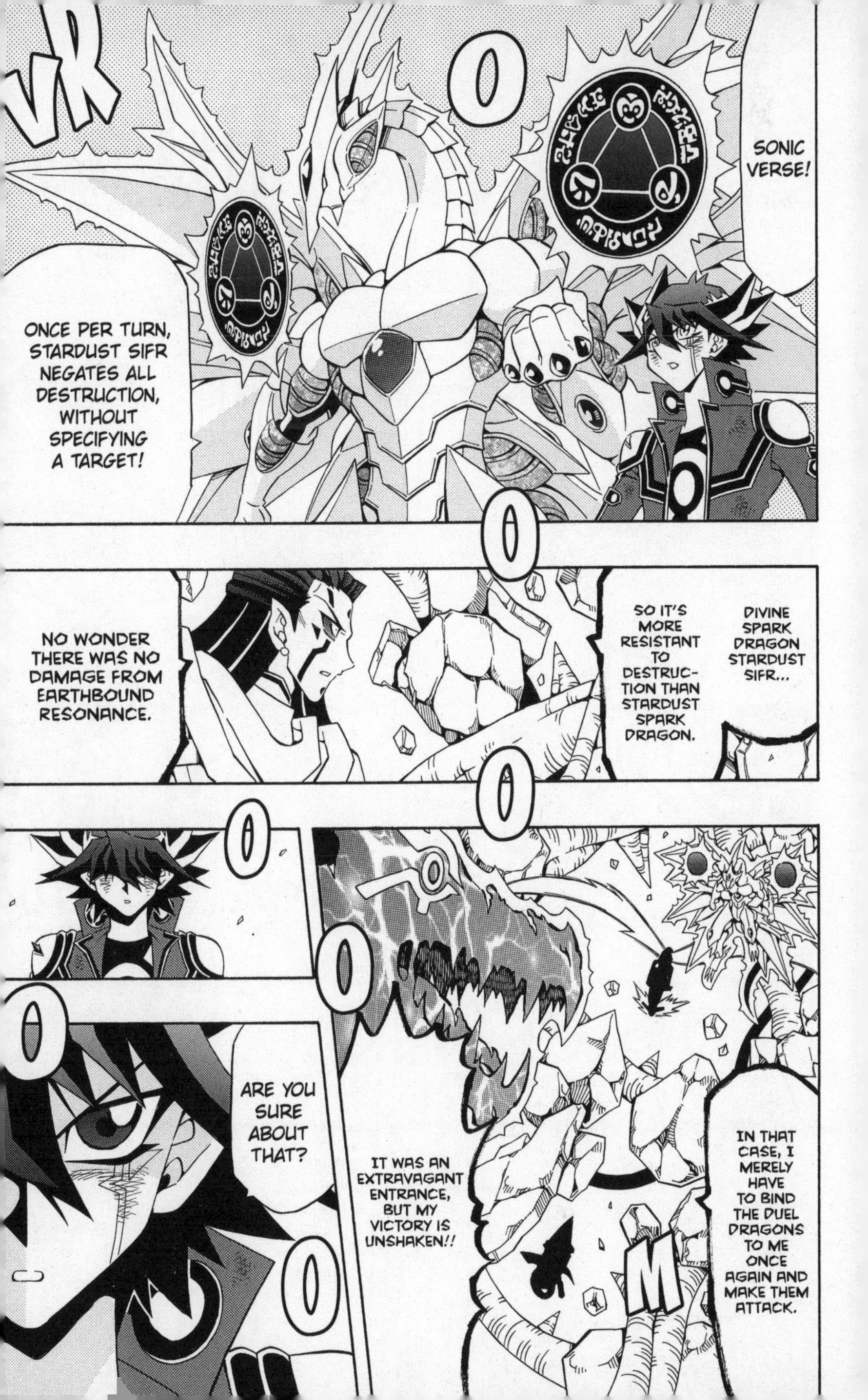
SONIC VERSE!
ONCE PER TURN, STARDUST SIFR NEGATES ALL DESTRUCTION, WITHOUT SPECIFYING A TARGET!
DIVINE SPARK DRAGON STARDUST SIFR...
SO IT'S MORE RESISTANT TO DESTRUCTION THAN STARDUST SPARK DRAGON.
NO WONDER THERE WAS NO DAMAGE FROM EARTHBOUND RESONANCE.
IN THAT CASE, I MERELY HAVE TO BIND THE DUEL DRAGONS TO ME ONCE AGAIN AND MAKE THEM ATTACK.
IT WAS AN EXTRAVAGANT ENTRANCE, BUT MY VICTORY IS UNSHAKEN!!
ARE YOU SURE ABOUT THAT?

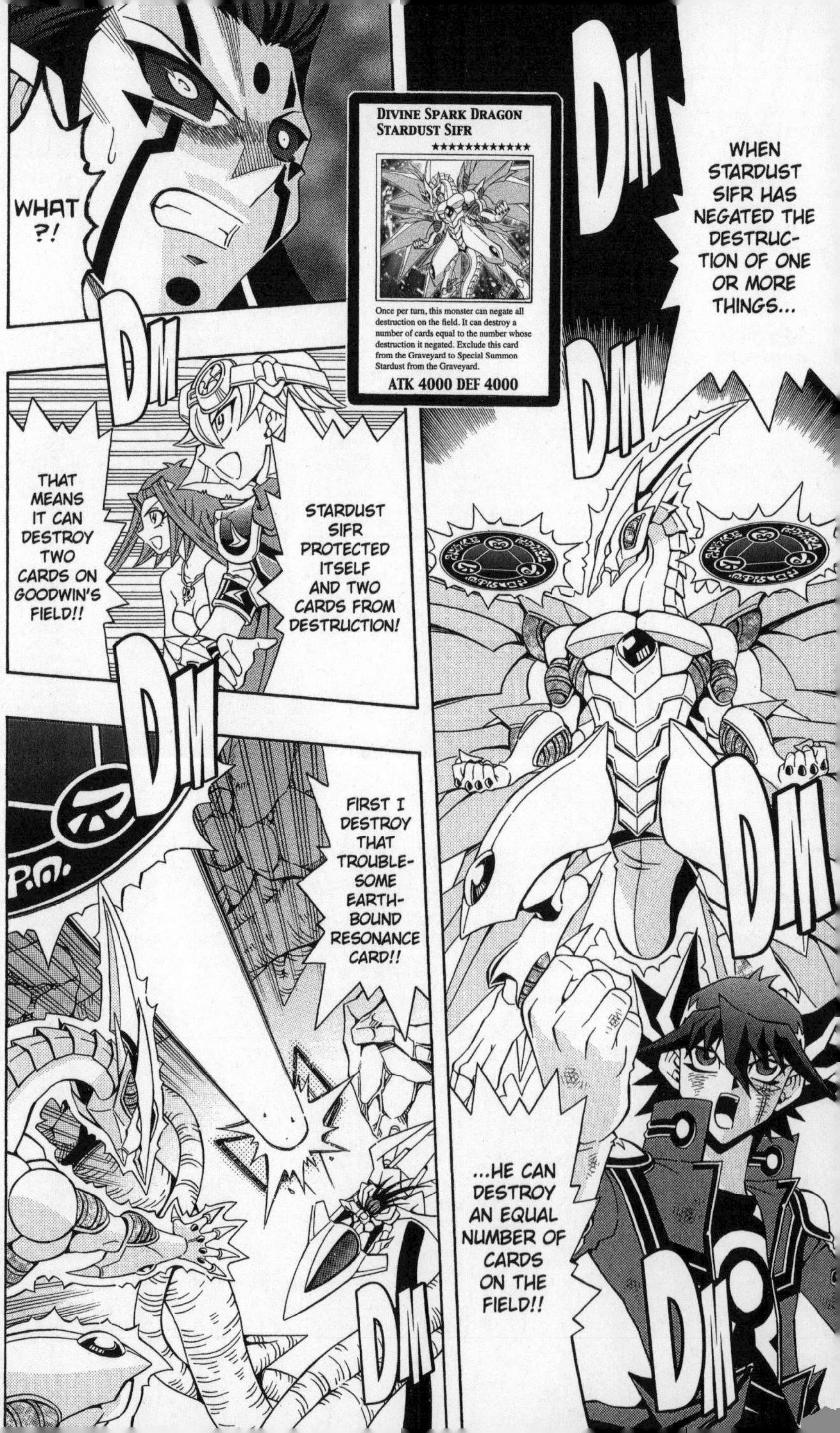
DM
WHEN STARDUST SIFR HAS NEGATED THE DESTRUC- TION OF ONE OR MORE THINGS...
DM
DM
...HE CAN DESTROY AN EQUAL NUMBER OF CARDS ON THE FIELD!!
DM
DIVINE SPARK DRAGON STARDUST SIFR
★★★★★★★★★★★★★
Once per turn, this monster can negate all destruction on the field. It can destroy a number of cards equal to the number whose destruction it negated. Exclude this card from the Graveyard to Special Summon Stardust from the Graveyard.
ATK 4000 DEF 4000
WHAT ?!
DM
STARDUST SIFR PROTECTED ITSELF AND TWO CARDS FROM DESTRUCTION!
THAT MEANS IT CAN DESTROY TWO CARDS ON GOODWIN'S FIELD!!
DM
FIRST I DESTROY THAT TROUBLE- SOME EARTH- BOUND RESONANCE CARD!!
DM

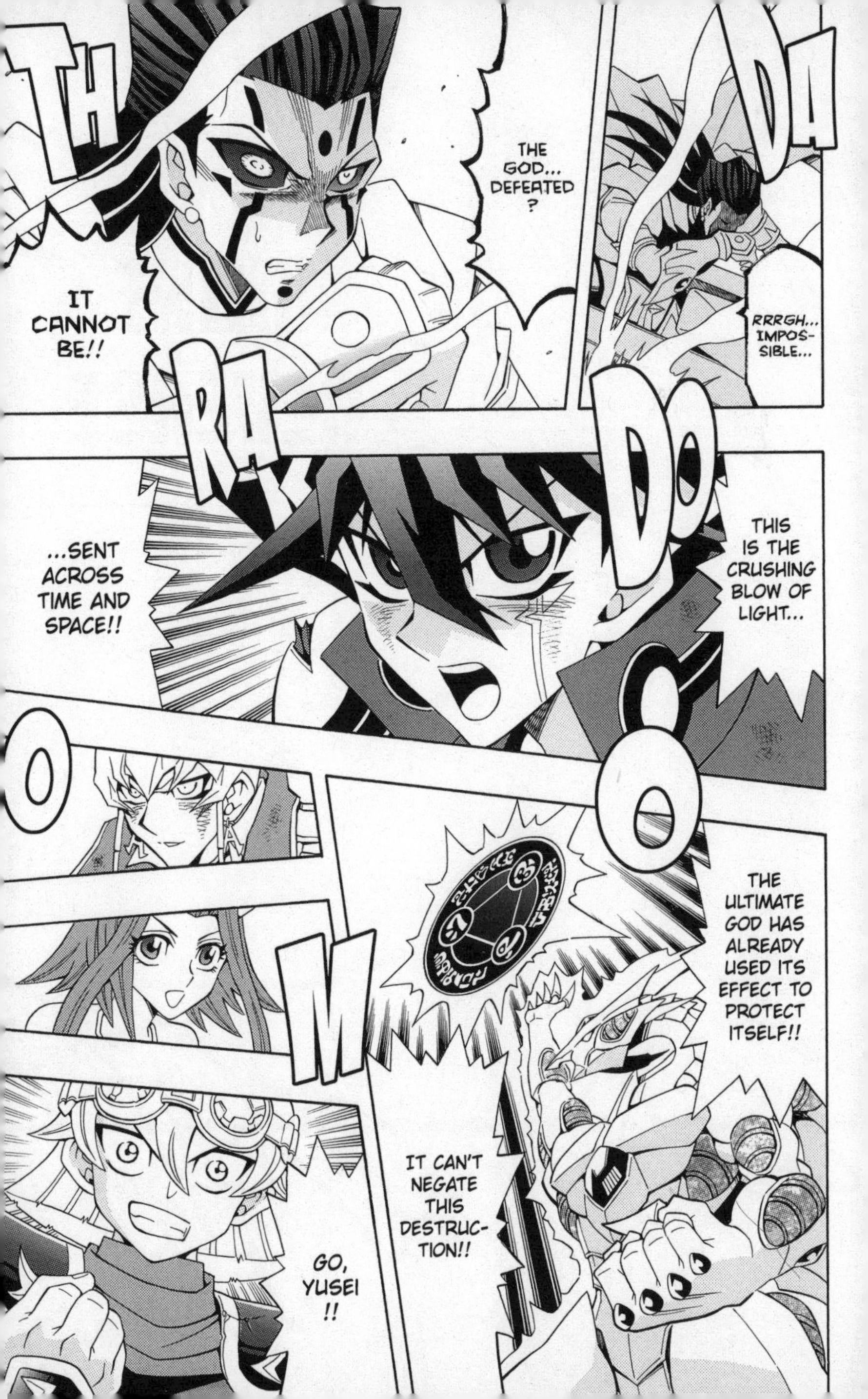
DA
RRRGH... IMPOSSIBLE...
THE GOD... DEFEATED?
TH
IT CANNOT BE!!
RA
DO
THIS IS THE CRUSHING BLOW OF LIGHT...
...SENT ACROSS TIME AND SPACE!!
O
THE ULTIMATE GOD HAS ALREADY USED ITS EFFECT TO PROTECT ITSELF!!
IT CAN'T NEGATE THIS DESTRUCTION!!
O
M
GO, YUSEI!!

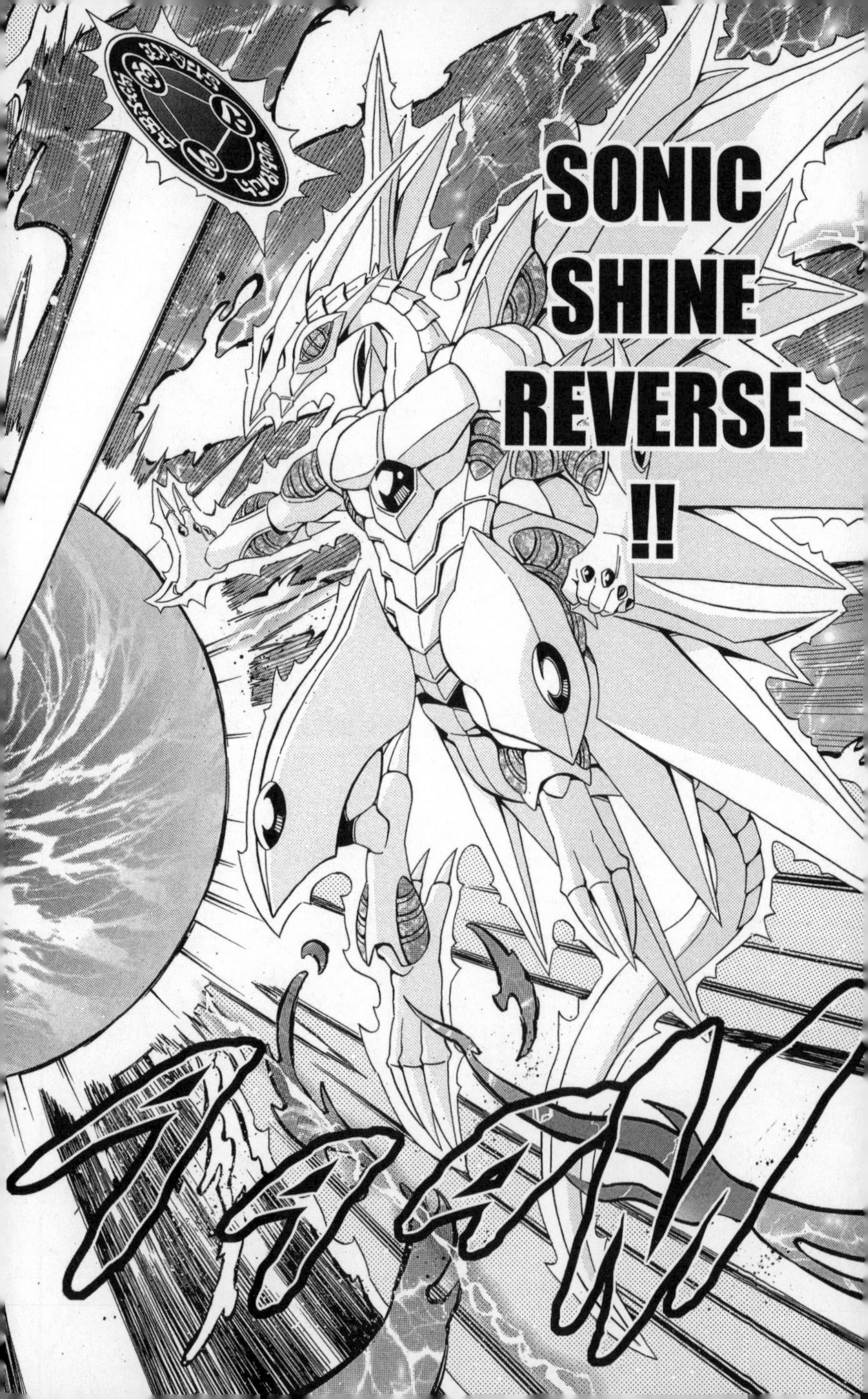
SONIC SHINE REVERSE !!

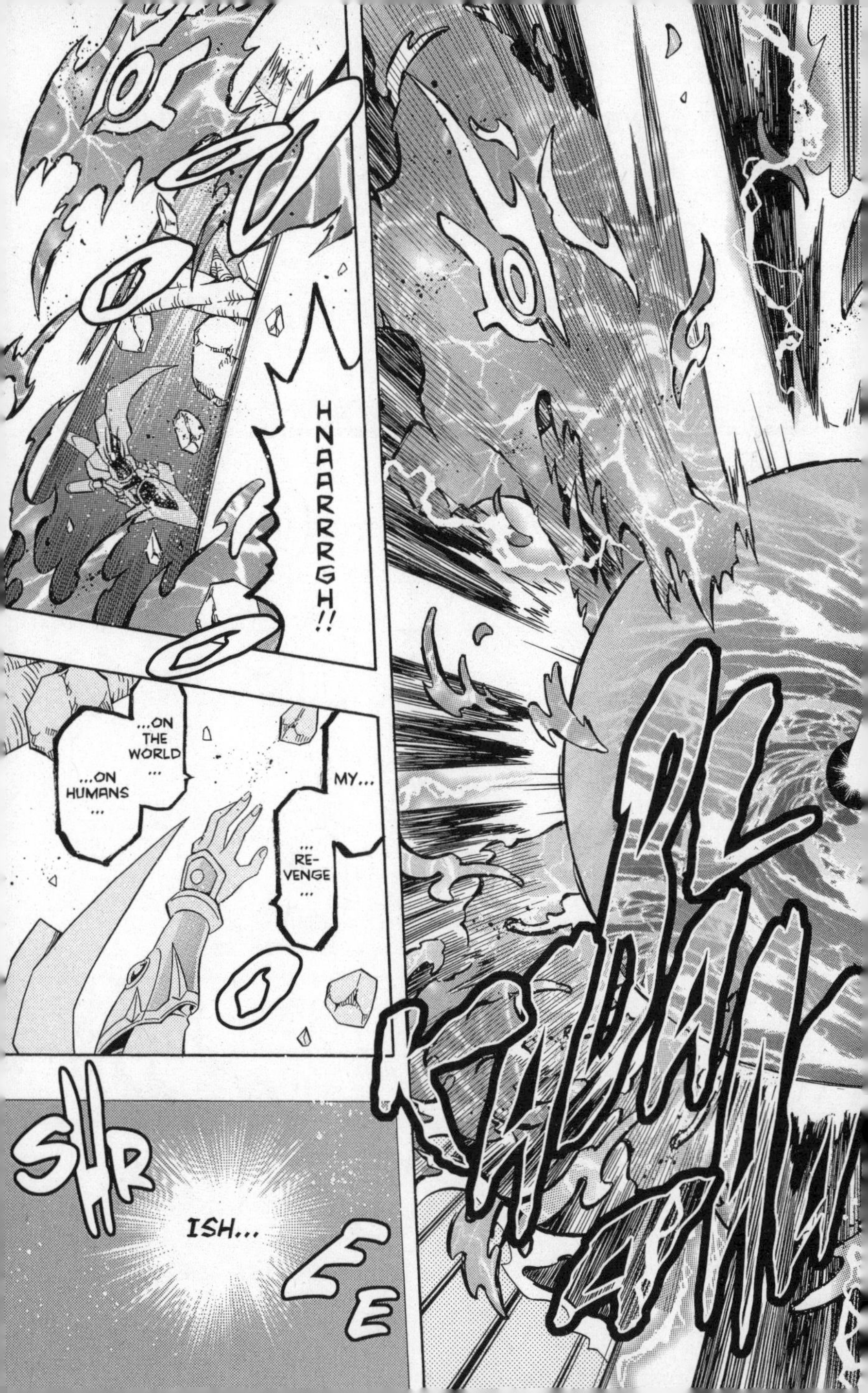
HNAARRRGH!!
MY... ...REVENGE...
...ON THE WORLD...
...ON HUMANS...
SHR
ISH...
EE

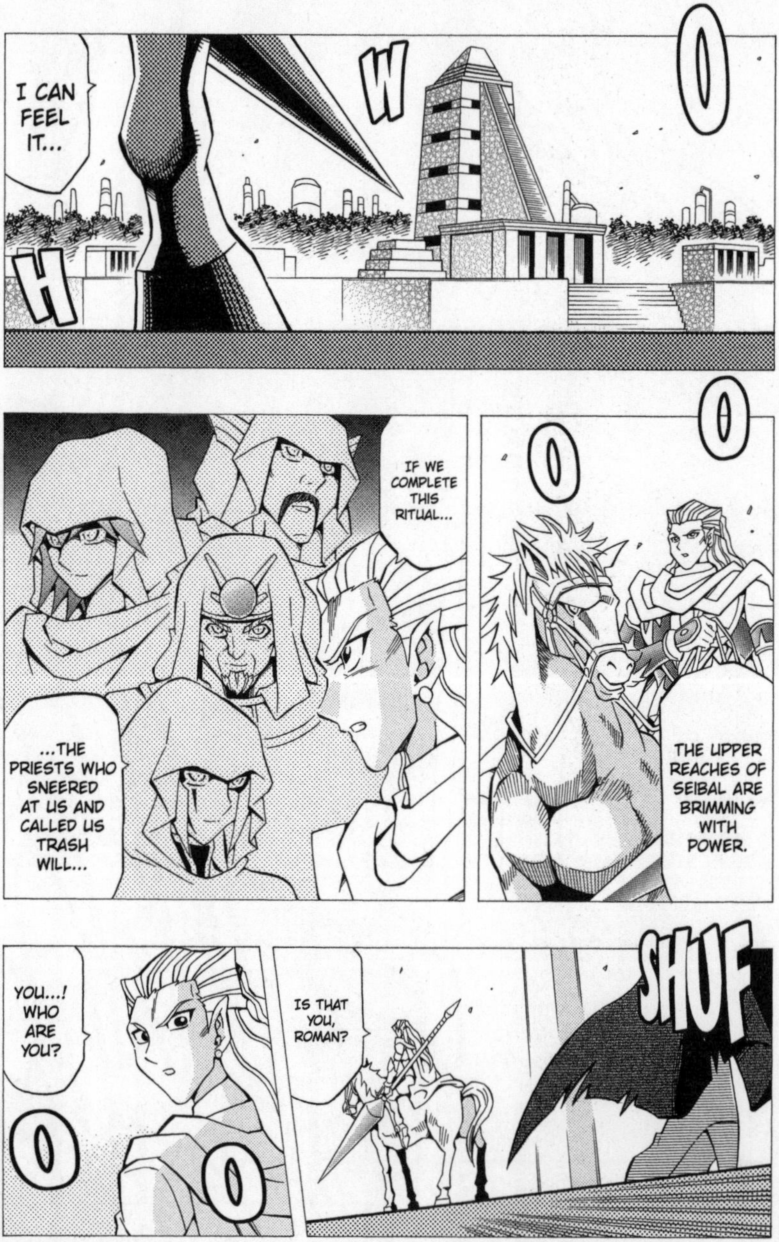
O
W
I CAN FEEL IT...
H
O
O
THE UPPER REACHES OF SEIBAL ARE BRIMMING WITH POWER.
IF WE COMPLETE THIS RITUAL...
...THE PRIESTS WHO SNEERED AT US AND CALLED US TRASH WILL...
SHUF
IS THAT YOU, ROMAN?
YOU...! WHO ARE YOU?
O
O

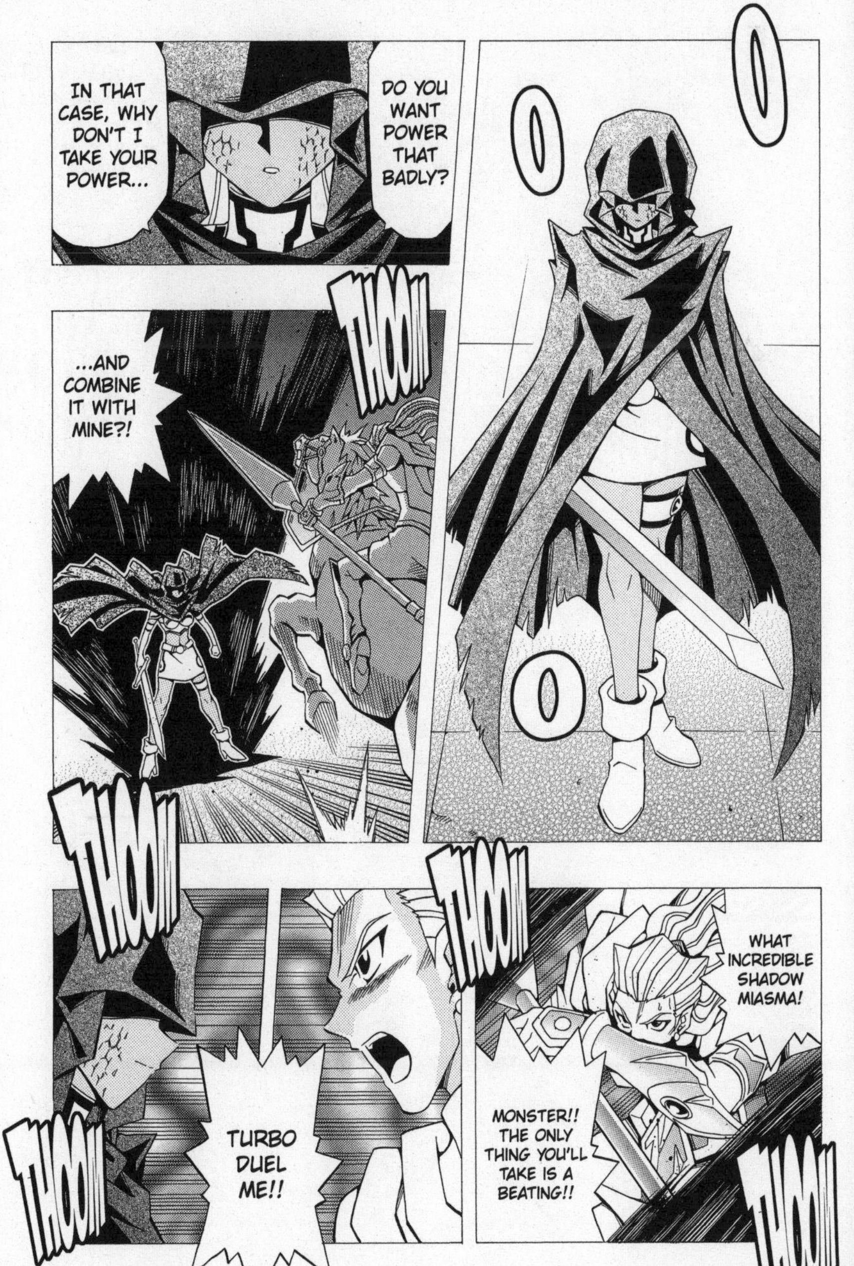
DO YOU WANT POWER THAT BADLY?
IN THAT CASE, WHY DON'T I TAKE YOUR POWER...
THOOM
...AND COMBINE IT WITH MINE?!
THOOM
THOOM
WHAT INCREDIBLE SHADOW MIASMA!
MONSTER!! THE ONLY THING YOU'LL TAKE IS A BEATING!!
THOOM
THOOM
TURBO DUEL ME!!

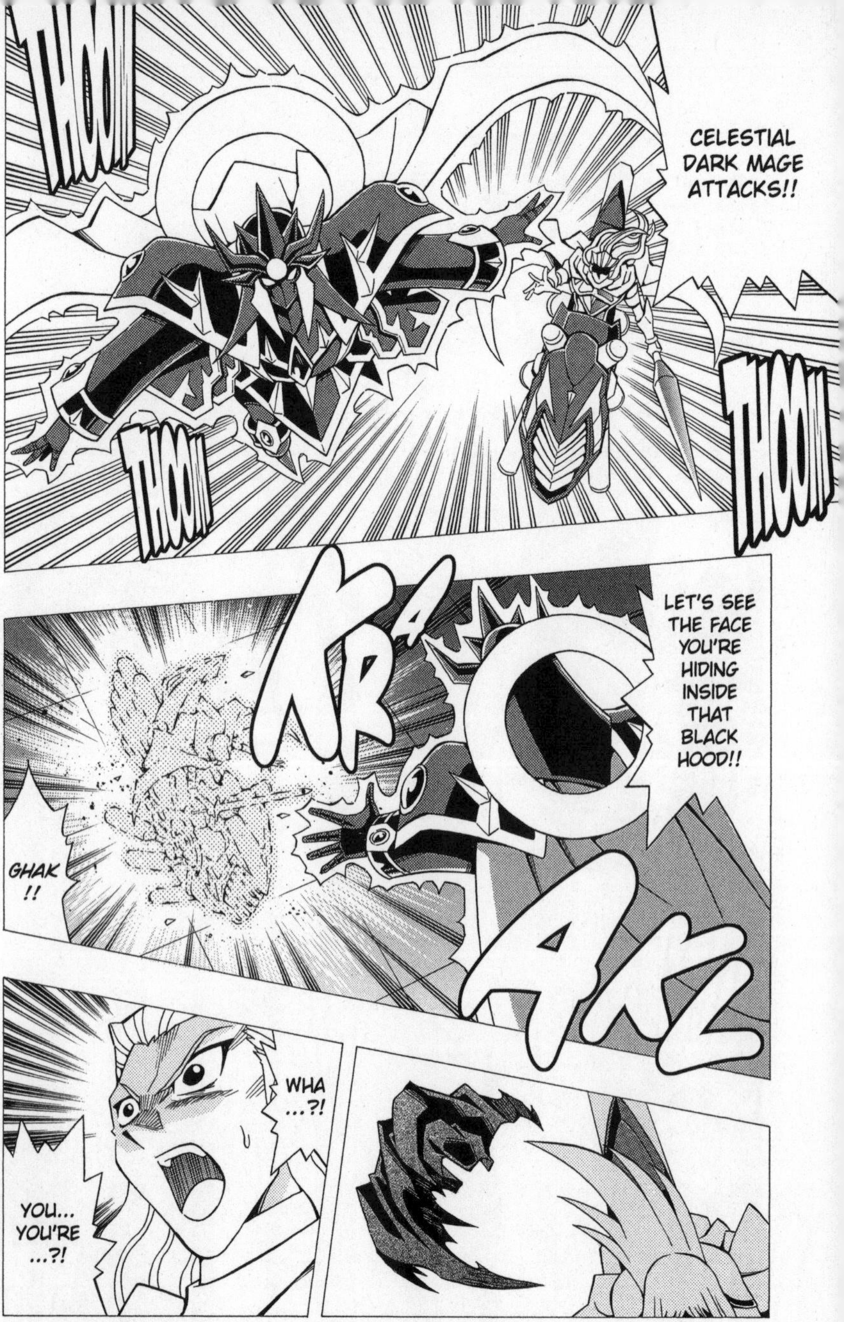
THOOM
CELESTIAL DARK MAGE ATTACKS!!
THOOM
THOOM
LET'S SEE THE FACE YOU'RE HIDING INSIDE THAT BLACK HOOD!!
GHAK !!
WHA ...?!
YOU... YOU'RE ...?!

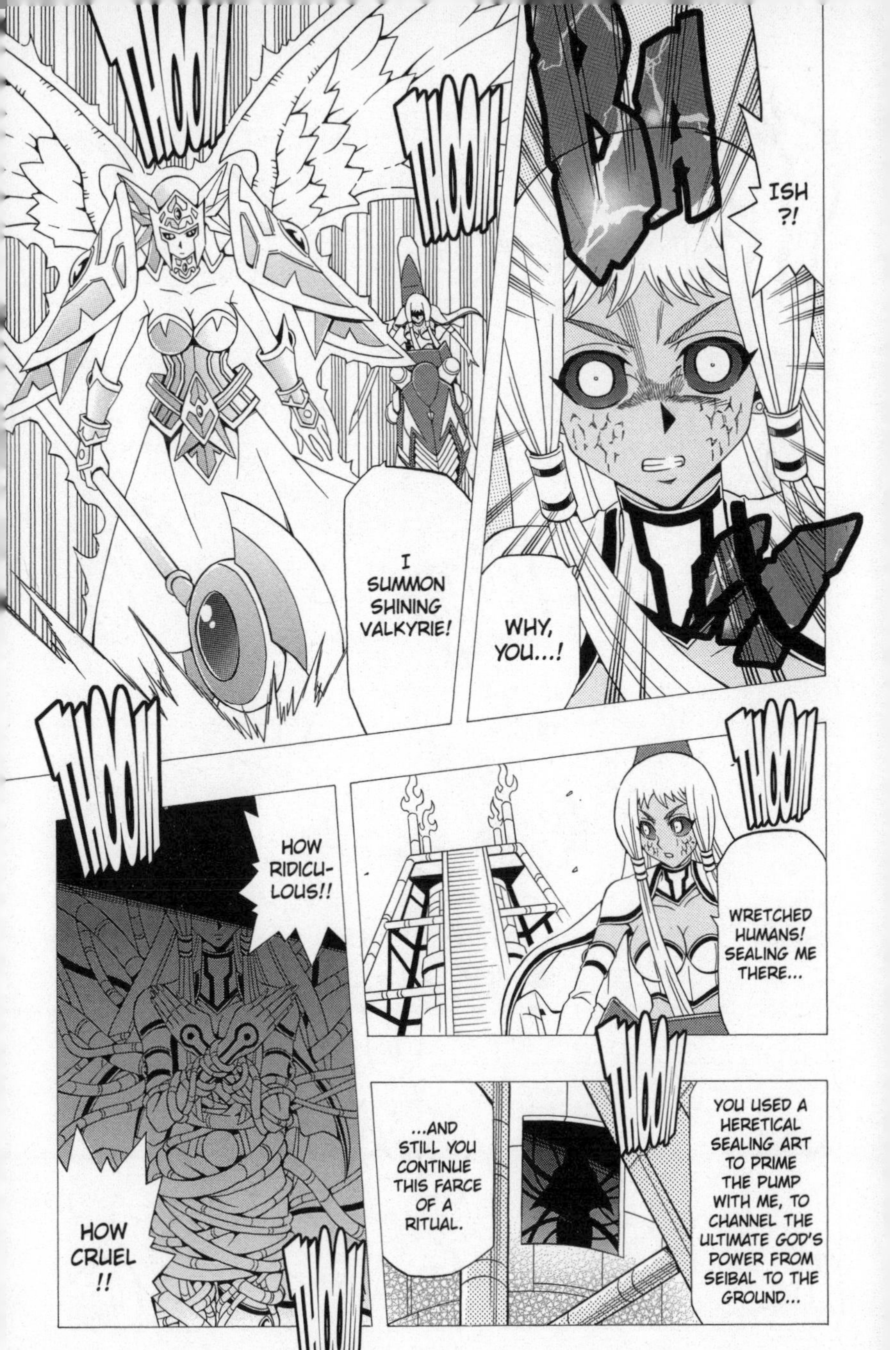
ISH ?!
WHY, YOU...!
THOOM
THOOM
I SUMMON SHINING VALKYRIE!
THOOM
WRETCHED HUMANS! SEALING ME THERE...
THOOM
YOU USED A HERETICAL SEALING ART TO PRIME THE PUMP WITH ME, TO CHANNEL THE ULTIMATE GOD'S POWER FROM SEIBAL TO THE GROUND...
...AND STILL YOU CONTINUE THIS FARCE OF A RITUAL.
THOOM
HOW RIDICULOUS!!
HOW CRUEL !!
THOOM

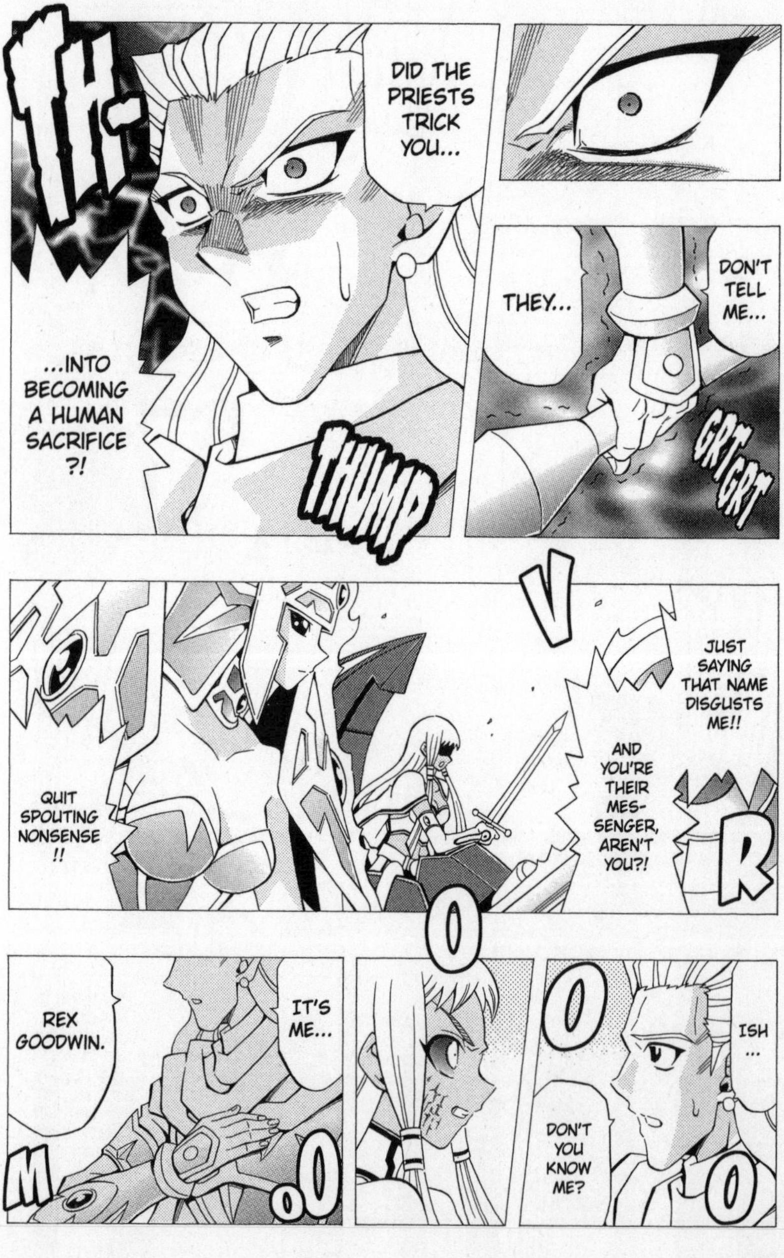
DON'T TELL ME...
THEY...
GRT GRT
TH-
DID THE PRIESTS TRICK YOU...
...INTO BECOMING A HUMAN SACRIFICE ?!
THUMP
V
JUST SAYING THAT NAME DISGUSTS ME!!
AND YOU'RE THEIR MES-SENGER, AREN'T YOU?!
R
QUIT SPOUTING NONSENSE !!
O
ISH ...
DON'T YOU KNOW ME?
O
O
O
IT'S ME...
REX GOODWIN.
O
O
M

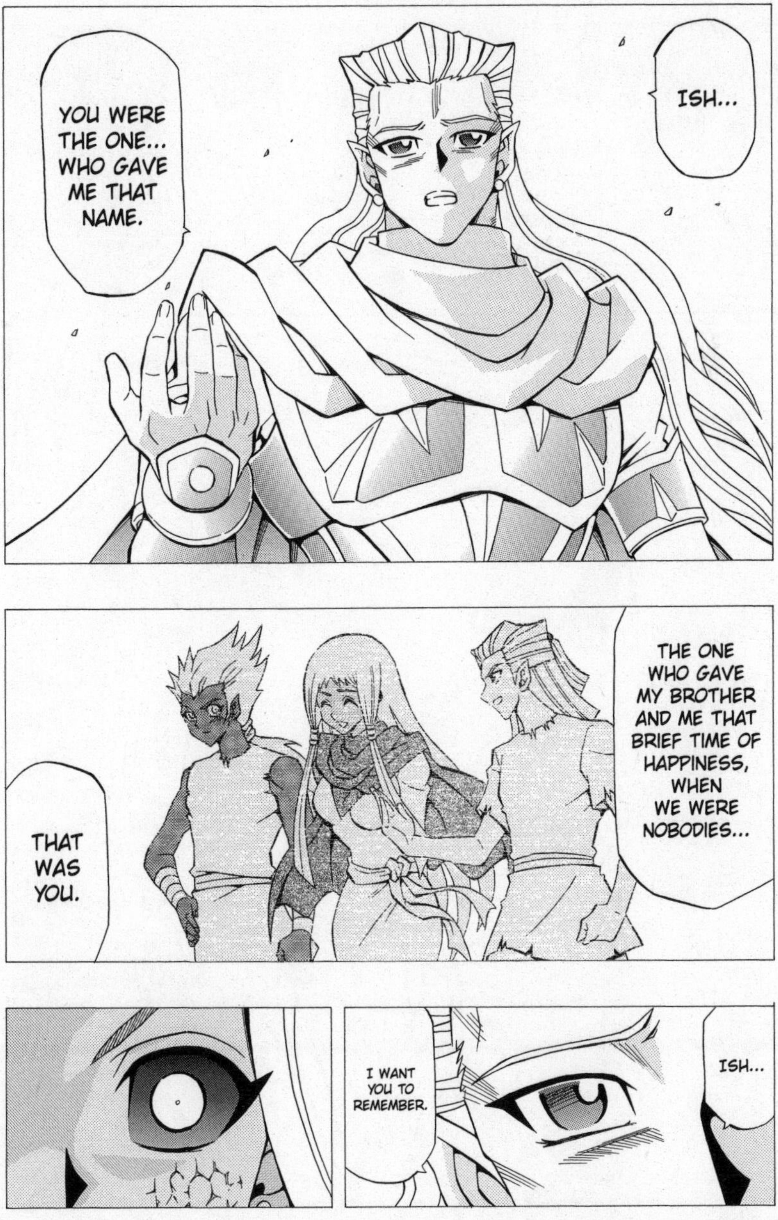
ISH...
YOU WERE THE ONE... WHO GAVE ME THAT NAME.
THE ONE WHO GAVE MY BROTHER AND ME THAT BRIEF TIME OF HAPPINESS, WHEN WE WERE NOBODIES...
THAT WAS YOU.
ISH...
I WANT YOU TO REMEMBER.

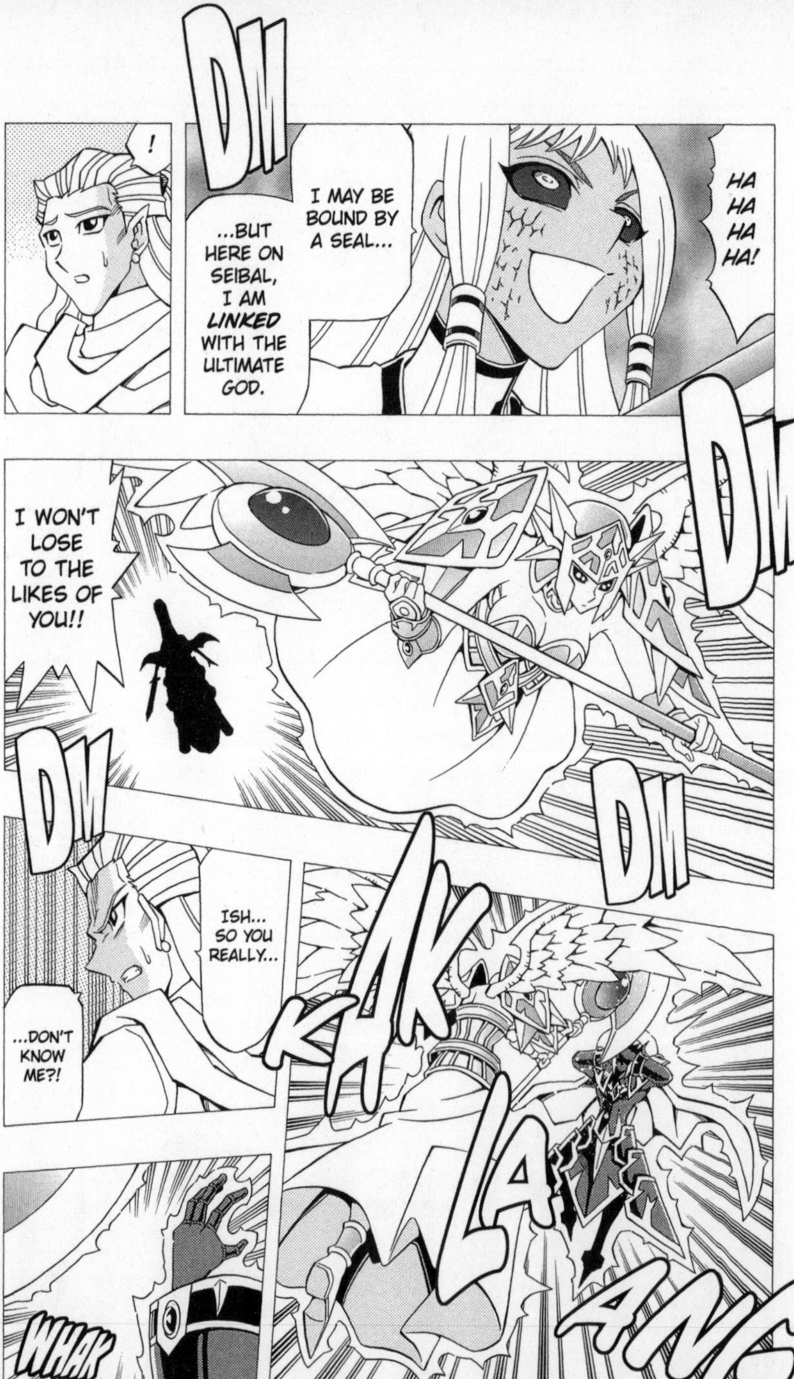
DM
HA HA HA HA!
I MAY BE BOUND BY A SEAL...
...BUT HERE ON SEIBAL, I AM *LINKED* WITH THE ULTIMATE GOD.
!
DM
I WON'T LOSE TO THE LIKES OF YOU!!
DM
DM
KAK
ISH... SO YOU REALLY...
...DON'T KNOW ME?!
LAANG
WHAK

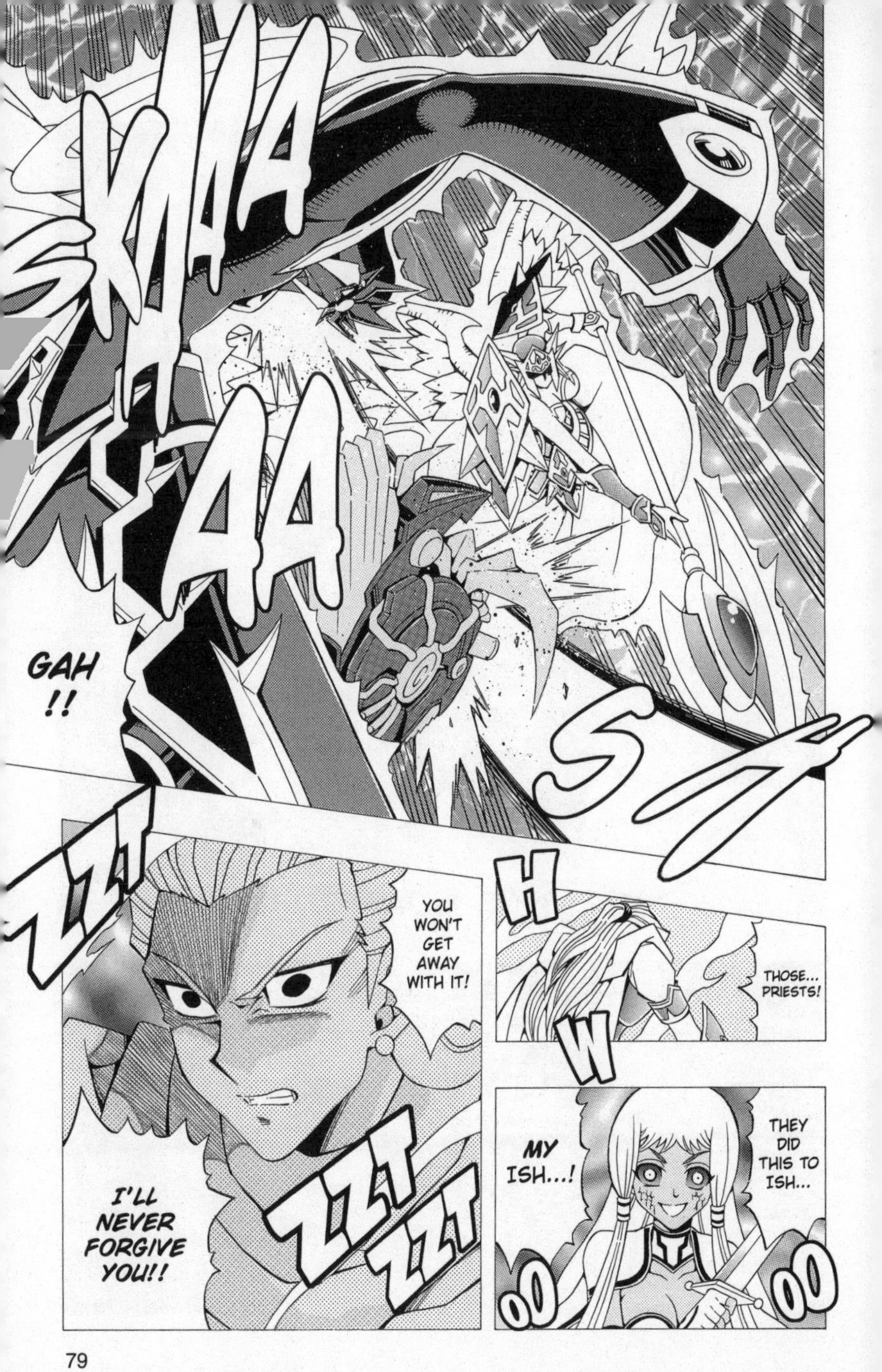
SKAAAAA
GAH!!
SH
H
THOSE... PRIESTS!
W
THEY DID THIS TO ISH...
MY ISH...!
OO
OO
YOU WON'T GET AWAY WITH IT!
I'LL NEVER FORGIVE YOU!!
ZZZT
ZZZT
ZZZT

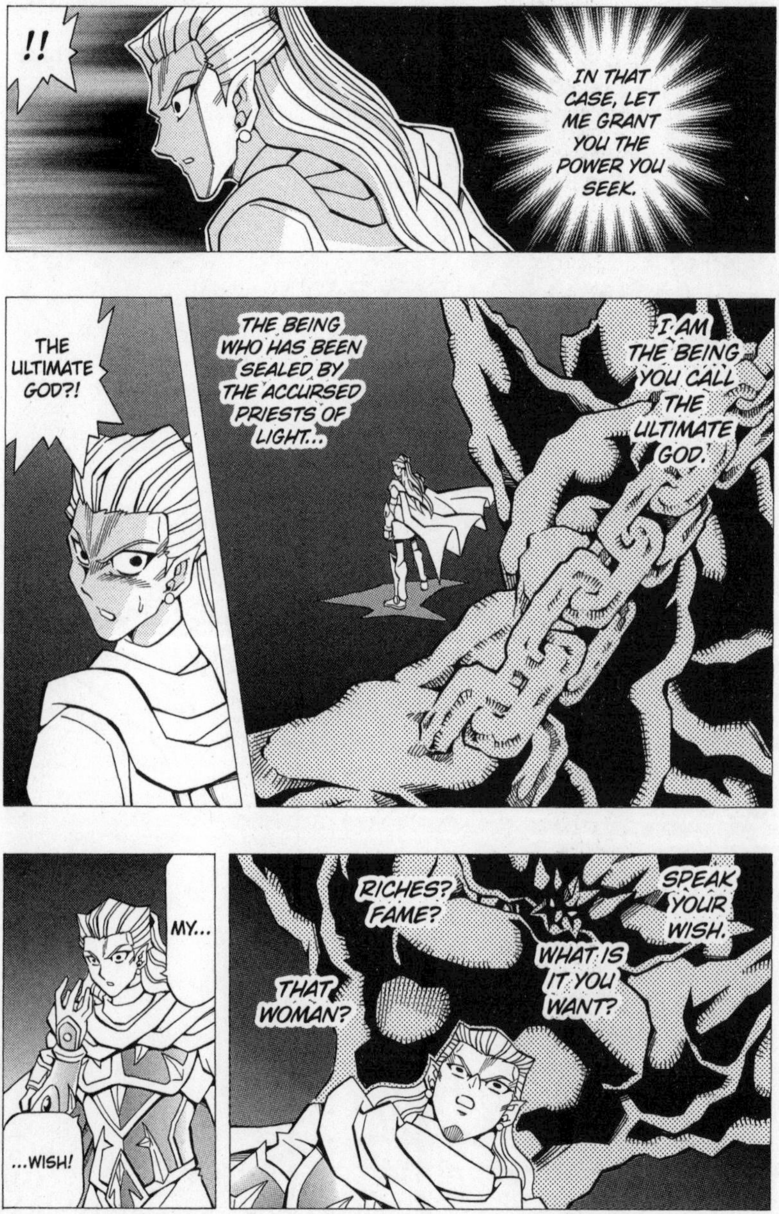

IN THAT CASE, LET ME GRANT YOU THE POWER YOU SEEK.
!!
I AM THE BEING YOU CALL THE ULTIMATE GOD.
THE BEING WHO HAS BEEN SEALED BY THE ACCURSED PRIESTS OF LIGHT...
THE ULTIMATE GOD?!
SPEAK YOUR WISH.
RICHES? FAME?
WHAT IS IT YOU WANT?
THAT WOMAN?
MY...
...WISH!

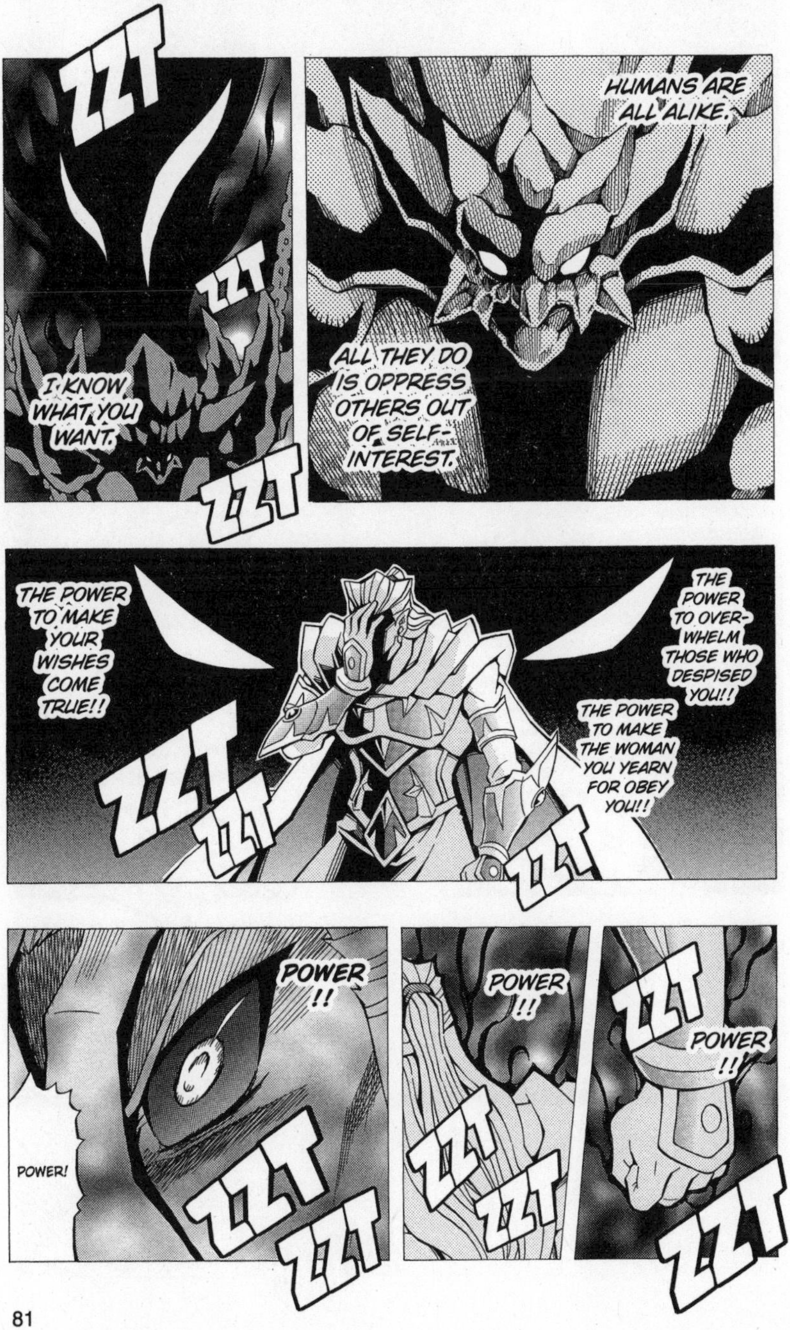
HUMANS ARE ALL ALIKE.
ALL THEY DO IS OPPRESS OTHERS OUT OF SELF-INTEREST.
ZZT
ZZT
I KNOW WHAT YOU WANT.
ZZT
THE POWER TO OVER-WHELM THOSE WHO DESPISED YOU!!
THE POWER TO MAKE THE WOMAN YOU YEARN FOR OBEY YOU!!
THE POWER TO MAKE YOUR WISHES COME TRUE!!
ZZT
ZZT
ZZT
ZZT
POWER!!
ZZT
POWER!!
ZZT
ZZT
POWER!!
POWER!
ZZT
ZZT

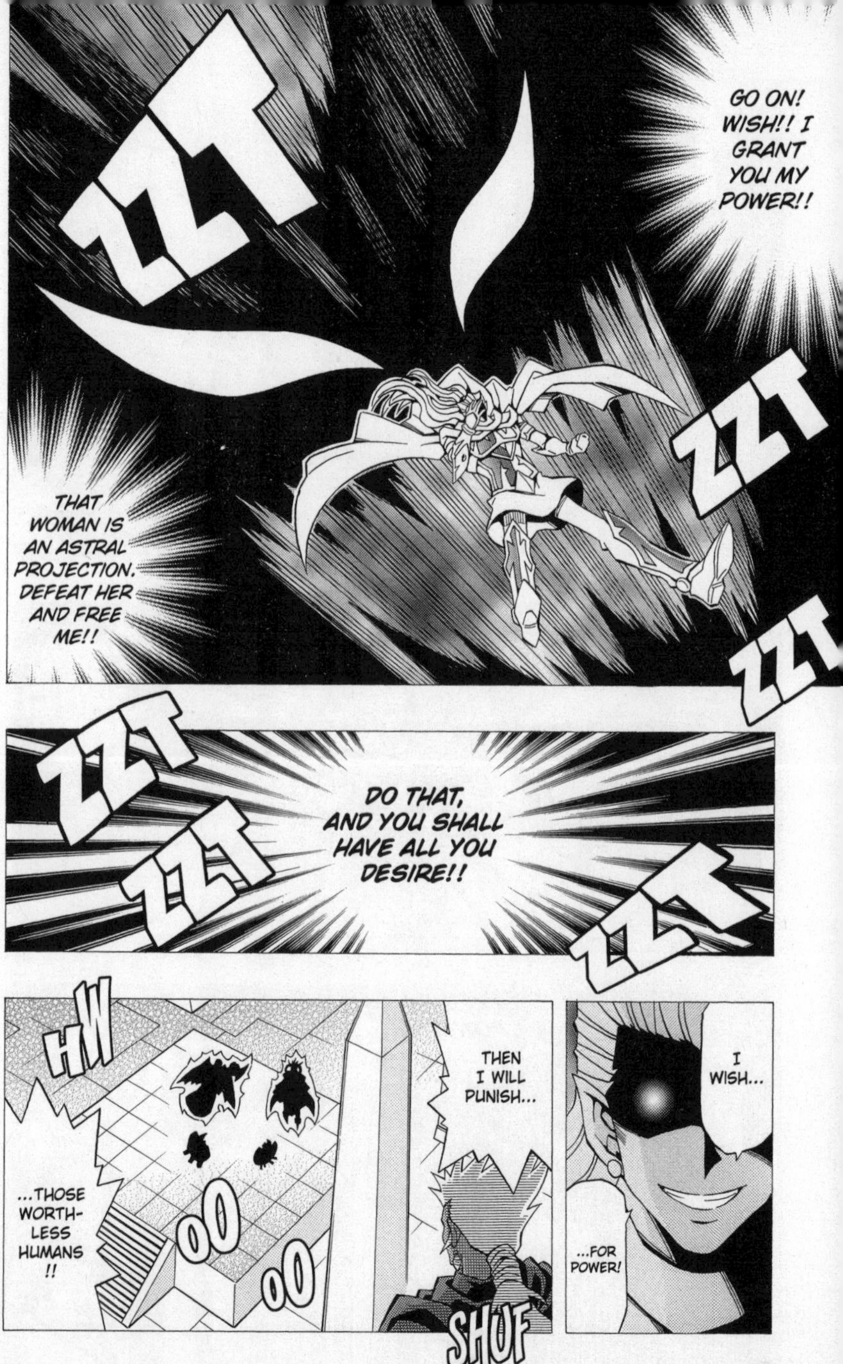
GO ON! WISH!! I GRANT YOU MY POWER!!
ZZZT
ZZZT
ZZZT
THAT WOMAN IS AN ASTRAL PROJECTION. DEFEAT HER AND FREE ME!!
ZZZT
ZZZT
DO THAT, AND YOU SHALL HAVE ALL YOU DESIRE!!
ZZZT
I WISH...
...FOR POWER!
THEN I WILL PUNISH...
SHUF
HW
OO
OO
...THOSE WORTH-LESS HUMANS !!

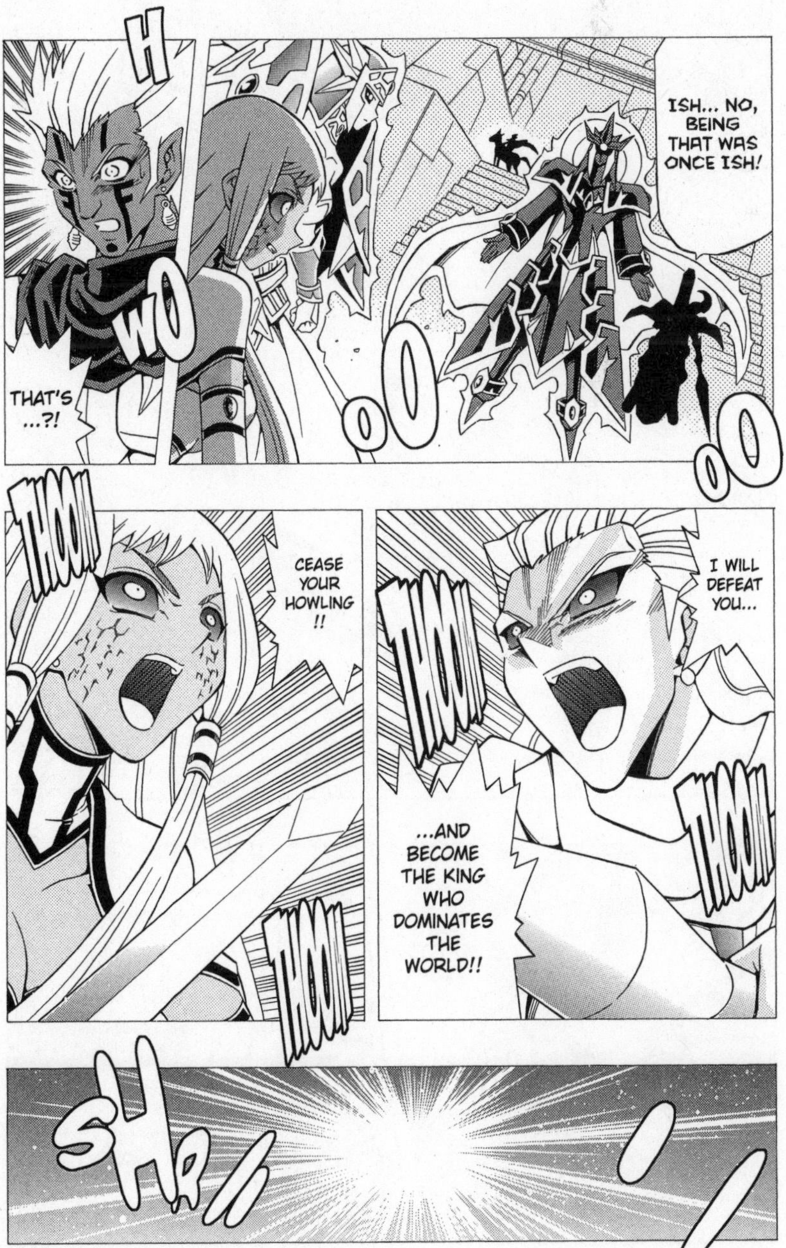
ISH... NO, BEING THAT WAS ONCE ISH!
H
WOOOOO
THAT'S ...?!
I WILL DEFEAT YOU...
THOOM
...AND BECOME THE KING WHO DOMINATES THE WORLD!!
THOOM
THOOM
CEASE YOUR HOWLING!!
THOOM
SHR

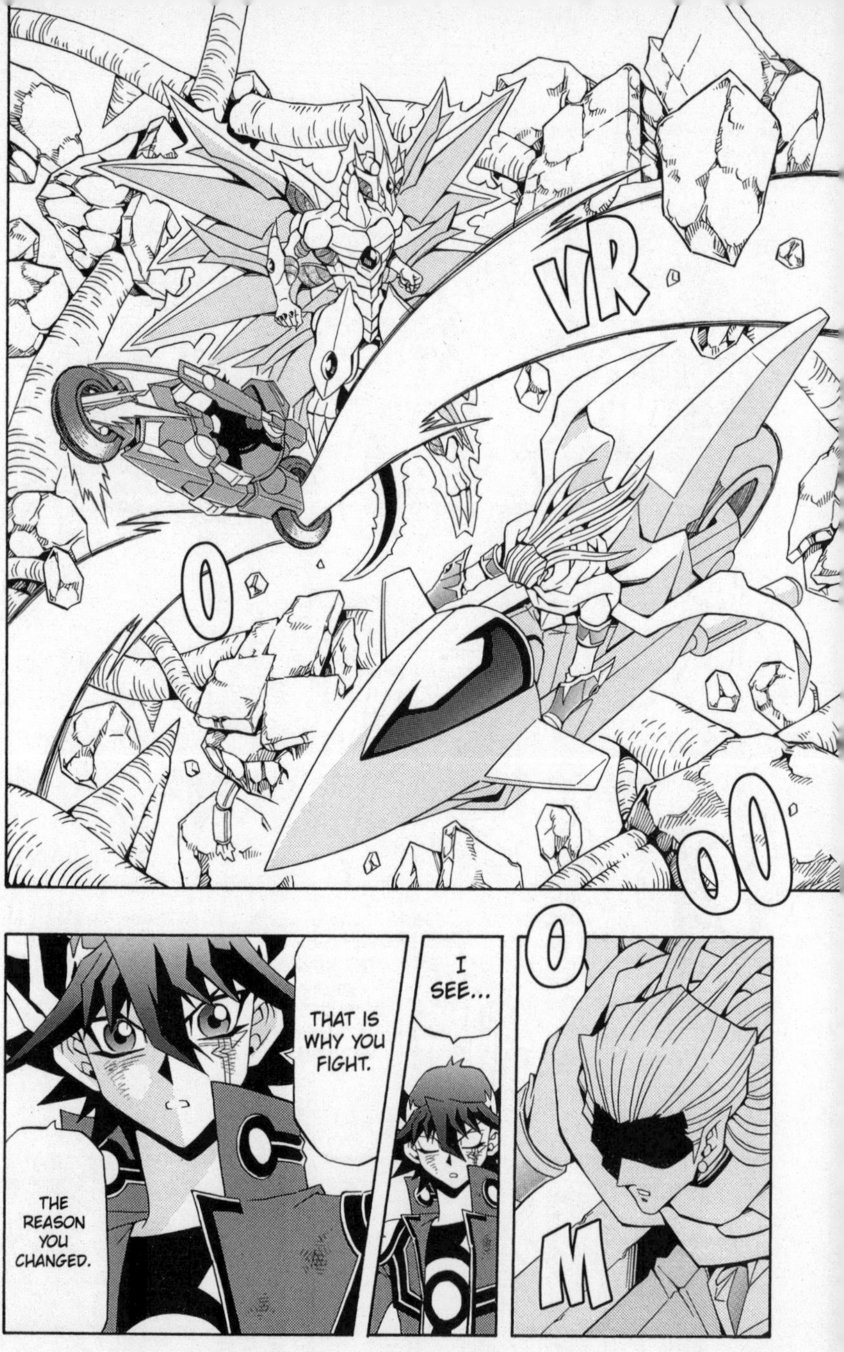
VR
O
OO
O
M
I SEE...
THAT IS WHY YOU FIGHT.
THE REASON YOU CHANGED.

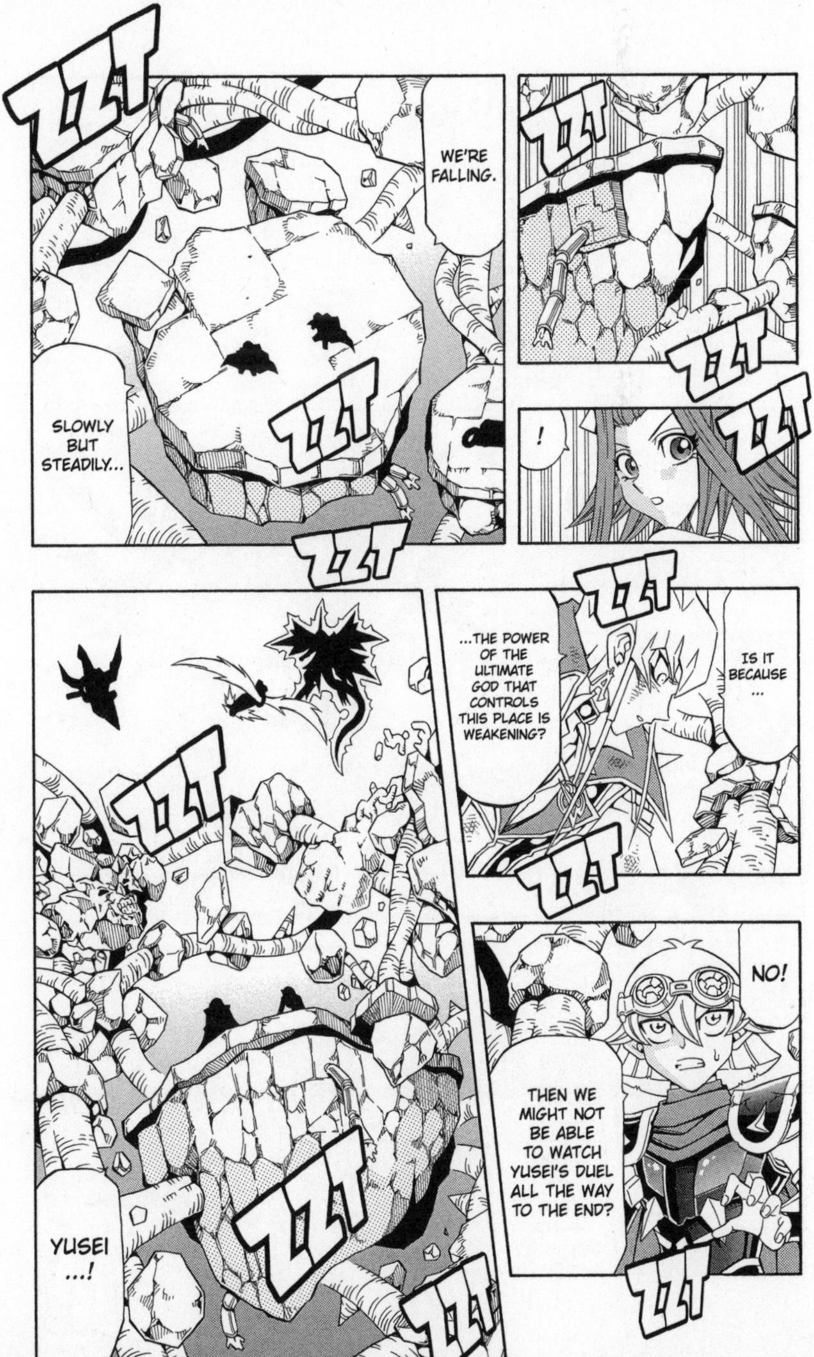
ZZZT
ZZZT
!
ZZZT
ZZZT
WE'RE FALLING.
SLOWLY BUT STEADILY...
ZZZT
ZZZT
ZZZT
IS IT BECAUSE ...
...THE POWER OF THE ULTIMATE GOD THAT CONTROLS THIS PLACE IS WEAKENING?
ZZZT
NO!
THEN WE MIGHT NOT BE ABLE TO WATCH YUSEI'S DUEL ALL THE WAY TO THE END?
ZZZT
ZZZT
ZZZT
YUSEI ...!
ZZZT

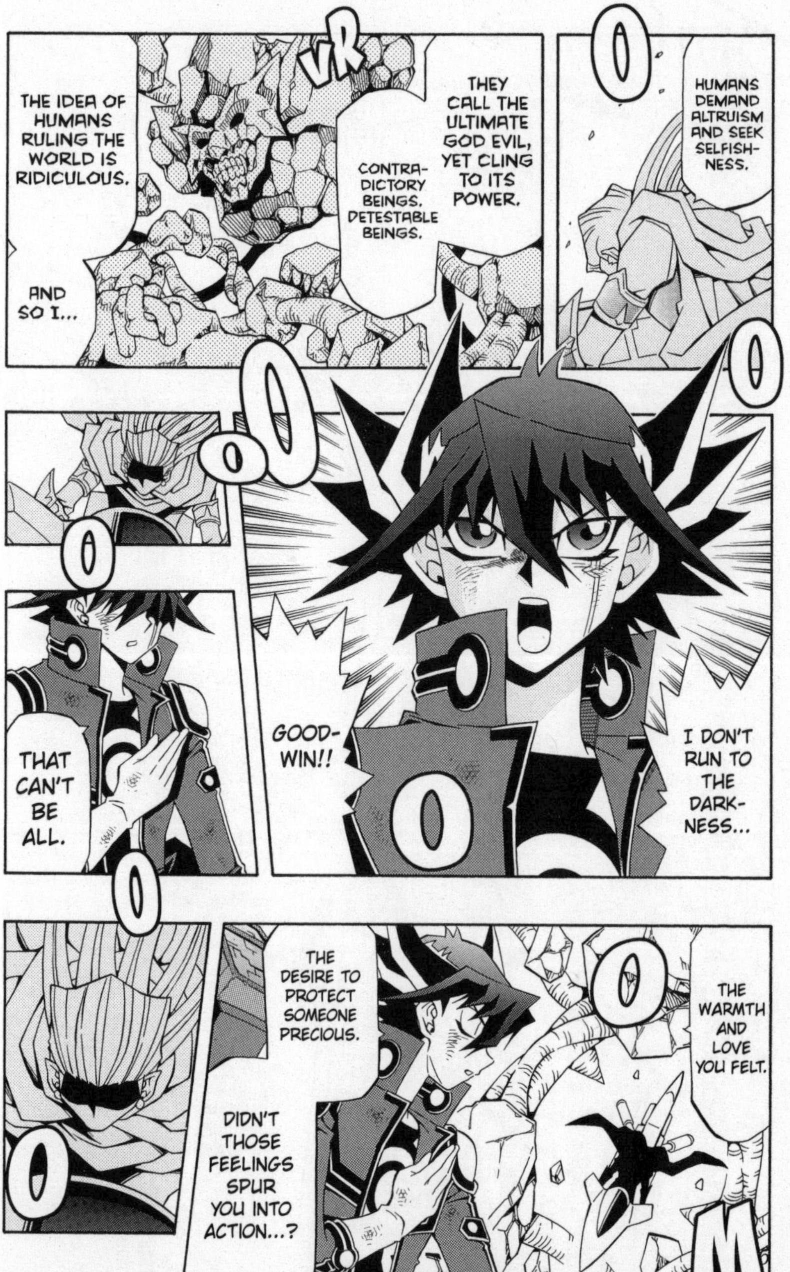
VR
HUMANS DEMAND ALTRUISM AND SEEK SELFISH-NESS.
THEY CALL THE ULTIMATE GOD EVIL, YET CLING TO ITS POWER.
CONTRA-DICTORY BEINGS. DETESTABLE BEINGS.
THE IDEA OF HUMANS RULING THE WORLD IS RIDICULOUS.
AND SO I...
OOOOOOOOO
I DON'T RUN TO THE DARK-NESS...
GOOD-WIN!!
THAT CAN'T BE ALL.
THE WARMTH AND LOVE YOU FELT.
THE DESIRE TO PROTECT SOMEONE PRECIOUS.
DIDN'T THOSE FEELINGS SPUR YOU INTO ACTION...?
M

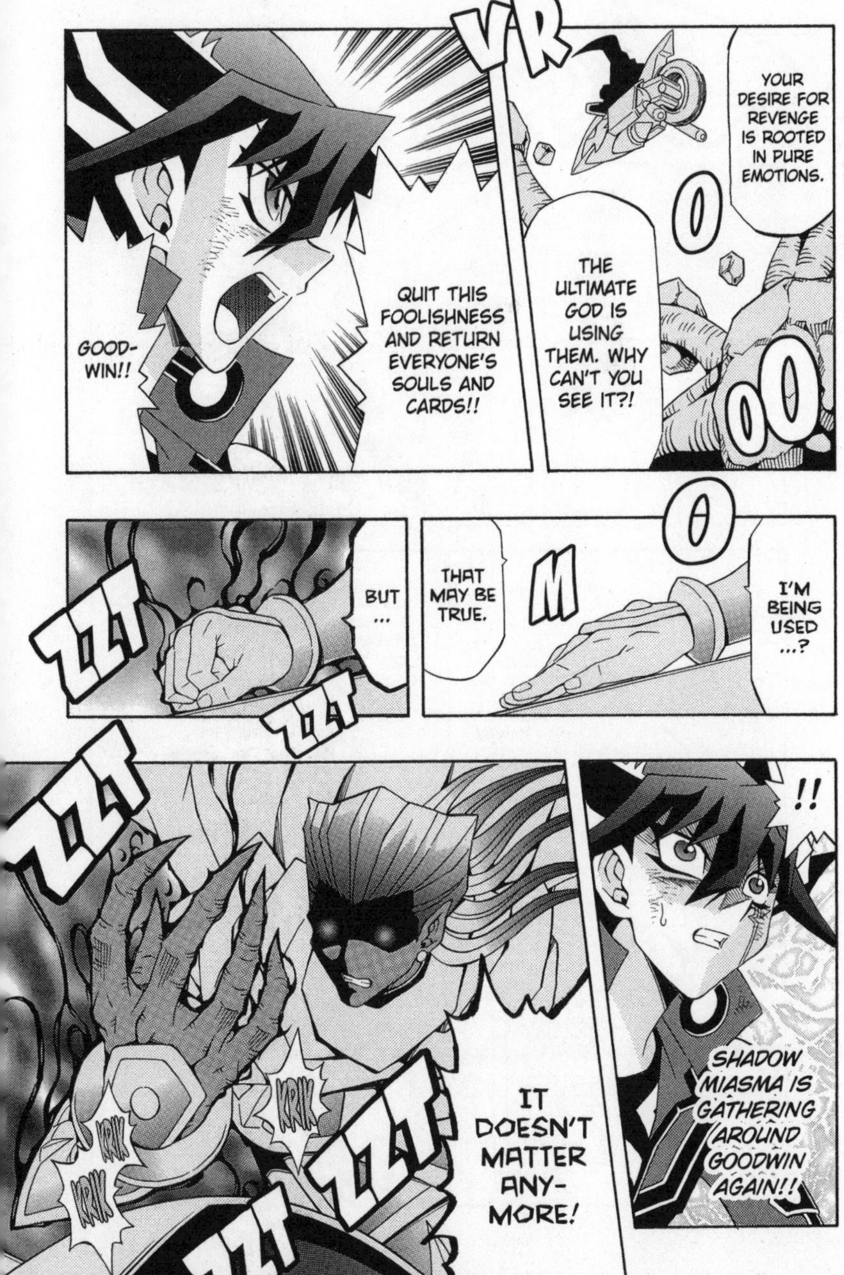
VR
YOUR DESIRE FOR REVENGE IS ROOTED IN PURE EMOTIONS.
O
OOO
THE ULTIMATE GOD IS USING THEM. WHY CAN'T YOU SEE IT?!
QUIT THIS FOOLISHNESS AND RETURN EVERYONE'S SOULS AND CARDS!!
GOOD-WIN!!
O
I'M BEING USED ...?
M
THAT MAY BE TRUE.
BUT ...
ZZZT
ZZZT
!!
SHADOW MIASMA IS GATHERING AROUND GOODWIN AGAIN!!
ZZZT
KRIK
KRIK
KRIK
IT DOESN'T MATTER ANY-MORE!
ZZZT
ZZZT

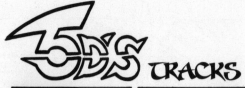

5D's TRACKS

THE 62ND

BY SATOMASA

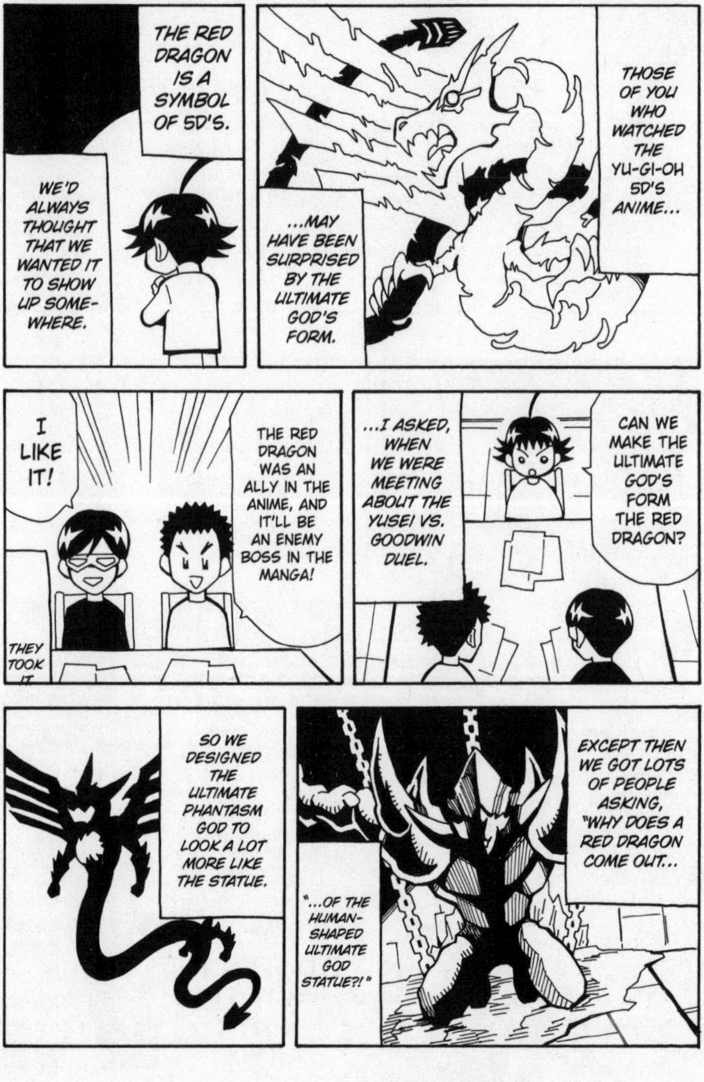

THOSE OF YOU WHO WATCHED THE YU-GI-OH 5D'S ANIME...
...MAY HAVE BEEN SURPRISED BY THE ULTIMATE GOD'S FORM.
THE RED DRAGON IS A SYMBOL OF 5D'S.
WE'D ALWAYS THOUGHT THAT WE WANTED IT TO SHOW UP SOME-WHERE.
CAN WE MAKE THE ULTIMATE GOD'S FORM THE RED DRAGON?
...I ASKED, WHEN WE WERE MEETING ABOUT THE YUSEI VS. GOODWIN DUEL.
THE RED DRAGON WAS AN ALLY IN THE ANIME, AND IT'LL BE AN ENEMY BOSS IN THE MANGA!
I LIKE IT!
THEY TOOK IT
EXCEPT THEN WE GOT LOTS OF PEOPLE ASKING, "WHY DOES A RED DRAGON COME OUT...
"...OF THE HUMAN-SHAPED ULTIMATE GOD STATUE?!"
SO WE DESIGNED THE ULTIMATE PHANTASM GOD TO LOOK A LOT MORE LIKE THE STATUE.

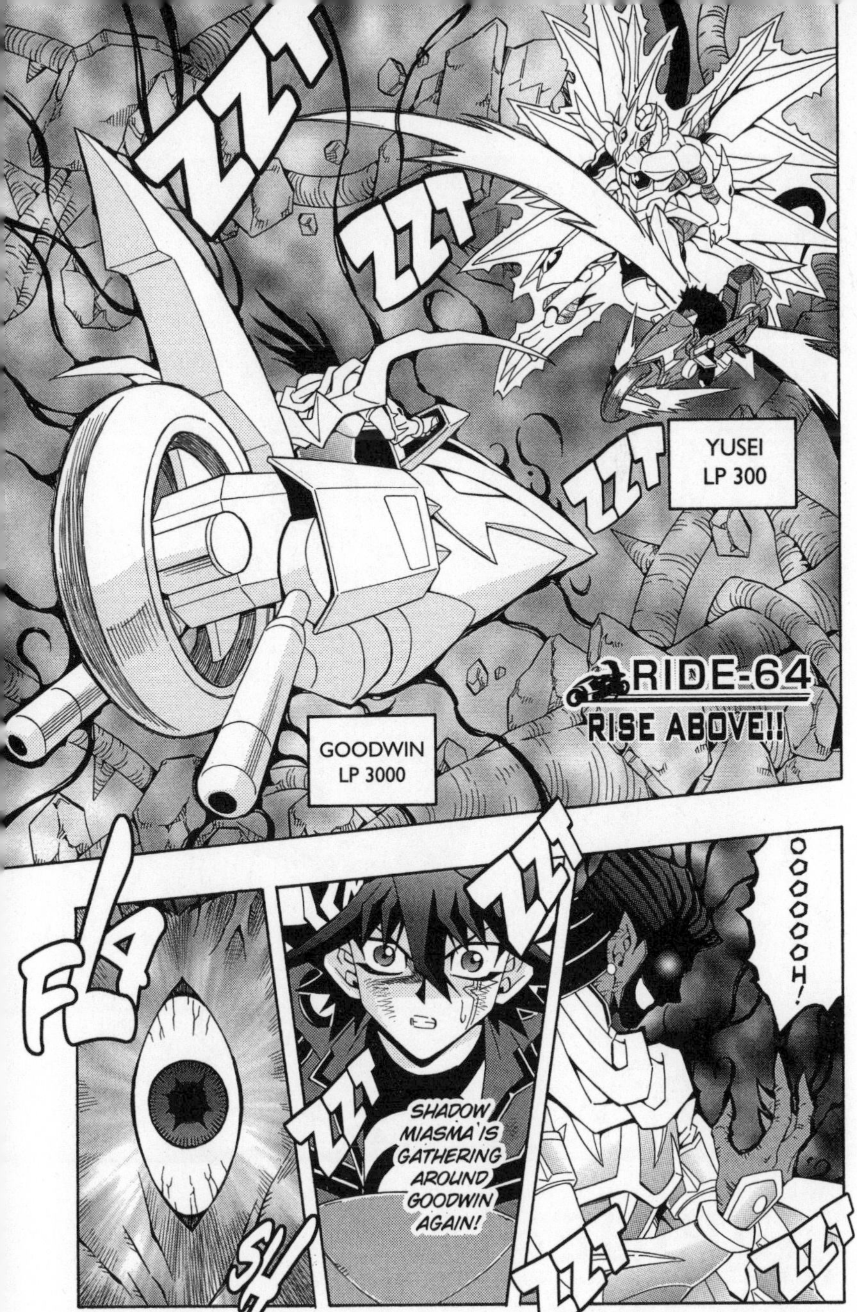
ZZZT
ZZZT
YUSEI
LP 300
ZZZT
RIDE-64
RISE ABOVE!!
GOODWIN
LP 3000
OOOOOOH!
ZZZT
ZZZT
ZZZT
ZZZT
SHADOW MIASMA IS GATHERING AROUND GOODWIN AGAIN!
ZZZT
FLA
SH

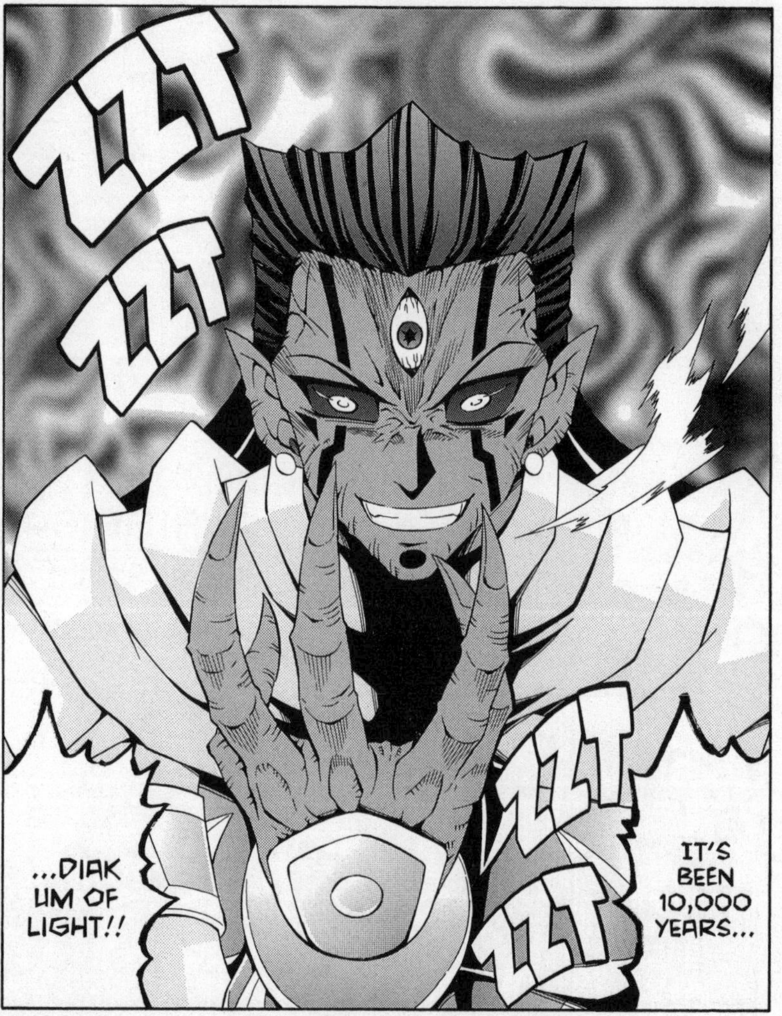
ZZZT
ZZZT
IT'S BEEN 10,000 YEARS...
...DIAK UM OF LIGHT!!
ZZZT
ZZZT

RIDE-64
RISE ABOVE!!

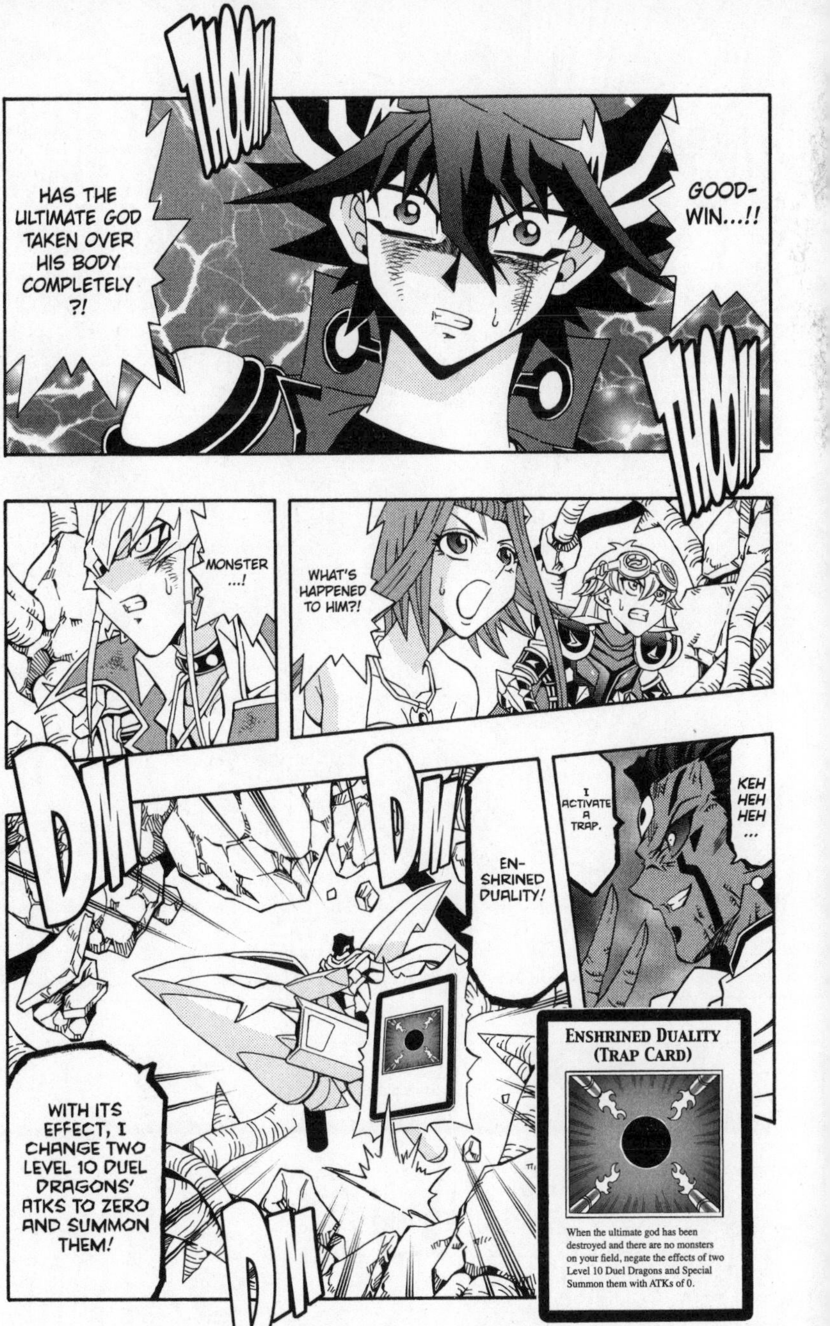
THOOM
GOOD-WIN...!!
HAS THE ULTIMATE GOD TAKEN OVER HIS BODY COMPLETELY?!
THOOM
WHAT'S HAPPENED TO HIM?!
MONSTER...!
KEH HEH HEH...
I ACTIVATE A TRAP.
EN-SHRINED DUALITY!
DM
DM
WITH ITS EFFECT, I CHANGE TWO LEVEL 10 DUEL DRAGONS' ATKS TO ZERO AND SUMMON THEM!
DM
ENSHRINED DUALITY (TRAP CARD)
When the ultimate god has been destroyed and there are no monsters on your field, negate the effects of two Level 10 Duel Dragons and Special Summon them with ATKs of 0.

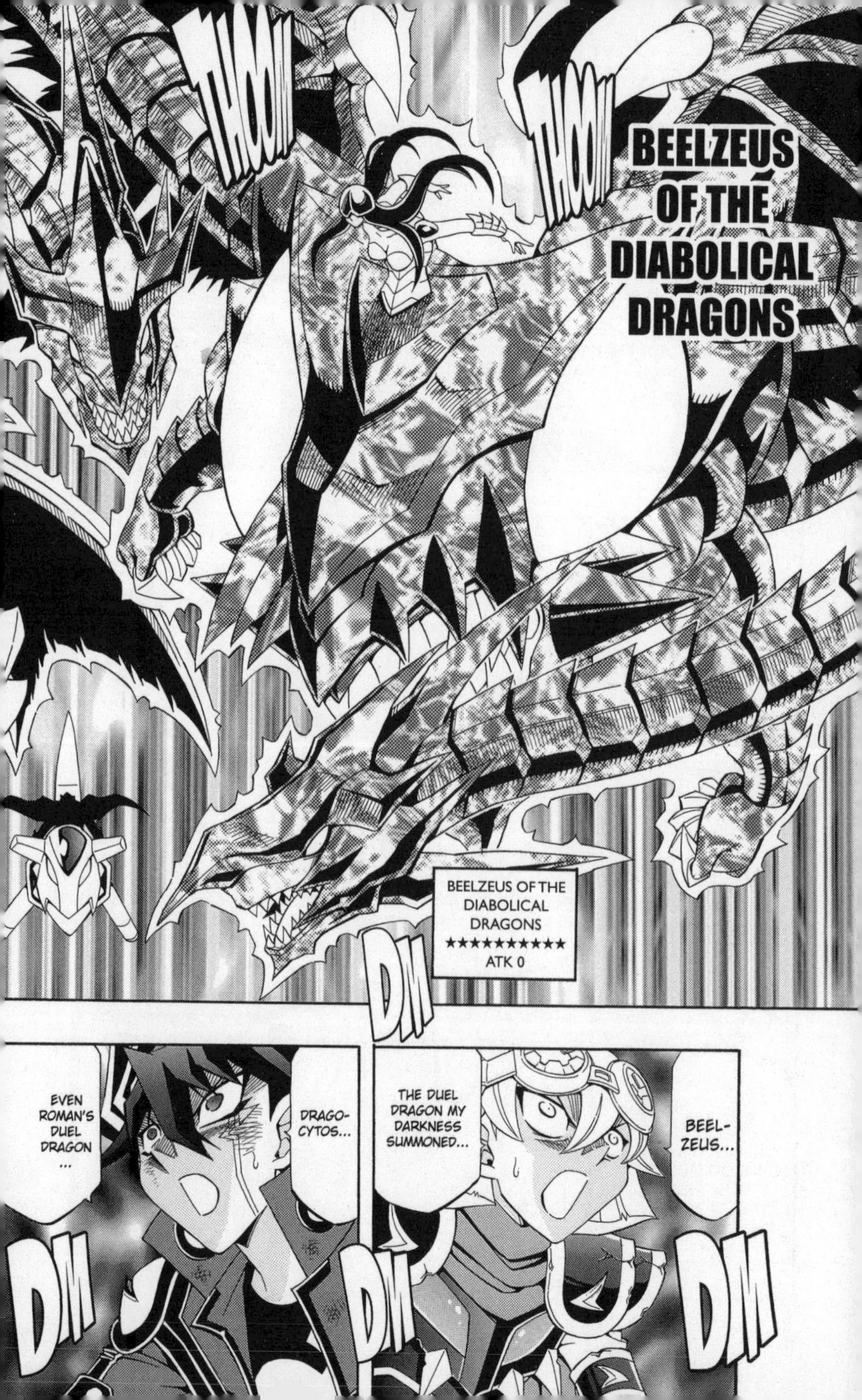
BEELZEUS OF THE DIABOLICAL DRAGONS
THOOM
THOOM
BEELZEUS OF THE DIABOLICAL DRAGONS ★★★★★★★★★★ ATK 0
DM
BEEL-ZEUS...
THE DUEL DRAGON MY DARKNESS SUMMONED...
DM
DRAGO-CYTOS...
EVEN ROMAN'S DUEL DRAGON ...
DM
DM

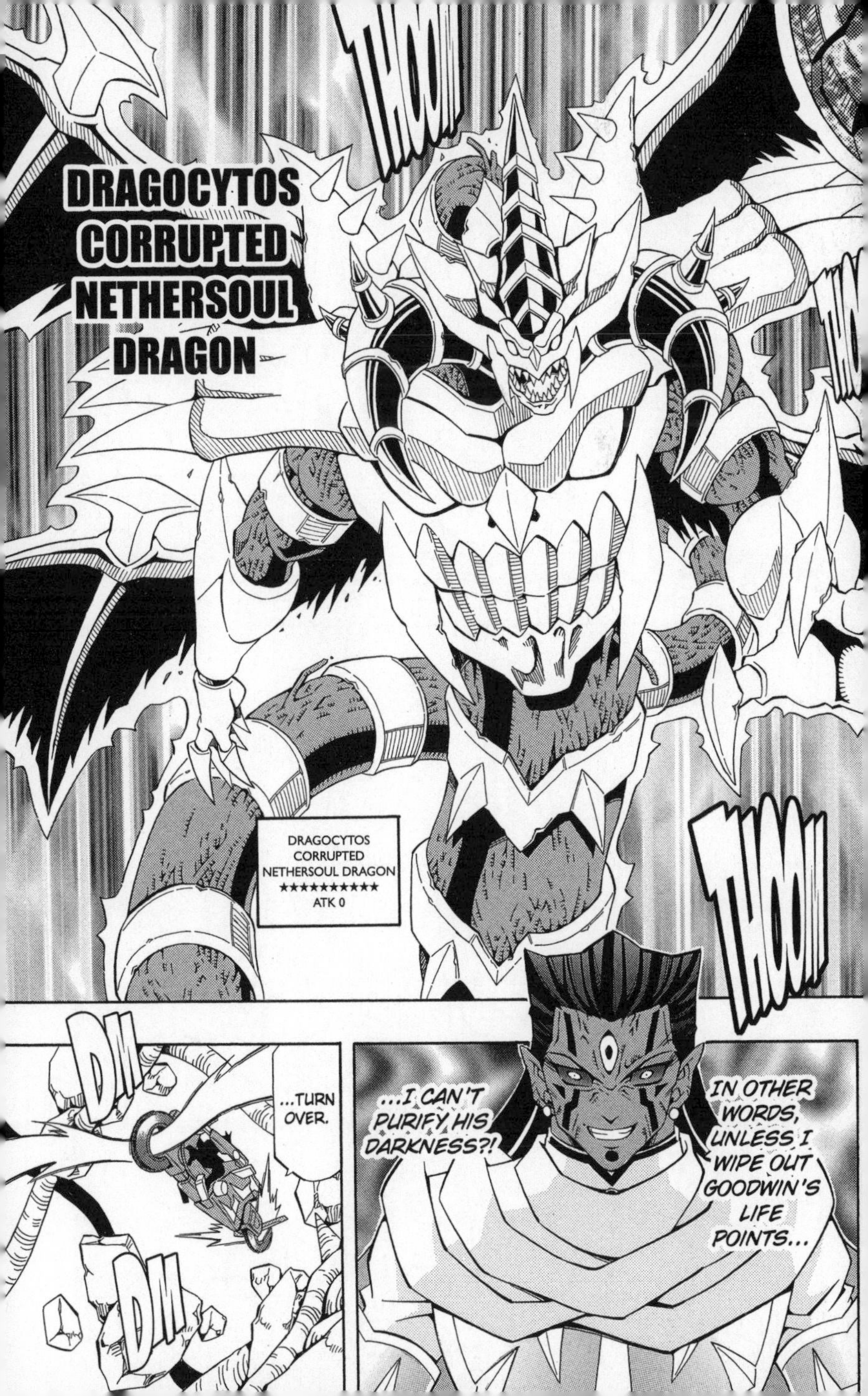
THOOM
DRAGOCYTOS CORRUPTED NETHERSOUL DRAGON
THOOM
DRAGOCYTOS CORRUPTED NETHERSOUL DRAGON ★★★★★★★★★★★ ATK 0
IN OTHER WORDS, UNLESS I WIPE OUT GOODWIN'S LIFE POINTS...
...I CAN'T PURIFY HIS DARKNESS?!
...TURN OVER.
DM
DM

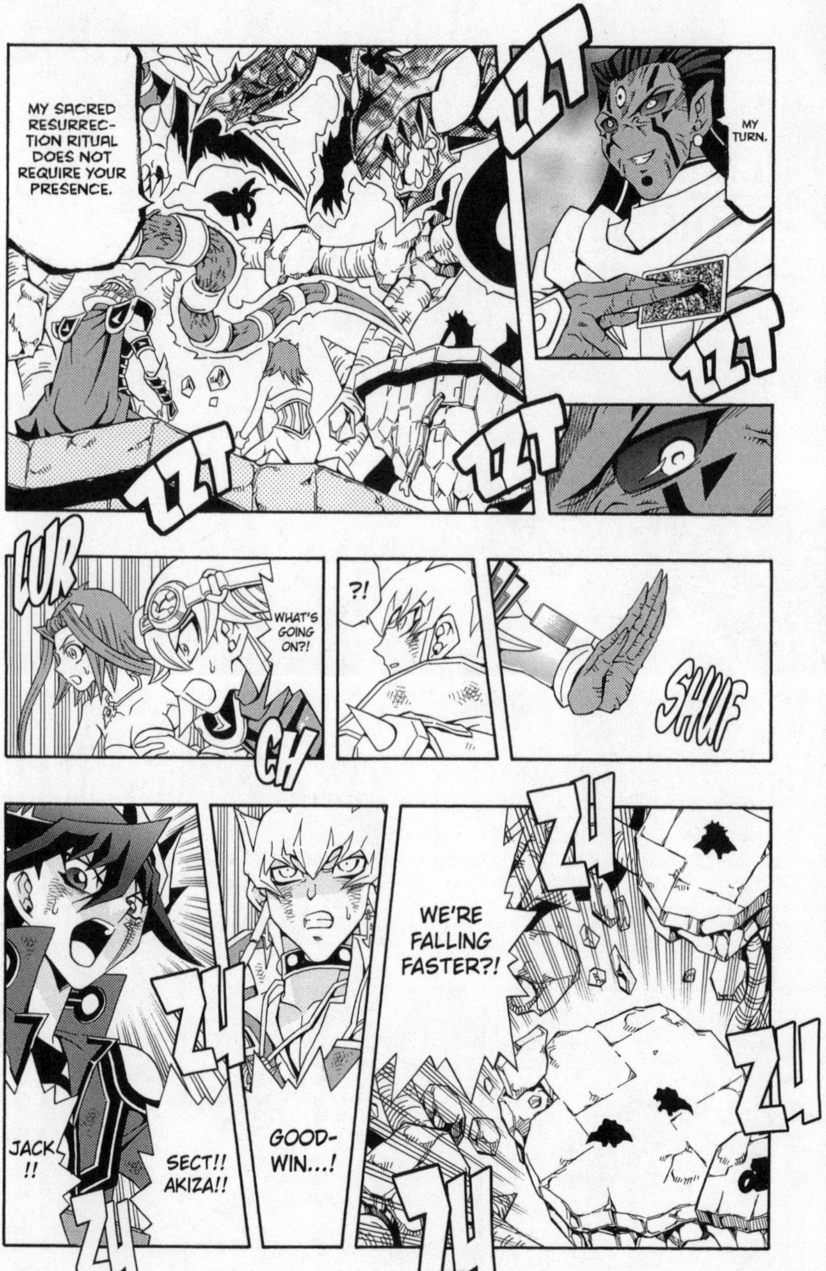
ZZT
MY TURN.
ZZT
ZZT
MY SACRED RESURRECTION RITUAL DOES NOT REQUIRE YOUR PRESENCE.
ZZT
SHUF
?!
LUR
WHAT'S GOING ON?!
CH
ZU
WE'RE FALLING FASTER?!
ZU
ZU
GOOD-WIN...!
ZU
SECT!! AKIZA!!
JACK!!
ZU

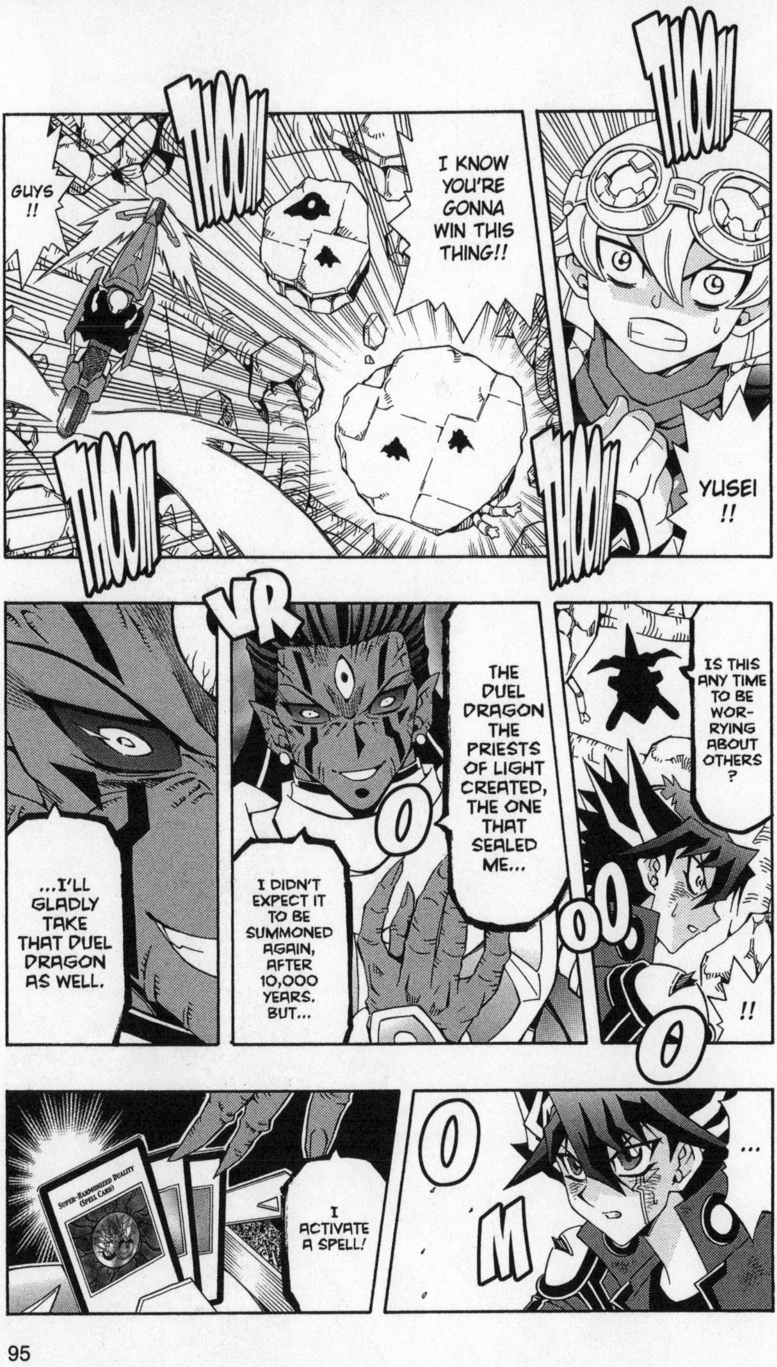
THOOM
YUSEI !!
THOOM
THOOM
I KNOW YOU'RE GONNA WIN THIS THING!!
GUYS !!
THOOM
IS THIS ANY TIME TO BE WOR-RYING ABOUT OTHERS?
!!
VR
THE DUEL DRAGON THE PRIESTS OF LIGHT CREATED, THE ONE THAT SEALED ME...
O
I DIDN'T EXPECT IT TO BE SUMMONED AGAIN, AFTER 10,000 YEARS. BUT...
...I'LL GLADLY TAKE THAT DUEL DRAGON AS WELL.
OOO
O
...
O
M
I ACTIVATE A SPELL!
SUPER-HARMONIZED DUALITY (SPELL CARD)

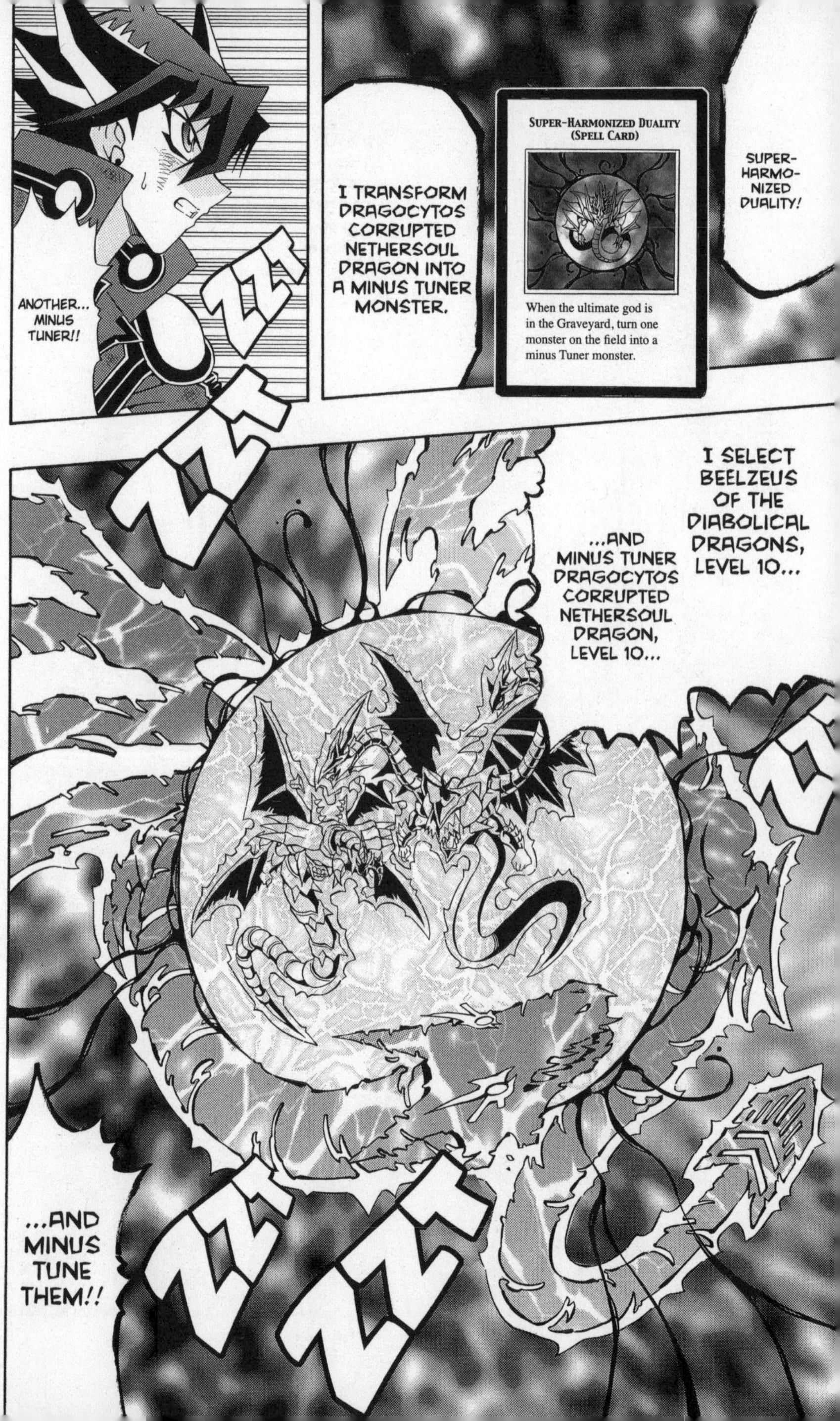
SUPER-HARMONIZED DUALITY!
SUPER-HARMONIZED DUALITY (SPELL CARD)
When the ultimate god is in the Graveyard, turn one monster on the field into a minus Tuner monster.
I TRANSFORM DRAGOCYTOS CORRUPTED NETHERSOUL DRAGON INTO A MINUS TUNER MONSTER.
ZZZT
ANOTHER... MINUS TUNER!!
ZZZT
I SELECT BEELZEUS OF THE DIABOLICAL DRAGONS, LEVEL 10...
...AND MINUS TUNER DRAGOCYTOS CORRUPTED NETHERSOUL DRAGON, LEVEL 10...
ZZZT
...AND MINUS TUNE THEM!!

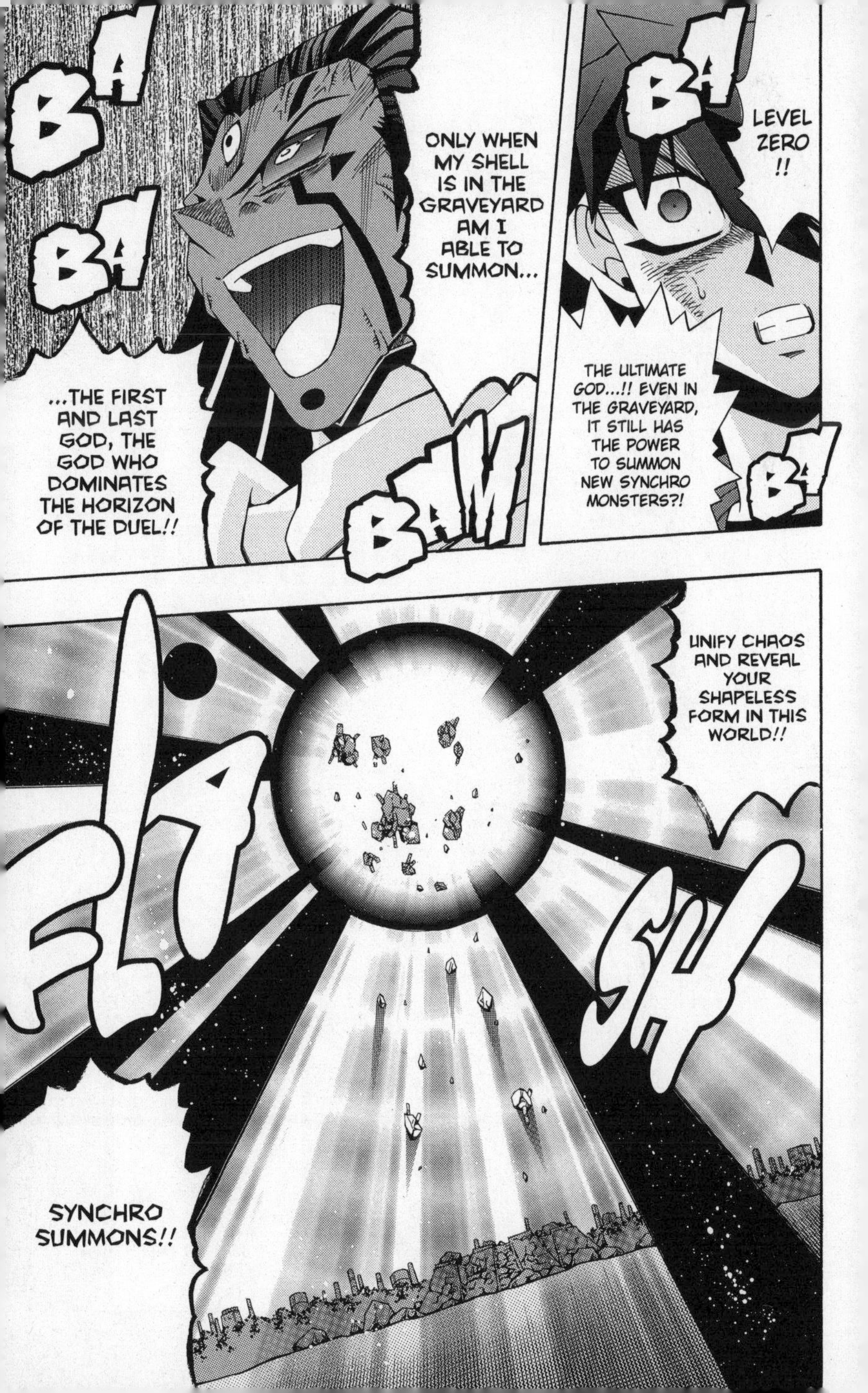
BAD
LEVEL ZERO!!
THE ULTIMATE GOD...!! EVEN IN THE GRAVEYARD, IT STILL HAS THE POWER TO SUMMON NEW SYNCHRO MONSTERS?!
BAD
BAD
BAD
ONLY WHEN MY SHELL IS IN THE GRAVEYARD AM I ABLE TO SUMMON...
...THE FIRST AND LAST GOD, THE GOD WHO DOMINATES THE HORIZON OF THE DUEL!!
BAM
UNIFY CHAOS AND REVEAL YOUR SHAPELESS FORM IN THIS WORLD!!
FLASH!
SYNCHRO SUMMONS!!

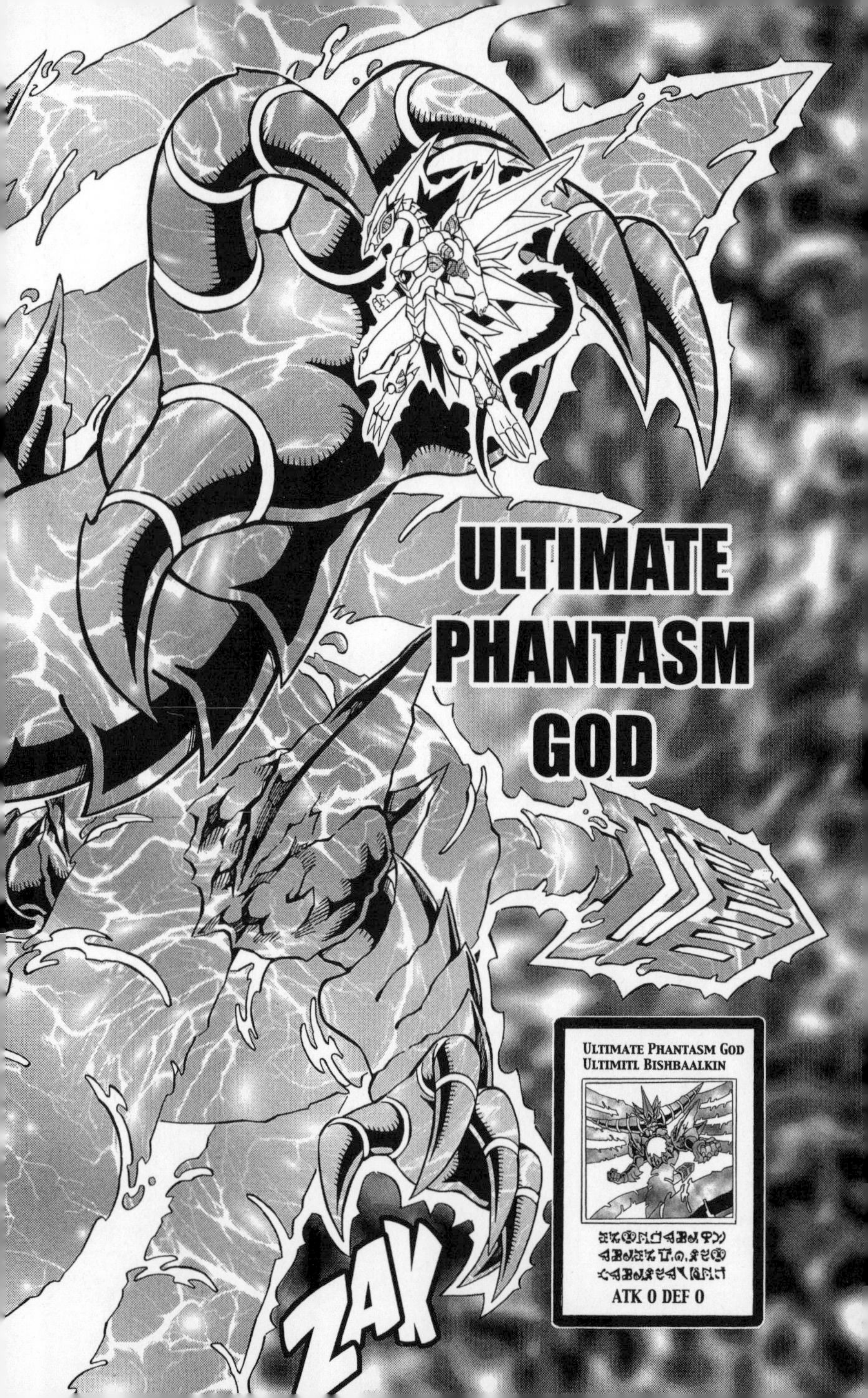
ULTIMATE PHANTASM GOD
ZAK
ULTIMATE PHANTASM GOD
ULTIMITL BISHBAALKIN
ATK 0 DEF 0

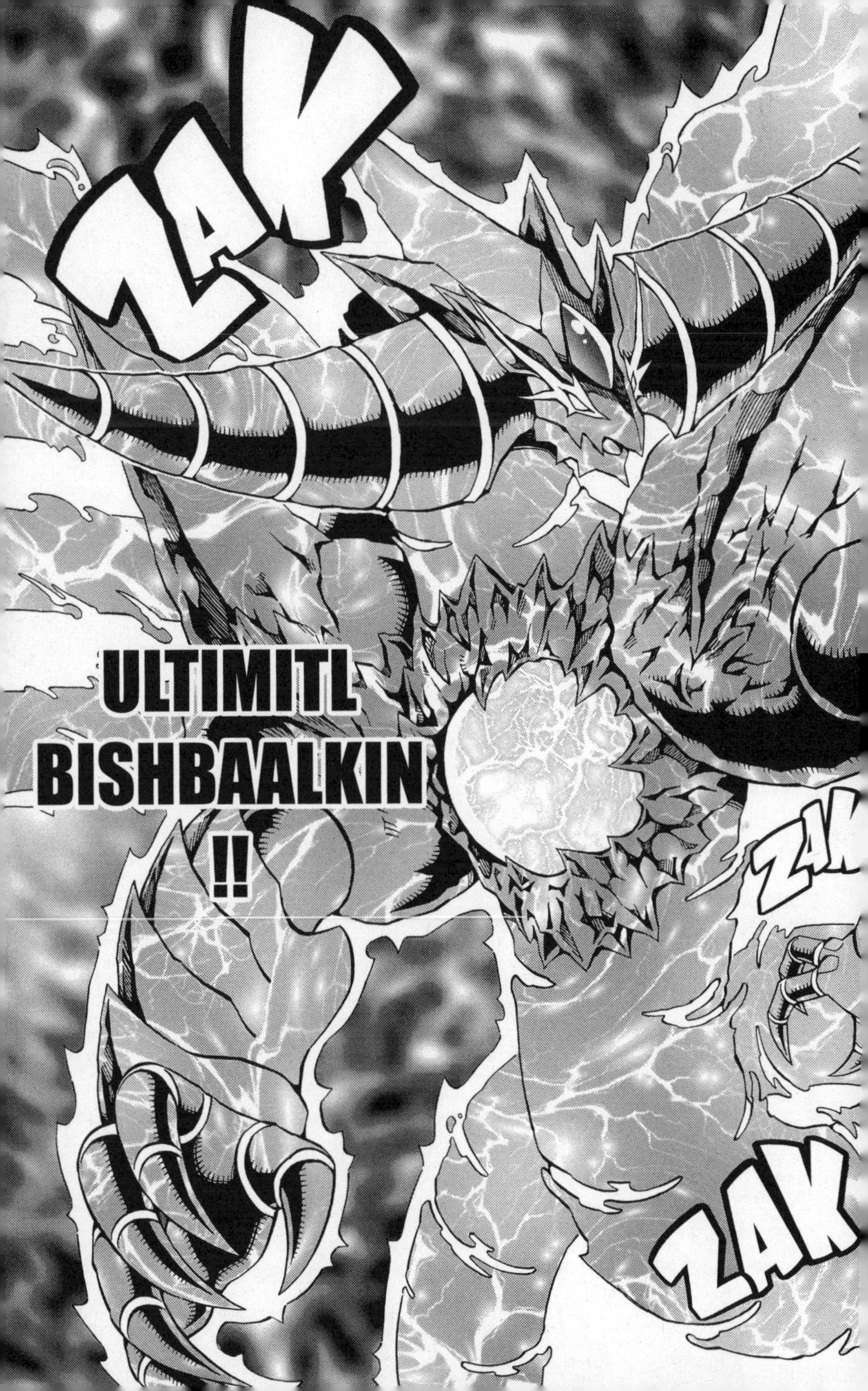
ZAK
ULTIMITL BISHBAALKIN!!
ZAK
ZAK

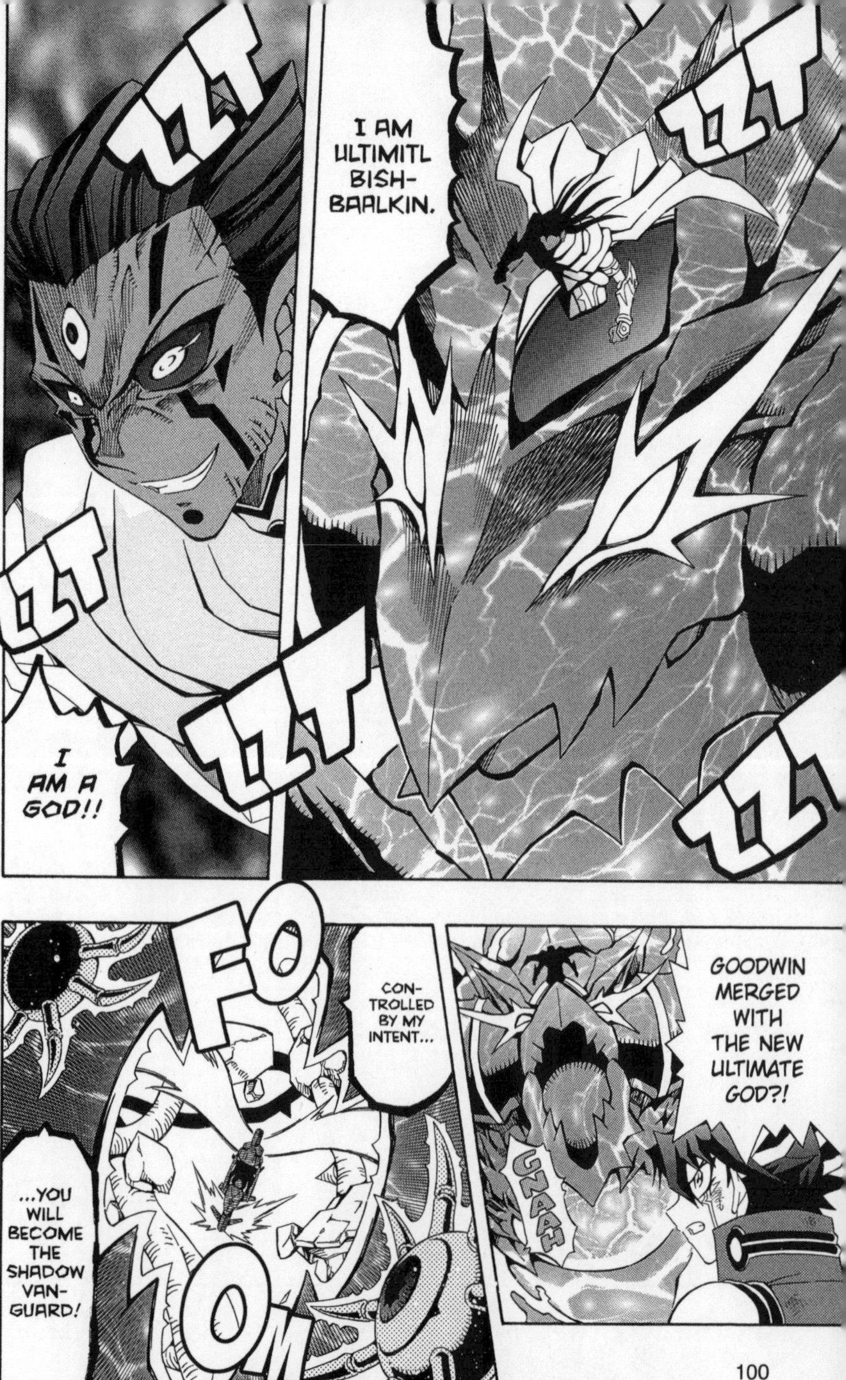
ZZT
I AM ULTIMITL BISH-BAALKIN.
ZZT
ZZT
ZZT
ZZT
I AM A GOD!!
GOODWIN MERGED WITH THE NEW ULTIMATE GOD?!
GNAAH
FOOOM
CON-TROLLED BY MY INTENT...
...YOU WILL BECOME THE SHADOW VAN-GUARD!

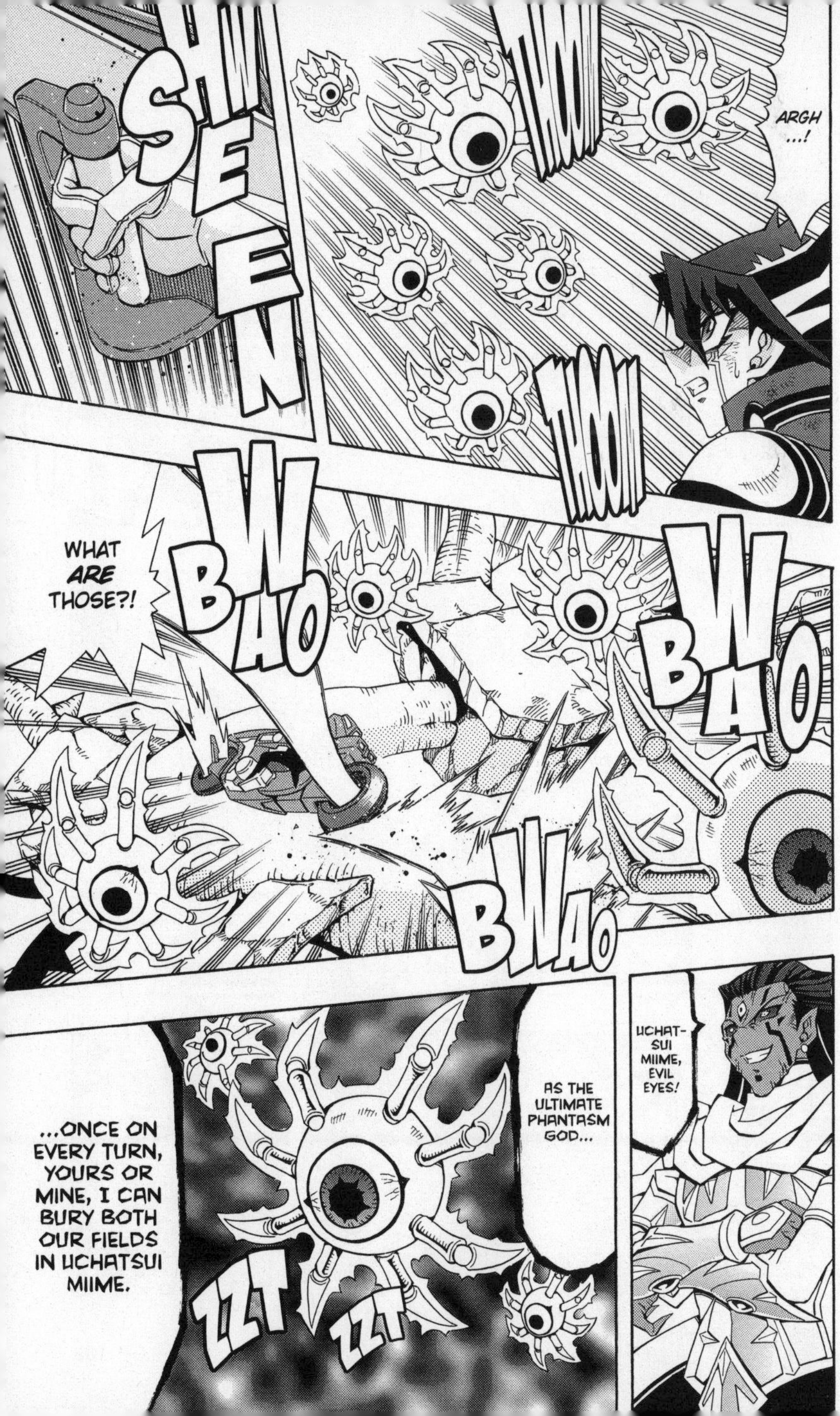
THOOM
ARGH ...!
THOOM
SHWEEN
BWAO
WHAT *ARE* THOSE?!
BWAO
BWAO
UCHAT-SUI MIIME, EVIL EYES!
AS THE ULTIMATE PHANTASM GOD...
...ONCE ON EVERY TURN, YOURS OR MINE, I CAN BURY BOTH OUR FIELDS IN UCHATSUI MIIME.
ZZT
ZZT

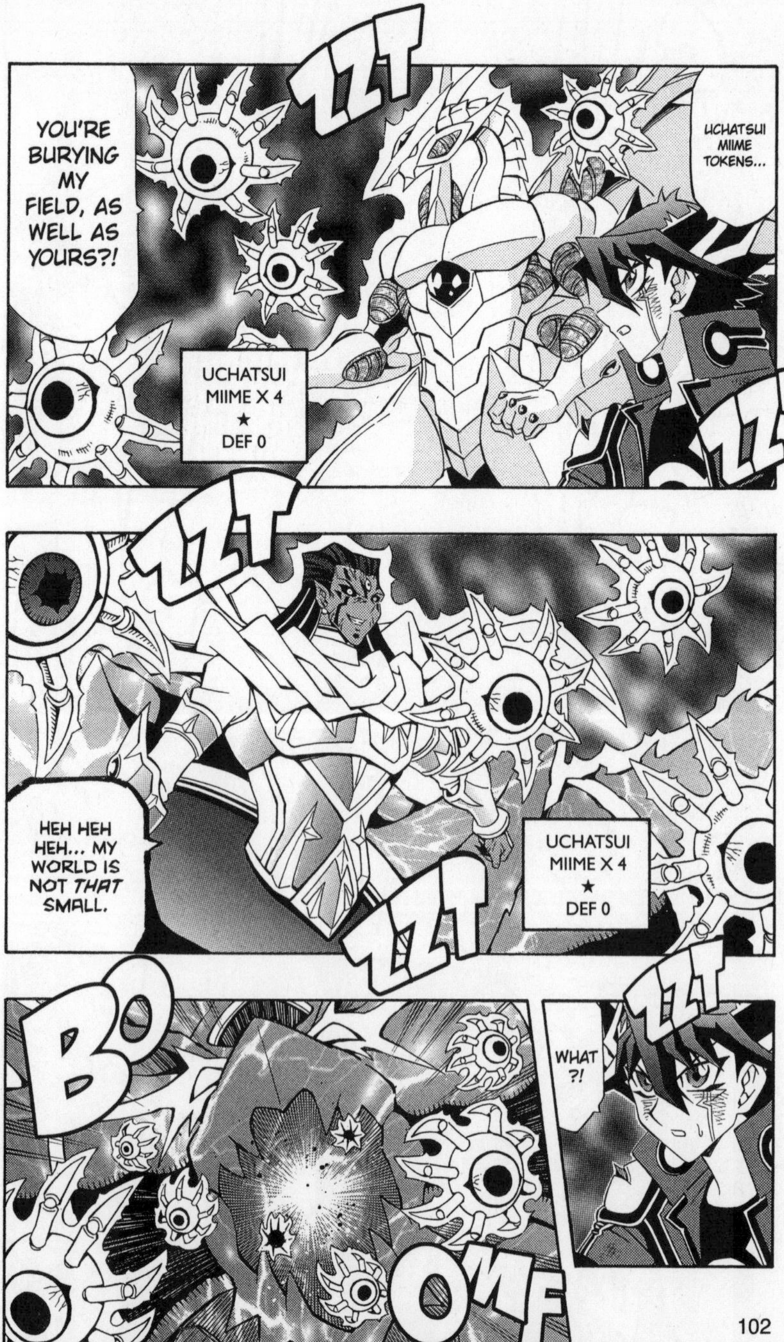
UCHATSUI MIIME TOKENS...
ZZT
YOU'RE BURYING MY FIELD, AS WELL AS YOURS?!
ZZT
UCHATSUI MIIME X 4 ★ DEF 0
ZZT
UCHATSUI MIIME X 4 ★ DEF 0
HEH HEH HEH... MY WORLD IS NOT *THAT* SMALL.
ZZT
ZZT
WHAT ?!
BOOMF

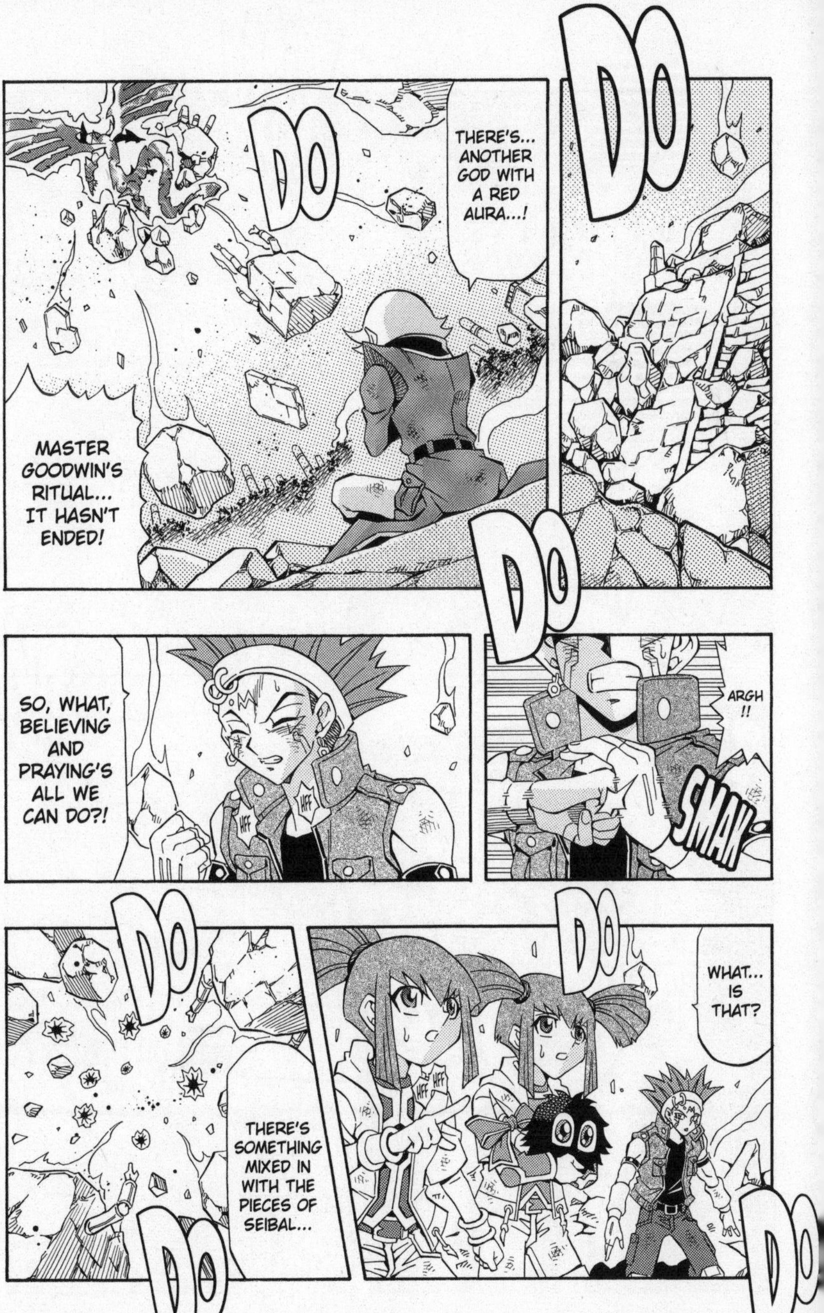
DO
DO
THERE'S... ANOTHER GOD WITH A RED AURA...!
DO
MASTER GOODWIN'S RITUAL... IT HASN'T ENDED!
DO
ARGH!!
SMAK
SO, WHAT, BELIEVING AND PRAYING'S ALL WE CAN DO?!
WHAT... IS THAT?
DO
DO
DO
THERE'S SOMETHING MIXED IN WITH THE PIECES OF SEIBAL...
DO

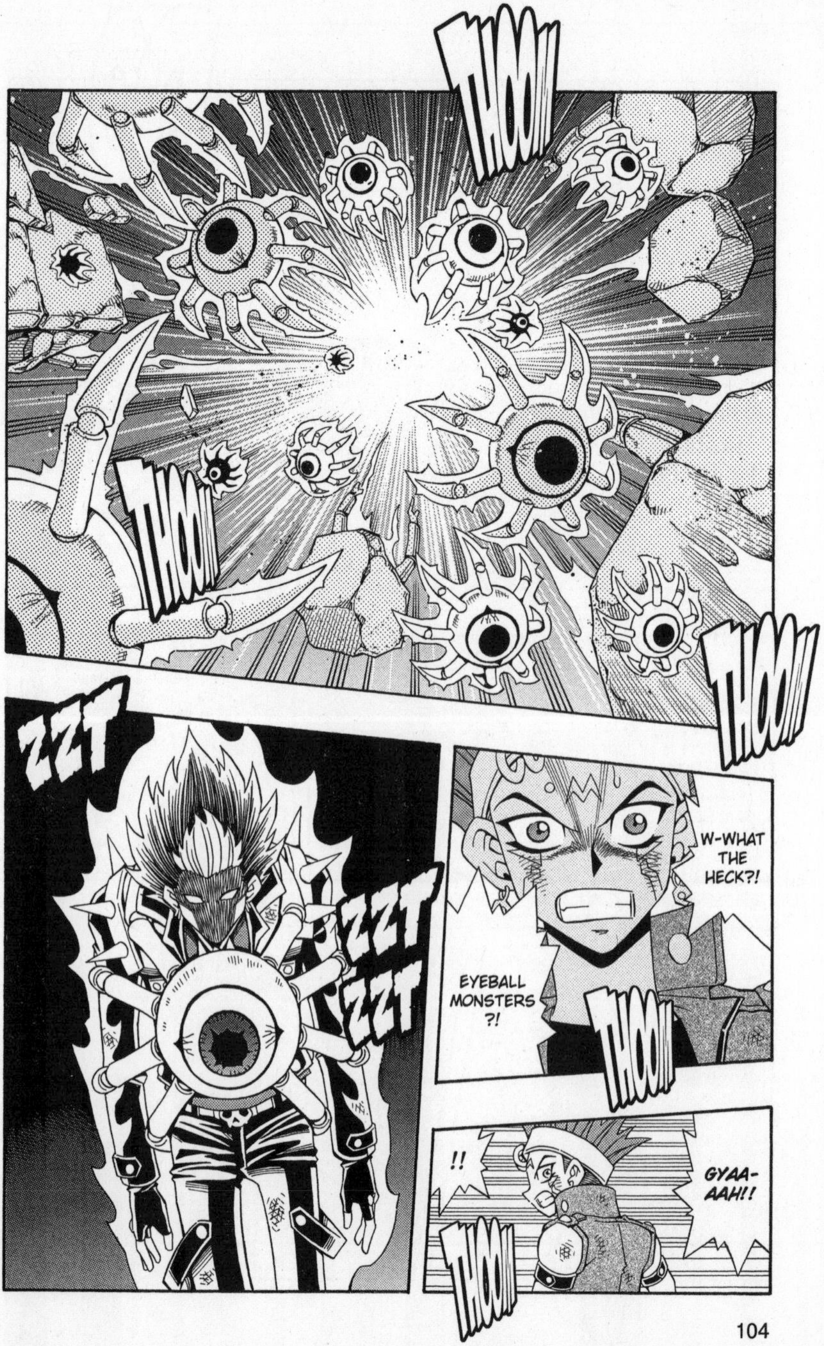
THOOM
THOOM
THOOM
W-WHAT THE HECK?!
EYEBALL MONSTERS ?!
THOOM
!!
GYAA-AAH!!
THOOM
ZZT
ZZT ZZT

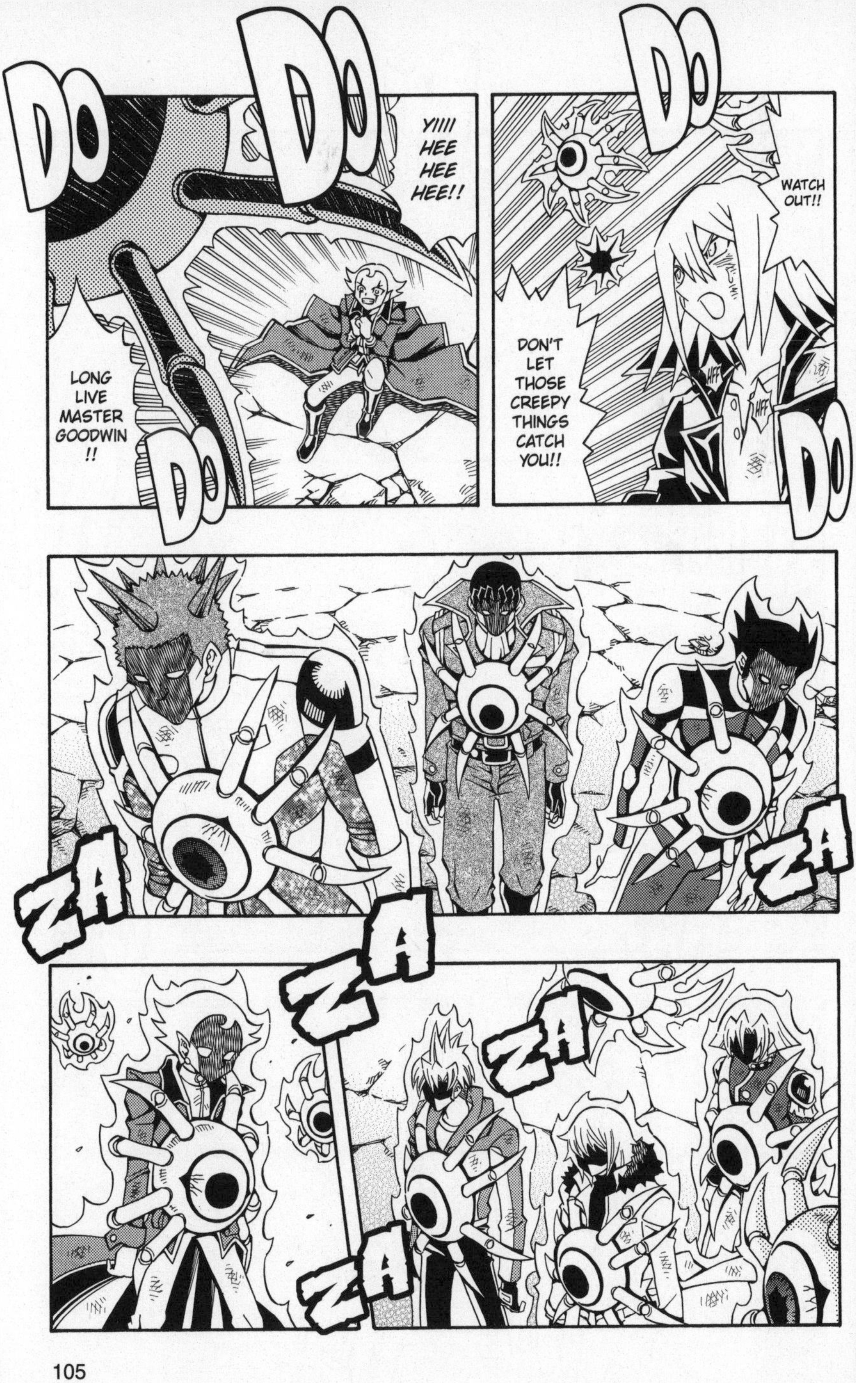
DO
WATCH OUT!!
DON'T LET THOSE CREEPY THINGS CATCH YOU!!
HFF
HFF
DO
DO
DO
YIIII HEE HEE HEE!!
LONG LIVE MASTER GOODWIN!!
DO
ZA
ZA
ZA
ZA
ZA

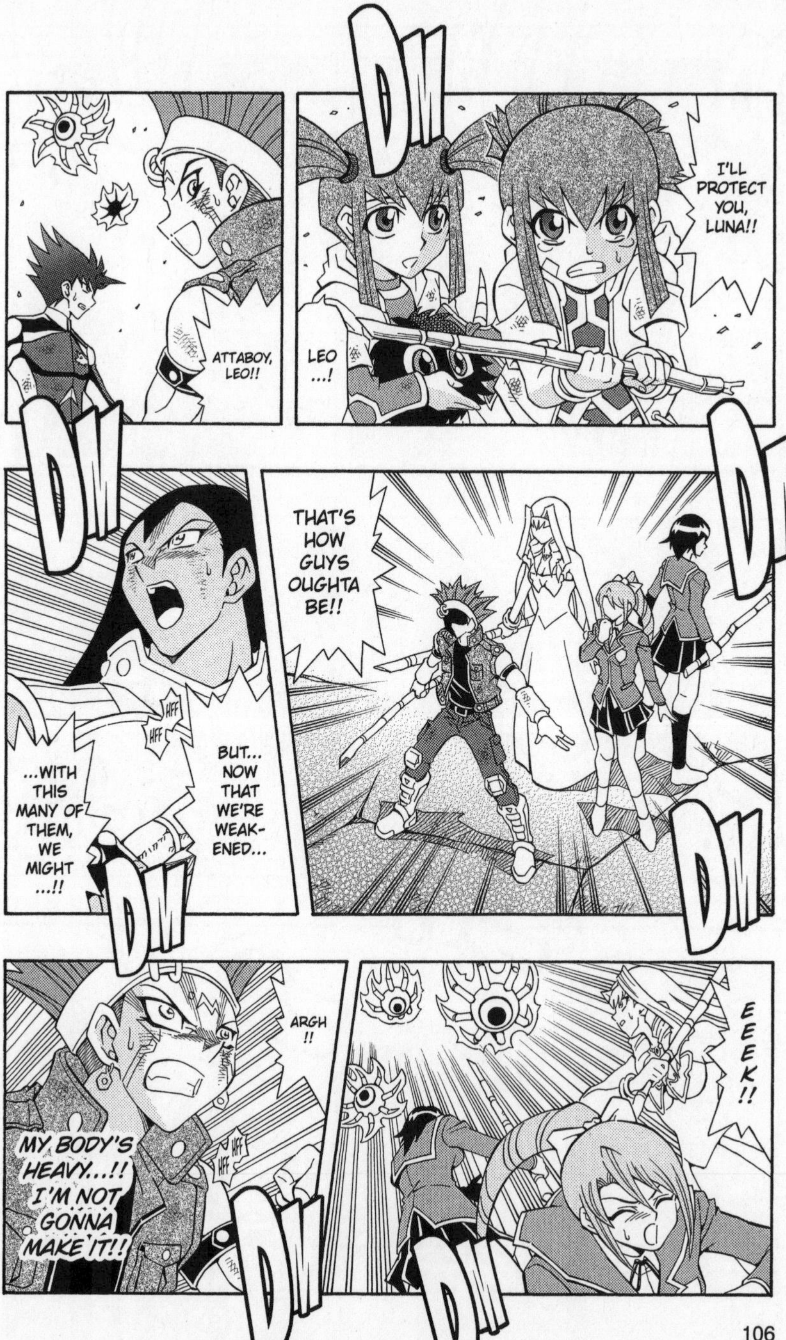
DM
I'LL PROTECT YOU, LUNA!!
LEO ...!
ATTABOY, LEO!!
DM
DM
THAT'S HOW GUYS OUGHTA BE!!
DM
DM
BUT... NOW THAT WE'RE WEAK-ENED...
...WITH THIS MANY OF THEM, WE MIGHT ...!!
HFF
HFF
DM
EEEEK!!
DM
ARGH!!
MY BODY'S HEAVY...!! I'M NOT GONNA MAKE IT!!
HFF
HFF
DM

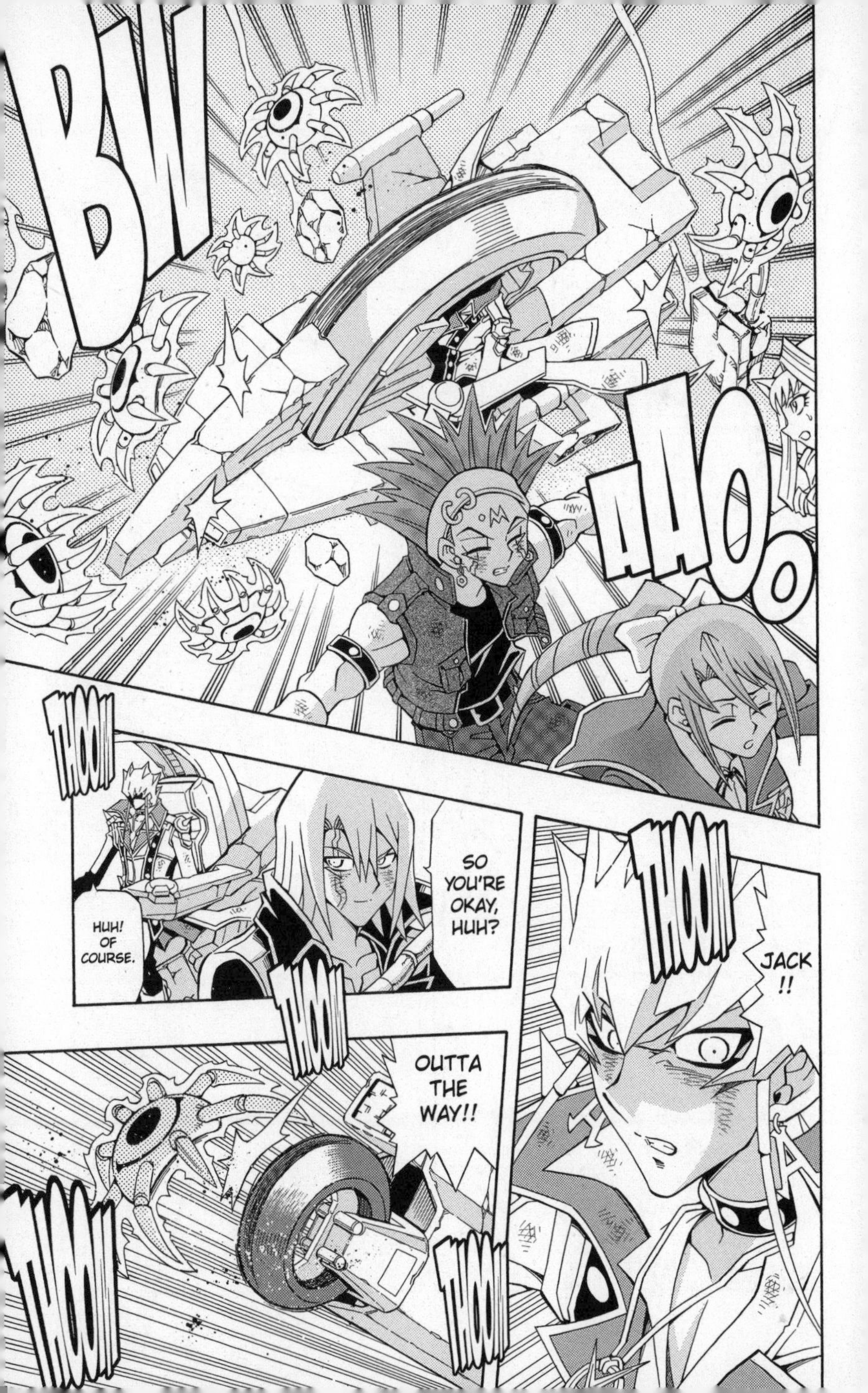
THOOM
JACK!!
THOOM
SO YOU'RE OKAY, HUH?
HUH! OF COURSE.
THOOM
OUTTA THE WAY!!
THOOM
THOOM

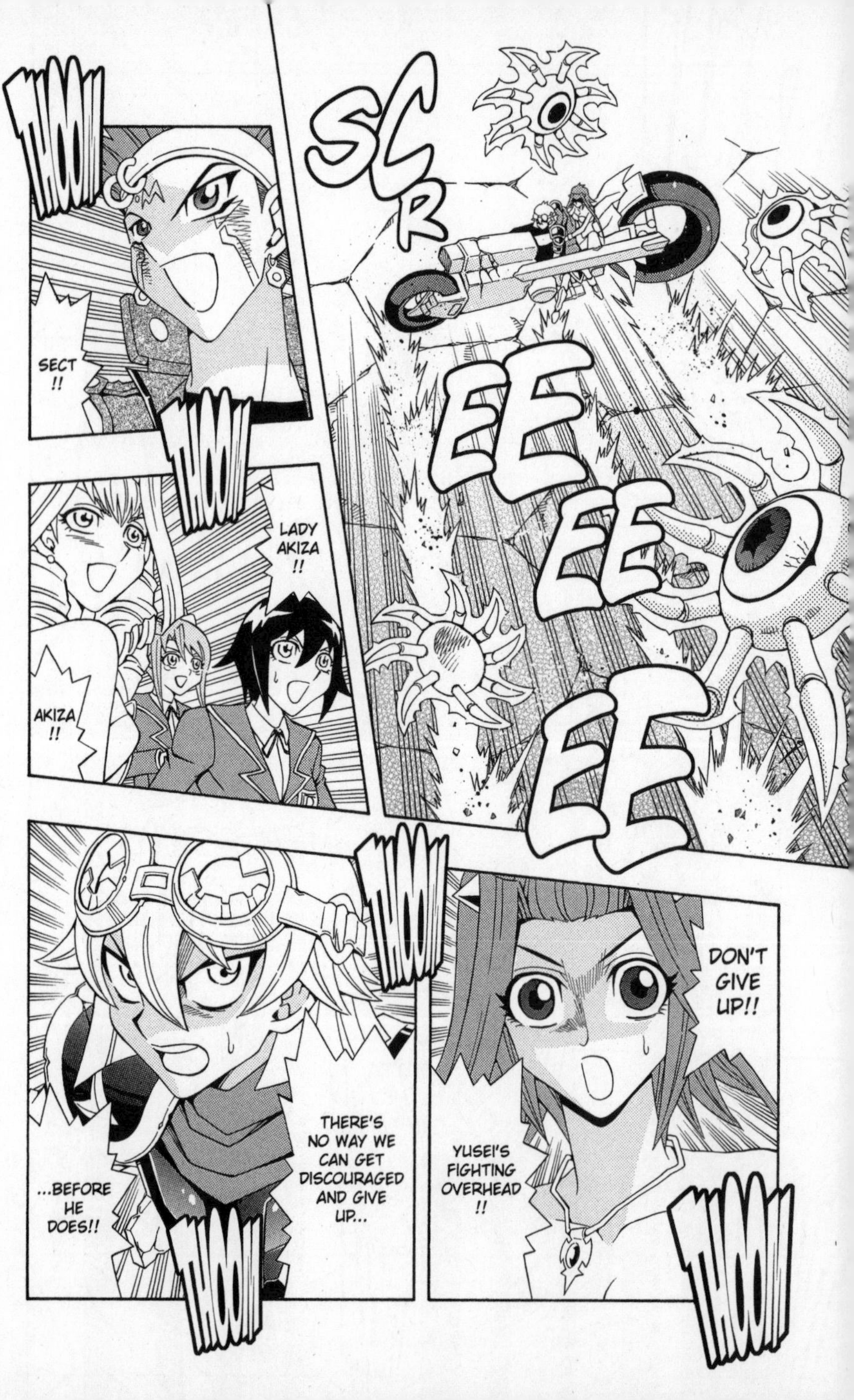
SCR
EEEEEE
THOOM
SECT!!
THOOM
LADY AKIZA!!
AKIZA!!
DON'T GIVE UP!!
YUSEI'S FIGHTING OVERHEAD!!
THOOM
THOOM
THERE'S NO WAY WE CAN GET DISCOURAGED AND GIVE UP...
...BEFORE HE DOES!!
THOOM

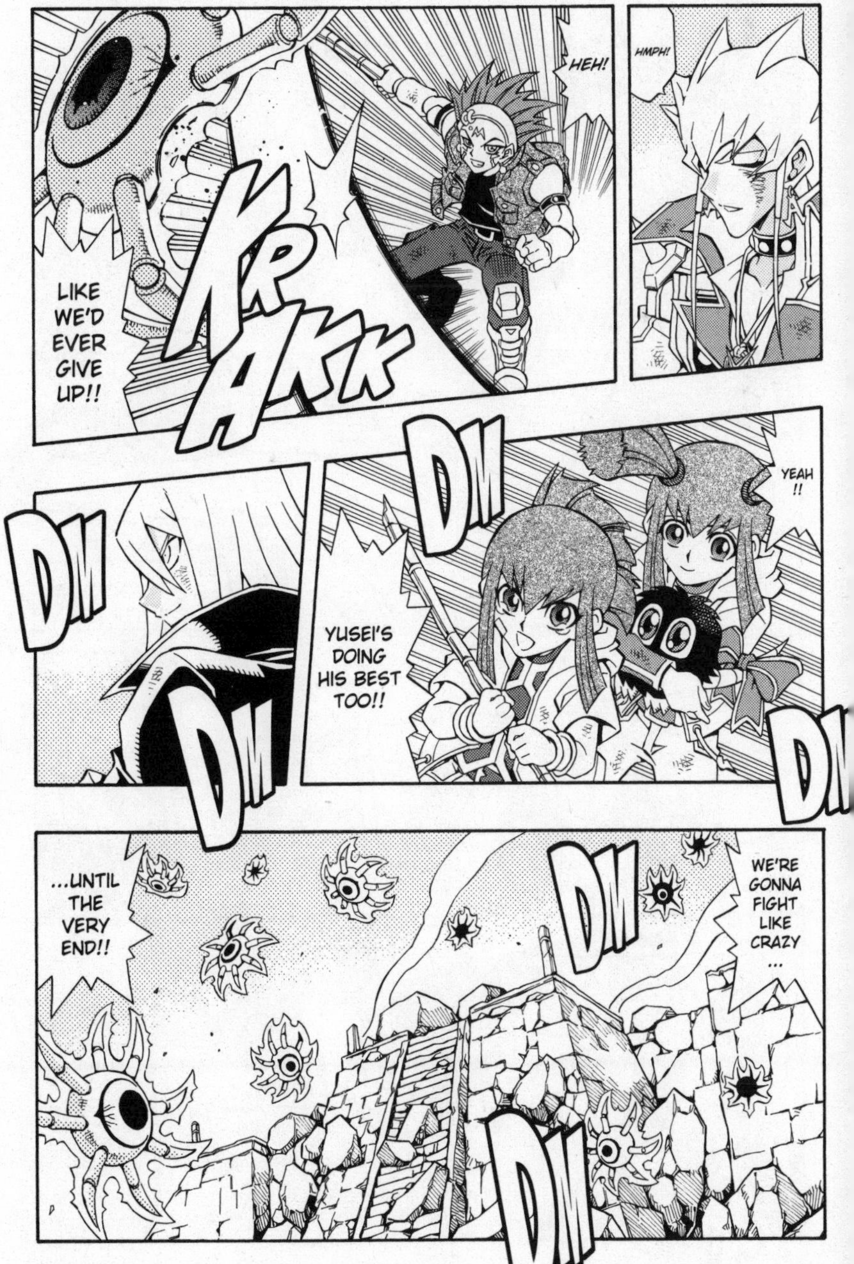
HMPH!
HEH!
KRAKK
LIKE WE'D EVER GIVE UP!!
YEAH!!
DM
YUSEI'S DOING HIS BEST TOO!!
DM
DM
DM
WE'RE GONNA FIGHT LIKE CRAZY...
DM
...UNTIL THE VERY END!!
DM

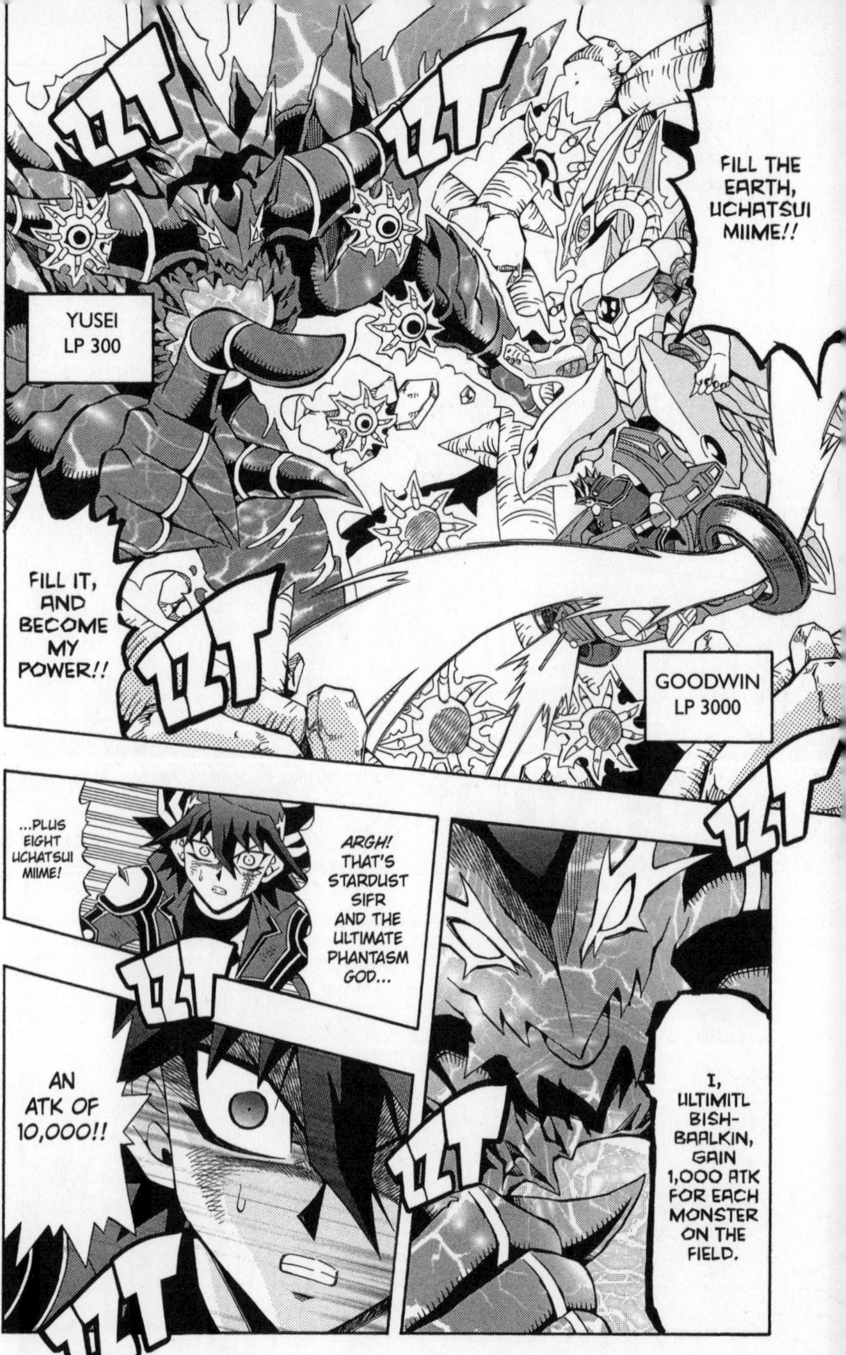
FILL THE EARTH, UCHATSUI MIIME!!
ZZT
ZZT
YUSEI LP 300
GOODWIN LP 3000
FILL IT, AND BECOME MY POWER!!
ZZT
ZZT
I, ULTIMITL BISH-BAALKIN, GAIN 1,000 ATK FOR EACH MONSTER ON THE FIELD.
ZZT
ARGH! THAT'S STARDUST SIFR AND THE ULTIMATE PHANTASM GOD...
...PLUS EIGHT UCHATSUI MIIME!
ZZT
AN ATK OF 10,000!!
ZZT

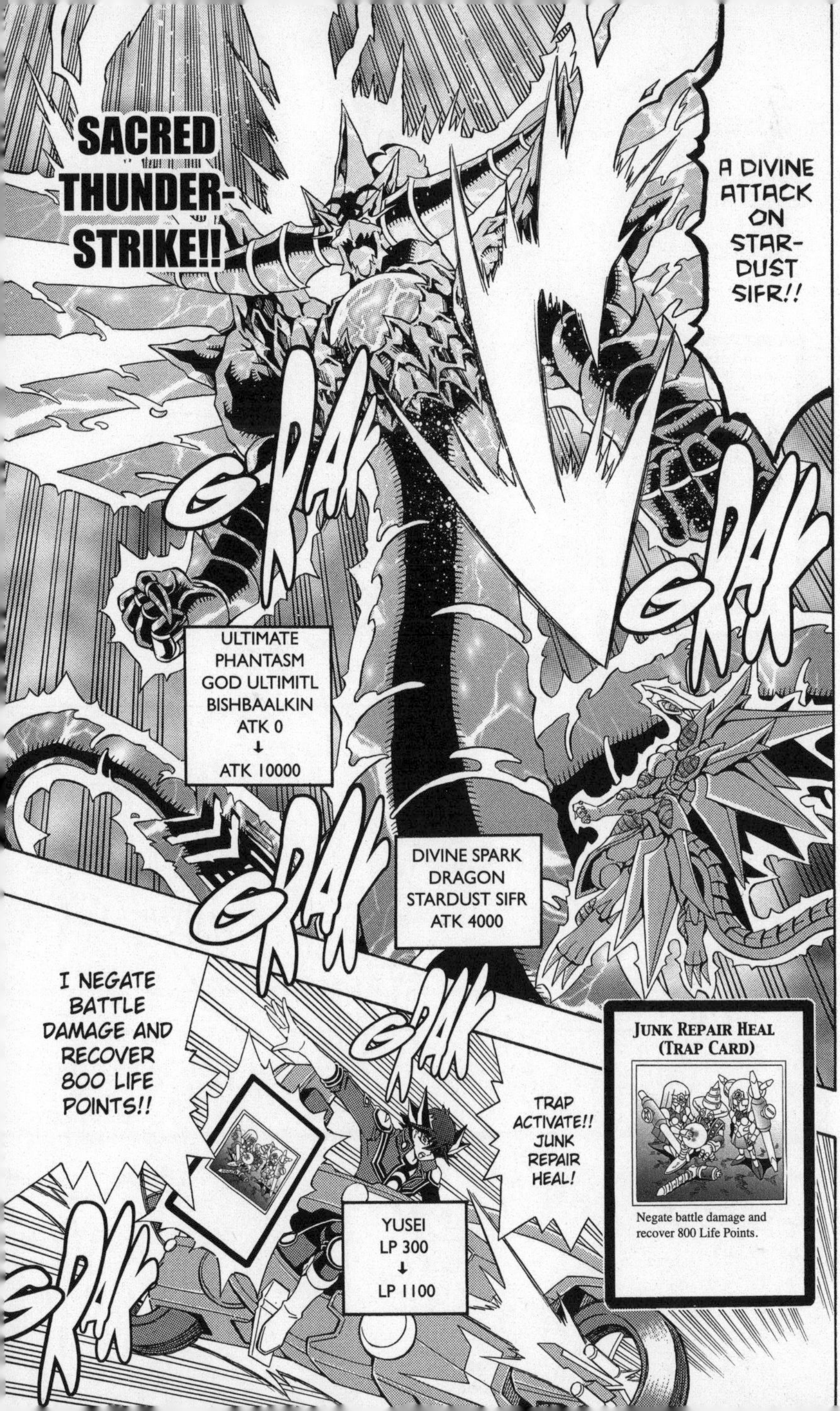
A DIVINE ATTACK ON STARDUST SIFR!!
SACRED THUNDER-STRIKE!!
GRAK
GRAK
ULTIMATE PHANTASM GOD ULTIMITL BISHBAALKIN ATK 0 ↓ ATK 10000
DIVINE SPARK DRAGON STARDUST SIFR ATK 4000
GRAK
JUNK REPAIR HEAL (TRAP CARD)
Negate battle damage and recover 800 Life Points.
TRAP ACTIVATE!! JUNK REPAIR HEAL!
GRAK
I NEGATE BATTLE DAMAGE AND RECOVER 800 LIFE POINTS!!
YUSEI LP 300 ↓ LP 1100
GRAK

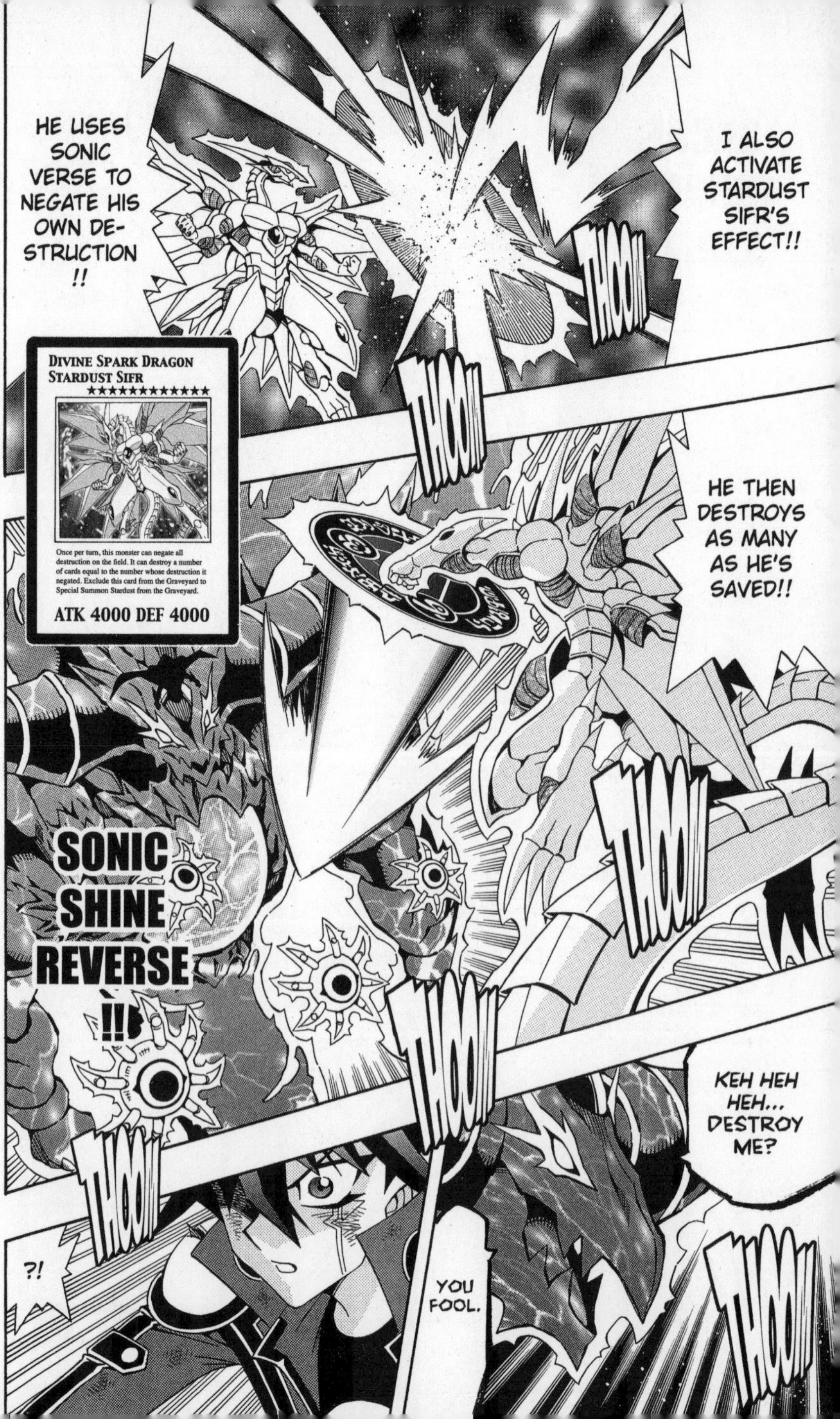
I ALSO ACTIVATE STARDUST SIFR'S EFFECT!!
THOOM
HE USES SONIC VERSE TO NEGATE HIS OWN DE-STRUCTION !!
THOOM
DIVINE SPARK DRAGON STARDUST SIFR
★★★★★★★★★★★★
Once per turn, this monster can negate all destruction on the field. It can destroy a number of cards equal to the number whose destruction it negated. Exclude this card from the Graveyard to Special Summon Stardust from the Graveyard.
ATK 4000 DEF 4000
HE THEN DESTROYS AS MANY AS HE'S SAVED!!
THOOM
SONIC SHINE REVERSE !!
THOOM
THOOM
KEH HEH HEH... DESTROY ME?
THOOM
YOU FOOL.
?!

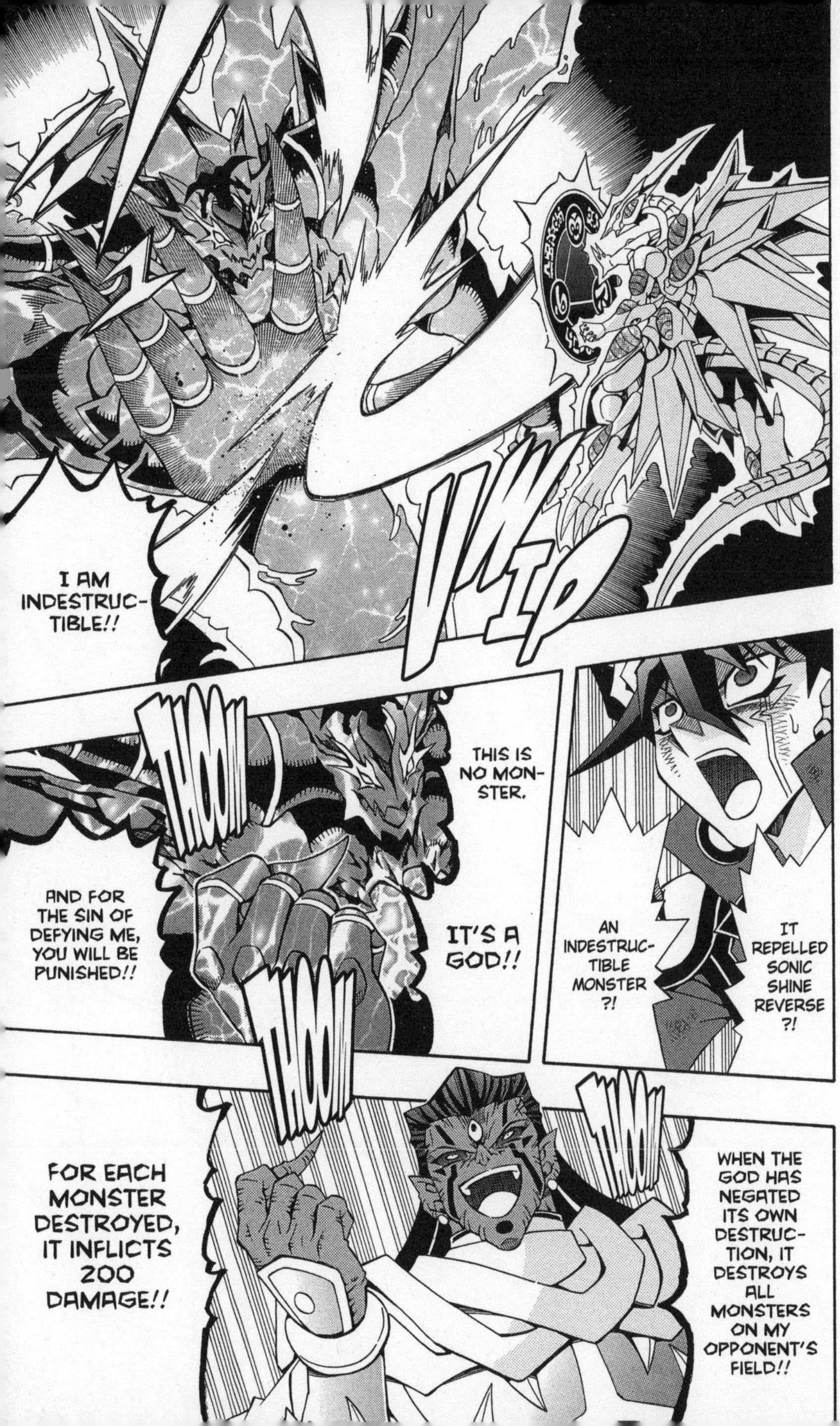
VWIP
I AM INDESTRUCTIBLE!!
IT REPELLED SONIC SHINE REVERSE?!
AN INDESTRUCTIBLE MONSTER?!
THIS IS NO MONSTER.
IT'S A GOD!!
THOOM
AND FOR THE SIN OF DEFYING ME, YOU WILL BE PUNISHED!!
THOOM
THOOM
WHEN THE GOD HAS NEGATED ITS OWN DESTRUCTION, IT DESTROYS ALL MONSTERS ON MY OPPONENT'S FIELD!!
FOR EACH MONSTER DESTROYED, IT INFLICTS 200 DAMAGE!!

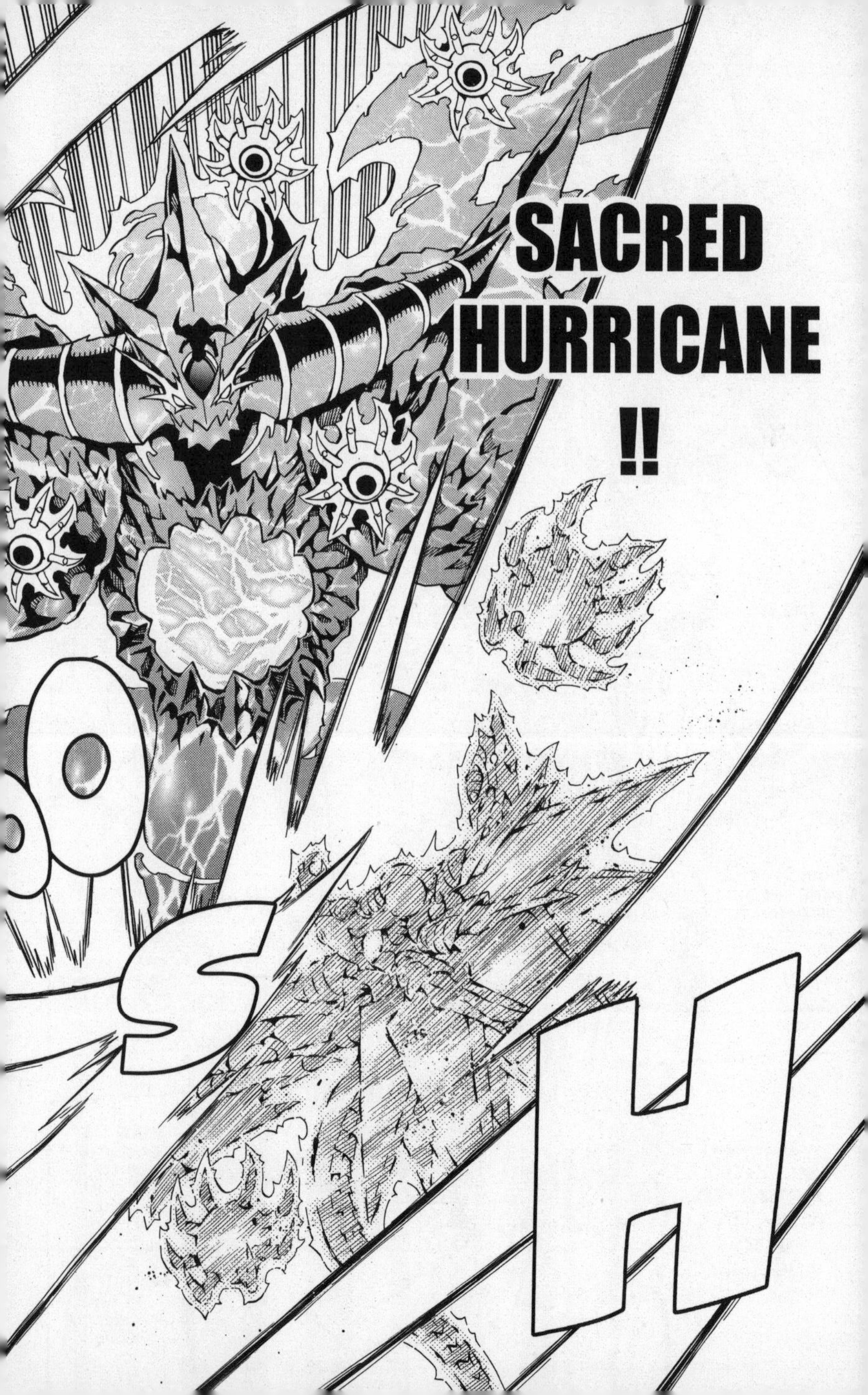
SACRED HURRICANE !!
SH

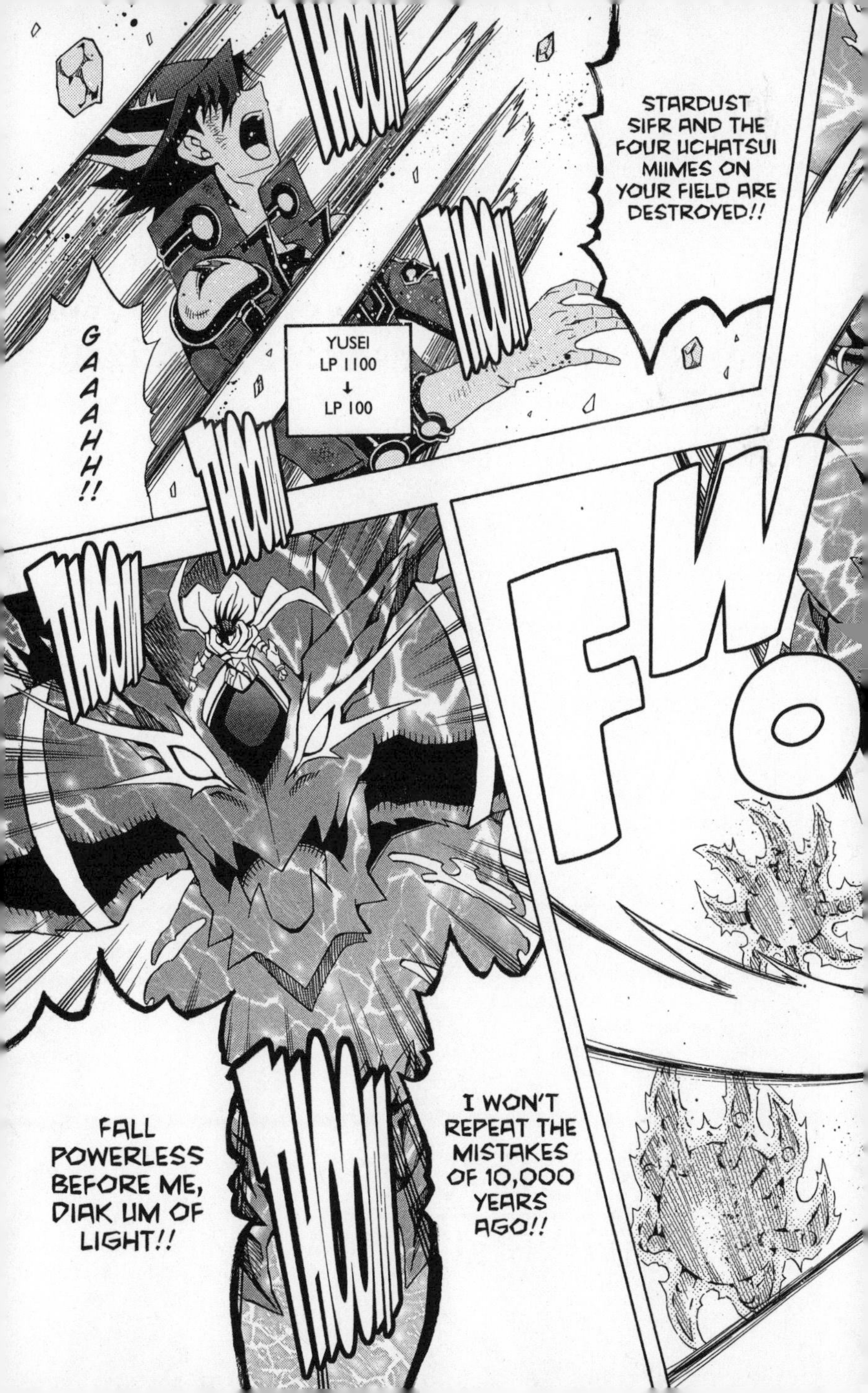
STARDUST SIFR AND THE FOUR UCHATSUI MIIMES ON YOUR FIELD ARE DESTROYED!!
THOOM
THOOM
YUSEI
LP 1100
↓
LP 100
THOOM
GAAAAHH!!
FWOO
THOOM
THOOM
I WON'T REPEAT THE MISTAKES OF 10,000 YEARS AGO!!
FALL POWERLESS BEFORE ME, DIAK UM OF LIGHT!!

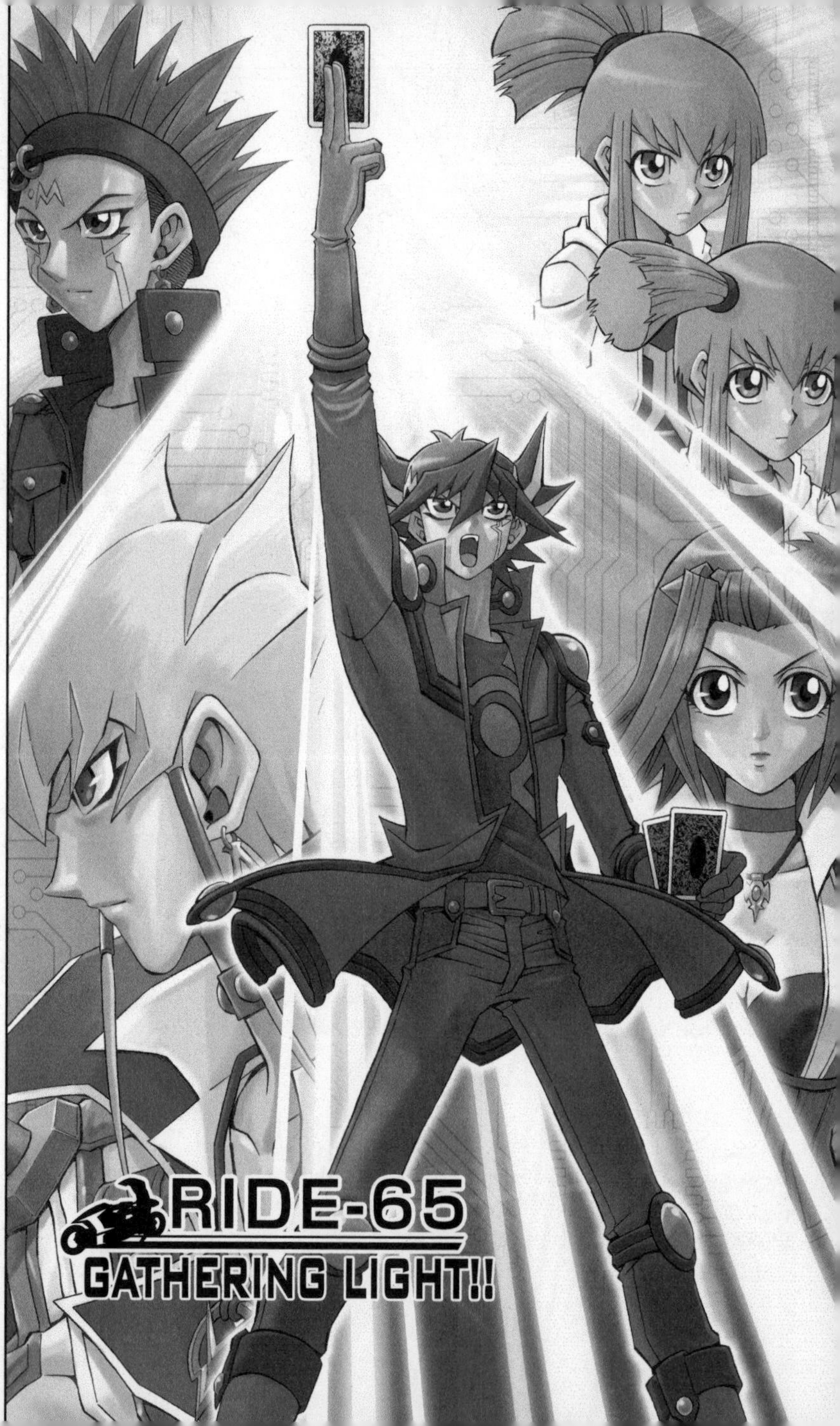
RIDE-65
GATHERING LIGHT!!

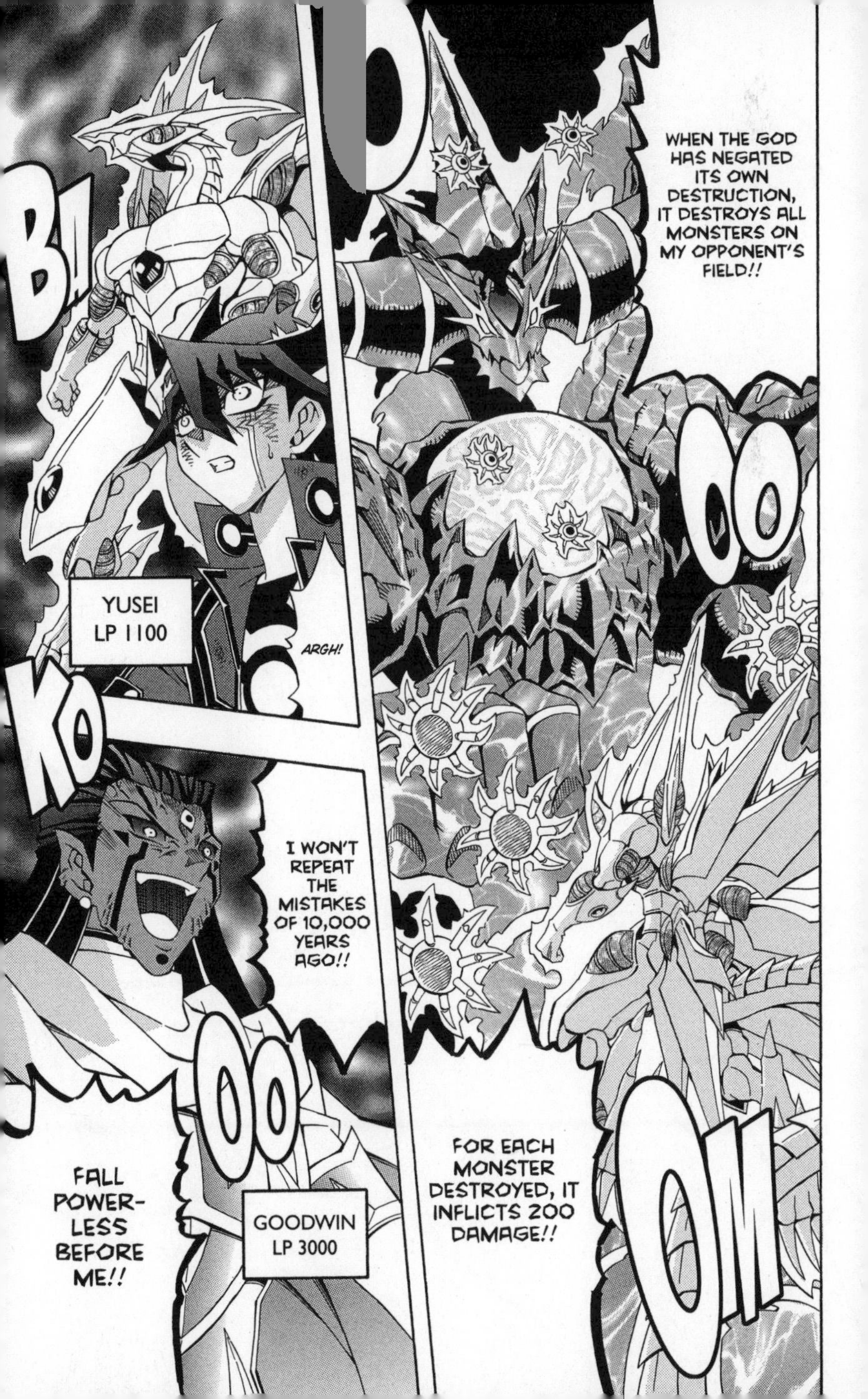
WHEN THE GOD HAS NEGATED ITS OWN DESTRUCTION, IT DESTROYS ALL MONSTERS ON MY OPPONENT'S FIELD!!
FOR EACH MONSTER DESTROYED, IT INFLICTS 200 DAMAGE!!
YUSEI LP 1100
ARGH!
I WON'T REPEAT THE MISTAKES OF 10,000 YEARS AGO!!
FALL POWER-LESS BEFORE ME!!
GOODWIN LP 3000

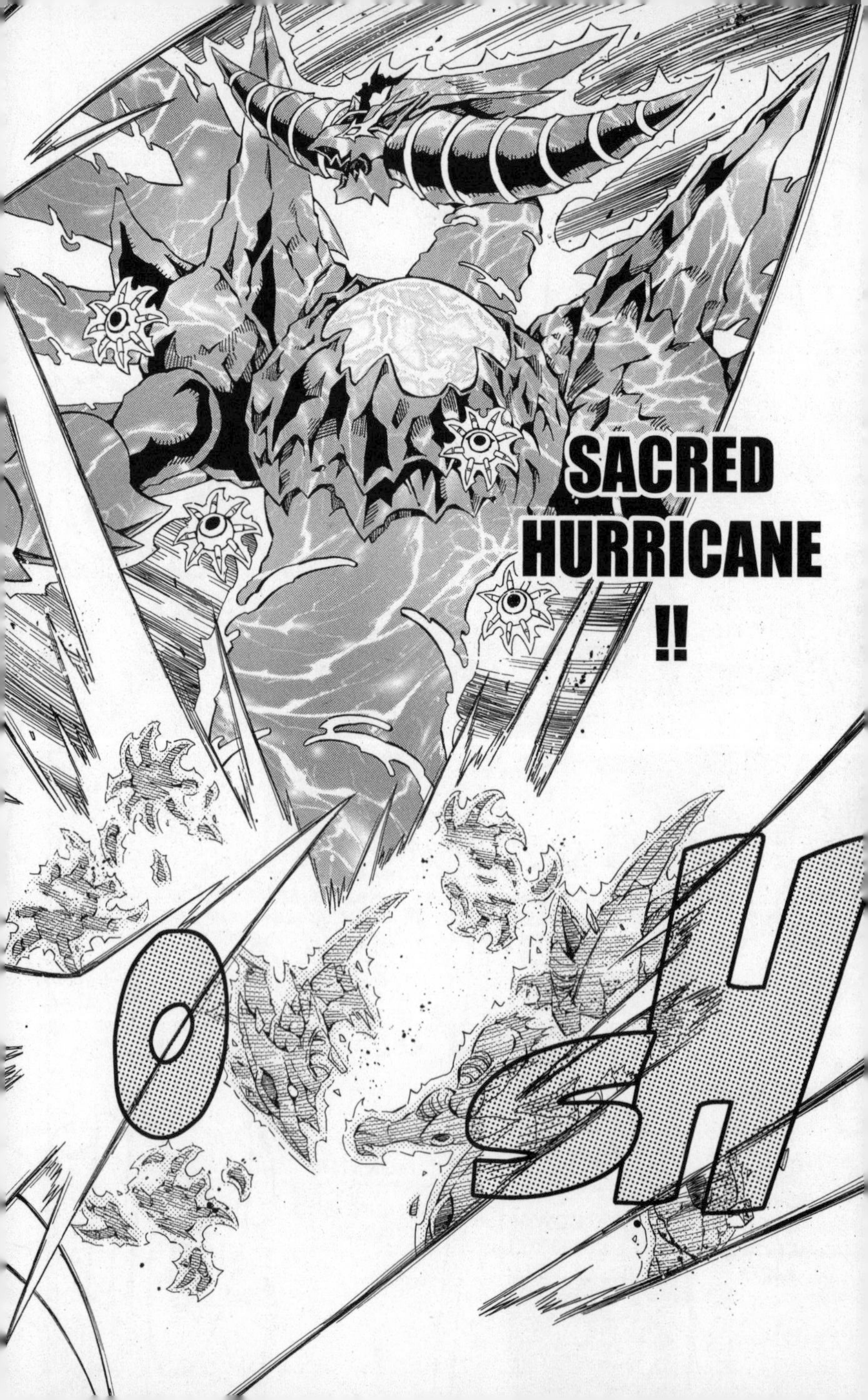
SACRED HURRICANE !!
WOOSH

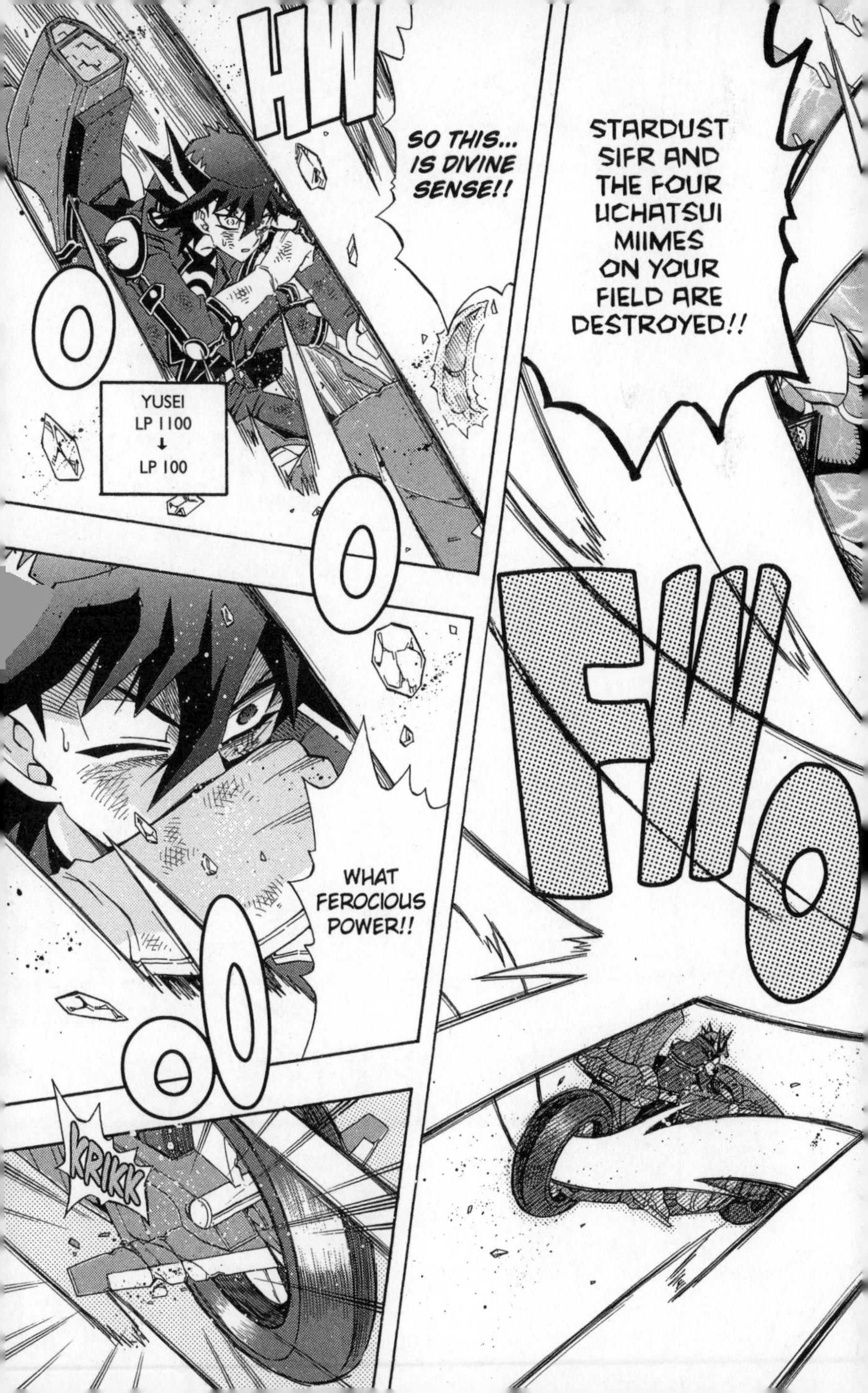
STARDUST SIFR AND THE FOUR UCHATSUI MIIMES ON YOUR FIELD ARE DESTROYED!!
FWO
HWOOOO
SO THIS... IS DIVINE SENSE!!
YUSEI
LP 1100
↓
LP 100
WHAT FEROCIOUS POWER!!
KRIKK

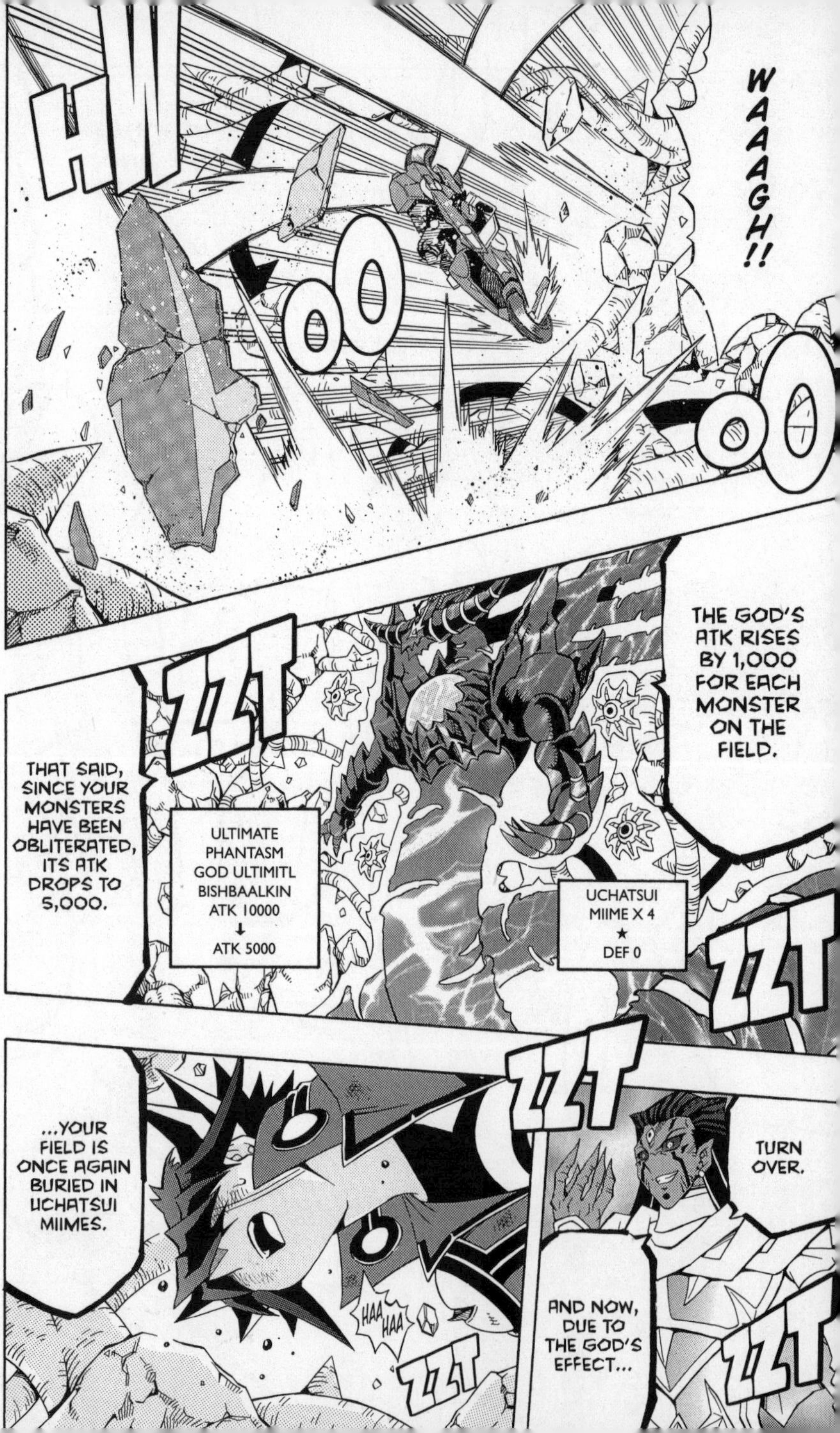
WAAAAGH!!
HWOOOOO
THE GOD'S ATK RISES BY 1,000 FOR EACH MONSTER ON THE FIELD.
UCHATSUI MIIME X 4 ★ DEF 0
ZZT
ULTIMATE PHANTASM GOD ULTIMITL BISHBAALKIN ATK 10000 ↓ ATK 5000
ZZT
THAT SAID, SINCE YOUR MONSTERS HAVE BEEN OBLITERATED, ITS ATK DROPS TO 5,000.
TURN OVER.
ZZT
AND NOW, DUE TO THE GOD'S EFFECT...
ZZT
...YOUR FIELD IS ONCE AGAIN BURIED IN UCHATSUI MIIMES.
HAA HAA
ZZT

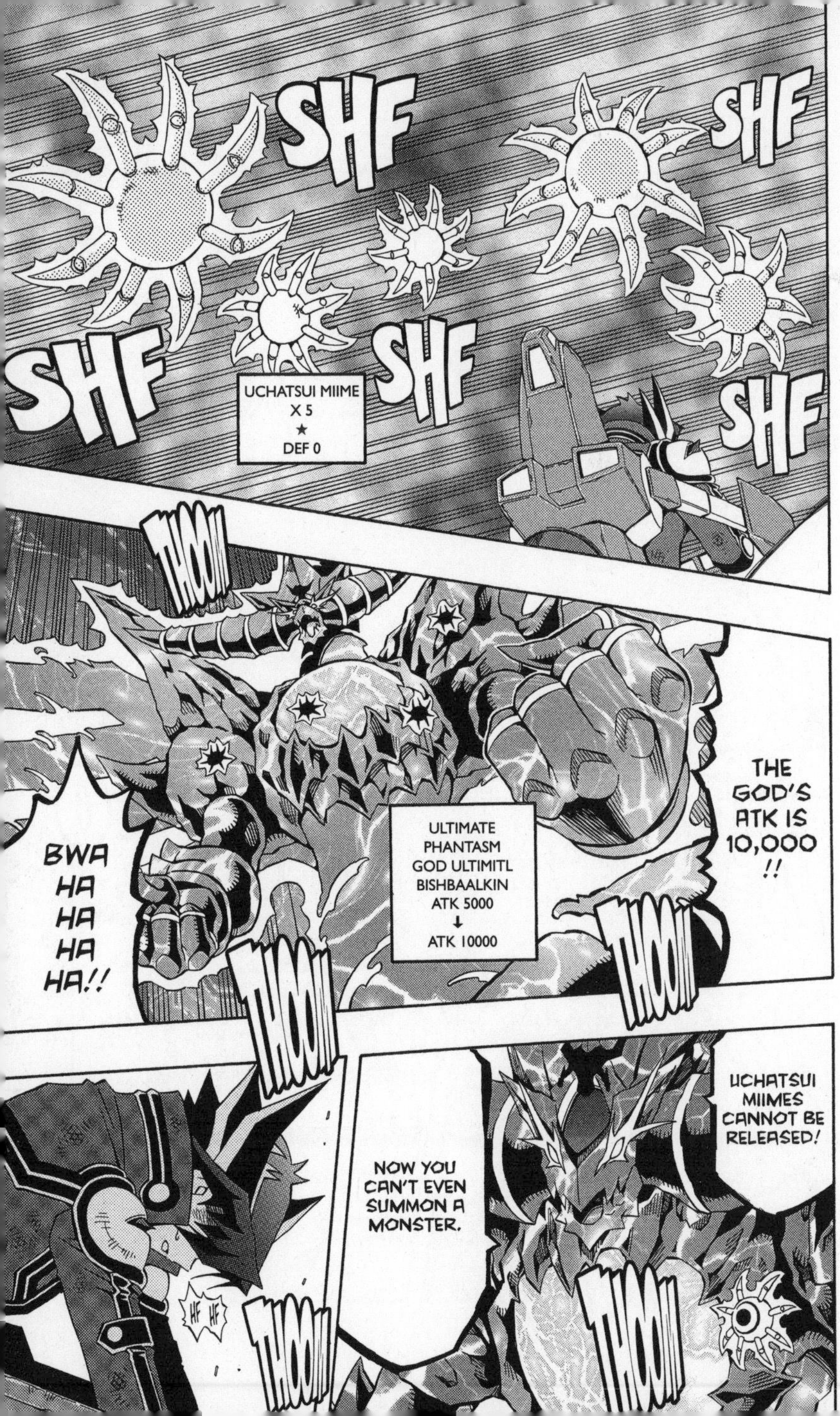
SHF
SHF
SHF
SHF
UCHATSUI MIIME
X 5
★
DEF 0
SHF
THOOM
THE GOD'S ATK IS 10,000!!
ULTIMATE PHANTASM GOD ULTIMITL BISHBAALKIN
ATK 5000
↓
ATK 10000
THOOM
BWA HA HA HA HA!!
THOOM
UCHATSUI MIIMES CANNOT BE RELEASED!
NOW YOU CAN'T EVEN SUMMON A MONSTER.
THOOM
HF HF
THOOM

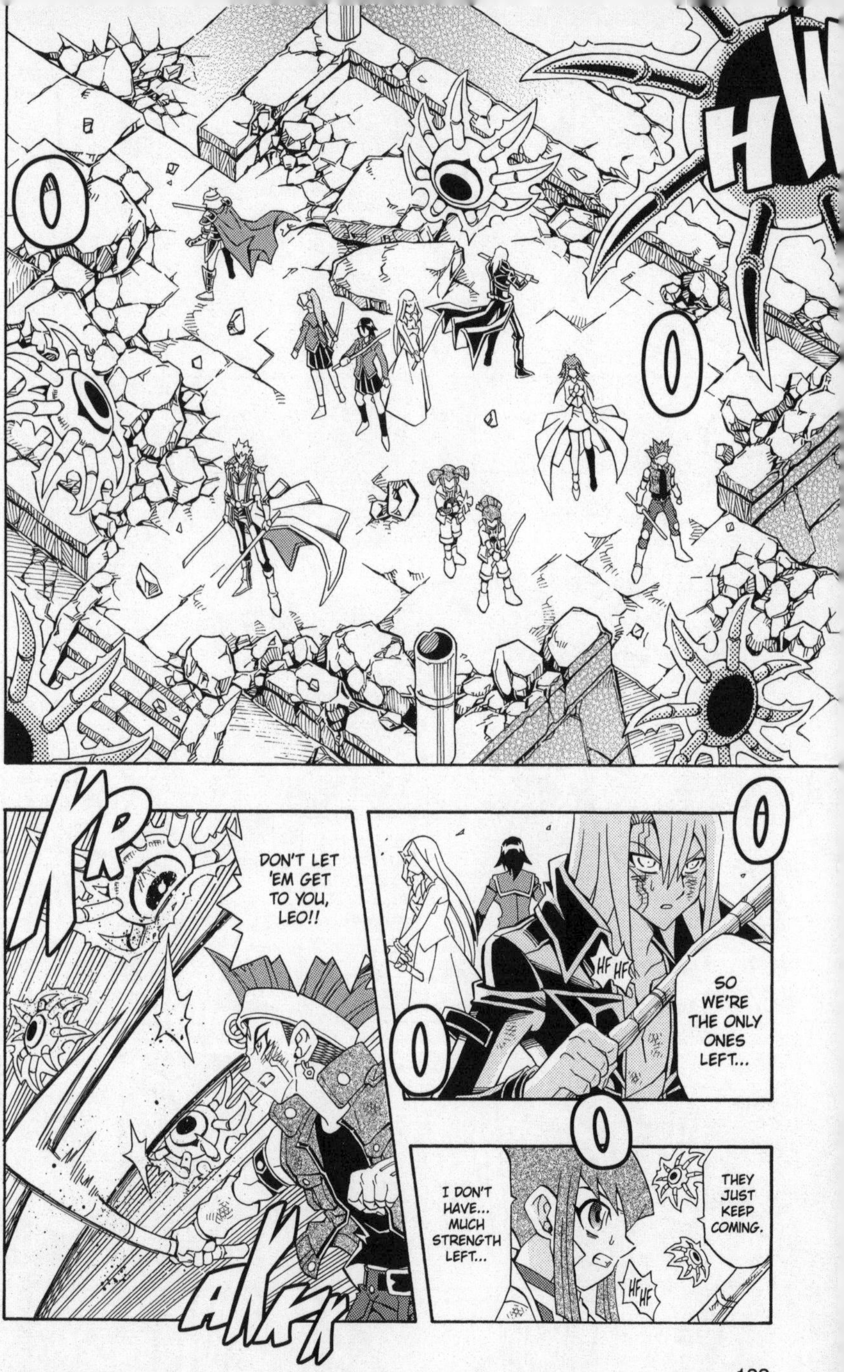
HW
O
O
O
O
SO WE'RE THE ONLY ONES LEFT...
HF HF
O
THEY JUST KEEP COMING.
I DON'T HAVE... MUCH STRENGTH LEFT...
HF HF
KR
DON'T LET 'EM GET TO YOU, LEO!!
AKKK

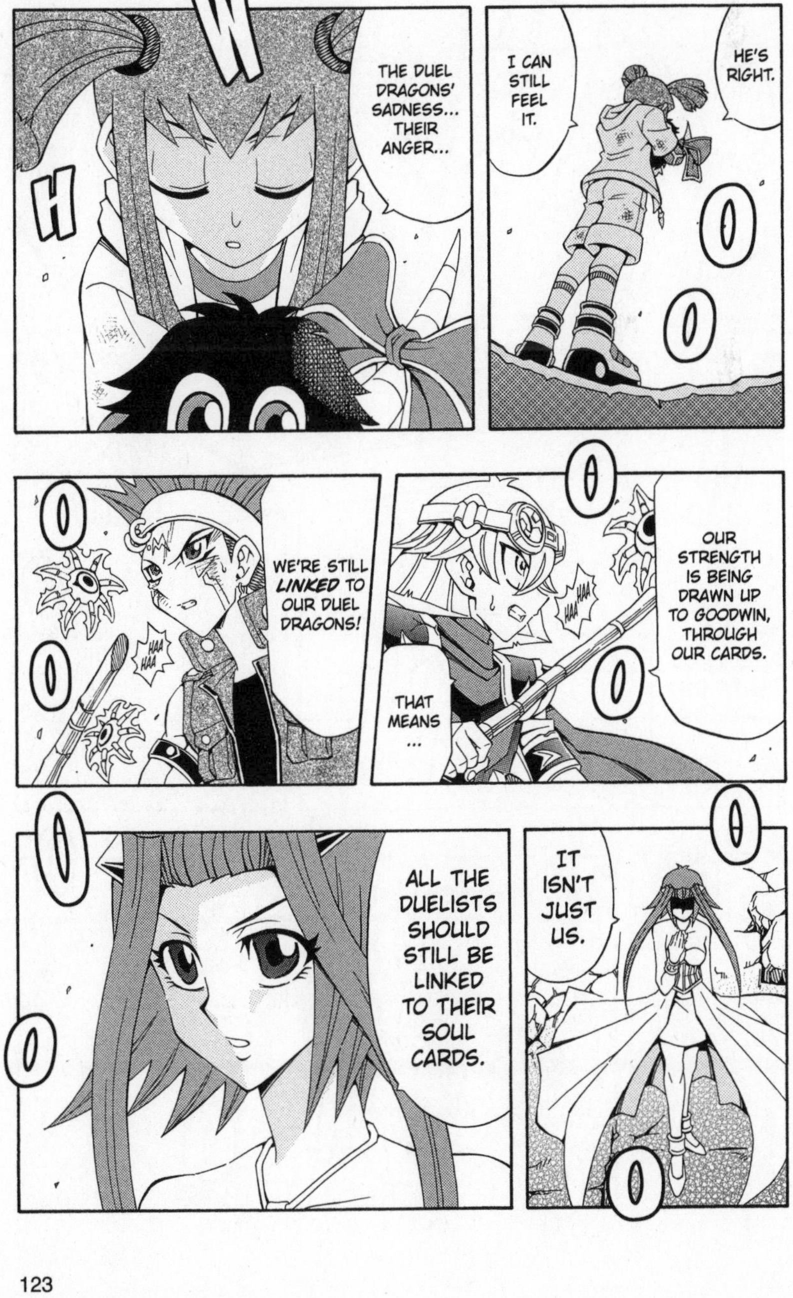
HE'S RIGHT.
I CAN STILL FEEL IT.
THE DUEL DRAGONS' SADNESS... THEIR ANGER...
OUR STRENGTH IS BEING DRAWN UP TO GOODWIN, THROUGH OUR CARDS.
HAA HAA
THAT MEANS ...
WE'RE STILL *LINKED* TO OUR DUEL DRAGONS!
HAA HAA
IT ISN'T JUST US.
ALL THE DUELISTS SHOULD STILL BE LINKED TO THEIR SOUL CARDS.

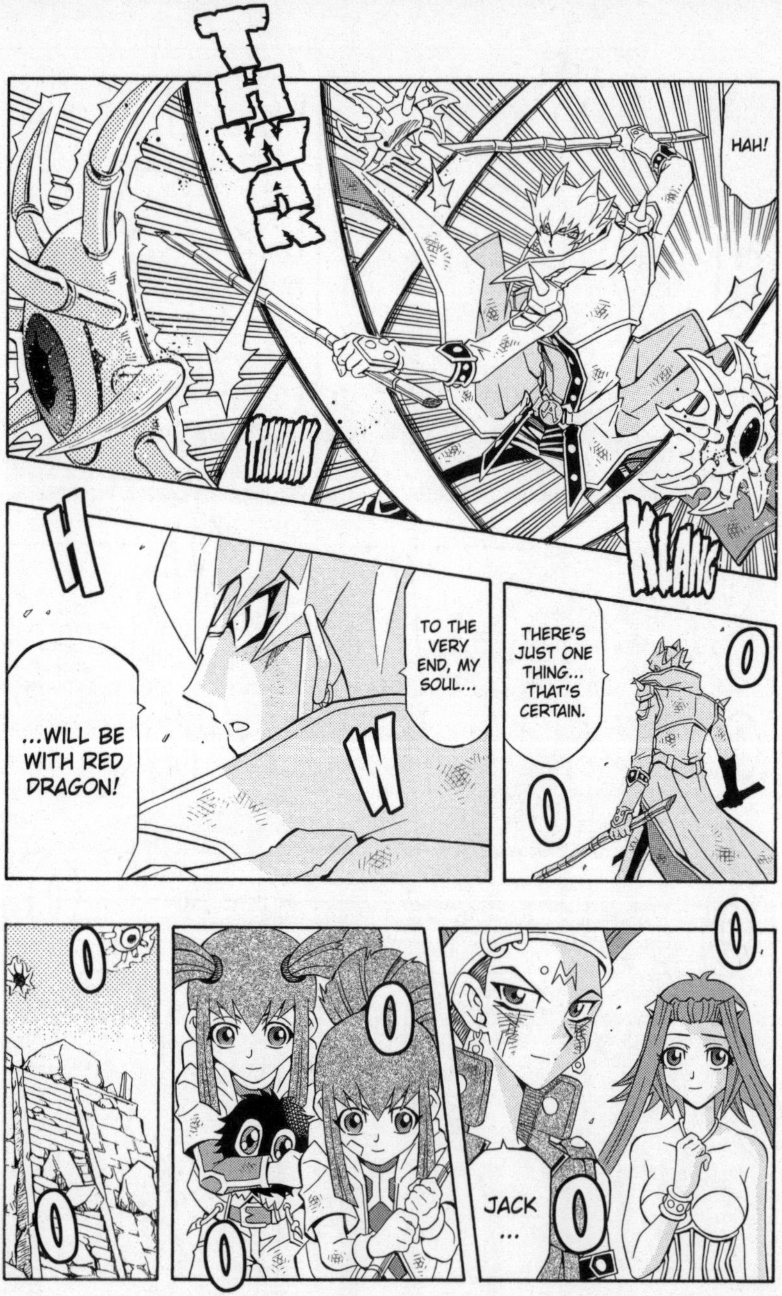
HAH!
THWAK
KLANG
THWAK
THERE'S JUST ONE THING... THAT'S CERTAIN.
O
O
H
TO THE VERY END, MY SOUL...
W
...WILL BE WITH RED DRAGON!
O
JACK ...
O
O
O
O
O
O

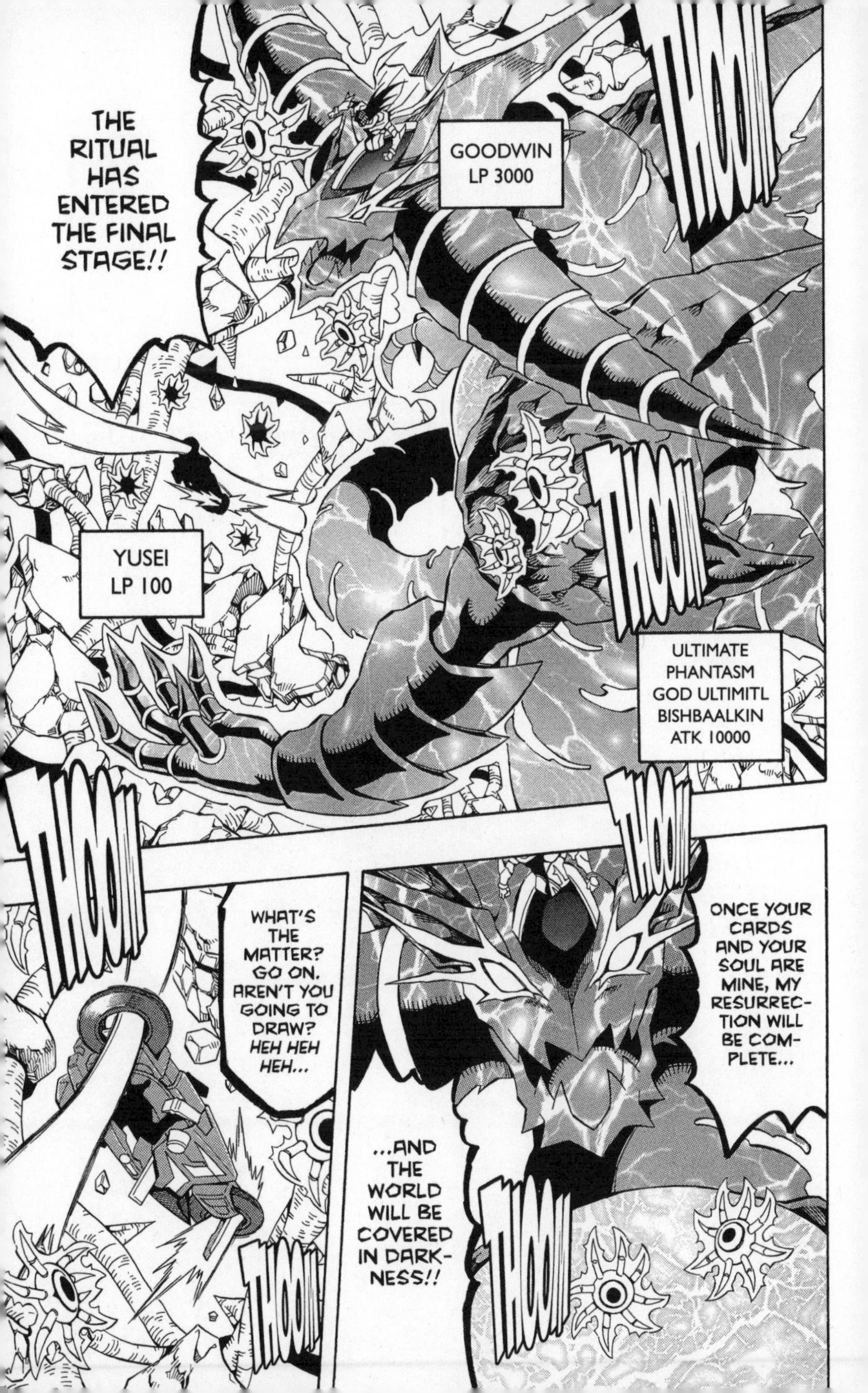
THOOM
GOODWIN LP 3000
THE RITUAL HAS ENTERED THE FINAL STAGE!!
THOOM
YUSEI LP 100
ULTIMATE PHANTASM GOD ULTIMITL BISHBAALKIN ATK 10000
THOOM
THOOM
ONCE YOUR CARDS AND YOUR SOUL ARE MINE, MY RESURRECTION WILL BE COMPLETE...
...AND THE WORLD WILL BE COVERED IN DARKNESS!!
THOOM
WHAT'S THE MATTER? GO ON. AREN'T YOU GOING TO DRAW? HEH HEH HEH...
THOOM

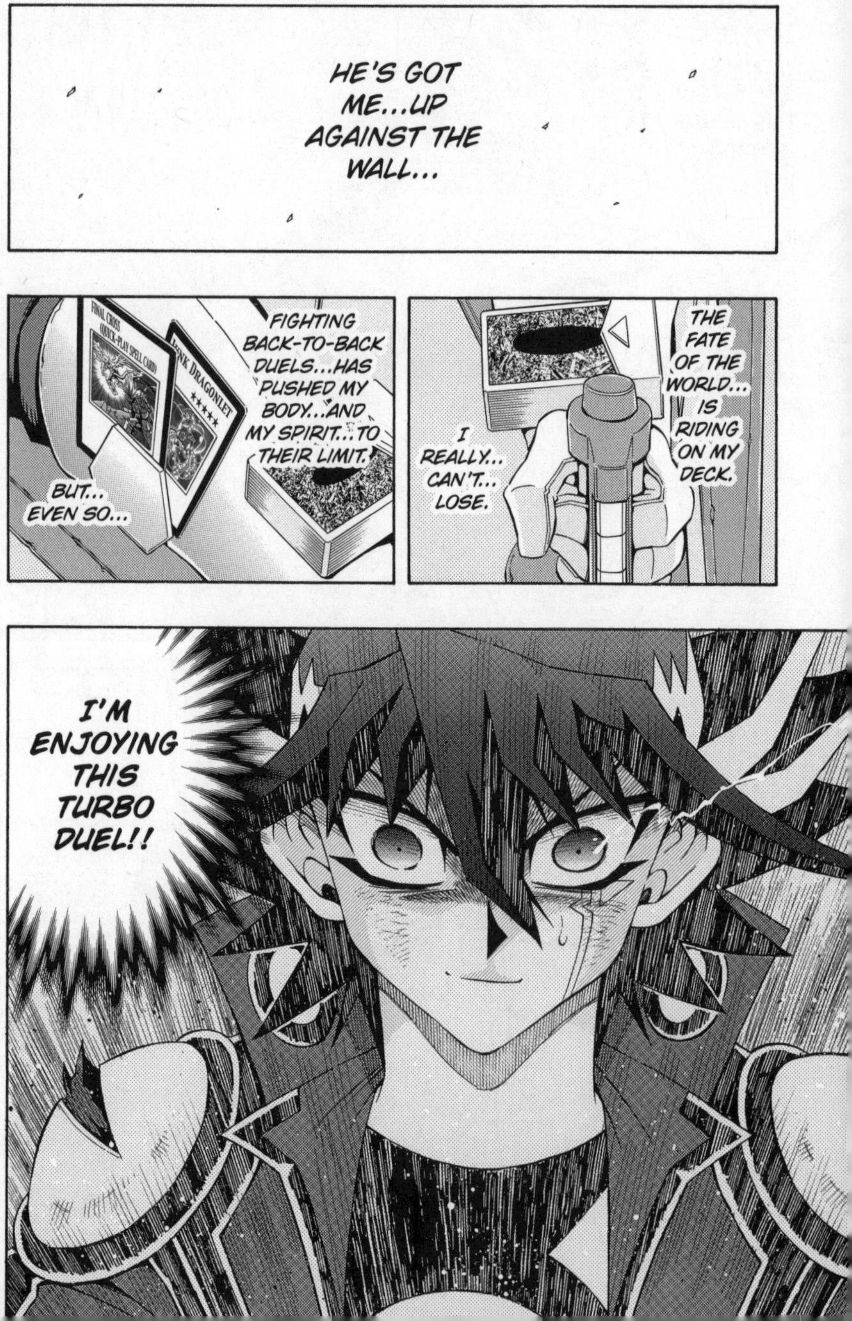
HE'S GOT ME...UP AGAINST THE WALL...
THE FATE OF THE WORLD... IS RIDING ON MY DECK.
I REALLY... CAN'T... LOSE.
FINAL CROSS
QUICK-PLAY SPELL CARD
FIGHTING BACK-TO-BACK DUELS...HAS PUSHED MY BODY...AND MY SPIRIT...TO THEIR LIMIT.
BUT... EVEN SO...
I'M ENJOYING THIS TURBO DUEL!!

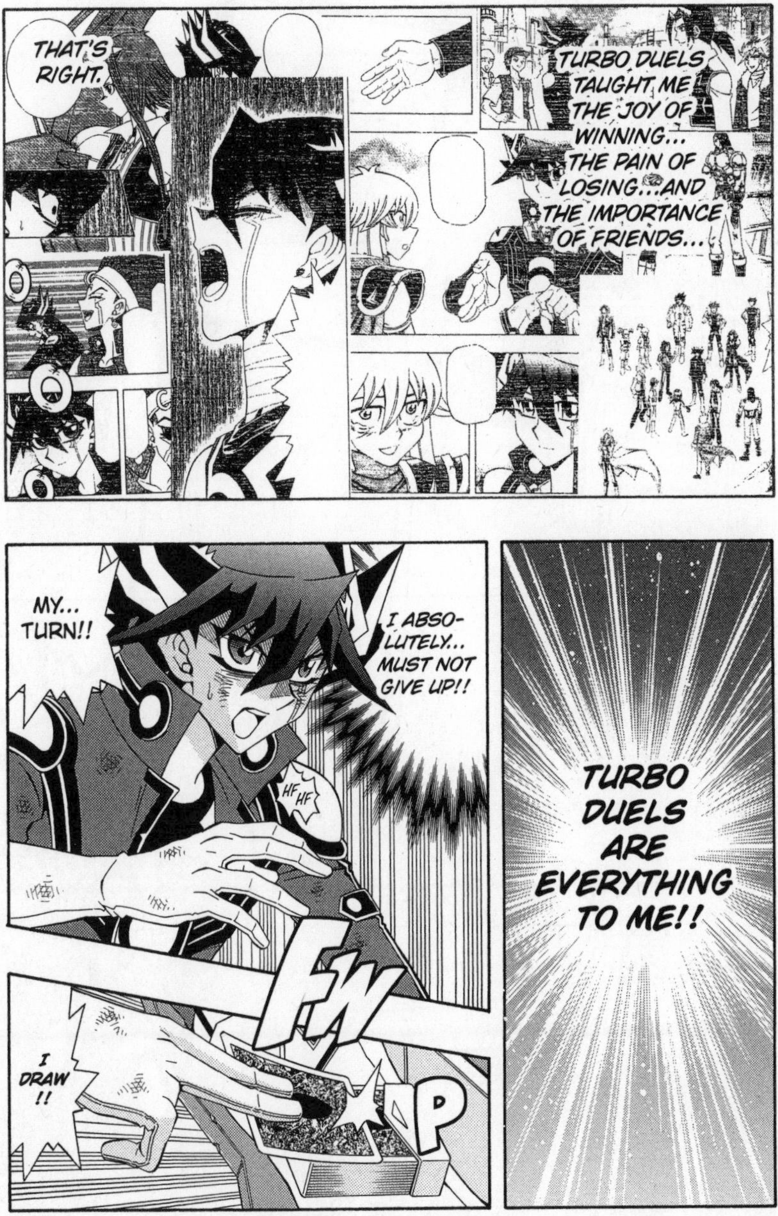
TURBO DUELS TAUGHT ME THE JOY OF WINNING... THE PAIN OF LOSING...AND THE IMPORTANCE OF FRIENDS...
THAT'S RIGHT.
TURBO DUELS ARE EVERYTHING TO ME!!
I ABSOLUTELY... MUST NOT GIVE UP!!
MY... TURN!!
HF HF
FW
I DRAW!!
P

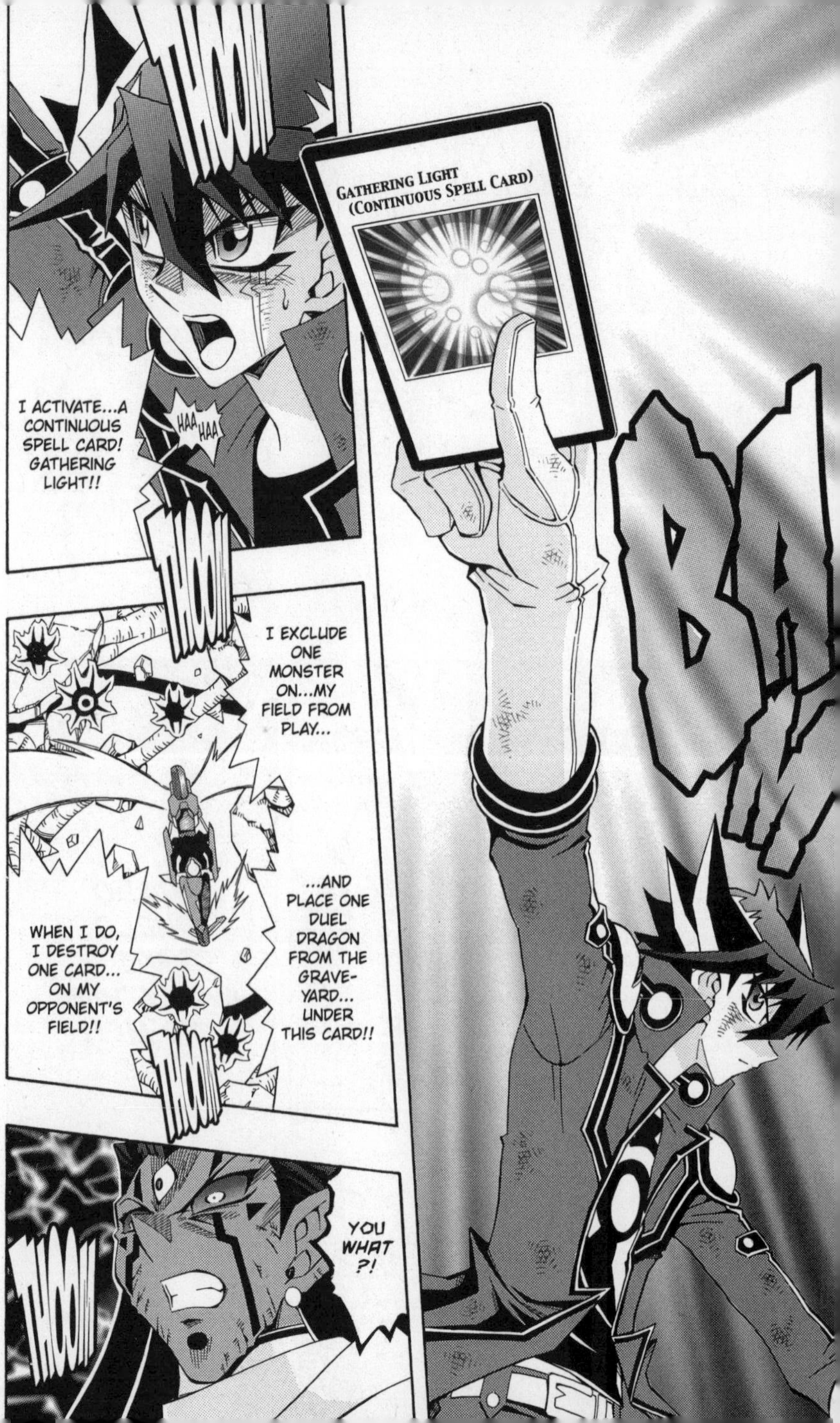
GATHERING LIGHT
(CONTINUOUS SPELL CARD)
BAM
THOOM
HAA HAA
I ACTIVATE...A CONTINUOUS SPELL CARD! GATHERING LIGHT!!
THOOM
I EXCLUDE ONE MONSTER ON...MY FIELD FROM PLAY...
...AND PLACE ONE DUEL DRAGON FROM THE GRAVE-YARD... UNDER THIS CARD!!
WHEN I DO, I DESTROY ONE CARD... ON MY OPPONENT'S FIELD!!
THOOM
YOU WHAT ?!
THOOM

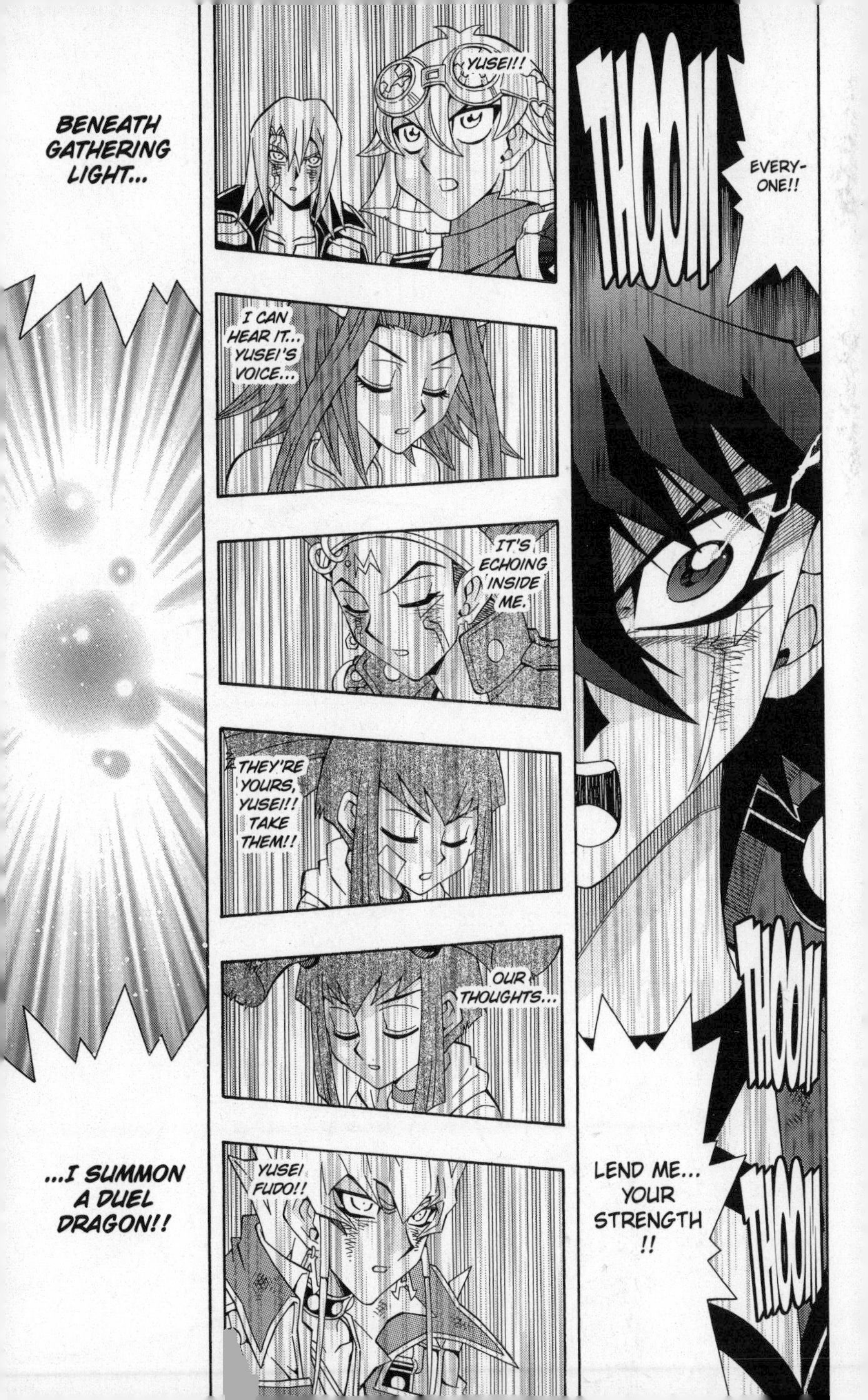
THOOM
EVERY-ONE!!
THOOM
THOOM
LEND ME... YOUR STRENGTH!!
YUSEI!!
I CAN HEAR IT... YUSEI'S VOICE...
IT'S ECHOING INSIDE ME.
THEY'RE YOURS, YUSEI!! TAKE THEM!!
OUR THOUGHTS...
YUSEI FUDO!!
BENEATH GATHERING LIGHT...
...I SUMMON A DUEL DRAGON!!

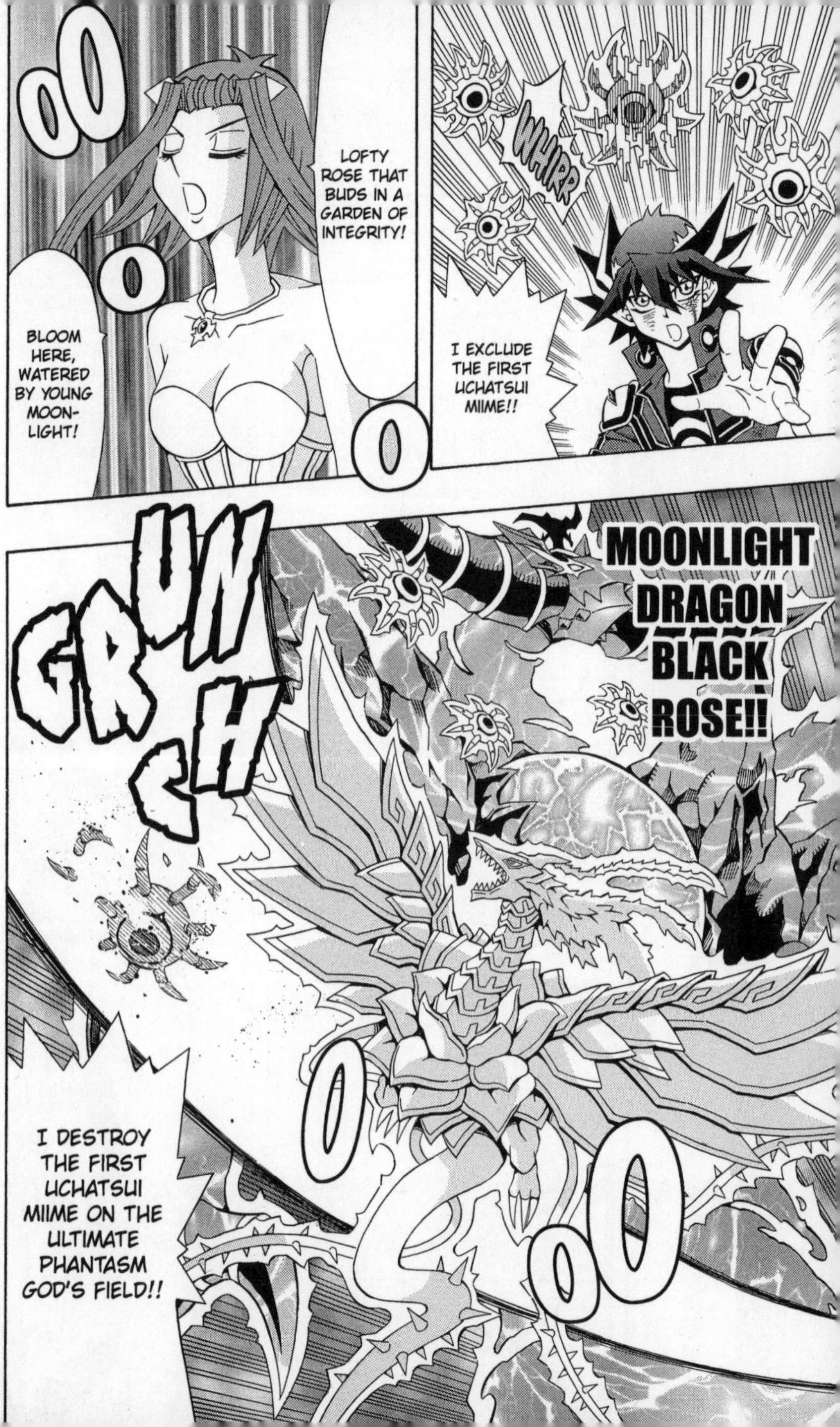
WHIRR
I EXCLUDE THE FIRST UCHATSUI MIIME!!
OO
LOFTY ROSE THAT BUDS IN A GARDEN OF INTEGRITY!
O
BLOOM HERE, WATERED BY YOUNG MOON-LIGHT!
O
MOONLIGHT DRAGON BLACK ROSE!!
GRUNCH
O
OO
I DESTROY THE FIRST UCHATSUI MIIME ON THE ULTIMATE PHANTASM GOD'S FIELD!!

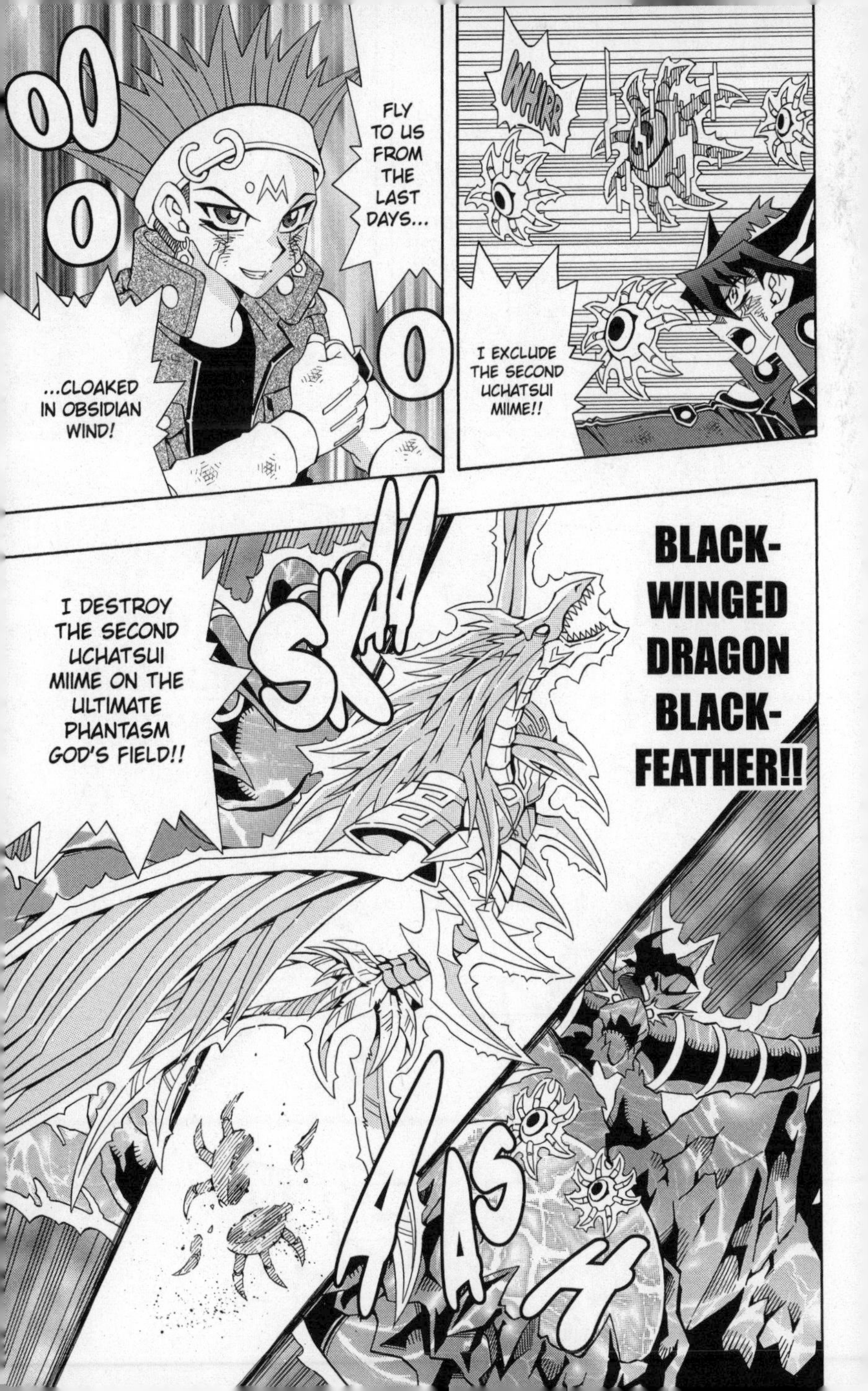
WHIRR
I EXCLUDE THE SECOND UCHATSUI MIIME!!
FLY TO US FROM THE LAST DAYS...
...CLOAKED IN OBSIDIAN WIND!
BLACK-WINGED DRAGON BLACK-FEATHER!!
I DESTROY THE SECOND UCHATSUI MIIME ON THE ULTIMATE PHANTASM GOD'S FIELD!!

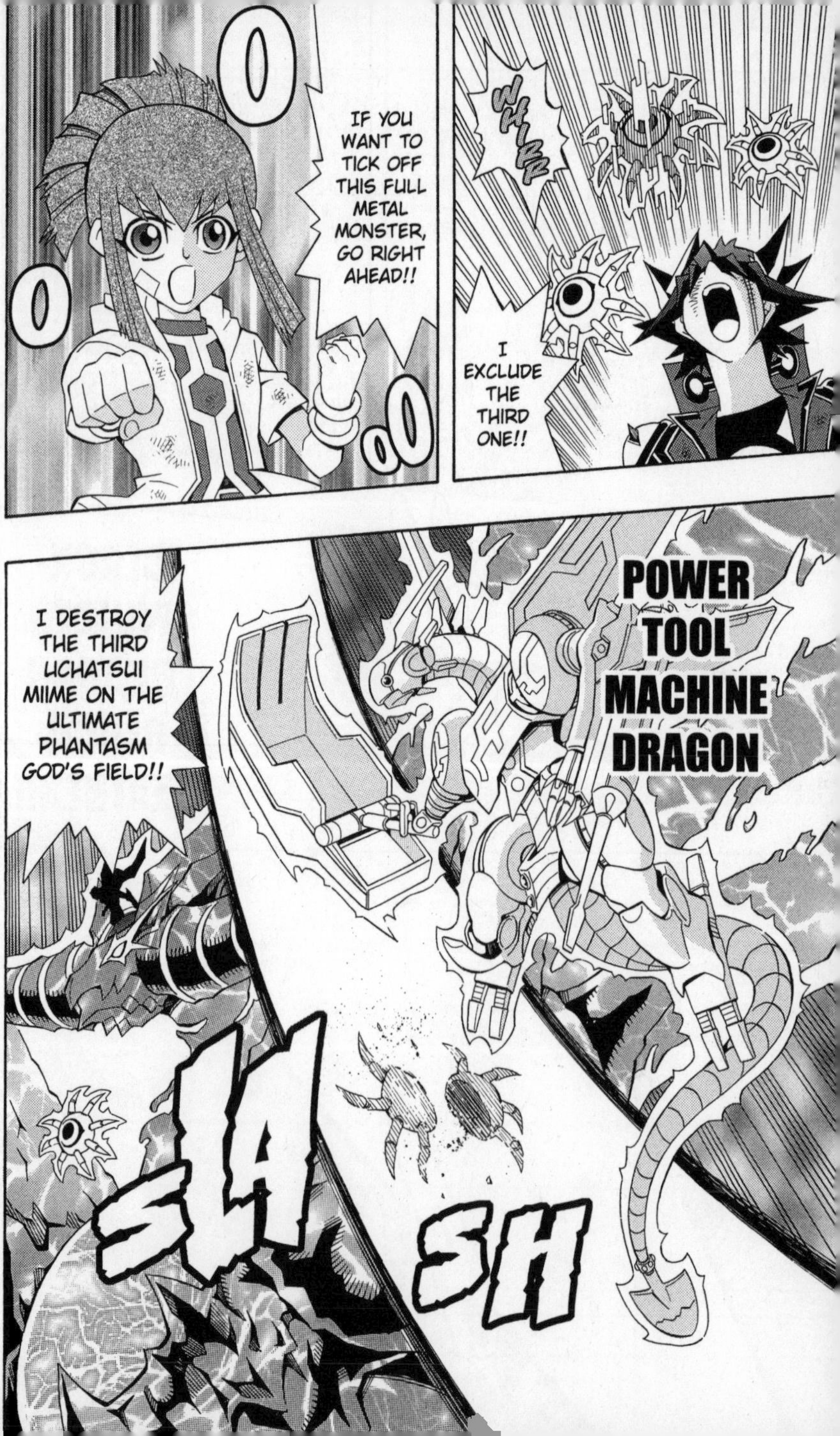
WHIRR
I EXCLUDE THE THIRD ONE!!
IF YOU WANT TO TICK OFF THIS FULL METAL MONSTER, GO RIGHT AHEAD!!
POWER TOOL MACHINE DRAGON
I DESTROY THE THIRD UCHATSUI MIIME ON THE ULTIMATE PHANTASM GOD'S FIELD!!
SLASH

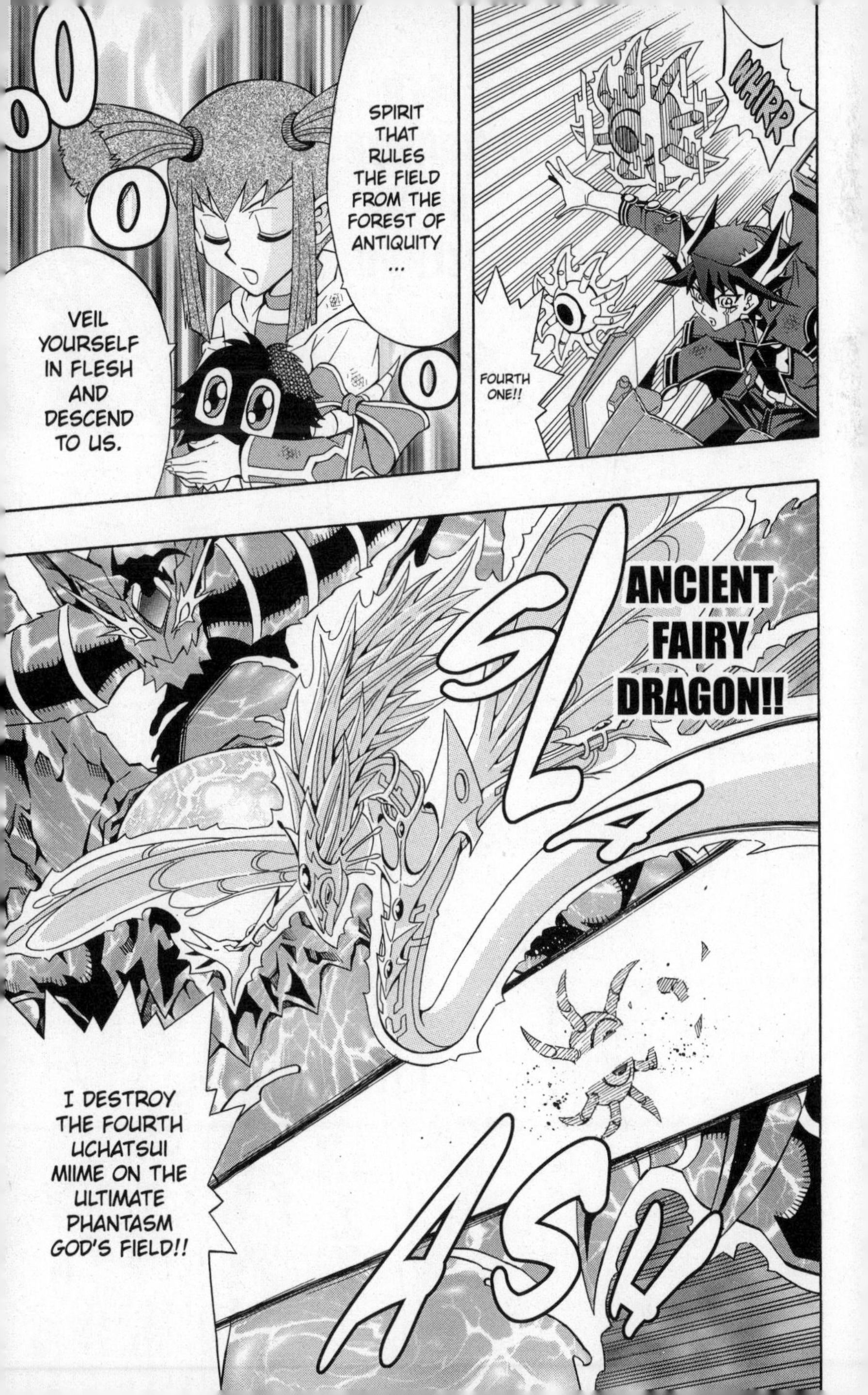
WHIRR
FOURTH ONE!!
OOOOO
SPIRIT THAT RULES THE FIELD FROM THE FOREST OF ANTIQUITY ...
VEIL YOURSELF IN FLESH AND DESCEND TO US.
ANCIENT FAIRY DRAGON!!
SLA
ASH
I DESTROY THE FOURTH UCHATSUI MIIME ON THE ULTIMATE PHANTASM GOD'S FIELD!!

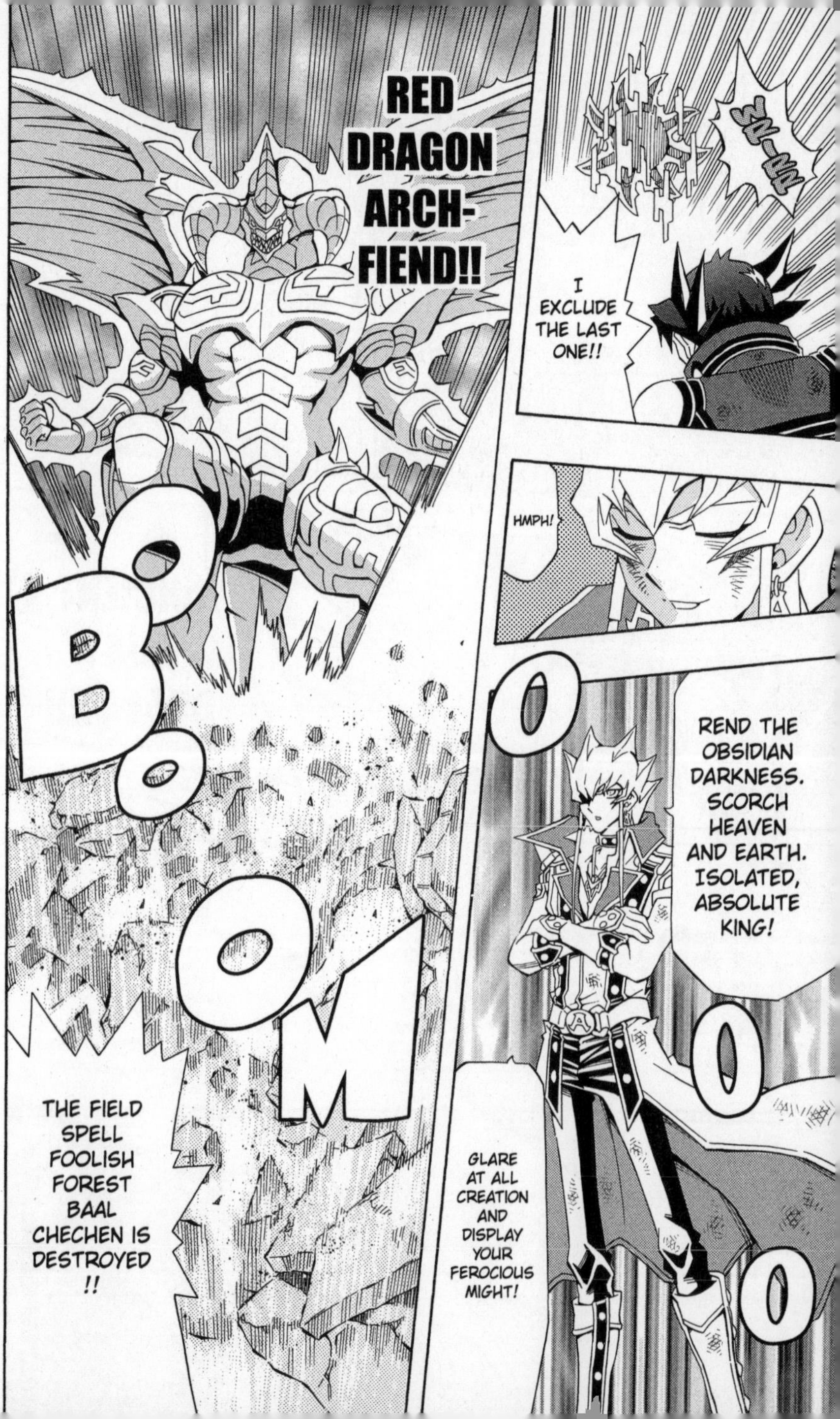
I EXCLUDE THE LAST ONE!!
HMPH!
REND THE OBSIDIAN DARKNESS. SCORCH HEAVEN AND EARTH. ISOLATED, ABSOLUTE KING!
GLARE AT ALL CREATION AND DISPLAY YOUR FEROCIOUS MIGHT!
OOO
RED DRAGON ARCH-FIEND!!
BOOOM
THE FIELD SPELL FOOLISH FOREST BAAL CHECHEN IS DESTROYED!!

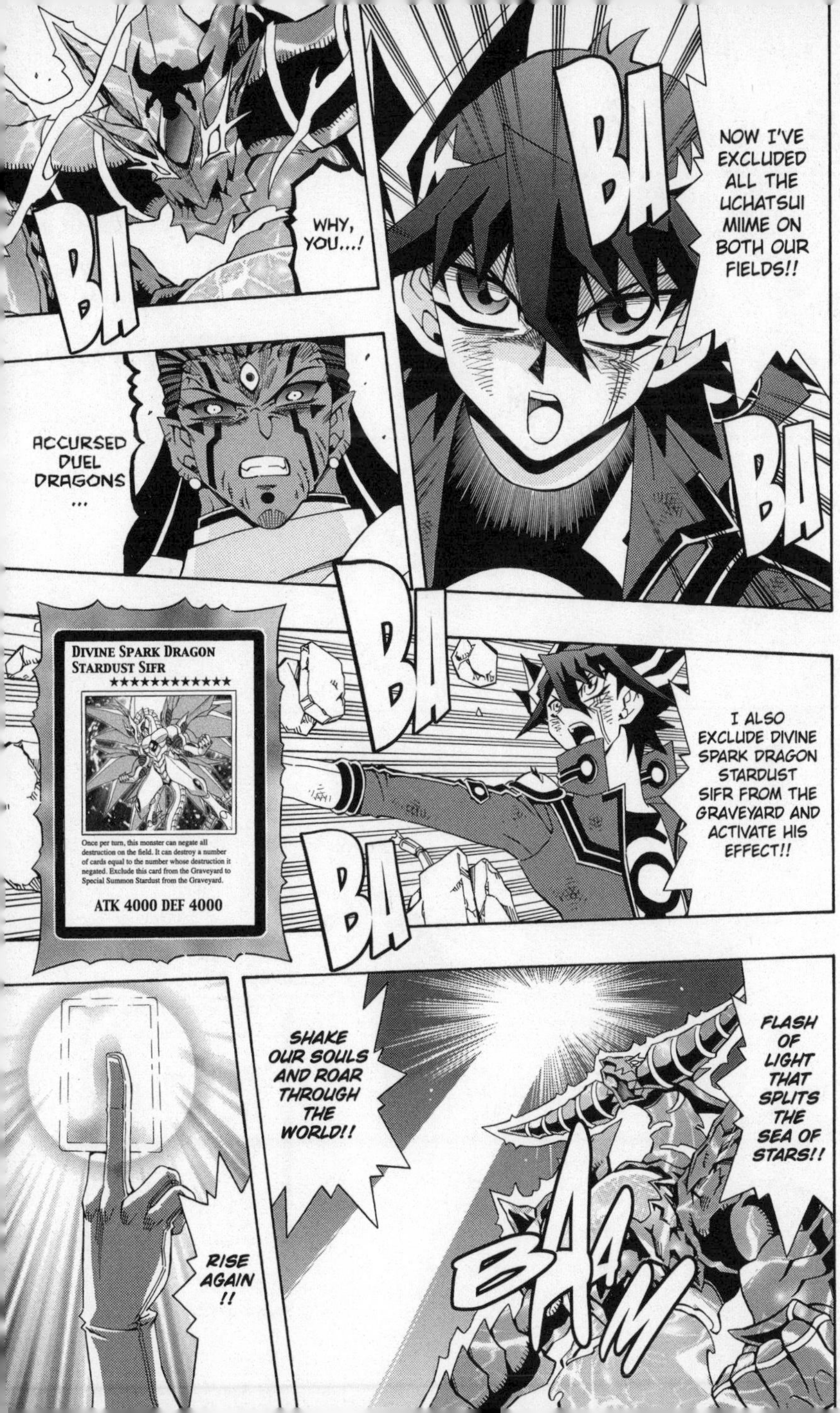

BA
NOW I'VE EXCLUDED ALL THE UCHATSUI MIIME ON BOTH OUR FIELDS!!
BA
BA
WHY, YOU...!
ACCURSED DUEL DRAGONS ...
BA
I ALSO EXCLUDE DIVINE SPARK DRAGON STARDUST SIFR FROM THE GRAVEYARD AND ACTIVATE HIS EFFECT!!
BA
DIVINE SPARK DRAGON STARDUST SIFR
★★★★★★★★★★★★
Once per turn, this monster can negate all destruction on the field. It can destroy a number of cards equal to the number whose destruction it negated. Exclude this card from the Graveyard to Special Summon Stardust from the Graveyard.
ATK 4000 DEF 4000
FLASH OF LIGHT THAT SPLITS THE SEA OF STARS!!
SHAKE OUR SOULS AND ROAR THROUGH THE WORLD!!
BAAAM
RISE AGAIN!!

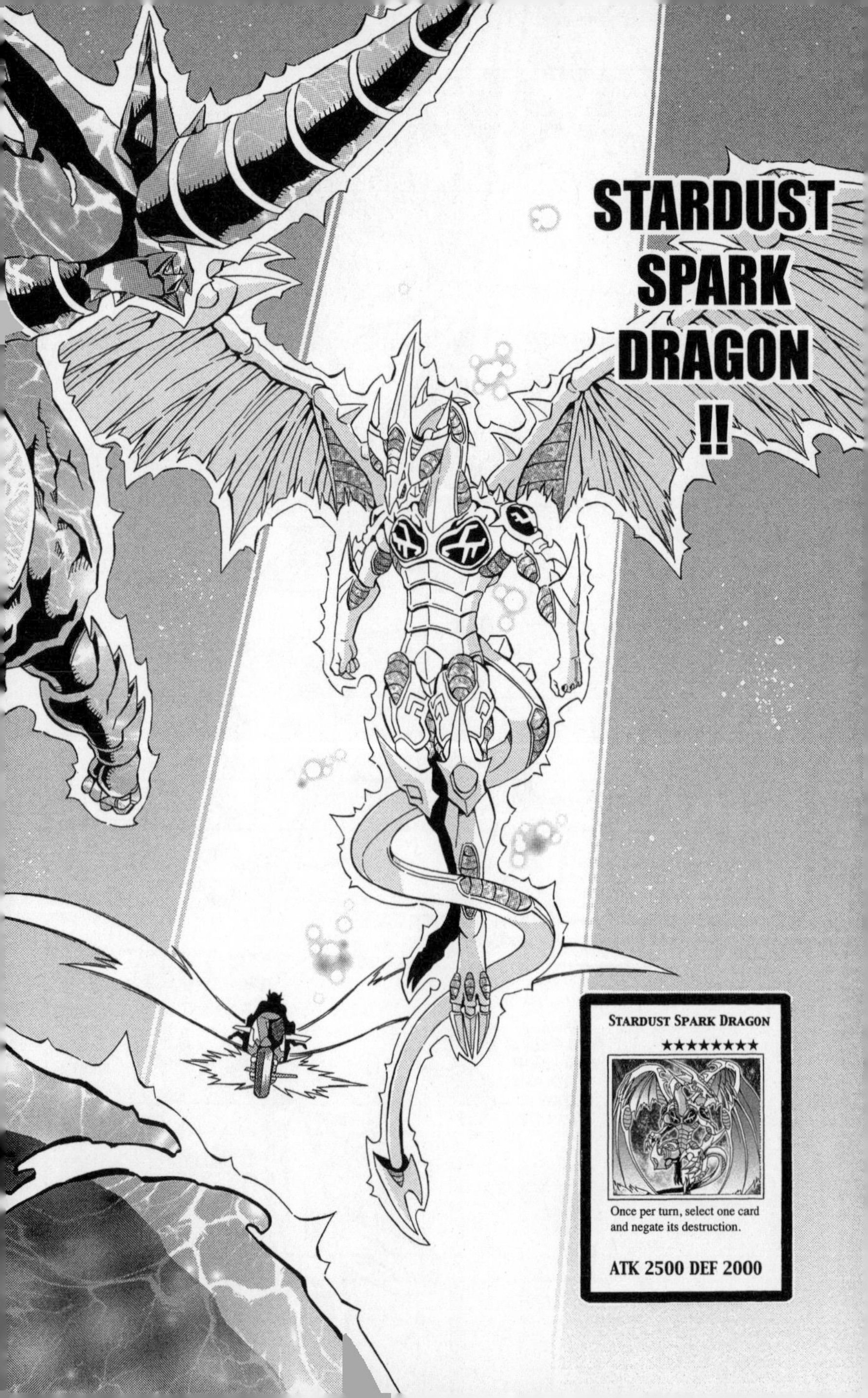
STARDUST SPARK DRAGON !!
STARDUST SPARK DRAGON
★★★★★★★★
Once per turn, select one card and negate its destruction.
ATK 2500 DEF 2000

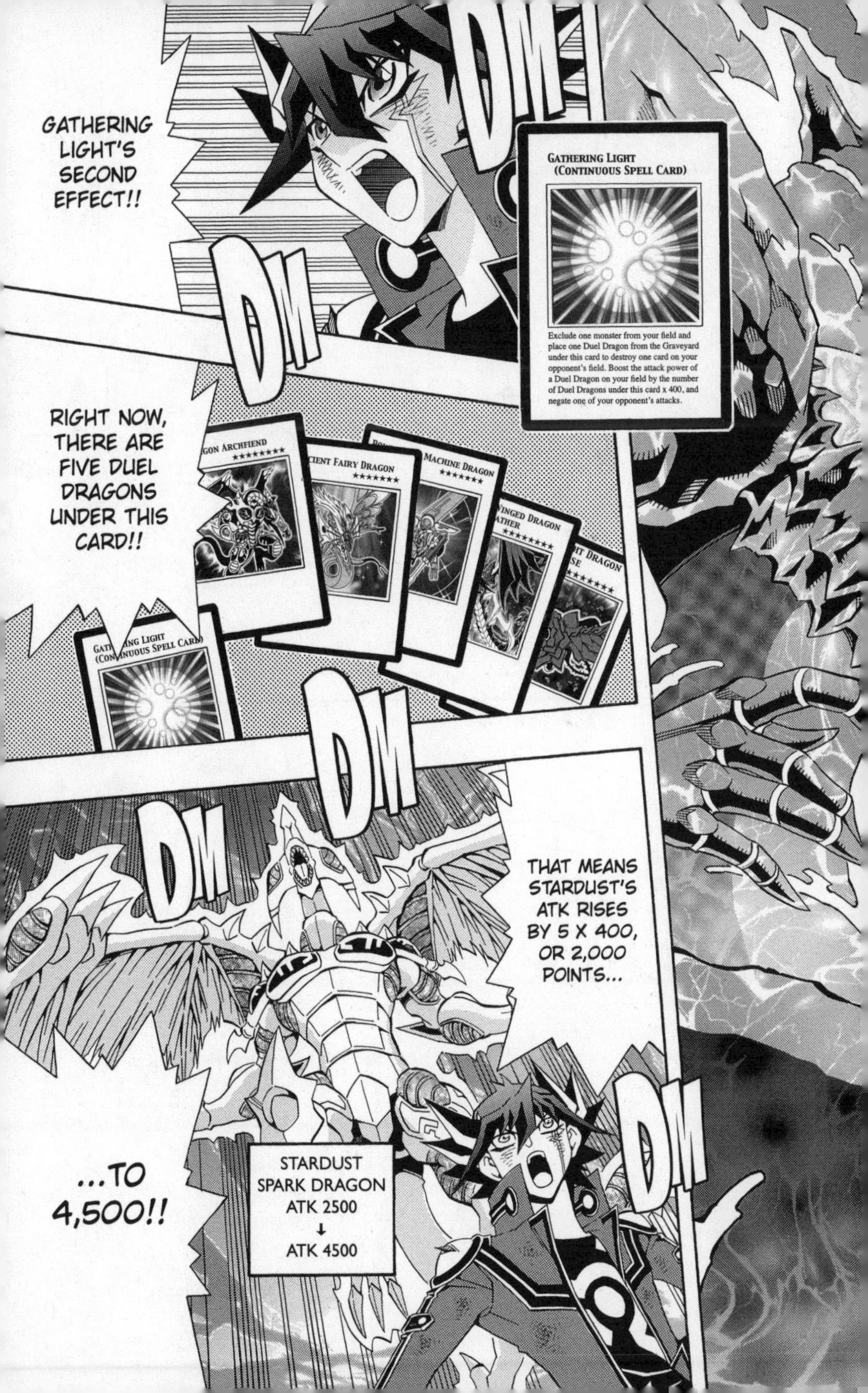

DM
GATHERING LIGHT (CONTINUOUS SPELL CARD)
Exclude one monster from your field and place one Duel Dragon from the Graveyard under this card to destroy one card on your opponent's field. Boost the attack power of a Duel Dragon on your field by the number of Duel Dragons under this card x 400, and negate one of your opponent's attacks.
GATHERING LIGHT'S SECOND EFFECT!!
DM
RIGHT NOW, THERE ARE FIVE DUEL DRAGONS UNDER THIS CARD!!
DM
DM
THAT MEANS STARDUST'S ATK RISES BY 5 X 400, OR 2,000 POINTS...
STARDUST SPARK DRAGON ATK 2500 ↓ ATK 4500
...TO 4,500!!
DM

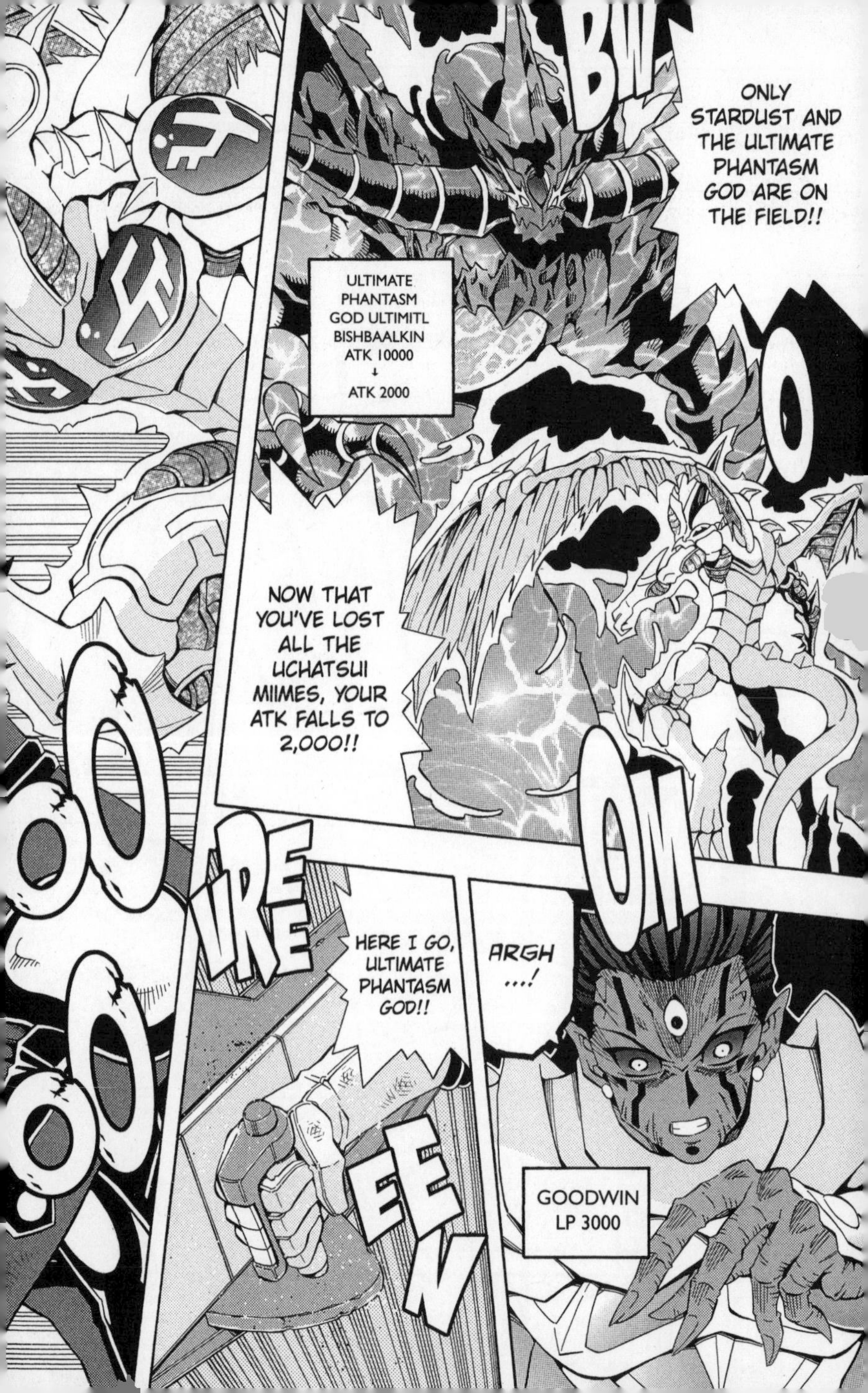
ONLY STARDUST AND THE ULTIMATE PHANTASM GOD ARE ON THE FIELD!!
ULTIMATE PHANTASM GOD ULTIMITL BISHBAALKIN ATK 10000 ↓ ATK 2000
NOW THAT YOU'VE LOST ALL THE UCHATSUI MIIMES, YOUR ATK FALLS TO 2,000!!
ARGH ...!
GOODWIN LP 3000
HERE I GO, ULTIMATE PHANTASM GOD!!

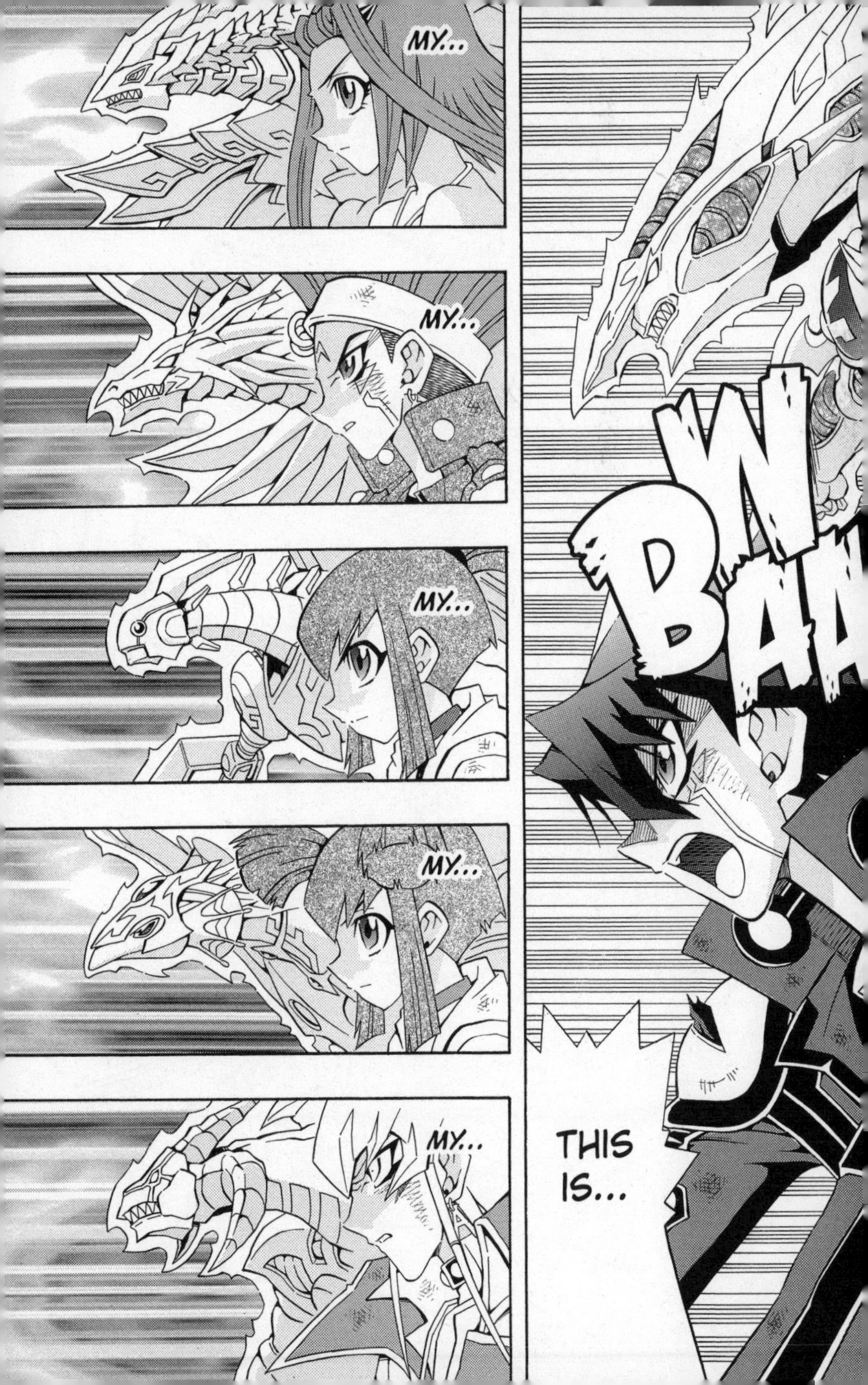
THIS IS...
MY...
MY...
MY...
MY...
MY...

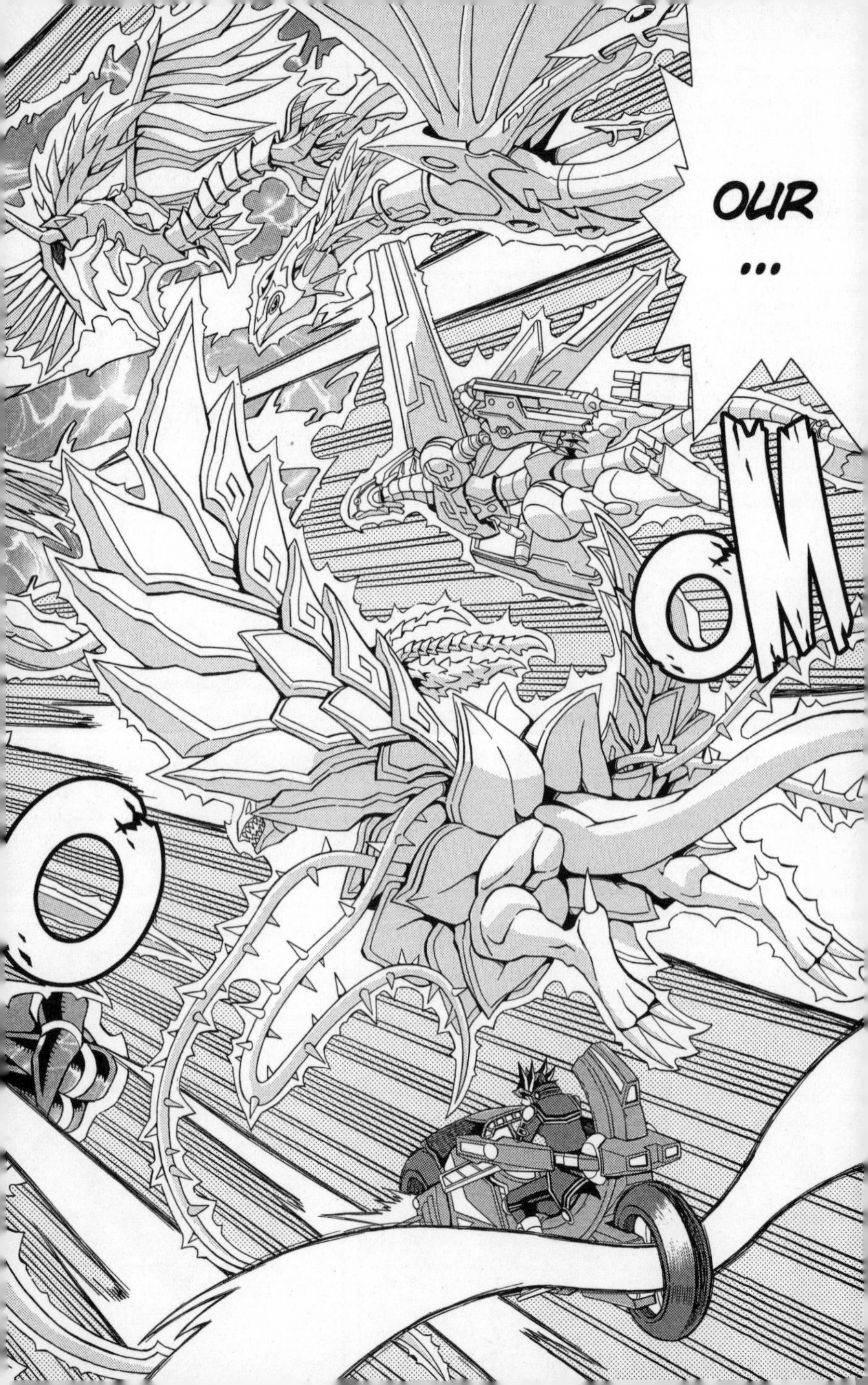
OUR ...
MWO
O

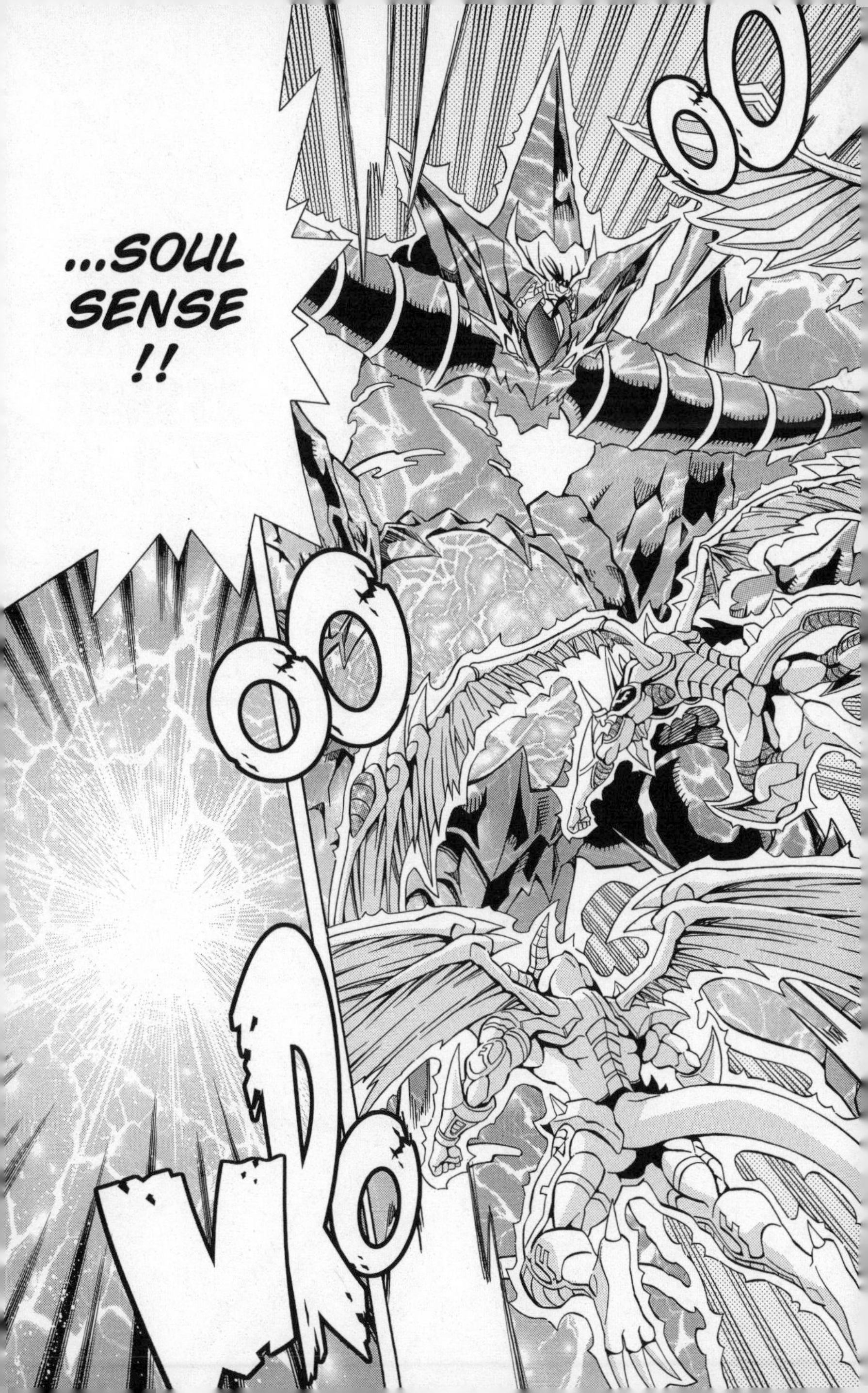
...SOUL SENSE !!

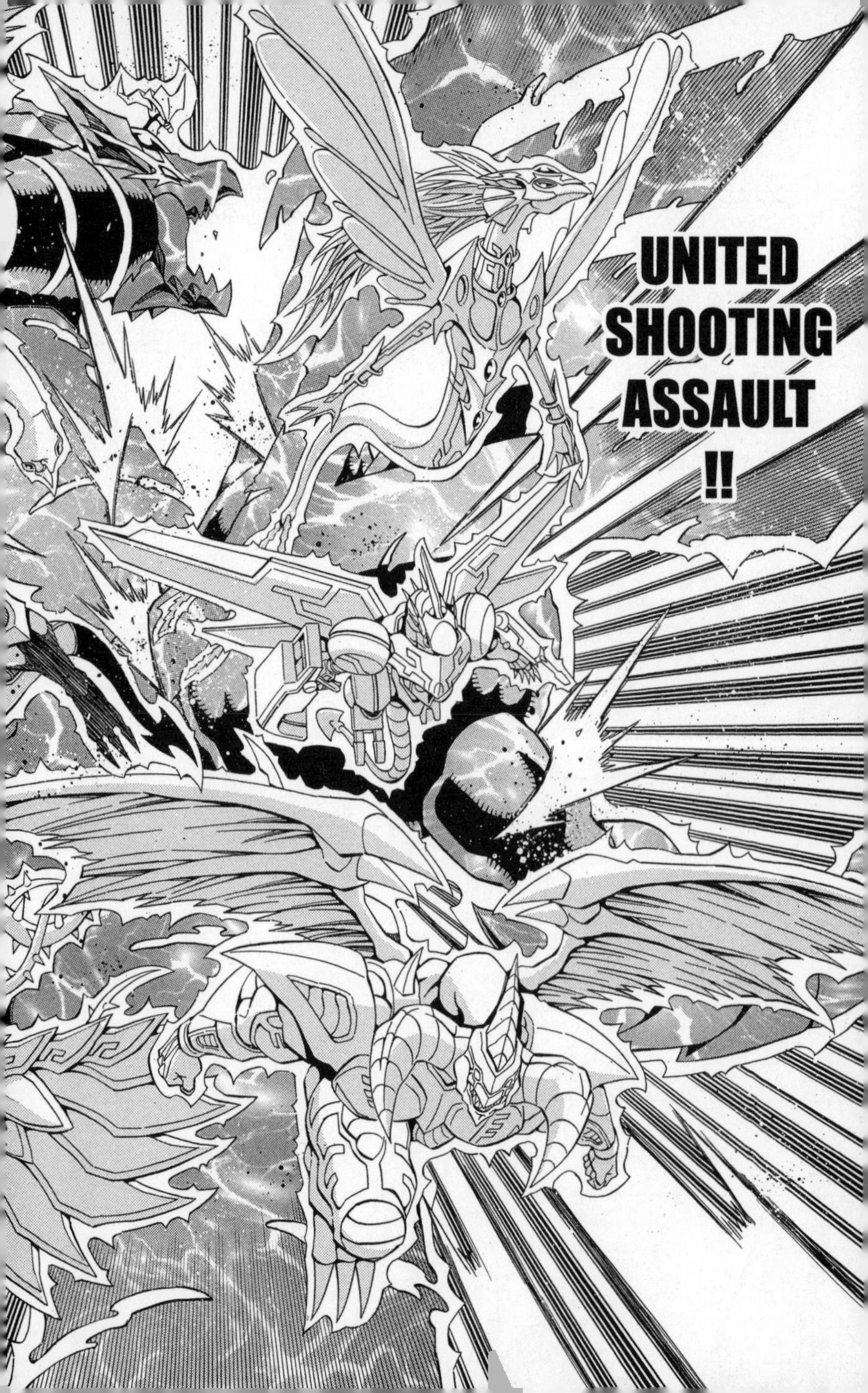
UNITED SHOOTING ASSAULT !!

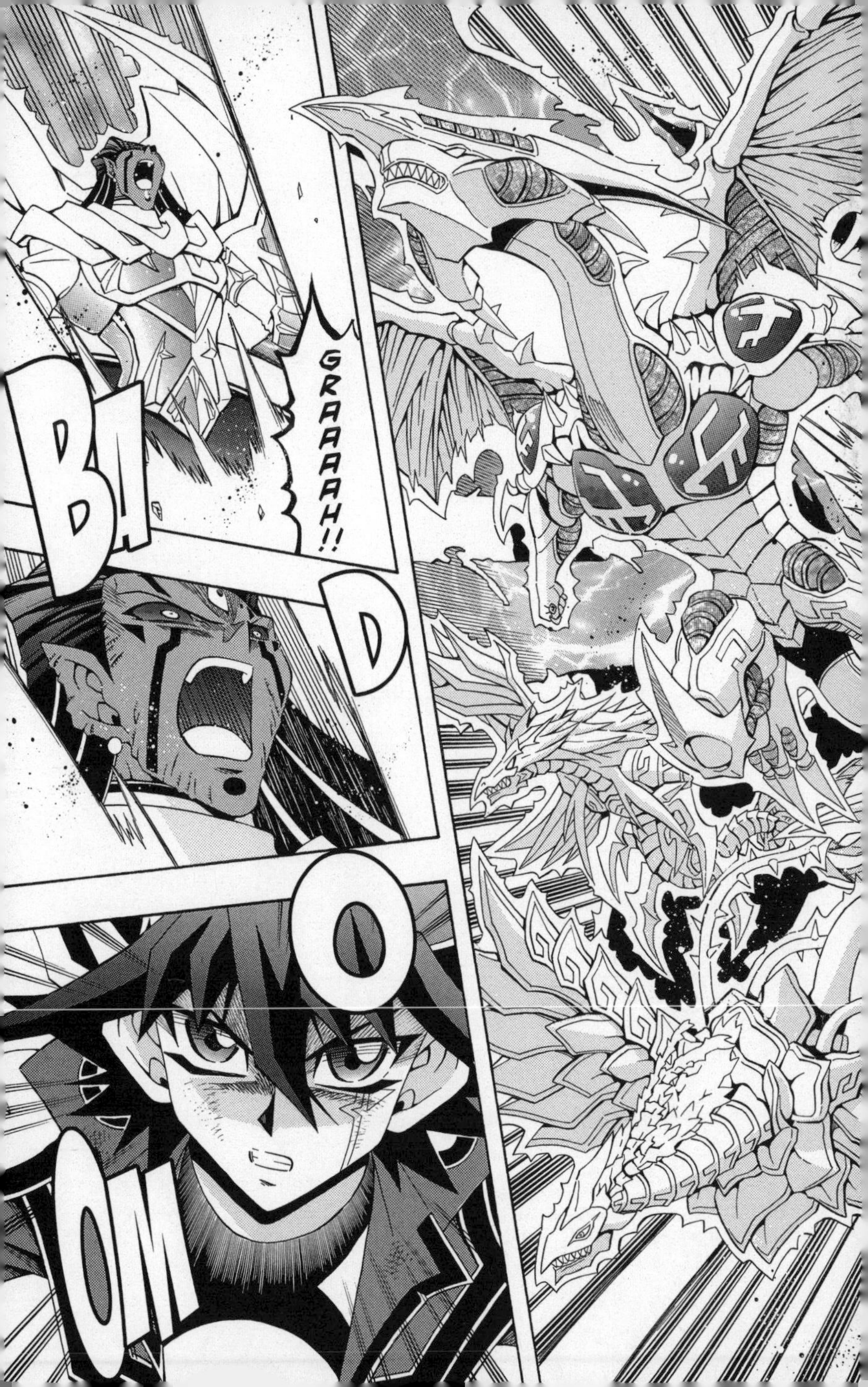
GRAAAAAH!!
BADOOOM

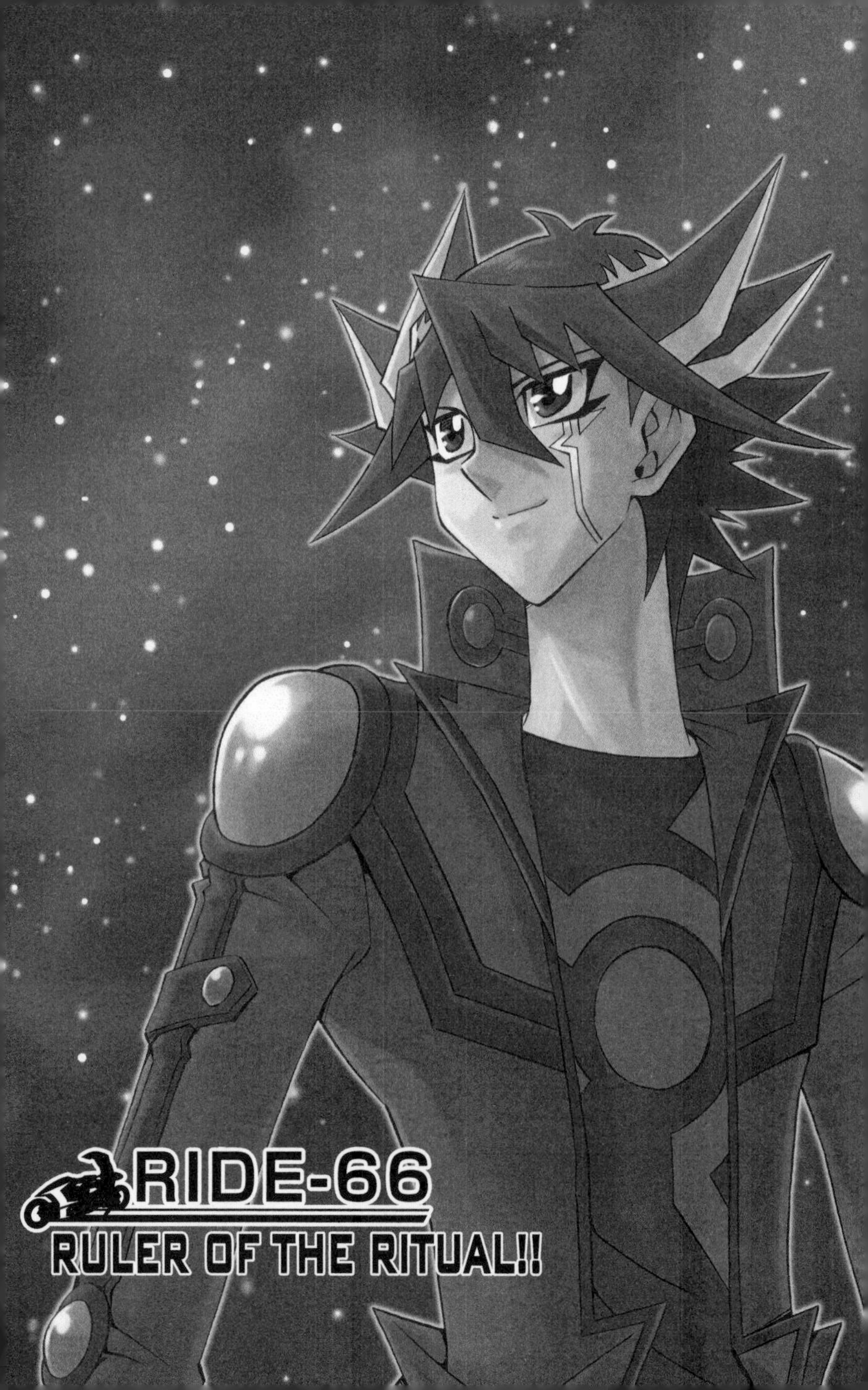
RIDE-66
RULER OF THE RITUAL!!

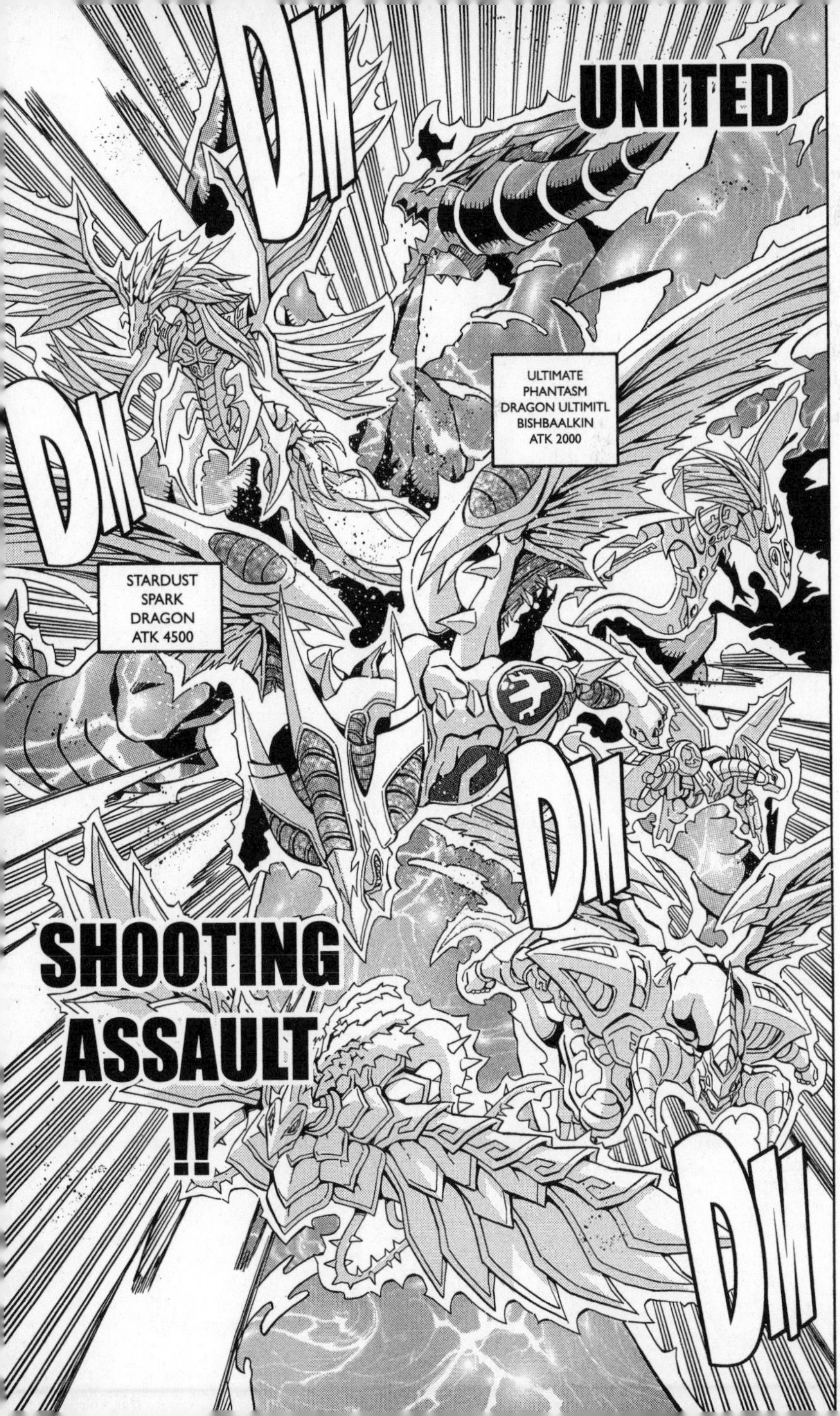
UNITED
DM
ULTIMATE PHANTASM DRAGON ULTIMITL BISHBAALKIN ATK 2000
DM
STARDUST SPARK DRAGON ATK 4500
DM
DM
SHOOTING ASSAULT!!

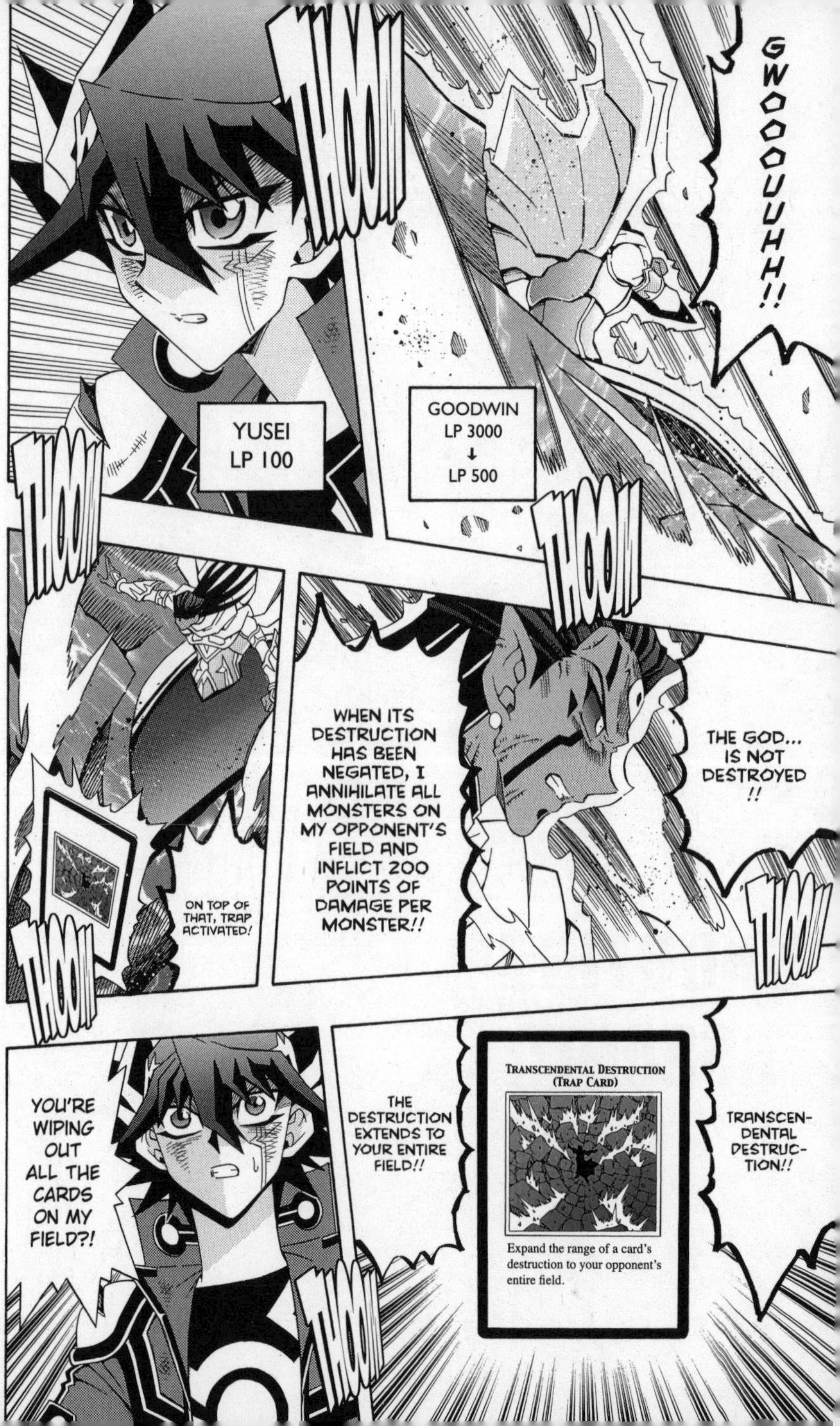
GWOOOOUUHH!!
GOODWIN
LP 3000
↓
LP 500
THOOM
THOOM
YUSEI
LP 100
THOOM
THOOM
THE GOD... IS NOT DESTROYED!!
WHEN ITS DESTRUCTION HAS BEEN NEGATED, I ANNIHILATE ALL MONSTERS ON MY OPPONENT'S FIELD AND INFLICT 200 POINTS OF DAMAGE PER MONSTER!!
THOOM
ON TOP OF THAT, TRAP ACTIVATED!
THOOM
TRANSCEN-DENTAL DESTRUC-TION!!
TRANSCENDENTAL DESTRUCTION
(TRAP CARD)
Expand the range of a card's destruction to your opponent's entire field.
THE DESTRUCTION EXTENDS TO YOUR ENTIRE FIELD!!
THOOM
YOU'RE WIPING OUT ALL THE CARDS ON MY FIELD?!

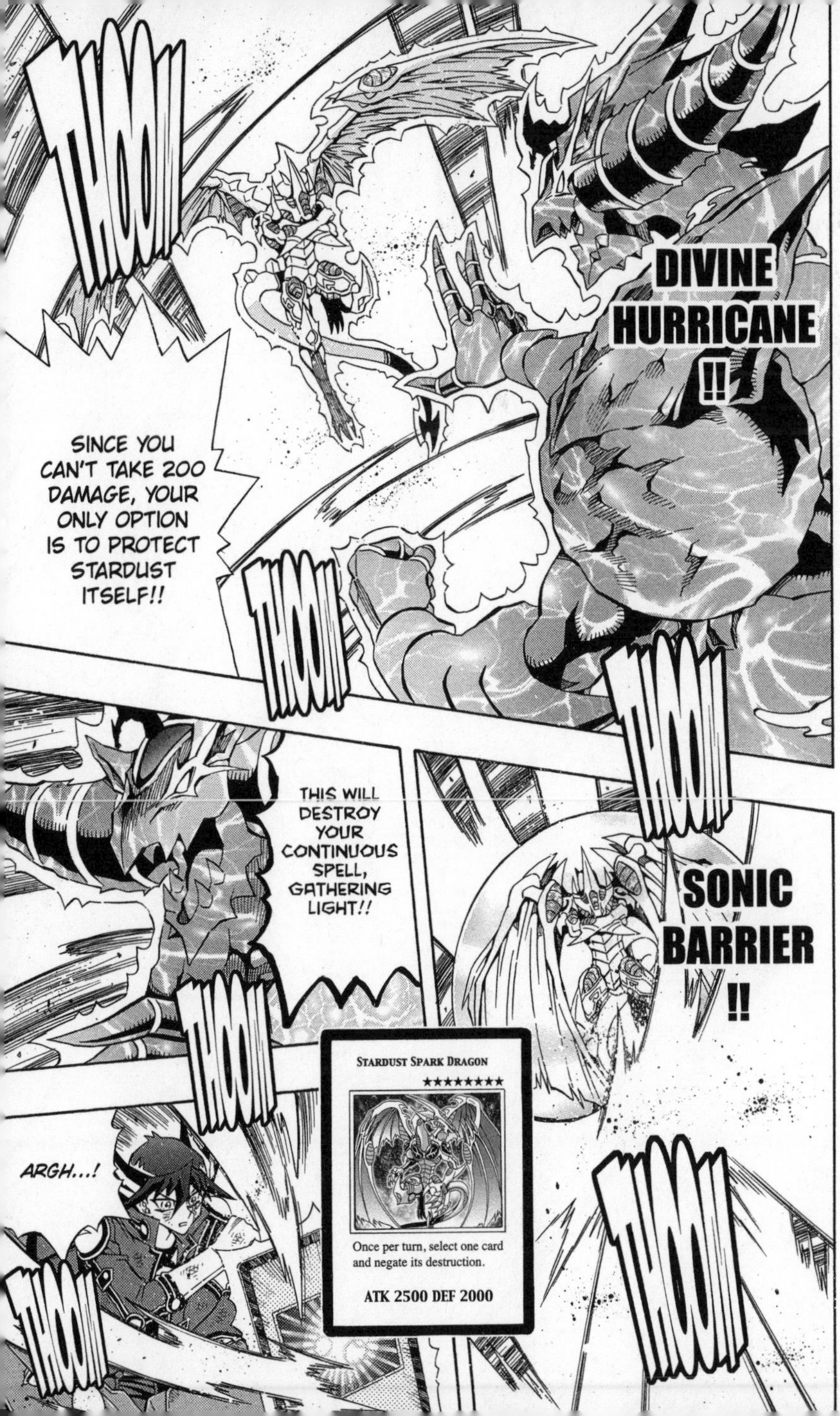
THOOM
DIVINE HURRICANE !!
SINCE YOU CAN'T TAKE 200 DAMAGE, YOUR ONLY OPTION IS TO PROTECT STARDUST ITSELF!!
THOOM
THOOM
SONIC BARRIER !!
THIS WILL DESTROY YOUR CONTINUOUS SPELL, GATHERING LIGHT!!
THOOM
THOOM
STARDUST SPARK DRAGON
Once per turn, select one card and negate its destruction.
ATK 2500 DEF 2000
ARGH...!
THOOM

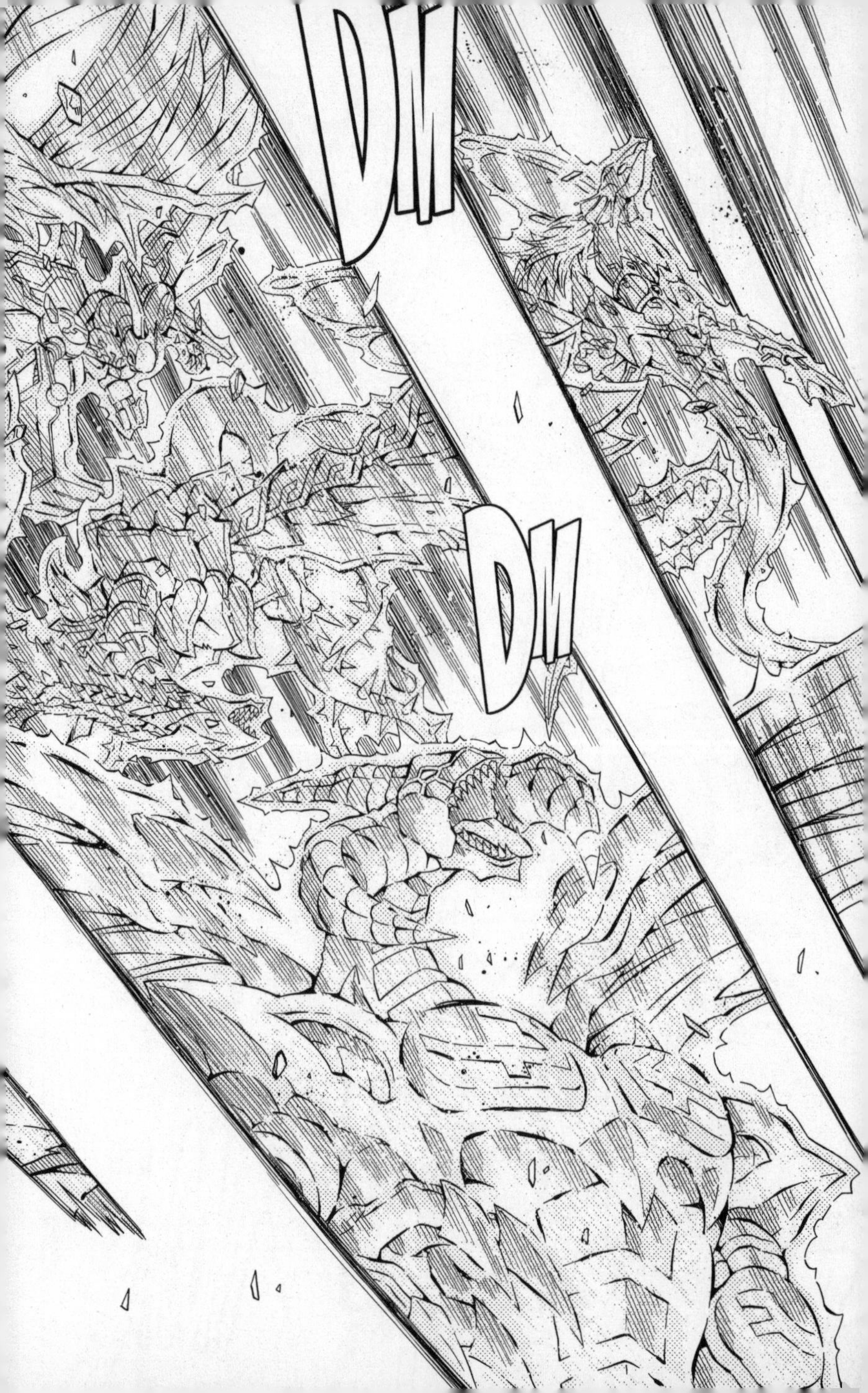
DM
DM

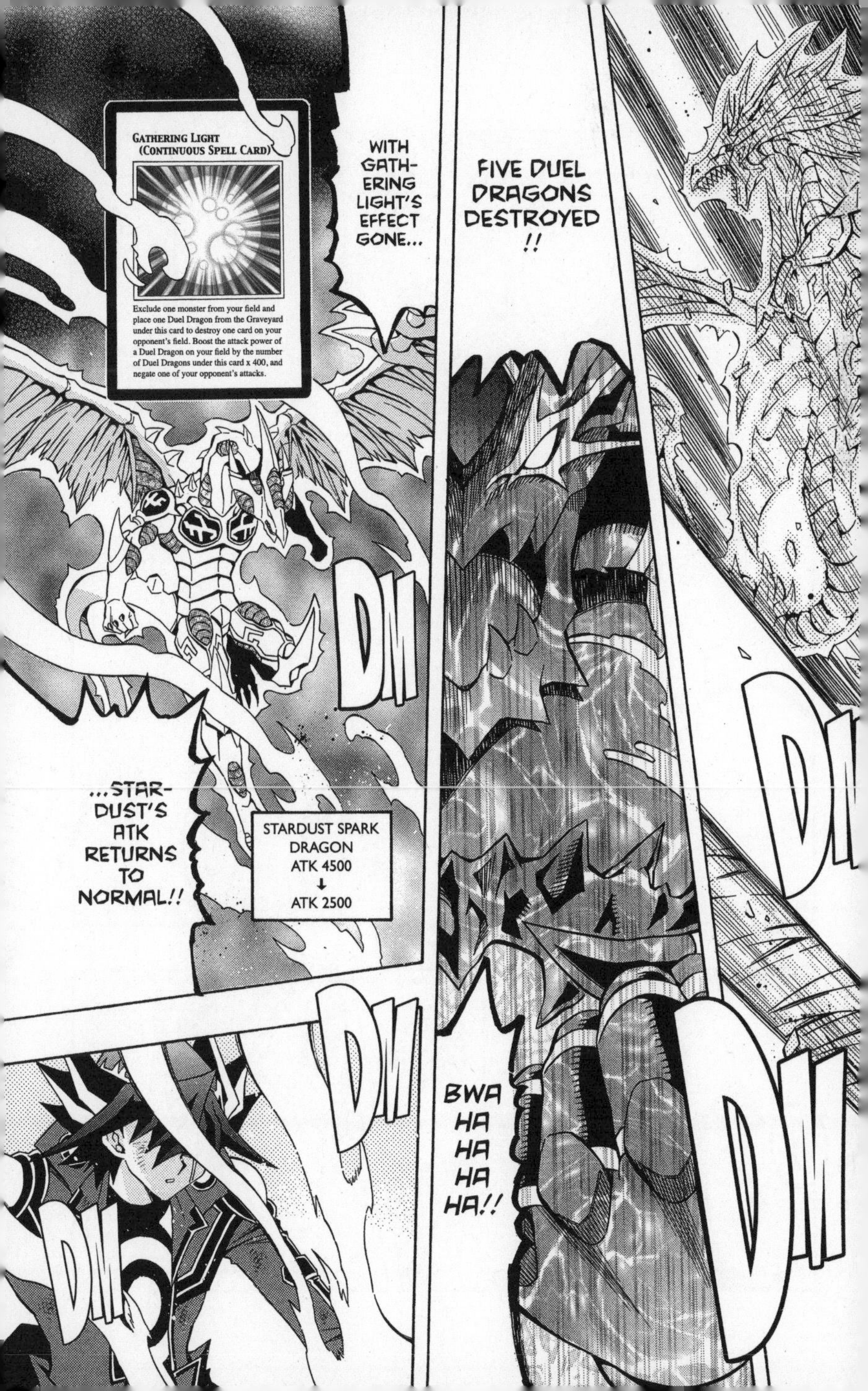

DM
DM
FIVE DUEL DRAGONS DESTROYED!!
BWA HA HA HA HA!!
WITH GATHERING LIGHT'S EFFECT GONE...
GATHERING LIGHT (CONTINUOUS SPELL CARD)
Exclude one monster from your field and place one Duel Dragon from the Graveyard under this card to destroy one card on your opponent's field. Boost the attack power of a Duel Dragon on your field by the number of Duel Dragons under this card x 400, and negate one of your opponent's attacks.
DM
...STARDUST'S ATK RETURNS TO NORMAL!!
STARDUST SPARK DRAGON ATK 4500 ↓ ATK 2500
DM
DM

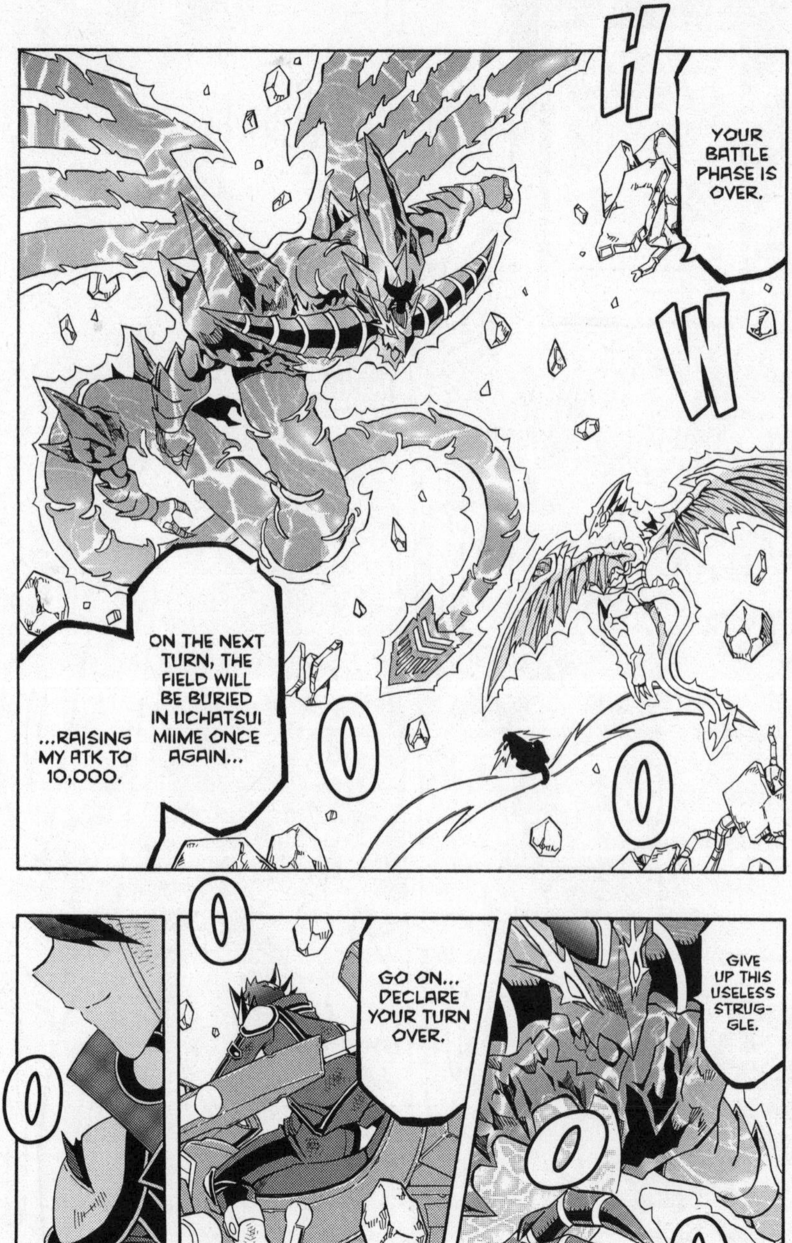
HWOOOOOO
YOUR BATTLE PHASE IS OVER.
ON THE NEXT TURN, THE FIELD WILL BE BURIED IN UCHATSUI MIIME ONCE AGAIN...
...RAISING MY ATK TO 10,000.
GIVE UP THIS USELESS STRUG-GLE.
GO ON... DECLARE YOUR TURN OVER.

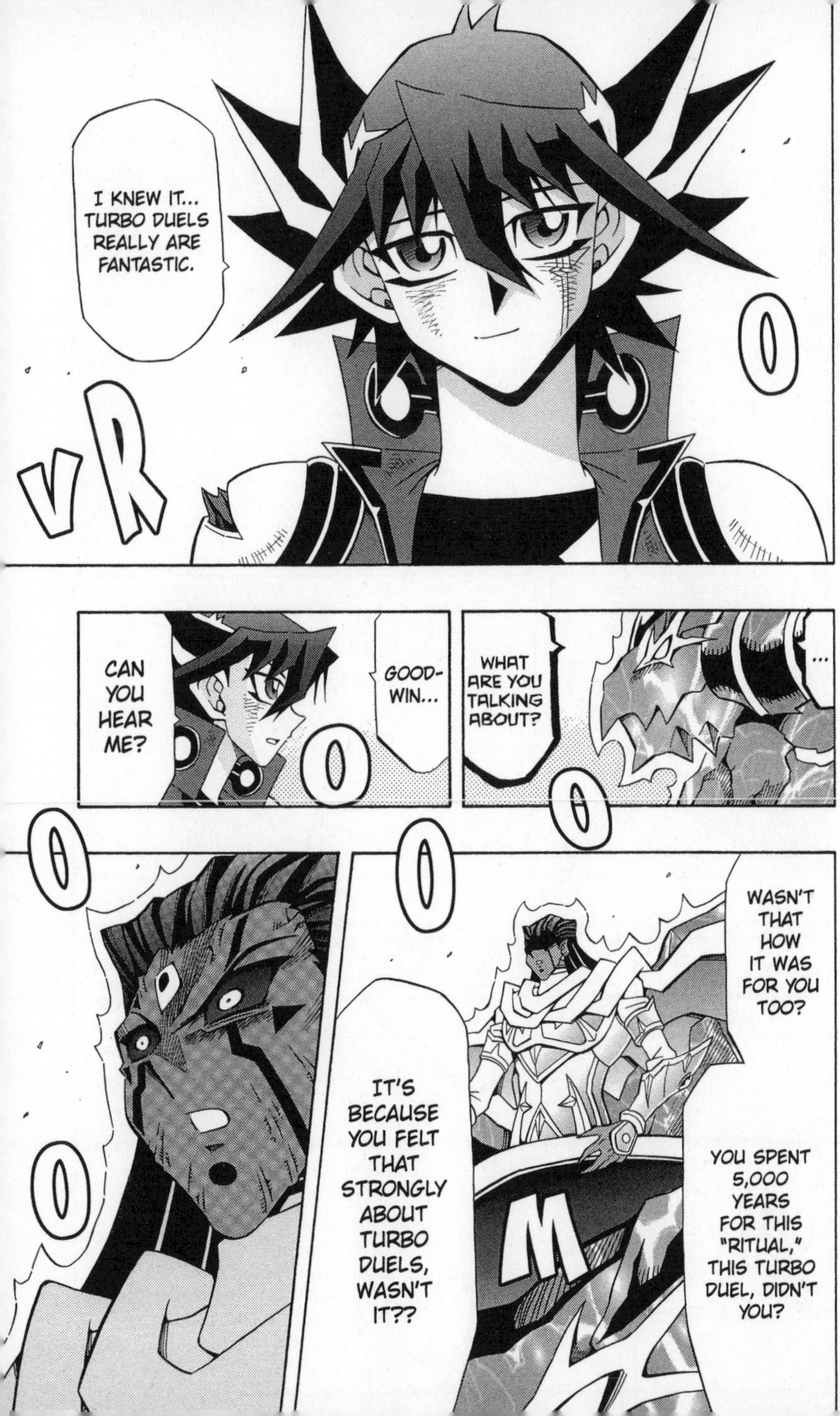
I KNEW IT... TURBO DUELS REALLY ARE FANTASTIC.
...
WHAT ARE YOU TALKING ABOUT?
GOOD-WIN...
CAN YOU HEAR ME?
WASN'T THAT HOW IT WAS FOR YOU TOO?
YOU SPENT 5,000 YEARS FOR THIS "RITUAL," THIS TURBO DUEL, DIDN'T YOU?
IT'S BECAUSE YOU FELT THAT STRONGLY ABOUT TURBO DUELS, WASN'T IT??

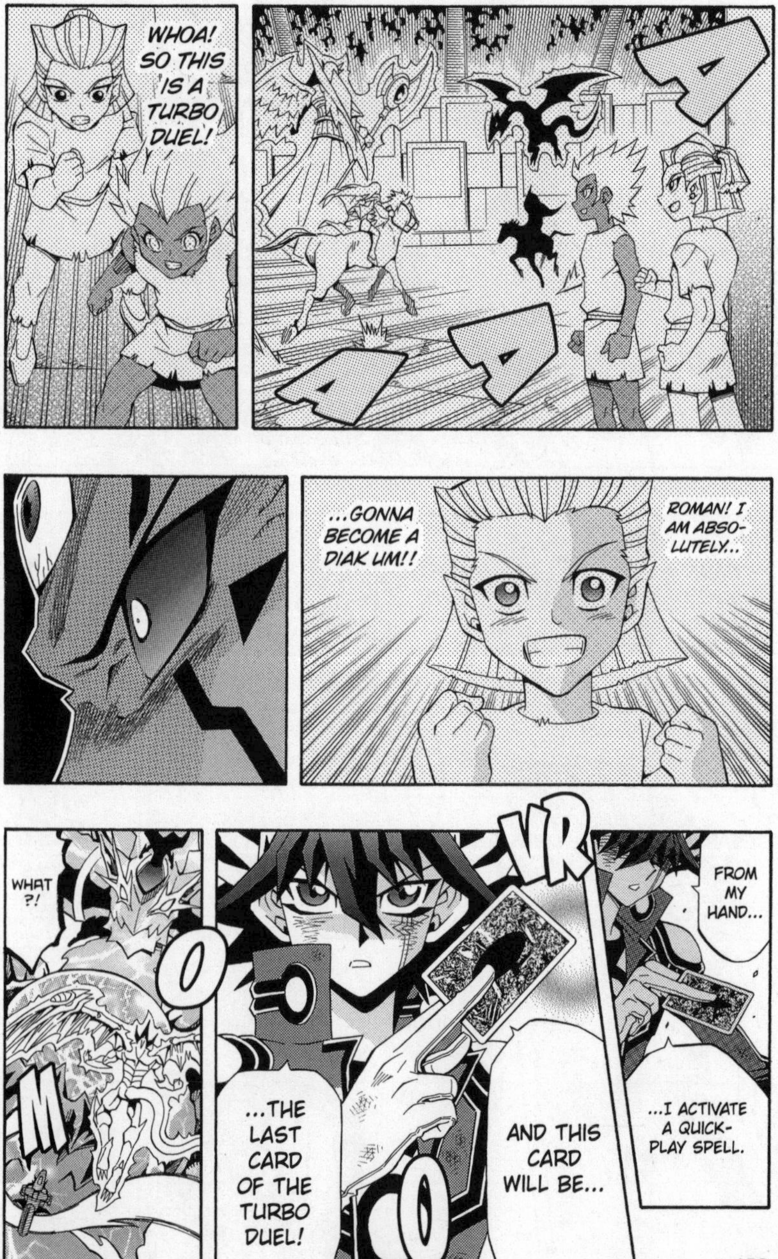
WHOA! SO THIS IS A TURBO DUEL!
ROMAN! I AM ABSOLUTELY...
...GONNA BECOME A DIAK UM!!
FROM MY HAND...
...I ACTIVATE A QUICK-PLAY SPELL.
VROOM
AND THIS CARD WILL BE...
...THE LAST CARD OF THE TURBO DUEL!
WHAT?!

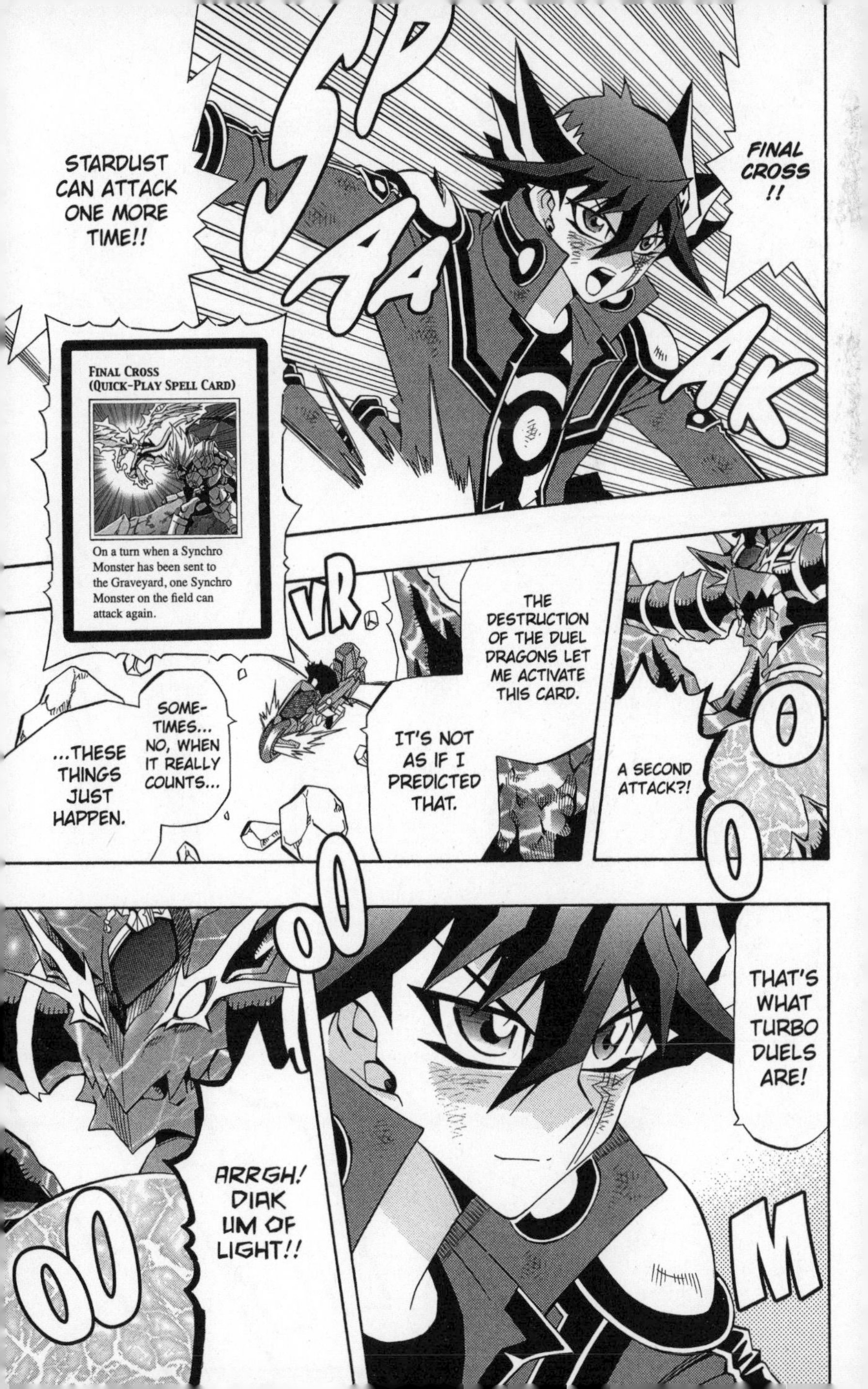
SPAAAK
FINAL CROSS!!
STARDUST CAN ATTACK ONE MORE TIME!!
FINAL CROSS (QUICK-PLAY SPELL CARD)
On a turn when a Synchro Monster has been sent to the Graveyard, one Synchro Monster on the field can attack again.
A SECOND ATTACK?!
THE DESTRUCTION OF THE DUEL DRAGONS LET ME ACTIVATE THIS CARD.
IT'S NOT AS IF I PREDICTED THAT.
VR
SOME-TIMES... NO, WHEN IT REALLY COUNTS...
...THESE THINGS JUST HAPPEN.
OOOOOOOM
THAT'S WHAT TURBO DUELS ARE!
ARRGH! DIAK UM OF LIGHT!!

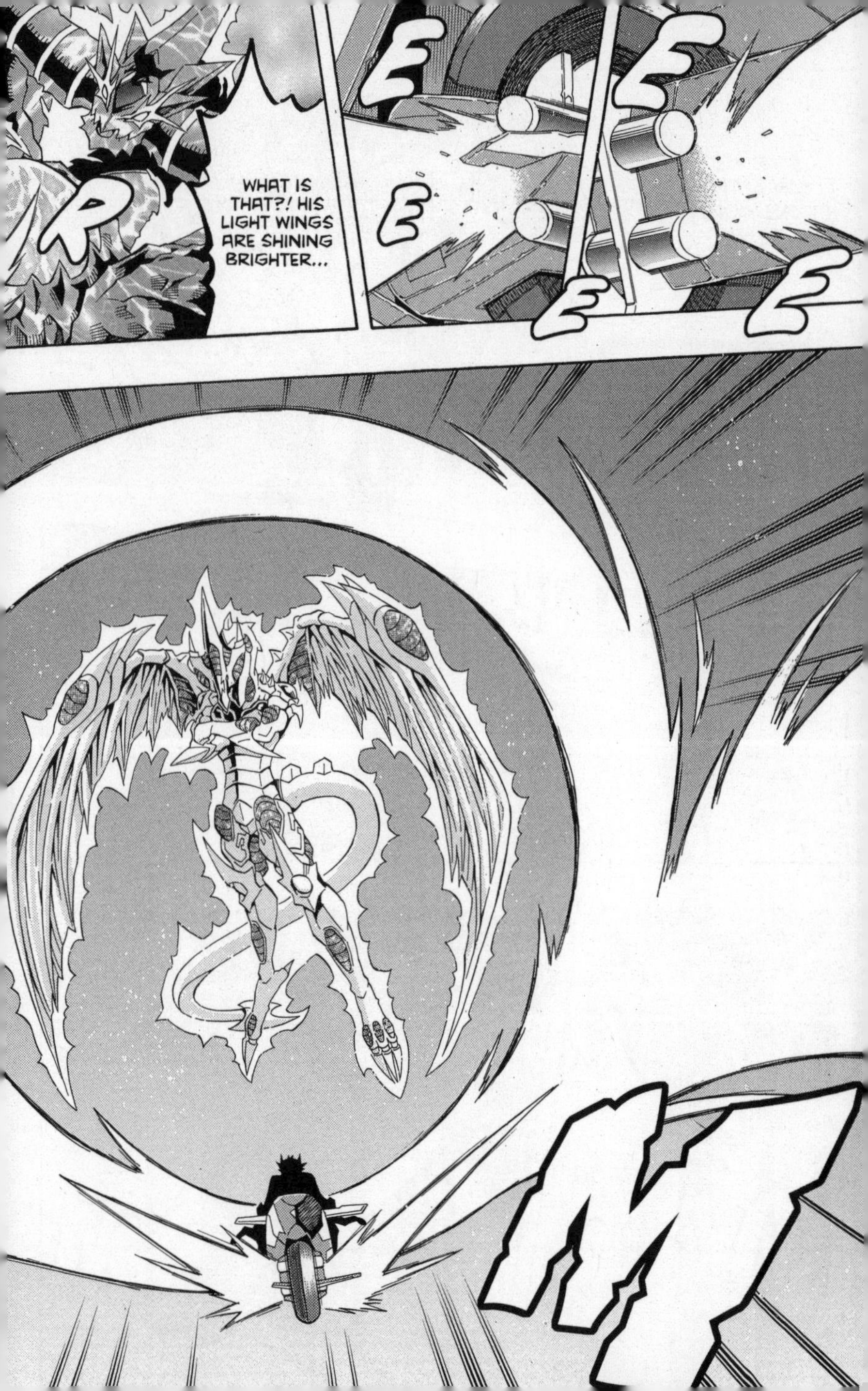
EEEEE
WHAT IS THAT?! HIS LIGHT WINGS ARE SHINING BRIGHTER...
P
M

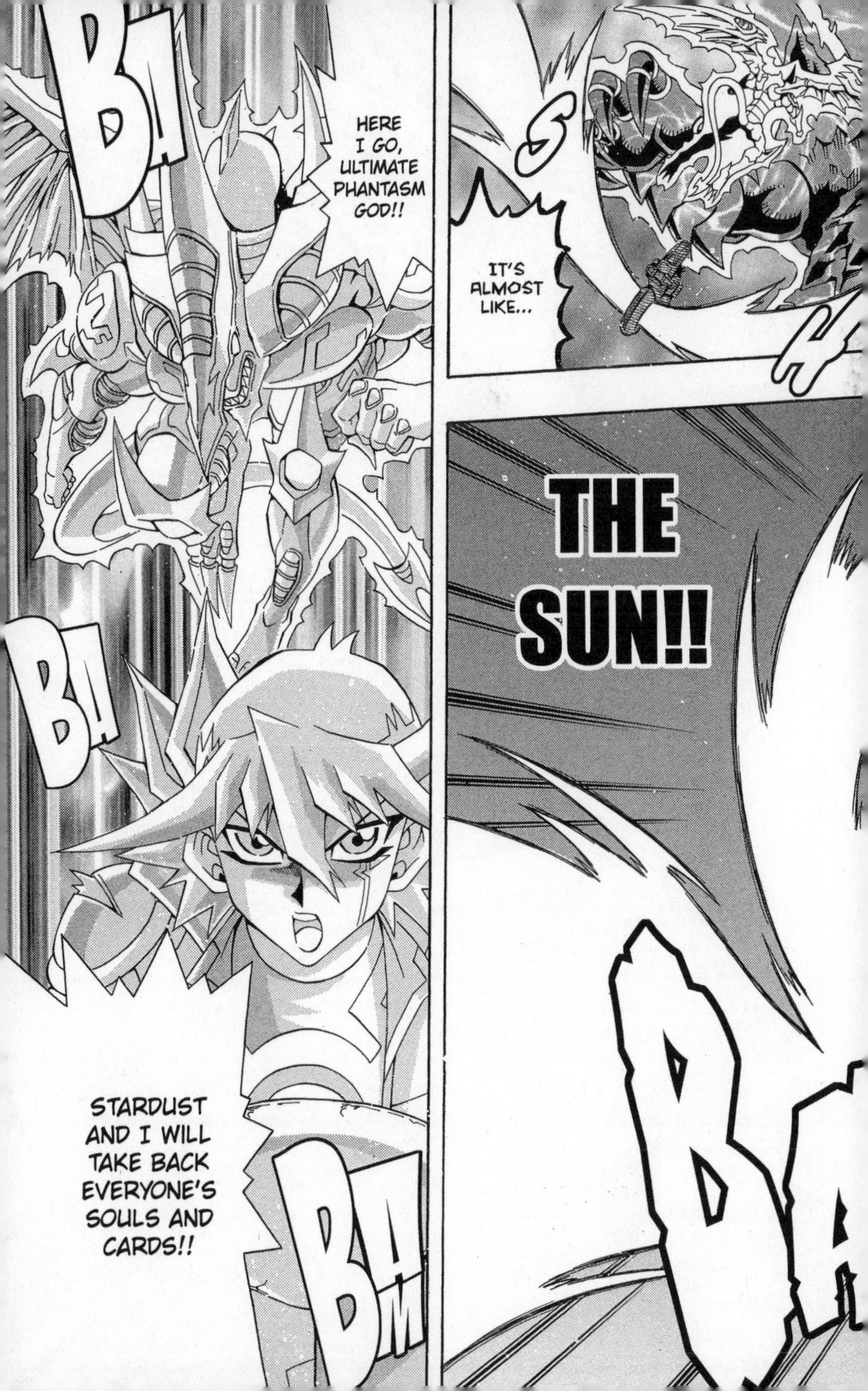
IT'S ALMOST LIKE...
THE SUN!!
BA
BA
HERE I GO, ULTIMATE PHANTASM GOD!!
BA
STARDUST AND I WILL TAKE BACK EVERYONE'S SOULS AND CARDS!!
BAM

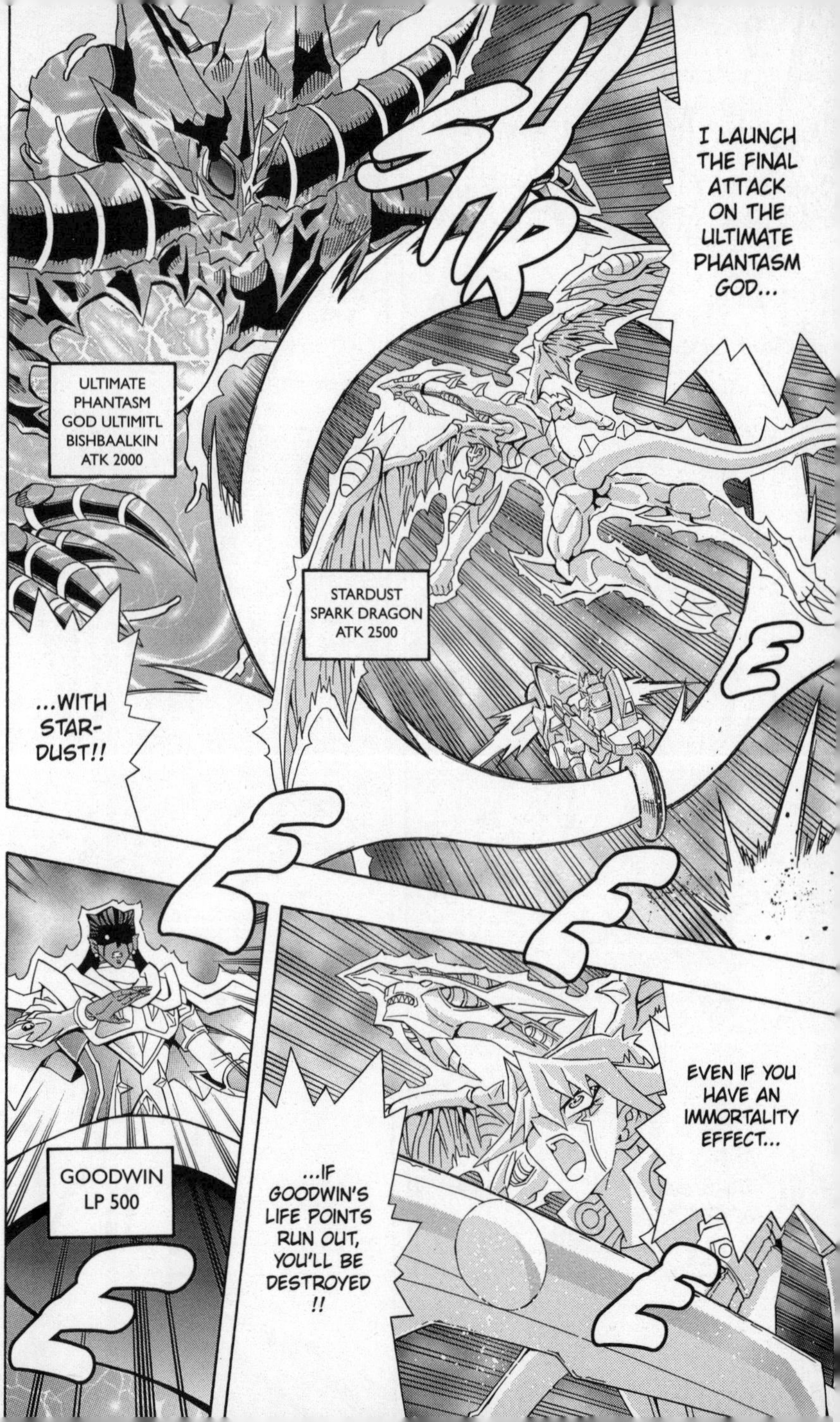
I LAUNCH THE FINAL ATTACK ON THE ULTIMATE PHANTASM GOD...
SHREEEEE
ULTIMATE PHANTASM GOD ULTIMITL BISHBAALKIN ATK 2000
STARDUST SPARK DRAGON ATK 2500
...WITH STAR-DUST!!
EVEN IF YOU HAVE AN IMMORTALITY EFFECT...
...IF GOODWIN'S LIFE POINTS RUN OUT, YOU'LL BE DESTROYED!!
GOODWIN LP 500

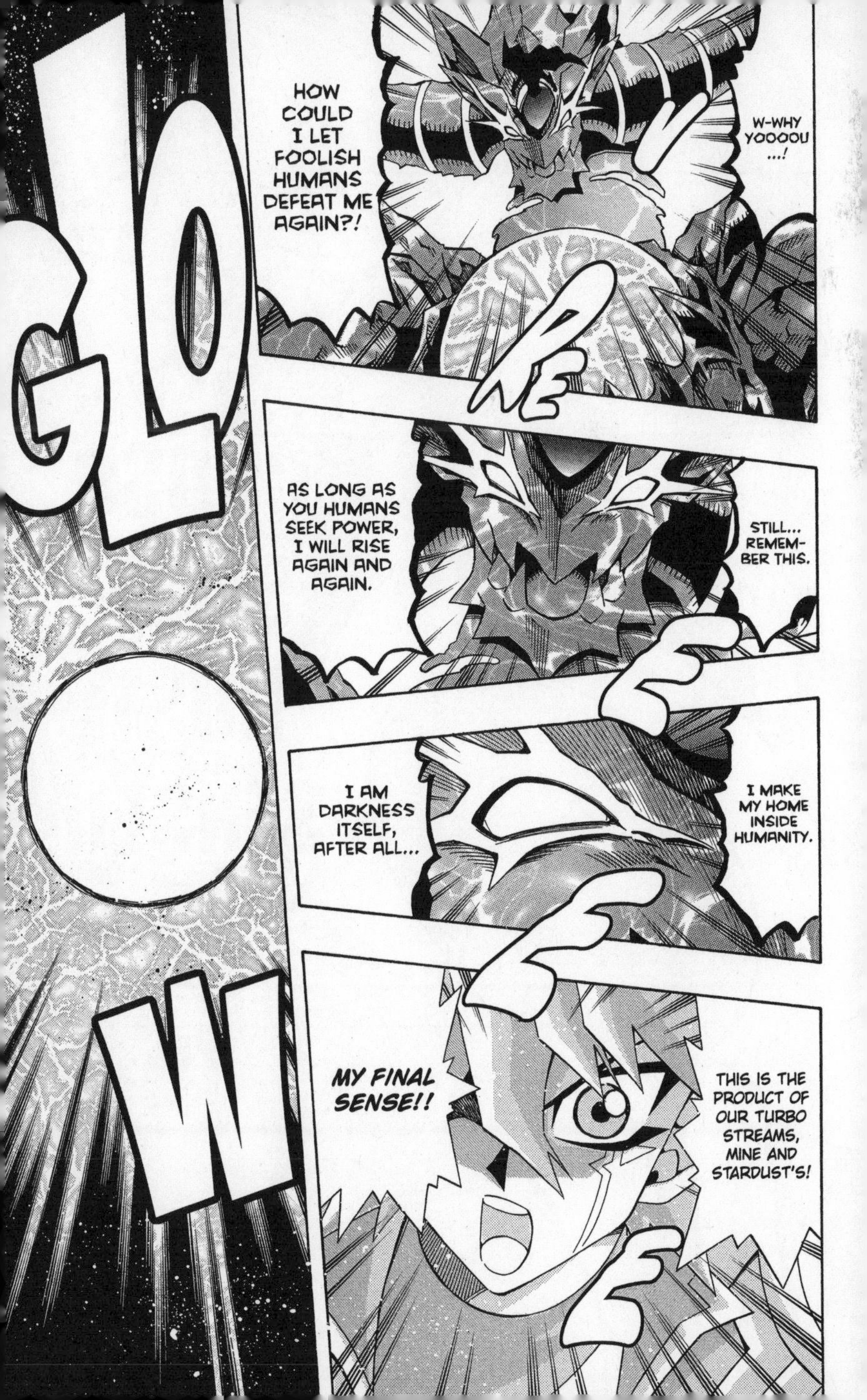
W-WHY YOOOOU ...!
HOW COULD I LET FOOLISH HUMANS DEFEAT ME AGAIN?!
STILL... REMEMBER THIS.
AS LONG AS YOU HUMANS SEEK POWER, I WILL RISE AGAIN AND AGAIN.
I MAKE MY HOME INSIDE HUMANITY.
I AM DARKNESS ITSELF, AFTER ALL...
THIS IS THE PRODUCT OF OUR TURBO STREAMS, MINE AND STARDUST'S!
MY FINAL SENSE!!
GLOW

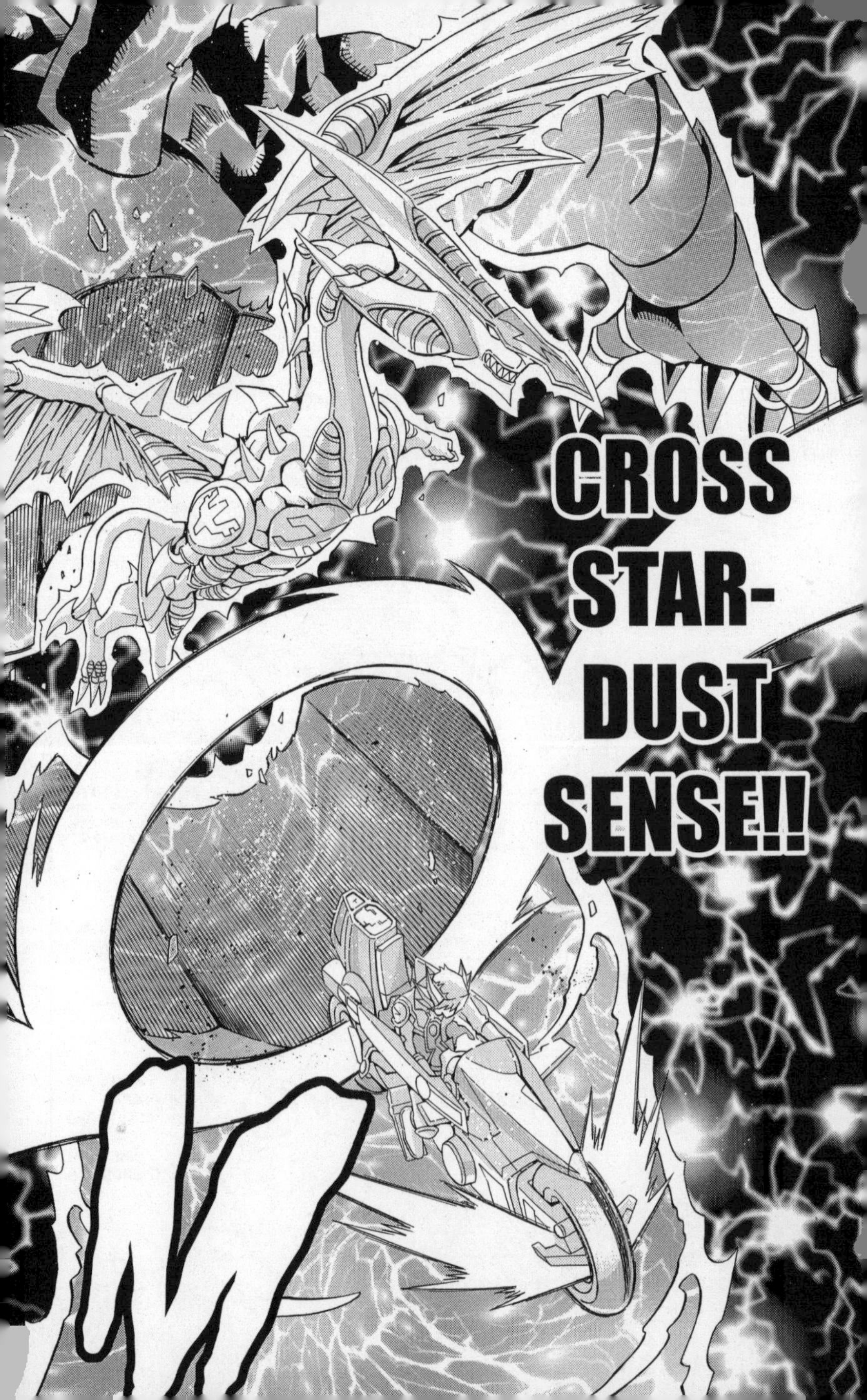
CROSS STAR-DUST SENSE!!

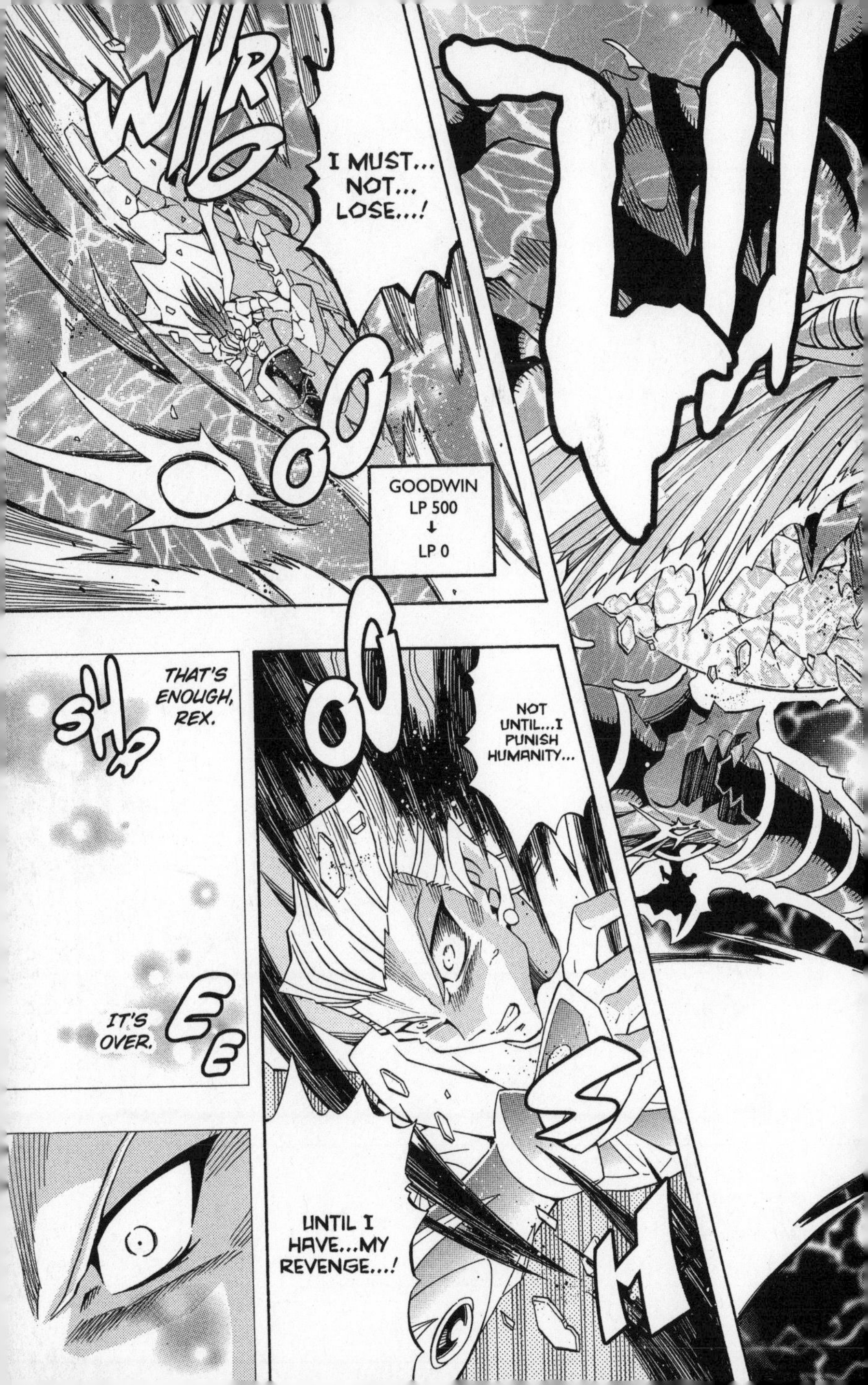
I MUST... NOT... LOSE...!
GOODWIN
LP 500
↓
LP 0
NOT UNTIL...I PUNISH HUMANITY...
UNTIL I HAVE...MY REVENGE...!
THAT'S ENOUGH, REX.
IT'S OVER.

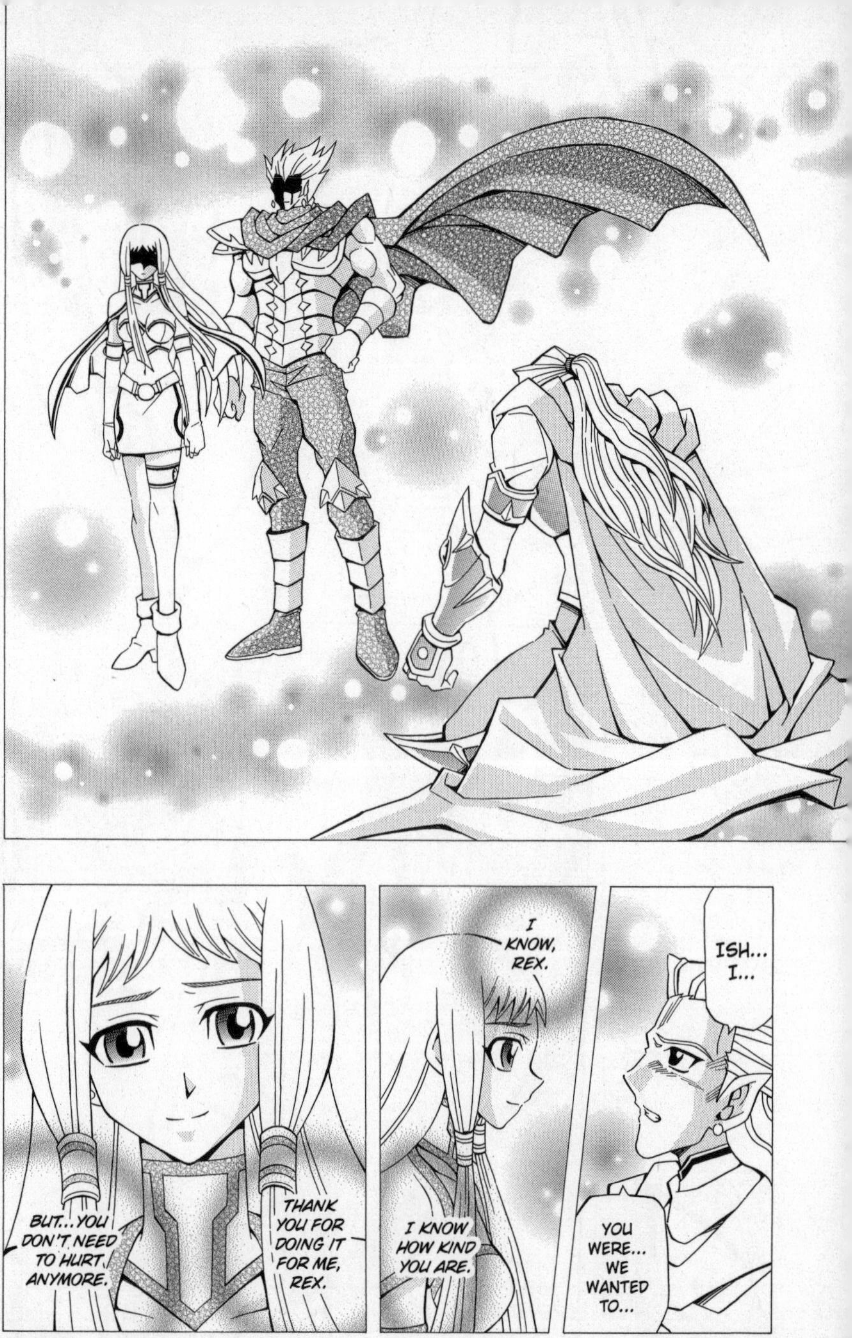
ISH... I...
YOU WERE... WE WANTED TO...
I KNOW, REX.
I KNOW HOW KIND YOU ARE.
THANK YOU FOR DOING IT FOR ME, REX.
BUT... YOU DON'T NEED TO HURT ANYMORE.

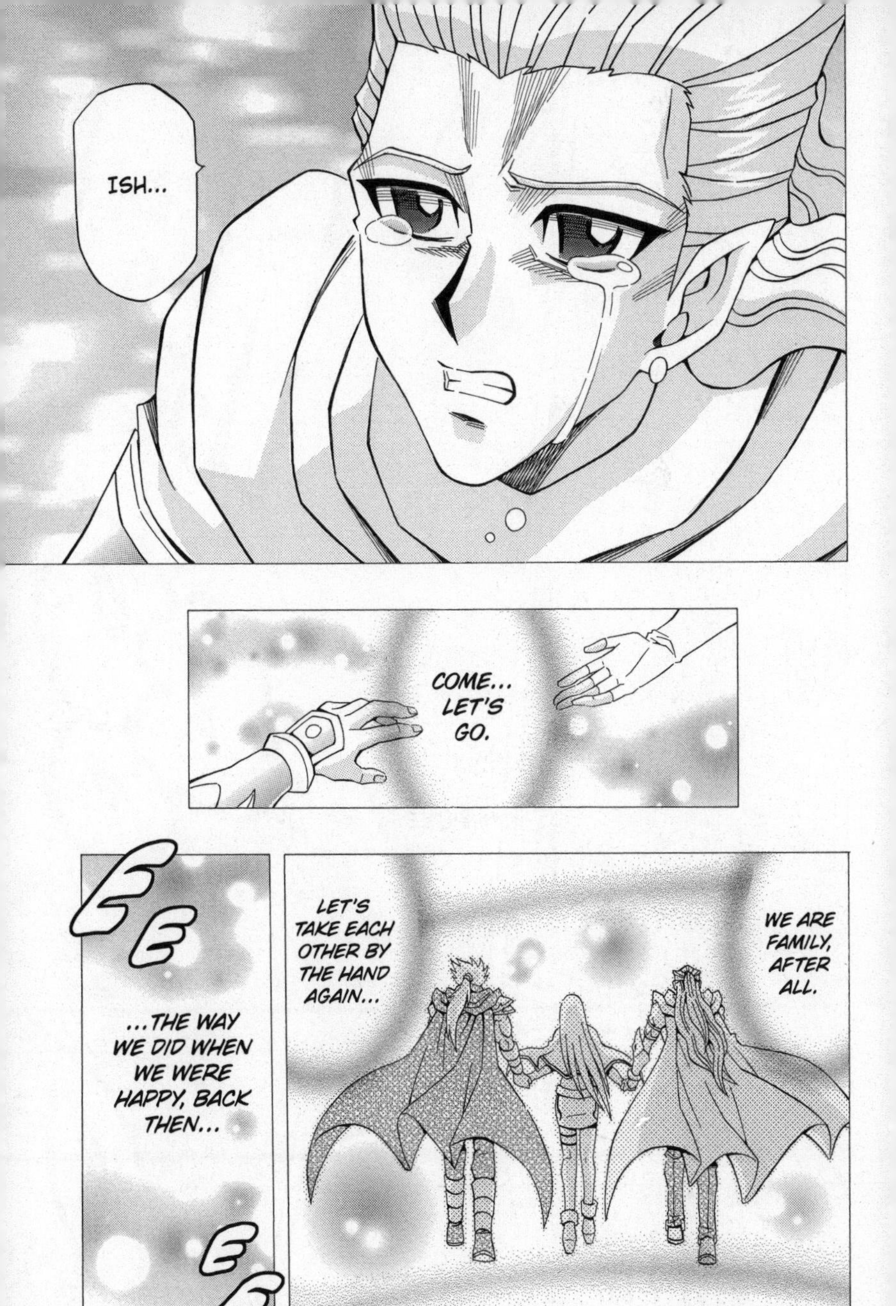
ISH...
COME... LET'S GO.
WE ARE FAMILY, AFTER ALL.
LET'S TAKE EACH OTHER BY THE HAND AGAIN...
...THE WAY WE DID WHEN WE WERE HAPPY, BACK THEN...

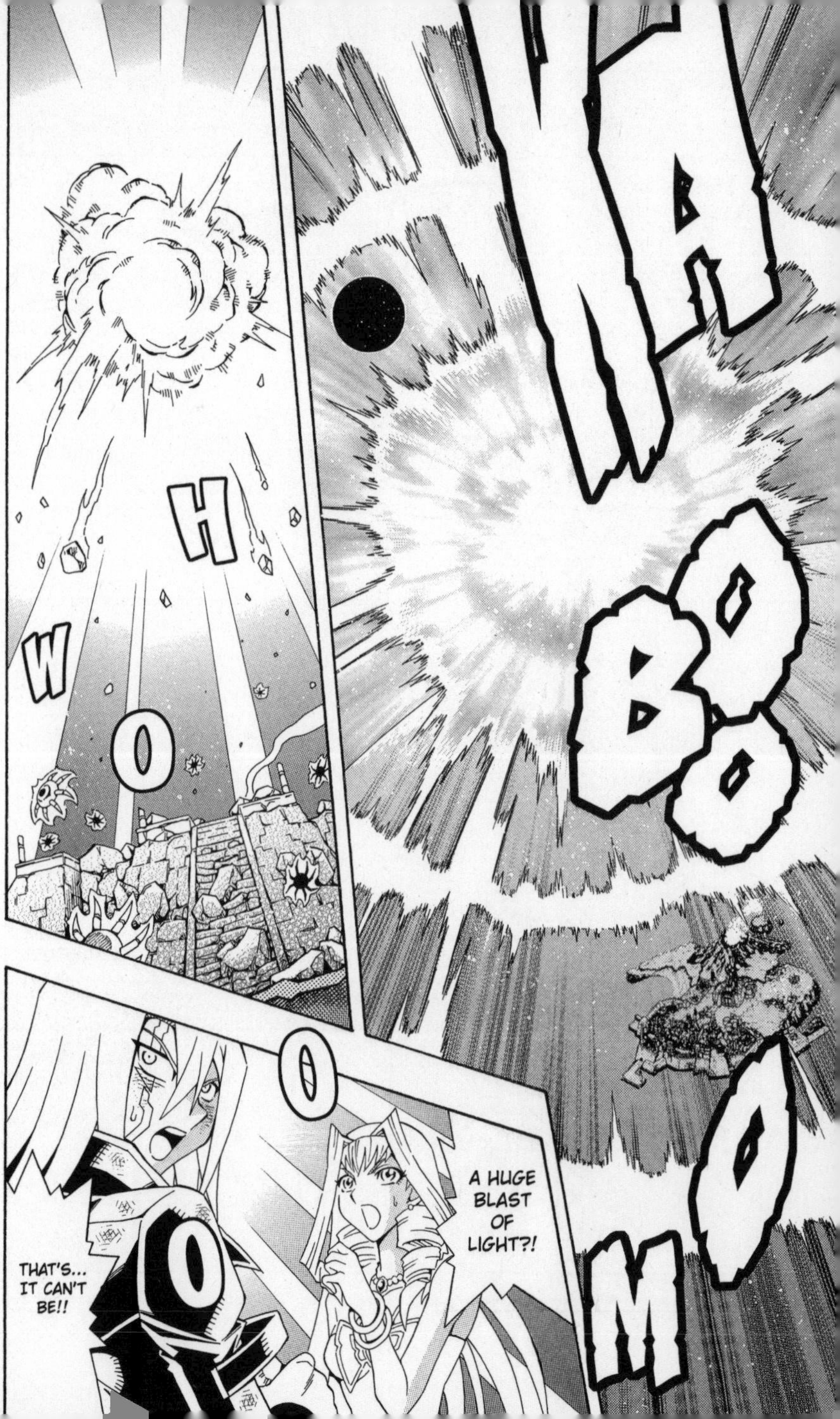

KABOOOM
WHOOO
A HUGE BLAST OF LIGHT?!
THAT'S... IT CAN'T BE!!

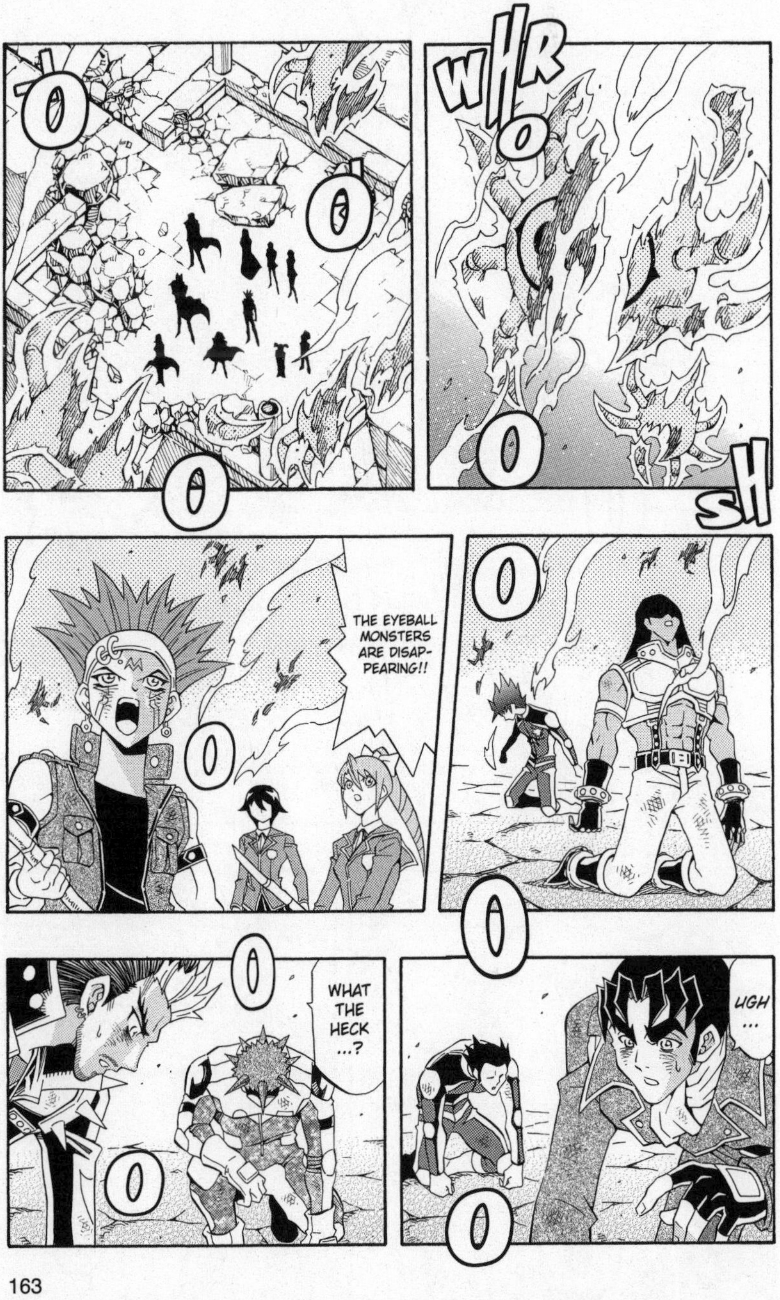
WHR
O
O
SH
O
O
O
O
THE EYEBALL MONSTERS ARE DISAP-PEARING!!
O
UGH ...
O
WHAT THE HECK ...?
O

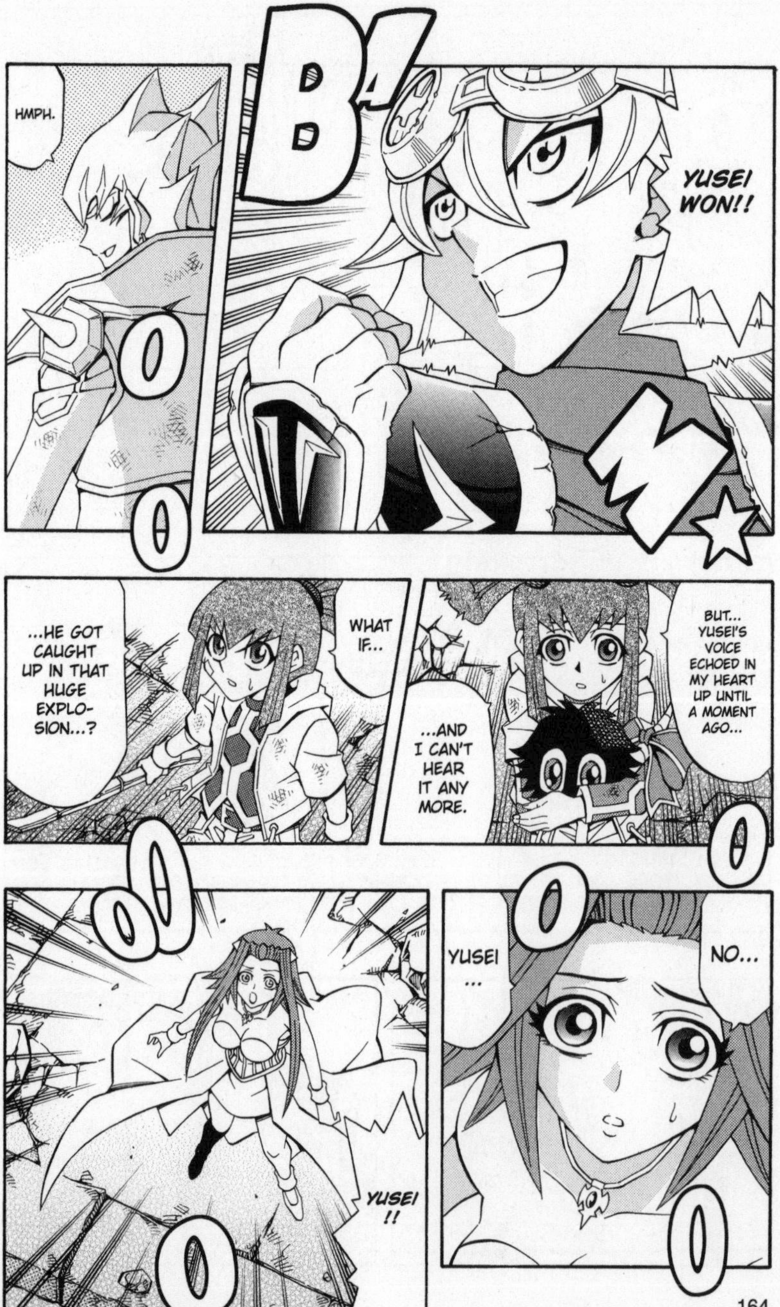

BOOM☆
YUSEI WON!!
HMPH.
BUT... YUSEI'S VOICE ECHOED IN MY HEART UP UNTIL A MOMENT AGO...
...AND I CAN'T HEAR IT ANY MORE.
WHAT IF...
...HE GOT CAUGHT UP IN THAT HUGE EXPLOSION...?
OOOOOO
NO...
YUSEI ...
YUSEI !!

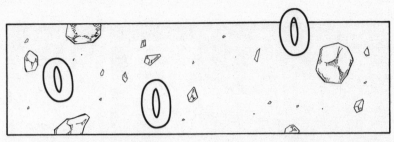

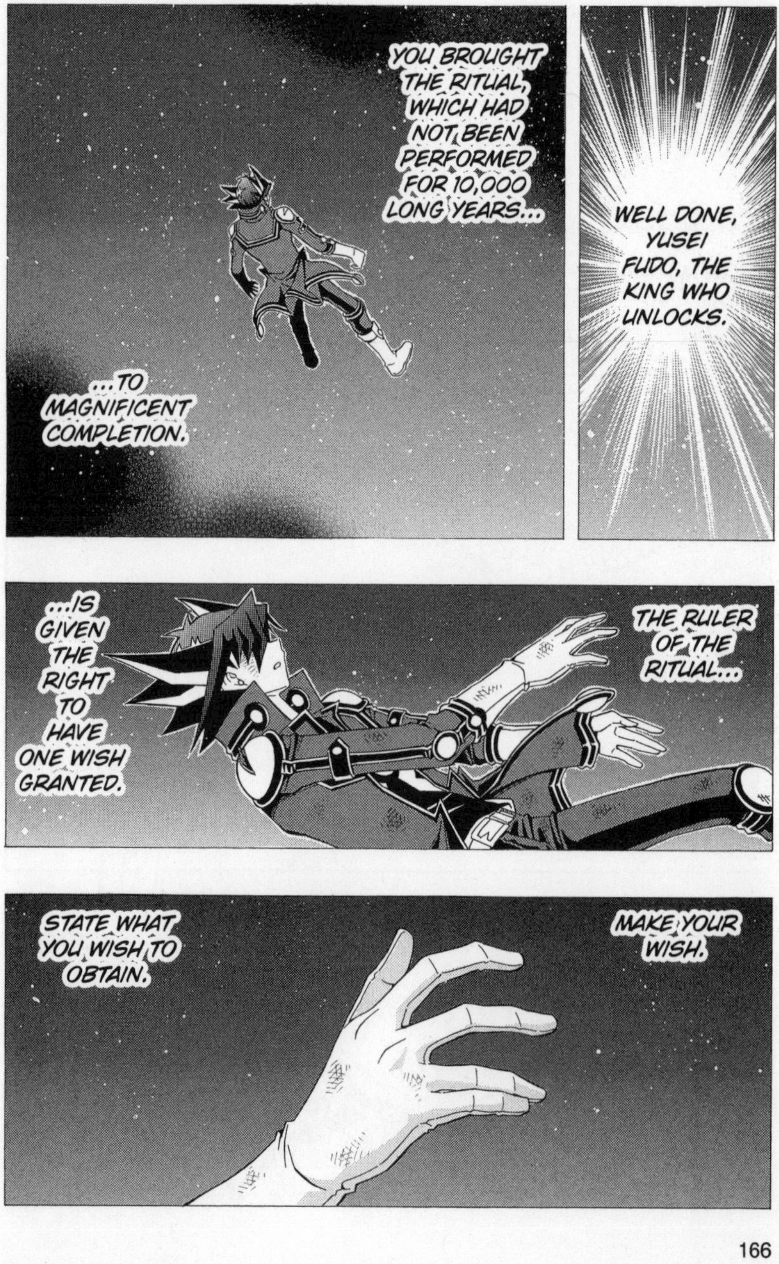
WELL DONE, YUSEI FUDO, THE KING WHO UNLOCKS.
YOU BROUGHT THE RITUAL, WHICH HAD NOT BEEN PERFORMED FOR 10,000 LONG YEARS...
...TO MAGNIFICENT COMPLETION.
THE RULER OF THE RITUAL...
...IS GIVEN THE RIGHT TO HAVE ONE WISH GRANTED.
MAKE YOUR WISH.
STATE WHAT YOU WISH TO OBTAIN.

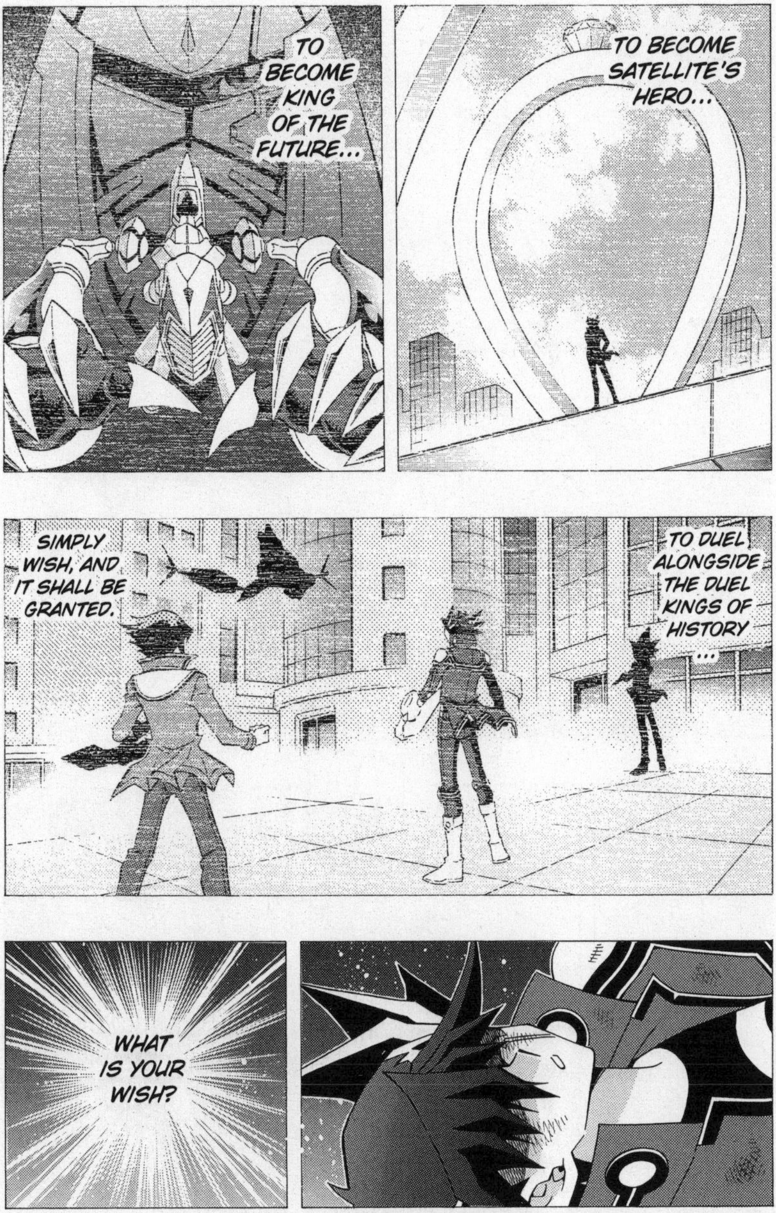
TO BECOME SATELLITE'S HERO...
TO BECOME KING OF THE FUTURE...
TO DUEL ALONGSIDE THE DUEL KINGS OF HISTORY...
SIMPLY WISH, AND IT SHALL BE GRANTED.
WHAT IS YOUR WISH?

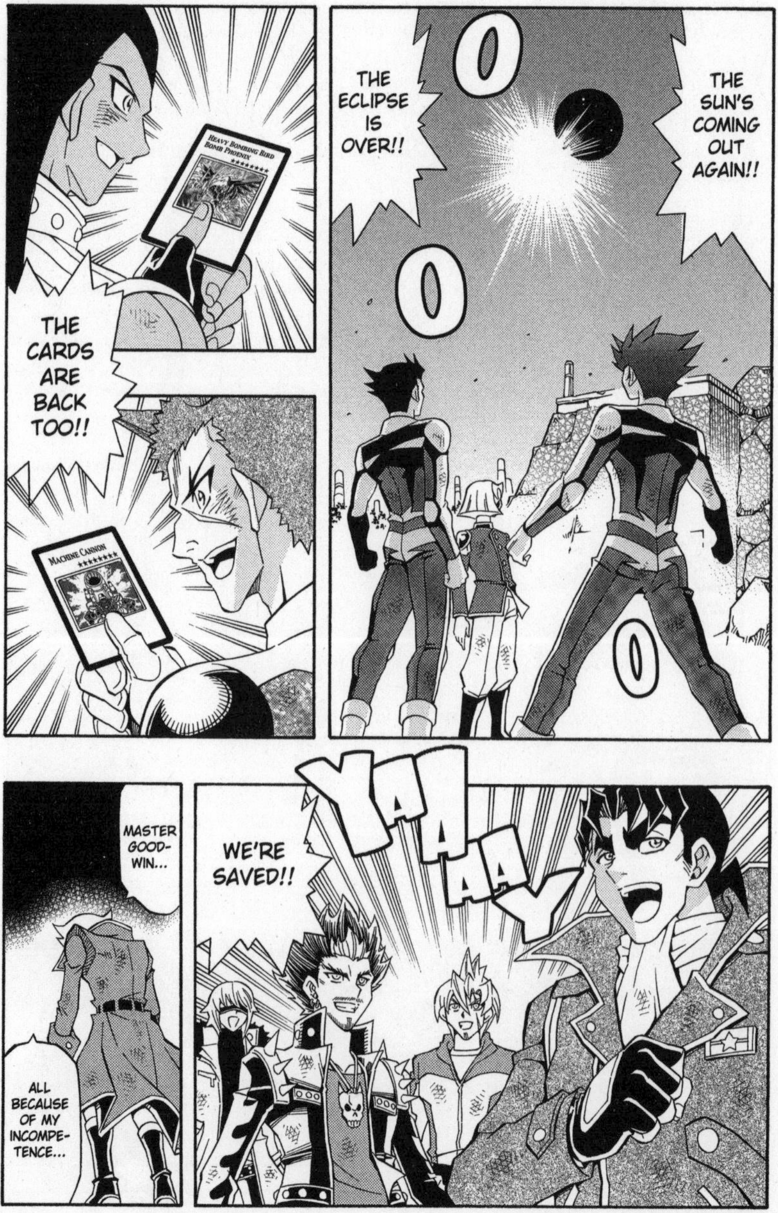
THE SUN'S COMING OUT AGAIN!!
THE ECLIPSE IS OVER!!
HEAVY BOMBING BIRD BOMB PHOENIX
THE CARDS ARE BACK TOO!!
MACHINE CANNON
YAAAAY
WE'RE SAVED!!
MASTER GOOD-WIN...
ALL BECAUSE OF MY INCOMPETE-TENCE...

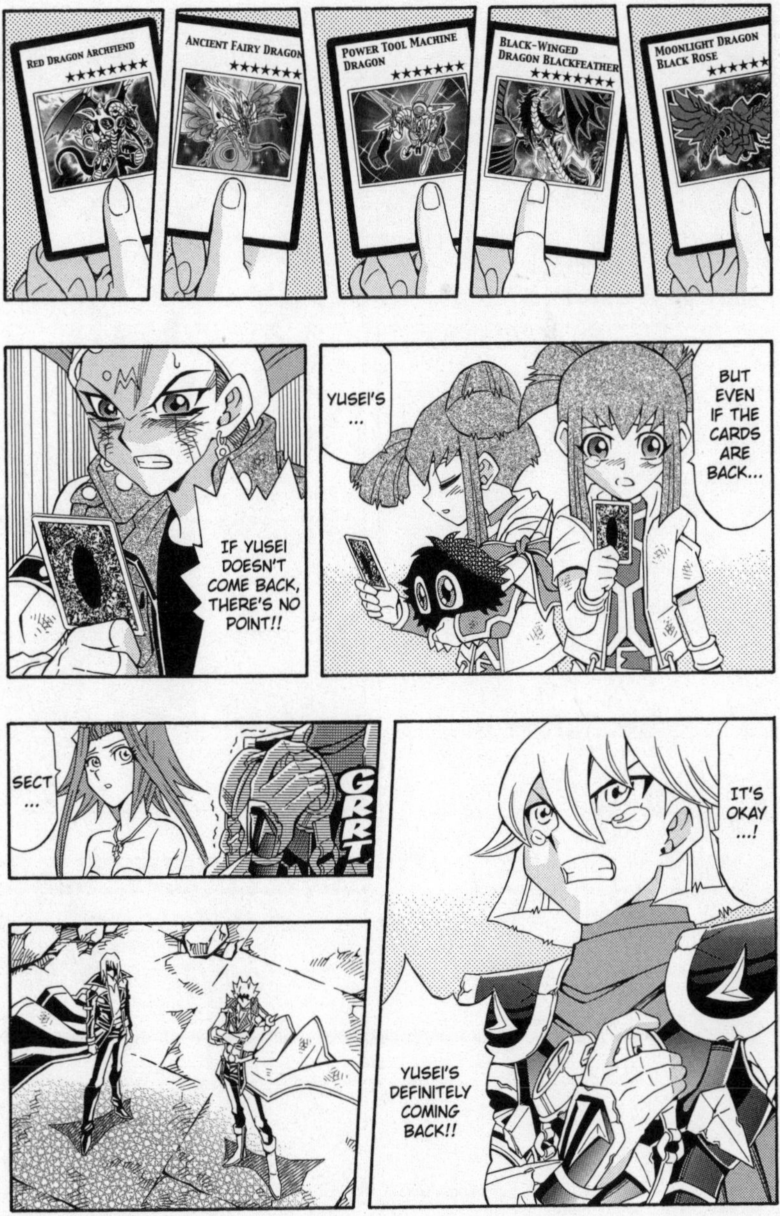
MOONLIGHT DRAGON BLACK ROSE
BLACK-WINGED DRAGON BLACKFEATHER
POWER TOOL MACHINE DRAGON
ANCIENT FAIRY DRAGON
RED DRAGON ARCHFIEND
BUT EVEN IF THE CARDS ARE BACK...
YUSEI'S ...
IF YUSEI DOESN'T COME BACK, THERE'S NO POINT!!
IT'S OKAY ...!
YUSEI'S DEFINITELY COMING BACK!!
SECT ...
GRRT

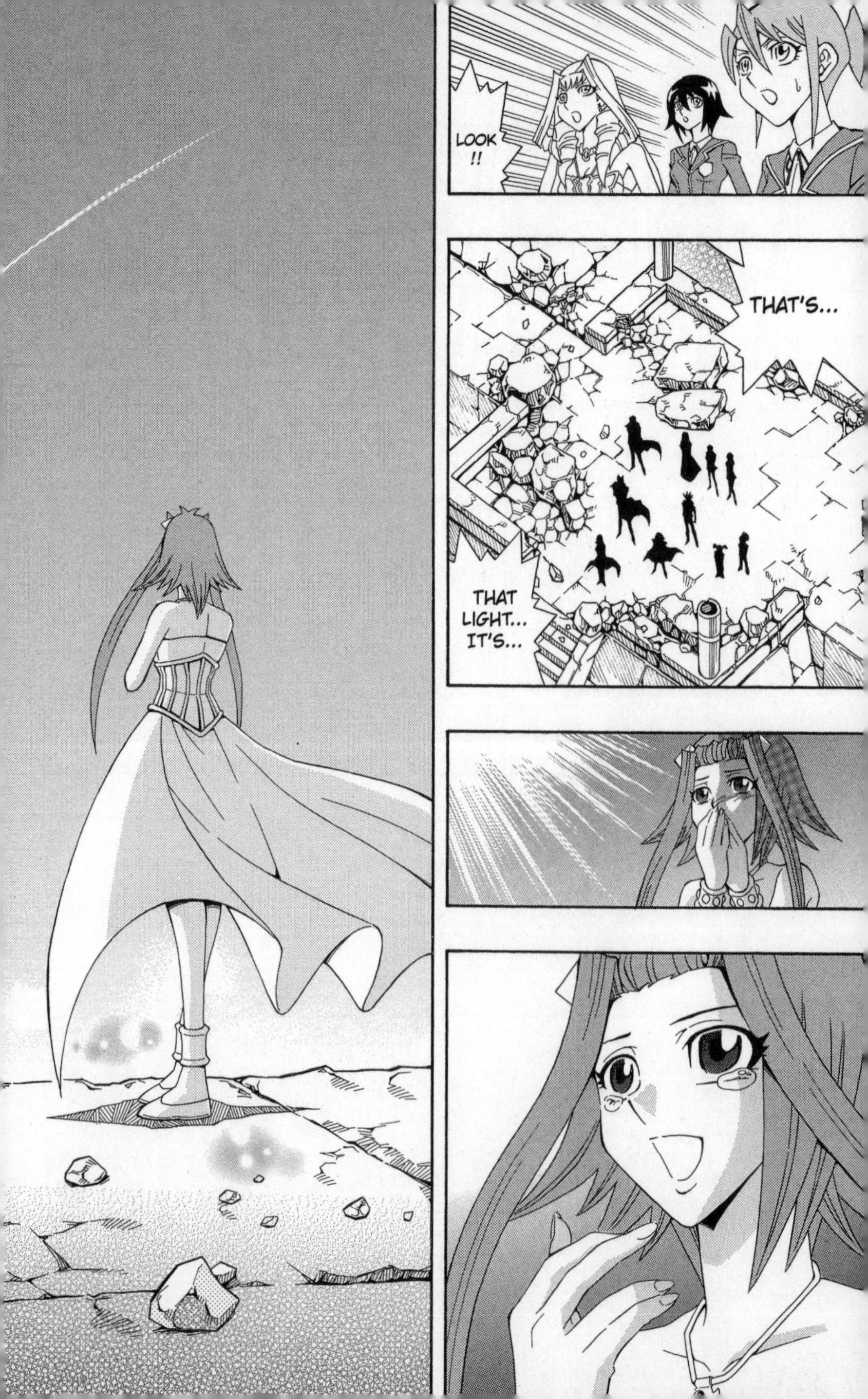
LOOK !!
THAT'S...
THAT LIGHT... IT'S...

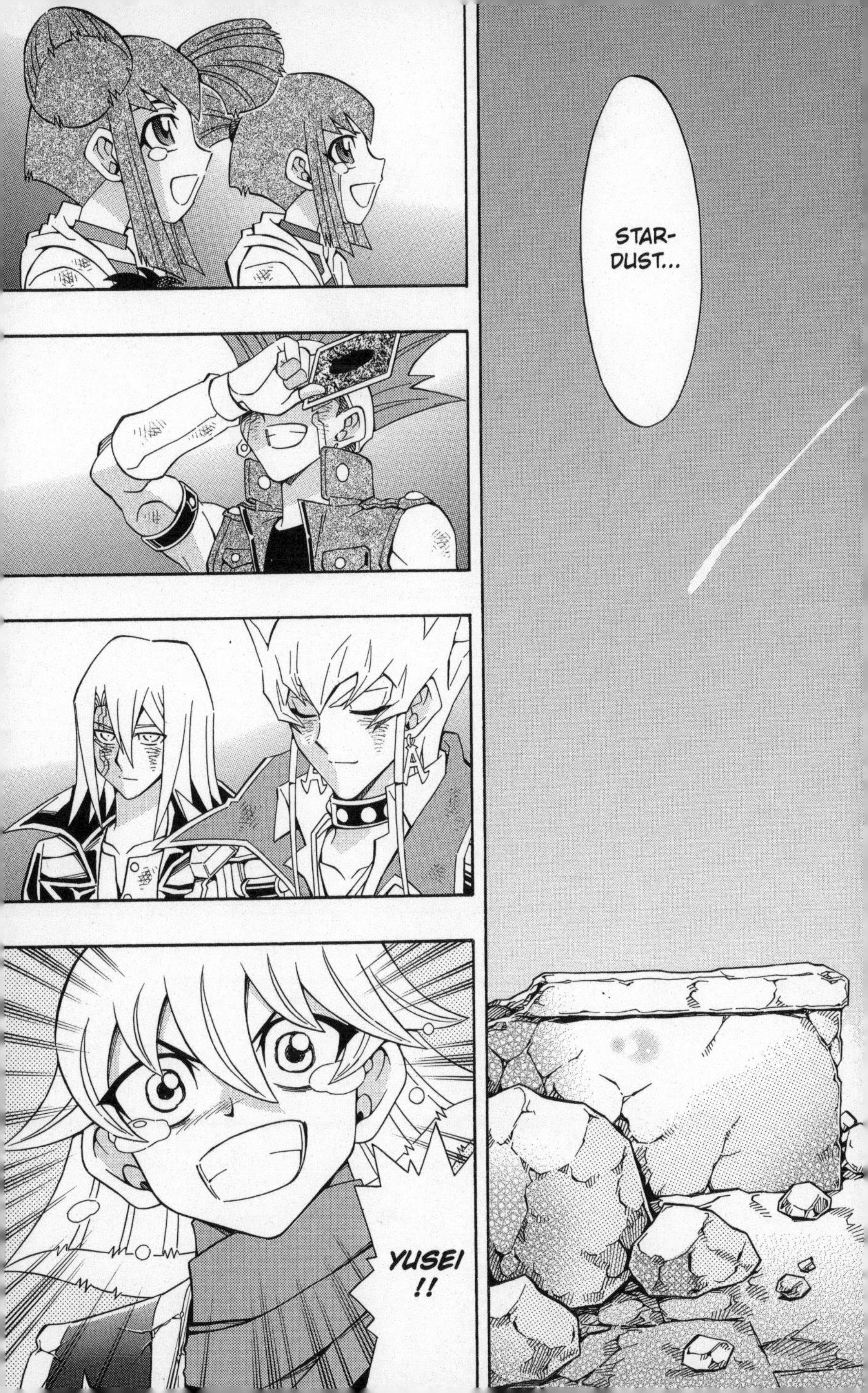
STAR-DUST...
YUSEI!!

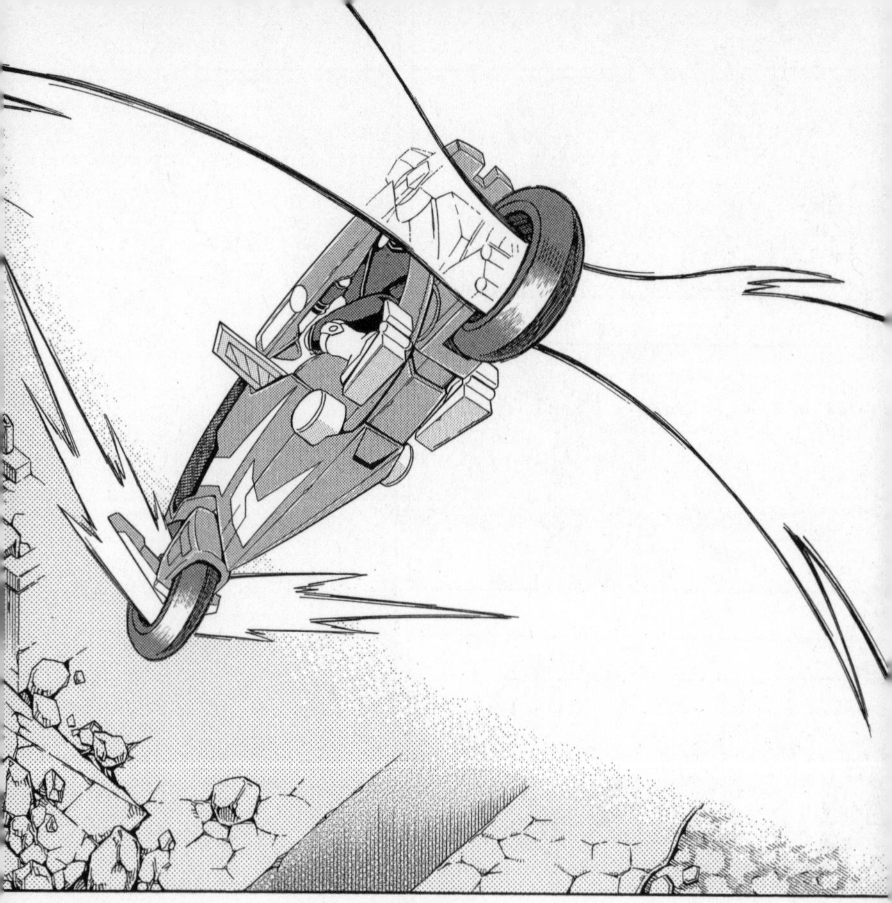

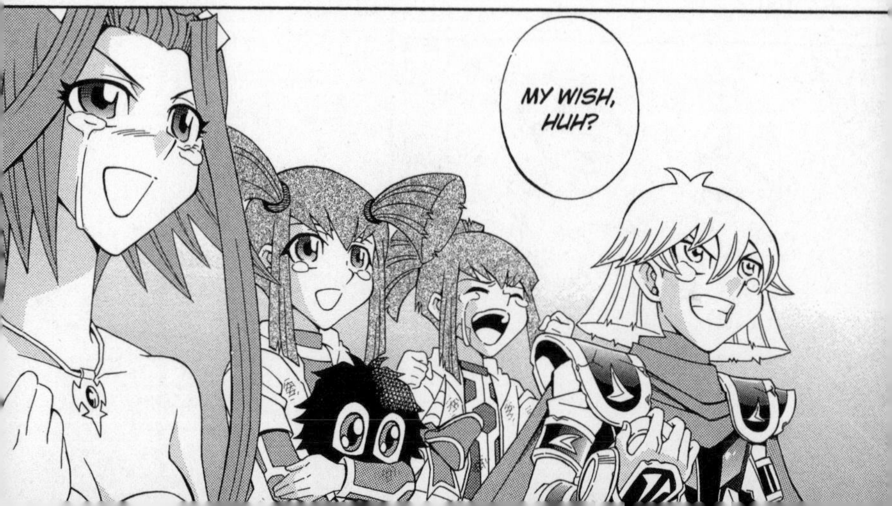
MY WISH, HUH?

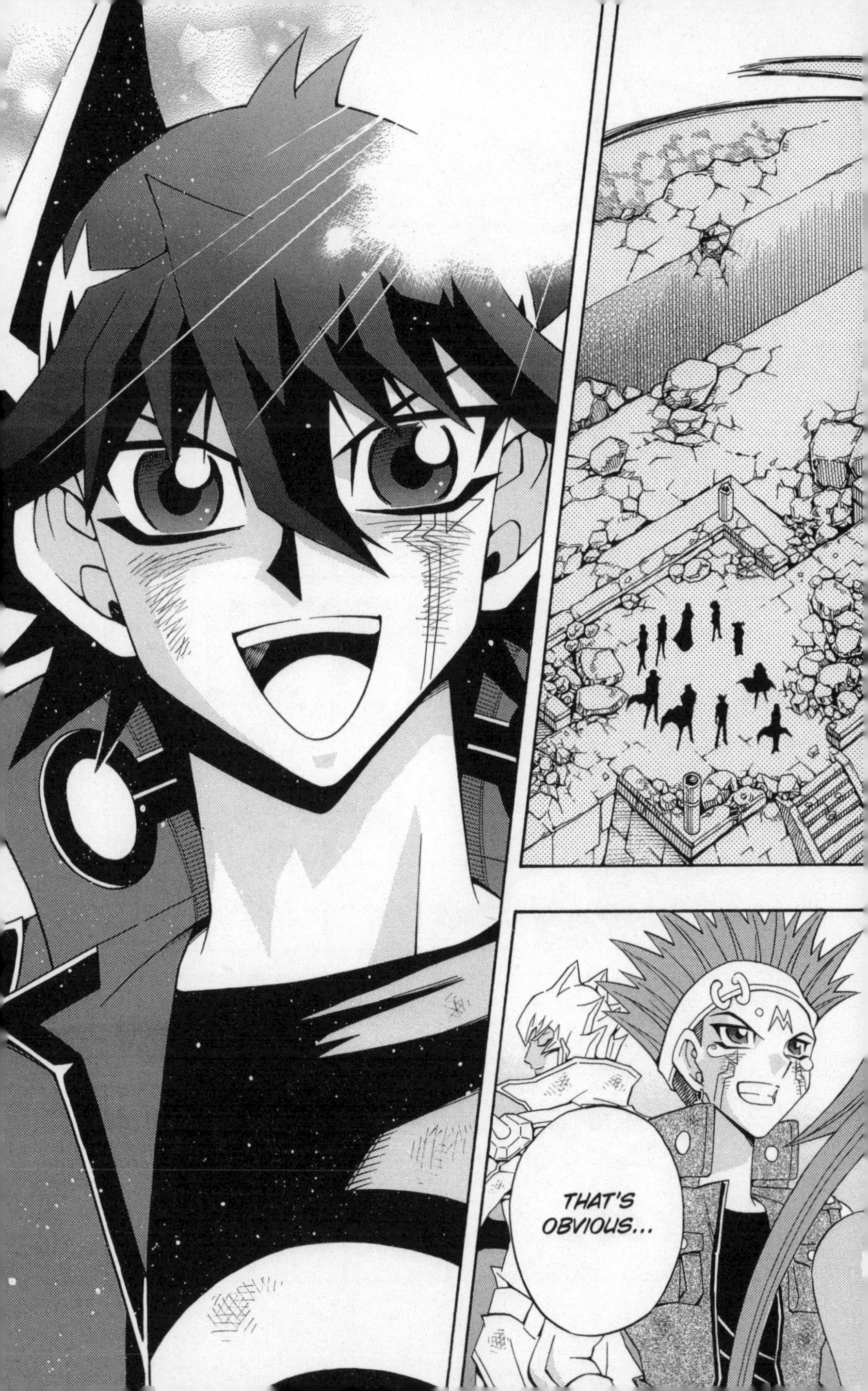
THAT'S OBVIOUS...

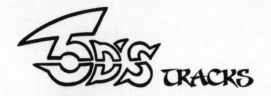

5D's TRACKS

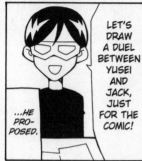

The 63rd

By Satomasa

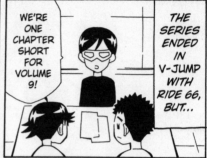

THE SERIES ENDED IN V-JUMP WITH RIDE 66, BUT...
WE'RE ONE CHAPTER SHORT FOR VOLUME 9!
LET'S DRAW A DUEL BETWEEN YUSEI AND JACK, JUST FOR THE COMIC!
...HE PROPOSED.
I WANTED TO DRAW A REMATCH WITH JACK, TOO, BUT...
WE CAN'T DRAW A WHOLE DUEL IN JUST ONE CHAPTER.
HE'S RIGHT!
IT'S FINE!
IF IT'LL MAKE THE MANGA THICKER, IT'S ABSOLUTELY NO PROBLEM!!
AND SO WE ASKED HIKOKUBO FOR A SCRIPT FOR TWO CHAPTERS, ROUGHLY 60 PAGES.
IT REALLY WON'T FIT...
IT TURNED OUT TO BE 78 PAGES.
ENJOY YUSEI'S LAST DUEL...
...STARTING ON THE NEXT PAGE.

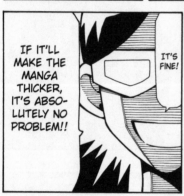

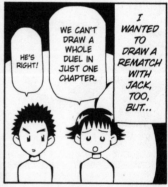

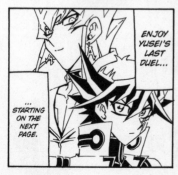

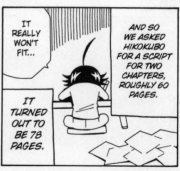

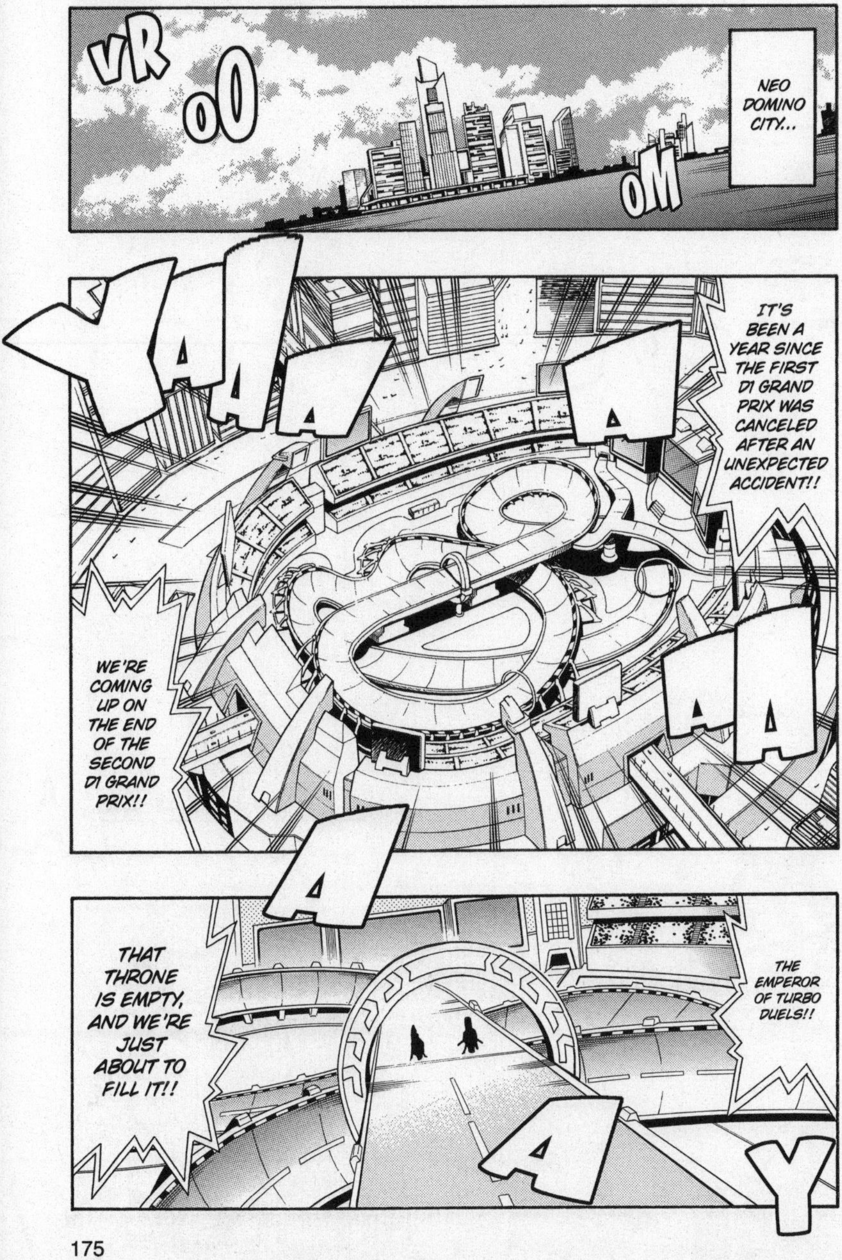
NEO DOMINO CITY...
VROOOM
IT'S BEEN A YEAR SINCE THE FIRST D1 GRAND PRIX WAS CANCELED AFTER AN UNEXPECTED ACCIDENT!!
YAAAAAAAAY
WE'RE COMING UP ON THE END OF THE SECOND D1 GRAND PRIX!!
THE EMPEROR OF TURBO DUELS!!
THAT THRONE IS EMPTY, AND WE'RE JUST ABOUT TO FILL IT!!

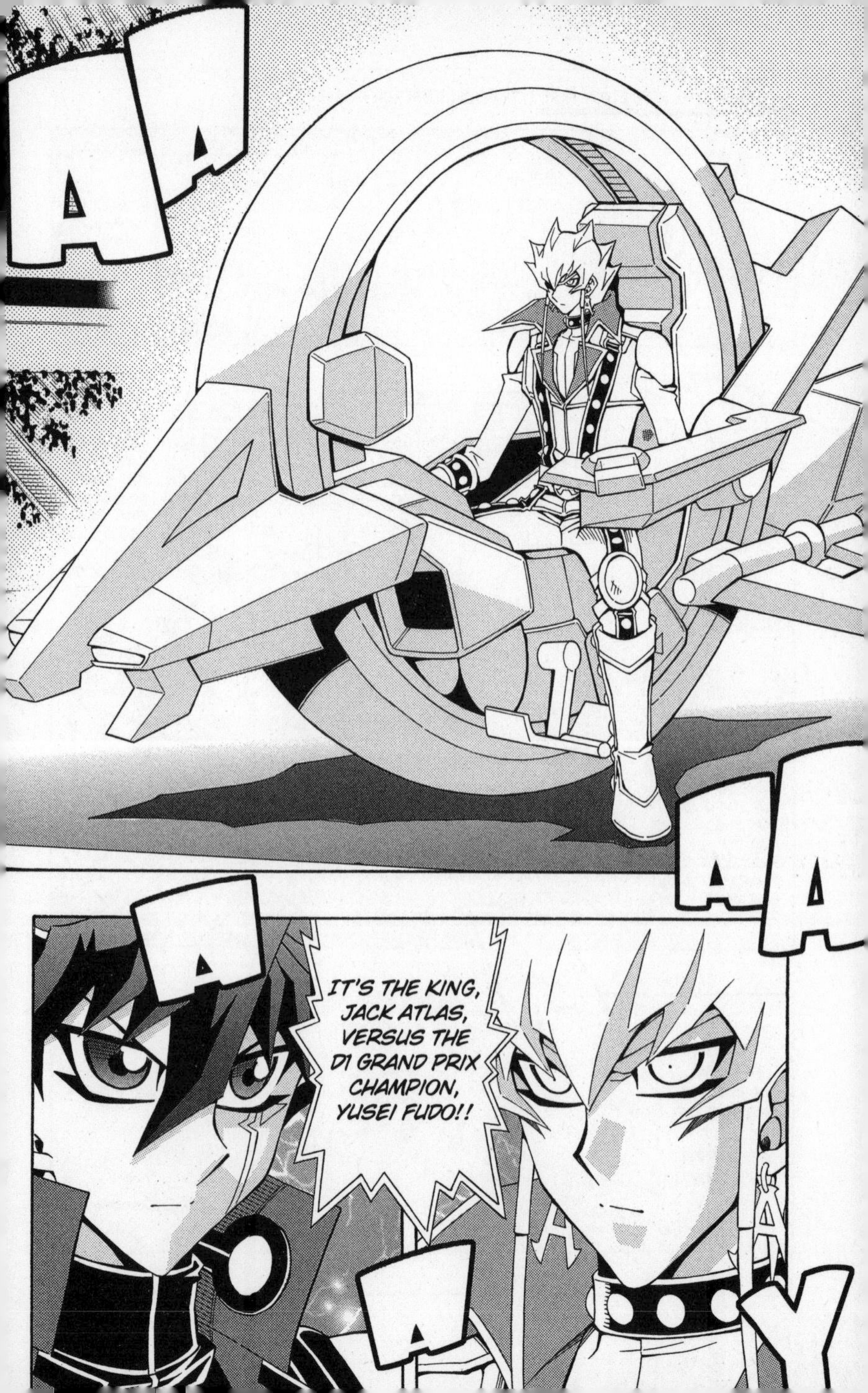
AA
AAA
IT'S THE KING, JACK ATLAS, VERSUS THE D1 GRAND PRIX CHAMPION, YUSEI FUDO!!

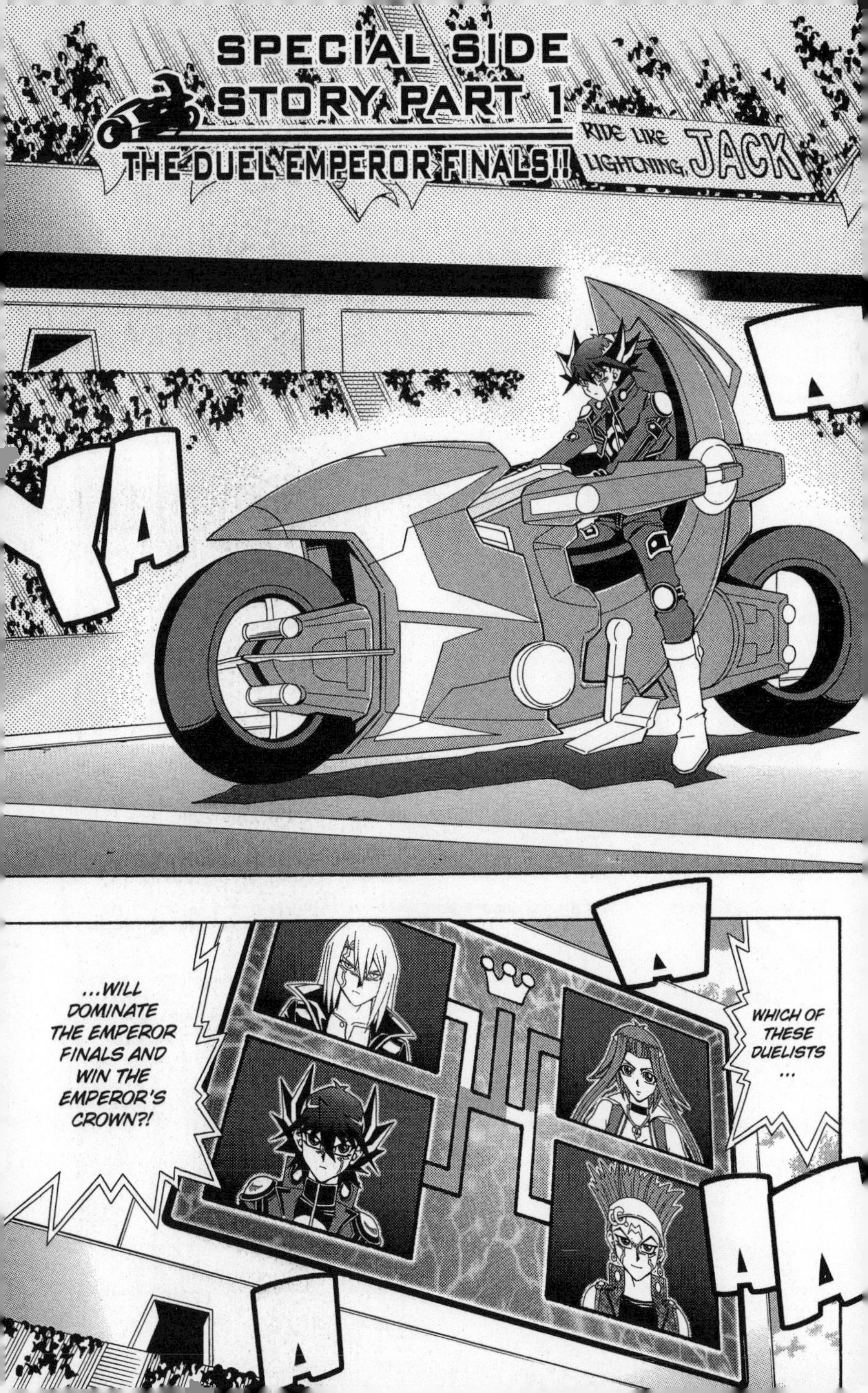
SPECIAL SIDE STORY PART 1
THE DUEL EMPEROR FINALS!!
RIDE LIKE LIGHTNING, JACK
A
YA
A
WHICH OF THESE DUELISTS ...
...WILL DOMINATE THE EMPEROR FINALS AND WIN THE EMPEROR'S CROWN?!
AA
A

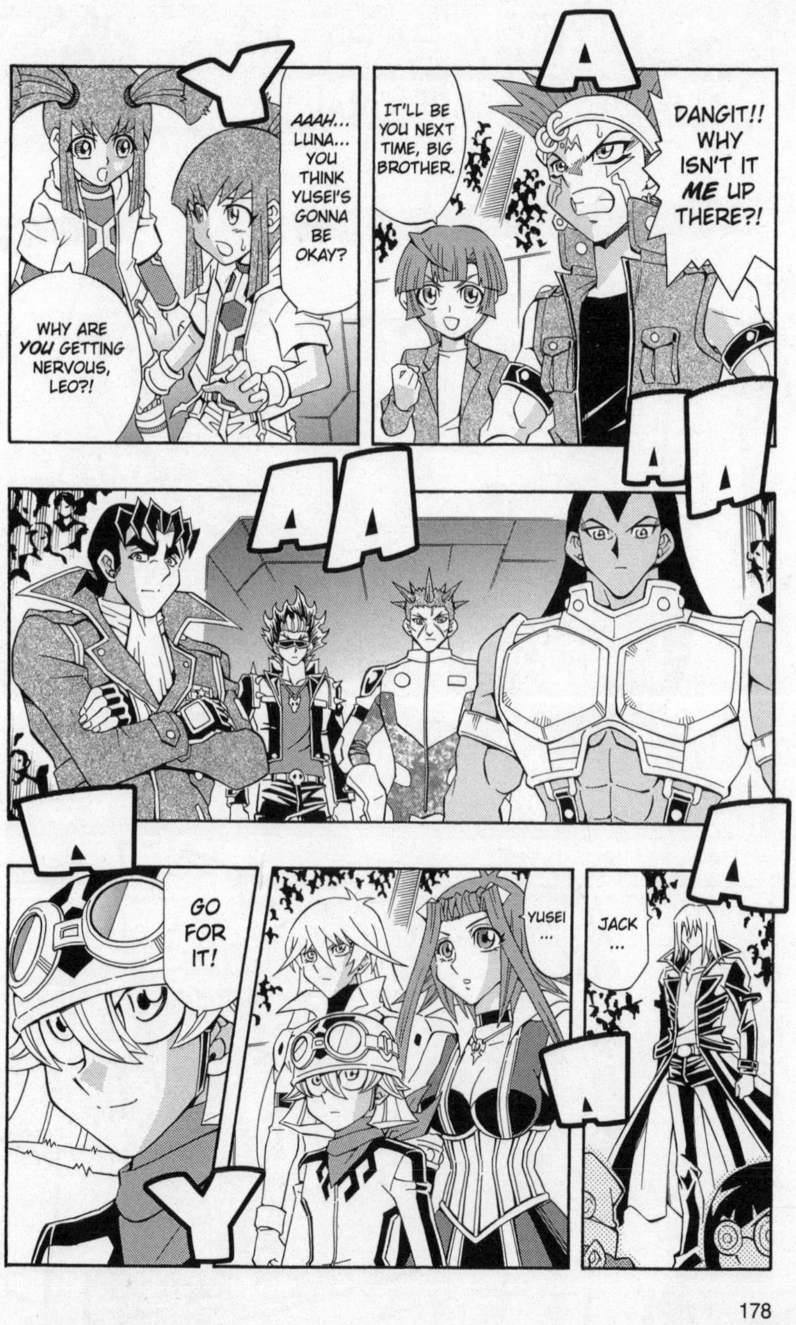
YAAAAAAAAY
DANGIT!! WHY ISN'T IT ME UP THERE?!
IT'LL BE YOU NEXT TIME, BIG BROTHER.
AAAH... LUNA... YOU THINK YUSEI'S GONNA BE OKAY?
WHY ARE YOU GETTING NERVOUS, LEO?!
JACK ...
YUSEI ...
GO FOR IT!

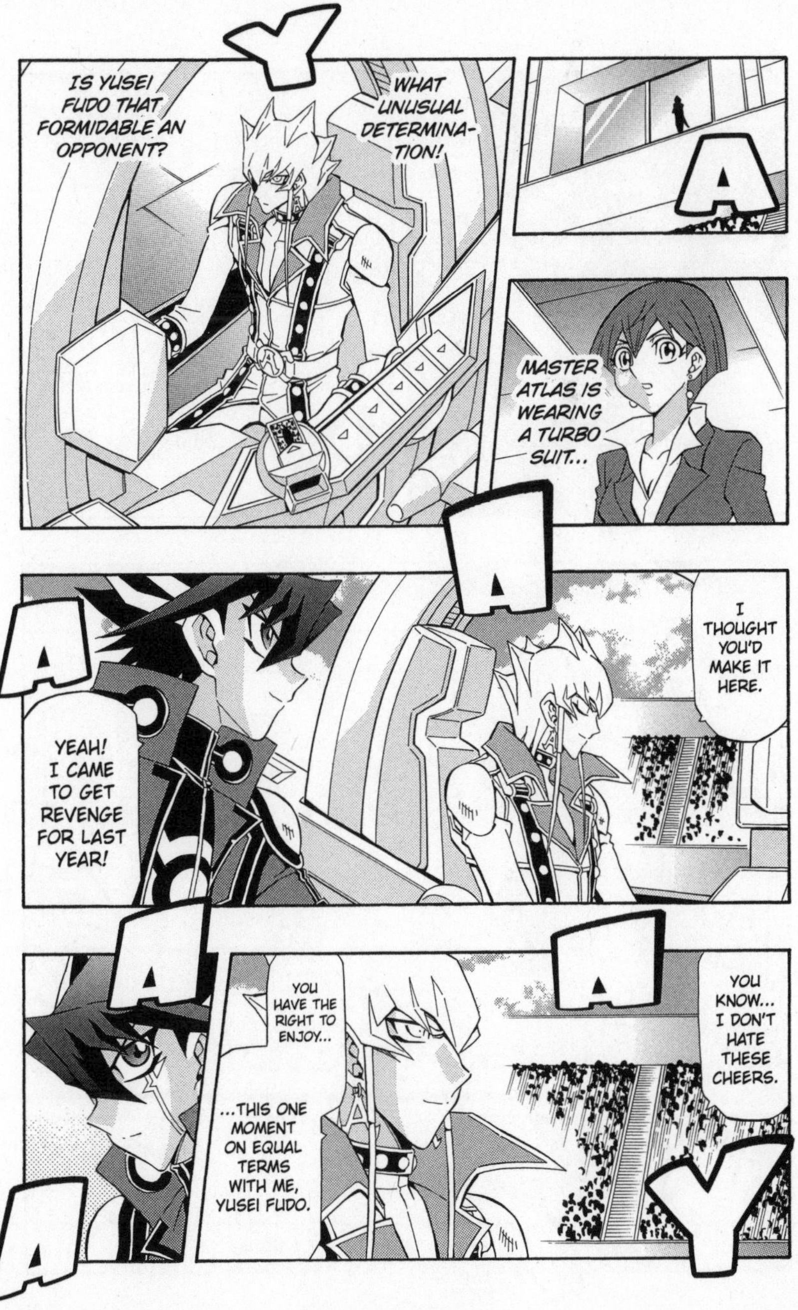
A
MASTER ATLAS IS WEARING A TURBO SUIT...
Y
WHAT UNUSUAL DETERMINA-TION!
IS YUSEI FUDO THAT FORMIDABLE AN OPPONENT?
A
I THOUGHT YOU'D MAKE IT HERE.
A
YEAH! I CAME TO GET REVENGE FOR LAST YEAR!
A
YOU KNOW... I DON'T HATE THESE CHEERS.
Y
YOU HAVE THE RIGHT TO ENJOY...
...THIS ONE MOMENT ON EQUAL TERMS WITH ME, YUSEI FUDO.
A
A

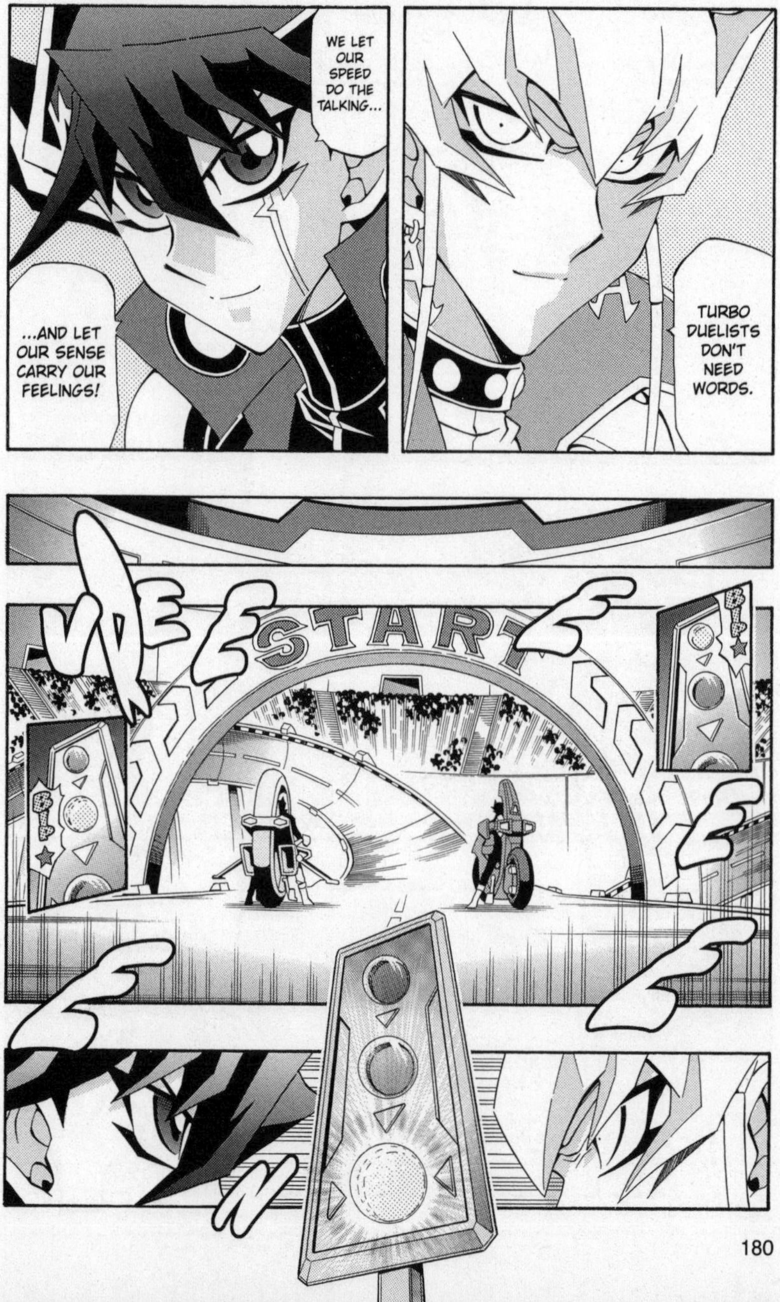
TURBO DUELISTS DON'T NEED WORDS.
WE LET OUR SPEED DO THE TALKING...
...AND LET OUR SENSE CARRY OUR FEELINGS!
START

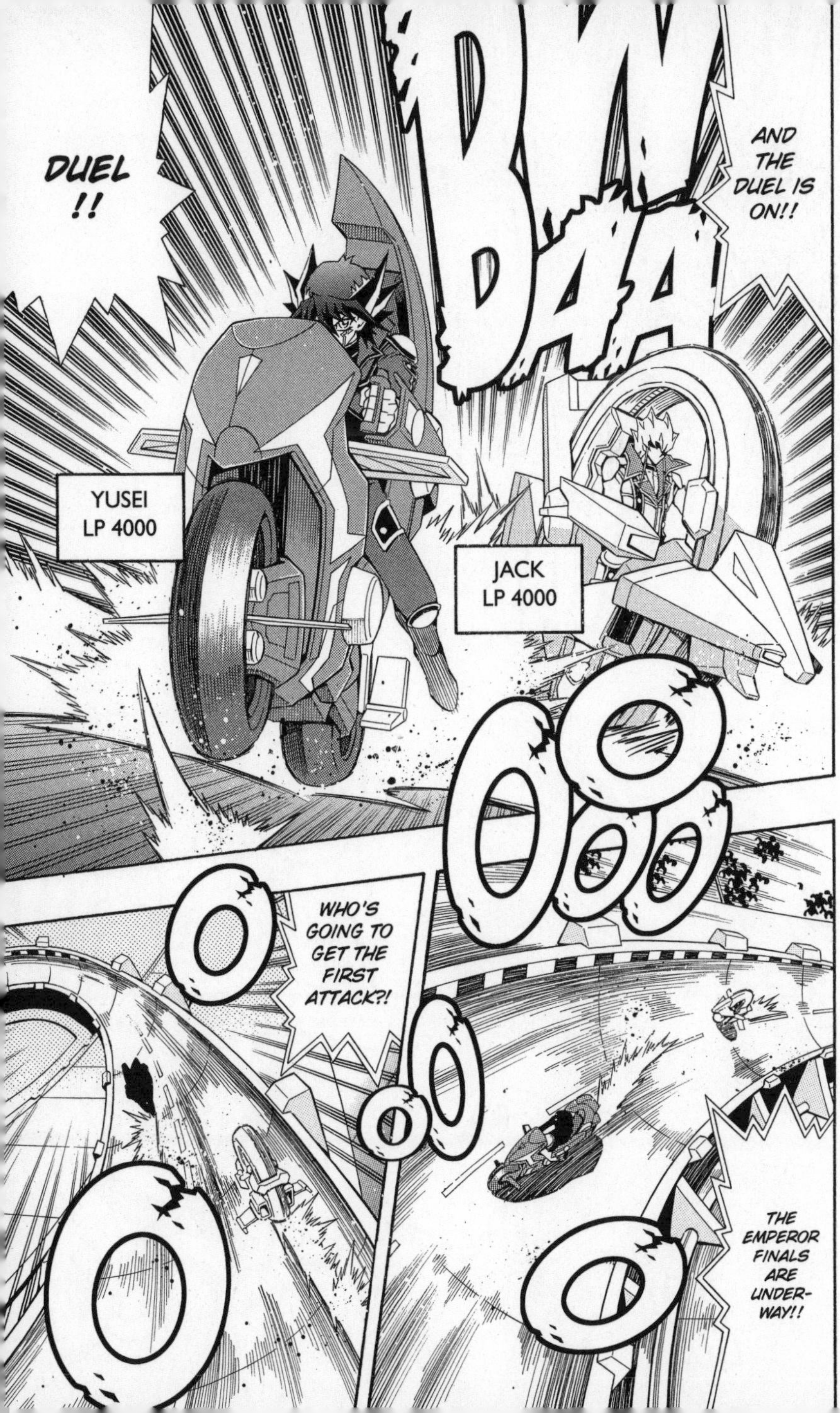
AND THE DUEL IS ON!!
DUEL !!
JACK LP 4000
YUSEI LP 4000
THE EMPEROR FINALS ARE UNDER-WAY!!
WHO'S GOING TO GET THE FIRST ATTACK?!

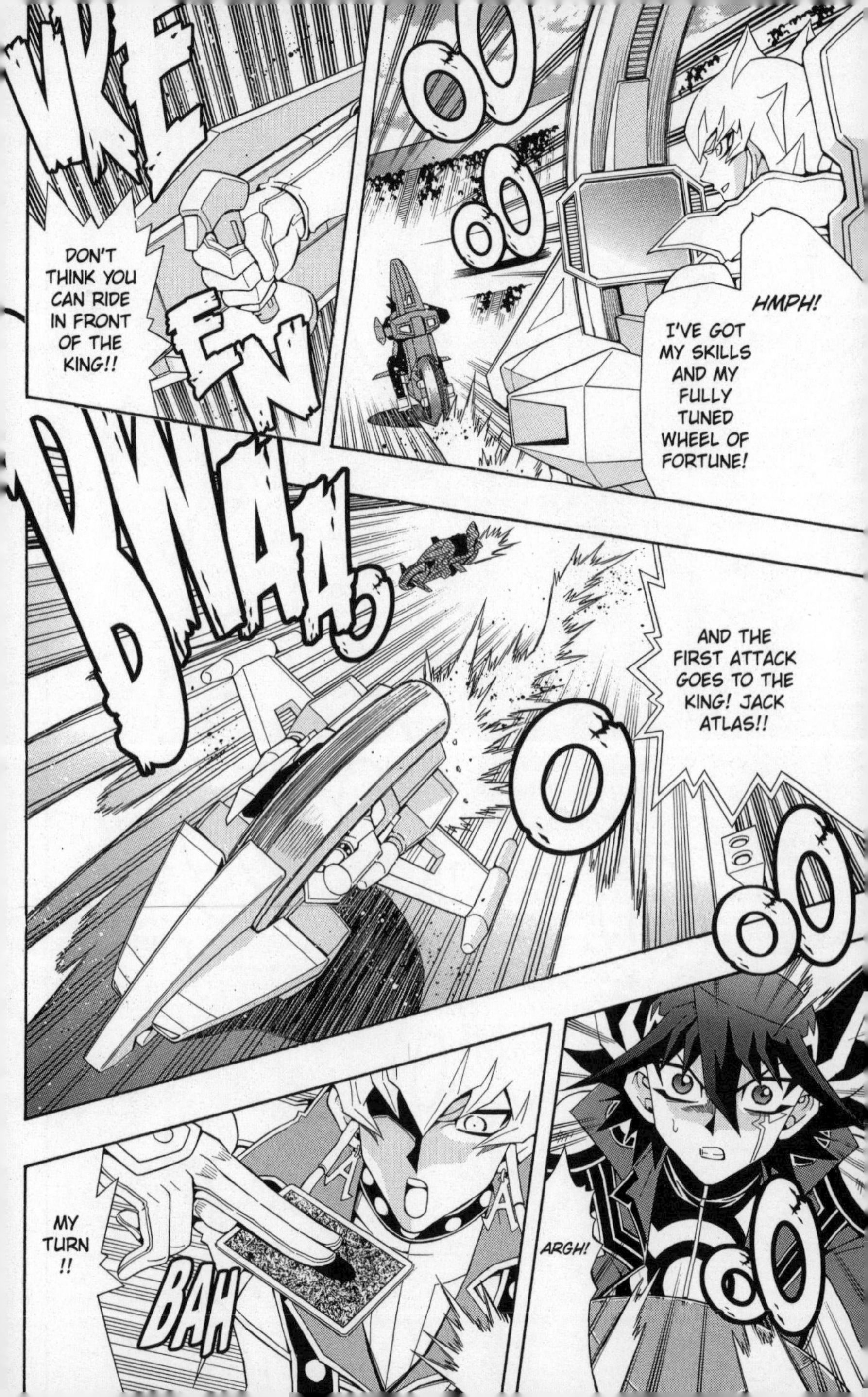
HMPH!
I'VE GOT MY SKILLS AND MY FULLY TUNED WHEEL OF FORTUNE!
DON'T THINK YOU CAN RIDE IN FRONT OF THE KING!!
BWAA
AND THE FIRST ATTACK GOES TO THE KING! JACK ATLAS!!
ARGH!
MY TURN !!
BAH

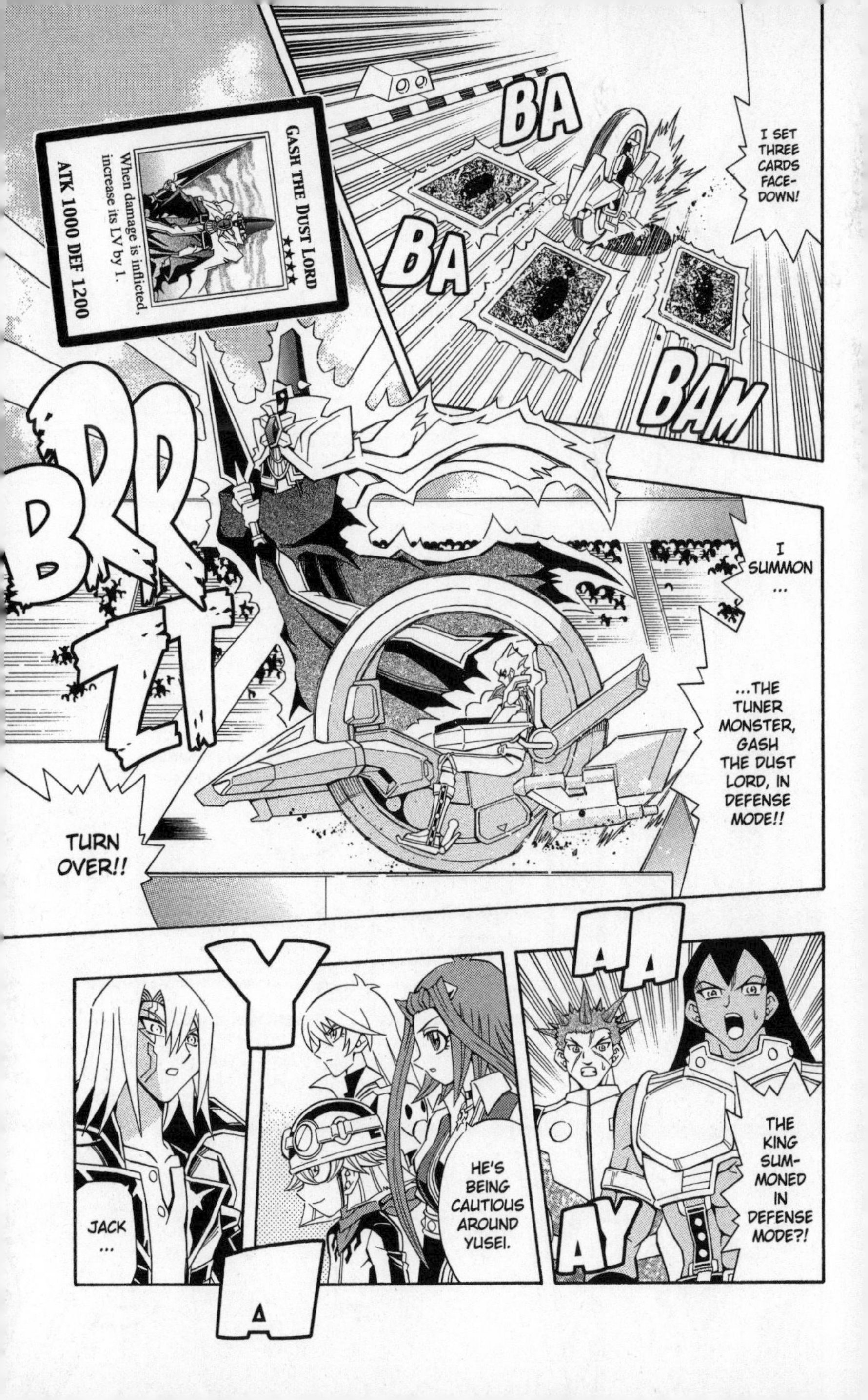
I SET THREE CARDS FACE-DOWN!
BA
BA
BAM
GASH THE DUST LORD
★★★★
When damage is inflicted, increase its LV by 1.
ATK 1000 DEF 1200
I SUMMON ...
...THE TUNER MONSTER, GASH THE DUST LORD, IN DEFENSE MODE!!
BRR
ZT
TURN OVER!!
AA
THE KING SUMMONED IN DEFENSE MODE?!
AY
Y
HE'S BEING CAUTIOUS AROUND YUSEI.
JACK ...
A

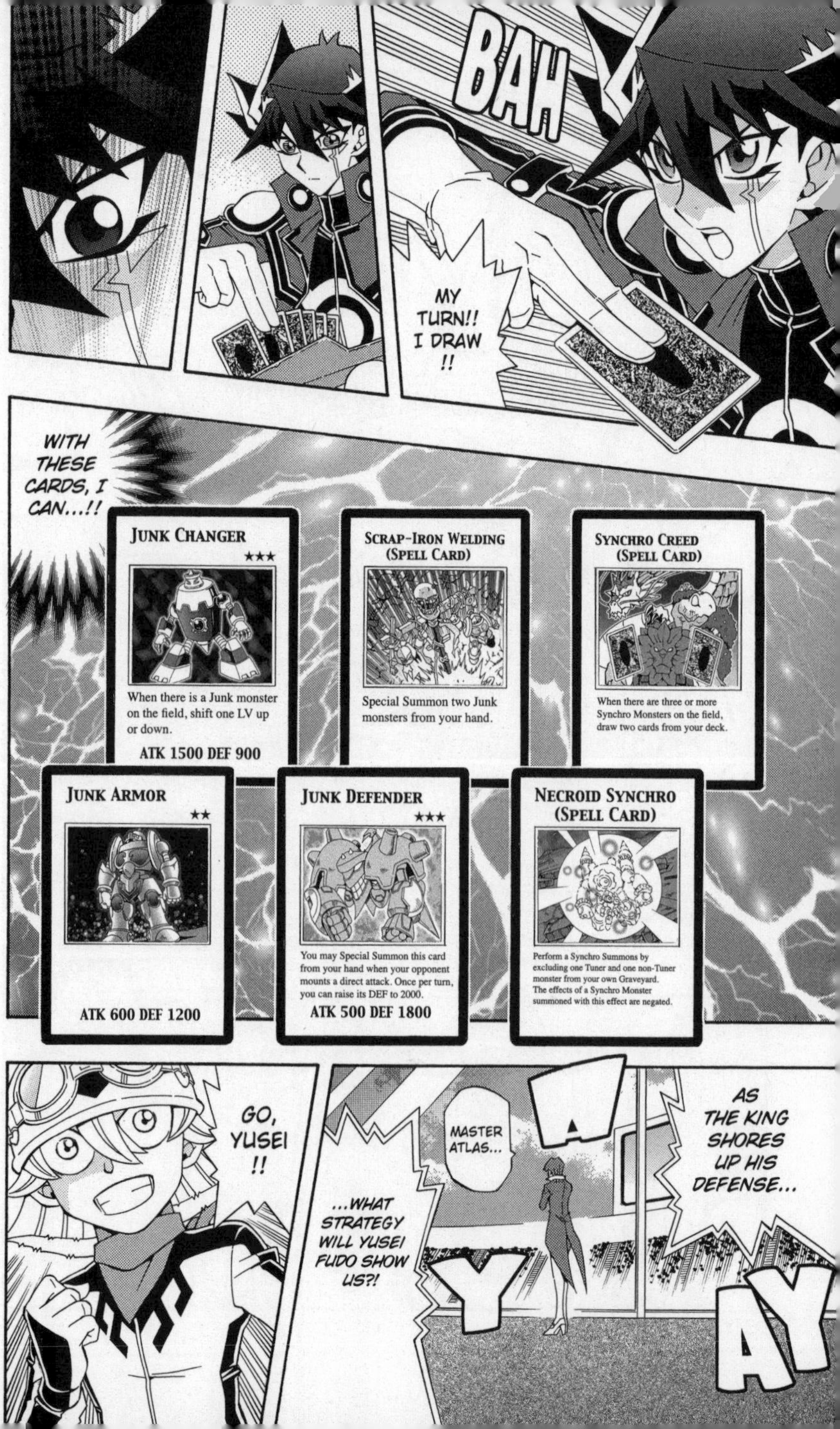
BAH
MY TURN!! I DRAW !!
WITH THESE CARDS, I CAN...!!
SYNCHRO CREED (SPELL CARD)
When there are three or more Synchro Monsters on the field, draw two cards from your deck.
SCRAP-IRON WELDING (SPELL CARD)
Special Summon two Junk monsters from your hand.
JUNK CHANGER
★★★
When there is a Junk monster on the field, shift one LV up or down.
ATK 1500 DEF 900
NECROID SYNCHRO (SPELL CARD)
Perform a Synchro Summons by excluding one Tuner and one non-Tuner monster from your own Graveyard. The effects of a Synchro Monster summoned with this effect are negated.
JUNK DEFENDER
★★★
You may Special Summon this card from your hand when your opponent mounts a direct attack. Once per turn, you can raise its DEF to 2000.
ATK 500 DEF 1800
JUNK ARMOR
★★
ATK 600 DEF 1200
AS THE KING SHORES UP HIS DEFENSE...
AY
A
MASTER ATLAS...
...WHAT STRATEGY WILL YUSEI FUDO SHOW US?!
Y
GO, YUSEI !!

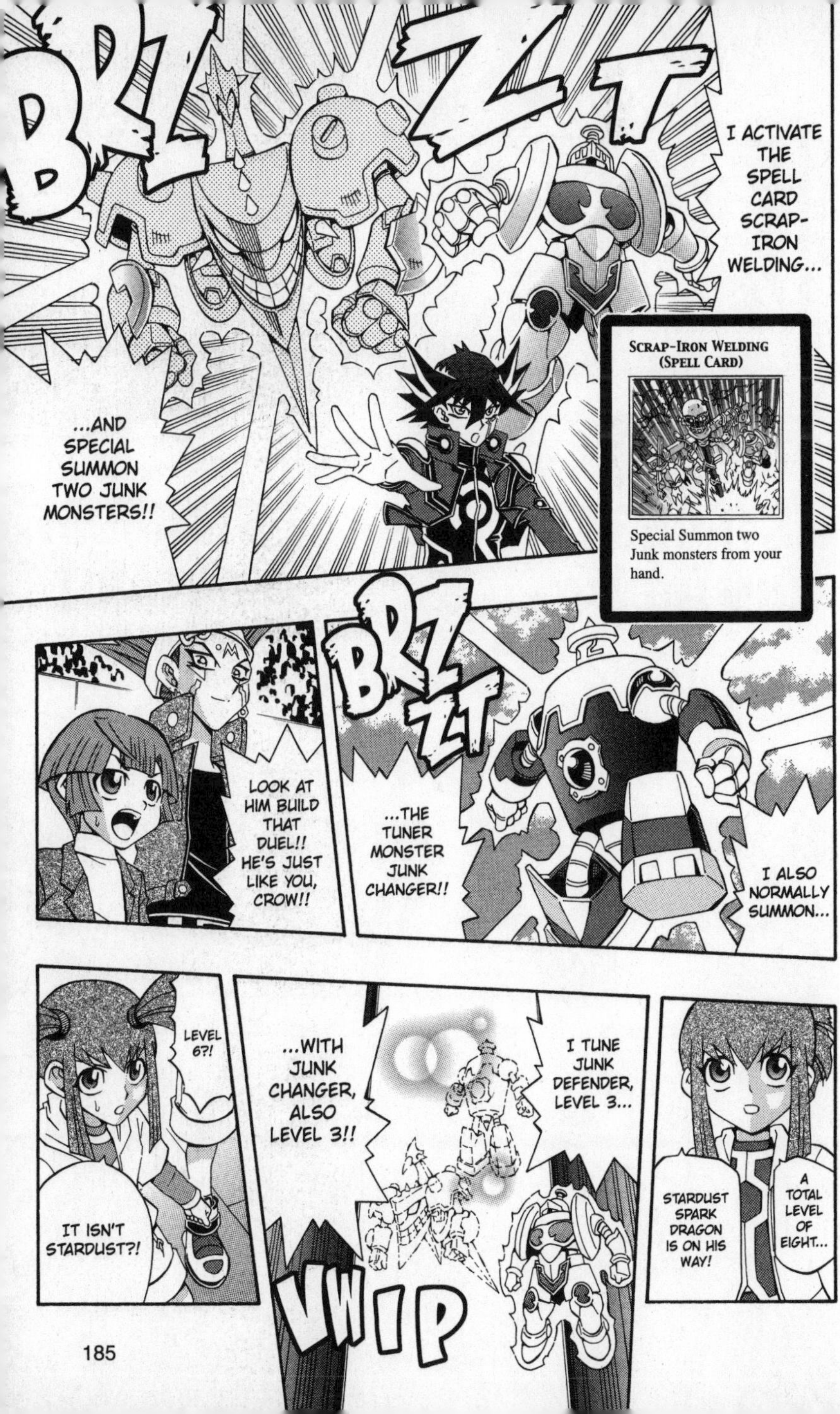
BRZZT
I ACTIVATE THE SPELL CARD SCRAP-IRON WELDING...
SCRAP-IRON WELDING (SPELL CARD)
Special Summon two Junk monsters from your hand.
...AND SPECIAL SUMMON TWO JUNK MONSTERS!!
BRZZT
I ALSO NORMALLY SUMMON...
...THE TUNER MONSTER JUNK CHANGER!!
LOOK AT HIM BUILD THAT DUEL!! HE'S JUST LIKE YOU, CROW!!
A TOTAL LEVEL OF EIGHT...
STARDUST SPARK DRAGON IS ON HIS WAY!
I TUNE JUNK DEFENDER, LEVEL 3...
...WITH JUNK CHANGER, ALSO LEVEL 3!!
VWIP
LEVEL 6?!
IT ISN'T STARDUST?!

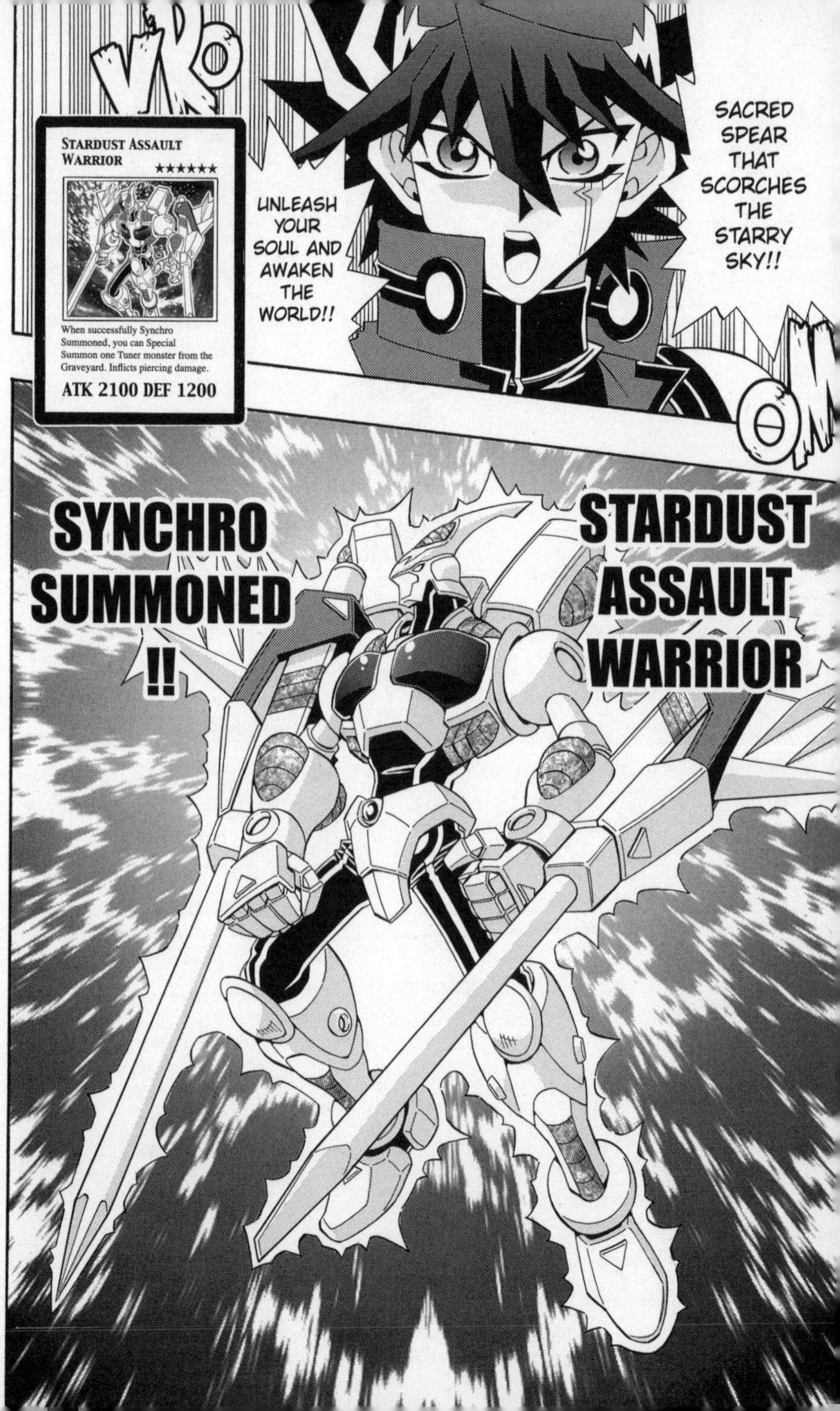
VRO
SACRED SPEAR THAT SCORCHES THE STARRY SKY!!
UNLEASH YOUR SOUL AND AWAKEN THE WORLD!!
OM
STARDUST ASSAULT WARRIOR ★★★★★★
When successfully Synchro Summoned, you can Special Summon one Tuner monster from the Graveyard. Inflicts piercing damage.
ATK 2100 DEF 1200
STARDUST ASSAULT WARRIOR
SYNCHRO SUMMONED!!

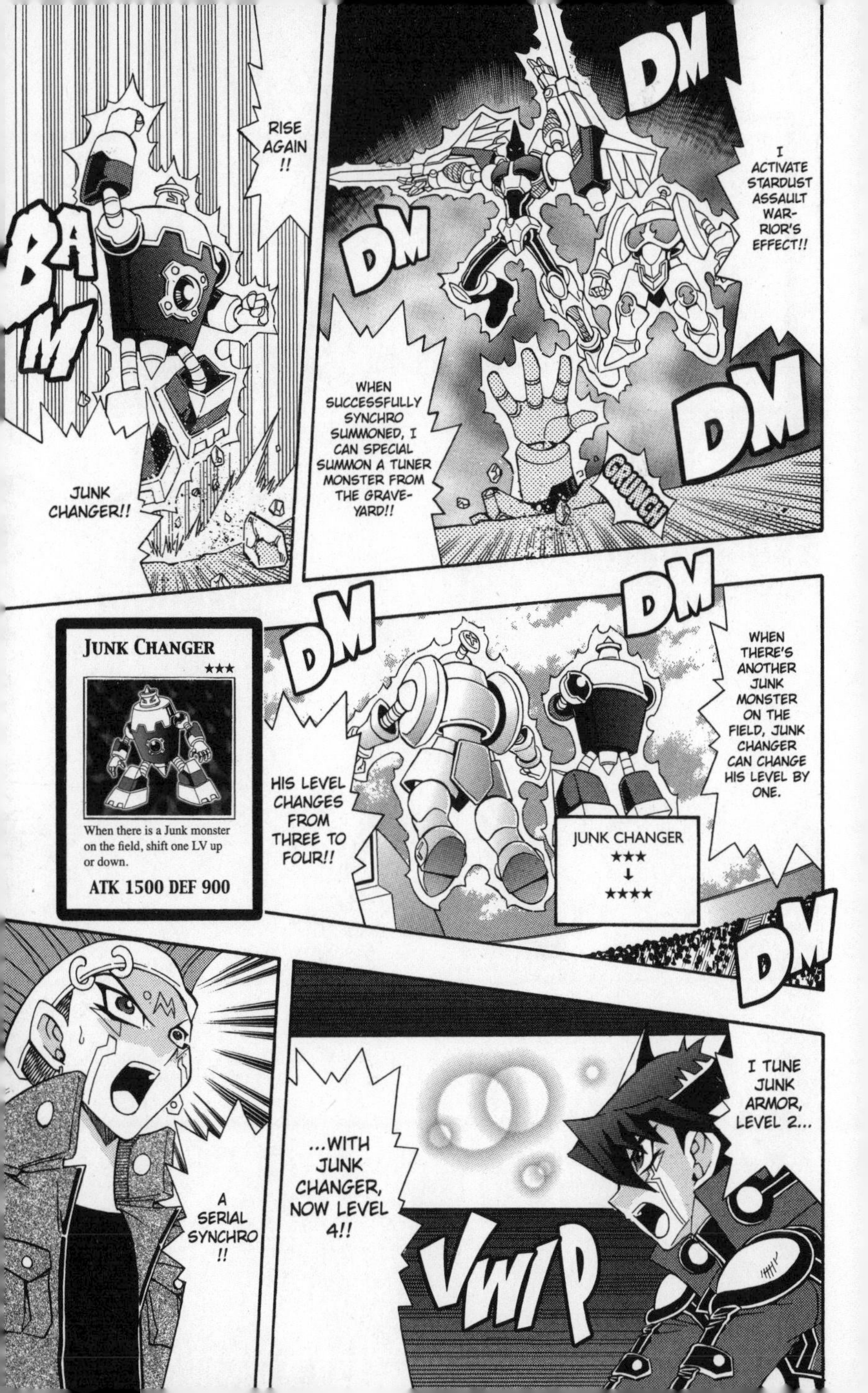
DM
I ACTIVATE STARDUST ASSAULT WAR-RIOR'S EFFECT!!
DM
DM
WHEN SUCCESSFULLY SYNCHRO SUMMONED, I CAN SPECIAL SUMMON A TUNER MONSTER FROM THE GRAVE-YARD!!
GRUNCH
RISE AGAIN!!
BAM
JUNK CHANGER!!
DM
DM
WHEN THERE'S ANOTHER JUNK MONSTER ON THE FIELD, JUNK CHANGER CAN CHANGE HIS LEVEL BY ONE.
HIS LEVEL CHANGES FROM THREE TO FOUR!!
JUNK CHANGER
★★★
↓
★★★★
DM
JUNK CHANGER
★★★
When there is a Junk monster on the field, shift one LV up or down.
ATK 1500 DEF 900
I TUNE JUNK ARMOR, LEVEL 2...
...WITH JUNK CHANGER, NOW LEVEL 4!!
VWIP
A SERIAL SYNCHRO!!

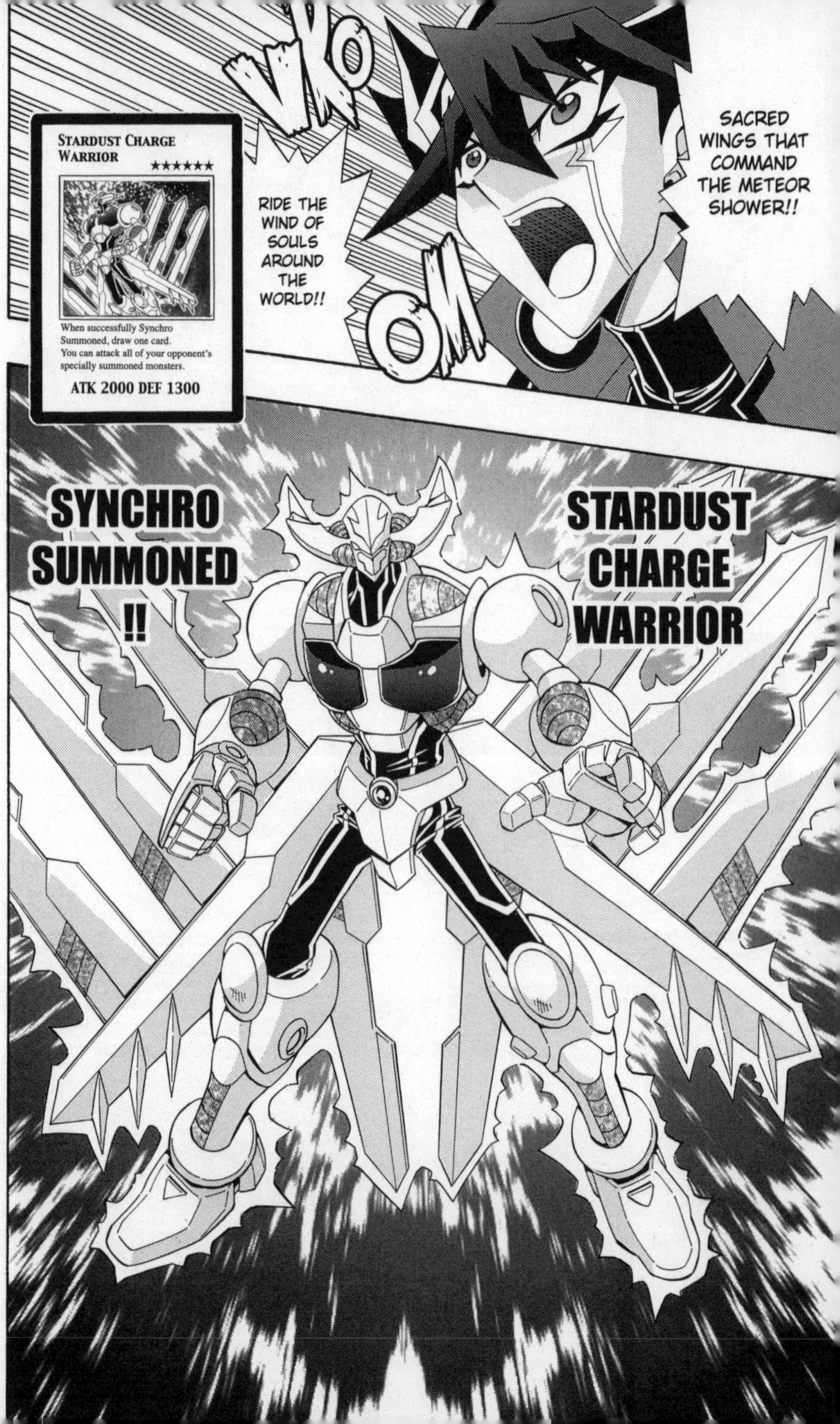
SACRED WINGS THAT COMMAND THE METEOR SHOWER!!
RIDE THE WIND OF SOULS AROUND THE WORLD!!
STARDUST CHARGE WARRIOR ★★★★★★
When successfully Synchro Summoned, draw one card. You can attack all of your opponent's specially summoned monsters.
ATK 2000 DEF 1300
STARDUST CHARGE WARRIOR
SYNCHRO SUMMONED!!

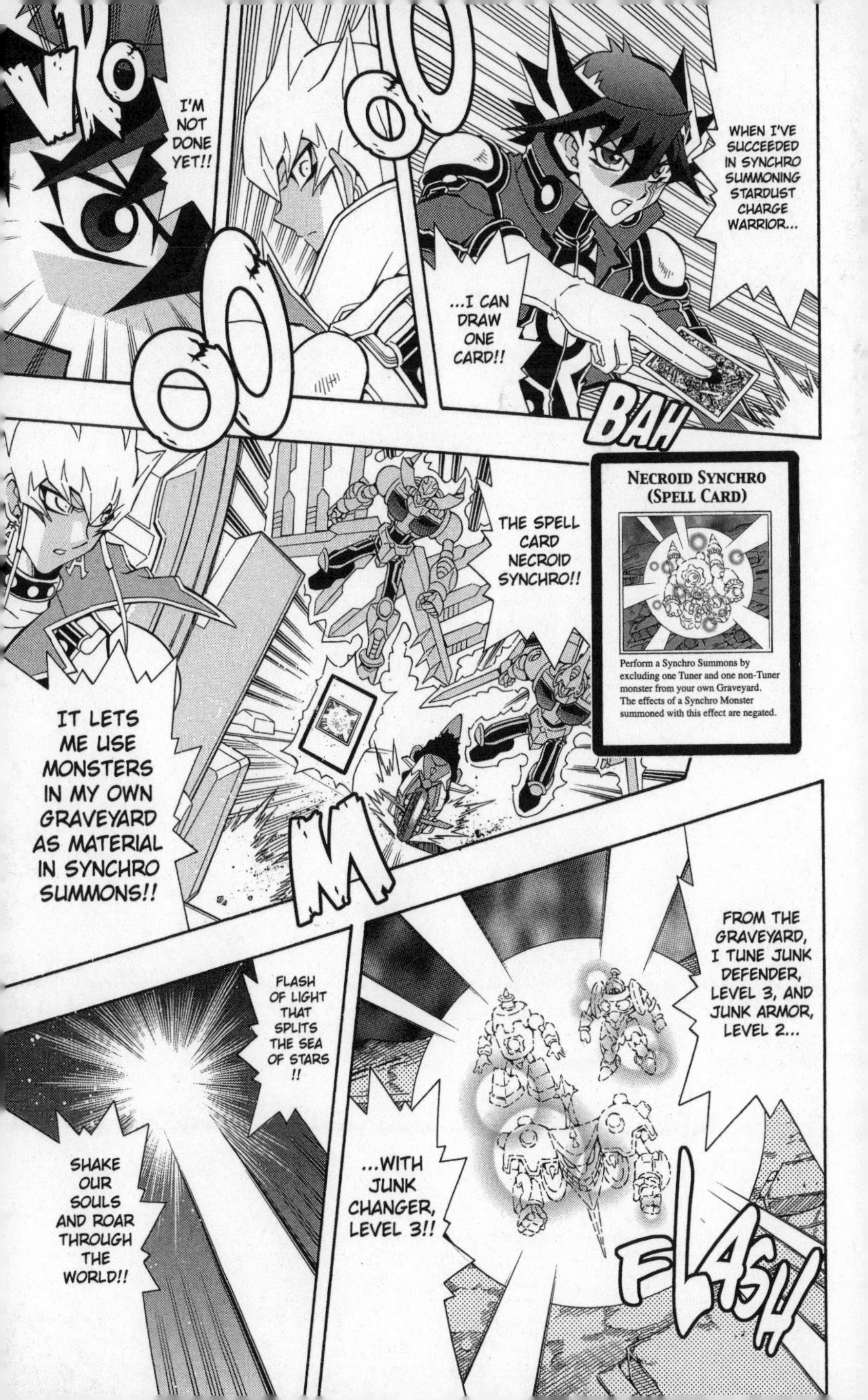

WHEN I'VE SUCCEEDED IN SYNCHRO SUMMONING STARDUST CHARGE WARRIOR...
...I CAN DRAW ONE CARD!!
BAH
I'M NOT DONE YET!!
NECROID SYNCHRO (SPELL CARD)
Perform a Synchro Summons by excluding one Tuner and one non-Tuner monster from your own Graveyard. The effects of a Synchro Monster summoned with this effect are negated.
THE SPELL CARD NECROID SYNCHRO!!
IT LETS ME USE MONSTERS IN MY OWN GRAVEYARD AS MATERIAL IN SYNCHRO SUMMONS!!
M
FROM THE GRAVEYARD, I TUNE JUNK DEFENDER, LEVEL 3, AND JUNK ARMOR, LEVEL 2...
...WITH JUNK CHANGER, LEVEL 3!!
FLASH
FLASH OF LIGHT THAT SPLITS THE SEA OF STARS!!
SHAKE OUR SOULS AND ROAR THROUGH THE WORLD!!

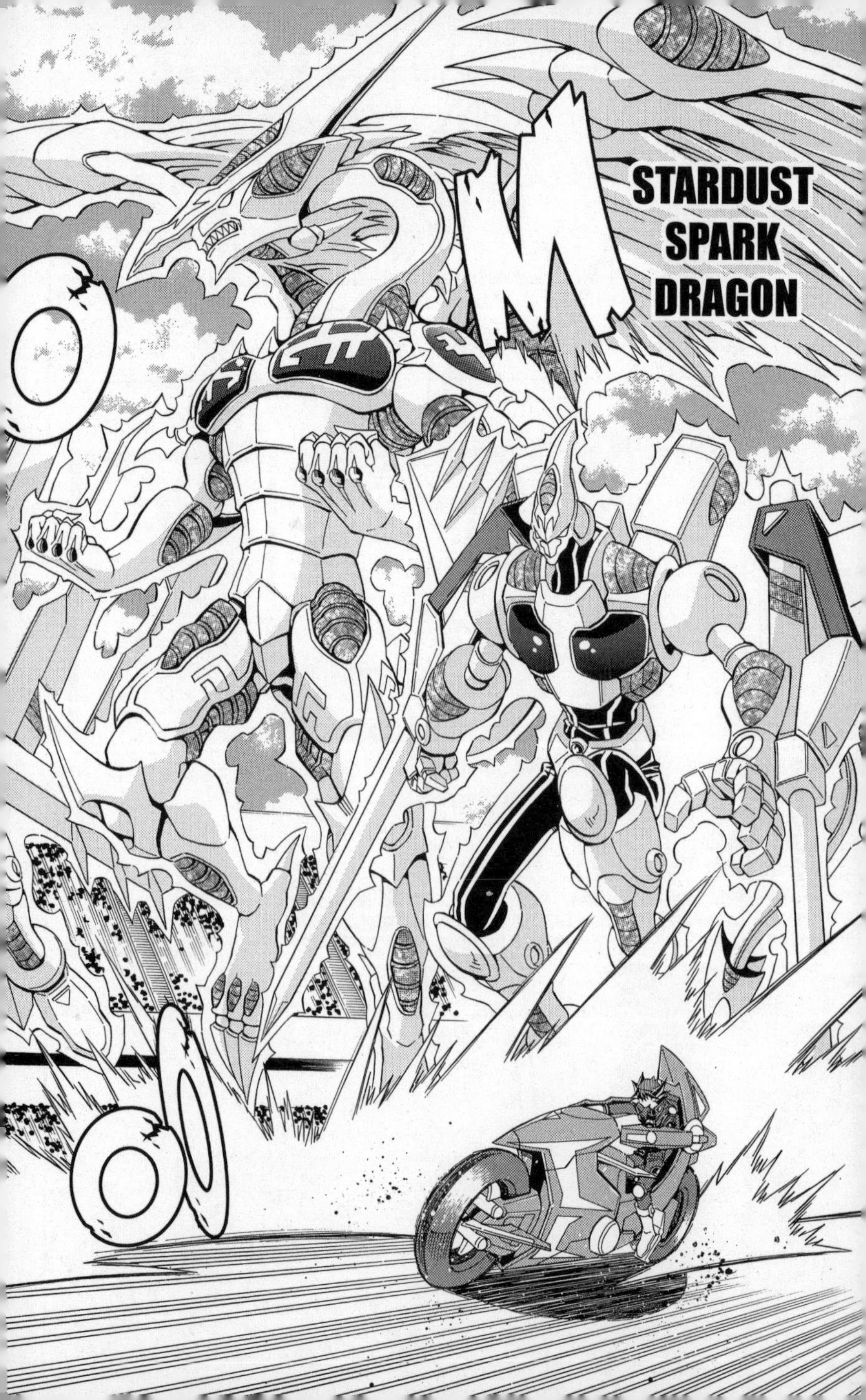
STARDUST SPARK DRAGON

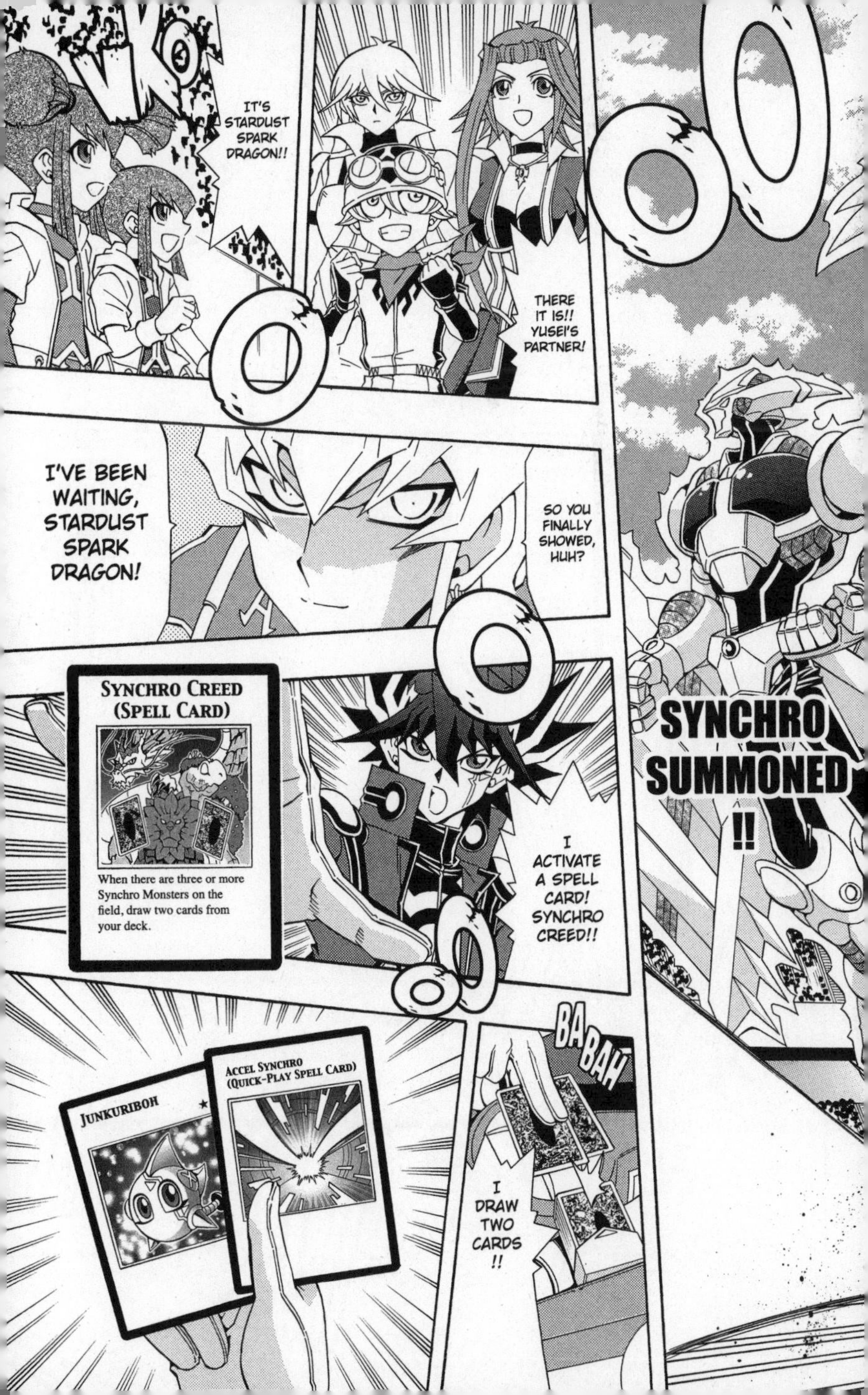
SYNCHRO SUMMONED!!
THERE IT IS!! YUSEI'S PARTNER!
IT'S STARDUST SPARK DRAGON!!
SO YOU FINALLY SHOWED, HUH?
I'VE BEEN WAITING, STARDUST SPARK DRAGON!
I ACTIVATE A SPELL CARD! SYNCHRO CREED!!
SYNCHRO CREED (SPELL CARD)
When there are three or more Synchro Monsters on the field, draw two cards from your deck.
BABAH
I DRAW TWO CARDS!!
ACCEL SYNCHRO (QUICK-PLAY SPELL CARD)
JUNKURIBOH

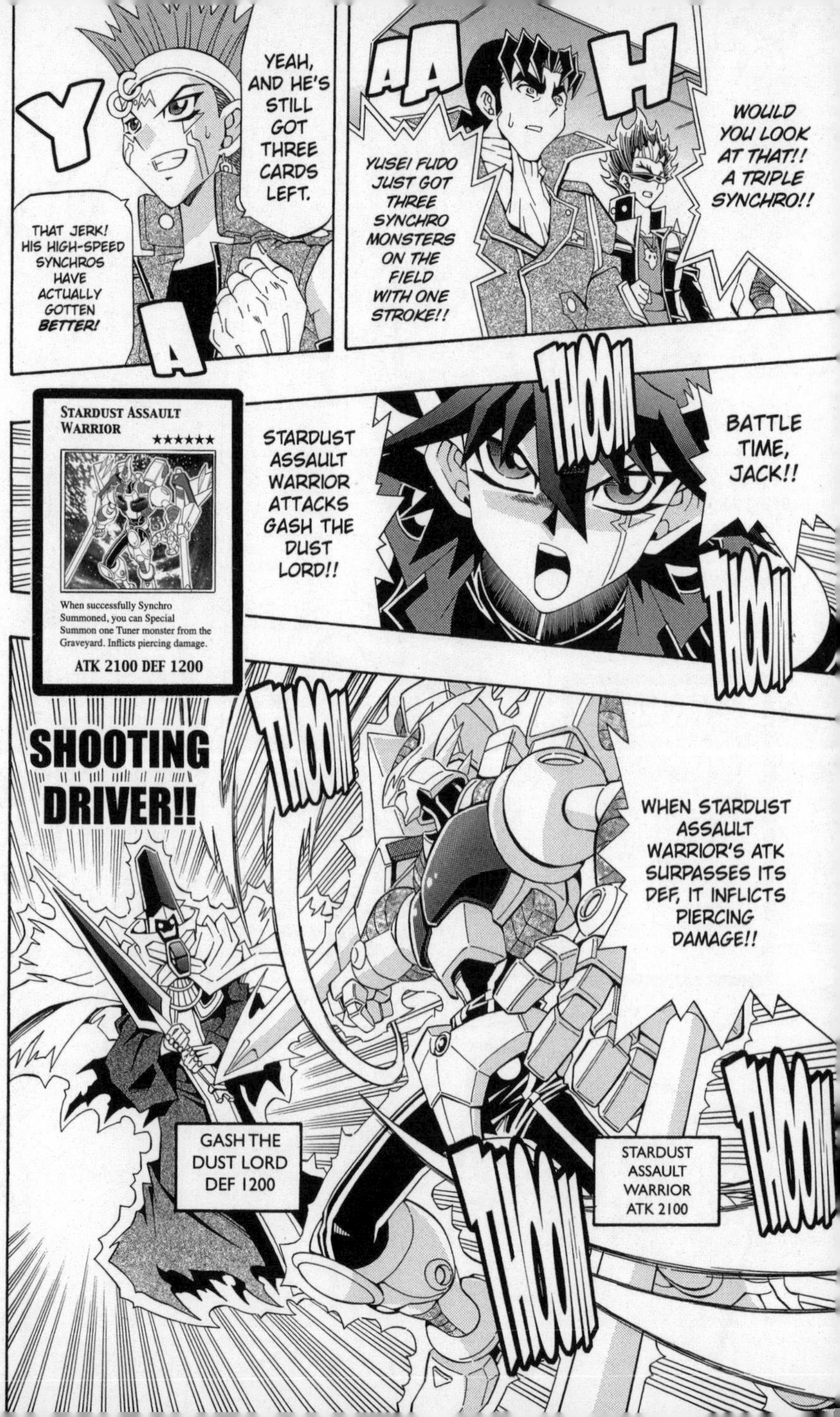
AA
H
WOULD YOU LOOK AT THAT!! A TRIPLE SYNCHRO!!
YUSEI FUDO JUST GOT THREE SYNCHRO MONSTERS ON THE FIELD WITH ONE STROKE!!
Y
YEAH, AND HE'S STILL GOT THREE CARDS LEFT.
THAT JERK! HIS HIGH-SPEED SYNCHROS HAVE ACTUALLY GOTTEN *BETTER!*
A
THOOM
BATTLE TIME, JACK!!
STARDUST ASSAULT WARRIOR ATTACKS GASH THE DUST LORD!!
THOOM
STARDUST ASSAULT WARRIOR
★★★★★★
When successfully Synchro Summoned, you can Special Summon one Tuner monster from the Graveyard. Inflicts piercing damage.
ATK 2100 DEF 1200
THOOM
WHEN STARDUST ASSAULT WARRIOR'S ATK SURPASSES ITS DEF, IT INFLICTS PIERCING DAMAGE!!
SHOOTING DRIVER!!
THOOM
STARDUST ASSAULT WARRIOR ATK 2100
THOOM
GASH THE DUST LORD DEF 1200

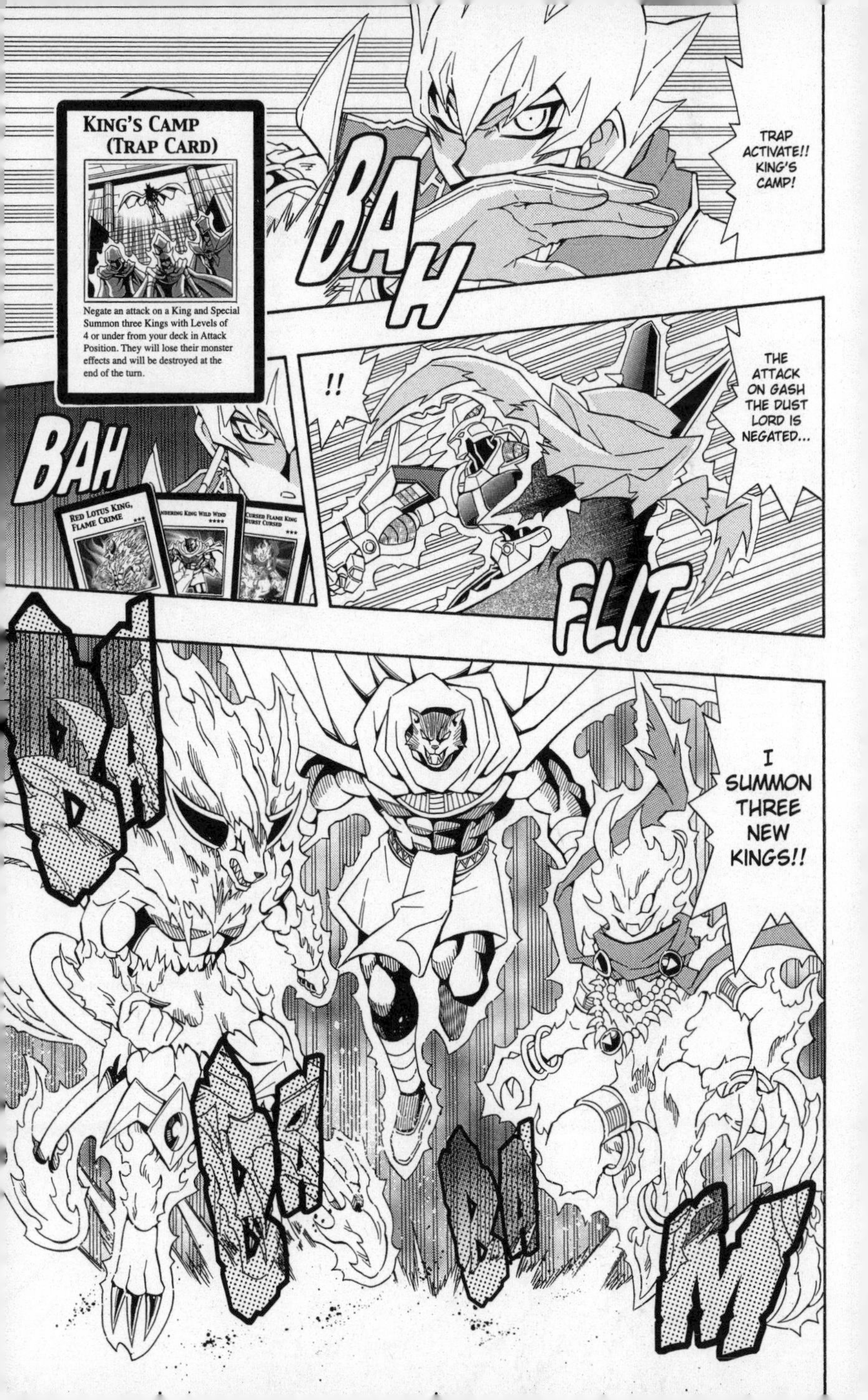
TRAP ACTIVATE!! KING'S CAMP!
BAH
KING'S CAMP
(TRAP CARD)
Negate an attack on a King and Special Summon three Kings with Levels of 4 or under from your deck in Attack Position. They will lose their monster effects and will be destroyed at the end of the turn.
THE ATTACK ON GASH THE DUST LORD IS NEGATED...
!!
FLIT
BAH
RED LOTUS KING, FLAME CRIME
NDERING KING WILD WIND
CURSED FLAME KING BURST CURSED
I SUMMON THREE NEW KINGS!!

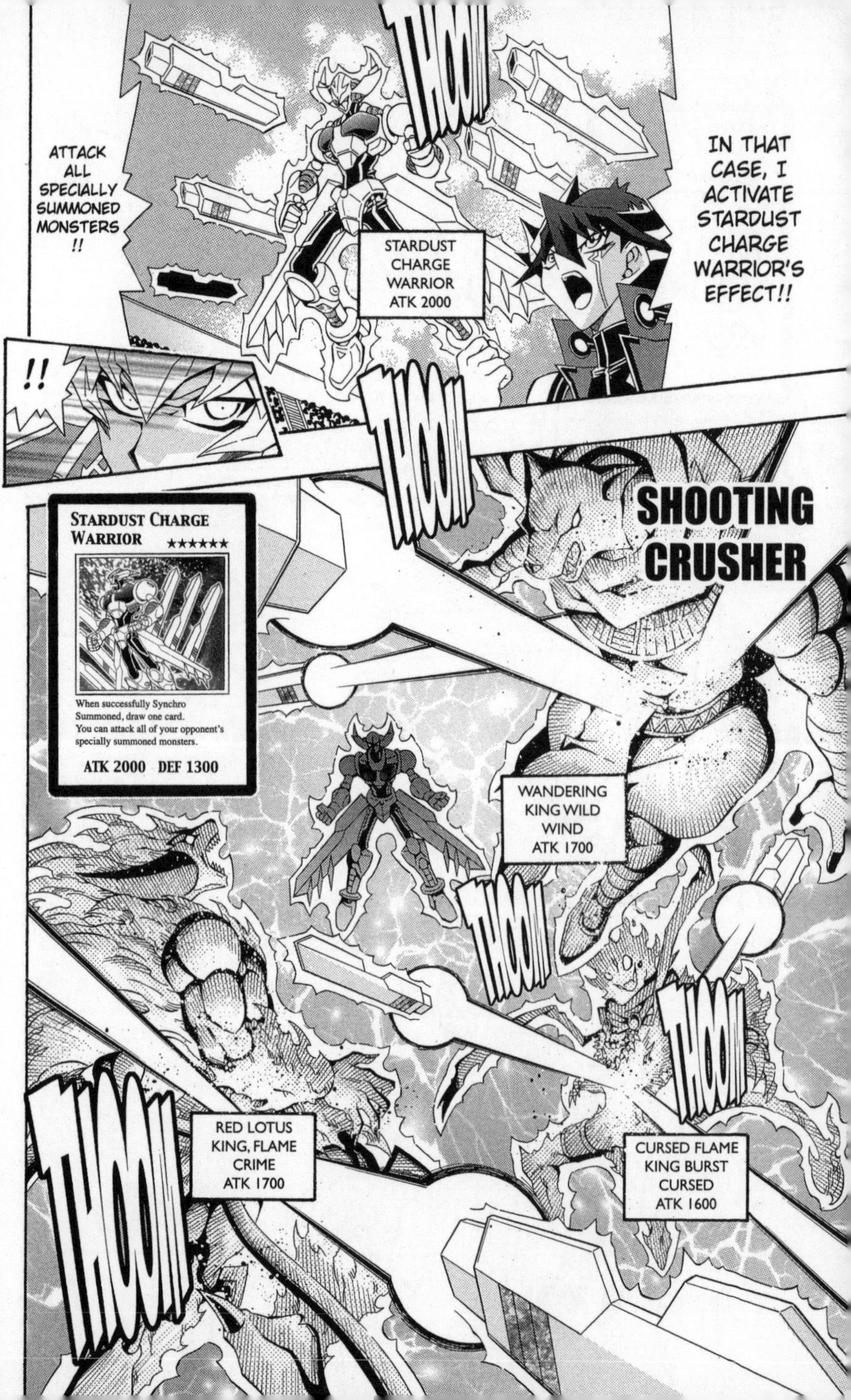
THOOM
IN THAT CASE, I ACTIVATE STARDUST CHARGE WARRIOR'S EFFECT!!
STARDUST CHARGE WARRIOR ATK 2000
ATTACK ALL SPECIALLY SUMMONED MONSTERS!!
!!
THOOM
SHOOTING CRUSHER
STARDUST CHARGE WARRIOR ★★★★★★
When successfully Synchro Summoned, draw one card. You can attack all of your opponent's specially summoned monsters.
ATK 2000 DEF 1300
WANDERING KING WILD WIND ATK 1700
THOOM
THOOM
CURSED FLAME KING BURST CURSED ATK 1600
THOOM
RED LOTUS KING, FLAME CRIME ATK 1700

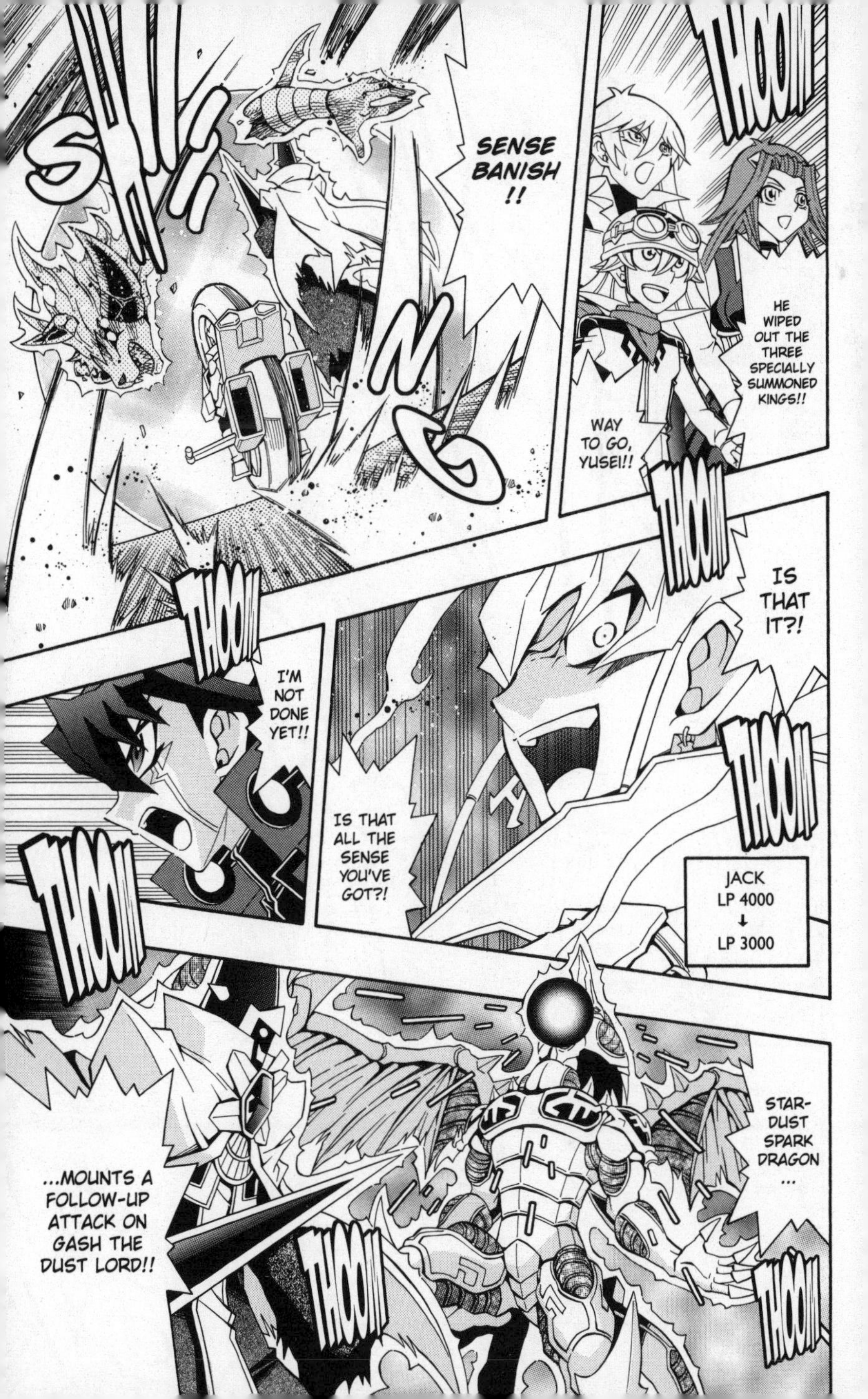
THOOM
HE WIPED OUT THE THREE SPECIALLY SUMMONED KINGS!!
WAY TO GO, YUSEI!!
THOOM
SENSE BANISH!!
SHING
THOOM
IS THAT IT?!
THOOM
IS THAT ALL THE SENSE YOU'VE GOT?!
JACK
LP 4000
↓
LP 3000
I'M NOT DONE YET!!
THOOM
THOOM
STARDUST SPARK DRAGON...
...MOUNTS A FOLLOW-UP ATTACK ON GASH THE DUST LORD!!
THOOM
THOOM

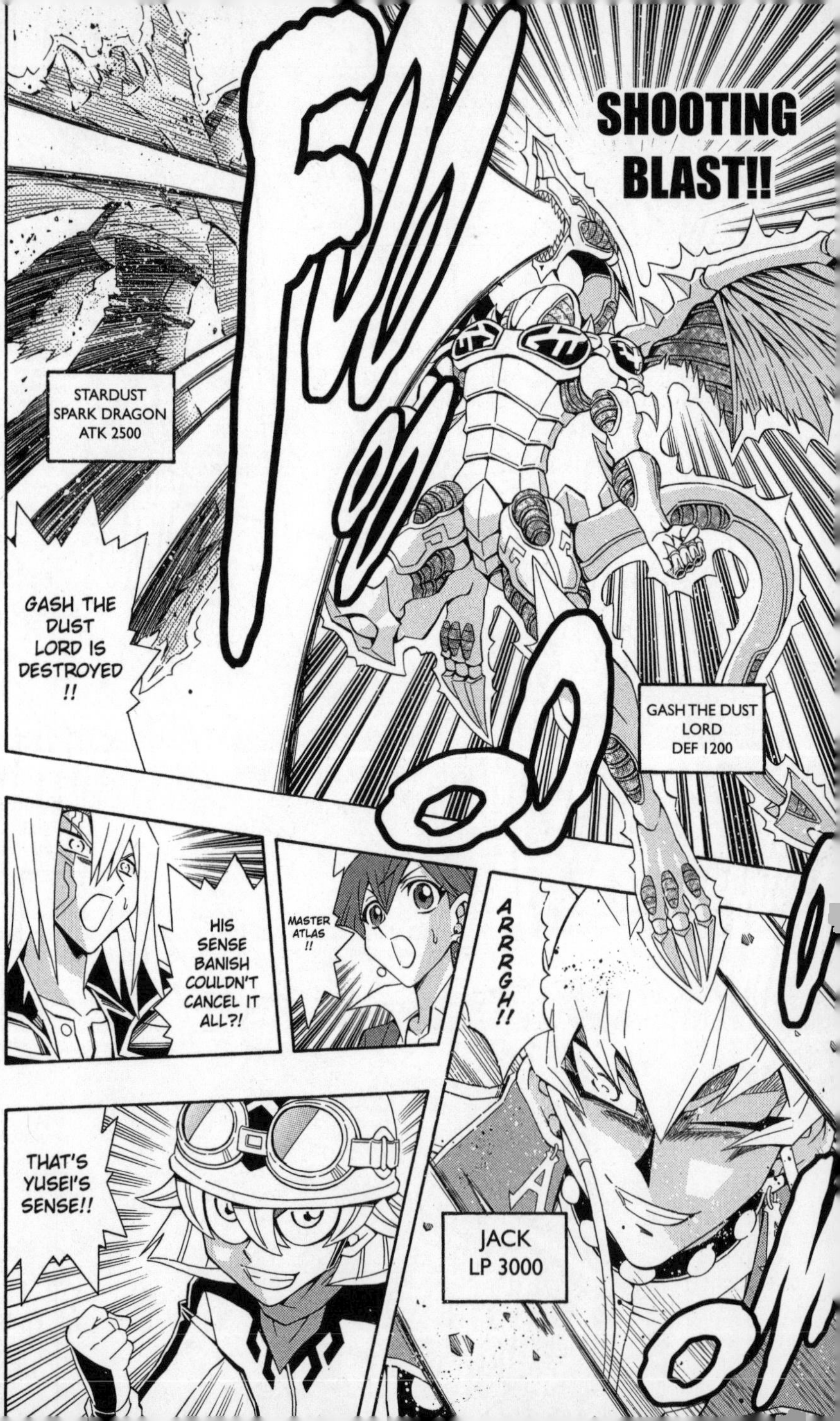
SHOOTING BLAST!!
GASH THE DUST LORD DEF 1200
STARDUST SPARK DRAGON ATK 2500
GASH THE DUST LORD IS DESTROYED!!
ARRRGH!!
MASTER ATLAS!!
HIS SENSE BANISH COULDN'T CANCEL IT ALL?!
JACK LP 3000
THAT'S YUSEI'S SENSE!!

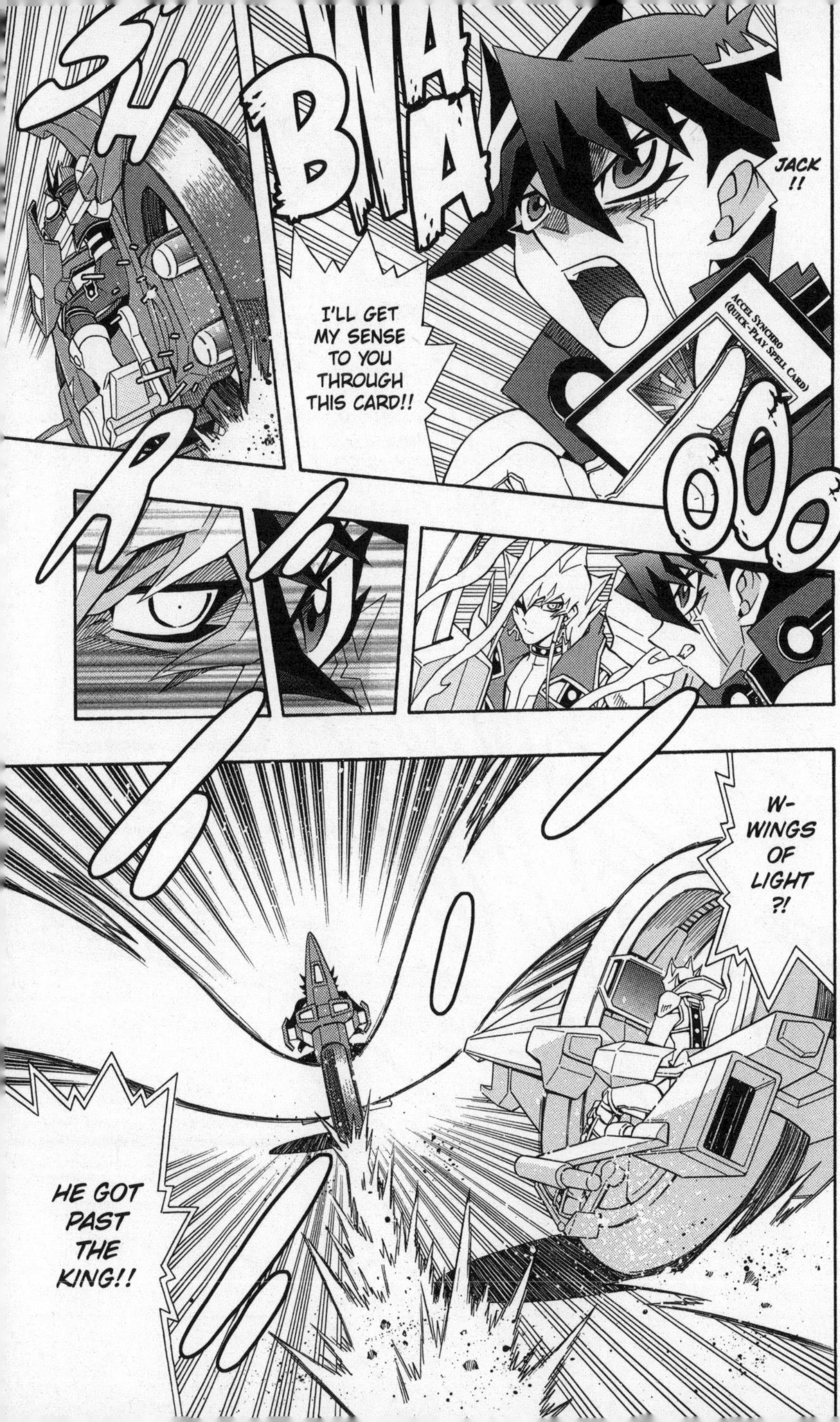
JACK !!
ACCEL SYNCHRO (QUICK-PLAY SPELL CARD)
I'LL GET MY SENSE TO YOU THROUGH THIS CARD!!
SH
W- WINGS OF LIGHT ?!
HE GOT PAST THE KING!!

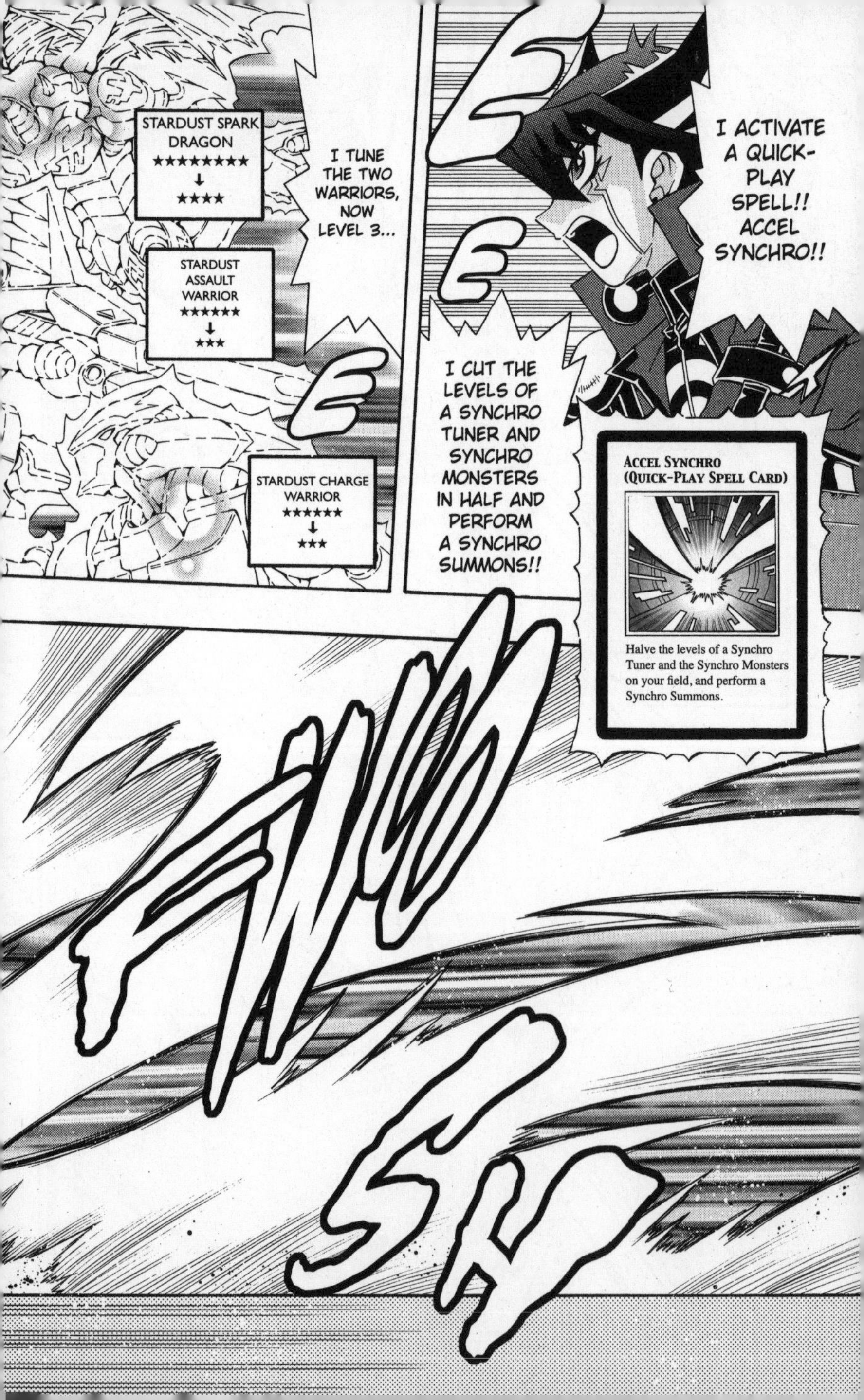
I ACTIVATE A QUICK-PLAY SPELL!! ACCEL SYNCHRO!!
I CUT THE LEVELS OF A SYNCHRO TUNER AND SYNCHRO MONSTERS IN HALF AND PERFORM A SYNCHRO SUMMONS!!
ACCEL SYNCHRO (QUICK-PLAY SPELL CARD)
Halve the levels of a Synchro Tuner and the Synchro Monsters on your field, and perform a Synchro Summons.
I TUNE THE TWO WARRIORS, NOW LEVEL 3...
STARDUST SPARK DRAGON ★★★★★★★★ ↓ ★★★★
STARDUST ASSAULT WARRIOR ★★★★★★ ↓ ★★★
STARDUST CHARGE WARRIOR ★★★★★★ ↓ ★★★

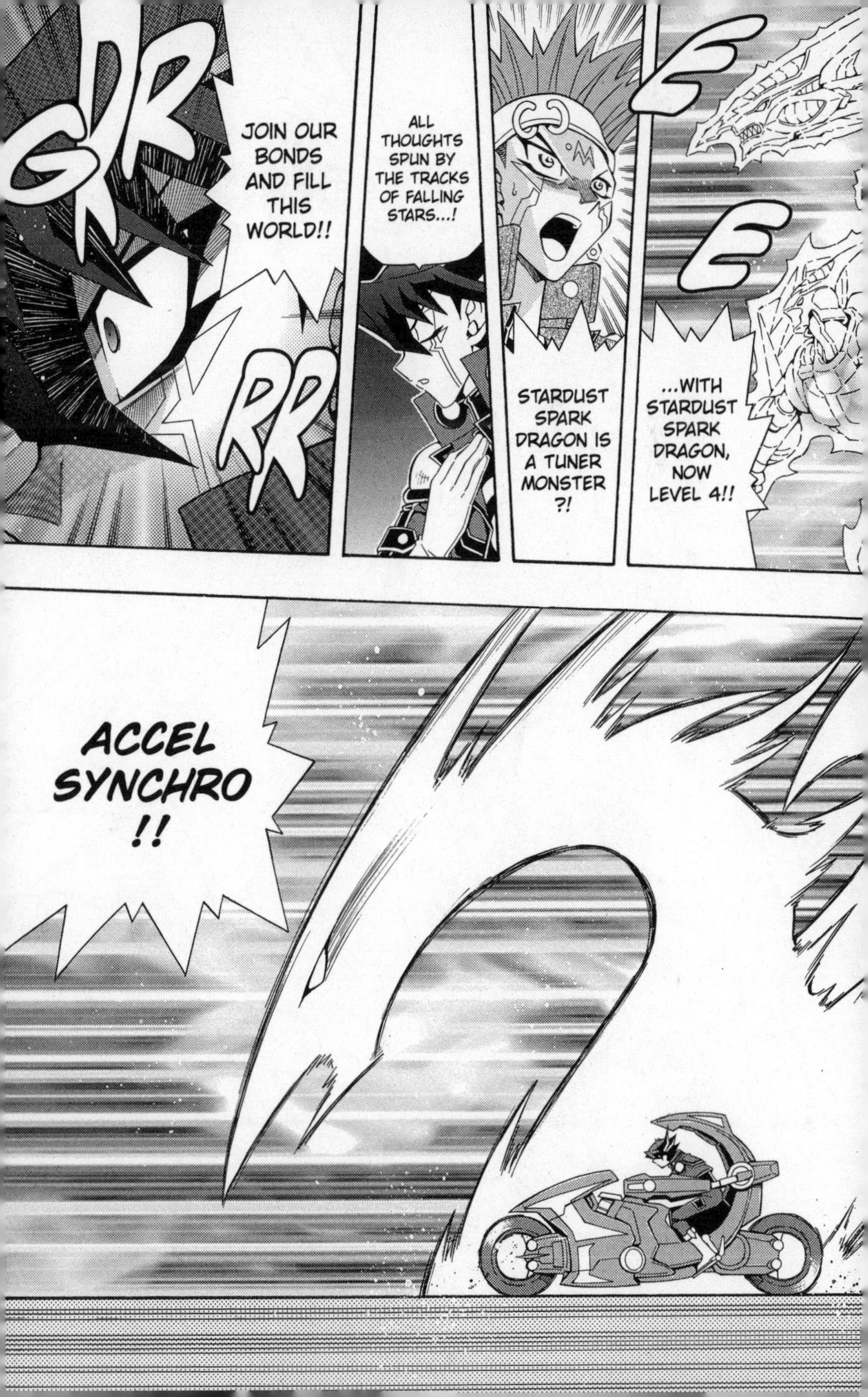

F
E
...WITH STARDUST SPARK DRAGON, NOW LEVEL 4!!
STARDUST SPARK DRAGON IS A TUNER MONSTER ?!
ALL THOUGHTS SPUN BY THE TRACKS OF FALLING STARS...!
GRR
JOIN OUR BONDS AND FILL THIS WORLD!!
RR
ACCEL SYNCHRO !!

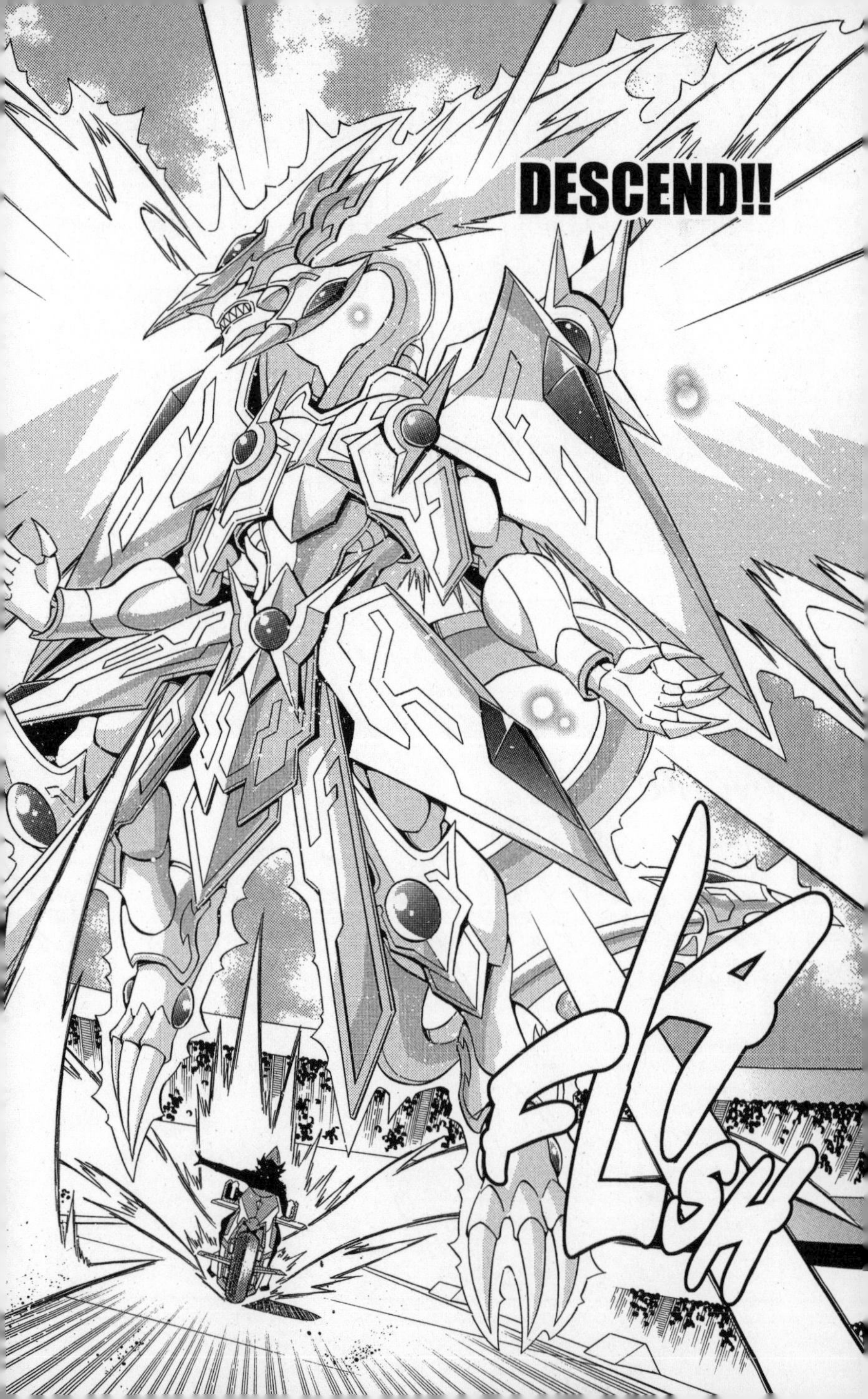
DESCEND!!
FLASH

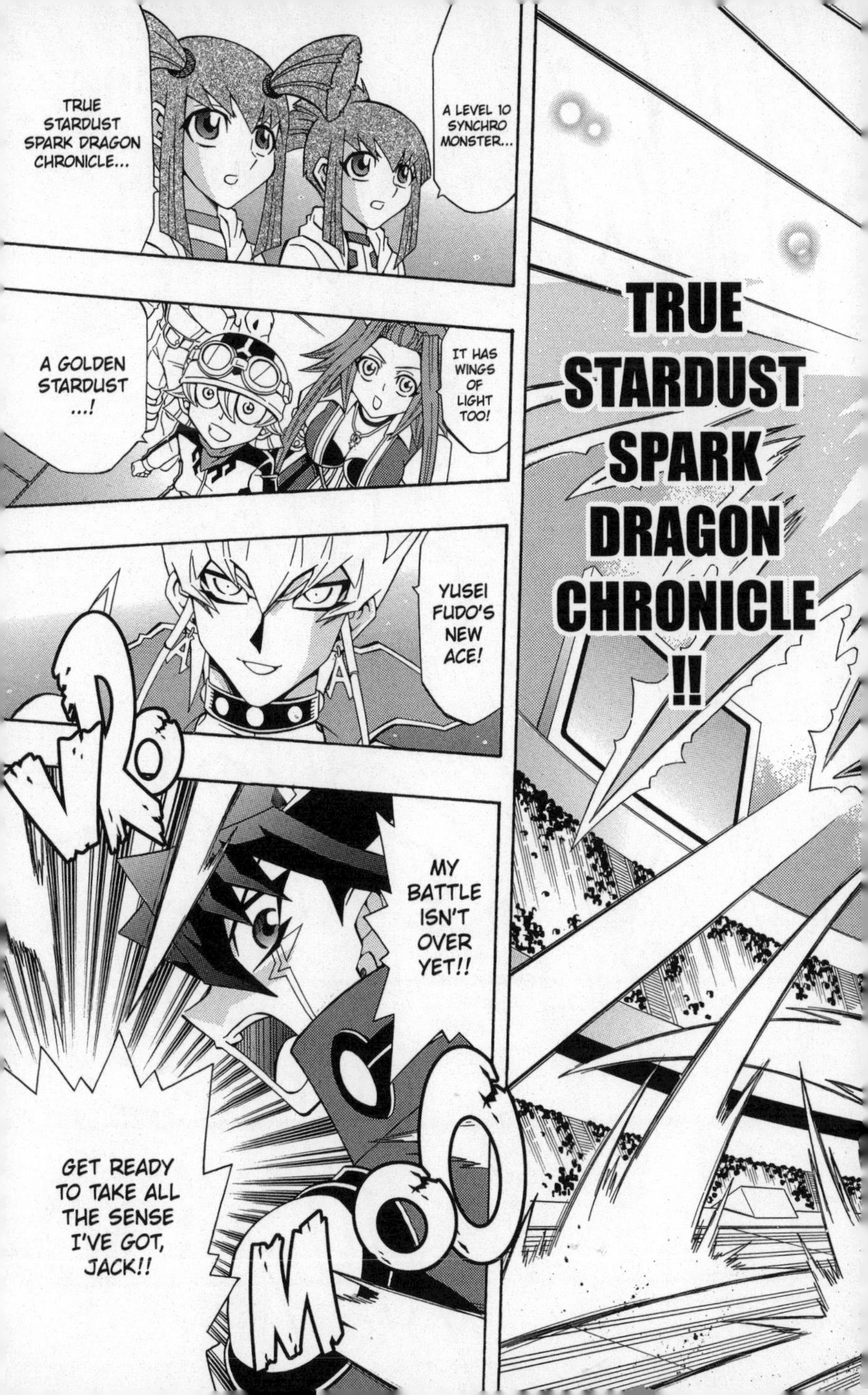
TRUE STARDUST SPARK DRAGON CHRONICLE!!
A LEVEL 10 SYNCHRO MONSTER...
TRUE STARDUST SPARK DRAGON CHRONICLE...
IT HAS WINGS OF LIGHT TOO!
A GOLDEN STARDUST ...!
YUSEI FUDO'S NEW ACE!
MY BATTLE ISN'T OVER YET!!
GET READY TO TAKE ALL THE SENSE I'VE GOT, JACK!!

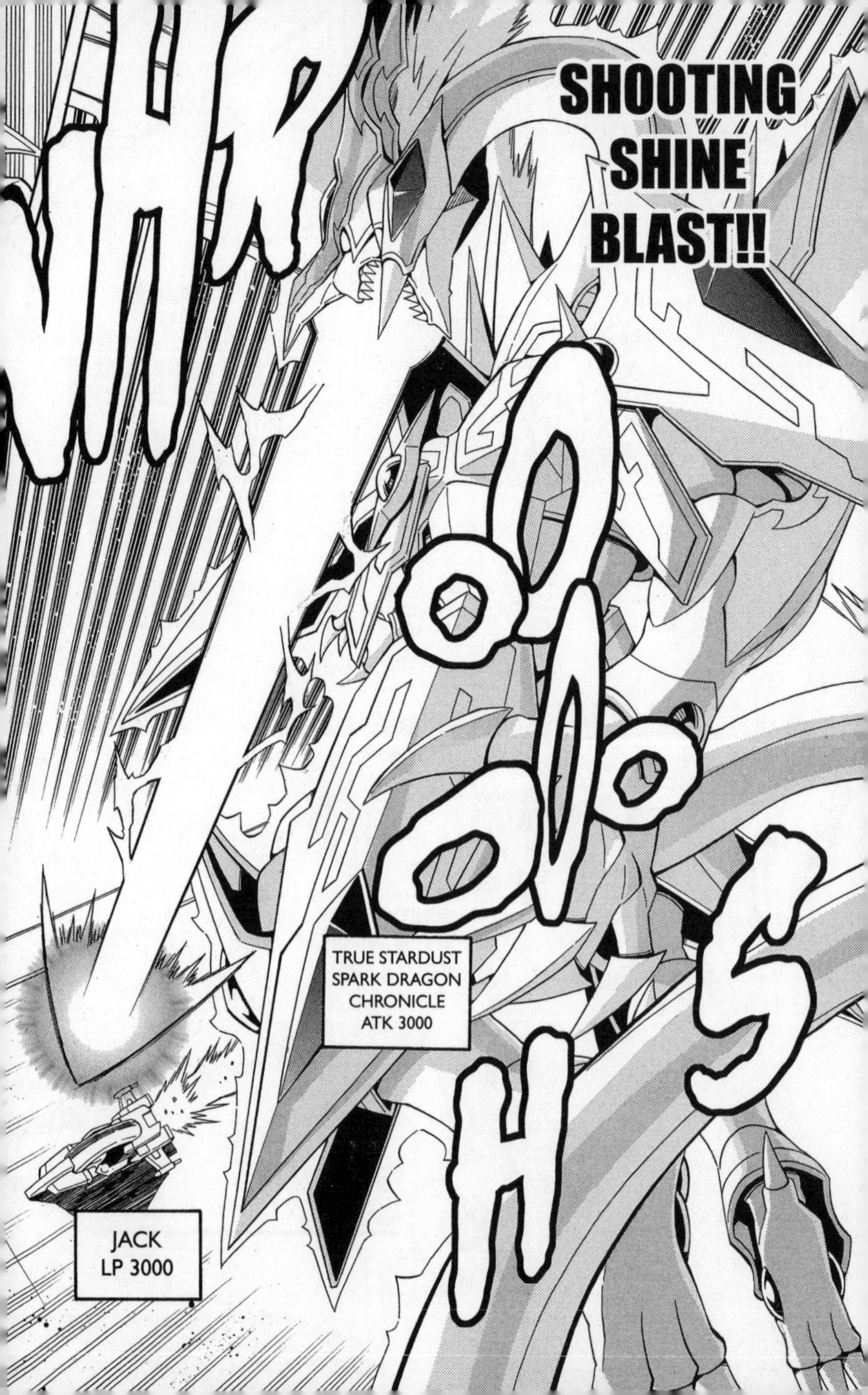
SHOOTING SHINE BLAST!!
TRUE STARDUST SPARK DRAGON CHRONICLE ATK 3000
JACK LP 3000

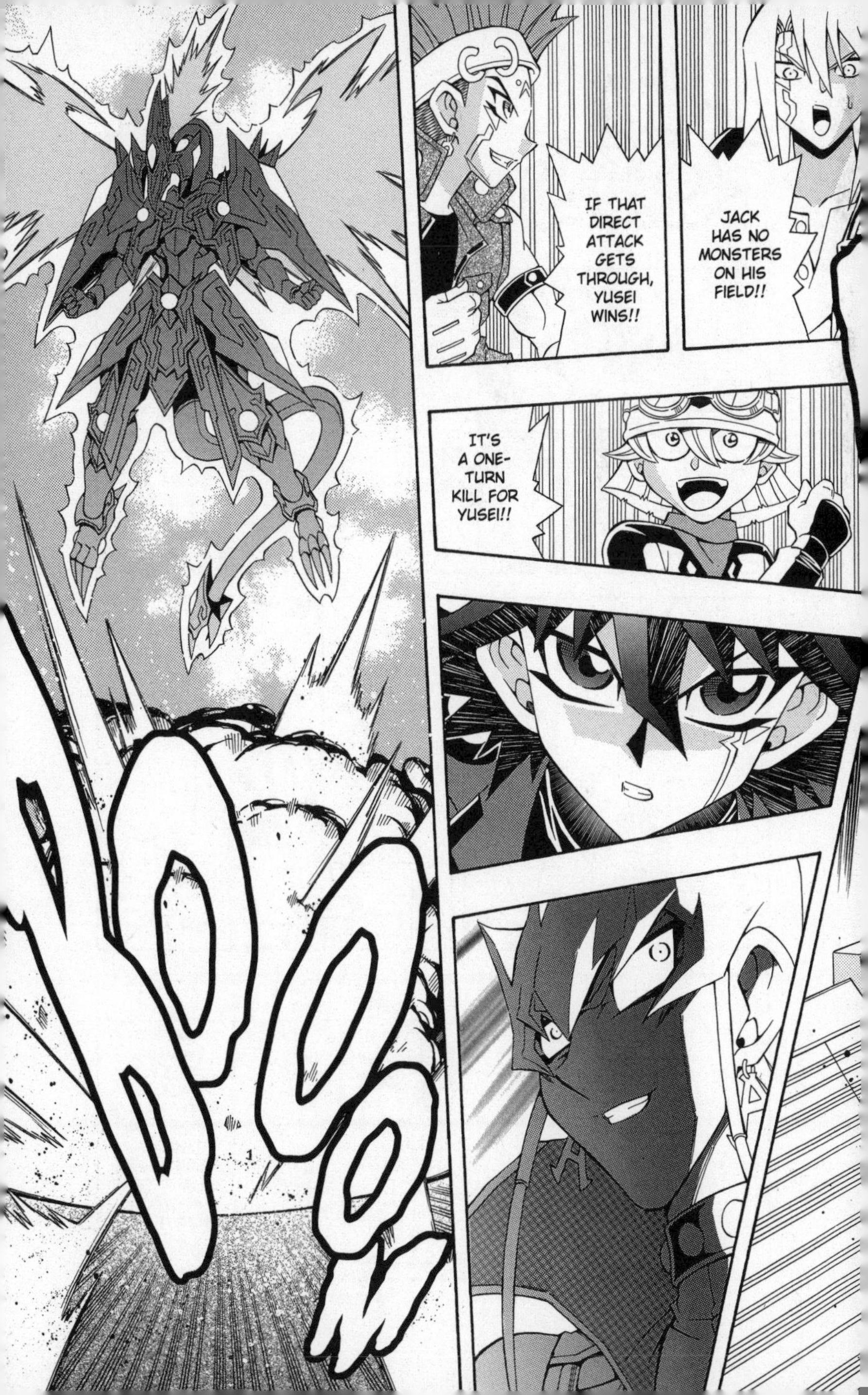
JACK HAS NO MONSTERS ON HIS FIELD!!
IF THAT DIRECT ATTACK GETS THROUGH, YUSEI WINS!!
IT'S A ONE-TURN KILL FOR YUSEI!!
BOOOM

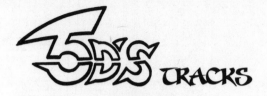

5D's TRACKS

THE 64TH

BY SATOMASA

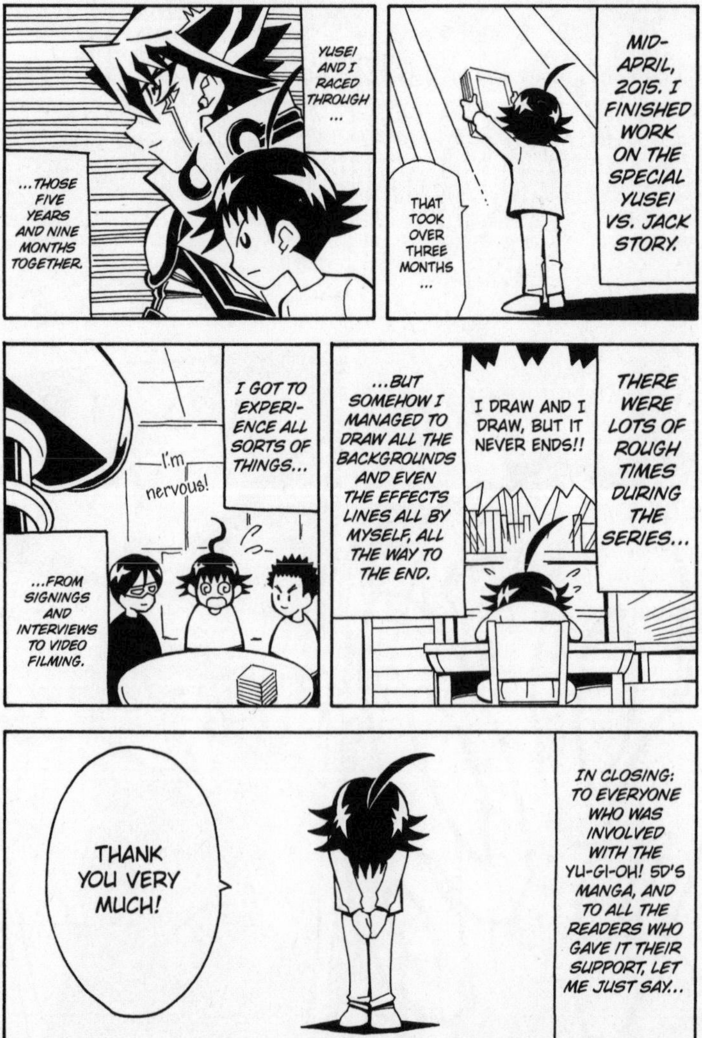
MID-APRIL, 2015. I FINISHED WORK ON THE SPECIAL YUSEI VS. JACK STORY.
THAT TOOK OVER THREE MONTHS...
YUSEI AND I RACED THROUGH...
...THOSE FIVE YEARS AND NINE MONTHS TOGETHER.
THERE WERE LOTS OF ROUGH TIMES DURING THE SERIES...
I DRAW AND I DRAW, BUT IT NEVER ENDS!!
...BUT SOMEHOW I MANAGED TO DRAW ALL THE BACKGROUNDS AND EVEN THE EFFECTS LINES ALL BY MYSELF, ALL THE WAY TO THE END.
I GOT TO EXPERIENCE ALL SORTS OF THINGS...
I'm nervous!
...FROM SIGNINGS AND INTERVIEWS TO VIDEO FILMING.
IN CLOSING: TO EVERYONE WHO WAS INVOLVED WITH THE YU-GI-OH! 5D'S MANGA, AND TO ALL THE READERS WHO GAVE IT THEIR SUPPORT, LET ME JUST SAY...
THANK YOU VERY MUCH!

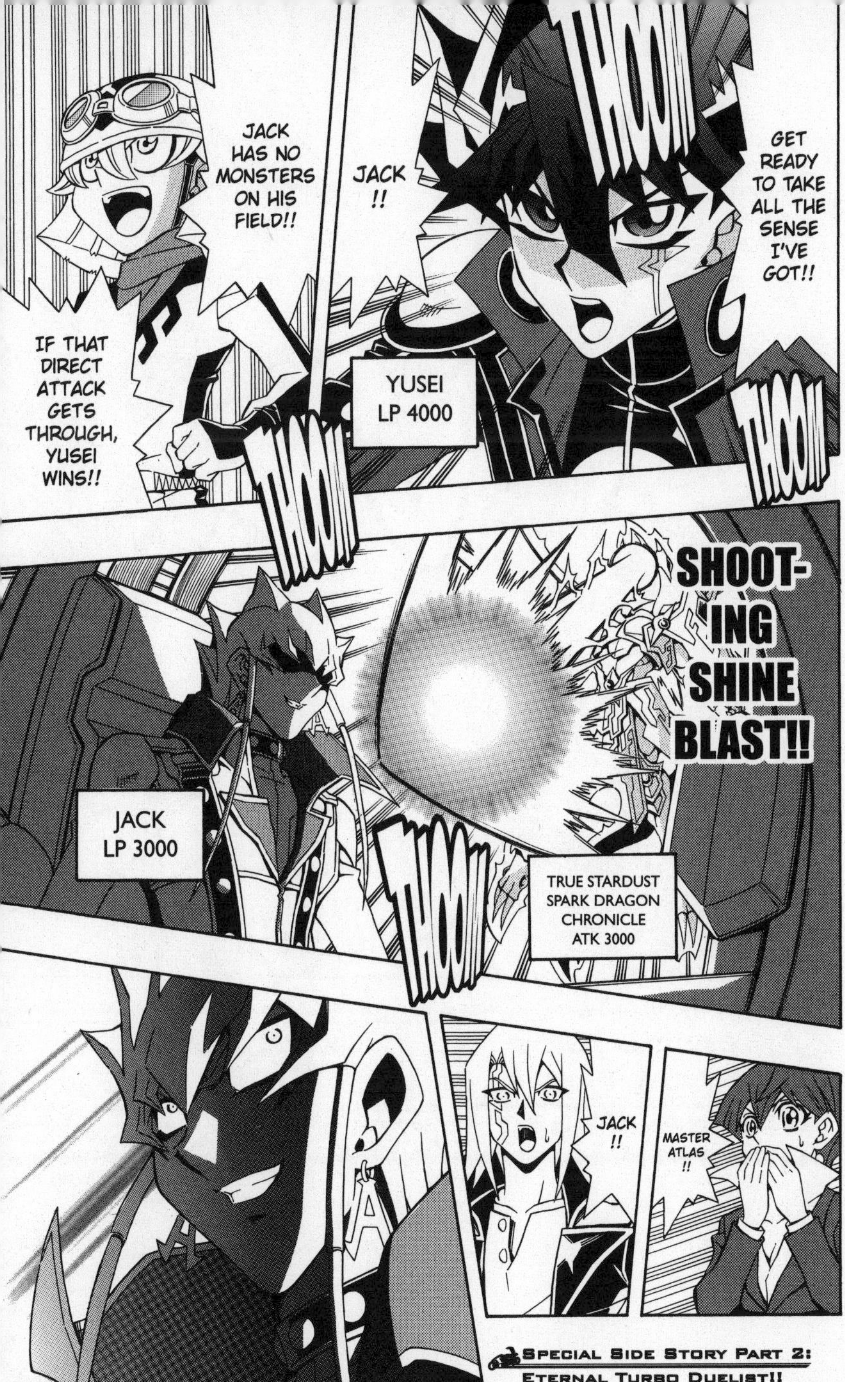
GET READY TO TAKE ALL THE SENSE I'VE GOT!!
THOOM
JACK !!
YUSEI LP 4000
THOOM
JACK HAS NO MONSTERS ON HIS FIELD!!
IF THAT DIRECT ATTACK GETS THROUGH, YUSEI WINS!!
THOOM
SHOOT-ING SHINE BLAST!!
TRUE STARDUST SPARK DRAGON CHRONICLE ATK 3000
THOOM
JACK LP 3000
MASTER ATLAS !!
JACK !!

Special Side Story Part 2: Eternal Turbo Duelist!!

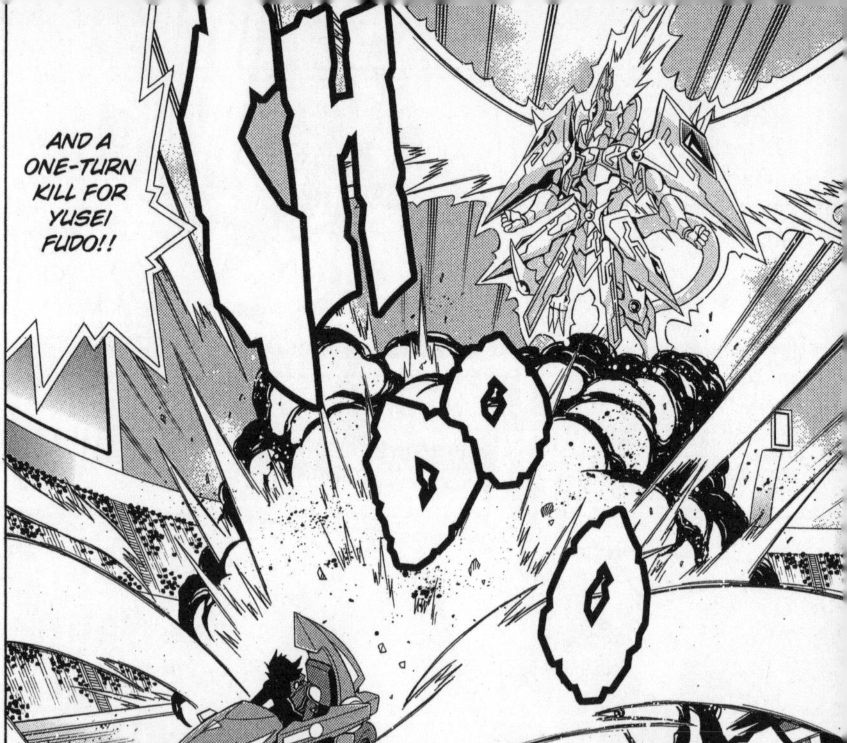
AND A ONE-TURN KILL FOR YUSEI FUDO!!

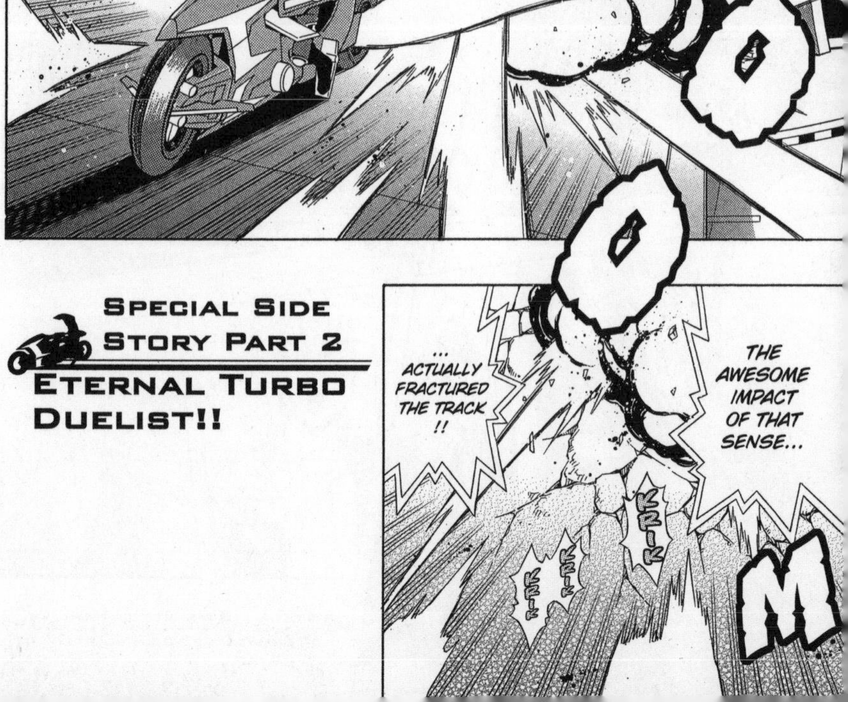
THE AWESOME IMPACT OF THAT SENSE...
...ACTUALLY FRACTURED THE TRACK!!

SPECIAL SIDE STORY PART 2
ETERNAL TURBO DUELIST!!

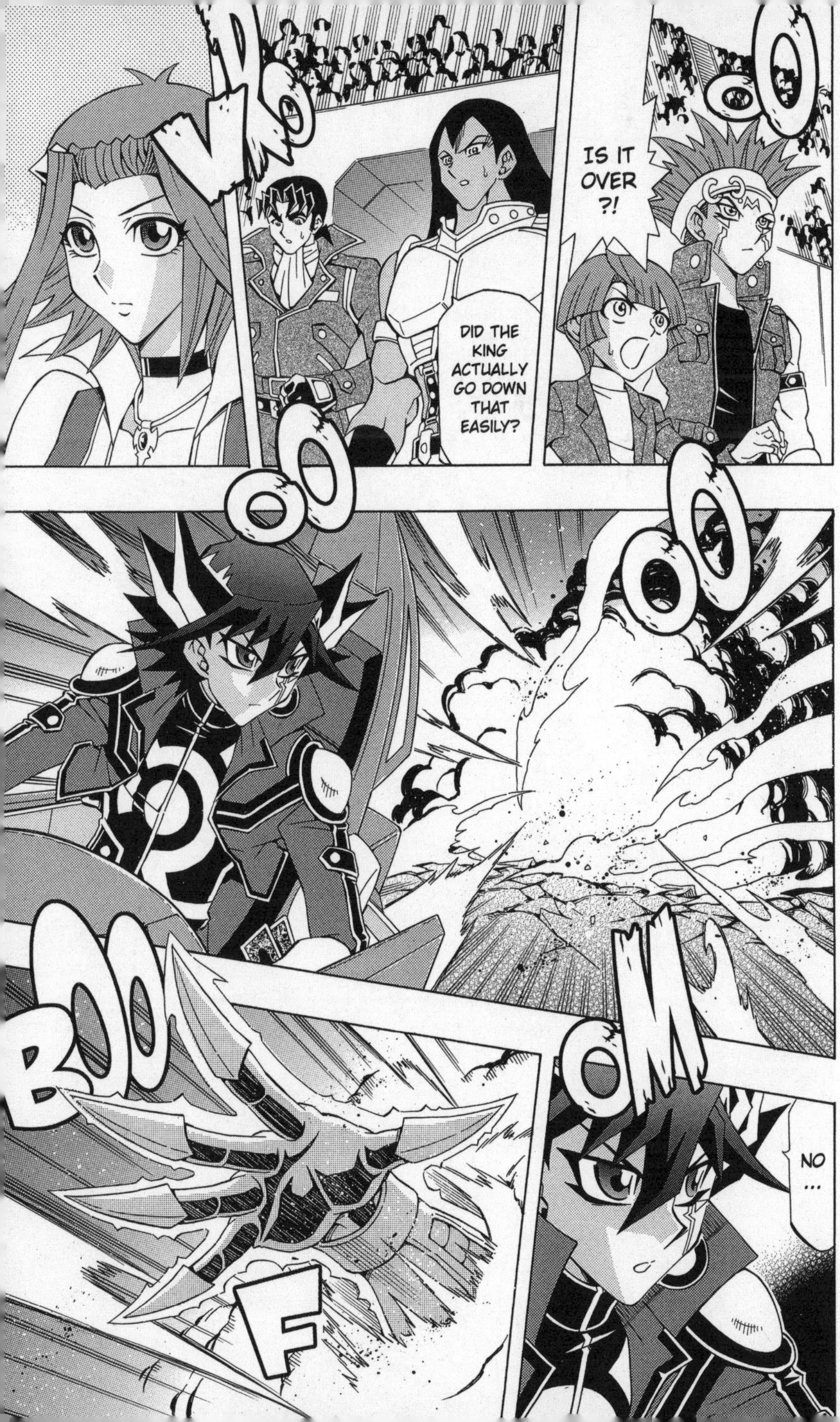
IS IT OVER ?!
DID THE KING ACTUALLY GO DOWN THAT EASILY?
NO ...

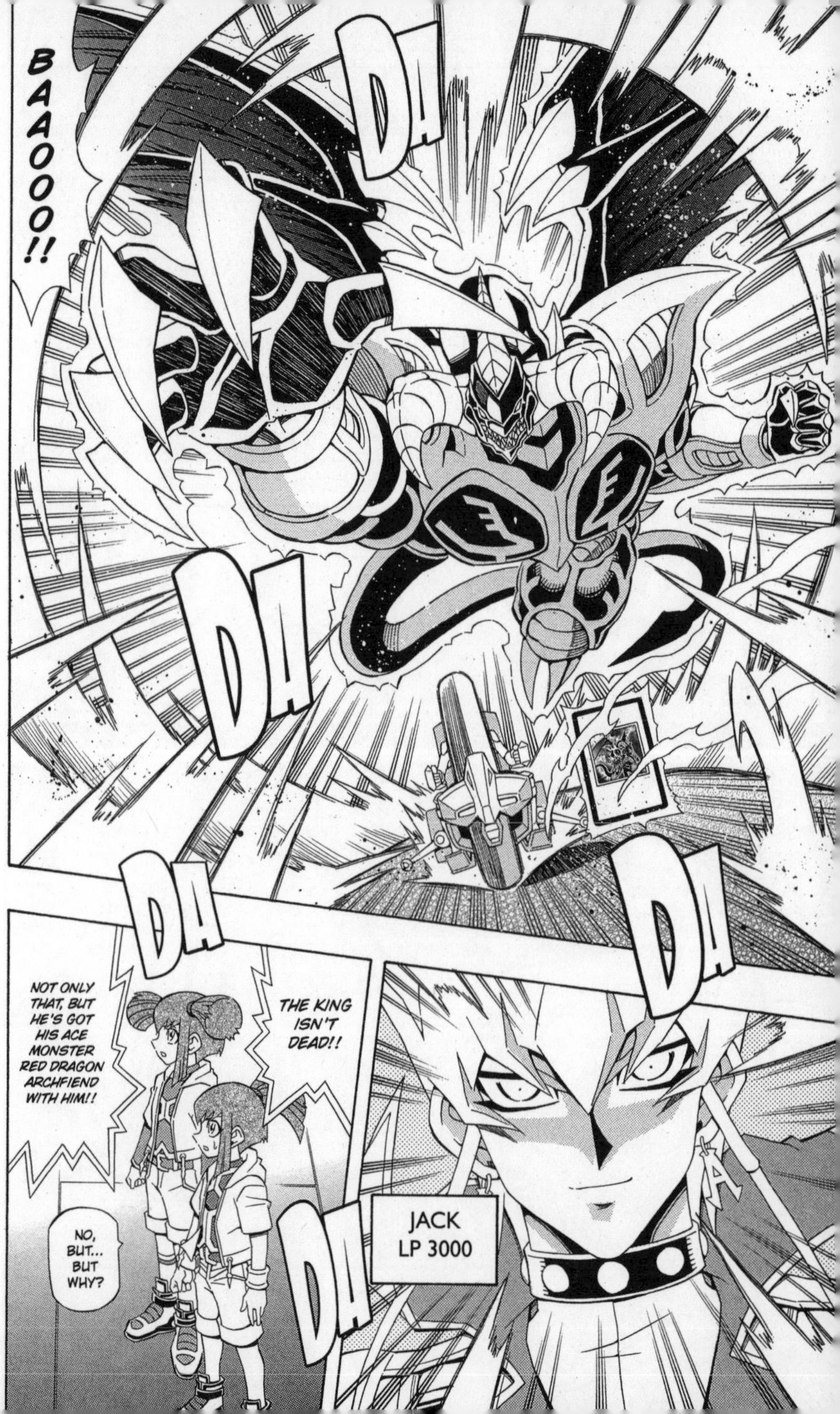
DA
BAAOOOO!!
DA
DA
JACK
LP 3000
DA
DA
THE KING ISN'T DEAD!!
NOT ONLY THAT, BUT HE'S GOT HIS ACE MONSTER RED DRAGON ARCHFIEND WITH HIM!!
NO, BUT... BUT WHY?

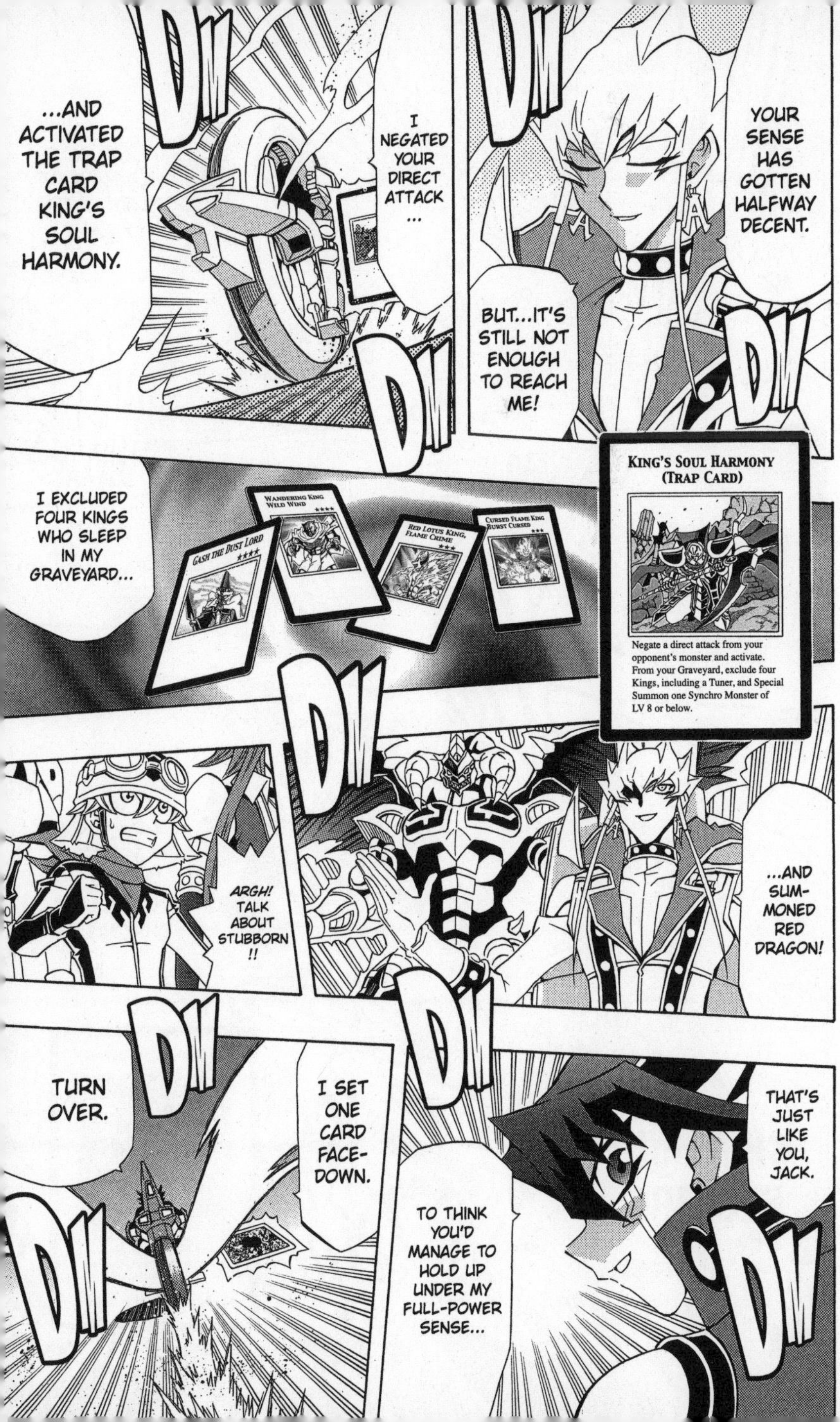
DM
YOUR SENSE HAS GOTTEN HALFWAY DECENT.
BUT...IT'S STILL NOT ENOUGH TO REACH ME!
DM
DM
I NEGATED YOUR DIRECT ATTACK...
...AND ACTIVATED THE TRAP CARD KING'S SOUL HARMONY.
DM
KING'S SOUL HARMONY (TRAP CARD)
Negate a direct attack from your opponent's monster and activate. From your Graveyard, exclude four Kings, including a Tuner, and Special Summon one Synchro Monster of LV 8 or below.
CURSED FLAME KING BURST CURSED
RED LOTUS KING, FLAME CRIME
WANDERING KING WILD WIND
GASH THE DUST LORD
I EXCLUDED FOUR KINGS WHO SLEEP IN MY GRAVEYARD...
DM
...AND SUMMONED RED DRAGON!
ARGH! TALK ABOUT STUBBORN!!
DM
THAT'S JUST LIKE YOU, JACK.
TO THINK YOU'D MANAGE TO HOLD UP UNDER MY FULL-POWER SENSE...
DM
DM
I SET ONE CARD FACE-DOWN.
TURN OVER.
DM

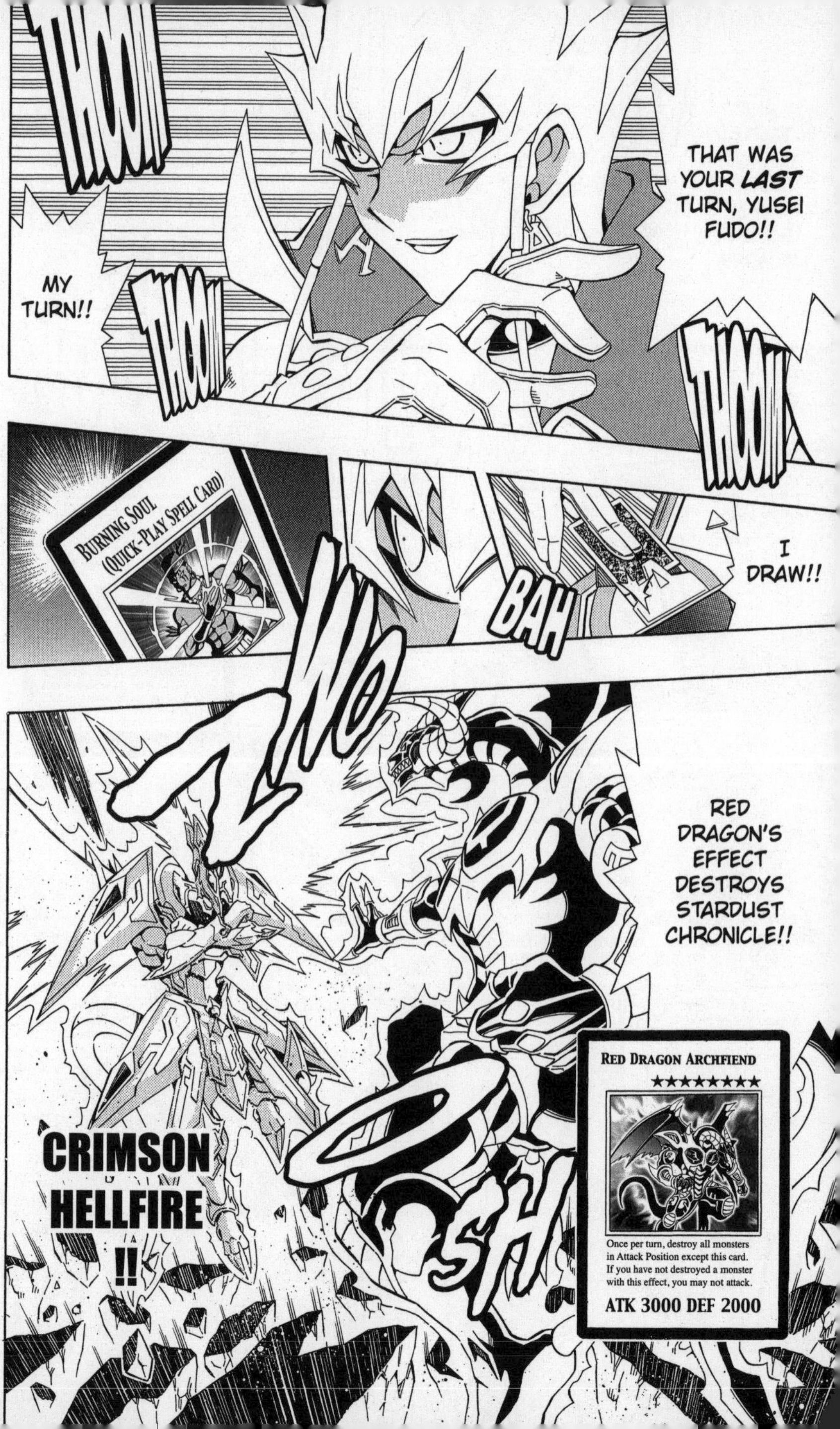
THOOM
THAT WAS YOUR LAST TURN, YUSEI FUDO!!
THOOM
MY TURN!!
THOOM
I DRAW!!
BAH
BURNING SOUL (QUICK-PLAY SPELL CARD)
RED DRAGON'S EFFECT DESTROYS STARDUST CHRONICLE!!
RED DRAGON ARCHFIEND
Once per turn, destroy all monsters in Attack Position except this card. If you have not destroyed a monster with this effect, you may not attack.
ATK 3000 DEF 2000
CRIMSON HELLFIRE!!

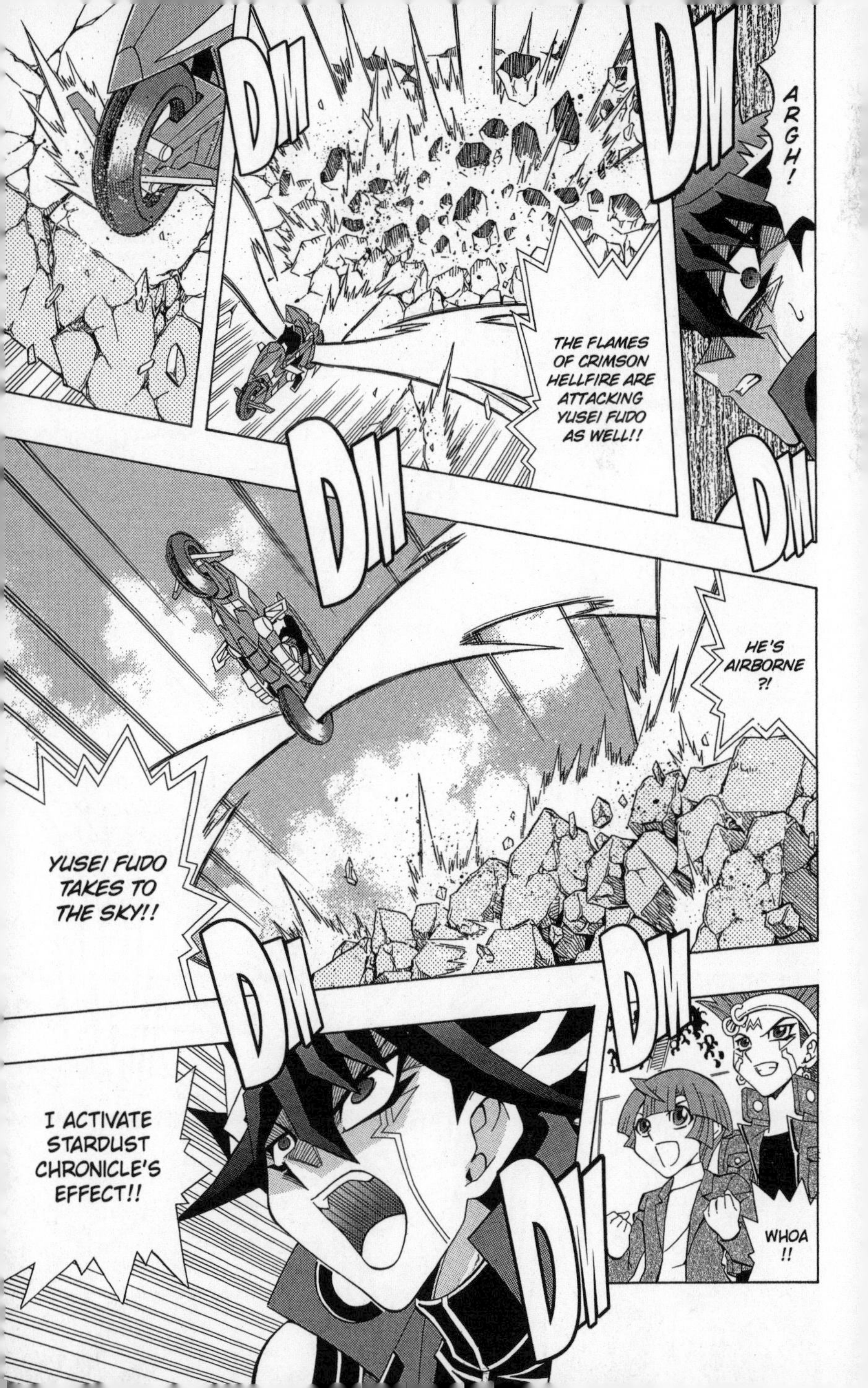
DM
ARGH!
DM
DM
THE FLAMES OF CRIMSON HELLFIRE ARE ATTACKING YUSEI FUDO AS WELL!!
DM
HE'S AIRBORNE?!
YUSEI FUDO TAKES TO THE SKY!!
DM
WHOA!!
DM
I ACTIVATE STARDUST CHRONICLE'S EFFECT!!
DM

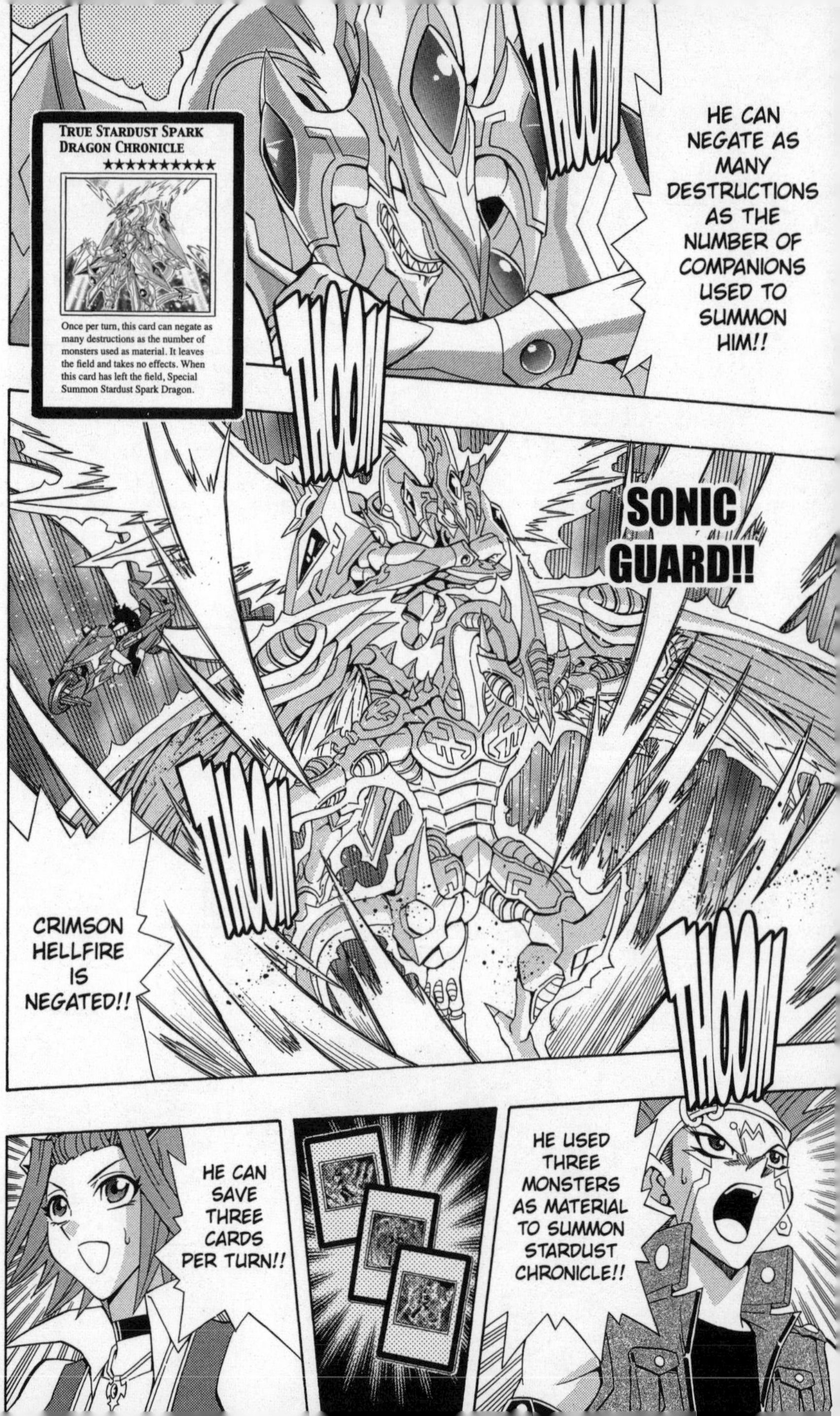
THOOM!!
HE CAN NEGATE AS MANY DESTRUCTIONS AS THE NUMBER OF COMPANIONS USED TO SUMMON HIM!!
TRUE STARDUST SPARK DRAGON CHRONICLE
★★★★★★★★★★★
Once per turn, this card can negate as many destructions as the number of monsters used as material. It leaves the field and takes no effects. When this card has left the field, Special Summon Stardust Spark Dragon.
THOOM!!
SONIC GUARD!!
THOOM!!
CRIMSON HELLFIRE IS NEGATED!!
THOOM!!
HE USED THREE MONSTERS AS MATERIAL TO SUMMON STARDUST CHRONICLE!!
HE CAN SAVE THREE CARDS PER TURN!!

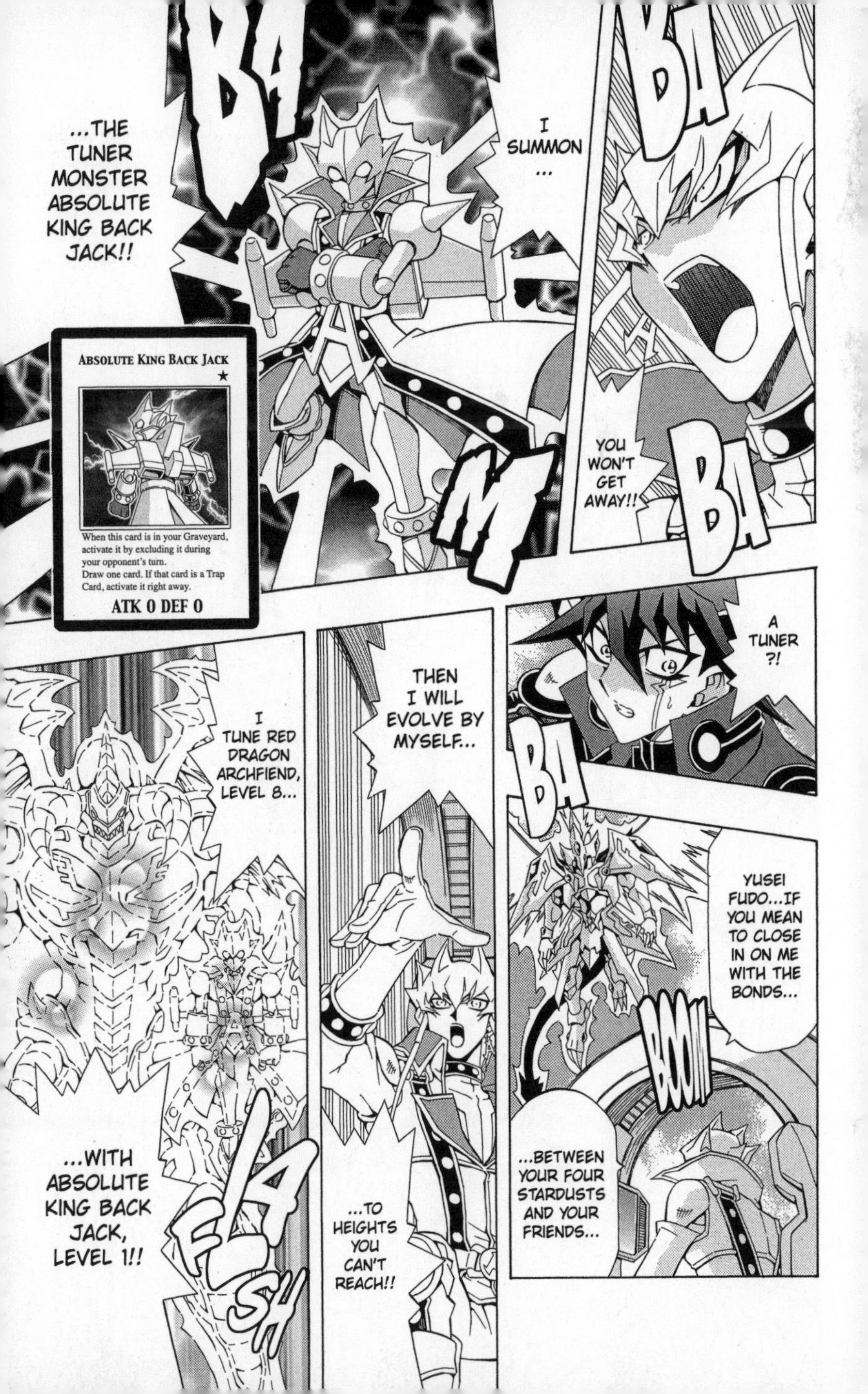
BA
I SUMMON ...
YOU WON'T GET AWAY!!
BA
BA
...THE TUNER MONSTER ABSOLUTE KING BACK JACK!!
ABSOLUTE KING BACK JACK
★
When this card is in your Graveyard, activate it by excluding it during your opponent's turn.
Draw one card. If that card is a Trap Card, activate it right away.
ATK 0 DEF 0
M
A TUNER ?!
BA
YUSEI FUDO...IF YOU MEAN TO CLOSE IN ON ME WITH THE BONDS...
BOOM
...BETWEEN YOUR FOUR STARDUSTS AND YOUR FRIENDS...
THEN I WILL EVOLVE BY MYSELF...
...TO HEIGHTS YOU CAN'T REACH!!
I TUNE RED DRAGON ARCHFIEND, LEVEL 8...
...WITH ABSOLUTE KING BACK JACK, LEVEL 1!!
FLASH

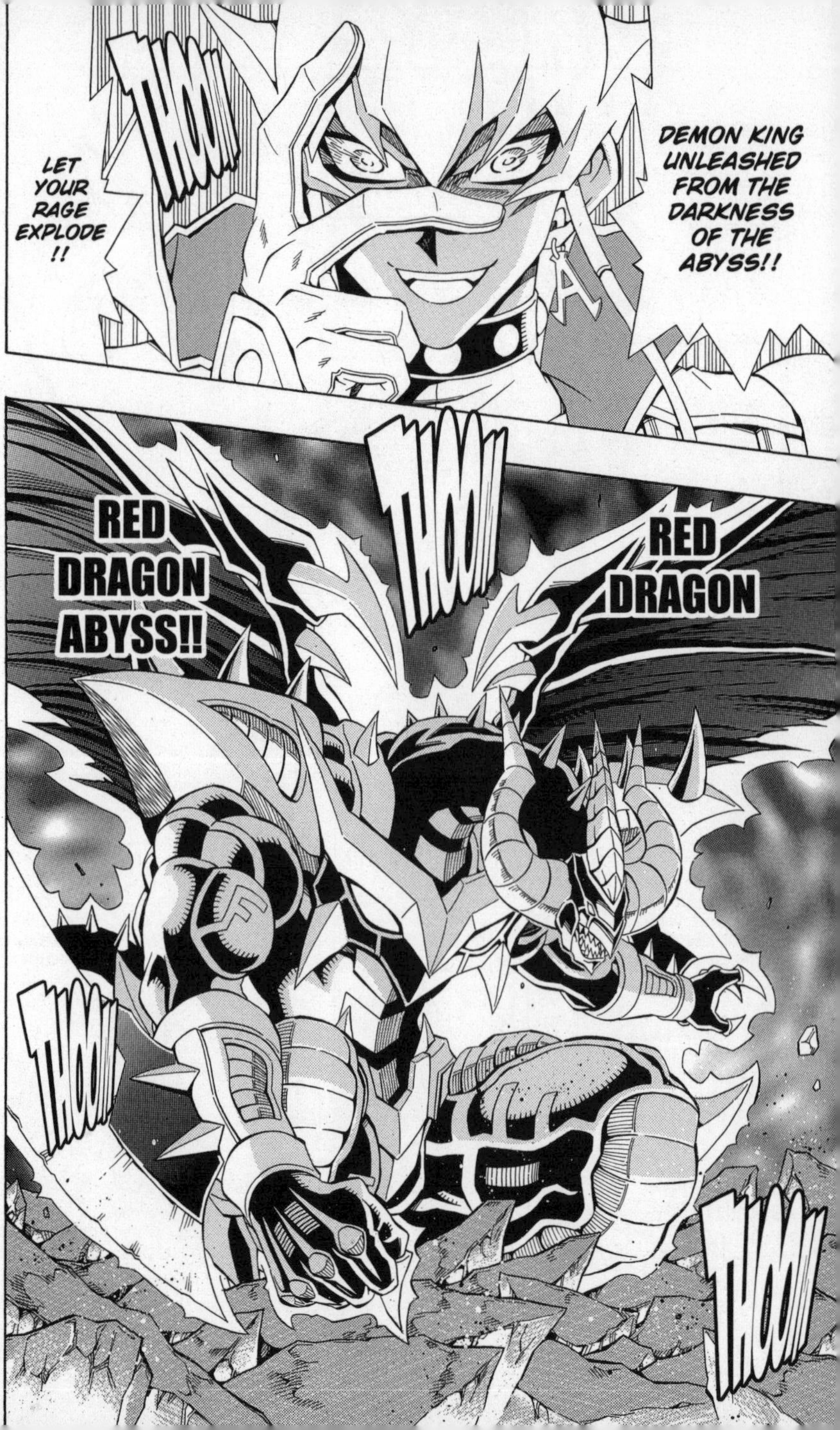
DEMON KING UNLEASHED FROM THE DARKNESS OF THE ABYSS!!
THOOM
LET YOUR RAGE EXPLODE!!
THOOM
RED DRAGON
RED DRAGON ABYSS!!!
THOOM
THOOM

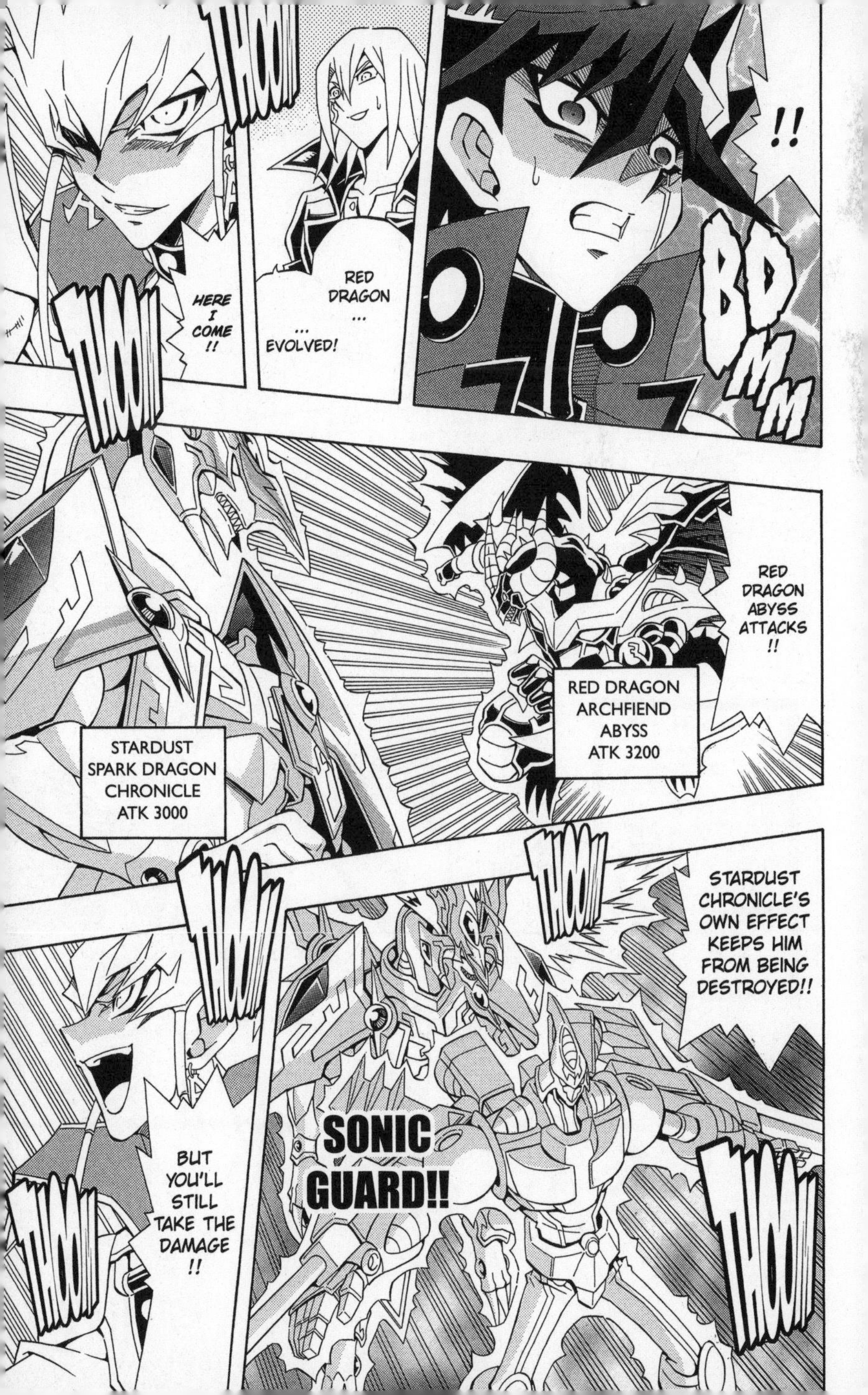
!!
BDMMM
RED DRAGON ...
... EVOLVED!
THOOM
HERE I COME !!
THOOM
RED DRAGON ABYSS ATTACKS !!
RED DRAGON ARCHFIEND ABYSS ATK 3200
STARDUST SPARK DRAGON CHRONICLE ATK 3000
THOOM
STARDUST CHRONICLE'S OWN EFFECT KEEPS HIM FROM BEING DESTROYED!!
THOOM
SONIC GUARD!!
THOOM
BUT YOU'LL STILL TAKE THE DAMAGE !!
THOOM

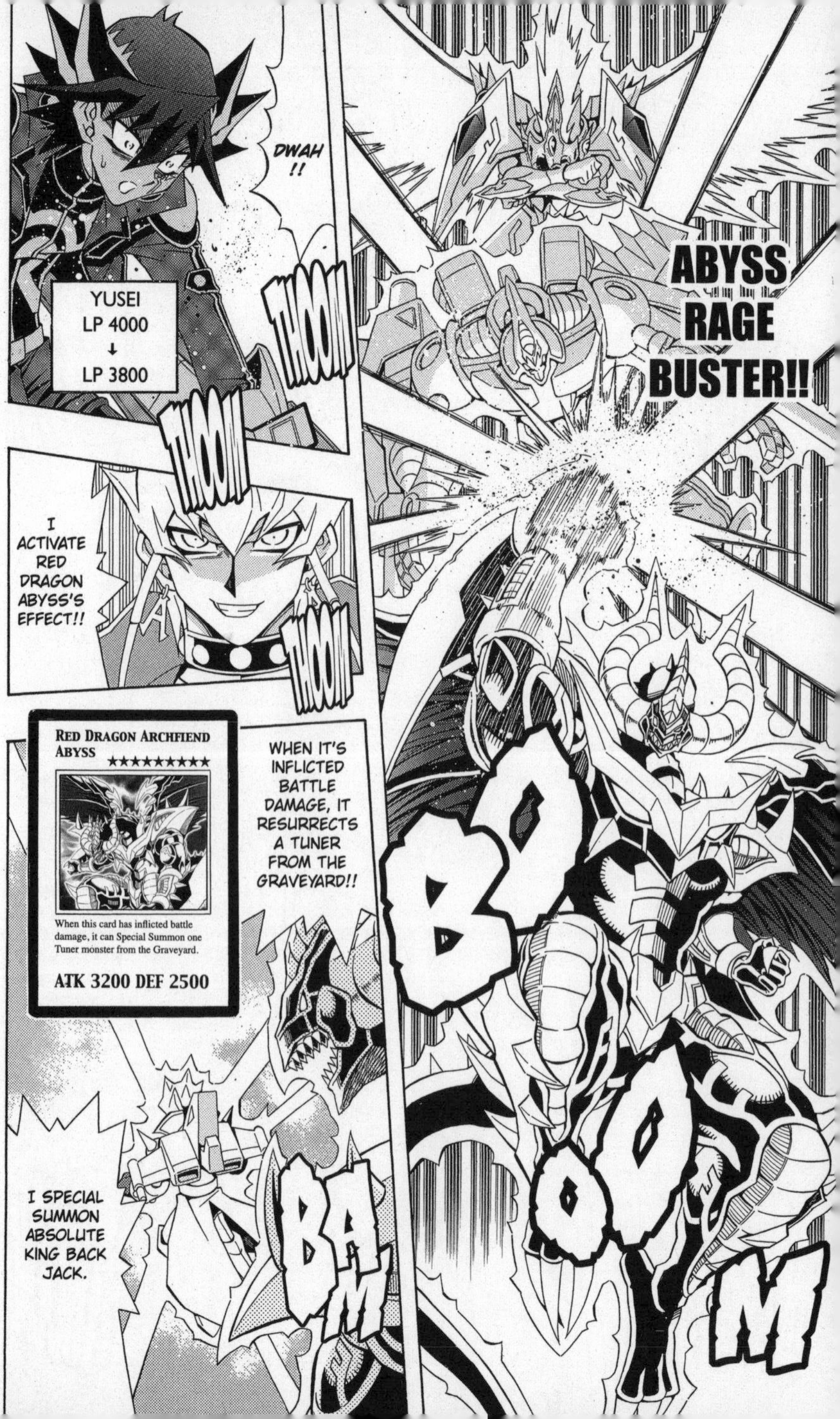
ABYSS RAGE BUSTER!!
BOOOM
DWAH !!
THOOM
YUSEI
LP 4000
↓
LP 3800
THOOM
I ACTIVATE RED DRAGON ABYSS'S EFFECT!!
THOOM
WHEN IT'S INFLICTED BATTLE DAMAGE, IT RESURRECTS A TUNER FROM THE GRAVEYARD!!
RED DRAGON ARCHFIEND ABYSS
★★★★★★★★★★
When this card has inflicted battle damage, it can Special Summon one Tuner monster from the Graveyard.
ATK 3200 DEF 2500
BAM
I SPECIAL SUMMON ABSOLUTE KING BACK JACK.

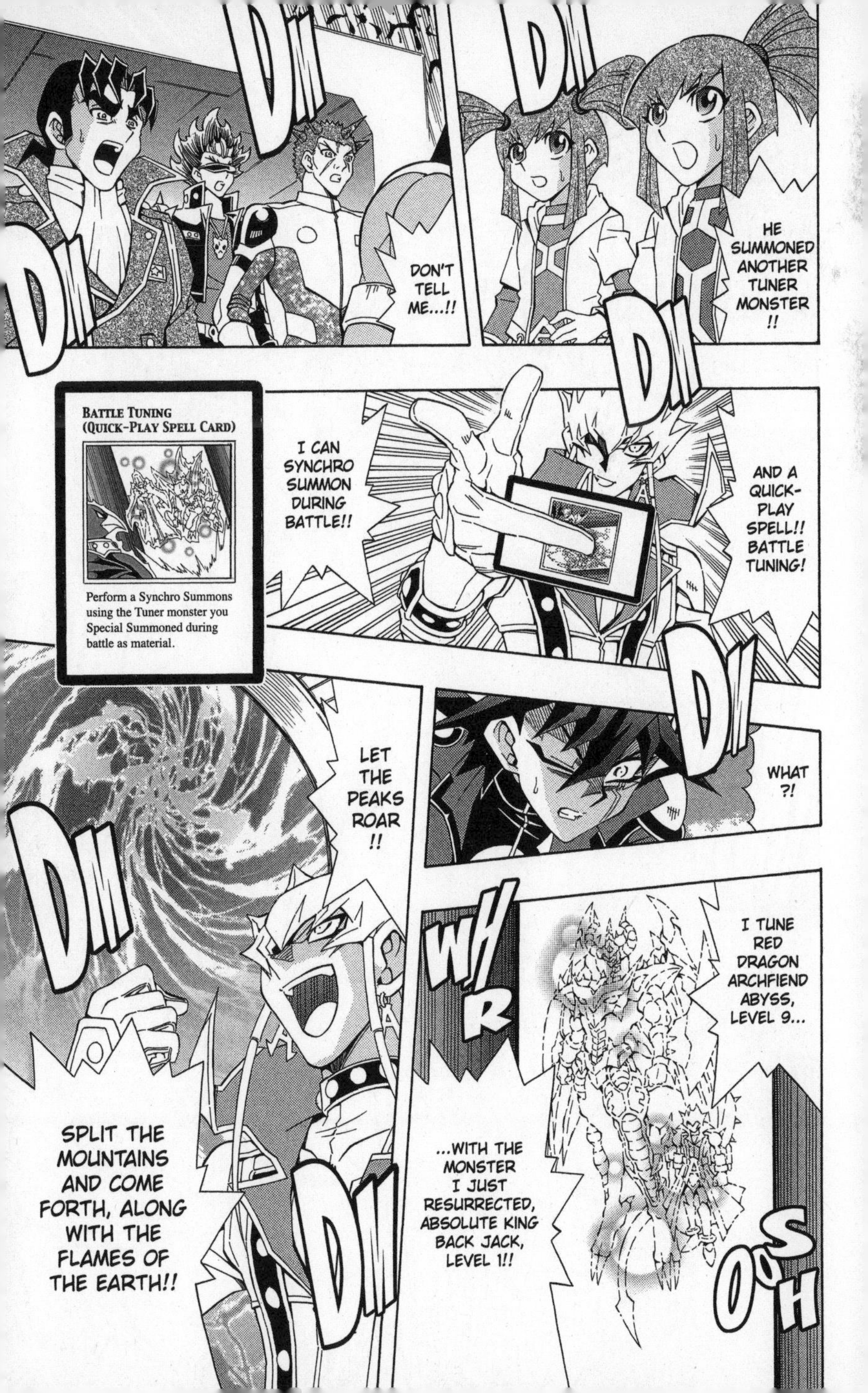
DM
DM
HE SUMMONED ANOTHER TUNER MONSTER !!
DON'T TELL ME...!!
DM
DM
AND A QUICK-PLAY SPELL!! BATTLE TUNING!
I CAN SYNCHRO SUMMON DURING BATTLE!!
BATTLE TUNING (QUICK-PLAY SPELL CARD)
Perform a Synchro Summons using the Tuner monster you Special Summoned during battle as material.
DM
WHAT ?!
I TUNE RED DRAGON ARCHFIEND ABYSS, LEVEL 9...
WHIR
...WITH THE MONSTER I JUST RESURRECTED, ABSOLUTE KING BACK JACK, LEVEL 1!!
WOOSH
LET THE PEAKS ROAR !!
DM
SPLIT THE MOUNTAINS AND COME FORTH, ALONG WITH THE FLAMES OF THE EARTH!!
DM

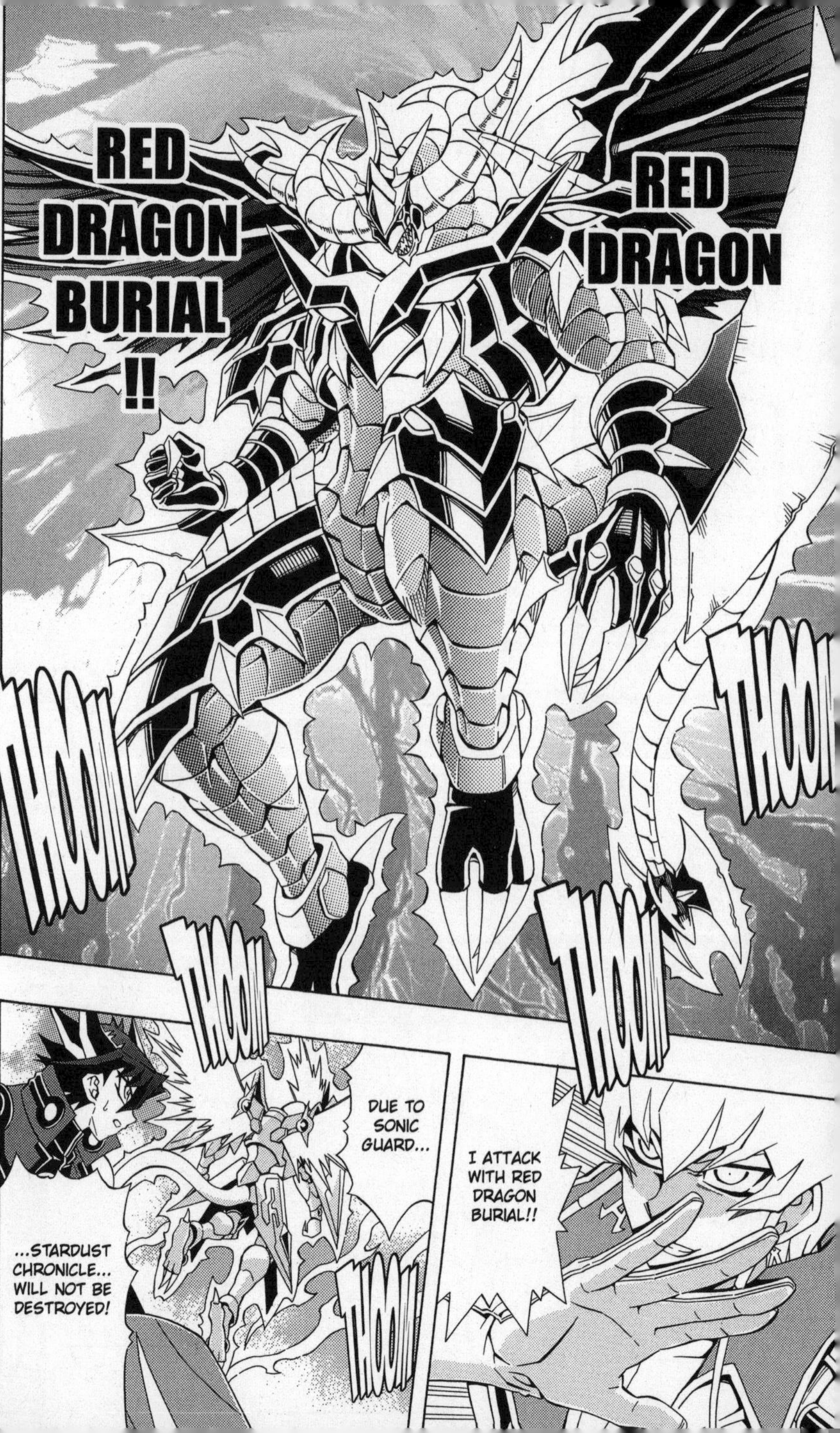
RED DRAGON
RED DRAGON BURIAL!!
I ATTACK WITH RED DRAGON BURIAL!!
DUE TO SONIC GUARD...
...STARDUST CHRONICLE... WILL NOT BE DESTROYED!

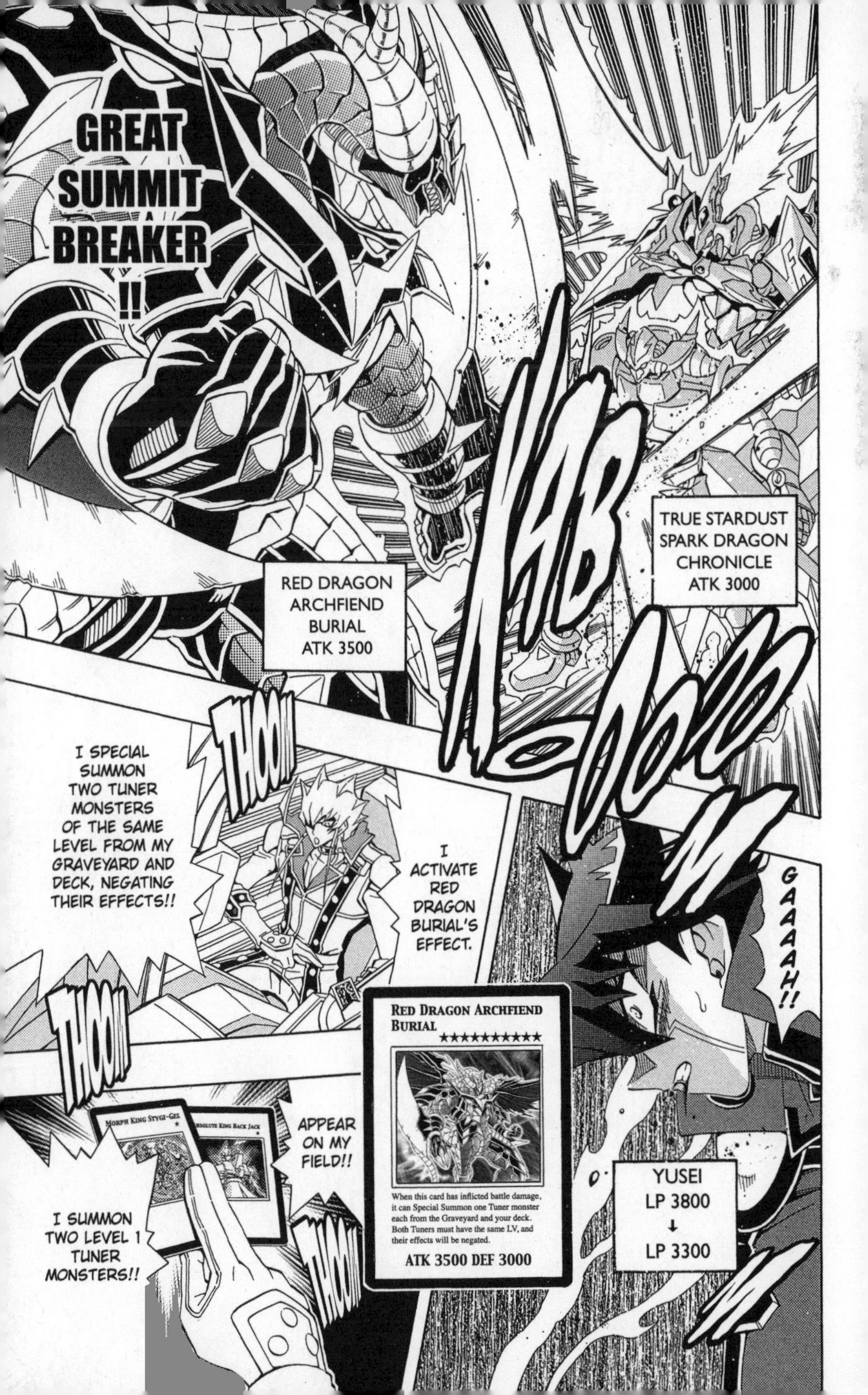
GREAT SUMMIT BREAKER!!
TRUE STARDUST SPARK DRAGON CHRONICLE ATK 3000
RED DRAGON ARCHFIEND BURIAL ATK 3500
GAAAAAH!!
YUSEI LP 3800 ↓ LP 3300
THOOM
I ACTIVATE RED DRAGON BURIAL'S EFFECT.
I SPECIAL SUMMON TWO TUNER MONSTERS OF THE SAME LEVEL FROM MY GRAVEYARD AND DECK, NEGATING THEIR EFFECTS!!
RED DRAGON ARCHFIEND BURIAL
When this card has inflicted battle damage, it can Special Summon one Tuner monster each from the Graveyard and your deck. Both Tuners must have the same LV, and their effects will be negated.
ATK 3500 DEF 3000
THOOM
THOOM
APPEAR ON MY FIELD!!
MORPH KING STYGI-GEL
I SUMMON TWO LEVEL 1 TUNER MONSTERS!!

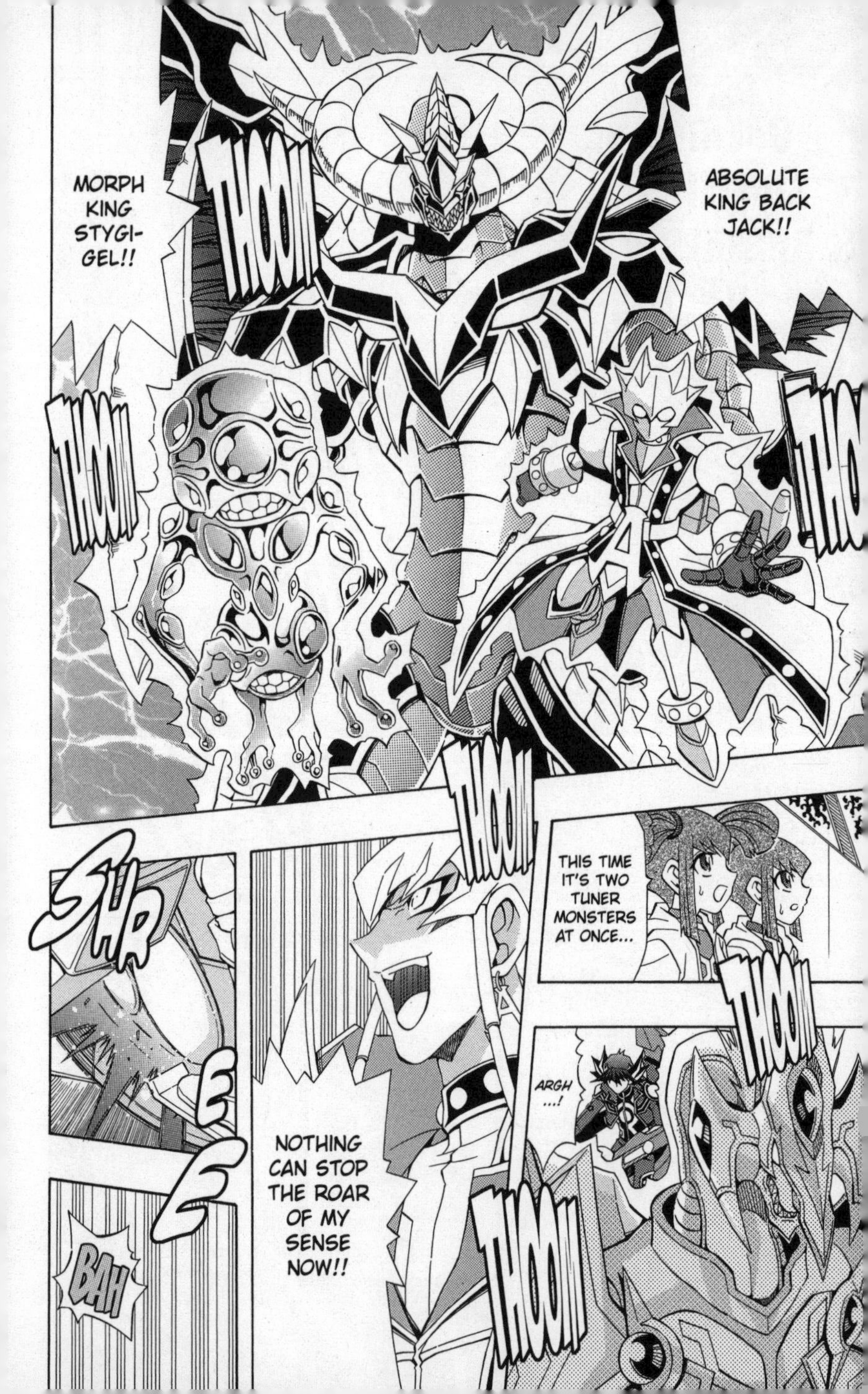
ABSOLUTE KING BACK JACK!!
THOOM
MORPH KING STYGI-GEL!!
THOOM
THOOM
THIS TIME IT'S TWO TUNER MONSTERS AT ONCE...
THOOM
ARGH ...!
THOOM
THOOM
NOTHING CAN STOP THE ROAR OF MY SENSE NOW!!
SHREE
BAH

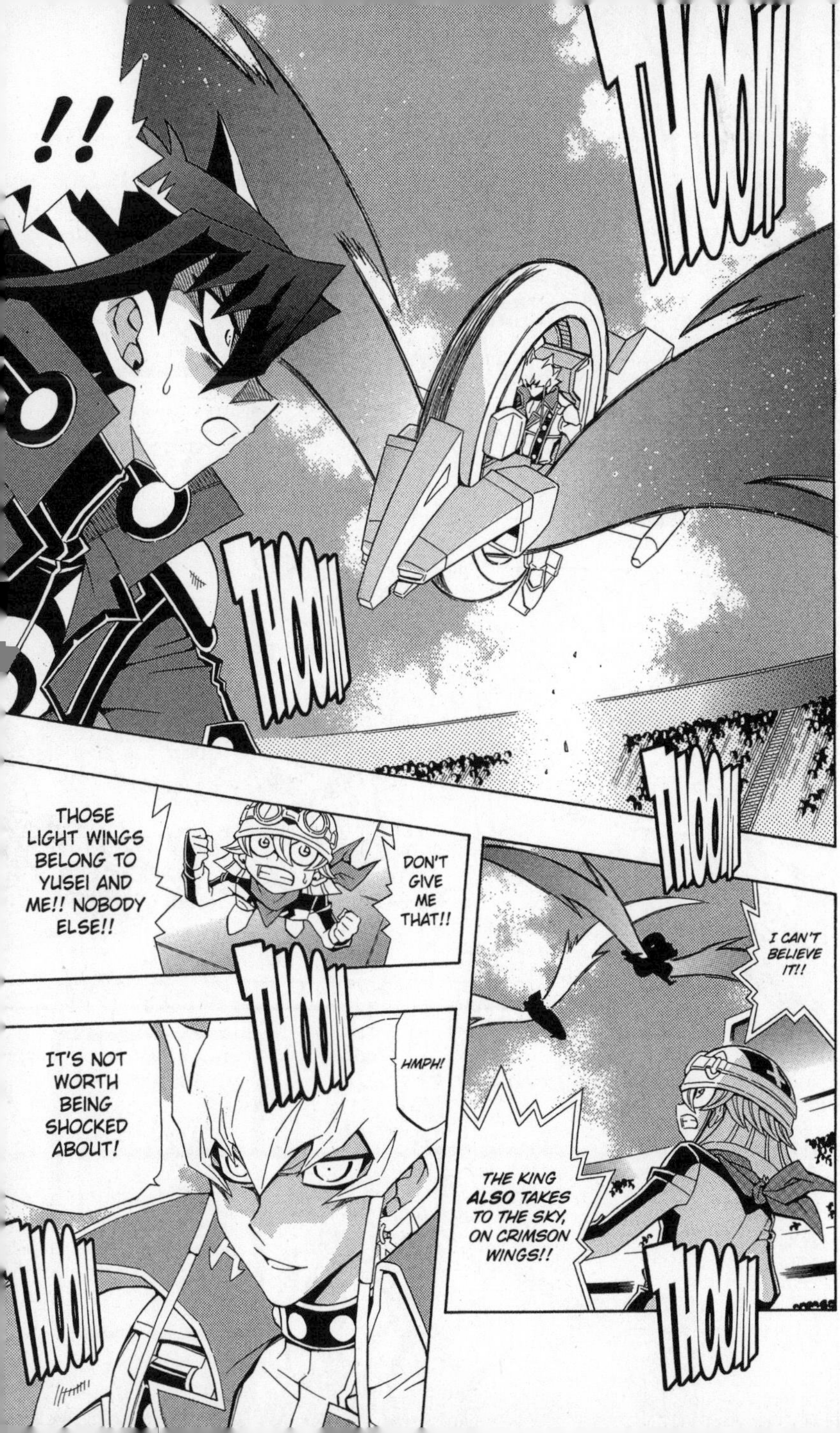
THOOM
!!
THOOM
THOOM
I CAN'T BELIEVE IT!!
THE KING ALSO TAKES TO THE SKY, ON CRIMSON WINGS!!
THOOM
DON'T GIVE ME THAT!!
THOSE LIGHT WINGS BELONG TO YUSEI AND ME!! NOBODY ELSE!!
THOOM
HMPH!
IT'S NOT WORTH BEING SHOCKED ABOUT!
THOOM

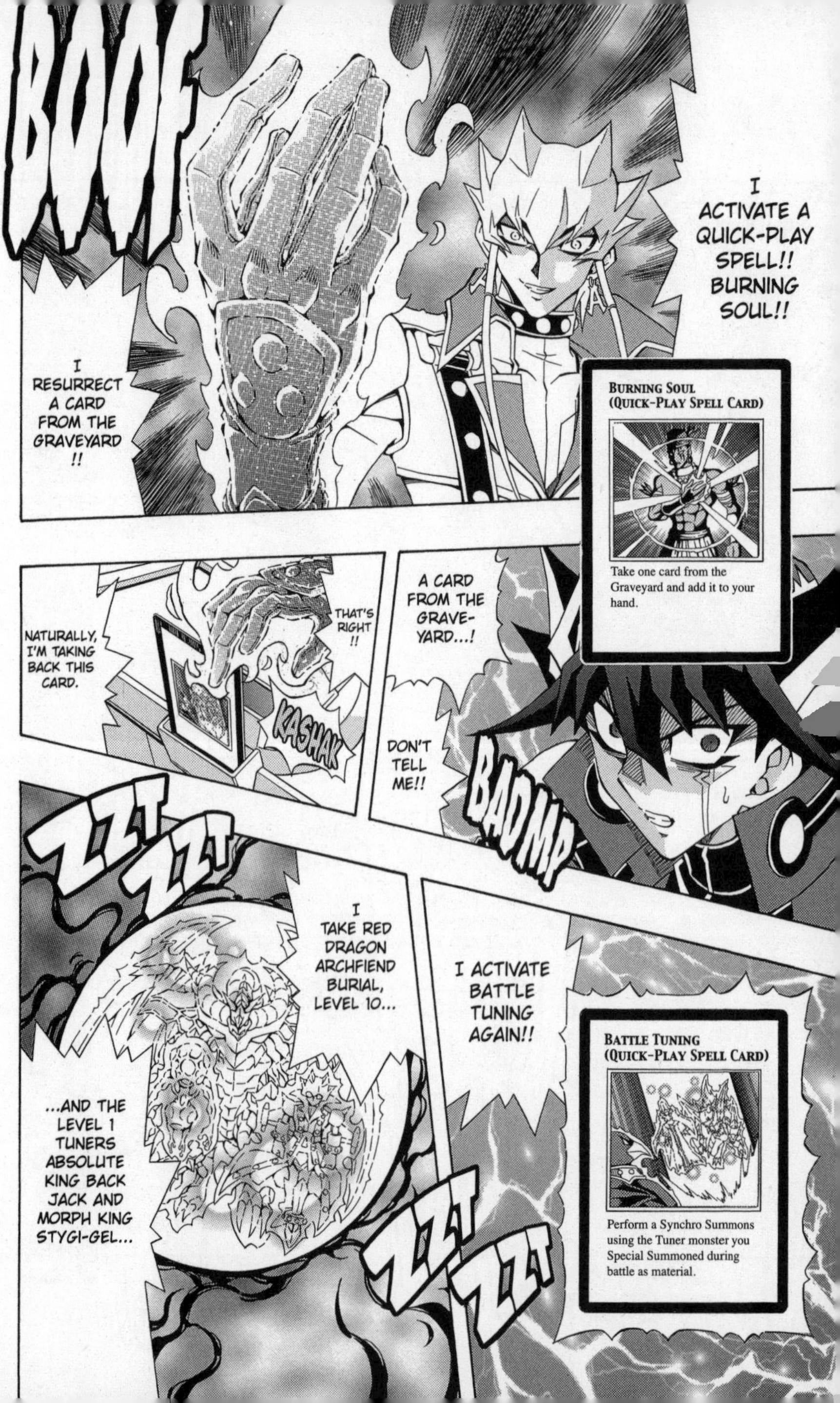
I ACTIVATE A QUICK-PLAY SPELL!! BURNING SOUL!!
BOOF
BURNING SOUL (QUICK-PLAY SPELL CARD)
Take one card from the Graveyard and add it to your hand.
I RESURRECT A CARD FROM THE GRAVEYARD!!
A CARD FROM THE GRAVE-YARD...!
DON'T TELL ME!!
BADMP
THAT'S RIGHT!!
NATURALLY, I'M TAKING BACK THIS CARD.
KASHAK
I ACTIVATE BATTLE TUNING AGAIN!!
BATTLE TUNING (QUICK-PLAY SPELL CARD)
Perform a Synchro Summons using the Tuner monster you Special Summoned during battle as material.
ZZZT ZZZT
I TAKE RED DRAGON ARCHFIEND BURIAL, LEVEL 10...
...AND THE LEVEL 1 TUNERS ABSOLUTE KING BACK JACK AND MORPH KING STYGI-GEL...
ZZZT ZZZT

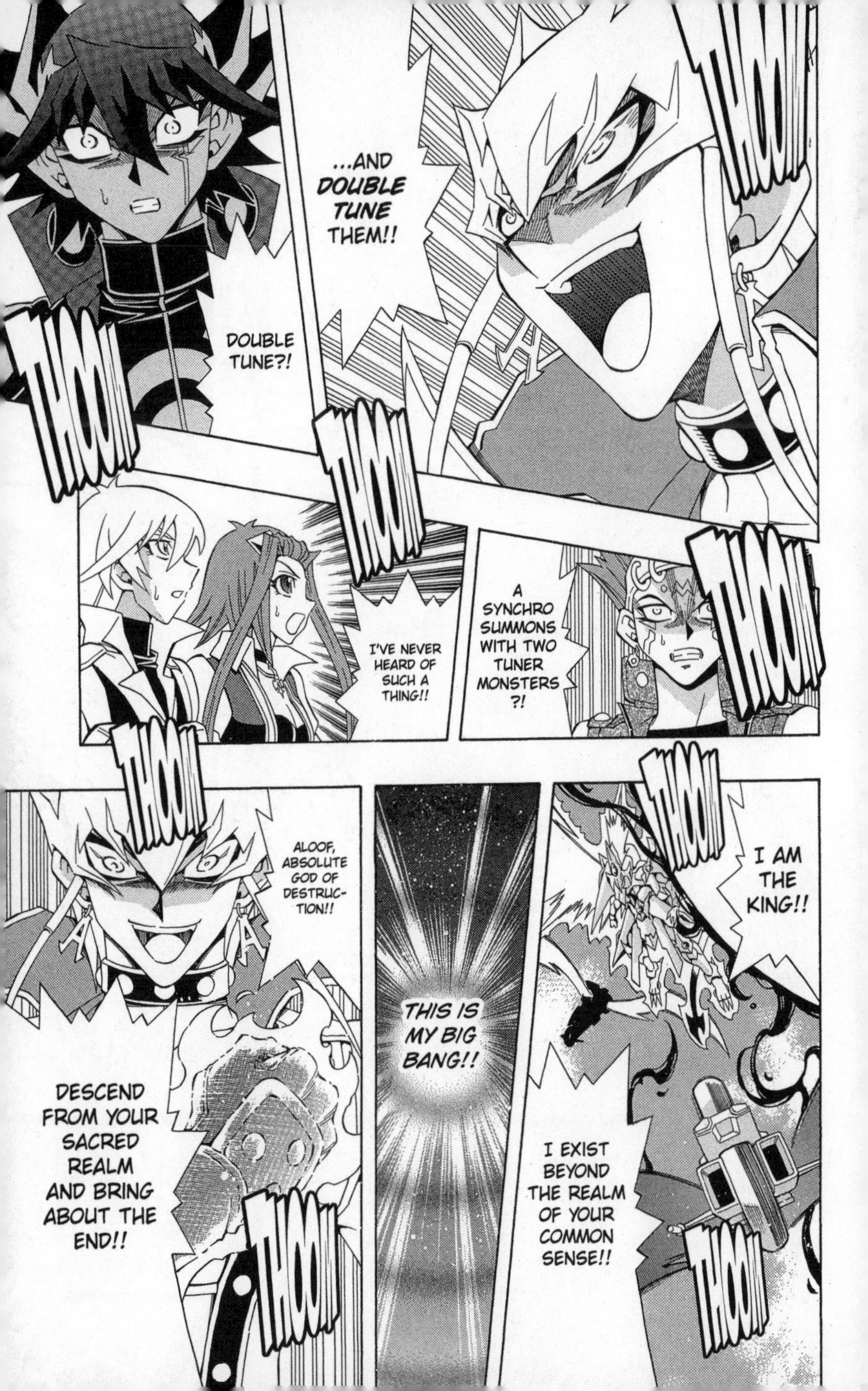
THOOM
...AND DOUBLE TUNE THEM!!
THOOM
DOUBLE TUNE?!
THOOM
THOOM
A SYNCHRO SUMMONS WITH TWO TUNER MONSTERS ?!
I'VE NEVER HEARD OF SUCH A THING!!
THOOM
THOOM
I AM THE KING!!
I EXIST BEYOND THE REALM OF YOUR COMMON SENSE!!
THOOM
THIS IS MY BIG BANG!!
THOOM
ALOOF, ABSOLUTE GOD OF DESTRUCTION!!
DESCEND FROM YOUR SACRED REALM AND BRING ABOUT THE END!!
THOOM

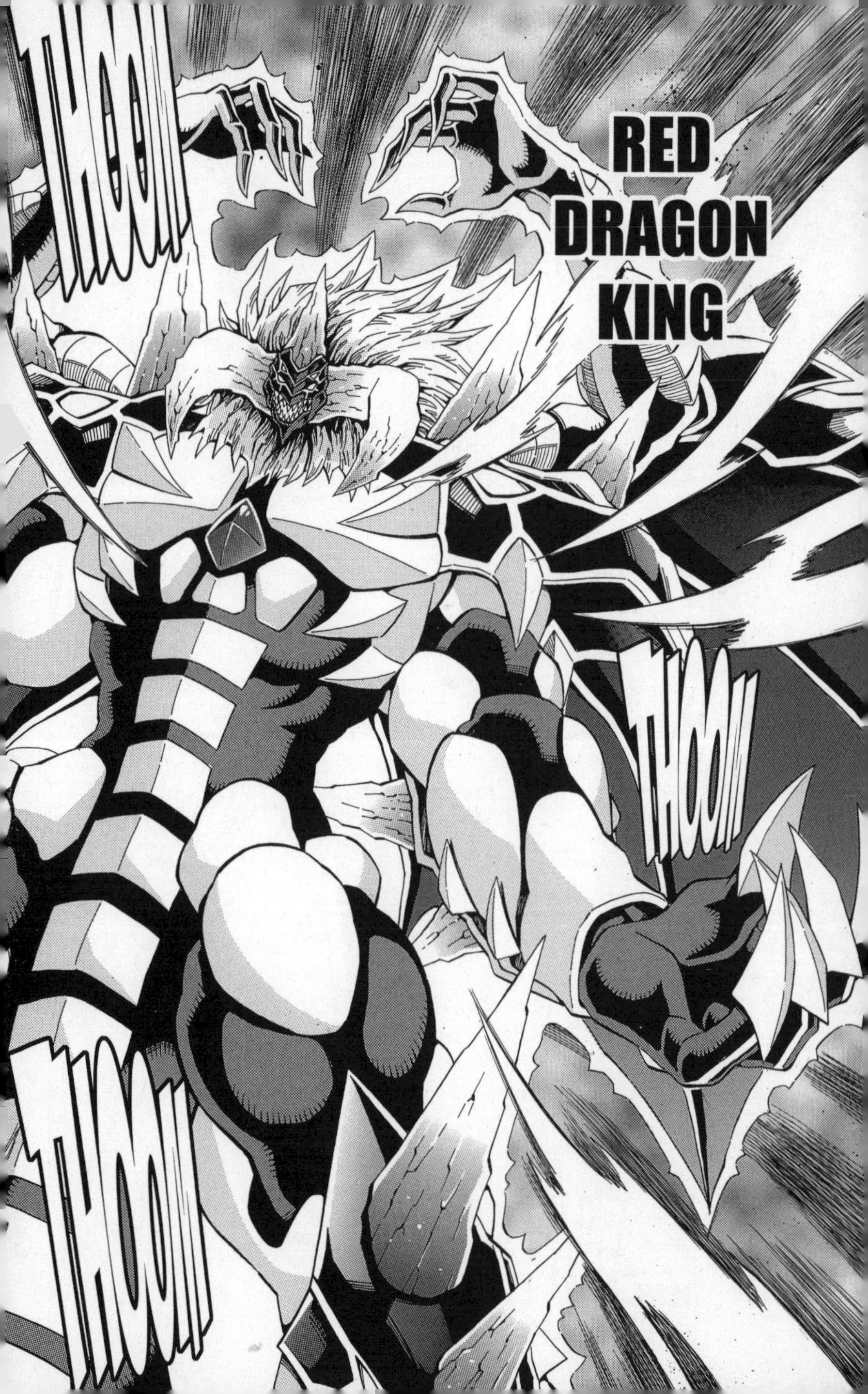
RED DRAGON KING
THOOM
THOOM
THOOM

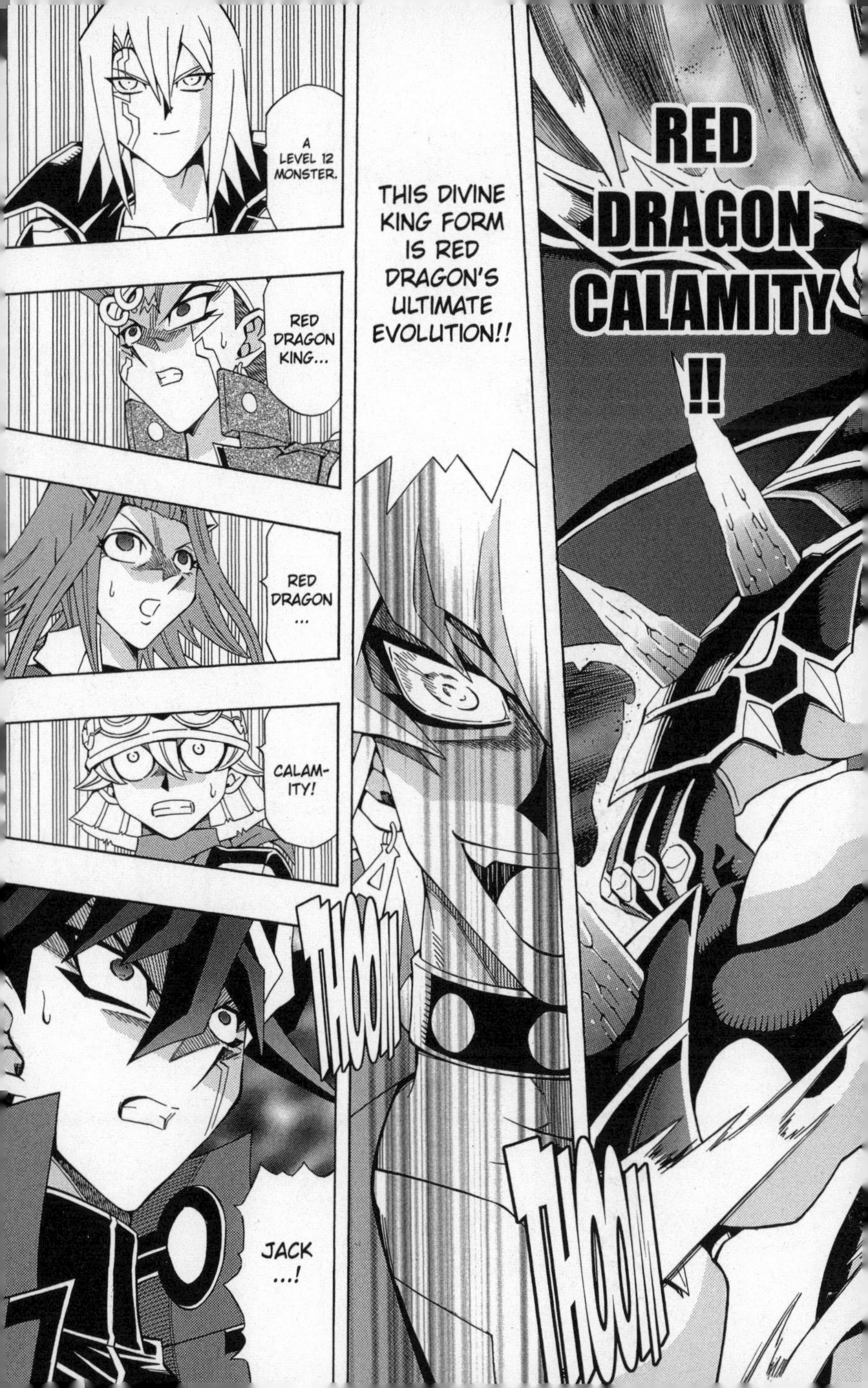
RED DRAGON CALAMITY!!
THOOM
THIS DIVINE KING FORM IS RED DRAGON'S ULTIMATE EVOLUTION!!
THOOM
A LEVEL 12 MONSTER.
RED DRAGON KING...
RED DRAGON...
CALAM-ITY!
JACK...!

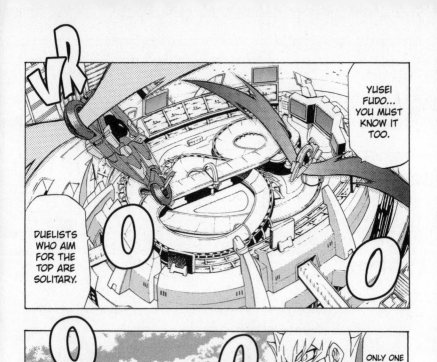

YUSEI FUDO... YOU MUST KNOW IT TOO.

DUELISTS WHO AIM FOR THE TOP ARE SOLITARY.

ONLY ONE PERSON IS GRANTED THIS LOFTY VIEW.

ONLY THE DUELIST WHO STANDS AT THE TOP!

THERE'S NO ROOM FOR TWO HEROES!!

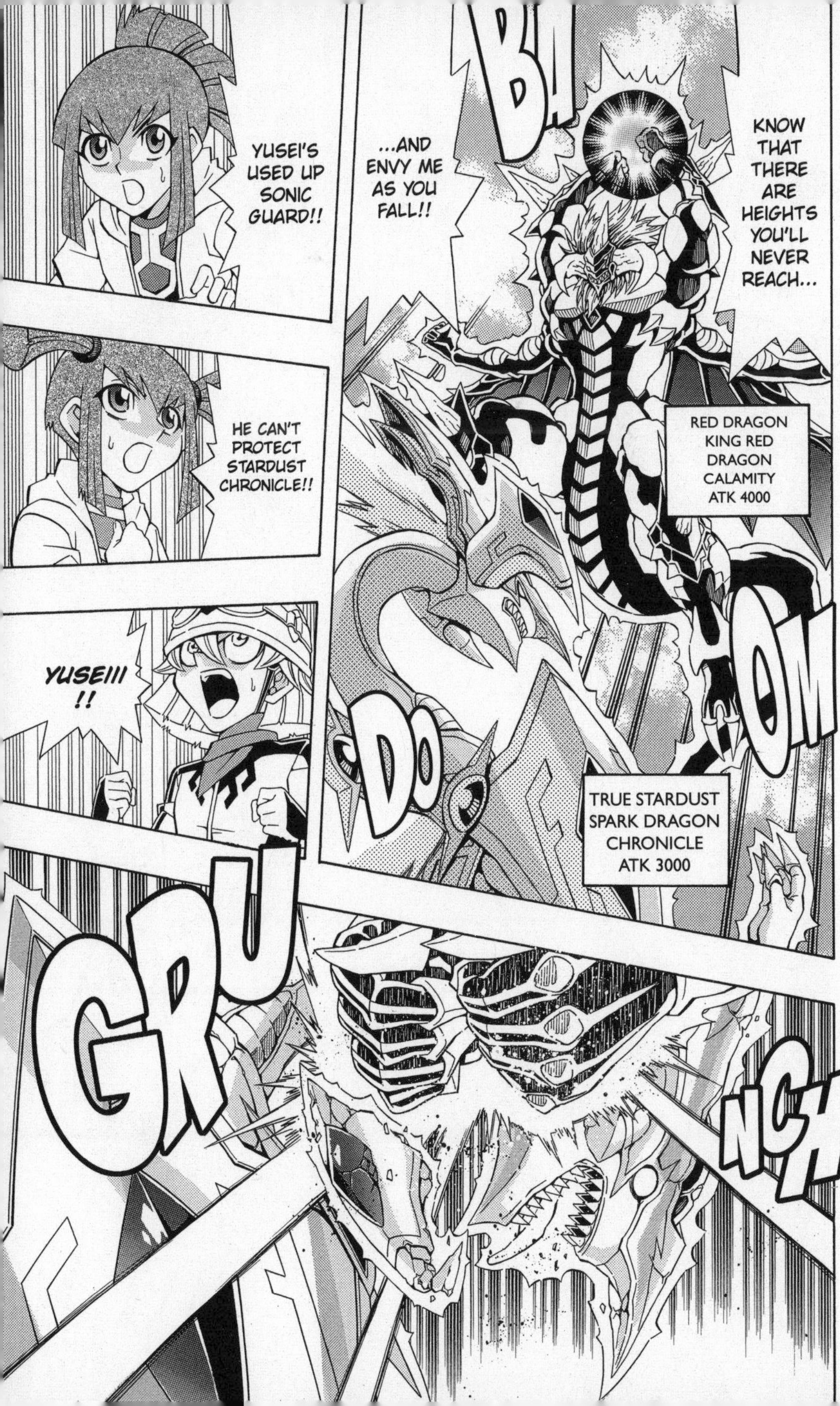
KNOW THAT THERE ARE HEIGHTS YOU'LL NEVER REACH...
BA
...AND ENVY ME AS YOU FALL!!
RED DRAGON KING RED DRAGON CALAMITY ATK 4000
DO
OM
TRUE STARDUST SPARK DRAGON CHRONICLE ATK 3000
YUSEI'S USED UP SONIC GUARD!!
HE CAN'T PROTECT STARDUST CHRONICLE!!
YUSEIII !!
GRU
NCH

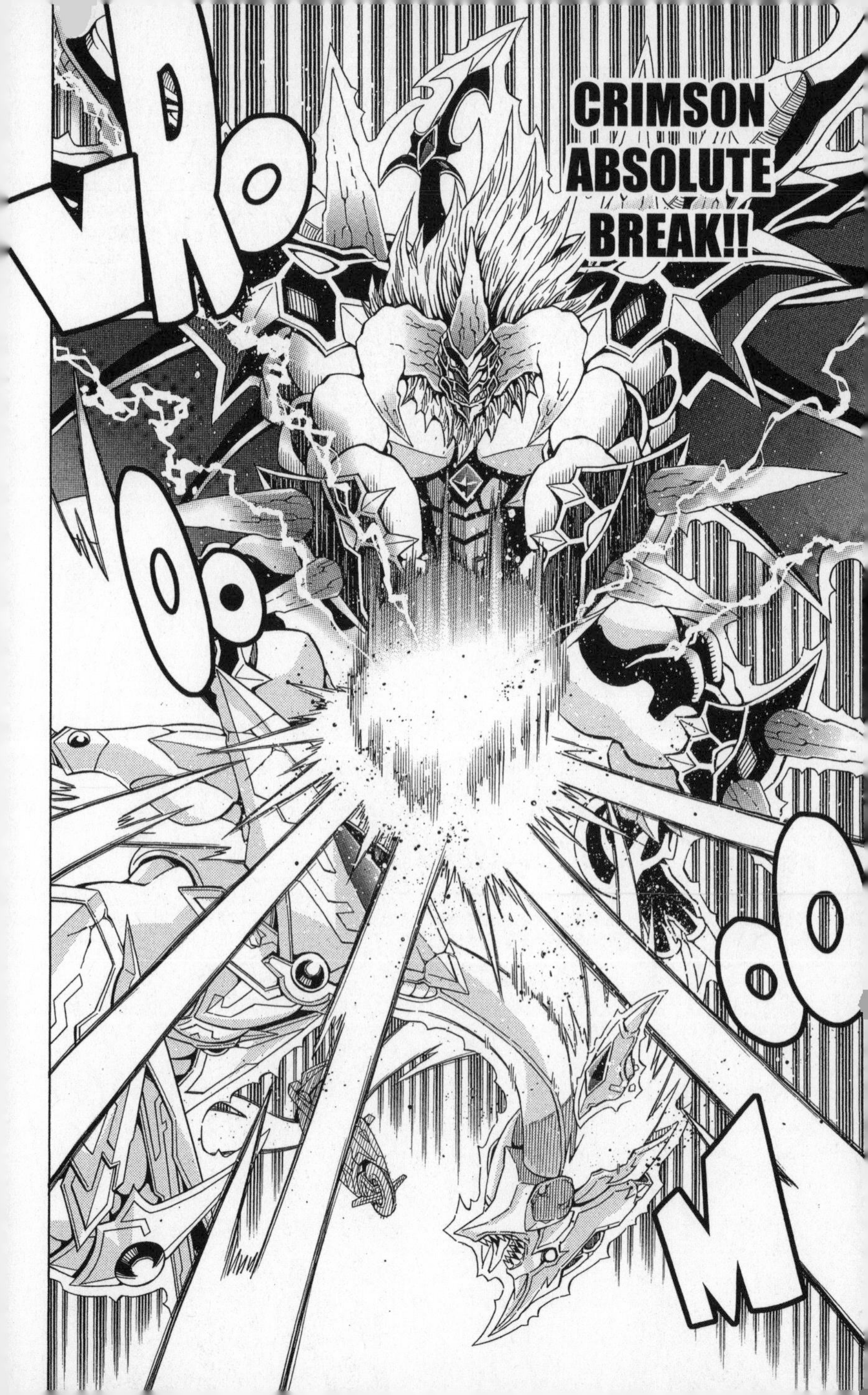
CRIMSON ABSOLUTE BREAK!!
VROOOOOM

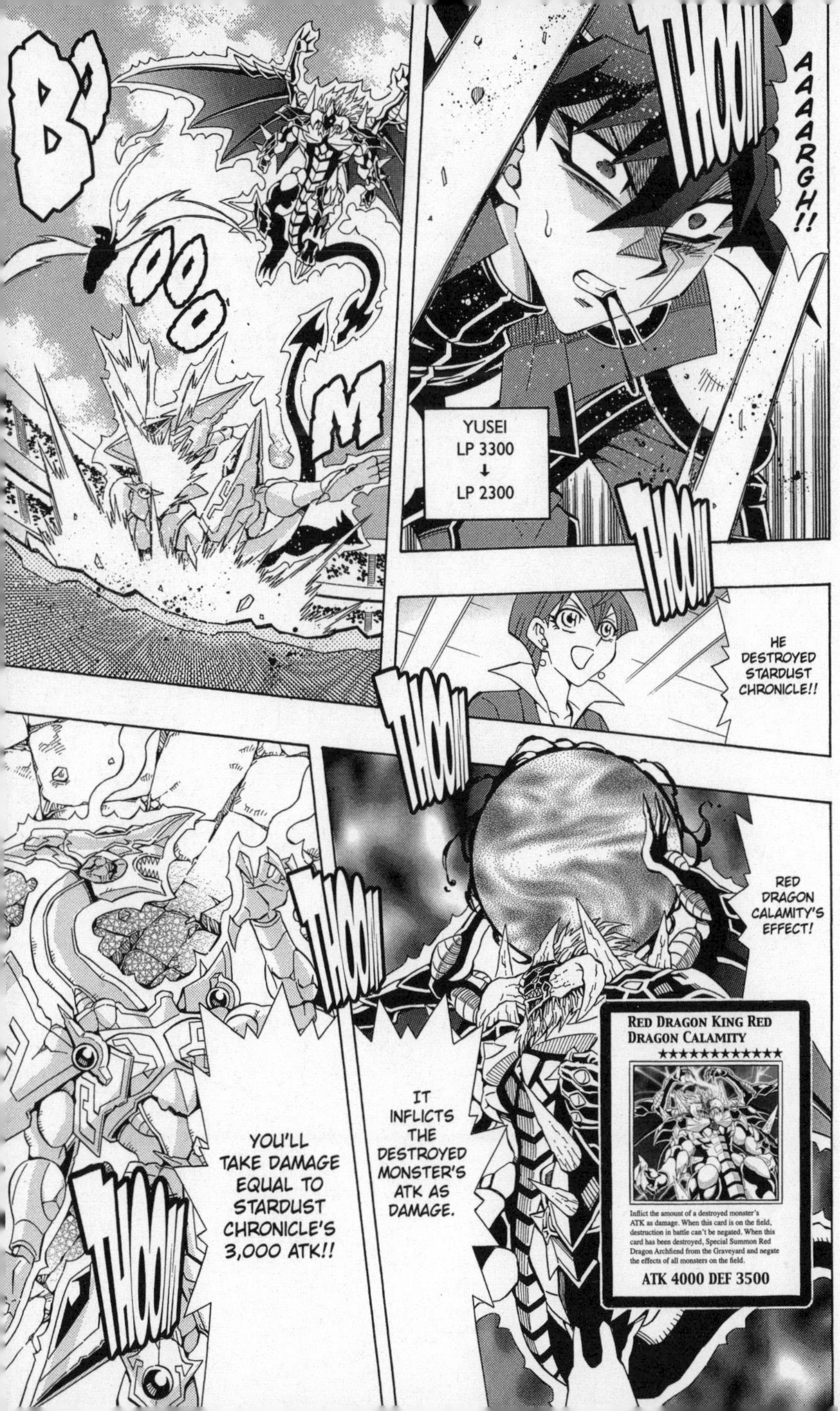
THOOM
AAAARGH!!
YUSEI
LP 3300
↓
LP 2300
THOOM
BOOOM
HE DESTROYED STARDUST CHRONICLE!!
THOOM
RED DRAGON CALAMITY'S EFFECT!
THOOM
RED DRAGON KING RED DRAGON CALAMITY
★★★★★★★★★★★★
Inflict the amount of a destroyed monster's ATK as damage. When this card is on the field, destruction in battle can't be negated. When this card has been destroyed, Special Summon Red Dragon Archfiend from the Graveyard and negate the effects of all monsters on the field.
ATK 4000 DEF 3500
IT INFLICTS THE DESTROYED MONSTER'S ATK AS DAMAGE.
YOU'LL TAKE DAMAGE EQUAL TO STARDUST CHRONICLE'S 3,000 ATK!!
THOOM

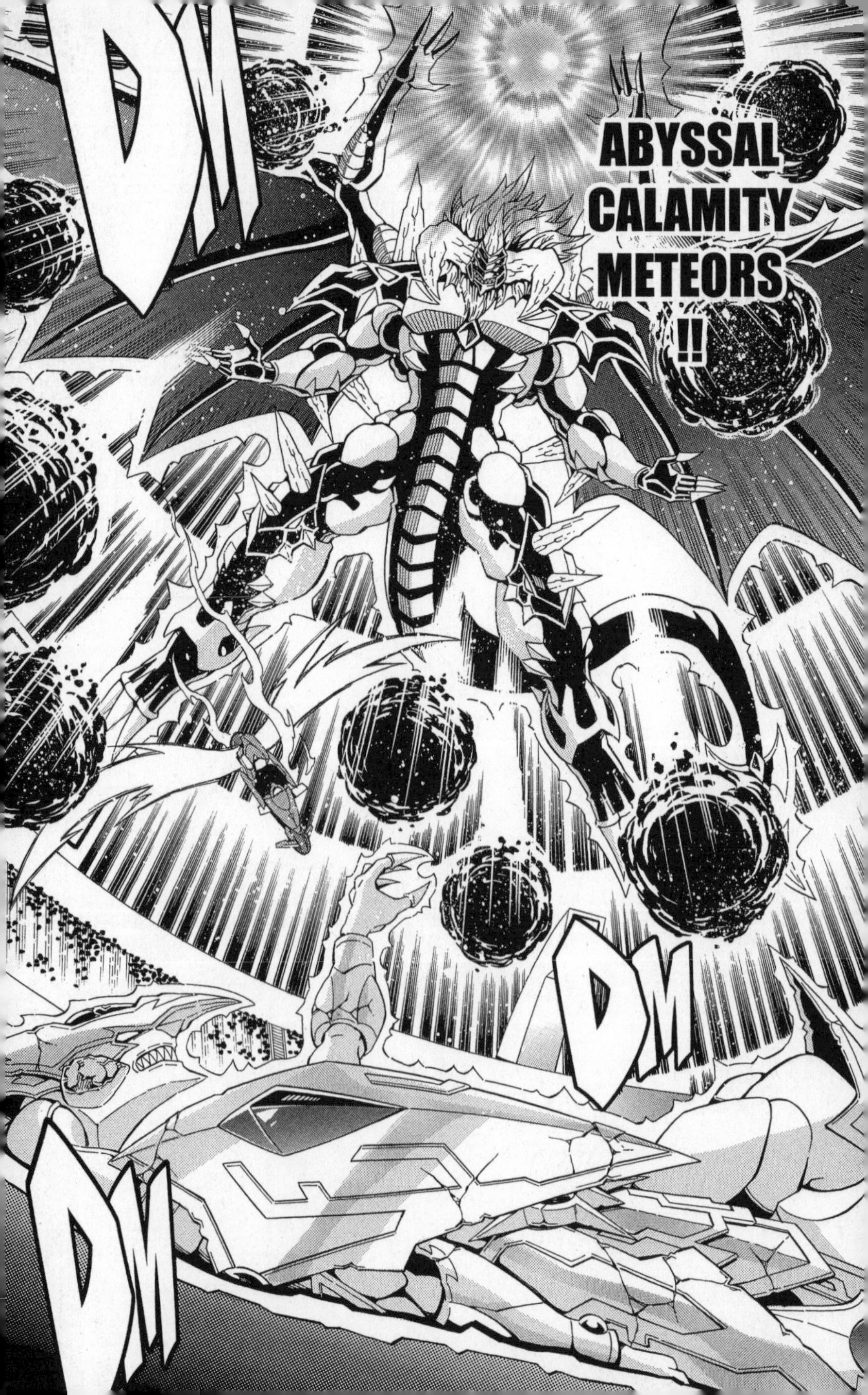
DM
ABYSSAL CALAMITY METEORS!!
DM
DM

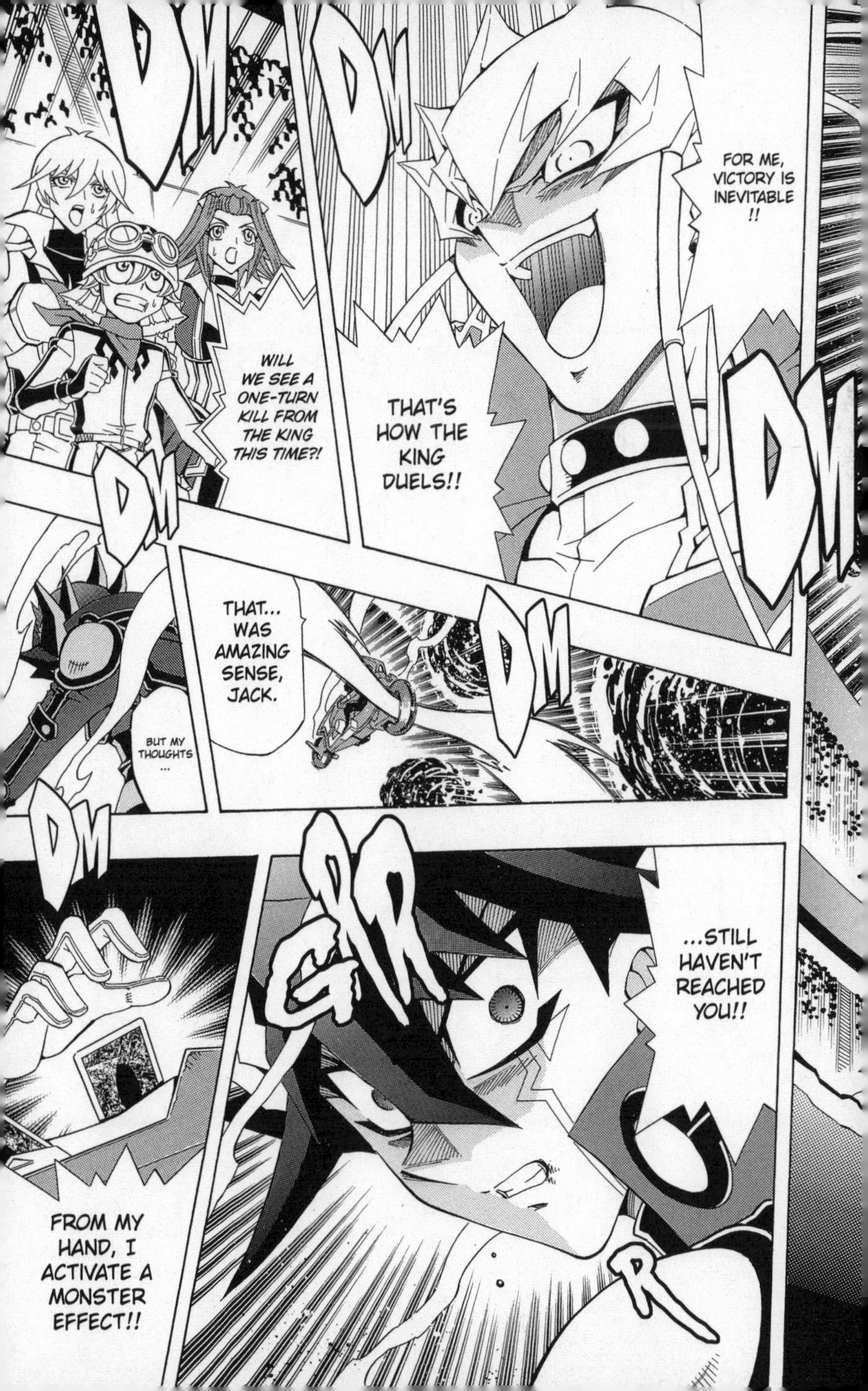
DM
DM
FOR ME, VICTORY IS INEVITABLE!!
THAT'S HOW THE KING DUELS!!
DM
DM
WILL WE SEE A ONE-TURN KILL FROM THE KING THIS TIME?!
DM
DM
THAT... WAS AMAZING SENSE, JACK.
BUT MY THOUGHTS...
DM
GRR
...STILL HAVEN'T REACHED YOU!!
R
FROM MY HAND, I ACTIVATE A MONSTER EFFECT!!

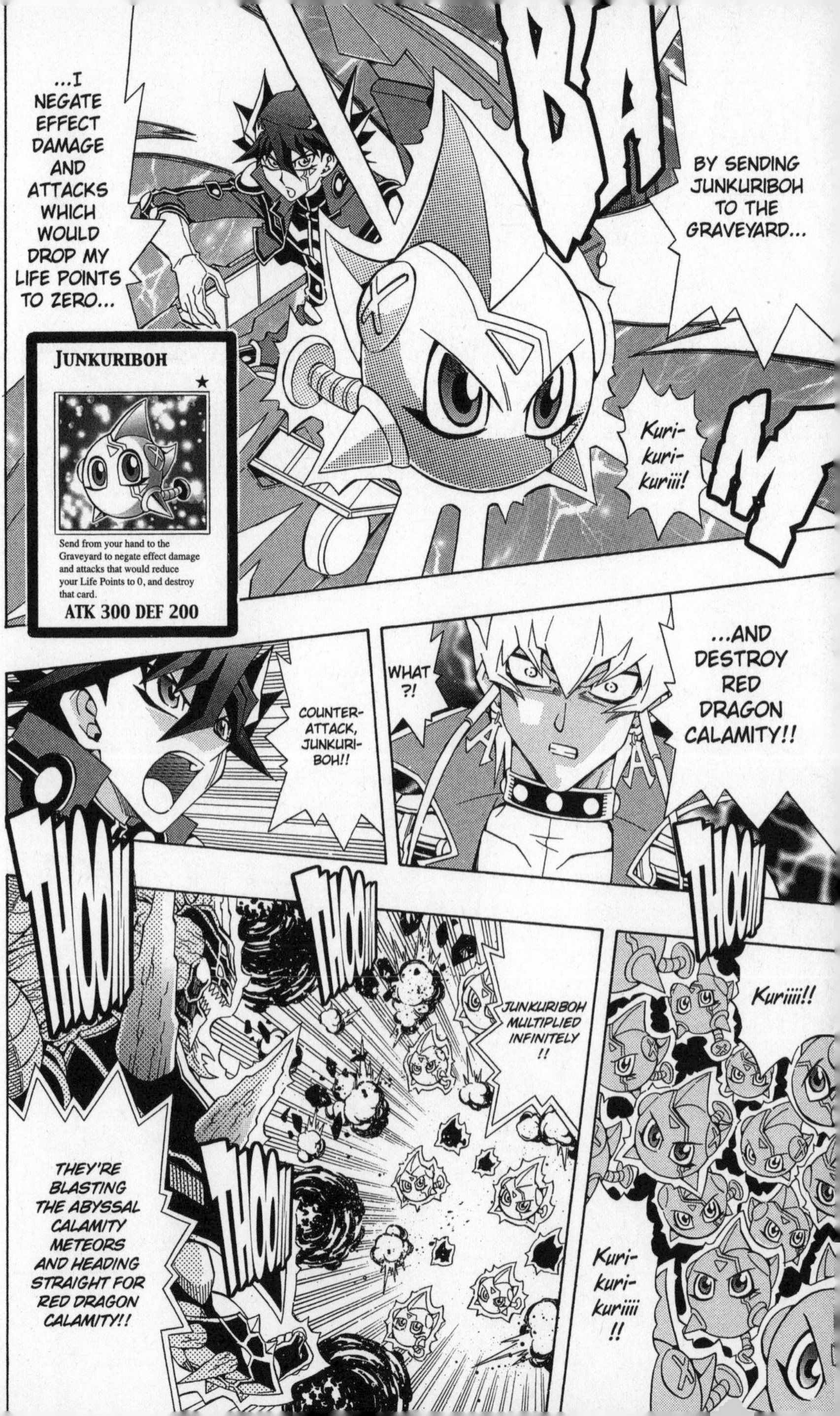
BAM
BY SENDING JUNKURIBOH TO THE GRAVEYARD...
Kuri-kuri-kuriii!
...I NEGATE EFFECT DAMAGE AND ATTACKS WHICH WOULD DROP MY LIFE POINTS TO ZERO...
JUNKURIBOH
Send from your hand to the Graveyard to negate effect damage and attacks that would reduce your Life Points to 0, and destroy that card.
ATK 300 DEF 200
...AND DESTROY RED DRAGON CALAMITY!!
WHAT?!
COUNTER-ATTACK, JUNKURIBOH!!
THOOM
THOOM
Kuriiii!!
Kuri-kuri-kuriiii !!
JUNKURIBOH MULTIPLIED INFINITELY !!
THOOM
THEY'RE BLASTING THE ABYSSAL CALAMITY METEORS AND HEADING STRAIGHT FOR RED DRAGON CALAMITY!!
THOOM
THOOM

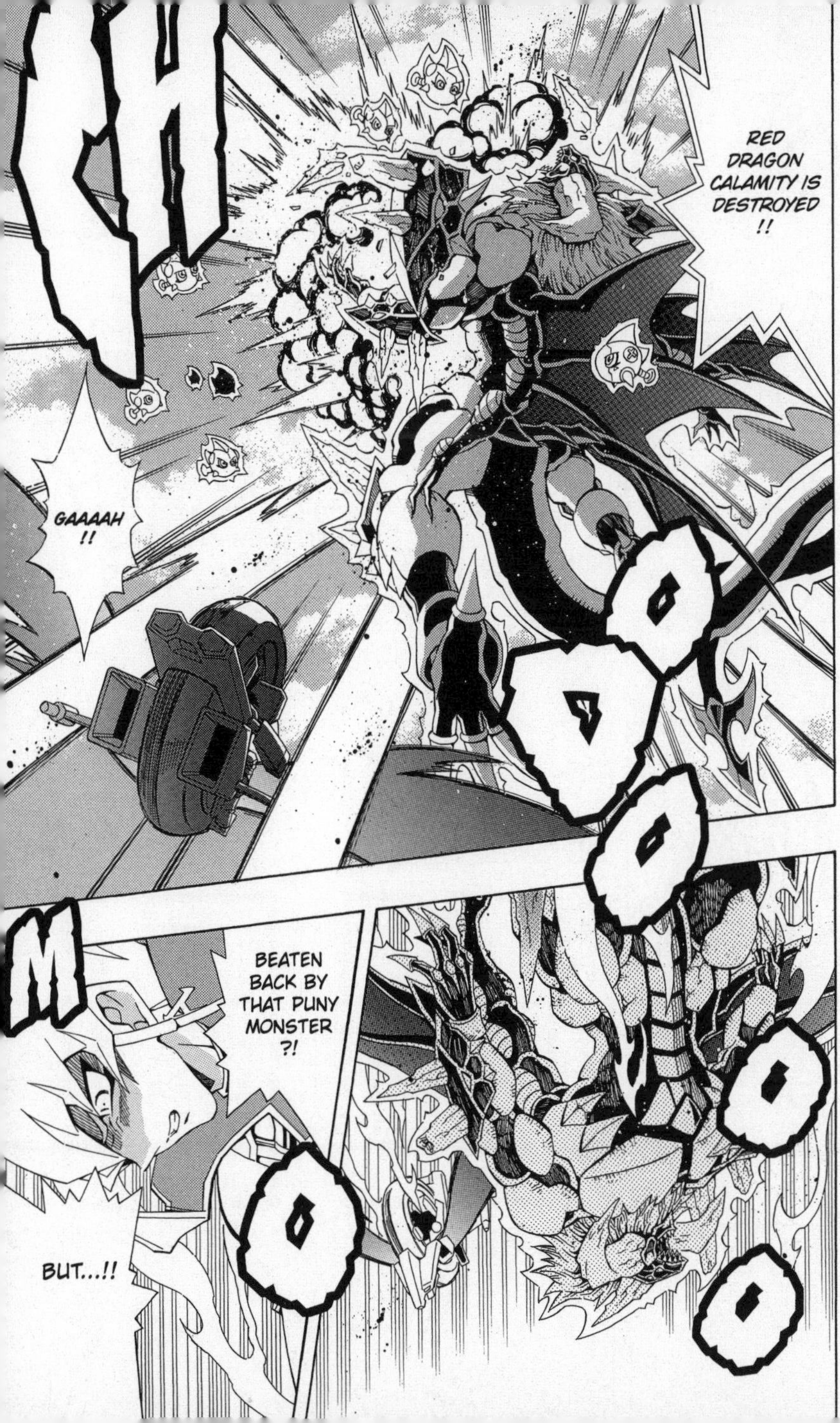
RED DRAGON CALAMITY IS DESTROYED !!
GAAAAH !!
BEATEN BACK BY THAT PUNY MONSTER ?!
BUT...!!

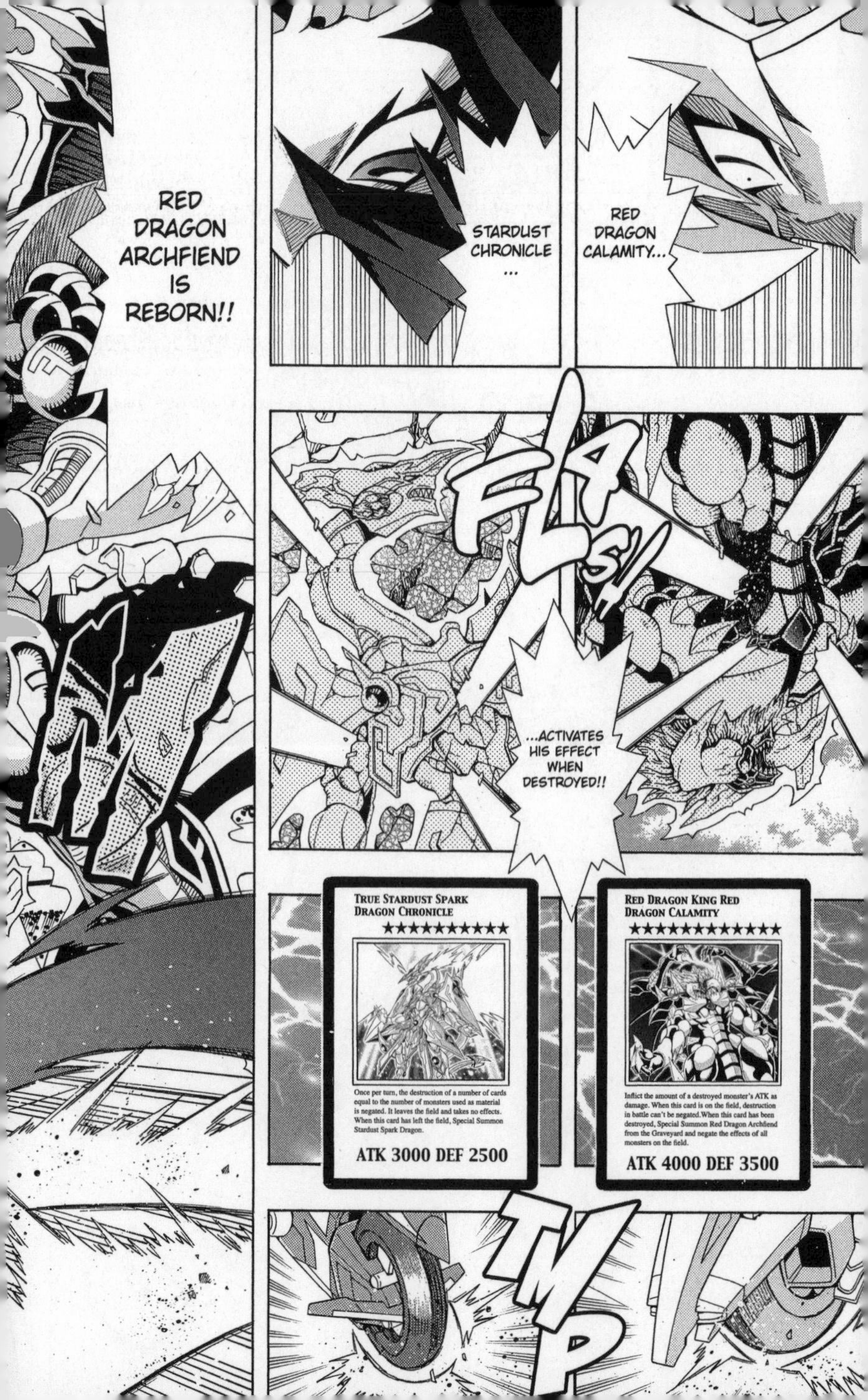
RED DRAGON CALAMITY...
STARDUST CHRONICLE ...
FLASH
...ACTIVATES HIS EFFECT WHEN DESTROYED!!
RED DRAGON KING RED DRAGON CALAMITY
Inflict the amount of a destroyed monster's ATK as damage. When this card is on the field, destruction in battle can't be negated. When this card has been destroyed, Special Summon Red Dragon Archfiend from the Graveyard and negate the effects of all monsters on the field.
ATK 4000 DEF 3500
TRUE STARDUST SPARK DRAGON CHRONICLE
Once per turn, the destruction of a number of cards equal to the number of monsters used as material is negated. It leaves the field and takes no effects. When this card has left the field, Special Summon Stardust Spark Dragon.
ATK 3000 DEF 2500
TMP
RED DRAGON ARCHFIEND IS REBORN!!

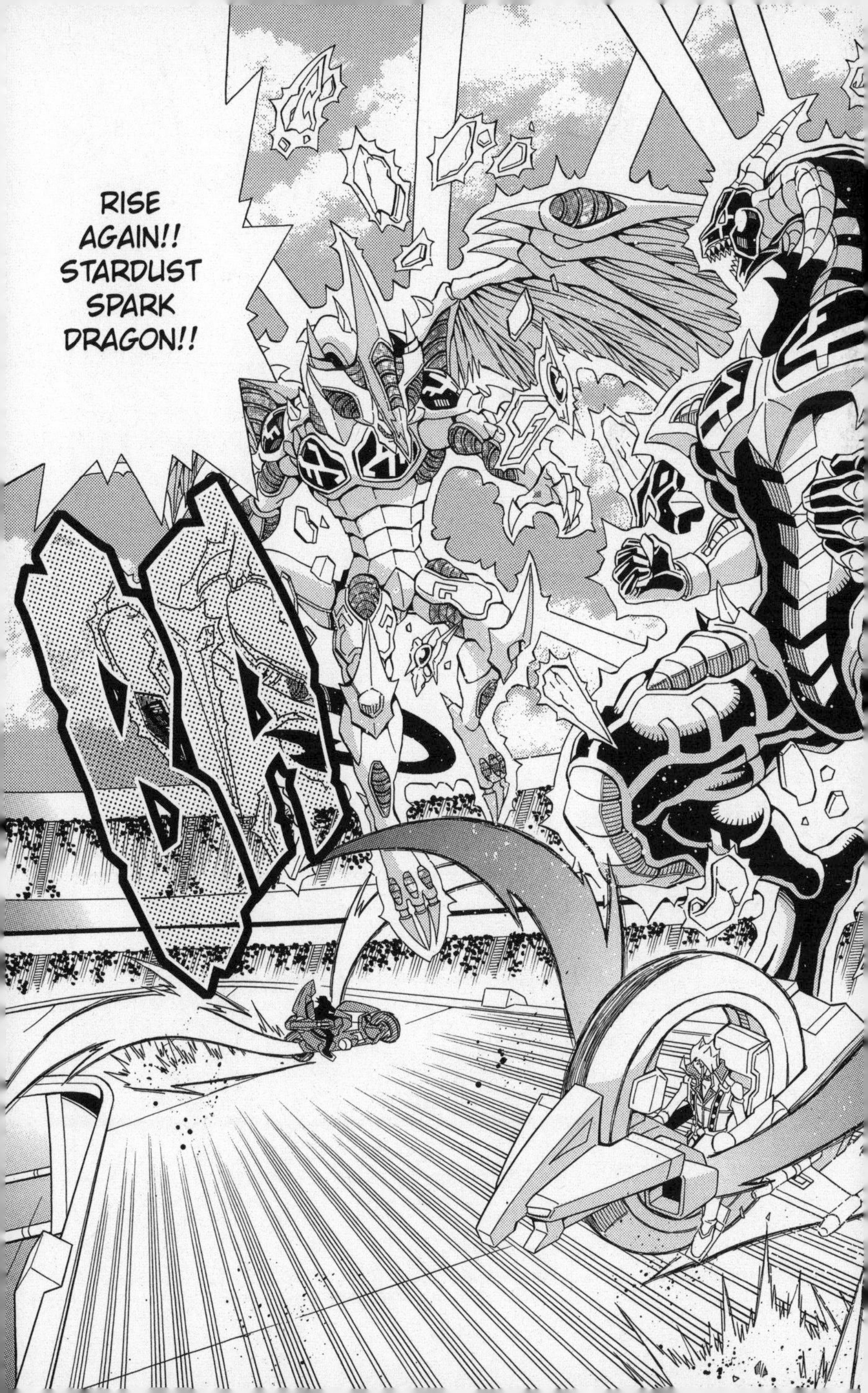
RISE AGAIN!! STARDUST SPARK DRAGON!!

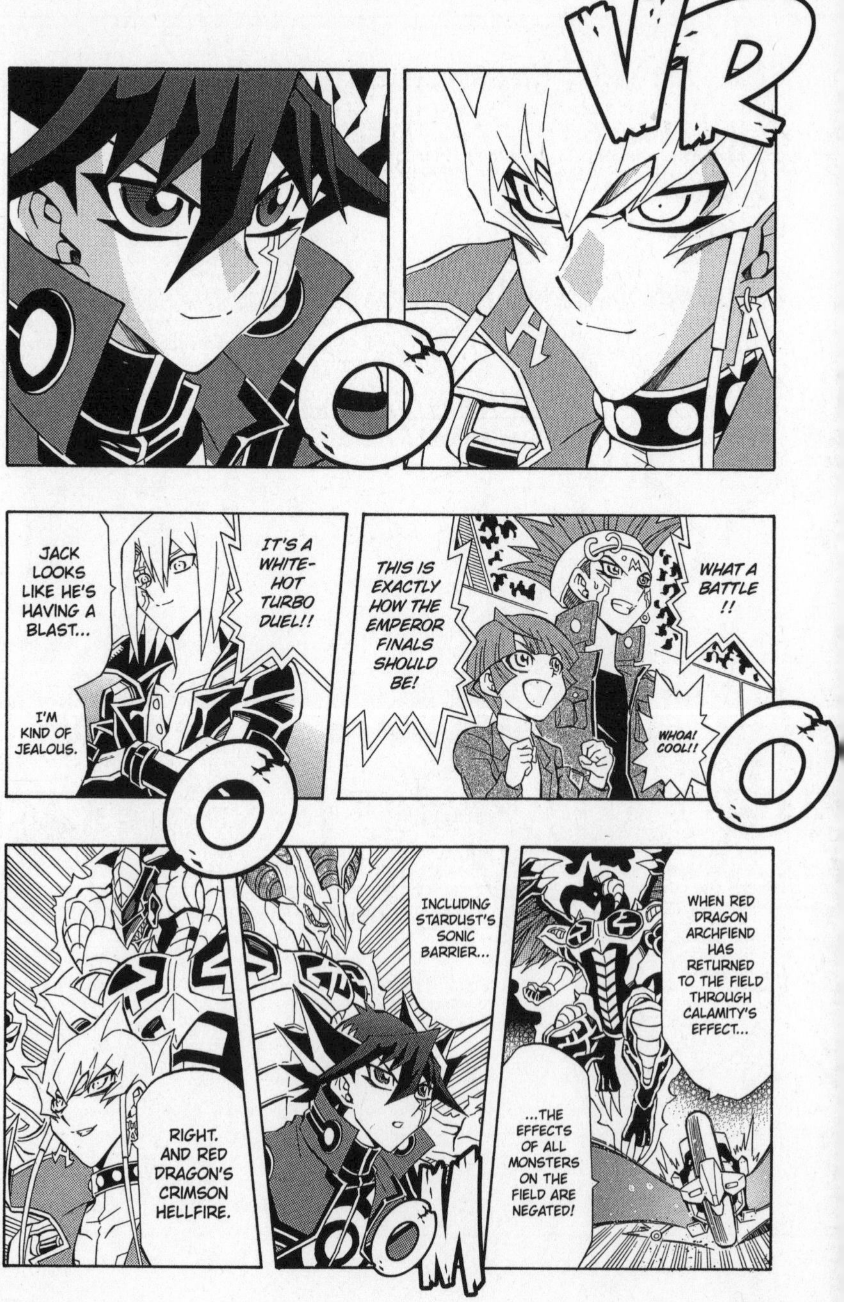
VROOOOOM
WHAT A BATTLE!!
THIS IS EXACTLY HOW THE EMPEROR FINALS SHOULD BE!
WHOA! COOL!!
IT'S A WHITE-HOT TURBO DUEL!!
JACK LOOKS LIKE HE'S HAVING A BLAST...
I'M KIND OF JEALOUS.
WHEN RED DRAGON ARCHFIEND HAS RETURNED TO THE FIELD THROUGH CALAMITY'S EFFECT...
...THE EFFECTS OF ALL MONSTERS ON THE FIELD ARE NEGATED!
INCLUDING STARDUST'S SONIC BARRIER...
RIGHT. AND RED DRAGON'S CRIMSON HELLFIRE.

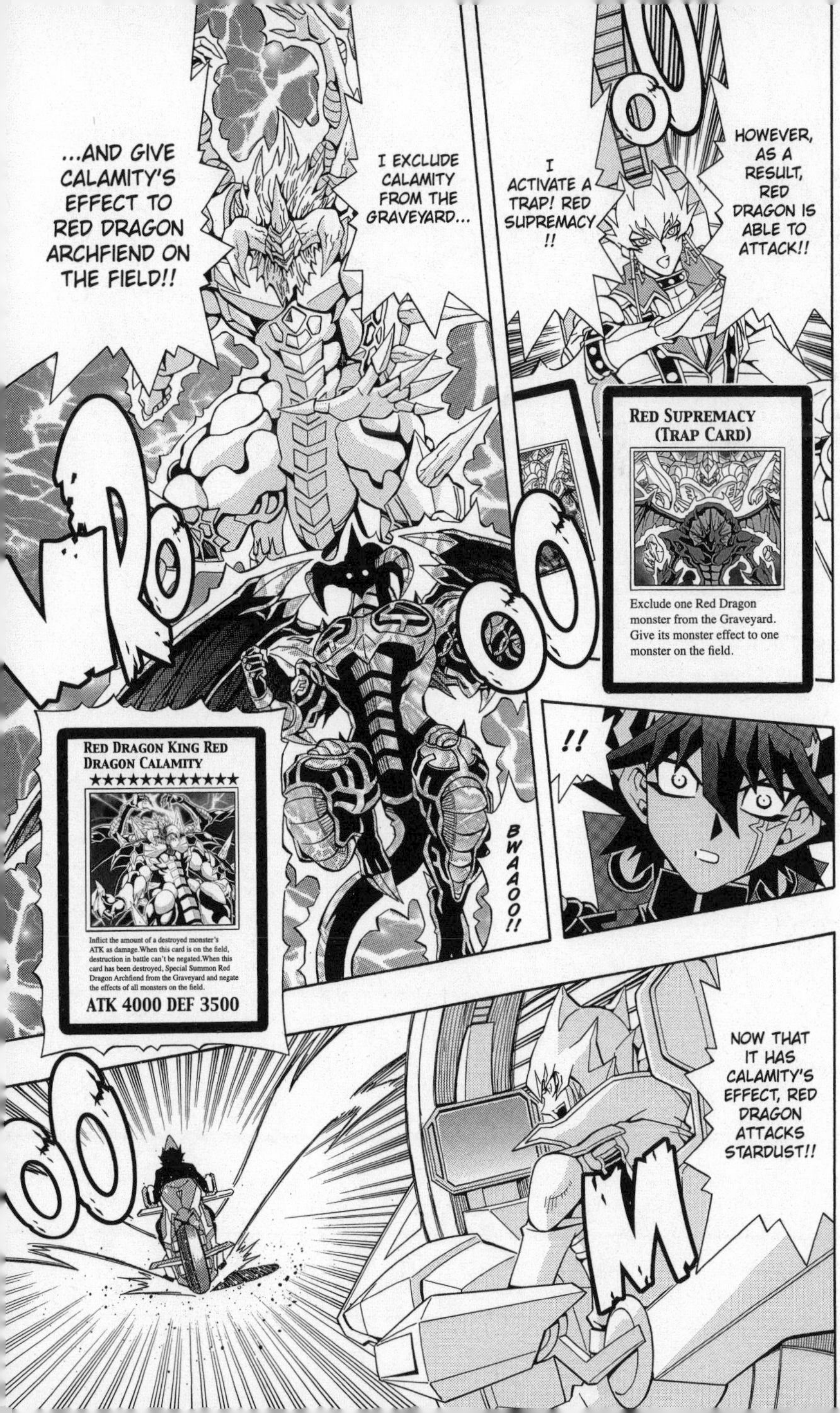
HOWEVER, AS A RESULT, RED DRAGON IS ABLE TO ATTACK!!
I ACTIVATE A TRAP! RED SUPREMACY!!
I EXCLUDE CALAMITY FROM THE GRAVEYARD...
...AND GIVE CALAMITY'S EFFECT TO RED DRAGON ARCHFIEND ON THE FIELD!!
RED SUPREMACY (TRAP CARD)
Exclude one Red Dragon monster from the Graveyard. Give its monster effect to one monster on the field.
!!
BWAAOOO!!
RED DRAGON KING RED DRAGON CALAMITY
★★★★★★★★★★★★
Inflict the amount of a destroyed monster's ATK as damage. When this card is on the field, destruction in battle can't be negated. When this card has been destroyed, Special Summon Red Dragon Archfiend from the Graveyard and negate the effects of all monsters on the field.
ATK 4000 DEF 3500
NOW THAT IT HAS CALAMITY'S EFFECT, RED DRAGON ATTACKS STARDUST!!

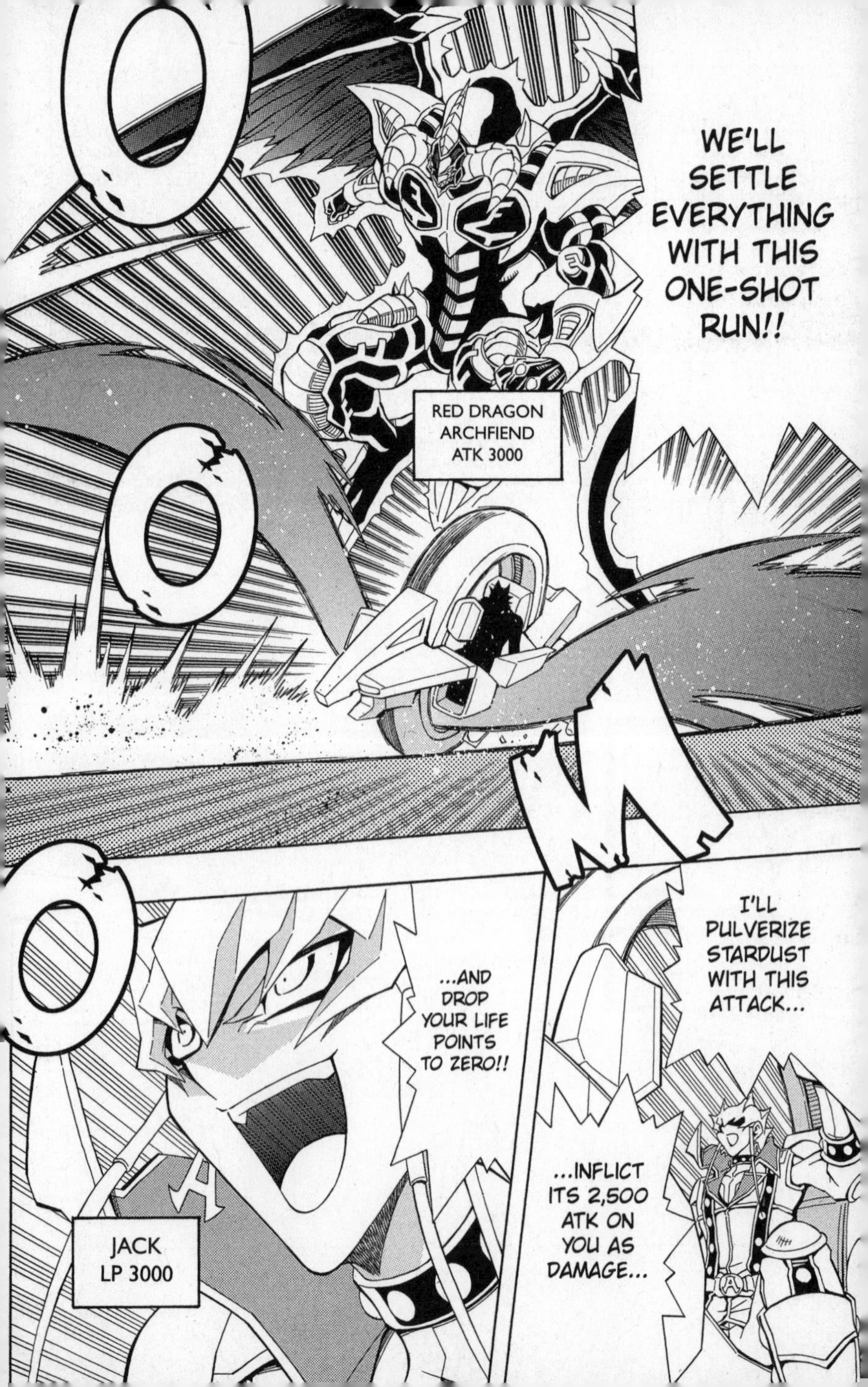
WE'LL SETTLE EVERYTHING WITH THIS ONE-SHOT RUN!!
RED DRAGON ARCHFIEND ATK 3000
I'LL PULVERIZE STARDUST WITH THIS ATTACK...
...INFLICT ITS 2,500 ATK ON YOU AS DAMAGE...
...AND DROP YOUR LIFE POINTS TO ZERO!!
JACK LP 3000

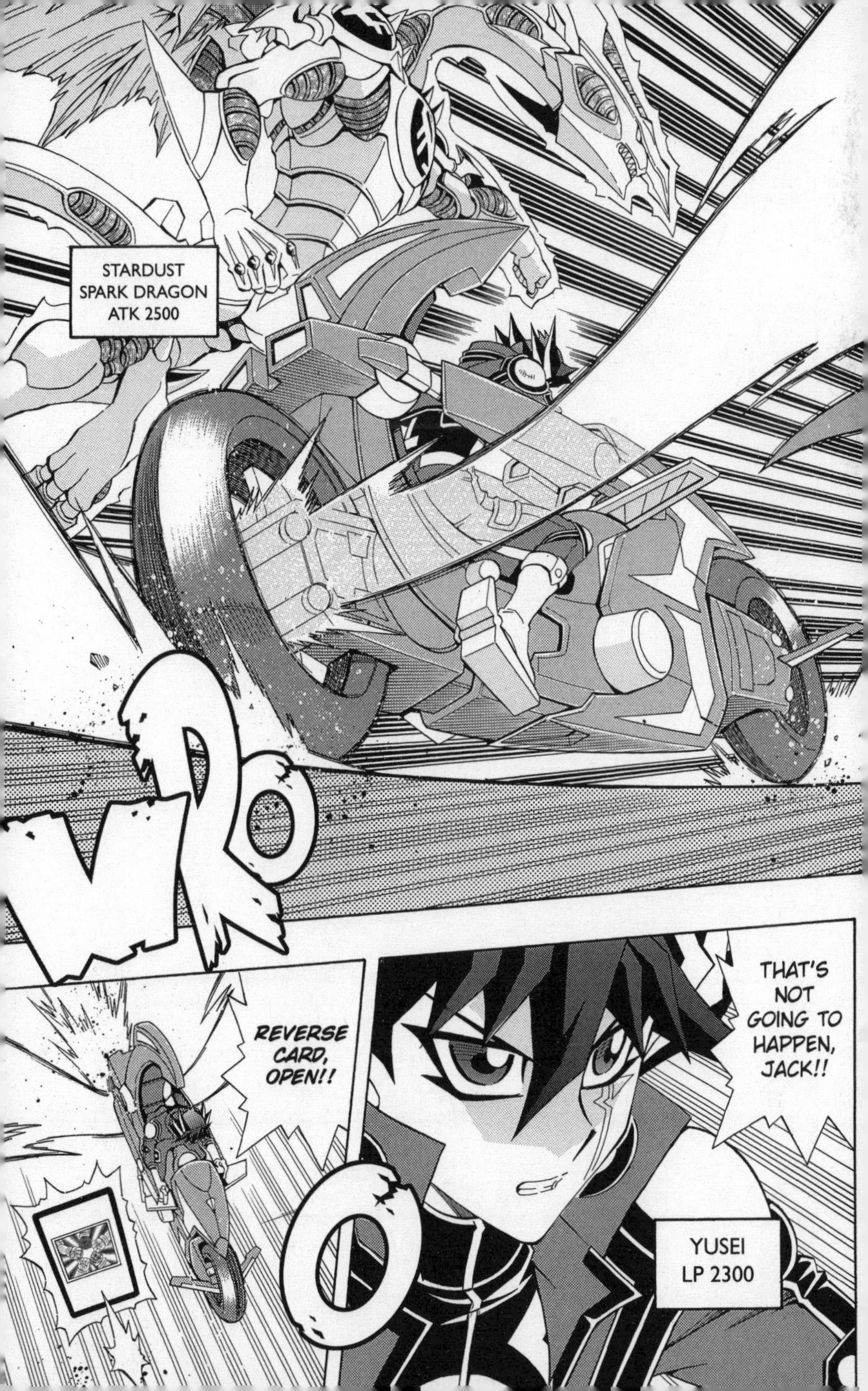
STARDUST SPARK DRAGON ATK 2500
THAT'S NOT GOING TO HAPPEN, JACK!!
YUSEI LP 2300
REVERSE CARD, OPEN!!

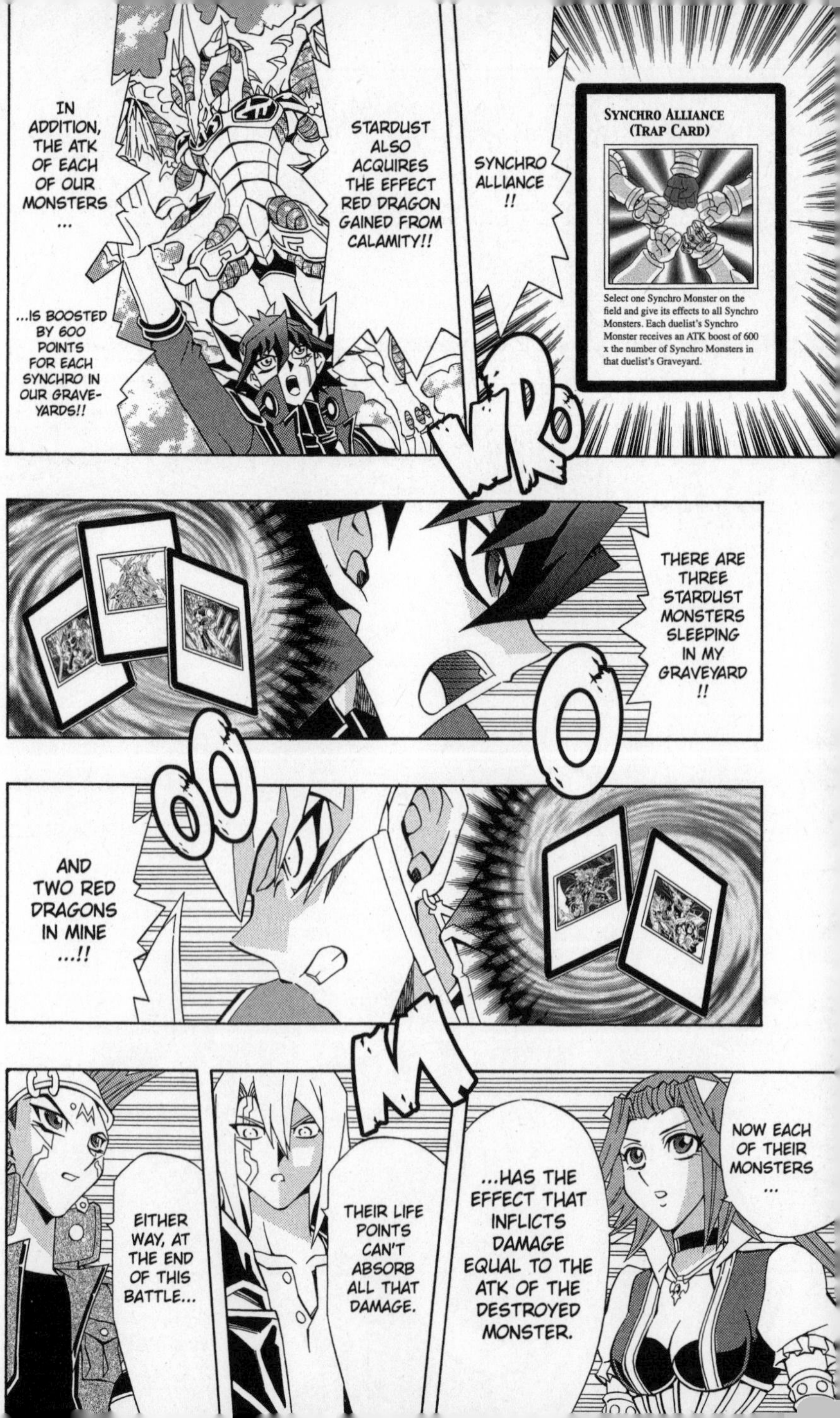
SYNCHRO ALLIANCE
(TRAP CARD)
Select one Synchro Monster on the field and give its effects to all Synchro Monsters. Each duelist's Synchro Monster receives an ATK boost of 600 x the number of Synchro Monsters in that duelist's Graveyard.
SYNCHRO ALLIANCE !!
STARDUST ALSO ACQUIRES THE EFFECT RED DRAGON GAINED FROM CALAMITY!!
IN ADDITION, THE ATK OF EACH OF OUR MONSTERS ...
...IS BOOSTED BY 600 POINTS FOR EACH SYNCHRO IN OUR GRAVE-YARDS!!
VROOOOM
THERE ARE THREE STARDUST MONSTERS SLEEPING IN MY GRAVEYARD !!
AND TWO RED DRAGONS IN MINE ...!!
NOW EACH OF THEIR MONSTERS ...
...HAS THE EFFECT THAT INFLICTS DAMAGE EQUAL TO THE ATK OF THE DESTROYED MONSTER.
THEIR LIFE POINTS CAN'T ABSORB ALL THAT DAMAGE.
EITHER WAY, AT THE END OF THIS BATTLE...

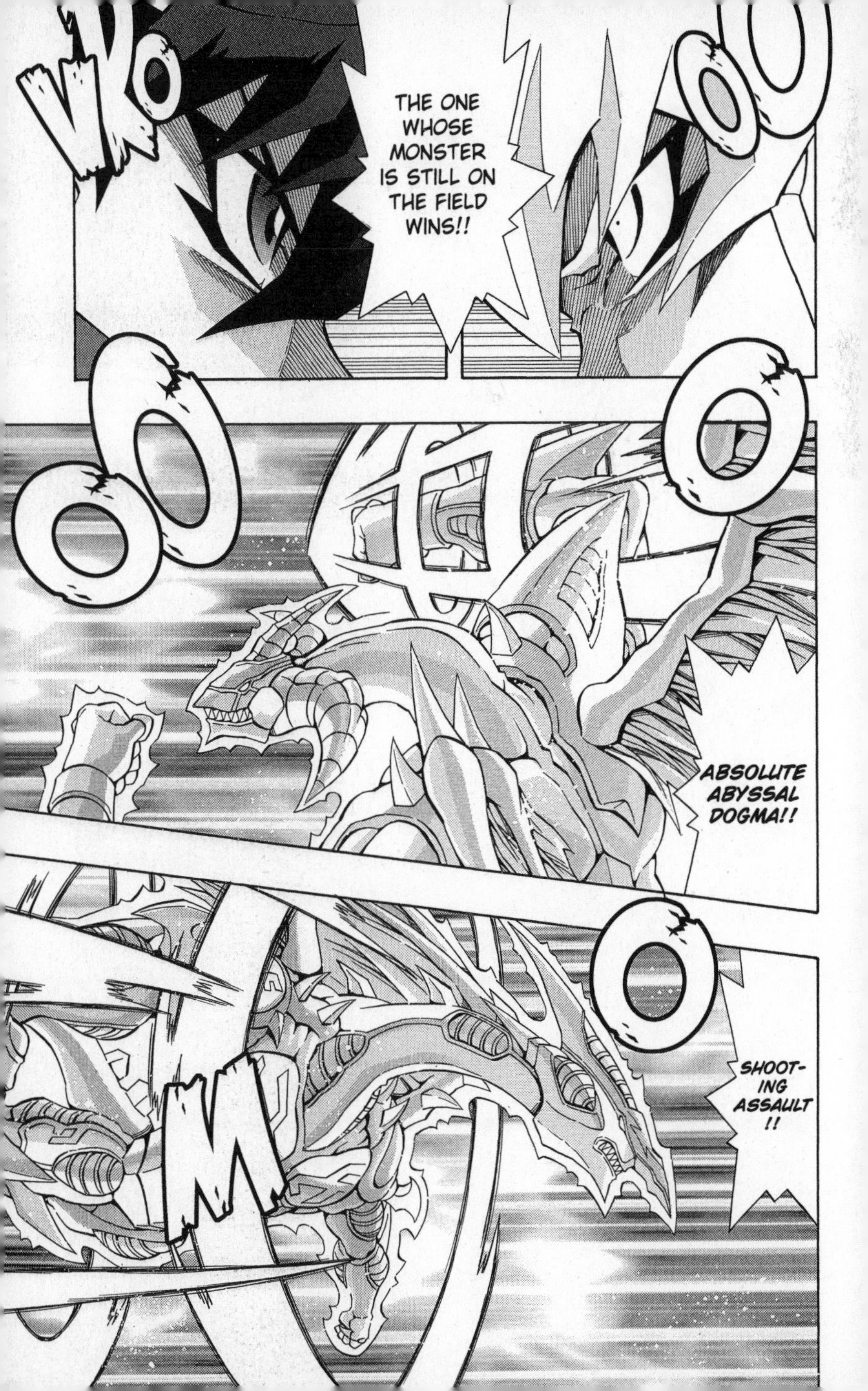
VOOO
THE ONE WHOSE MONSTER IS STILL ON THE FIELD WINS!!
VOOO
ABSOLUTE ABYSSAL DOGMA!!
VOOM
SHOOT-ING ASSAULT !!

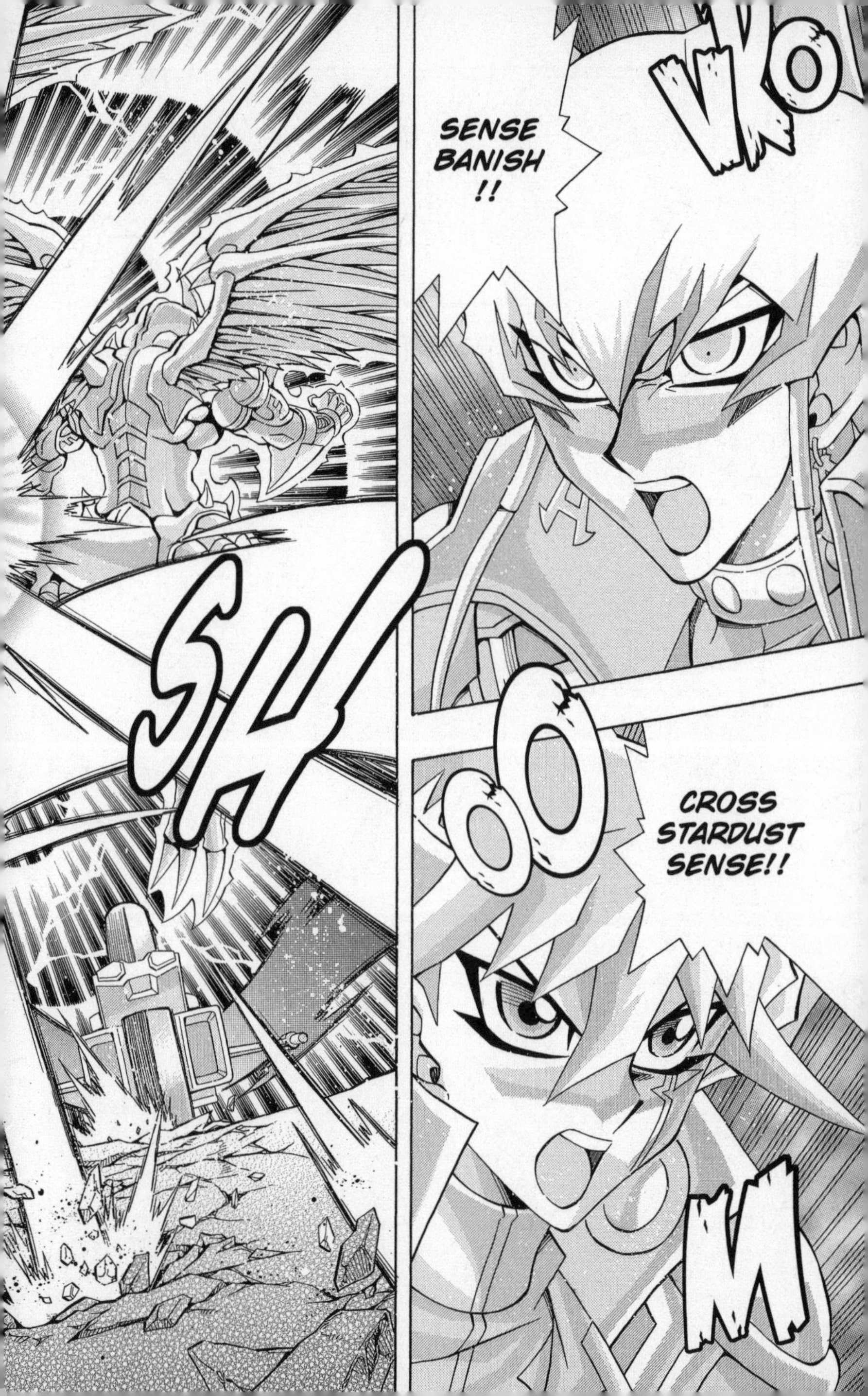
VO
SENSE BANISH!!
OO
CROSS STARDUST SENSE!!
M
SH

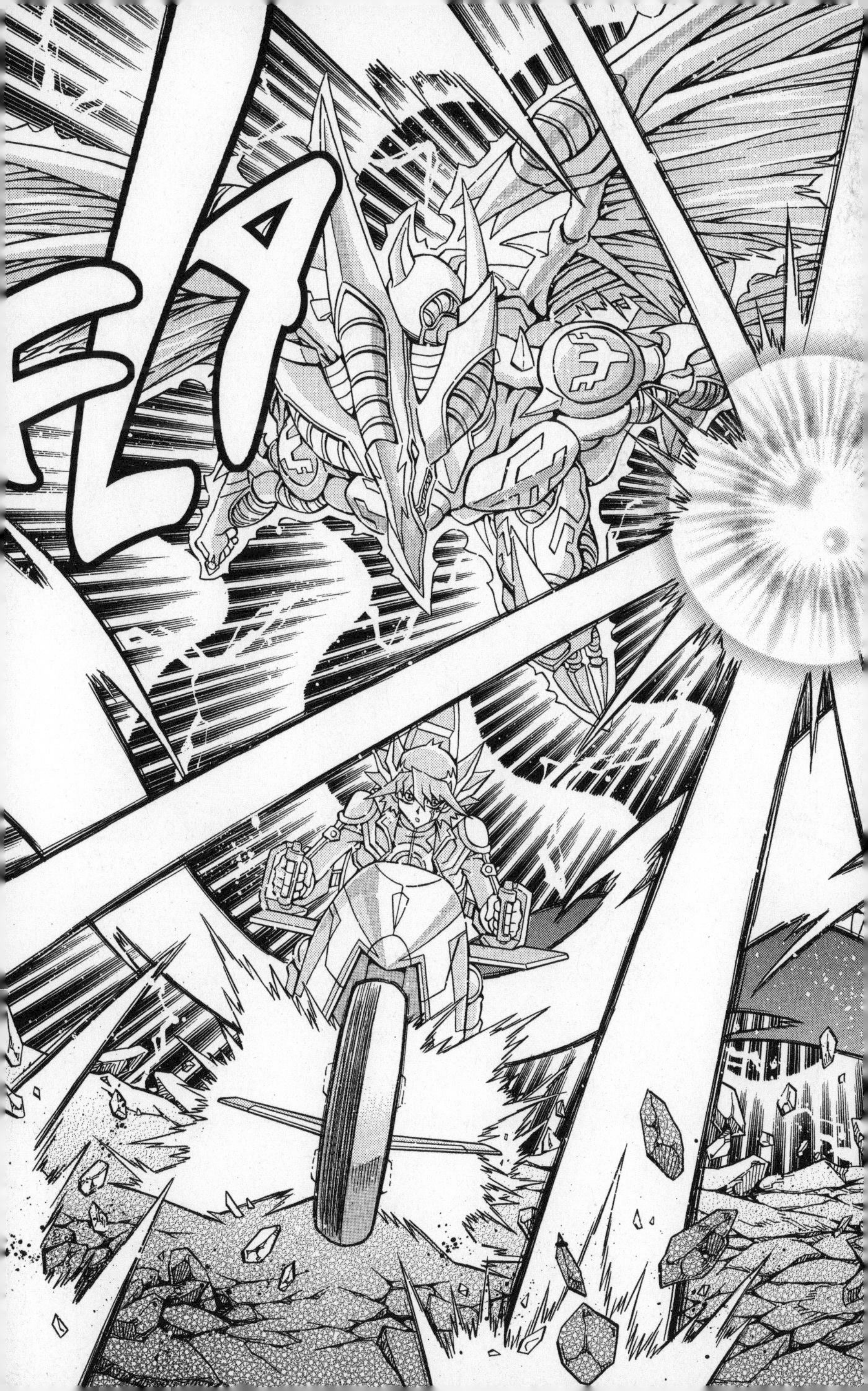

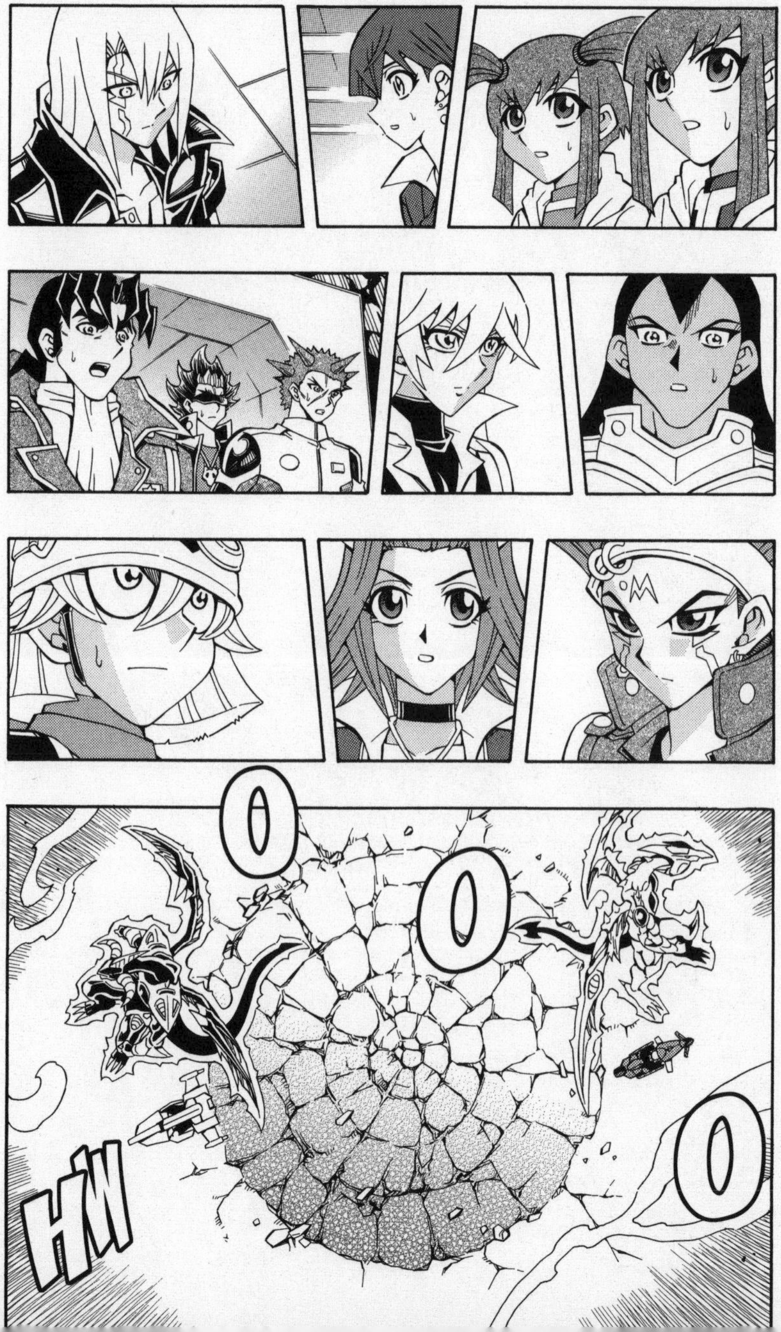
HWOOO

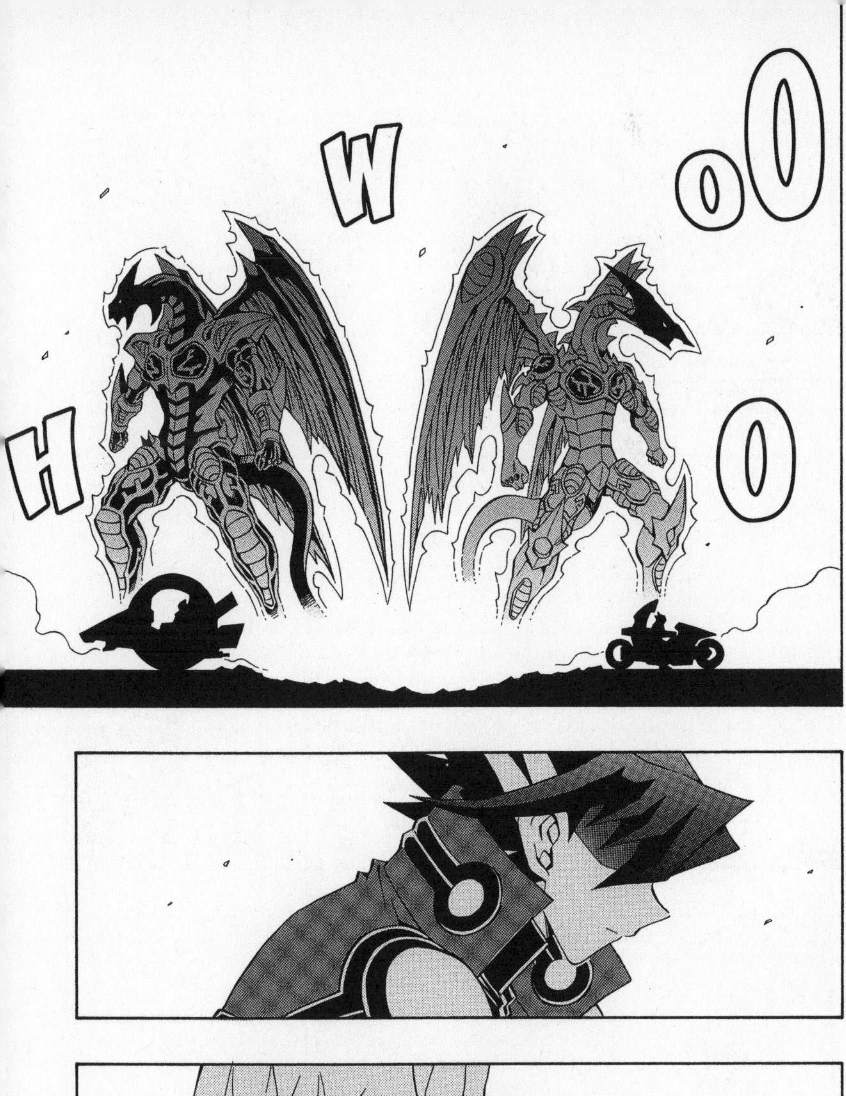
HWOOO

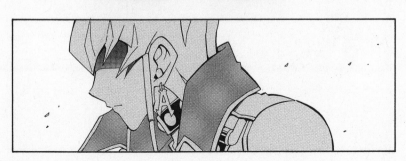

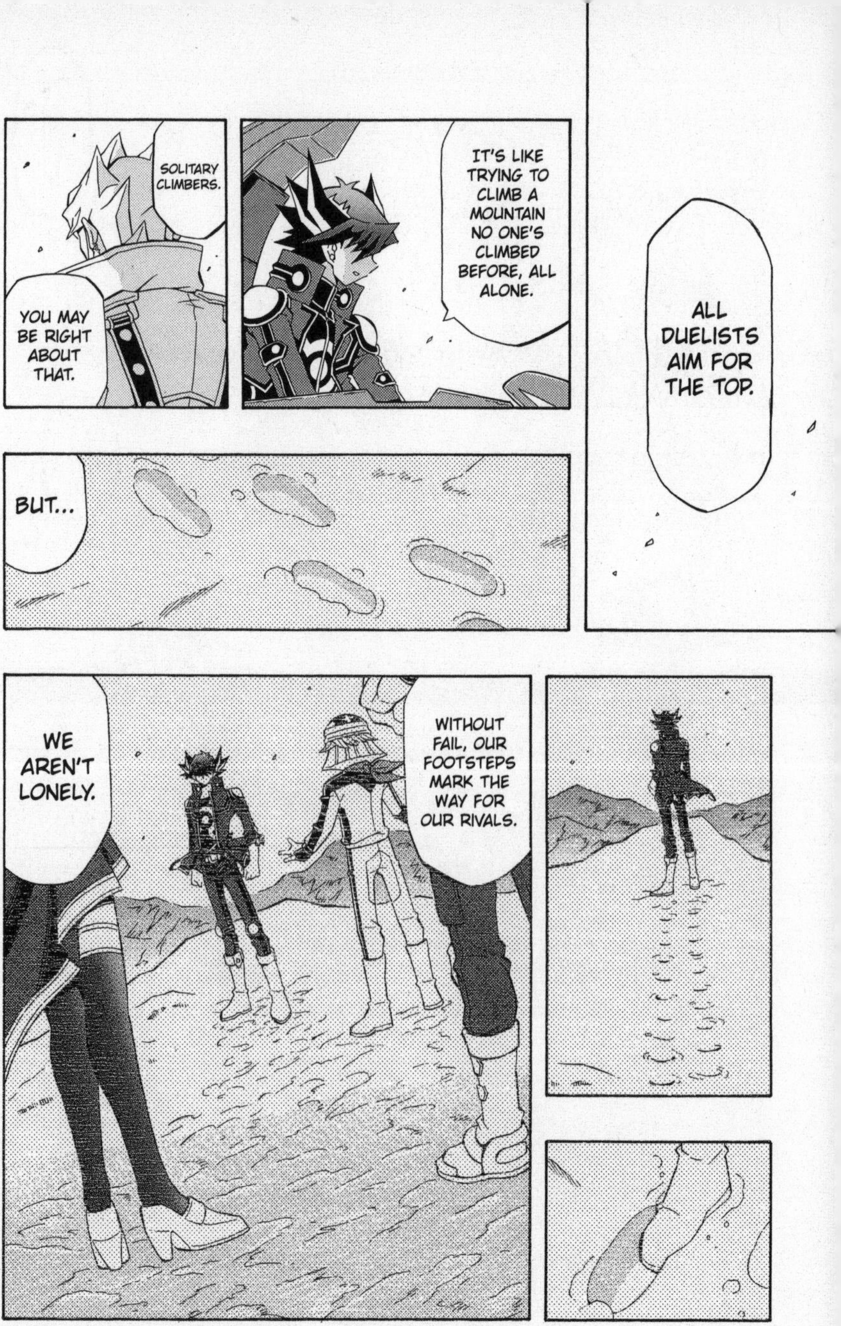
ALL DUELISTS AIM FOR THE TOP.
IT'S LIKE TRYING TO CLIMB A MOUNTAIN NO ONE'S CLIMBED BEFORE, ALL ALONE.
SOLITARY CLIMBERS.
YOU MAY BE RIGHT ABOUT THAT.
BUT...
WITHOUT FAIL, OUR FOOTSTEPS MARK THE WAY FOR OUR RIVALS.
WE AREN'T LONELY.

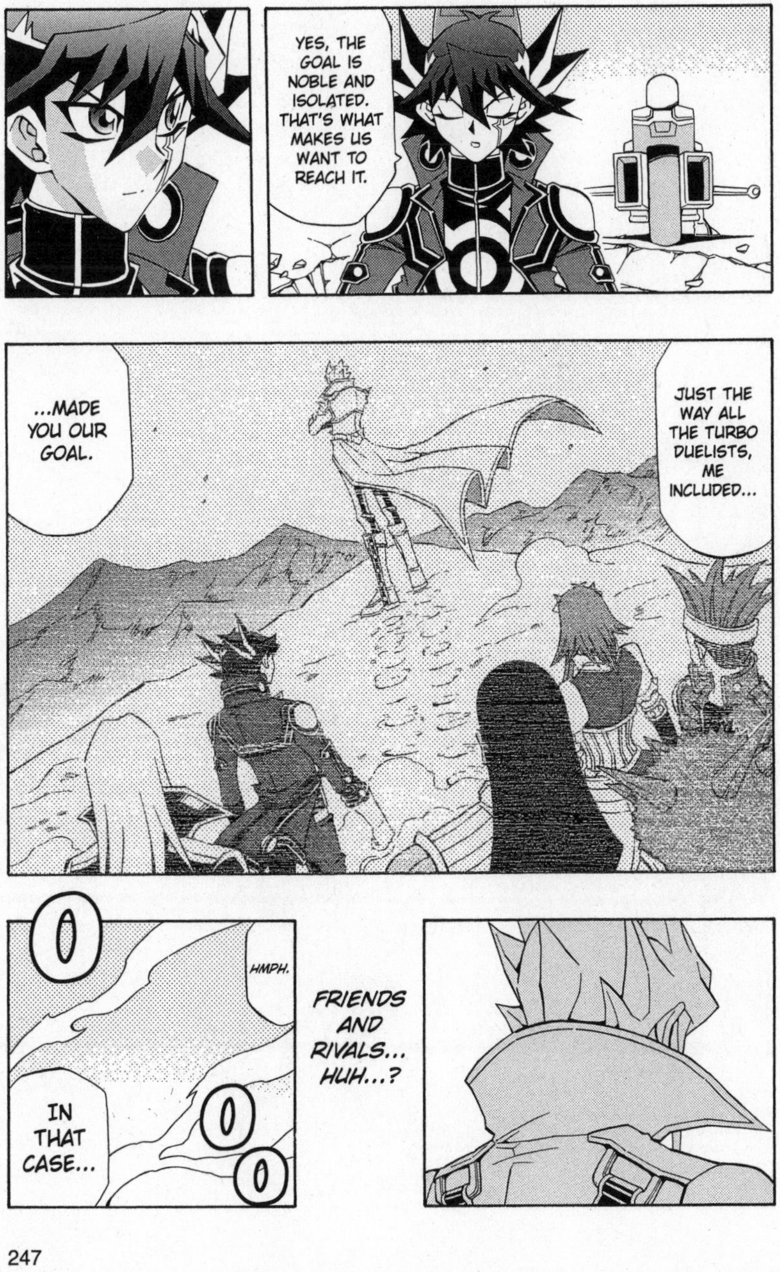
YES, THE GOAL IS NOBLE AND ISOLATED. THAT'S WHAT MAKES US WANT TO REACH IT.
JUST THE WAY ALL THE TURBO DUELISTS, ME INCLUDED...
...MADE YOU OUR GOAL.
FRIENDS AND RIVALS... HUH...?
HMPH.
IN THAT CASE...

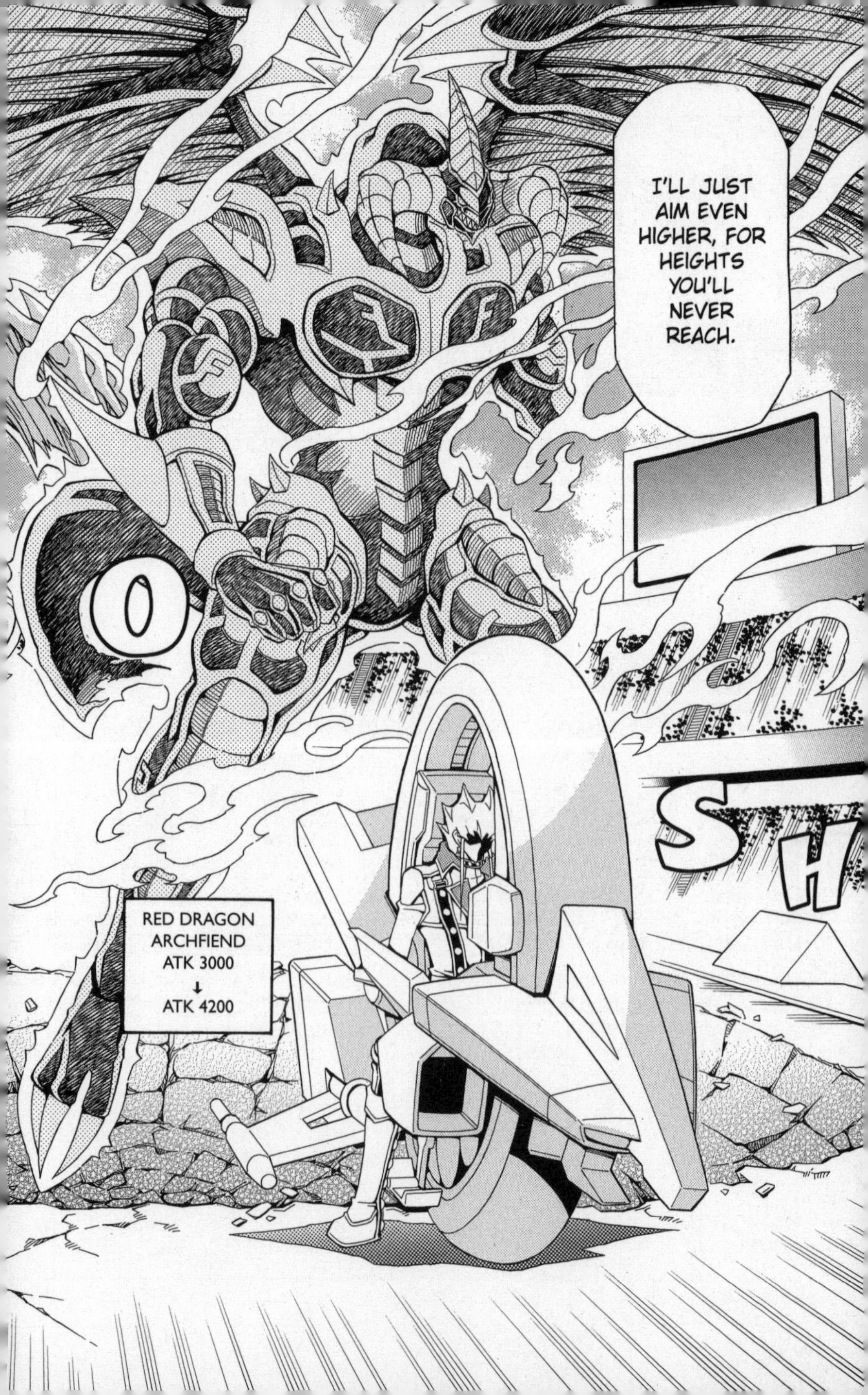
I'LL JUST AIM EVEN HIGHER, FOR HEIGHTS YOU'LL NEVER REACH.
RED DRAGON ARCHFIEND ATK 3000 ↓ ATK 4200
SH

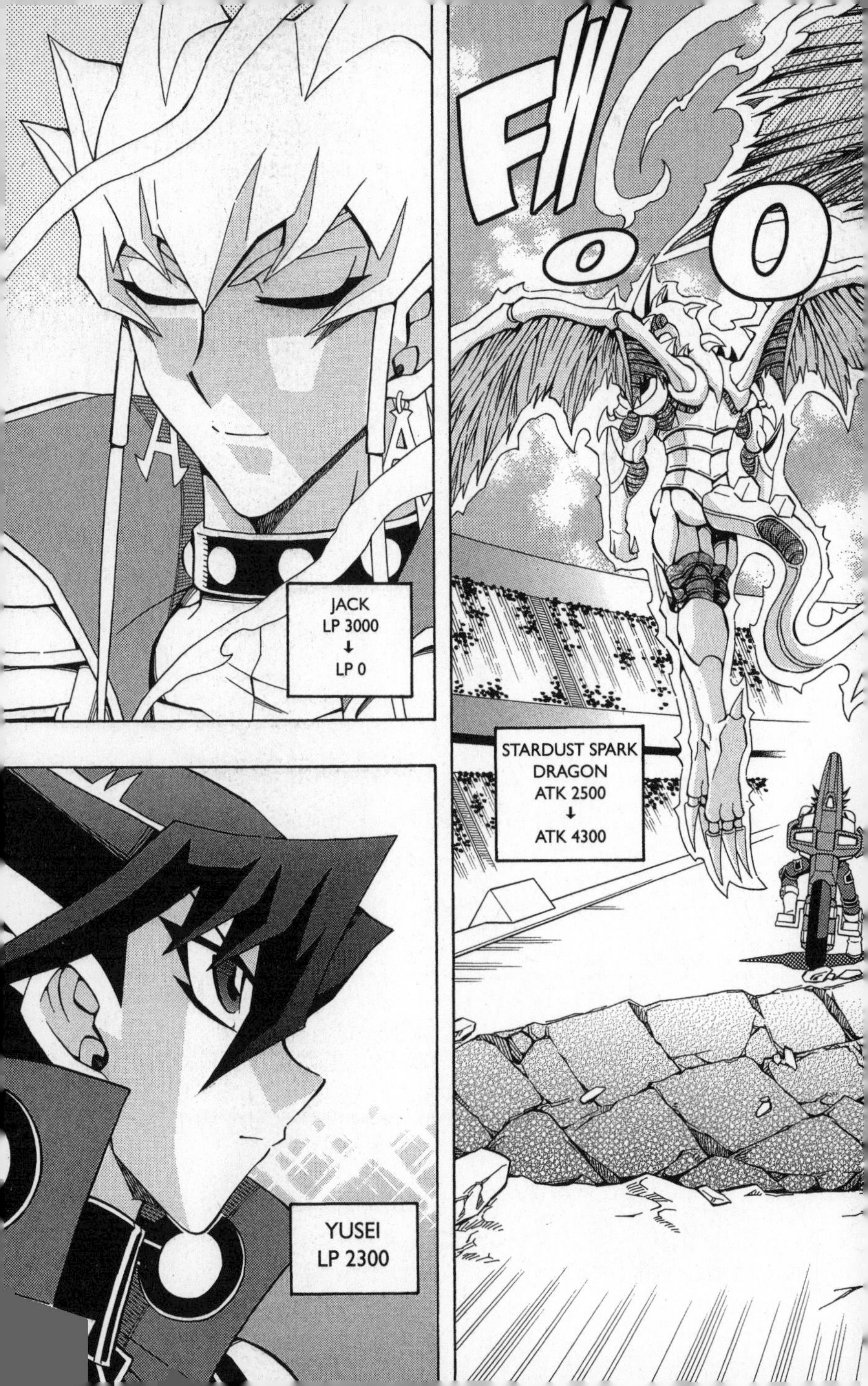
FWOO
STARDUST SPARK DRAGON
ATK 2500
↓
ATK 4300
JACK
LP 3000
↓
LP 0
YUSEI
LP 2300

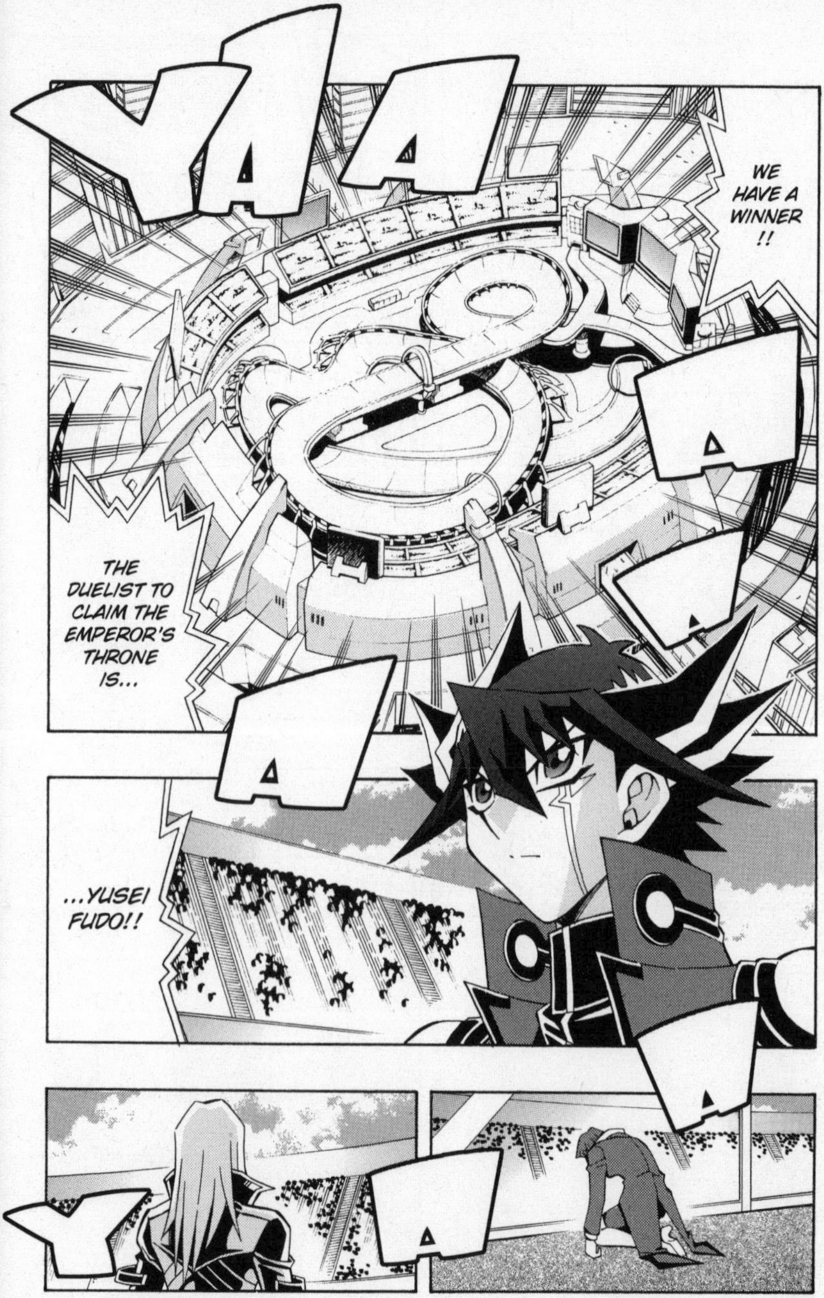
YAA
WE HAVE A WINNER!!
A
A
THE DUELIST TO CLAIM THE EMPEROR'S THRONE IS...
A
...YUSEI FUDO!!
A
YA

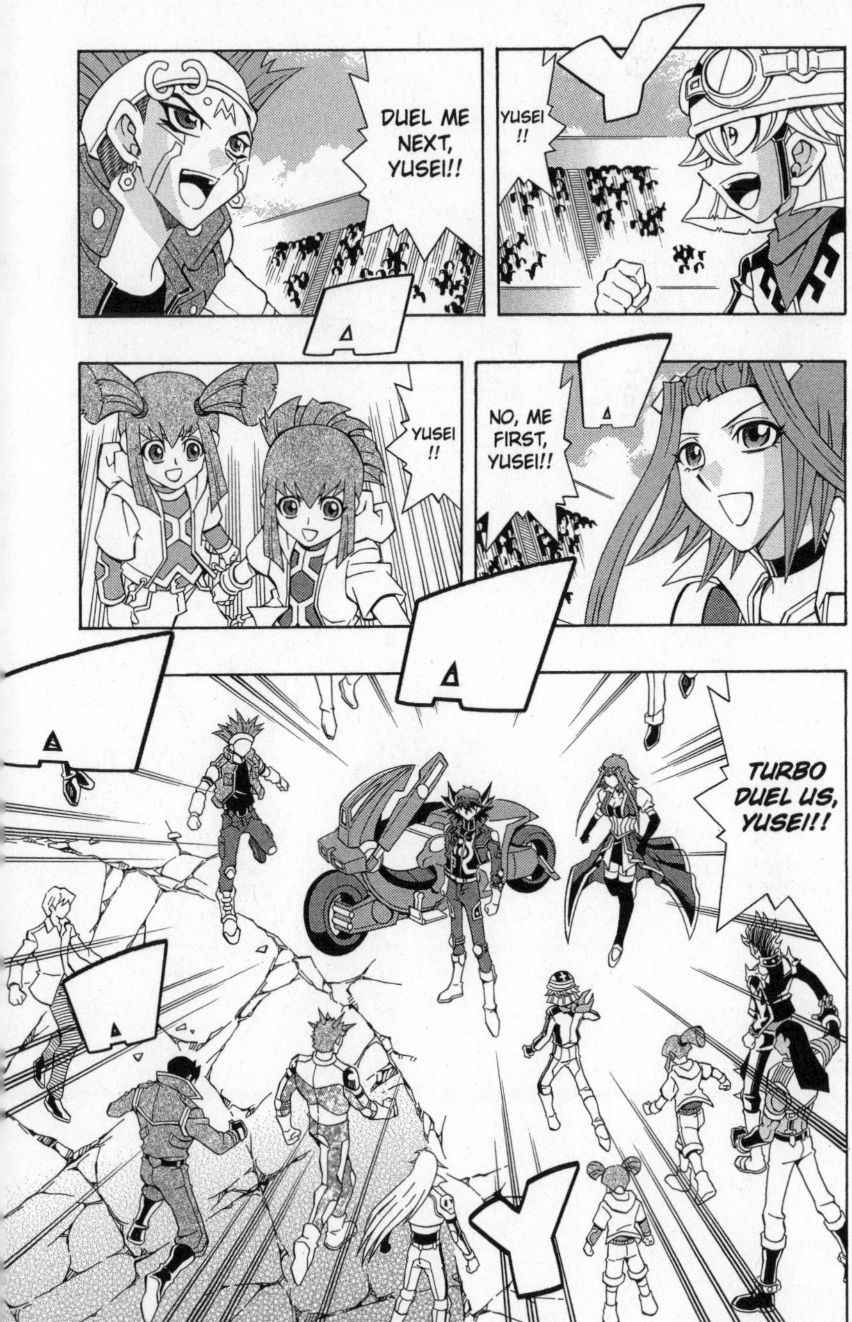
YUSEI !!
DUEL ME NEXT, YUSEI!!
NO, ME FIRST, YUSEI!!
YUSEI !!
TURBO DUEL US, YUSEI!!

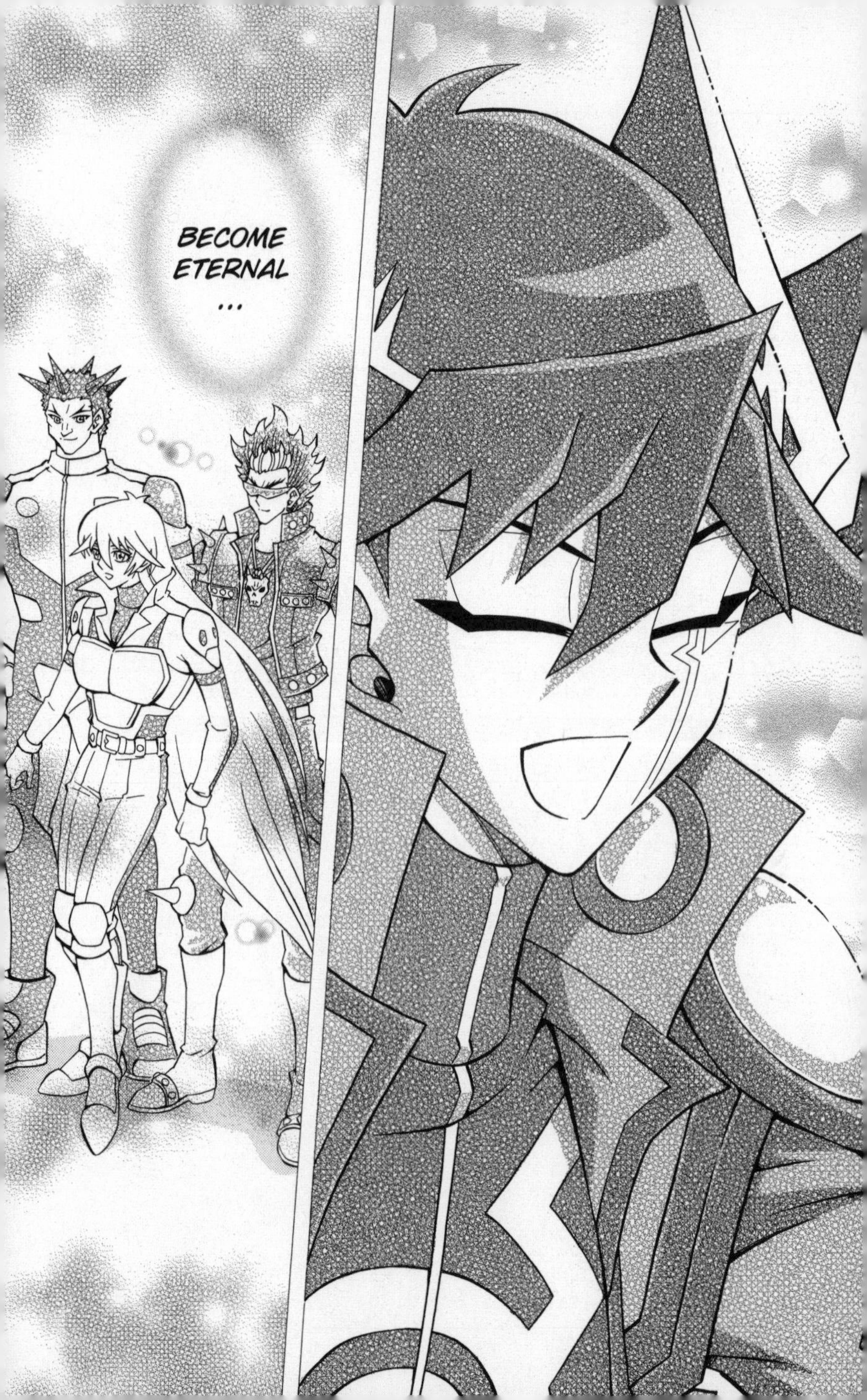
BECOME ETERNAL ...

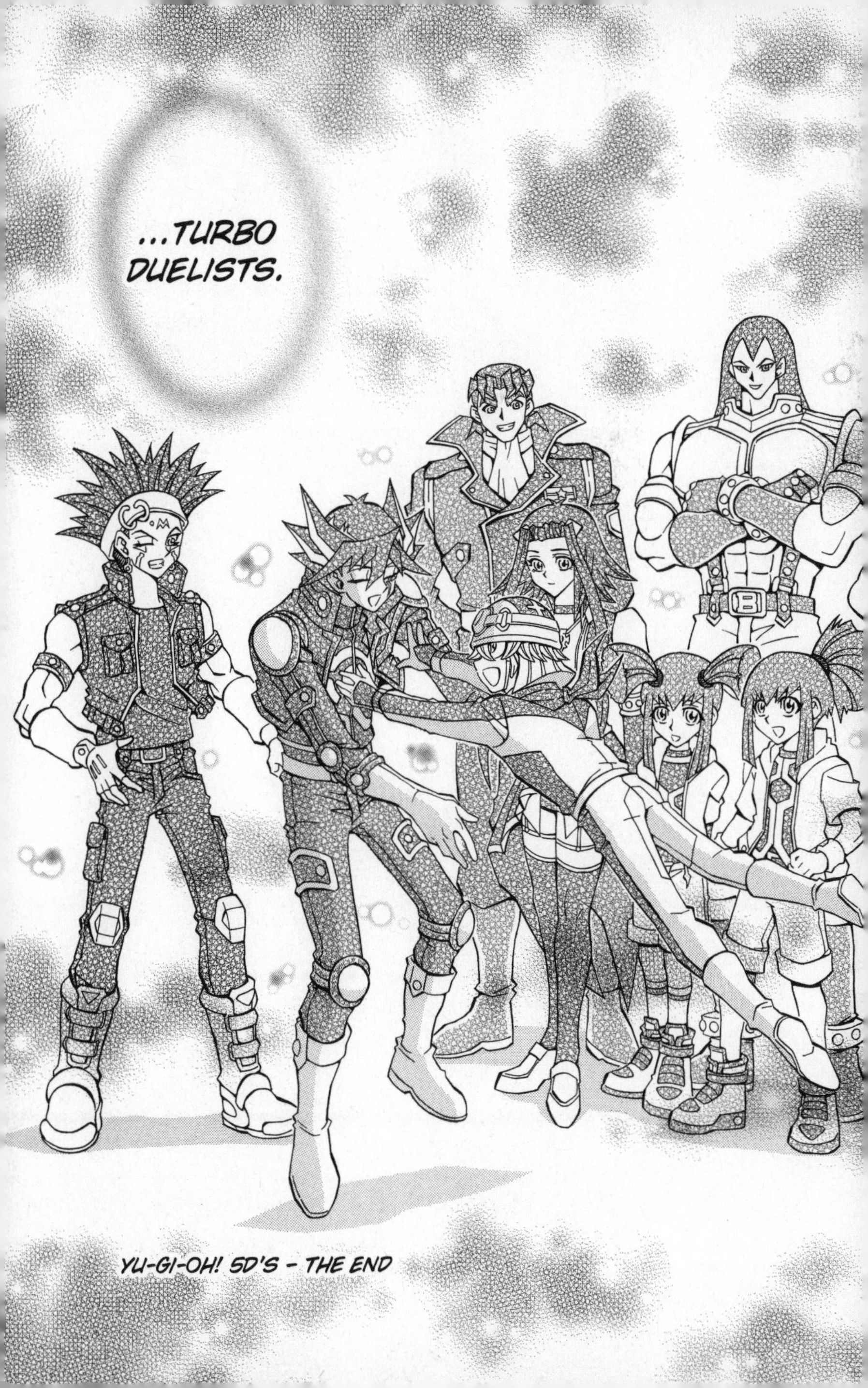
...TURBO DUELISTS.
YU-GI-OH! 5D'S - THE END

NARUTO

Story and Art by
Masashi Kishimoto

Naruto is determined to become the greatest ninja ever!

Twelve years ago the Village Hidden in the Leaves was attacked by a fearsome threat. A nine-tailed fox spirit claimed the life of the village leader, the Hokage, and many others. Today, the village is at peace and a troublemaking kid named Naruto is struggling to graduate from Ninja Academy. His goal may be to become the next Hokage, but his true destiny will be much more complicated. The adventure begins now!

WORLD'S BEST SELLING MANGA!

www.shonenjump.com

www.viz.com

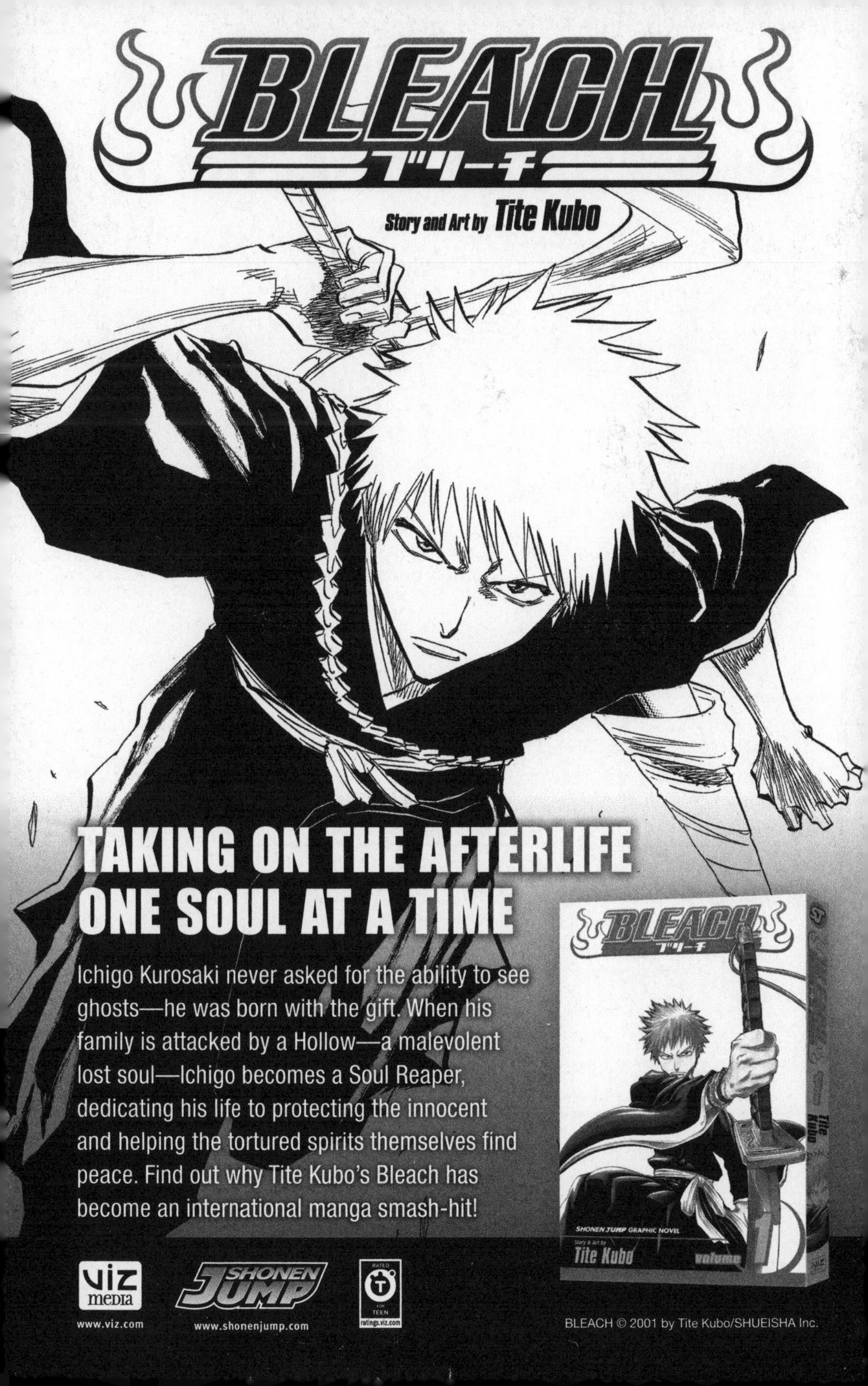
BLEACH
ブリーチ
Story and Art by Tite Kubo
TAKING ON THE AFTERLIFE ONE SOUL AT A TIME
Ichigo Kurosaki never asked for the ability to see ghosts—he was born with the gift. When his family is attacked by a Hollow—a malevolent lost soul—Ichigo becomes a Soul Reaper, dedicating his life to protecting the innocent and helping the tortured spirits themselves find peace. Find out why Tite Kubo's Bleach has become an international manga smash-hit!
BLEACH
ブリーチ
SHONEN JUMP GRAPHIC NOVEL
Story & Art by Tite Kubo
volume 1
viz media
www.viz.com
SHONEN JUMP
www.shonenjump.com
RATED T FOR TEEN
ratings.viz.com
BLEACH © 2001 by Tite Kubo/SHUEISHA Inc.

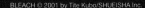

IN THE WRONG DIRECTION!!

Whoops!
Guess what?
You're starting at
the wrong end
of the comic!

...It's true! In keeping with the original Japanese format, *Yu-Gi-Oh! 5Ds* is meant to be read from right to left, starting in the upper-right corner.

Unlike English, which is read from left to right, Japanese is read from right to left, meaning that action, sound effects and word-balloon order are completely reversed... something which can make readers unfamiliar with Japanese feel pretty backwards themselves. For this reason, manga or Japanese comics published in the U.S. in English have sometimes been published "flopped"—that is, printed in exact reverse order, as though seen from the other side of a mirror.

By flopping pages, U.S. publishers can avoid confusing readers, but the compromise is not without its downside. For one thing, a character in a flopped manga series who once wore in the original Japanese version a T-shirt emblazoned with "M A Y" (as in "the merry month of") now wears one which reads "Y A M"! Additionally, many manga creators in Japan are themselves unhappy with the process, as some feel the mirror-imaging of their art alters their original intentions.

We are proud to bring you Masahiro Hikokubo and Masashi Sato's *Yu-Gi-Oh! 5D's* in the original unflopped format. For now, though, turn to the other side of the book and let the duel begin...!

—Editor